016.071 Faib
Faibisoff
Bibliography of newspapers in
fourteen New York State counties

DATE DUE

A Bibliography of Newspapers
In Fourteen New York Counties

PRODUCTION STAFF

DATA COLLECTORS

Marion Brophy	Linda L. Hillman
Sylvia G. Faibisoff	Andrew A. Hritz
Susan E. Feldman	Abigail S. Kelly
Evelyn Hand	June Lang
Shirley Heppell	Lois O'Connor

Fatinitza Smith

COMPILERS

Sylvia G. Faibisoff	Linda L. Hillman
Susan E. Feldman	Abigail S. Kelly

Lois O'Connor

EDITORIAL ASSISTANTS

Amy Barnum	Deborah Nichols

MANAGING EDITOR

Anne Bland

A BIBLIOGRAPHY
of NEWSPAPERS
In Fourteen New York Counties

EDITED BY

SYLVIA G. FAIBISOFF and WENDELL TRIPP

COOPERSTOWN and ITHACA

SOUTH CENTRAL RESEARCH LIBRARY COUNCIL

NEW YORK STATE HISTORICAL ASSOCIATION

1978

Library of Congress Catalog Card Number: 78-71392
ISBN: 0-917334-02-7
Printed in the United States of America

CONTENTS

Preface   vi

Use of the Bibliography   viii

Abbreviations   ix

Allegany County   1

Broome County   17

Cayuga County   37

Chemung County   68

Chenango County   89

Cortland County   112

Delaware County   137

Otsego County   156

Schuyler County   177

Seneca County   189

Steuben County   206

Tioga County   232

Tompkins County   251

Yates County   273

Supplement   285

Selected Bibliography   292

Index   295

Preface

Hundreds of newspapers were founded in New York State in the nineteenth and twentieth centuries. A few survive to the present day, but most of them have died. Complete holdings of the deceased newspapers are rare, and for many not a single copy survives. For the remainder there exist either long series of issues, with an occasional hiatus, or a few scattered issues—surviving in libraries and newspaper offices or in private collections through sheer good fortune and the wisdom of a few individuals.

The losses through the years are most unfortunate and the surviving materials are treasures, for newspapers are truly "the diary of the community," and for some communities they are the only significant historical source. Recognizing the importance of newspapers as resources for history and other disciplines, and aware of the lack of bibliographic references, the South Central Research Library Council began, nearly a decade ago, to compile a newspaper bibliography for the fourteen counties that it serves—Allegany, Broome, Cayuga, Chemung, Chenango, Cortland, Delaware, Otsego, Schuyler, Seneca, Steuben, Tioga, Tompkins, and Yates.

The South Central Research Library Council, with headquarters in Ithaca, is geographically the second largest of nine research library councils chartered by New York State in the 1960s. One of its major objectives is to facilitate the use of research materials by locating such materials, making them more accessible to the public, and working toward their preservation. With this in mind, the Council's board of trustees recommended a newspaper bibliographic project that would serve as a model in collecting information about community newspapers and providing standardized bibliograpic citations to include the basic information needed by researchers, libraries, and historical societies.

In 1969, a committee representing the library, archival, and historical fields (Selby Gration, Susanne Beaudry, C. Herbert Finch, Harry Stanley, and Sylvia Faibisoff) further defined the scope and details of the project. They determined that the bibliography would include information on all newspapers published in each village, town, and city of the fourteen counties, and that for each newspaper the compilers would include not only complete bibliograpical information—volumes, dates, frequency, pages, page sizes, location—but also information on publishers and editors, politics, noteworthy events in the development of the newspaper. Giles Shepherd of the Cornell University Libraries saw the bibliography as the first step in a state-wide compilation.

That same year they initiated a survey to list all newspapers ever published in each county and to locate surviving issues. Lois

O'Connor and Sylvia Faibisoff gathered complete information on newspapers in Tompkins County, the first to be surveyed, and the Council then approached the New York State Historical Association regarding a cooperative effort to publish the entire bibliography. It was agreed that the material would be published in installments in the Association's quarterly journal, *New York History*. Format and other details were worked out with the journal's editor, Wendell Tripp. The Council's staff and individual compilers gathered data for all the counties, and these were assembled and edited by the staff. The bibliography appeared in *New York History* between April 1971 and April 1974.

The bibliography was extremely well received, but its publication in serial form did present users with the problem of locating and consulting several separate issues of *New York History*. The present volume, which presents all the county bibliographies under one cover, fulfills an original hope of the staff.

To reduce costs, we have re-used the photo-offset negatives used in the original publication. It has thus not been possible to update the bibliography, though newly-detected errors have been corrected. The major addition to the bibliography is a complete name and subject index for all communities and all newspapers mentioned in the bibliography. This has been an arduous task, but one that makes the bibliography much more usable. A number of illustrations have also been added to the reprint, partly for esthetic purposes, but also as makeweights in recasting certain pages.

The decision to use the original offset negatives was influenced by the fact that major collections have not changed hands and that few additional titles have been discovered in the past three years. More important is the work of several organizations in microfilming a number of newspapers cited in the bibliography. These projects do not effect a change in depository of the original newspapers; they do provide additional depositories for copies of the newspapers. It is beyond the capacity of the present work to deal with this continuing process except to note a few of the recent projects affecting the newspapers of the fourteen-county area: The Southern Tier Library System and the South Central Research Library Council have microfilmed newspapers of Allegany, Schuyler, Steuben, and Yates Counties; the New York State Historical Association and the State University College at Oneonta have microfilmed newspapers of Delaware and Otsego Counties; the Finger Lakes Library System and Cornell University have microfilmed newspapers of Chemung, Seneca, Schuyler, and Tioga Counties. Information about specific newspapers may be obtained from these institutions.

The work of preparing this volume has been interrupted by a variety of responsibilities in Ithaca and Cooperstown. On several occasions it rested on the launching pad, the countdown held up for months by a variety of factors. Edmond Menegaux, executive director of the South Central Research Library Council and Minor Wine Thomas, director of the New York State Historical Association, and their respective boards, have been paragons of patience and understanding. The moral and financial support of the boards reflects their awareness of the needs of seekers of information—a vast and heterogeneous group who, in ways large and small, work toward a better understanding of the human condition.

Use of the Bibliography

Newspapers are grouped by county and listed alphabetically by title. For each entry the following information is provided:

Title of newspaper: As it appears on the front page banner. *Frequency of issue:* Indicated by the abbreviation for daily (d), weekly (w), etc. *Place of publication. Dates of publication:* Dates for first and last issues, when verified, with volumes and numbers in parentheses. When no issues have been found to verify date of publication, question marks are inserted. *Changes of title:* When a newspaper changed hands, the title was sometimes changed, though the volume and number remained consecutive. Title changes have been included as well as cross references to the title under which the newspaper's history is given. *Editors and publishers:* The names and dates of editors and publishers, and sometimes printers, as ascertained from extant issues. *Political affiliation:* Included when it can be definitely determined, including neutral or independent positions. *Address of publication:* This appears under the heading "Comment." *Format:* Variations in size and number of pages. *Subscription price and circulation. Location:* The name of each institution or individual holding issues of the newspaper, with inclusive dates of holdings. Examples:

NCortHi: [My 24, 1900–Mr 5, 1925 (2:51–27:42)]; Ap 9–23, My 7–Jl 24, 1931 (1:17–19, 21–26). This indicates that the Cortland County Historical Society holds issues of May 24, 1900 through March 5, 1925 (vol. 2, no. 51 through vol. 27, no. 42) [brackets show that the run is incomplete], and issues of April 9 through 23 and May 7 through July 24, 1931 (vol. 1, no. 17 through vol. 1, no. 19; vol. 1, no. 21 through vol. 1, no. 26).

NIC/MMN: Ja 21, 1857–D 3, 1862//(1:1–5:52). This indicates that the Maps, Microtext, and Newspaper Division of Cornell University Libraries holds issues of the newspaper for the dates January 21, 1857 through December 3, 1862 (vol. 1, no. 1 through vol. 5, no. 52). The slanted lines (//), indicate that holdings for those dates are complete.

Abbreviations

Abbreviations of Locations

Cortland, N.Y.; **NCortD**—Cortland Democrat Office, Cortland, N.Y.; **NCort/ Heppell**—Roger C. Heppell, Cortland, N.Y.; **NCortHi**—Cortland County Historical Society, Cortland, N.Y.; **NCort/Kenyon**—Floyd Kenyon, Higgins Supply Co., McGraw, N.Y.; **NCort/Mullen**—Mr. and Mrs. Harry Mullen, 2 Glyndon Ave., Cortland, N.Y.; **NCortSt**—Cortland Standard Office, Cortland, N.Y.; **NCortUC**— State University College at Cortland, Cortland, N.Y.; **NCu/Patriot Office**—Cuba Patriot and Free Press Office, Cuba, N.Y.; **NDe**—Cannon Free Library, Delhi, N.Y.; **NDeD**—The Delaware Republican Express Office, Delhi, N.Y.; **NDeHi**—The Delaware County Historical Association, Delhi, N.Y.; **NDep**—Deposit Free Library, Deposit, N.Y.; **NDrS**—Southworth Public Library, Dryden, N.Y.; **NDun**—Women's Study Club and Library, Dundee, N.Y.; **NDun/Observer**— Dundee Observer Office, Dundee, N.Y.; **NEd**—Edmeston Public Library, Edmeston, N.Y.; **NEm**—Steele Memorial Library, Elmira, N.Y.; **NEm/Hardeman**—Edward Hardeman, Elmira, N.Y.; **NEmHi**—Chemung County Historical Society, Elmira, N.Y.; **NEmS**—Star-Gazette, Elmira, N.Y.; **NEn**—George F. Johnson Memorial Library, Endicott, N.Y.; **NFi**—Fillmore Wide-Awake Club Library, Fillmore, N.Y.; **NFi/Observer**—Northern Allegany Observer Office, Fillmore, N.Y.; **NFl/Kelly**— Mrs. Iva M. Kelly, Main St., Fleischmanns, N.Y.; **NFra**—Franklin Free Library, Franklin, N.Y.; **NFra/Finch**—Mrs. Lynn Finch, 61 Main St., Franklin, N.Y.; **NFri**—Friendship Free Library, Friendship, N.Y.; **NFri/Marilyn Lester**— Marilyn Lester, Friendship, N.Y.; **NGeno/Cummings**—Gordon J. Cummings, King Ferry, N.Y.; **NGil/Gilbertsville** Free Library, Gilbertsville, N.Y.; **NGr**— Moore Memorial Library, Greene, N.Y.; **NGro**—Groton Public Library, Groton, N.Y.; **NGro/Town Clerk's Office**—Town Clerk's Office, Groton, N.Y.; **NHa**— Hammondsport Public Library, Hammondsport, N.Y.; **NHan**—Louise Adelia Read Memorial Library, Hancock, N.Y.; **NHanH**—Hancock Herald Office, Hancock, N.Y.; **NHar**—Kinney Memorial Library, Hartwick, N.Y.; **NHom**— Phillips Free Library, Homer, N.Y.; **NHor**—Hornell Public Library, Hornell, N.Y.; **NHorT**—The Evening Tribune Office, Hornell, N.Y.; **NHrC**—Chemung Valley Reporter, Horseheads, N.Y.; **NI/Gazette**—The Good Times Gazette Office, Ithaca, N.Y.; **NI/TCB Office**—TCB Office, Ithaca, N.Y.; **NIC/ILR**—Industrial and Labor Relations Library, Cornell University, Ithaca, N.Y.; **NIC/Mann**—Albert R. Mann Library, Cornell University, Ithaca, N.Y.; **NIC/MMN**—Maps, Microtexts and Newspaper Division, Cornell University Libraries, Ithaca, N.Y.; **NIC/Rare**—Rare Books Division, Cornell University Libraries, Ithaca, N.Y.; **NIC/RHA**—Regional History and Archives Division, Cornell University Libraries, Ithaca, N.Y.; **NIDeW**—DeWitt Historical Society, Ithaca, N.Y.; **NIn**—Interlaken Public Library, Interlaken, N.Y.; **NJoh**—Your Home Public Library, Johnson City, N.Y.; **NLi**—Lisle Free Library, Lisle, N.Y.; **NMac**—Lamont Memorial Library, McGraw, N.Y.; **NMara**—Peck Memorial Library, Marathon, N.Y.; **NMara/Grunfeld**—Walter Grunfeld, 10 Main St., Marathon, N.Y.; **NMargC**—Catskill Mountain News Office, Margaretville, N.Y.; **NMill**— Veteran's Branch of Steele Memorial Library, Millport, N.Y.; **NMn**—Montour Falls Memorial Library, Montour Falls, N.Y.; **NMnHi**—Schuyler County Historical Society, Montour Falls, N.Y.; **NMor**—Powers Library, Moravia, N.Y.; **NMor/ MoR**—Moravia Republican Register Office, Moravia, N.Y.; **NMrr**—Village Library of Morris, Morris, N.Y.; **NNb**—New Berlin Library, New Berlin, N.Y.; **NNbG**— New Berlin Gazette Office, New Berlin, N.Y.; **NNfPl**—Newfield Public Library, Newfield, N.Y.; **NNich/Burtis Everett**—Burtis Everett, Nichols, N.Y.; **NNich/John Edsall**—John Edsall, Nichols, N.Y.;**NNo**—Guernsey Memorial Library, Norwich, N.Y.; **NNoHi**—Chenango County Historical Museum, Norwich, N.Y.;

NNoUn—Chenango Union Office, Norwich, N.Y.; NOn—Huntington Public Library, Oneonta, N.Y.; NOnHC—Hartwick College Library, Oneonta, N.Y.; NOnHi—Upper Susquehanna Historical Society, Oneonta, N.Y.; NOnHS—Oneonta High School Library, Oneonta, N.Y.; NOnStar—The Oneonta Star Office, Oneonta, N.Y.; NOnSUCO—Milne Library, State University College at Oneonta, Oneonta, N.Y.; NOt—Otego Free Library, Otego, N.Y.; NOt/Connor—Mrs. Chris Connor, Otego, N.Y.; NOv—Edith B. Ford Memorial Library, Ovid, N.Y.; NOwHi—Tioga County Historical Society Museum, Owego, N.Y.; NOx—Oxford Memorial Library, Oxford, N.Y.; NPP/Town of Erwin Museum—Town of Erwin Museum, Painted Post, N.Y.; NPy—Penn Yan Public Library, Penn Yan, N.Y.; NPyC—Chronicle Express Office, Penn Yan, N.Y.; NPyCl—County Clerk's Office, Yates County Court House, Penn Yan, N.Y.; NPyHi—Yates County Genealogical Historical Society, Penn Yan, N.Y.; NRC/Wayuga—Wayuga Community News, Inc., Red Creek, N.Y.; NRo—Roxbury Public Library, Roxbury, N.Y.; NRS/Palmer—Mr. and Mrs. LeRoy Palmer, Richfield Springs, N.Y.; NRu/Mable Blodgett—Mable Blodgett, Rushville, N.Y.; NRu/Robert Moody—Robert Moody, Rushville, N.Y.; NRU—Rush Rhees Library, University of Rochester, Rochester, N.Y.; NRU/Rare Books Division—Rare Books Division, University of Rochester, Rochester, N.Y.; NRus/Mrs. Oliver J. Williams—Mrs. Oliver J. Williams, Rushford, N.Y.; NSenHi—Seneca Falls Historical Society, Seneca Falls, N.Y.; NSen/Reveille—Waterloo Reveille Office, Waterloo, N.Y.; NShe—Sherburne Public Library, Sherburne, N.Y.; NShw/Cleaveland—Mrs. Eleanor Cleaveland, Sherwood, N.Y.; NSi—Sidney Public Library, Sidney, N.Y.; NSiHi—Sidney Historical Association, Sidney Public Library Building, Sidney, N.Y.; NSiT—Tri-Town News Office, Sidney, N.Y.; NSNB—South New Berlin Free Library, South New Berlin, N.Y.; NSpe—Spencer Library, Spencer, N.Y.; NSpe/Alice B. Pope—Alice B. Pope, Spencer, N.Y.; NSpe/Payne Museum—George Payne Museum, Spencer, N.Y.; NSpe/Theresa Cortright—Theresa Cortright, Spencer, N.Y.; NSt—Stamford Village Library, Stamford, N.Y.; NStM—Mirror-Recorder Office, Stamford, N.Y.; NStV/Cooper—Mrs. Clara H. Cooper, Sterling Valley, N.Y.; NSyU—Syracuse University Libraries, Syracuse, N.Y.; NT—Ulysses Philomathic Society, Trumansburg, N.Y.; NTu/Jacob—Mrs. R. Leone Jacob, Tunnel, N.Y.; NUS—Springport Free Library, Union Springs, N.Y.; NUS/Stryker—Mr. and Mrs. Harold E. Stryker, Union Springs, N.Y.; NVes—Vestal Free Library, Vestal, N.Y.; NVes/News Office—The Vestal News Office, Vestal, N.Y.; NWa—William B. Ogden Free Library, Walton, N.Y.; NWaHi—Walton Historical Society, William B. Ogden Free Library Building, Walton, N.Y.; NWaR—Walton Reporter Office, Walton, N.Y.; NWat—Waterloo Library and Historical Society, Waterloo, N.Y.; NWav—Waverly Free Library, Waverly, N.Y.; NWee/Finley—Howard Finley, Weedsport, N.Y.; NWel—David A. Howe Public Library, Wellsville, N.Y.; NWelHi—Thelma Rogers Genealogical and Historical Society, Wellsville, N.Y.; NWel/Mrs. Herbert Bliss—Mrs. Herbert D. Bliss, Wellsville, N.Y.; NWel/Reporter Office—Wellsville Daily Reporter Office, Wellsville, N.Y.; NWhit—Whitesville Free Library, Whitesville, N.Y.; NWhP—Mary Wilcox Memorial Library, Whitney Point, N.Y.; NWi—Windsor Free Library, Windsor, N.Y.; NWi/Standard Office—Windsor Standard Office, Windsor, N.Y.

GILBERTSVILLE EAGLE
AND TRUE
DEMOCRATIC AND
PATRIOTIC REFLECTOR

[COPYRIGHT SECURED.]

VOL. II. No. 2   DATED AT SATAN'S HOLLYHAWK DEN, GILBERTSVILLE, 1897.   PRICE, ONE DOLLAR.

In the year 1897 of the Christian Era, and year 75 of the Satanic Era.

Second Epistle of a Son of His Satanic Majesty's True Creator or Devil (all one) to Jew, Christian, Mormon and all other Heathen Sects of this little Globe. Greeting.

Published only as necessity seems to require at
ONE DOLLAR PER YEAR IN ADVANCE.

All orders for same and subscriptions must be addressed to
J. LAKIN GILBERT, Gilbertsville, Otsego Co., N. Y.
Editor and Proprietor.

The true creator and one only spiritual power has seen fit to reveal to me that Heaven, Earth and Hell are all one and the Christian Bible also proves this as it was said to the Apostle that the Kingdom of Heaven was within you, showing it was with us here. It says also of Christ that he was crucified dead and buried, descended into Hell (the grave) and rose again—all of course here else bible and reason of no account.

Some thirty years ago I was inspired to pray to the all wise Creator for a peep into the Hell of the Scriptures. After a sound sleep of three hours I was awakened by the village church fire-bells. The fire destroyed twenty-eight buildings in our small village and since that prayer I have never doubted where Hell was, though I have contended at times that it was a much more desirable place than Heaven, but later communion with my Creator convinces me that Heaven, Earth and Hell are all one, and so it is a waste of time to pray for a passport to Hell or Heaven, so long as they are both here same as the earth.

In my first epistle I had assurances from unexpected quarters that my position as to the true religion of reason and good works was sound and would eventually sweep the whole earth, but I soon found it was the Creator's will to make my work slow and in the end the more sure.

The trouble I now see is with the great and only spiritual power which has pleased this power to give success to Judaism, Christianity, Mormonism, Mahomedanism and all other abominable systems of belief in Moses, Holy God, ghosts, witches, &c., and so I conclude that Reason is no where when confronted with spiritual power of the Creator that he deemed necessary so long as the world was in such gross ignorance and heathenism. But it is revealed to me that a change is coming that will satisfy all that this world is not "all a fleeting show," and so eventually will be worth a short life in.

That our Creator has given spiritual power to all the false religions of all nations and great peace to all accepting them as true though all of them have been revealed with miracles holy men, holy Gods and holy witches and holy ghosts.

As to creeds in our own land this same spiritual power has been given so that the ministry of all creeds have a good show for followers in that they have learned to denounce and renounce Satan and the Devil.

But our Creator having given reason to mankind makes half our race reject these creeds, notwithstanding all the doom of fire and brimstone threatened, so I conclude that a little spiritual power is given these rejectors with reason so that they also have peace in believing as they do, so none so happy as they who have a witness within their breasts—'he spirit)—convincing them that all is well &c. Our Trinity then consisting of true Creator, Satan and the Devil all one, the same as snow, ice and water are one, is at war with that of the Christian, theirs being made up of Moses, Holy God, Jesus and a Ghost, all of which are only imaginary. The new War of Reason is to be carried on by the sword (bloodless) out of the mouth—plain language—scriptural phrases meaning more and with the aid of the true spirit will in our Creator's own time overcome that sword of Mahomet and Christ that they would have us believe is the key to Heaven and Hell.

And now as to Heaven and Hell so generally believed in by the world I have to say that during my long life of more than three score years, I have been converted to belief in the christian religion several times and aver that in all these conversions I had great peace in believing, until through reason and spiritual power I was converted back to Satan where I found still more peace in believing.

Though brought up in the Orthodox religion, I have

been directed by my maker to examine well all the bibles and text books of the different nations and sects, and while I have found in all some good moral teachings, I am satisfied that all of them have been gotten up for the benefit of Monarchs, Kings, Popes and Bishops, and aspirants to honors in every age, and the murder system of war has been the great protector of these nations and their biblical religions.

On reconversion to Satan I was inclined to believe that Hell the supposed residence of my master, the Devil, was far more desirable than Moses, Heaven, and hence my prayers to be admitted there. But upon allowing reason (the best of nature's gifts) to aid me in communion with my maker, I have found that Heaven and Hell, both are really only conditions, and not to be found in the universe.

Our Jew Scripture novelists knowing nothing of astronomy only taught of two places besides the earth—the one Heaven and the other Hell.

Knowing my Creator has so many worlds fit for residence, I have not lifted a prayer to know which is the more desirable feeling satisfied that none of them will be cursed with military and religious systems, so cruel and heathen as in this. In all I trust the religion of Reason and works will be the only true, and plain language, the sword out of the mouth, will take the place of cannon and powder magazines.

Reason should teach all that he who gives life only should be allowed to take it again, and all the nations and individuals who indulge in it must be defying the Almighty and may expect little mercy at his hands. If punishment in this world is not meeted out sufficiently, surely it will come hereafter. Many born white in this world I conclude are black in the next, being born again of black parents, and who of white race will not shudder at such a doom ahead for sins here. When this world was first populated four pairs of human beings were placed here, by the Almighty. And so we have the Black race, the White, the Yellow and the Red, and I am satisfied many worlds have these same races and our inhabitors by good works here will have choice of the best race on the planet awaiting them.

That many of the yellow and red races, will by good works here will be added to the white race hereafter, as in all reason it must be the most desirable.

The tale of Adam and Eve, in the garden of Eden, places beyond doubt, Satan's claims as maker and ruler of the universe. Moses God declared that Adam

---

A number of exotic and short-lived newspapers were published in central New York in the nineteenth century. This issue of a Satanic newspaper published in Gilbertsville is among the sole survivors. From the collections of the New York State Historical Association, Cooperstown.

ALLEGANY COUNTY

THE ABOUT TOWN (semi-m) Alfred. O 15, 1970 to date (1:1 to date). *Pub*: Alfred Seventh Day Baptist Youth Fellowship. *Ed*: David Snyder. *Format*: Four pages 8½" x 14". *Price and Circ*: Delivered free to all village residents. *Comment*: Address: P.O. Box 1191, Alfred. *Loc*: NAlf/Baptist Parish House: O 15, 1970 to date (1:1 to date).

THE ACADEMIC GAZETTE (m) Wellsville. Je 1885–? (1:1–?). *Format*: Sixteen pages 10" x 15". *Loc*: NWel: Je 1885 (1:1).

THE ALFRED SUN (w) Alfred. D 6, 1883–Je 25, 1970// (1:1–87:26). *Title changes*: Alfred Sun D 6, 1883–S 28, 1885; Daily Alfred Sun S 29–O 1, 1885; The Alfred Sun O 8, 1885–Je 25, 1970. *Pub*: Sun Publishing Co. 1883–1907 (Lewis W. Niles Ja 1–Ja 8, 1885; Frank A. Crumb Ja 15, 1885–?; W. H. Satterlee O 6, 1887–Ja 12, 1888; Frank A. Crumb and F. S. Whitford 1896–1907); Sun Publishing Assoc., Ltd. 1907–1951; Eugene T. Van Horn and Aurabeth E. Van Horn 1951–Je 1970. *Ed*: John M. Mosher 1883–1884, 1894–1895; L. E. Livermore 1885–1888; W. H. Satterlee 1888–1889; J. J. Merrill 1890, 1894–1895; Frank A. Crumb and F. S. Whitford 1896–1907; Frank A. Crumb 1907–1951; Eugene T. Van Horn 1951–Je 25, 1970. *Pol*: Started as a weekly non-partisan newspaper then became Republican. *Format*: Four to eight pages, varying sizes 15" x 20", 17" x 24", 19½" x 25", 10½" x 14½", 15" x 22", 12" x 17½". *Price*: $3.50 per year. *Circ*: 746 (1960); 677 (1963). *Comment*: Published at Sabbath Recorder Building, Alfred Centre until 1895, then 11 South Main Street, Alfred. *Loc*: NAlfAU: microfilm 1958–1970 (75:1–87:26); [bound 1900–1968]. NAlfAg: microfilm Ja 5, 1956–D 1967 (73:1–8:52); D 6, 1883–N 19, 1885 (1:1–2:?); O 1887–1899; 1927–Je 25, 1970. NAlf/Sun Publishing Co.: microfilm D 1967–Je 25, 1970.

ALLEGANY COUNTY ADVOCATE see *ALLEGANY REPUBLICAN* 1842–1856

1

THE ALLEGANY COUNTY DEMOCRAT (w) Wellsville, Genesee.
S 16, 1867–1965// (1:1–98:?). *Title changes*: *Allegany Democrat* S
16, 1867–Ja 1882; *The Allegany County Democrat* F 8, 1882–1965.
Pub and Ed: Myron E. Eddy and Charles F. White 1867–1874; William W. Nichols Ag 21, 1874–F 9, 1887; William W. Nichols and
A. E. Cowles 1882–F 2, 1887; A. E. Cowles F 2, 1887–?; Hubert D.
Bliss 1940–Ap 1963; Julia Bliss 1963–1965. *Pol*: Democrat. *Format*:
Four to eight pages, varying sizes 17½" x 23", 20" x 23½", 20" x 26".
Price: $1.50 per year. *Circ*: 350 (1867); 1,800 (1879). *Comment*:
"The Allegany Democrat was founded on the 16th of September, 1867,
by Williams & Barton, at Wellsville. . . . Previous to its publication
there was no Democratic paper in the county. . . . The Democrat
started with a circulation of three hundred and fifty copies, and was
kept alive at first by the private purses of Hon. Martin Grover, Hon.
M. D. Champlain and other leading Democrats of the county. The
material of the office consisted of one old Washington hand press, upon which the newspaper and job work was printed, about four hundred pounds of metal type, a few fonts of wood letter, two imposing
stones and a small number of other articles, the cash value of which
would not exceed $600. The Democratic Party in the county was
greatly in the minority and the paper struggled along under adverse
circumstances appearing occasionally, as the publisher had means to
purchase blank paper. In consequence its circulation fell off rather than
increased. The proprietors became discouraged, and made this remark, which many of the old time Democrats will remember, 'For
Napoleon to have crossed the Alps was an easy matter, compared
with an attempt to establish a Democratic paper in Allegany County'."
(F. W. Beers & Company, *History of Allegany County*, p. 86) Published at Barnes Block, Main Street, Genesee and then Sprague Block,
Main Street, Wellsville. *Loc*: NAng: Ja 2, 1880–N 5, 1890 (29:8–
30:52). NBelC: O 29, 1931 (64:43); F 6, 1936 (69:6); Ap 12, 1951
(84:15); Je 30, 1955 (88:26); D 24, 1959 (92:52); [F 16–D 28, 1961
(94:7–52)]. NBelHi: S 4, 1874 (6:12). NIC/RHA: Ap 26, S 27,
1956 (89:17, 39); Ag 22, 1957 (90:34). NWel: O 6, 1871–O 2, 1874
(3:16–6:16); Ja 4, 1882–Ap. 19, 1893 (22:10–33:24). NWel/Mrs.
Herbert D. Bliss: Ja 3–D 26, 1883 (23:10–24:8); Ja 5–D 28, 1887
(27:8–28:7); Ja 6, 1909–D 29, 1910 (40:29–42:28); Ja 5–D 28,
1950 (83:1–52).

ALLEGANY COUNTY NEWS see *WHITESVILLE NEWS*

ALLEGANY COUNTY REPORTER (w) Angelica, Belmont and
Wellsville. Je 1837–? (1:1–?). *Title changes*: *Angelica Reporter* (Je
1837 (n.s.)–Ag 1856; *Angelica Reporter and Allegany Republican* Ag
26, 1856–1861; *Angelica Reporter* 1862–1870; *Allegany County Reporter* O 1870–?   *Pub and Ed*: William Pitt Angel Je–D
1837; Samuel C. Wilson D 1837–1841; Horace E. Purdy 1841–1844;
Charles Horton 1844–1864; C. F. Dickinson 1864–1865; C. F. Dickinson and G. W. Dickinson 1865–1870; Enos W. Barnes 1875–1888;
The Reporter Co. (Charles M. Barnes and E. Willard Barnes) 1888–
1930. *Pol*: Republican. *Format*: Four to eight pages, varying sizes

20″ x 25½″, 22″ x 28½″, 15″ x 22″. *Price*: $2.00 per year (1837); $1.50 per year (1848); $2.00 per year (1927). *Circ*: 1,200 (1871); 2,500 (1874). *Comment*: Published at Arnold's Brick Block (1868) then at the Reporter Printing House, Wellsville (1874). From 1872 until January 17, 1874 the paper was published in Belmont, and then moved to Wellsville and the *Wellsville Times* (q.v.) was combined with it. *Loc*: NAng: Ag 16, 1837 (n.s. 1:11); D 4, 1839 (3:26); Ap 26, 1843 (6:45); N 20, 1844 (8:23); S 1, 1847 (11:12); Mr 12–19, Ap 3, N 20, D 3, 1850 (13:39, 40, 42; 14:24, 25). NBelC: Je 17, 1862 (26:11); F 1, Mr 15–22, D 13, 1865 (28:32, 38–39; 29:25); Ja 9–16, 30, F 13, 27, Mr 20, Ap 24, My 8, 1867 (30:26–27, 29, 31, 33, 36, 41, 43). NIC/MMN: microfilm Ag 16, 1837 (1:11); D 4, 1839 (3:26); Ap 26, 1843 (6:45); N 20, 1844 (8:23); S 1, 1847 (11:12); S 11, 1849 (13:13); F 26, Mr 12–19, Ap 2, N 26–D 3, 1850 (13:37, 39–40, 42; 14:24, 25); [Jl 25, 1854–D 6, 1859 (18:6–23:27)]; Ap 17, 1860 (23:45); Ap 23, 1861 (24:46); My 27, Je 24, N 11, 1862 (25:50; 26:2, 21); [Ja 13, 1863–O 12, 1870 (26:29–34:15)]. NWel: microfilm: Ag 16, 1837 (n.s. 1:11); D 4, 1839 (3:26); Ap 26, 1843 (6:45); N 20, 1844 (8:23); S 1, 1847 (11:12); S 11, 1849 (13:13); F 26, Mr 12–19, Ap 2, N 26–D 3, 1850 (13:37; 39–40, 42; 14:24, 25); [Jl 25, 1854–D 6, 1859 (18:6–23:27)]; Ap 17, 1860 (23:45); Ap 23, 1861 (24:46); My 27, Je 24, N 11, 1862 (25:50; 26:2, 21); [Ja 13, 1863–Je 25, 1930 (26:29–86th year)].

ALLEGANY COUNTY REPUBLICAN (w) Angelica. Ap 26, 1877–? (1:1–?). *Title changes*: *Angelica Advertiser* Ap 26, 1877–Jl 31, 1879; *Allegany County Republican and Angelica Advertiser* Ag 8, 1879–Ja 9, 1880; *Allegany County Republican* Ja 16, 1880–? *Pub and Ed*: H. C. Scott Ap 1877–Jl 1879; LaMonte Gardiner Raymond Ag 8, 1879–Ap 1898. *Pol*: Republican. *Format*: Four pages, varying sizes 20″ x 25″, 17″ x 24″. *Price*: $1.50 per year. *Comment*: Motto: "Our Country First; Party Afterward." Published from the Angelica Court House. Once each year, Raymond issued a "red letter edition" devoted entirely to one story or issue, such as "The Evolution of the Railway." He embellished these issues frequently with woodcuts he carved himself with his jacknife. On January 7, 1881 LaMonte Raymond switched series numbering from volume four to volume sixty-one without apology or explanation. On January 14, he explained that the new numbering reflected the continuous publication of a newspaper at the Angelica Court House since January 1820. *Loc*: NIC/MMN: microfilm: [My 3, 1877–Ja 14, 1881 (1:2–61:2)]. NNang: [My 3, 1877–Mr 18, 1898 (1:2–78:11)]. NWel: microfilm: My 3, 1877–Jl 31, 1879 (1:2–3:15); Ag 15, 1879–Mr 25, 1898 (3:17–78:12).

ALLEGANY COUNTY REPUBLICAN, Friendship, N. Y., see *FRIENDSHIP REGISTER*

ALLEGANY DEMOCRAT see *ALLEGANY COUNTY DEMOCRAT*

ALLEGANY REPUBLICAN (w) Angelica. Je 1826–? (1:1–?). *Pub and Ed*: Samuel C. Wilson. *Pol*: Republican. *Format*: Four pages 12″ x 20½″. *Price*: $2.50 per year. *Loc*: NAng: N 22, 1826 (1:24).

ALLEGANY REPUBLICAN (w) Angelica. Ja 1842–Ag 21, 1856// (1:1–14:2). *Title changes*: *Allegany County Advocate* Ja 1842–Ja 20, 1853; *Whig and Advocate* Ja 27, 1853–Ap 24, 1856; *Allegany Republican* My 1, 1856–Ag 21, 1856. *Pub and Ed*: Erastus S. Palmer 1842–1850; Ellroy and S. Churchill 1851; Peter S. Norris 1852; William H. and Charles M. Beecher Ja 27, 1853–Ag 24, 1854; William H. Beecher Ag 31, 1854–Ap 24, 1856; Charles M. Beecher My 1–Ag 21, 1856. *Pol*: Republican. *Format*: Four pages, varying sizes 17½″ x 23½″, 16″ x 23½″. *Price*: $1.50 per year (1849); $2.00 per year (1850–1853); $1.00 per year (1853–1854); $1.50 per year (1854). *Comment*: Published from the North Side of Main Street, "a few rods west of the Exchange Hotel." Motto of the *Whig and Advocate*: "Freedom of Speech, and Freedom of Press, for the Sake of Freedom." According to William J. Doty (*Historic Annals of Southwestern New York*, 1940), *The Allegany County Advocate* was founded in 1842 by Erastus S. Palmer. *Loc*: NAng: Ja 11, Jl 26, S 6, 1850 (8:30; 9:6, 11); Mr 21, Ag 1, 1851 (9:39; 10:6); F 27, Ap 29, Jl 15, S 9, 1852 (10:34, 43; 11:2, 10); Ja 27, My 5, 1853 (11:28, 42). NBel/William C. Green: Ag 2, S 6, 1848 (7:4, 12); My 30, Je 20, 1849 (7:50; 8:1). NWel: microfilm: Ap 18, 1849 (7:44); Ja 11, Jl 26, Ag 2, S 6, 1850 (8:30; 9:6, 7, 11); Mr 21, Ag 1, 1851 (9:39; 10:6); F 27, Ap 29, Jl 15, S 9, 1852 (10:34, 43; 11:2, 10); Ja 27, My 5, 1853 (11:28, 42).

ALMOND GLEANER (w) Almond. Ap 24, 1901–? (1:1–?). *Pub and Ed*: F. W. Ames. *Format*: Eight pages 15″ x 22″. *Loc*: NAl: D 31, 1902 (2:37); Mr 25, 1903 (2:49).

THE AMATEUR COURIER (m) Cuba. Jl 1877–Je 1878//(?) (1:1–2:6). *Pub and Ed*: R. W. Burnett 1877–1878. *Format*: Four to eight pages 4¾″ x 7″. *Price*: 10¢ per year. *Comment*: *The Amateur Courier* announced a six month suspension of publication in its June 1878 issue. It is not known if it did resume publication, as promised, in January 1879. *Loc*: NCu: Jl 1877–Je 1878 (1:1–2:6).

ANDOVER ADVERTISER see *ANDOVER ADVERTISER AND FREE PRESS*

ANDOVER ADVERTISER AND FREE PRESS (w) Andover. 1868–? (1:1–?). *Title changes*: *The Andover Advertiser* 1868–Mr 6, 1873; *Andover Weekly Advertiser* Mr 13, 1873–My 7, 1874; *Andover Advertiser and Free Press* My 14, 1874–? *Pub and Ed*: E. S. Barnard 1868–1870; E. S. Barnard and Underhill 1870; E. S. Barnard 1871–1874; E. B. Galatian and E. S. Barnard My 14, 1874–? *Pol*: Republican. *Format*: Four to eight pages, varying sizes 13″ x 18½″, 18½″ x 25″, 20½″ x 26¾″. *Comment*: Published from an office over Russell and Wolcott's Auction Rooms, Andover. When the *Andover Weekly Advertiser* merged with the *Free Press* on May 14, 1874, two serial numbers appear, volume 6 number 21 (*The Advertiser*) and volume

22 number 9 (the *Free Press*). *Loc*: NAn: Je 3, 1869–N 12, 1874 (1:28–6:47 or 22:34).

ANDOVER NEWS (w) Andover. Ag 31, 1887 to date (1:1 to date). *Pub and Ed*: Hamilton C. Norris and George L. Tucker, Jr. 1887–1888; Hamilton C. Norris and John M. Mosher 1889–1890; John M. Mosher and Sidney H. Greene 1890–1899; J. Harvey Backus 1899–1916; J. Harvey and Claire C. Backus 1916–1934; Claire C. Backus 1934–1961; Ralph A. and Jean Backus Allen Ja 1, 1961 to date. *Pol*: Independent, then Republican, then Progressive, then Democrat. *Format*: Four to eight pages, varying sizes 14½″ x 19½″, 13″ x 19½″, 14½″ x 21½″, 12½″ x 17½″. *Price*: $3.00 per year (1960); $3.50 per year (1970). *Circ*: 1,000 (1896); 649 (1960); 800 (1970). *Comment*: Published at Snyder and Clark Building, corner of Main and Elm Streets (1887–1903); The News Printing House, Main Street (1904 to date). *Loc*: NAn: S 7, 1887–O 26, 1892 (1:2–6:12). NAn/ News Office: Ag 31, 1887 to date (1:1 to date).

ANDOVER WEEKLY ADVERTISER see *ANDOVER ADVERTISER AND FREE PRESS*

ANGELICA ADVERTISER see *ALLEGANY COUNTY REPUBLICAN*

ANGELICA ADVOCATE (w) Angelica. Jl 1901–Je 12, 1958// (1:1–59:52). *Pub and Ed*: Edwin P. Mills Ag 6, 1908–O 27, 1921; J. G. Lauritzen N 3, 1921–Ap 26, 1923; L. L. Stillwell My 3, 1923–1956; Dorothea C. Stillwell and L. L. Stillwell 1956–Je 1958. *Pol*: Republican. *Format*: Eight pages, varying sizes 15″ x 21″, 12″ x 18½″. *Price*: $1.00 per year (1914); $1.25 per year (1917); $2.00 per year (1925); $2.50 per year (1948). *Comment*: Merged with the *Belmont Dispatch* July 3, 1958. *Loc*: NAng: Ag 8, 1908–Je 29, 1939 (8:2–40:52); Jl 3, 1941–My 29, 1958 (43:1–58:52). NWelHi: F 26, 1948 (48:36).

ANGELICA REPORTER (w) Angelica. 1834–1836// (volumes 1–3). *Pub and Ed*: William Pitt Angel. *Format*: Four pages 14½″ x 21½″. *Price*: $2.50 per year. *Comment*: We have located only one issue of this edition of the *Angelica Reporter* published by William Pitt Angel. The paper allegedly lasted for a brief period. Angel started a new series of the newspaper under the same title on June 8, 1837, which became the *Allegany County Reporter* (q.v.). *Loc*: NAng: (O) ?, 1836 (v. 3). See also *Allegany County Reporter*.

ANGELICA REPORTER AND ALLEGANY REPUBLICAN see *ALLEGANY COUNTY REPORTER*

ANGELICA REPUBLICAN (w) Angelica. O 3, 1820–? *Pub*: Franklin Coudery. *Comment*: Although referred to as the *Allegany Republican* by William J. Doty in *Historic Annals of Southwestern New York*, p. 933, Brigham, in *History and Bibliography of American Newspapers*, 1690–1820, located the November 1 and December issues for 1820 in the American Antiquarian Society and cited the paper as the *Angelica Republican.* Possibly continued until 1822. No issues located in Allegany County.

ANGELICA REPUBLICAN (w) Angelica. D 6, 1837–? (1:1–?). *Loc*: NAng: D 6, 1837; F 3, Mr 10, 1838 (1:1, 7, 10).

THE ANGELICA REPUBLICAN (w?) Angelica. D 22, 1871–? (1:1–?). *Pub and Ed*: Peter S. Norris D 22, 1871–Ap 1875; A. W. Phillips and Co.; A. W. Phillips and Clark. *Pol*: Republican. *Format*: Four pages 13" x 17½". *Comment*: The beginning date of this newspaper is based on information taken from William J. Doty's *Historic Annals of Southwestern New York.* Doty also states that the plant was destroyed by fire in June 1876. *Loc*: NAng: S 29, 1876 (5:41).

ANGELICA REPUBLICAN AND ALLEGANY WHIG (irregular) Angelica. Je 1883–? (1:1–?). *Pub and Ed*: Thomas Carrier. *Pol*: Whig. *Format*: Four pages 14½" x 21". *Loc*: NAng: Je 14, Je 21, S 20, O 20, 1837 (4:1, 2, 8, 12).

ANGELICA REPUBLICAN AND FARMERS' and MECHANICS' PRESS (w) Angelica. Je 23, 1831–? (1:1–?). *Pub and Ed*: Benjamin Franklin Smead Je 23, 1831–? *Pol*: Republican. *Format*: Four pages 14½" x 21". *Price*: $2.50 per year. *Loc*: NAl: Ja 30, 1833 (2:32). NAng: Je 30, Jl 7, S 15, 29, 1831 (1:2, 3, 13, 15).

THE BELFAST BLAZE (w) Belfast. 1899–Ag 26, 1970// (1:1–69:35). *Pub and Ed*: Peter J. Quinn 1899–1900; E. Chandler Bristol 1900–1935; Edgar L. Miller 1936; W. Oran Hall 1937–Ag 1, 1940; John L. Kee Ag 1940–1953; Robert W. Nesbit 1953–O 17, 1957; Sanders Publications O 25, 1957–Ag 26, 1970 (William B. Sanders, ed., 1957–1966; Donald R. Sanders, ed., 1966–Ag 26, 1970). *Pol*: Independent. *Format*: Four to eight pages, varying sizes 20" x 26", 17" x 22", 12" x 17", 14" x 21½", 16" x 21½". *Price*: $1.25 per year (1900); $1.50 per year (1919); $2.50 per year (1951); $3.00 per year (1956); $4.00 per year (1960); $5.00 per year (1970). *Circ*: 560 (1960); 470 (1970). *Comment*: First published at the Bristol Block, Main Street and then by the Northern Allegany Observer Printing Office in Geneseo. The *Northern Allegany Observer* maintained a news office in Fillmore. Except for the difference in title and volume numbers, the *Belfast Blaze* was identical in content to the *Northern Allegany Observer. Loc*: NBe: Ja 11, F 15, 1900 (1:15, 20); Mr 6, 1902 (3:23); Je 1, 1916–Ag 26, 1970 (17:35–68:52). NFi/Observer Office: Ja 2, 1958–Ag 26, 1970 (58:1–69:35). *See also* p. 285

BELFAST BULLETIN (w) Belfast. My 4, 1910–? (1:1–?). *Pub and Ed*: E. Paul Markham. *Format*: Eight pages 14" x 22". *Price*: $1.25 per year (1910). *Loc*: NBe: Je 8, 1910 (1:6).

THE BELFAST CHAMPION (w) Belfast. Mr 26, 1891–? (1:1–?). *Pub and Ed*: Mrs. M. L. Rumpff. *Format*: Four pages 17½" x 24". *Comment*: Probably a temperance newspaper. Mrs. Rumpff, a member of the Women's Christian Temperance Union, also published *Every Week* (q.v.) in Angelica. *Loc*: NBe: My 28, 1891 (1:10).

THE BELFAST PATRIOT see *THE CUBA PATRIOT AND FREE PRESS*

BELMONT COURIER (w) Belmont. Ja 1, 1898–? (1:1–?). *Pub and Ed*: Virgil A. Willard Ja 1, 1898–? *Pol*: Prohibition. *Format*: Eight pages 13″ x 20″. *Price*: $1.00 per year. *Loc*: NBel: Ja 28, 1898–D 29, 1899 (1:4–2:52). NBelC: Ap 11, My 2, 1902 (5:15, 18). NBel/William C. Green: S 2, 1898 (1:35); Ap 19, 1901 (4:16).

BELMONT DISPATCH see *THE DISPATCH*

BELMONT WEEKLY DISPATCH see *THE DISPATCH*

BOLIVAR BREEZE (w) Bolivar. Ag 29, 1891–O 14, 1965// (1:1–76:8). *Pub*: John P. Herrick Ag 29, 1891–Jl 27, 1911; Bolivar Breeze, Inc. Ag 3, 1911–O 16, 1924; Frank A. Herrick O 23, 1924–N 6 1946; Mr. and Mrs. Glen W. McCoy N 6, 1946–O 29, 1953; Jack B. Moore, N 5, 1953–Jl 1, 1954; Breeze Publishing Co. Jl 8, 1954–Mr 13, 1958; Allegany Printing Co. Mr 13, 1958– O 14, 1965. *Ed*: John P. Herrick Ag 29, 1891–O 16, 1923; Frank A. Herrick Ag 13, 1911—N 6, 1946; Mr. and Mrs. Glen W. McCoy N 6, 1946–O 29, 1953; Jack B. Moore N 5, 1953–Jl 1, 1954; Jack B. Moore and Robert J. Wilson Jl 8, 1954–Ja 10, 1957; Robert J. Wilson Ja 17, 1957–Mr 6, 1958; Robert Schnettler Mr 13, 1958–Jl 11, 1963; Marilyn L. Lester Jl 18, 1963–O 14, 1965. *Pol*: Independent. *Format*: Four to eight pages, varying sizes 13″ x 19″, 14″ x 22″, 17″ x 23″, 15″ x 21″, 16″ x 21″, 12″ x 17″. *Comment*: The paper was published from the second floor of the Hoyt Building, the Masonic Temple (1899), and the Allegany Printing Co., Main Street. *Loc*: NBelC: Ap 8, 29, 1965 (75th year). NBo: [Ag 27, 1892–O 14, 1965 (21:1–76:8)].

CANASERAGA TIMES (w) Canaseraga. N 29, 1873–O 29, 1942// (1:1–75:27). *Pub and Ed*: H. C. Scott 1873–1877; William H. Barnum 1877–Mr 1885; Frank S. Miller Ap 3, 1885–1911; Allegany Printing Co. 1911–1921 (Frank S. Miller, Manager and Ed.); Guy Chilson Mr 4, 1921–1925; H. N. Jeffries 1925–1931; Russell J. Brewer 1933–1936; Burt's Printing Service 1936–O 29, 1942 (William R. Burt, Ed.). *Pol*: Democrat. *Format*: Four to twelve pages, varying sizes 19″ x 23″, 20″ x 25½″, 15″ x 22″. *Price*: $1.00 per year (thru 1909); $1.50 per year (1920); $2.00 per year (1921); $1.50 per year (early 1930's); $1.00 per year (1936–1942). *Circ*: 600 (1875). *Comment*: Published at Boyd's Block, Canaseraga (1873)then moved to Main Street, Canaseraga in the 1920s. In 1936 published at Burt's Printing Service, Dalton, New York, Livingston County. From 1936 through 1942 the paper was printed in Dalton and mailed to subscribers. William Burt maintained a news office and a reporter in Canaseraga. The paper was discontinued because his help left to join the armed services. *Loc*: NCans: N 29, 1873–Ap 24, 1903 (1:1–30:52); My 5, 1905–O 26, 1906 (33:1–34:26); My 7, 1909–Ap 1918 (34 [sic]:1–43:35); My 14, 1920–Ap 29, 1921 (46:2–52); F 12, 1925 (52:41).

CHRONICLE JOURNAL, CATTARAUGUS STAR AND RUSHFORD SPECTATOR see *NEWS TIME*

CUBA DAILY NEWS (d) Cuba. Ag 23, 1880–? (1:1–?). *Pub and Ed*: R. W. Burnett and C. W. Nash Ag 1880–F 1881; C. W. Nash Mr 1881–?. *Pol*: Independent. *Format*: Four pages, varying sizes 4¾" x 7", 5¾" x 8", 11½" x 14½". *Price*: 25¢ per month, 2¢ per copy (1881). *Circ*: 3,000 (1881). *Comment*: Published at Banfield Block, Main Street, then Palmer Block, Cuba. On May 7, 1881 the *Daily News* announced "Owing to other business fully occupying our attention for a short time, the *Daily News* will be temporarily suspended next week. The suspension will be of short duration and the paper will reappear in an enlarged and improved form. . . ." Publication resumed August 1881. *Loc*: NCu: Ag 8, 1880–My 7, 1881 (1:1–220). NCu/Patriot Office: Ag 19, S 20, 1881 (1:231, 258).

CUBA EVENING REVIEW (d) Cuba. My 8, 1881–? (1:1–?). *Pub*: The Peerless Printing Co. *Ed*: R. W. Burnett My 1881– D 30, 1882. *Format*: Four pages 8½" x 11". *Price*: 25¢ per month. *Comment*: Published in the Palmer Block, second floor, Cuba. *Loc*: NCu: Ag 9, 1881–D 30, 1882 (1:79–2:200). NCu/Patriot Office: D 30, 1881 (1:201); Ja 3, Jl 20, 1882 (1:205; 2:61).

CUBA FREE PRESS (w) Cuba. Ap 1903–1909// (1:1–?). *Pub*: Robert J. Tuite 1905–1907; Edwin M. Park 1908–1909. *Ed*: Edwin M. Park 1903–1909. *Format*: Eight pages 17½" x 24". *Comment*: In 1909, the *Free Press* consolidated with *The Cuba Patriot* and became *The Cuba Patriot and Free Press*. *Loc*: NCu/Patriot Office: F 9, 1905 (2:42); My 10, 1906 (4:?); O 24, 1907 (5:27); Mr 19, 1908 (5:48); Ap 1, 1909 (6:50).

THE CUBA PATRIOT see *THE CUBA PATRIOT AND FREE PRESS*

THE CUBA PATRIOT AND FREE PRESS (w) Cuba, Belfast. Jl 1862 to date (1:1 to date). *Title changes*: *The Cuba True Patriot* 1862–1872; *Cuba Weekly Herald* O 1872–Ja 1875; *The Cuba Patriot* Ja 1875–1908; *The Cuba Patriot and Free Press* 1909 to date. *Pub*: Frank G. Stebbins 1862–D 1874 and F 28, 1875–Ap 23, 1880; Cuba Herald Assoc. 1872–1875; Erastus Stearns Barnard Ja 1–F 28, 1875; Miles A. Davis Ap 30, 1880–1882; W. J. Beecher and W. J. Glenn 1882–Ja 27, 1887; W. J. Glenn and Co. F 10, 1887–Mr 26, 1891 and Ap 30, 1893–1902; Stanley C. Swift Ap 16, 1891–Ap 28, 1892; H. Moulton and Co. My 5–D 1892; H. Moulton Printing Co. Ja–Ap, 1893; Lewis H. Thornton 1903–1906; J. R. Childs 1907–1908; Arthur A. Norton 1909–1910; F. C. Dean 1911–Ap 9, 1914; Elmer E. Conrath Ap 16, 1914–Jl 18, 1929; Cassar Rodney Adams 1929–S 14, 1945; L. L. Schuyler S 21, 1945–Ja 1950; Clare Trenkle Ja 19, 1950–My 29, 1952; John J. Crowley Je 5, 1952–Ja 9, 1964; David H. C. Crowley Ja 16, 1964 to date. *Ed*: Frank G. Stebbins 1862–1871 and 1873–1880; James A. McKibbin 1872; Miles A. Davis Ap 30, 1880–1882; W. J. Beecher and W. J. Glenn 1882–Ja 27, 1887; W. J. Glenn and Co. F 10, 1887–Mr 26, 1891; Stanley C. Swift Ap 16, 1891–Ap 28, 1892; W. D. Moulton My 5,–D 1892; H. S. Wagoner D 1892–Ap

6, 1893; W. J. Glenn Ap 30, 1893–Ap 1902; Edwin M. Park Ap 1902–1903; Lewis H. Thornton 1903–1906; J. R. Childs 1907–1908; John W. Sticker 1909–1910; F. C. Dean 1911–Ap 9, 1914; Elmer E. Conrath Ap 16, 1914–Jl 18, 1929; Cassar Rodney Adams Ag 1, 1929–Jl 13, 1939; Lena E. Todd Jl 13, 1939–S 14, 1945; Mr. and Mrs. Lewis Schuyler S 21, 1945–Ap 1947; Clare Trenkle My 5, 1947–Ag 4, 1949 and Ja 19, 1950–My 29, 1952; R. J. Hooks Ag 25–D 8, 1949; Hal Shapiro D 8, 1949–Ja 12, 1950; John J. Crowley Je 5, 1952–Ap 1954; Irene H. Crowley My 6, 1954 to date. *Pol*: Republican. *Format*: Four to eight pages, varying sizes 15″ x 20½″, 15″ x 22″, 17″ x 22½″, 20″ x 25¼″, 22″ x 28″. *Price*: $1.50 per year (1893); $4.00 per year (1968). *Circ*: about 2,127 (1880); 1,115 (1968). *Comment*: We have located only one issue of the *Cuba Weekly Herald*. Its numbering and the following statement by J. Minard in *Allegany County and Its People* (Alfred, New York, 1896) indicate that it, too, was part of the *Cuba Patriot and Free Press*. "In October, 1872, *The Patriot* was sold to The Cuba Herald Association, its name changed to the *Cuba Herald*, which was placed under the editorial management of James A. McKibbin. About January 1, 1875, it was sold to E. S. Barnard, who associated Mr. Stebbins with him as associate editor and changed the name back to *The Patriot*." Currently published from 45 West Main Street, Cuba, the newspaper was published at a number of addresses: In Belfast over B. T. Willis and Sons' Store, and at the H. Moulton Printing Co. in Cuba during the early 1890s. Then in the Mead Block (1893), and the Patriot Block (1894). From 1893–? the last page of each issue of the *Cuba Patriot* was titled *The Belfast Patriot*, with its dateline at Belfast. The masthead for this period carried both a Cuba and a Belfast address. In 1909, the *Cuba Free Press* (q.v.) merged with the *Patriot*. *Loc*: NCu: Ja 7, 1875–D 31, 1880 (14:1–19:52); F 2, 1883–D 1904 (22:5–44:?). NCu/Patriot Office: My 18, 1876 (14:41); Ja 6–D 22, 1887 (26:1–51); My 4, 1893 (32:18); Ag 10, 1899 (38:32); Ja 2–D 25, 1902 (41:1–52); D 26, 1907 (46:45); Ja 2, Ja 9, 1908 (46:46, 47); Ap 30, S 8, 1909 (48:9, 27); Mr 25, 1910 (49:4); Mr 9, My 4, 1911 (50:2, 10); Je 13, 1912 (51:15); Mr 4, 1913 (52:4); Ja 1, 1914 to date (52:44 to date). NIC/MMN: Ap 25, 1924 (63:17); NIC/RHA: Ja 5, 1888–D 25, 1890 (27:1–29:52); Ja 5–D 28, 1893 (32:1–52); Ja 3, 1895–D 27, 1900 (34:1–39:52); [O 7, 1943–F 18, 1954 (82:40–93:7)]. NWel: microfilm Ja 5, 1866–Ap 20, 1893 (4:27–32:16).

THE CUBA POST (w) Belmont, Cuba. Ap 13, 1881–? (1:1–?). *Title changes*: *Genesee Valley Post* 1881–1888; *The Genesee Valley Post* 1888–My 16, 1895; *The Cuba Post* My 23, 1895–?. *Pub*: James E. Norton Ap 13, 1881–D 1891; Genesee Valley Post Publishing Assoc. 1891–1895; John F. Coad 1895–?. *Ed*: James E. Norton Ap 13, 1881–Ja 4, 1888; V. A. Willard Ja 11, 1888–1895; John F. Coad 1895–? *Pol*: Republican. *Format*: Four pages, varying sizes 20″ x 26″, 13″ x 19½″. *Price*: $1.00 per year. *Comment*: James E. Norton purchased the *Genesee Valley Free Press* on April 6, 1881 from A. N. Cole and changed its name to the *Genesee Valley Post* with new series numbering. On January 3, 1895 the *Genesee Valley Post* moved to Cuba. The banner of the newspaper was changed to *The Cuba Post,* although the masthead still read *Genesee Valley Post.* On May 30, 1895 the masthead was changed to *The Cuba Post. Loc*: NCu/Patriot Office: Ja 3–D 19, 1895 (14:27–15:24). NWel: Ap 13, My 25, S 21–D 28, 1881 (1:1, 7, 24–38); [Ja 4, 1882–D 31, 1884 (1:39–4:37)]; Ap 28, 1886–Jl 7, 1892 (6:1–12:9).

THE CUBA TRUE PATRIOT see *THE CUBA PATRIOT AND FREE PRESS*

CUBA WEEKLY HERALD see *THE CUBA PATRIOT AND FREE PRESS*

DAILY ALFRED SUN see *THE ALFRED SUN*

DAILY ALLEGANIAN (d) Belmont. N 10, 1874–? (1:1–?). *Pub and Ed*: B. D. Southworth. *Pol*: Republican. *Format*: Four pages 13½″ x 20″. *Comment*: The *Daily Alleganian* was the official Republican paper for Allegany County. *Loc*: NBelHi: N 13, 1874 (1:3).

THE DAILY REPORTER see *WELLSVILLE DAILY REPORTER*

DAILY REPORTER AND DEMOCRAT (d) Wellsville. 1876–1877//. *Pub and Ed*: Not given. *Format*: Four pages 11″ x 15″. *Price*: 5¢ per copy. *Circ*: 5,448. *Comment*: This newspaper, subtitled the *Wellsville Enterprise,* was probably the combined effort of the staffs of the *Wellsville Daily Reporter* (q.v.) and the *Allegany County Democrat* (q.v.). It ran for only a few weeks during 1876 and 1877 during the trial of one Hendryx. It carried only news of the trial. *Loc*: NBelC: Ja 25–30, 1877. NIC/RHA: Ja 26, 29–31, F 2, 1877.

THE DEMOCRATIC TIMES (w) Cuba. 1881–? (1:1–?). *Pub and Ed*: Wright and Holbrook 1901. *Pol*: Democrat. *Format*: Four pages 20″ x 26″. *Price*: $1.00 per year. *Comment*: Published at the Times Building listed at Genesee Street in 1898 and South Street in 1901. *Loc*: NCu/Patriot Office: F 24, 1898 (17:8); Je 14, 1900 (18:34); Ap 11, 1901 (19:27).

THE DISPATCH (w) Belmont. Mr 3, 1889–D 22, 1966// (1:1–n.s. 10:25). *Title changes*: *Belmont Weekly Dispatch* Mr 3, 1889–?; *The Dispatch* 1904; *Belmont Dispatch* F 5, 1904–Je 26, 1958; *The Dispatch* Jl 3, 1958–D 22, 1966. *Pub and Ed*: R. R. and F. G. Helme 1889–N 18, 1891; W. M. Barnum N 1891–Mr 1893; William E. Smith Mr–Ap 1893; William E. Smith and Roger Stillman 1983–?; L. H. Thornton 1898–1914; Russell E. Pierson D 4, 1914–N 1947; Janet P. Bush (Grace Young, ed.) N 1947–F 26, 1948; Clifford G. and Rosemary S. Grastorf Mr 1, 1948–D 22, 1966. *Pol*: Republican. *Format*: Four to eight pages, varying sizes 20½″ x 26½″, 17½″ x 23½″, 15″ x 21½″, 13½″ x 20″. *Price*: $1.00 per year (1892); $2.00 per year (1948); $3.00 per year (1958); $3.50 per year (1966). *Circ*: 1,455 (1960). *Comment*: Published at 50 Schuyler Street. *The Friendship Register* (q.v.) and the *Angelica Advocate* (q.v.) merged with the *Belmont Dispatch* on June 27 and July 3, 1958 respectively. The title of the three papers was then changed to *The Dispatch*. *Loc*: NAlfAg: S 20, 1901 (13:29); O 24, 1935 (46:43). NBel: Ja 3, 1902–D 22, 1966 (13:44–n.s. 10:25). NIC/RHA: Ap 5, 1956–D 22, 1966 (68:14–n.s. 10:25). NWel: [Mr 26, 1889–Mr 8, 1893 (1:3–5:6)].

EVERY WEEK (w) Angelica. D 8, 1885–1901// (1:1–?). *Pub*: Angelica Womens' Christian Temperance Union. *Ed*: Mrs. M. L. Rumpff. *Pol*: Temperance. *Format*: Eight pages 8" x 11". *Price*: 25¢ per year. *Comment*: The Womens' Christian Temperance Union Office was located "over Joholes store, a few rods from the park." The last date of publication for this paper was listed as 1901 in Doty, *The Historic Annals of Southwestern New York*. *Loc*: NAng: O 26, 1886–D 27, 1887 (1:47–3:4).

FILLMORE ENTERPRISE see *NORTHERN ALLEGANY OBSERVER*

FREE PRESS see *GENESEE VALLEY FREE PRESS*

FRIENDSHIP CHRONICLE (w) Friendship. F 11, 1880–Ag 31, 1881// (1:1–2:30). *Pub and Ed*: Raymond C. Hill F 11–Ag 4, 1880; Raymond C. Hill and J. Welland Hendrick Ag 18–D 29, 1880; J. Welland Hendrick Ja 5–Ag 31, 1881. *Pol*: Democrat. *Format*: Four pages 17½" x 23½". *Loc*: NFri: Ap 28–Jl 28, 1880 (1:12–25). NWel: Ap 7, 1880–Ag 31, 1881 (1:9–2:30).

FRIENDSHIP REGISTER (w) Friendship. D 30, 1869–Je 26, 1958// (1:1–89:26). *Title changes*: Friendship Register 1869–1874; Friendship Weekly Register 1874–1900; Allegany County Republican O 18, 1900–Ja 2, 1903; Friendship Register 1904–1958. *Pub*: J. J. Barker D 1869–1870; L. H. Bailey 1870–1871; R. R. Helme 1871–N 8, 1888; George W. Fries N 15, 1888–1899; Lewis C. Rice 1899–1903; F. L. Steenrod 1904–Ap 4, 1907; Register Publishing Co. Ap 11, 1907–My 23, 1907; Anna Steenrod My 30, 1907–1916; D. M. and M. H. Todd 1916–N 16, 1916; Charles Raymond Stout N 23, 1916–Ag 1, 1927; Frank W. LeClere Ag 1, 1927–Mr 28, 1946; Mrs. Frank W. LeClere Ap 4, 1946–Je 26, 1958. *Ed*: Same as publisher until 1946, then Walter J. Baker Jl 18, 1946–O 14, 1948; Merlin A. Pitt F 24, 1949–Ap 13, 1950; Grace Youngs N 30, 1950–Je 26, 1958. *Pol*: Republican. *Format*: Four to eight pages, varying sizes 13" x 20", 17½" x 23½", 15" x 21", 20½" x 28", 20" x 26½", 19" x 24". *Price*: $1.00 per year (1869–1879); $1.20 per year (1880–1882); $1.50 per year (1882); $2.00 per year (1927). *Circ*: 1,200 (1881). *Comment*: Published at R. R. Helme's Job Printing Office. Merged with the *Belmont Dispatch* (q.v.) Je 26, 1958. *Loc*: NFri: [Ja 6, 1872–D 12, 1895 (3:1–26:50)]; Ja 6–D 29, 1898 (29:1–52); O 11, 1900–Ja 2, 1903 (31:41–83 [sic] : 1); Ja 3, 1907–D 31, 1908 (37:1–38:53); Ja 6, 1916–Je 26, 1958 (46:1–89:26). NIC/MMN: Ag 12, 1943 (74:32). NWel: [Ja 20, 1872–Ap 20, 1893 (3:3–24:16)].

THE FRIENDSHIP VOLUNTEER (w) Friendship, Bolivar. Jl 14,

1960–O 14, 1965// (no series numbers). *Pub*: Friendship Advancement Assoc. Inc. Jl 14, 1960–Je 1964; Allegany Printing Co., Bolivar, Jl 9, 1964–O 14, 1965. *Ed*: Marilyn L. Lester. *Pol*: Independent. *Format*: Eight pages 12" x 17". *Price*: $3.00 per year. *Circ*: 1350 (1963). *Comment*: Published in the Barron Building, Main Street, Friendship 1960–1964), then Allegany Printing Co., Bolivar (1964–1965). *The Friendship Volunteer* began as a volunteer paper to take the place of the *Friendship Register* which ceased publication in 1958. *Loc*: NBelC: [Jl 14, 1960–O 14, 1965 (1:1–6:15)]. NFri: Jl 14, 1960–F 11, 1965 (1:1–5:32). NFri/Marilyn Lester: Jl 14, 1960–O 14, 1965 (1:1–6:15).

FRIENDSHIP WEEKLY REGISTER see *FRIENDSHIP REGISTER*

GENESEE VALLEY FREE PRESS (w) Belfast, Wellsville, Genesee, Belmont, Belfast. 1852–D 20, 1883// (1:1–?). *Title changes*: *Genesee Valley Free Press* 1852–1853; *Wellsville Free Press* 1853–1875; *Genesee Valley Free Press*, Belmont 1877–D 20, 1883. *Pub*: Asa N. Cole 1852–1864; J. B. Bray 1864; Henry C. Fiske 1866–1869; Henry C. Fiske and James H. Fish 1869–Jl 1870; Charles M. and William H. Beecher 1870; Charles M. Beecher 1871–?; Asher P. Cole 1879; Asher P. and Asa N. Cole 1879–1880; Horace E. Purdy 1881–D 20, 1883. *Ed*: Asa N. Cole 1852–1865; Henry C. Fiske 1866–1869; Henry C. Fiske and James H. Fish 1869–Jl 1870; Charles M. and William H. Beecher 1870; Charles M. Beecher 1871–Ja 1872; Asa N. Cole 1872–1879; Asher P. Cole 1880; Horace E. Purdy D 1881–D 20, 1883. *Pol*: "Republican Independence." *Format*: Four pages 18" x 23½". *Price*: $1.50 per year (1871); $1.00 per year (1881). *Comment*: "Founded in Belfast by A. N. Cole, assisted by General James S. Wadsworth, in the autumn of 1852, and nine issues published at various intervals. Moved to Wellsville in February 1853, and published there until 1875 under four managements: A. N. Cole its founder; Henry C. Fiske; Fiske and Fish (under whose regime its name was changed to the *Wellsville Free Press*); and Charles M. Beecher. Suspended in 1875; revived in Belmont in 1877 by A. N. Cole in an office purchased from the Alleganian and continued there until 1881, when the paper was discontinued." (Thornton, *Historic Annals of Southwestern New York*, Vol. II) In 1881 James E. Norton purchased part of the *Free Press* and started the *Genesee Valley Post* in Belmont. He considered this a continuation of the *Genesee Valley Free Press*, but commenced a new volume series number. At the same time Horace E. Purdy also seems to have bought a piece of the *Genesee Valley Free Press* and started the newspaper again in Belfast under the same title with a new series numbering. He suspended publication by December 20, 1883. A. N. Cole, not to be outdone reestablished the *Genesee Valley Free Press* in Wellsville and published it as the *Wellsville Daily Free Press* through the boom decade ending with 1890. "The paper is recognized as having been the pioneer Republican Journal of America." (*Allegany County History,* 1806–1879, pp. 83–85). *Loc*: NAng: N 18, 1857 (5:46 whole no. 254); Je 8, 1864 (12:23); F 14–21, Mr 14, 1866

(14:7, 8, 11). NBe: D 7, 1881; Mr 1, 1882 (n.s. 1:1; 30:9). NIC/ MMN: D 4, 1872 (20:48). NWel: [Mr 7–D 26, 1866 (14:10–52)]; [My 29, 1867–D 31, 1873 (15:6–21:50)]; [Ja 22, 1879–D 29, 1880 (27:4–28:52)].

THE GENESEE VALLEY POST see *THE CUBA POST*

HUME ENTERPRISE see *NORTHERN ALLEGANY OBSERVER*

MY LADY (m) Cuba. *Pub and Ed*: W. J. Glenn. *Format*: Twenty pages 10″ x 14½″. *Price*: 50¢ per year. *Comment*: A magazine supplement to the *Cuba Patriot* for which only three issues have been located. NCu/Patriot Office: Ja, F, Mr, 1902.

NEWS TIME (w) Rushford, Franklinville. 1878–Ap 15, 1970// (1:1–?). *Title changes*: *Rushford Spectator* 1878–1882, *The Spectator* 1883–1926; *Rushford Spectator* (Franklinville, New York, Cattaraugus County) 1926–?; *Chronicle-Journal, Cattaraugus Star and Rushford Spectator* ?–1968; *News Time* 1968–Ap 15, 1970. *Pub and Ed*: Frank B. Smith 1878–F 19, 1885; William F. Benjamin F 26, 1885–1912; Abram P. Benjamin 1912–1916; Harlan H. Woods 1916–1917 and 1920–1926; Cassar Rodney Adams 1926–1927; C. R. and Max Stout 1927–?; Raymond K. Wieloszynski. *Pol*: Independent, then Republican. *Format*: Four to eight pages, varying sizes 19″ x 25″, 20″ x 26″, 15″ x 21½″. *Price*: $4.00 per year. *Circ*: 2,650 (1885–1912); 1,437 (1969). *Comment*: Published over Pratt and Colburns, Main Street. From 1917 until 1920 the *Rushford Spectator* was suspended because Mr. Woods, publisher and editor was drafted into the army and Rushford was journalistically served by the *Cuba Patriot*. After 1926 the *Spectator* was moved from Rushford to Franklinville, Cattaraugus County, where it was published in connection with the *Chronicle-Journal and Cattaraugus Star* until 1968. In 1969 the title of the newspaper became the *News Time*. The *News Time* suspended publication on April 15, 1970. *Loc*: NBelC: F 17, 1881 (3:20). NCu/Patriot Office: Jl 26, 1894 (16:42). NRus/Mrs. Oliver J. Williams: N 11, 1880 (3:6); S 29, 1881 (3:52); F 23, 1882 (4:21); O 12, 1882–O 1, 1891 (5:2–13:52); O 11, 1894– D 26, 1912 (17:1– 35:19); D 7, 1915 (38:16); S 30, 1927 (49:13).

NORTHERN ALLEGANY OBSERVER (w) Fillmore, Geneseo. 1880 to date (1:1 to date). *Title changes*: *Hume Enterprise* 1880– 1882; *Fillmore Enterprise* Mr 1882–My 4, 1888; *Northern Allegany Observer* My 11, 1888 to date. *Pub and Ed*: H. C. Scott 1880–1888; J. L. Howden My 11, 1888–Ap 8, 1932; Melvine P. Howden 1932– 1949; Robert G. and Evelyn I. Aldrich 1949–1957; Sanders Publications 1958 to date (Editors: Donald R. Sanders 1958–D 1960; 1964 to date; Yvonne C. Barnes 1960–1963). *Pol*: Republican. *Format*: Four to eight pages, varying sizes 20″ x 25½″, 15″ x 21″, 8″ x 11″, 11½″ x 15″. *Price*: $1.25 per year (1888); $2.00 per year (1930); $3.00 per year (1950); $4.00 per year (1968). *Circ*: 1,374 (1968). *Comment*: "The *Northern Allegany Observer*, republican weekly now issued at Fillmore by Judson Howden and Son, began in 1880, when H. C. Scott printed the first number of the *Hume Enterprise*. In March, 1882, the paper was moved to Fillmore, and in 1888 Judson Howden bought the plant and changed the name to the present form." (Doty, Lockwood R., Editor, *History of the Genesee County*, Vol. II) The *Observer* was published at the newspaper office on Main Street in Fillmore until Donald L. Sanders purchased the paper in 1958 and moved the printing to Geneseo. Only a news collecting office was maintained in Fillmore. *Loc*: NBelC: My 24, Je 7, 1895 (16:23, 25); 0 6, 1899 (20:40). NFi: Ja 3, 1952–D 27, 1956 (63:1–67:52); [Ja 5, 1961–D 29, 1965 (72:1–77:51)]; Ag 26, 1970 (69 [*sic*] :35)]. NFi/Observer Office: My 4, 1888 to date (9:18 to date).

THE NORTHERN SPY (q) Almond. S 1904–? (1:1–?). *Pub*: Hopkins and Allen Nursery. *Format*: About 36 pages 5½" x 8½". *Price*: 15¢ per year. *Comment*: Primarily an advertising medium filled with pictures and historical sketches of Almond. *Loc*: NAl/John Reynolds: Ap 1905 (1:3).

THE PATRIOT see *THE CUBA PATRIOT AND FREE PRESS*.

REPUBLICAN ERA (w) Rushford, Oramel. D 1846–? (1:1–?). *Pub and Ed*: Horace E. Purdy. *Pol*: Republican. *Format*: Eight pages, varying sizes 16" x 22", 14" x 20". *Price*: $1.50 per year (1846); $1.00 per year (1848). *Comment*: First published from the second story of Gordon's Block, Main Street, Rushford, and then moved to Oramel about 1848. *Loc*: NAng: Mr 3, 1847 (1:33); S 21, 1885 (10:11). NBe: Ap 6, 1855 (9:38).

THE RUSHFORD SPECTATOR see *NEWS TIME*

THE SABBATH RECORDER (w) Alfred Centre, N. Y.; Plainfield, N. J. Je 13, 1844 to date. (1:1 to date). *Pub*: American Sabbath Tract Society Je 1872— *Ed*: N. V. Hull 1872–S 5, 1881; Reverend Stephen Burdick S 22, 1881–O 1882; L. A. Platts O 1882–Ja 26, 1893; John P. Mosher F 2–F 16, 1893; Reverend L. E. Livermore F 22, 1893–1894. *Format*: Four to sixteen pages, varying sizes 21½" x 28", 15" x 20", 10" x 15". *Price*: $2.50 per year (1872); $2.00 per year (1899). *Comment*: Although currently published in New Jersey, this newspaper was published in Alfred Centre from 1872 through 1894. In addition to religious news, it carried news items and ads of local interest. *Loc.*: NAlf/7th Day Baptist Church: Je 27, 1872–D 1894 (28:27–50:52).

SESQUICENTENNIAL TIMES Friendship. Jl 25–31, 1965// *Ed*: Mrs. Arlene Hess. *Format*: Ten pages 14¾" x 21½". *Comment*: Only one issue of this newspaper was published. It commemorated Friendship's 150th anniversary. *Loc*: NAlfAg: Jl 25–31, 1965.

THE SPECTATOR see *NEWS TIMES*

TRUE PATRIOT see *THE CUBA PATRIOT AND FREE PRESS*

WELLSVILLE DAILY FREE PRESS (d) Wellsville. Ja 1884–?
Pub and Ed: George Howe and Asa N. Cole. *Pol*: Republican. *Format*: Four pages 15½" x 20". *Price*: $2.00 per year. *Comment*: Published by the Daily Free Press, River Street, Wellsville. "It (*Wellsville Free Press*) was revived in Belmont in 1877 by A. N. Cole in an office purchased from the *Alleganian,* and continued until 1881 when the paper was again discontinued and the plant sold to the *Genesee Valley Post.* Re-established in Wellsville in the early part of the 1880's by A. N. Cole, it was published as a daily through the boom decade ending with 1890, when it was discontinued because Wellsville could not support two daily papers." (Martha Elson Howe, *A History of the Town of Wellsville,* New York, 1963). *Loc*: NWelHi: My 12, 1885 (2:106).

WELLSVILLE DAILY REPORTER (d) Wellsville. N 1, 1880 to date (1:1 to date). *Title changes*: *Wellsville Daily Reporter* N 1, 1880–F 6, 1881; *The Daily Reporter* F 7, 1881–late 1881; *Wellsville Daily Reporter* 1881 to date. *Pub*: Enos W. Barnes N 1, 1880–Ja 9, 1888; E. Willard Barnes Ja 9, 1888–D 3, 1925; Charles M. Barnes Ja 9, 1888–N 19, 1927; The Reporter Co. N 20, 1929–Jl 9, 1964 (E. Willard Barnes and Lillian Barnes, publishers); Wellsville Daily Reporter, Inc. (John J. Waterbury publisher and president) Jl 9, 1964 to date. *Ed*: Enos W. Barnes N 1, 1880–Ja 9, 1888; E. Willard Barnes Ja 9, 1888–D 3, 1925; Charles M. Barnes Ja 9, 1888–N 19, 1929; E. Willard Barnes N 20, 1929–Jl 9, 1964; J. J. Waterbury Jl 9, 1964 to date. *Pol*: Republican. *Format*: Four pages 13¼" x 17½". *Price*: $3.00 per year (1882–1883); $18.50 per year (1968). *Circ*: 2,000 (1925); 4,682 (1960); 4,559 (1963). *Comment*: Published at the Reporter Printing House, The Reporter Building, 141 North Main Street and then 159 North Main Street; currently by the Wellsville Daily Reporter, Inc., 213 Pine Street. *Loc*: NIC/RHA: D 27, 1882–Mr 17, 1883 (3:47–3:115). NWel: microfilm N 1, 1880 to date (1:1 to date). NWel/Reporter Office: Latest issues only.

WELLSVILLE FREE PRESS see *GENESEE VALLEY FREE PRESS*

THE WELLSVILLE TIMES (w) Wellsville. Ag 8, 1872–1874// (1:1–2:?). *Pub*: George Howe Ag 8, 1872–N 20, 1873. *Ed*: Benton C. Rude Ag 8, 1872—N 20, 1873. *Pol*: Republican. *Format*: Four pages. *Price*: $1.50 per year. *Comment*: Published at Plum's Block, second floor, Main Street. This paper was established because George Howe felt that the editor of the *Genesee Valley Free Press,* Charles M. Beecher, "had repudiated the Republican Party" by sponsoring Horace Greeley. He was joined by F. G. Stebbins, editor of the *Cuba True Patriot* for the same reason. When the *Angelica County Republican* was moved to Wellsville, *The Wellsville Times* combined with it on January 21, 1874 and no longer appeared as a separate paper. *Loc*: NIC/MMN: microfilm: Ag 8, 1872–N 20, 1873 (1:1–2:16). NWel: microfilm: Ag 8, 1872–N 20, 1873 (1:1–2:16).

WHIG AND ADVOCATE see *ALLEGANY REPUBLICAN* 1842–1856

THE WHITESVILLE NEWS (w) Whitesville. Ap 3, 1895–My 7, 1953// (1:1–57:51). *Title changes*: *The Whitesville News* Ap 3, 1895–S 1913; *Allegany County News* O 9, 1913–Mr 9, 1916; *The Whitesville News* Mr 16, 1916–My 7, 1953. *Pub*: Lester J. Fortner and W. D. Dexter Ap 3–17, 1895; Lester J. Fortner and LaBert Davie Ap 24, 1895–Ja 1987; Lester J. Fortner Ja 1897–D 7, 1899; E. A. Blair D 1899–D 1900; Lester J. Fortner D 1900–1907; Crescent Press Ja 1908–Ag 1913; Alleco Printing Co. S 1, 1913–F 1916; Glen J. Robbins F 1916–1944; Bi-State Printing Co. 1944–S 1952; Herrick Newspapers O 1952–My 7, 1953. *Ed*: Lester J. Fortner and W. D. Dexter Ap 3–17, 1895; Lester J. Fortner and LaBert Davie Ap 24, 1895–Ja 1897; Lester J. Fortner Ja 1897–D 7, 1899; E. A. Blair D 1899–D 1900; Lester J. Fortner D 1900–1907; William D. Fish Ja 1908–Ag 1, 1911, Glen J. Robbins S–D 1911; Herbert Martin Peet D 1911–F 1916; Glen J. Robbins F 1916–1944; Scott Thurston Ag 1944–Ap 1945; Robert J. Wilson Ap 1945– O 1952; Mrs. Lera Coleman O 1952–1953. *Pol*: Independent until 1908; Democratic 1908–1916; Republican 1916–1953. *Format*: Four to eight pages, varying sizes 13″ x 19½″, 15″ x 21½″, 12″ x 17″, 14″ x 21½″. *Price*: $2.50 per year (1947); $3.00 per year (1953). *Loc*: NAlfAg: Ap 3, 1895–My 7, 1953 (1:1–57:51). NWhit: [N 20, 1947–Ap 30, 1953 (52:26–57:50)]. *See also* p. 285

THE AXE (w) Binghamton. Ag 8, 1885–? (1:1–?). *Title changes*: *The Binghamton Axe* Ag 8, 1885–?; *The Axe* 1886(?)–? *Pub and Ed*: O. E. Briggs and O. S. Bishop. *Pol*: Organ of Prohibition Party in Broome County. *Format*: Four pages 17″ x 24″. *Comment*: Published at 7 Myrtle Avenue (O 1885); 157 Water Street (1886). *Loc*: NBiHi: Ag 15, O 24, 1885 (1:2, 11); Mr 20, 1886 (1:29).

THE BINGHAMTON ADVOCATE (d) Binghamton. Mr 10–Jl 9, 1921// (1:1–103). *Pub*: Binghamton Typographical Union #232. *Ed*: Harry V. Casey. *Format*: Four to eight pages 17″ x 22½″. *Comment*: A labor newspaper published at 46 Commercial Avenue. *Loc*: NIC/ILR: Mr 10–Jl 9, 1921 (1:1–103).

THE BINGHAMTON ADVOCATE (w?) Binghamton. O 17, 1895–D 12, 1895// (1:1–1:9). *Format*: Four pages 12″ x 19″. *Loc*: NBiHi: D 12, 1895 (1:9).

THE BINGHAMTON AXE see *THE AXE*

BINGHAMTON CHRONICLE (w) Binghamton. 1887(?)–? (1:1–?). *Title changes*: *Saturday Call* 1887(?)–1896(?); *Binghamton Chronicle* 1896(?)–? *Pol*: Republican. *Format*: Sixteen to twenty pages 13″ x 18″. *Comment*: "The *Saturday Call* was founded in 1887 by J. W. Hagar. Edward H. Freeman acquired an interest in the paper in 1889 and was in charge of the editorial and news departments. In 1893 the paper was purchased by Perry P. Rogers and A. J. Dibble. They continued it until Mr. Rogers' death in 1894, when Mr. Dibble became sole proprietor. The *Call* was sold to a stock company in 1896 and continued under the name of *The Chronicle*, with Francis Curtis as editor." (From William F. Seward's *Binghamton and Broome County*, p. 281.) We are assuming from the only issue located of the *Sunday Morning Star and Binghamton Chronicle*, September 15, 1901 (15:38), published at 70 State Street, that the *Binghamton Chronicle* was also issued on Sunday in combination with the *Morning Star* (no issues located). *Loc*: NBiHi: S 26, 1896 (10:23); Ag 20, D 31, 1898 (12:18, 37); Je 3, 1899 (13:22); D 15, 1900 (14:50); S 15, 1901 (15:38).

BINGHAMTON COMMERCIAL REVIEW (m?) Binghamton. D 1897–? (1:1–?). *Format*: Eight pages 15½″ x 22″. *Loc*: NBiHi: D 1897 (1:1).

BINGHAMTON COURIER (w) Binghamton. Ag 4, 1831–1849// (1:1–?). *Title changes*: *Broome County Courier and Country Literary Gazette* Ag 4, 1831–F 21, 1833; *Broome County Courier* F 28, 1833–Je 22, 1837; *The Binghamton Courier and Broome County Democrat* Jl 6, 1837–1846; *Binghamton Courier* 1847–1849. *Pub and Ed*: Jason R. Orton Ag 4, 1831–Je 1837; J. S. Getch Je 1837–?; Thomas Johnson and J. W. Marble 1839–?; Charles J. Orton and J. W. Hotchkiss Je 10, 1841–Je 9, 1842; Charles J. Orton Je 9, 1842–?; Jeremy T. Brodt

1849. *Pol*: Democrat. *Format*: Four pages 17″ x 23″. *Comment*: "The *Broome County Courier* . . . was weekly with Democratic proclivities. It was published by Mr. Orton until 1837. During the next five years it changed hands several times. Among the successive owners were Sheldon and Marble, Isaac C. Sheldon, E. P. Marble, Marble and Johnson. J. R. and C. Orton became proprietors in 1847. In that year John L. Burtis bought the *Courier* and abridged the title to the *Binghamton Courier*. Jeremy T. Brodt then became the owner and continued the publication until 1849, when John R. Dickinson and a party of prominent Democrats in the village purchased the paper and merged it into the *Binghamton Democrat* (q.v.). . . ." (Seward, *Binghamton and Broome County,* p. 279.) The paper was first published three doors west of the Broome County Court House; then at Court Street at the Book Store; then published from the Publisher's Bookstore; then from the second story of J. A. Collier's new building, two doors west of the Phoenix and then from the second story of the Odd Fellows Hall, South End on Washington Street. *Loc*: NBi: microfilm Ag 4, 1831–Jl 20, 1837 (1:1–6:52); Ap 4, 1839–S 25, 1839 (n.s. 1:1–26); Je 17, 1841–Mr 21, 1844 (3:12–5:52). NBiHi: Je 10, 1841–Je 2, 1842 (n.s. 3:11–4:10); Ag 2, 1849 (n.s. 2:49).

BINGHAMTON COURIER AND BROOME COUNTY DEMO-CRAT see *BINGHAMTON COURIER*

BINGHAMTON DAILY DEMOCRAT (d) Binghamton. F 8, 1864–? (1:1–?). *Pub and Ed*: W. S. Lawyer 1864–1869; William S. and George L. Lawyer 1869–? *Pol*: Democrat. *Format*: Four pages 15½″ x 22″. *Comment*: There is some question regarding the first date of the *Binghamton Daily Democrat*. Although the February 8, 1864 issue is numbered volume 1, number 1, the January 4, 1869 issue which was numbered volume 2, number 1 is called the "first number of the new *Daily Democrat.*" The newspaper became the official city paper in 1876. From 1861 to 1869 the paper was published at 61 Court Street, Sisson's Granite Block; then 89 Water Street, north of the American Hotel. Many errors in numbering and dating. *Loc*: NBi: F 8, 1864–F 27, 1865 (1:1–no number given); Ja 4, 1869–D 31, 1881 (2:1–14:307). NBiHi: F 1, 1871 (4:26).

BINGHAMTON DAILY LEADER see *BINGHAMTON LEADER*

THE BINGHAMTON DAILY REPUBLICAN see *SUN-BUL-LETIN*

THE BINGHAMTON DAILY TIMES (d) Binghamton. D 1, 1863–Ag 1864// (1:1–?). *Pub and Ed*: C. B. Gould. *Pol*: Republican. *Format*: Four pages 12½″ x 18¼″. *Comment*: Published at Brigham Hall, second story, corner of Court and Collier Streets, Binghamton. We have based the final date of the paper on a statement by Seward, *Binghamton and Broome County,* p. 279, "*The Binghamton Times,* daily, was started December 1, 1863. C. B. Gould was the publisher, and the editorial department was then in charge of Edward K. Clark, father of Roger and Lewis C. Clark, now practicing attorneys in

Binghamton. The *Times* was a Republican paper, well edited and well managed, but failed to survive the keen competition that existed in the village at that time and was not a financial success. It suspended in August, 1864." *Loc*: NIC/MMN: My 21, 1864 (1:156). NBiHi: D 15, 1863 (1:18).

THE BINGHAMTON DAILY TIMES (d) Binghamton. D 4, 1872–Ja 19, 1878// (1:1–6:44). *Pub*: David E. Cronin D 4, 1872–Ap 7, 1873; Binghamton Times Assoc. Ap 7–Ag 1874; (J. C. Truman, Frank A. Bassler Ag 11–O 2, 1873; David E. Cronin O 2–N 1873, Pub.); F. W. Halsey and Frederick G. Mather Ag 10, 1874–S 1875; George B. Edwards S 28, 1875–Ja 1877; P. L. Tucker Ja 23, 1877–1878. *Ed*: David E. Cronin D 4, 1872–Je 2, 1875; 1875–1878 no editor listed. *Pol*: Independent. *Format*: Four pages, varying sizes 7" x 9", 12½" x 18¼", 17¼" x 23¾", 19½" x 27". *Price*: $7.50 per year. *Circ*: 3,000 (1874). *Comment*: Motto: "Independent but not neutral." Published at 38 Court Street until April 7, 1873, then the Lewis Block, 89 Washington Street. Moved to the Republican Building, 98 Water Street on January 14. 1878, merged with the *Binghamton Republican* January 22, 1878, and issued as a morning paper, the *Binghamton Republican and Morning Times* (q.v.). *Loc*: NBi: [D 4, 1872–Ja 19, 1878 (1:1–6:44)]. NBiHi: Ja 6, My 5, 1873 (1:27, 128); Je 9, 1874 (2:148); Mr 2, 1877 (5:76).

BINGHAMTON DEMOCRAT (w) Binghamton. D 15, 1846–? (1:1–?). *Pub and Ed*: Robert C. Whitmore D 15, 1846–Ag 30, 1847; Hiram L. Shaw S 1847–D 6, 1849; John R. Dickinson 1849–?; Dickinson and Lawyer D 21, 1854–1857; J. M. Adams and William S. Lawyer S 17, 1857–1860; William S. Lawyer N 27 1860–1863; William S. and George L. Lawyer 1863–N 23, 1865. *Pol*: Democrat. *Format*: Four pages, varying sizes 15" x 22", 21" x 27". *Price*: $1.50 per year. *Comment*: Motto: "Principles—Not Men." First published east side of Franklin Street directly over the jewelry store of Alfred J. Evans. Then from Wickham's New Building over Wickham and Bennett's store, opposite Post Office (1853); 53 Court Street (1862); 61 Court Street, Sisson's Granite Block (1865); 89 Water Street, three doors north of the American Hotel (1895). The *Binghamton Democrat* was founded by R. C. Whitmore "assisted by several of the leading Democrats of the village, who issued a statement giving their political attitude, showing the founding of the paper was due to alleged 'defection of the editor and proprietor of the *Courier* and their union with the Whigs for the purpose of defeating a portion of the Democratic ticket'." (Seward, *Binghamton and Broome County*, p. 280.) In 1849, Mr. John R. Dickinson, who had assumed control of the *Binghamton Democrat,* also purchased the *Binghamton Courier* (q.v.) and consolidated the two under the name of the *Binghamton Democrat*. *Loc*: NBi: Ja 20, 1853–N 25, 1858 (7:7–12:52); N 27, 1862–D 7, 1865 (17:1–20:3); Jl 11, 1878–O 5, 1882 (32:36–36:49). NBiHi: D 15, 1846 (1:1); Mr 20, 1862 (16:17); Ja 12, 1871 (25:9). NIC/RHA: D 15, 1846–D 5, 1848 (1:1–2:52).

BINGHAMTON EVENING HERALD see *EVENING HERALD*

THE BINGHAMTON JOURNAL (w) Binghamton. Ap 1869–?
(1:1–?). *Pub and Ed*: J. E. Williams. *Format*: Four pages. *Comment*:
Published at 65 Court Street on the second floor of the McNamara
Building. *Loc*: NBiHi: Ag 5, 1869 (1:19).

BINGHAMTON LEADER (d) Binghamton. Ap 19, 1878–S 11, 1905
(1:1–"28th year"). *Title changes*: *Binghamton Daily Leader* 1878–
1888; *Daily Leader* 1889–S 20, 1890; *Binghamton Leader* S 27, 1890–
S 11, 1905. *Pub*: A. W. Carl 1878–?; Leader Publishing Co. 1893–?.
Ed: A. W. Carl 1878–? *Pol*: Democrat. *Format*: Four to twenty-four
pages, varying sizes 19½ " x 25½ ", 15" x 21⅝ ", 17½ " x 24", 18¼ " x
25½". *Comment*: The *Binghamton Leader* united with the *Binghamton Press* (q.v.) in September 1905. The *Press*, which had been publishing for a year and a half, picked up the volume numbering of the
Leader. It was published at various addresses on Water Street. *Loc*:
NBi: [Ap 26, 1878–Je 29, 1905 (1:2–28:?)]. NBiHi: My 18, S 30, 1878
(1:21, 135); Mr 12, 21, My 15, 1879 (1:272, 280; 2:18); O 5, 1880
(3:140); Je 25, N 2, 1881 (4:54, 165); Ja 28, 1882 (4:240); D 22,
1883 (6:207); Ag 29, 1884 (7:109); Mr 16, Ap 11, 1888 (10:280,
302); N 4, 1896; My 3, 1889 (12:8).

BINGHAMTON MESSAGE (w and Sunday) Binghamton. 1893–?
(1:1–?). *Pub*: The Message Printing Company. *Ed*: "Anonymous."
Format: Eight pages 17½" x 22¾ ". *Price*: $2.00 per year. *Comment*:
Published at 128 Washington Street. The only issue located was a sou-
venir edition on the opening of the Commercial Travelers' Home on
South Mt. *Loc*: NBiHi: O 9, 1894 (2:11).

BINGHAMTON MORNING HERALD (d) Binghamton. N 7,
1894–? (1:1–?). *Pub*: Evening Herald Co. (M. A. Stanley, President
and General Manager 1894–?). *Ed*: G. W. Blakeslee, managing editor; G. C. Richardson, night editor, Frank W. Spaulding, day and
news editor. *Pol*: Independent. *Format*: Four pages. *Loc*: NBi: microfilm N 7–D 5, 1894 (1:1–25).

BINGHAMTON MORNING REPUBLICAN see *SUN-BULLETIN*

BINGHAMTON PHOENIX (w) Binghamton. Jl 1814–Jl 15, 1819//
(1:1–?). *Title changes*: *The Phoenix* 1814–?; *Binghamton Phoenix*. *Pub*:
Tracy Robinson 1814–1816; Tracy Robinson and Augustus Morgan
1817–? *Pol*: Federalist. *Format*: Four pages, varying sizes 11⅝ " x
18⅜", 12" x 19¾ ". *Comment*: So few issues of the newspaper have
been located we can only estimate that the paper was established
about July 1814. We do not know when the title change took place
except that the May 20, 1817 issue is called the *Binghamton Phoenix*.
"In 1818 the paper was sold to Anson M. Howard and was discontinued about 1820" (Lawyer, *Binghamton*, p. 448), but in the Nor-
folk (Va.) "American Beacon" of August 17, 1819, is reprinted A. M.
Howard's valedictory, stating that the paper was discontinued with
the issue of July 15, 1819." *Loc*: NBiHi: Jl 29, 1815–Jl 16, 1816

(2:2–52, also numbered 53 to 104). NBiU: My 20, 1817 (3:44).

BINGHAMTON PRESS see *THE EVENING PRESS*

BINGHAMTON PRESS AND LEADER see *THE EVENING PRESS*

BINGHAMTON REPUBLICAN [*Ap 1889–My 3, 1889*] see *SUN-BULLETIN*

BINGHAMTON REPUBLICAN AND MORNING TIMES see *SUN-BULLETIN*

BINGHAMTON REPUBLICAN-HERALD see *SUN-BULLETIN*

THE BINGHAMTON STANDARD (w) Binghamton. O 19, 1853–Ja 20, 1869// (1:1–?). *Pub and Ed*: James Van Valkinburgh O 19, 1853–?; George W. Reynolds 1859; Franklin N. Chase 1861–?; Alvin Sturtevant 1868; M. L. Hawley and Co. *Pol*: Independent. *Format*: Four to eight pages, varying sizes 20″ x 26½″, 18½″ x 24″, 14″ x 20½″. *Comment*: Published at Le Roy Place over J. Cornwall's clothing store, one door east of the Canal Bridge (1853–1856); New Exchange Block (1857–1860); Bacon's Block, 63 Court Street (September 1860–?); 7 Collier Street, third floor (1867–1868). In 1867 it called itself the "Official County Paper." It merged with the *Broome Republican* (q.v.) to become *The Republican and Standard* (q.v.). *Loc*: NBi: O 19, 1853–O 11, 1854 (1:1–52). NBiHi: Ja 14, 1857 (4:14); Ap 7–My 19, Je 16–30, Jl 21–N 10, N 24, D 8–29,1858 (5:26–32, 36–38, 41–52; 6:1–5, 7, 9–12); [Ja 19–N 23, 1859 (6:15–7:7)]; [Mr 21–D 26, 1860 (7:24–8:12)]; Ap 18, 1866 (13:?); Je 5, Jl 31, O 2, 1867 (14:36, 44; 15:1); F 19, 1868 (15:21). NIC/MMN: Jl 25, 1860 (7:42); D 3, 1862 (10:9); O 16, 1867 (15:3); Mr 11, 1868 (15:24). NIC/RHA: Ap 19, 1865 (12:29). NLi: [Je 27–O 17, 1860 (7:38–8:2)]; Ja 30, F 6, 27, Mr 12–27, 1861 (8:17, 18, 21, 23–25).

BINGHAMTON STANDARD AND SEMI-WEEKLY REPUBLICAN (semi-w) Binghamton. Jl 2, 1870–? (1:1–?). *Pub*: James Malette and George J. Reid Jl 2, 1870–D 1870; George J. Reid D 14, 1870–? *Ed*: James Malette 1870–? *Pol*: Republican. *Format*: Four pages 19″ x 24½″. *Comment*: Published at the Republican Building on Water Street. An item in the *Republican and Standard* July 1870 stated "The *Binghamton Standard* is in effect a revival from our press of *The Standard*, now consolidated with the *Broome Republican*, with more frequent publication. It will supply a want of many persons in this part of the state—well educated and well-to-do people who cannot regularly obtain and read a daily journal and for whom a weekly home paper scarcely suffices." The *Republican and Standard* (q.v.), a weekly, was published at the same time as the *Binghamton Standard and Semi-Weekly Republican*. *Loc*: NBi: microfilm [Jl 2, 1870–Je 29, 1872 (1:1–4:104)]. NBiHi: Jl 3, 1872–Je 28, 1873 (3:1–3:104).

THE BINGHAMTON SUN see *SUN-BULLETIN*

BINGHAMTON SUN AND DAILY BULLETIN see *SUN-BULLETIN*

BINGHAMTON SUNDAY TRIBUNE (w) Binghamton. Je 15, 1879–? (1:1–?). *Pub and Ed*: William T. Baker 1881; William T. and Thomas F. Baker Mr 6–Ap 23, 1881; Peter D. Van Vradenburg and Frank Mantz Ap 24, 1881–? *Format*: Four pages, varying sizes 18″ x 24″, 12½″ x 15⅞″. *Comment*: Published at Court and Wall Streets. *Loc*: NBiHi: Je 22, 1879 (1:2); S 12, 1880 (2:14); Ja 16, Mr 6, Ap 24, 1881 (2:31, 38, 45).

THE BINGHAMTON SUNDAY WASP (w) Binghamton. My 5, 1878–? (1:1–?). *Pub and Ed*: Will S. Secor and Storten. *Pol*: Republican. *Format*: Four pages 13″ x 20″. *Comment*: Published over Stryker's Store on Court Street. *Loc*: NBiHi: My 26, 1878 (1:4).

THE BINGHAMTON TIMES (w) Binghamton. Ap 6, 1871–Ja 17, 1878// (1:1–7:42). *Pub*: The Binghamton Times Assoc. Ap 1871–My 1872; A. L. Watson My 2–Ag 1872–; E. H. Purdy and A. L. Watson Ag 8–28, 1872; E. H. Purdy and David E. Cronin Ag 29–D 1872; David E. Cronin D 12, 1872–My 22, 1873; J. C. Truman My 22–Ag 14, 1873; Binghamton Times Assoc. O 9, 1873–1874; Frank A. Bassler, David E. Cronin; George B. Edwards S 30, 1875–Ja 25, 1877; P. L. Tucker Ja 23, 1877–Ja 17, 1878. *Ed*: David E. Cronin 1871–1878. *Pol*: Independent. "The best proof of the absolute independence of *The Times* is to be found in the fact that its Democratic contemporaries classify it as Republican, while the Republicans insist that it has gone over to the Democrats." *Format*: Four to eight pages, varying sizes 21¾″ x 28″, 13¼″ x 20¼″. *Comment*: Published at 38 Court Street, third floor, then the Lewis Block, 89 Washington Street. Although the address is no longer listed after 1873, they probably moved to the Republican Building, 98 Water Street. *Loc*: NBi: microfilm [Ap 6, 1871–Ja 17, 1878 (1:1–7:42)]. NBiHi: N 9, 23, D 21, 28, 1871 (1:32, 34, 38, 39); F 1–22, Mr 7–Ap 11, Ap 25, 1872 (1:44–47, 49–52; 2:1, 2, 4); S 4, O 23, N 6, 20, 1873 (3:21, 30, 32, 34); Ja 15, Mr 5, My 7–14, 1874 (3:40, 47, 52, 53). NWi: Mr 27, 1873 (2:52). NIC/RHA: S 8, N 2, 16, 30, D 7–14, 1871 (1:26, 31, 33, 35–37); Ja 4–11, 25, F 15, 29, Ap 18, 1872 (1:40, 41, 43, 46, 48; 2:3); S 11, 25, O 2, 1873 (3:24, 26, 27); F 5, 26, Mr 12–19, 1874 (3:43, 46, 48, 49).

THE BINGHAMTON WEEKLY HERALD (w) Binghamton. F 28, 1889–N 7, 1900// (1:1–?). *Pub and Ed*: The Herald Publishing Company 1889–1893; The Evening Herald Company 1893–1900. *Price*: $1.00 per year. *Comment*: Published at 277 Washington Street. Early issues of the newspaper are numbered volume one, number, etc., but no numbers appear on issues of 1900. *Loc*: NBi: microfilm S 11, 1890–N 7, 1900 (1:33–no numbers given).

BROOME COUNTY COURIER see *BINGHAMTON COURIER*

BROOME COUNTY COURIER AND COUNTRY LITERARY GAZETTE see *BINGHAMTON COURIER*

BROOME COUNTY HERALD (w) Chenango Forks My 2, 1888–?
(1:1–?). *Title changes: Chenango Forks Herald* My 2, 1888–Ag 28,
1889; *Broome County Herald* S 4, 1889–? *Pub and Ed*: Fred D. Van
Amburg My 2, 1888–?; William E. Ames 1894–? *Format*: Eight pages
15″ x 22″. *Price*: $1.00 per year. *Comment*: "Official Organ of Pa-
trons of Husbandry." *Loc*: NBiHi: [My 2, 1888–Mr 1, 1893 (1:1–
5:43)]. NWhP: Mr 18, Ap 22, 1891 (3:46, 51); S 5, 1894 (7:19).

BROOME COUNTY REPUBLICAN see *BROOME REPUBLICAN*

BROOME GAZETTE (w) Whitney Point. Ja 1858–1871// (1:1–?).
Pub and Ed: Gilbert A. Dodge 1858–?; Milo B. Eldredge and C. A.
Van Vradenburg 1865. *Pol*: Independent. *Format*: Four pages, varying sizes 13″ x 19″, 13″ x 21″, 15¼″ x 24¼″. *Circ*: 440. *Comment*:
Predecessor of *Nioga Reporter* (q.v.) and *Whitney's Point Reporter*
(q.v.). It was published in the basement of Patterson's Building at
Whitney Point in the "Nioga" Block. "About the latter part of the
war, Mr. Dodge sold the office to Charles A. Heath, who subsequently
retired and the office was bought by Colonel Milo B. Eldredge who
in turn sold to Teller and Foote. Mr. Foote subsequently purchased
his partner's interest, and soon after the office was burned, and for
two years Whitney Point was without a publication." (H. P. Smith,
History of Broome County, 1885, p. 366.) *Loc*: NWhP: Ja 13, 1859
(1:27); Ap 14, 1864 (6:41). NBiHi: Je 16, 1859 (1:49); F 2, 1860
(2:30); Ag 4, 1864 (7:5); Ja 26, 1865 (7:30). NIC/MMN: My 4,
1865 (7:44); Mr 22, 1866 (8:38).

BROOME REPUBLICAN (w) Binghamton. Je 1822–? (1:1–?) *Title
changes: Broome County Republican* 1822; *Broome Republican; The
Broome Republican; Broome Weekly Republican* Jl 16, 1862–Ja 12,
1869; *Republican and Standard* Ja 20, 1869–Jl 15, 1871; *Broome
Republican* 1871–?; *Broome Republican and Weekly Times* 1872–
1879; *Broome Republican. Pub*: Augustus Morgan 1822–?; Abiel C.
Canoll 1824–1828; Abiel C. Canoll and Thomas Collier; Abiel C.
Canoll and Edwin T. Evans 1830–Ap 30, 1835; Benjamin T. Cooke
and Abiel C. Canoll Ap 30, 1835–Je 21, 1841; Benjamin T. Cooke
Je 21–N 10, 1841, also Ag 7, 1844–Ag 1849; Francis B. Penniman
N 10, 1841–?; Edwin T. Evans Ag 1, 1849–Ag 1850; William Stuart
Ag 1850–Ap 1863; William Stuart and James S. Cary Ap 1, 1863–
1864; Carl Brothers and Taylor My 25, 1864; James Malette and
George J. Reid Ap 3, 1867–1874; Binghamton Republican Assoc. O
1874–? (George Reid, President); Binghamton Republican Printing Co.
Ja 17, 1878–?; Binghamton Publishing Co. O 14, 1878. *Ed*: Augustus
Morgan 1822–?; Abiel C. Canoll and Edwin T. Evans 1830–Ap
23, 1835; Abiel C. Canoll and Benjamin T. Cooke Ap 30, 1835–
Je 14, 1841; Benjamin T. Cooke Je 21–N 10, 1841; Francis Penniman Ag 7, 1844–?; Edwin T. Evans Ag 1, 1849; William Stuart
Ag 1850–Jl 25, 1866; James Malette. *Pol*: Republican. *Format*: Four
to ten pages, varying sizes 11½″ x 19¼″, 21″ x 27″, 18″ x 23″,
13½″ x 19″, 15″ x 20″, 18″ x 26″. *Price*: $2.00 per year (1850) in
village, $1.50 per year to all others. *Comment*: This newspaper was

the oldest predecessor to *The Sun-Bulletin.* From 1849 it was published by the publishers of the *Binghamton Daily Republican.* Published from a number of different locations: Mr. F. Whitney's new three story brick store, one door east of Muzzy's Binghamton Hotel, Court Street (August 7, 1844); 11 Franklin Street (August 1, 1849); Third Floor over Fish and Squires' opposite Binghamton Hotel (1851); 27–29 Court Street (1862); 72 Court Street (March 30, 1864–?); Corner of Court and Exchange Streets (May 10, 1865); Republican Building, 98 Water Street (December 14, 1870); 166 Water Street (1890); Corner of State and Henry Streets (1894). Follow volume numbering at your own risk. The volume numbering for 1879 and subsequent issues is generally inconsistent with the year of issue and does not seem to bear any relationship to previous numbers. *Loc*: NBiHi: D 17–31, 1829 (7:393–395); F 11, Mr 4, 1830 (7:401, 404); My 6, 1830–Ap 25, 1833 (8:1–10:52); Ap 27, 1837–Ap 19, 1838 (15:1–52); [Ja 4, 1838–D 13, 1838 (15:39–16:34)]; Ja 3, 17–F 14, 1839 (16:37, 39, 40–43); My 16, Je 6, 13, 27, Jl 4–18, Ag 1–15, 1839 (17:4, 7, 8, 10, 11–13, 2 [*sic*]–4); Ja 16, 1840 (17:26); S 10, 17, 1845 (24:6, 11); Ja 21, 1846 (24:25); Je 9, 1847 (25:45); Jl 2–16, 1851 (30:49–51); Ap 22, 1857 (35:40); Ap 25, 1860 (38:41) [Jl 9, 1862– Jl 1, 1863 (41:1–52)]; Ag 16, 1865 (44:7); S 29, 1869 (48:22); My 24, 1871 (49:47); My 27, 1874 ("Extra Extra" edition); Ja 14, 1878 (no volume or number printed on issue); Ja 22, 1879 (60:31); F 5, 1879 (62:33); Je 18, 1879 (70:52); S 17, O 15–22, 1879 (72:13, 17, 18); Ja 7, 1880 (62:29); S 30, 1886 (45:14); Ja 5, 1893 (62:26). NLi: Ja 30, F 6, Mr 13, My 22, 1850 (28:27, 28, 33, 43); Ja 29, 1851 (29:27); Ap 16, 23, 1851 (30:38, 39); Je 9, 16, 30, 1880 (72:51), 52; 73:2); Ap 29, 1886 (54:?); Ap 19, 1888 (46:42). NIC/ MMN: S 20, 1822 (1:14); Je 19, 1872; My 7, S 24–O 8, 1879 (65: 46; 72:14–16).

BROOME REPUBLICAN AND WEEKLY TIMES see *BROOME REPUBLICAN*

BROOME WEEKLY REPUBLICAN see *BROOME REPUBLICAN*

CHENANGO AMERICAN AND WHITNEY POINT REPORTER (w) Whitney Point, Greene. O 1, 1873 to date (1:1 to date). *Title changes*: *Nioga Reporter* O 1, 1873–1877; *Whitney's Point Reporter* ?–Mr 4, 1943; *Whitney Point Reporter* Mr 11, 1943–O 6, 1960; *Chenango American and Whitney Point Reporter* O 1960 to date. *Pub and Ed*: Milo B. Eldredge 1873–1877; Mark D. Branday 1877–1879; Mark D. and F. C. Branday 1879–1893; F. C. Branday 1893–My 27, 1948; Charles M. Branday 1948–N 5, 1957; John H. Gardiner N 1957–O 1960; Twin Valley Publishers, Inc., Greene, N. Y. O 6, 1960 to date. *Pol*: Independent. *Format*: Four to twenty-four pages, varying sizes 20½" x 26¾", 15" x 28½",18" x 24". *Circ*: 1,500. *Comment*: After the *Broome Gazette* office burned in 1871, Whitney Point was without a paper for two years. Milo Eldredge called his newspaper the *Nioga Reporter* in order to induce the people to change the name of the place to Nioga. It remained Whitney's Point until March 1943, when the Post Office changed the name to Whitney Point. Published at 510 Main Street in Whitney Point until a fire in 1897, then moved publishing operation temporarily to Chenango Forks. In 1960 moved to Greene, N. Y., Chenango County, and combined with the *Chenango American*. *Loc*: NBiHi: S 22, 1876 (3:51); My 11, Ag 17, 1877 (4:32, 46); Ja 4, 11, 1878 (5:14, 15); Mr 11, D 30, 1881 (8:24; 9:14); Ap 27, 1883 (10:31); Je 14, Jl 26, 1889 (16:38, 44); Je 19, 1891 (18:39); My 1, 1897 (24:33). NWhP: N 5, 1873 (1:6); F 28, Mr 21, 1874 (1:21, 24); Je 30, 1876 (3:39); F 2, 1877 (4:18); Ja 4–11, 1878 (5:14, 15); Mr 11, D 30, 1881 (8:24; 9:14); Ap 27, Je 8, S 7, 1883 (10:31, 37, 50); Ap 19, Je 14, Jl 26, 1889 (16:30, 38, 44); Je 19, 1891 (18:39); Je 2, 1893 (20:37); Ap 23, 1897 (extra); [My 1, 1897 to date (24:33 to date)]. NIC/RHA: Ja 14, 1960 (99:28).

CHENANGO FORKS HERALD see *BROOME COUNTY HERALD*

THE COURIER see *THE BINGHAMTON COURIER*

THE DAILY BULLETIN (w then d) Endicott. Ag 20, 1914–1960// (1:1–?). *Title changes*: *The Endicott Bulletin* Ag 20, 1914–My 13, 1915; *Endicott Bulletin* My 20, 1915–S 1937; *Endicott Daily Bulletin* O 4, 1937–O 23, 1950; *The Daily Bulletin* O 30, 1950–1960. *Pub*: The Free Land Press Ag 20–O 15, 1914 (H. J. Freeland, Manager); H. J. Freeland 1914–Mr 1918; The Bulletin Publishing Company (H. J. Freeland, Business Manager) D 1914–D 1918; Harry J. Freeland D 5, 1918–My 1, 1919; Harry and H. M. Freeland My 1, 1919–1933; The Endicott Bulletin, Inc. (Harry J. Freeland, President) Ja 3, 1933–1936; The Endicott Bulletin, Inc. (James H. Ottoway, President) N 20, 1936–1946; Empire Newspapers-Radio Inc. (James H. Ottoway, Publisher) Ap 1, 1946–D 3, 1953; Ottoway Newspapers-Radio, Inc. D 4, 1953–1960. *Ed*: Harry J. Freeland Ag 20, 1914–Ap 24, 1919; Jesse F. Relyea Ap 24–N 3, 1919; L. N. English N 4, 1919–Ap 4, 1921; William I. Engle Ap 5, 1921–My 19, 1930; Paul L. Hooper My 20, 1930–Ag 1943; John S. Remaly S 1, 1943–Je 29, 1946; Harvey W. Travis Je 30, 1946–1949; Byron E. French Je 30, 1949–Jl 1950; Donald F. Munro Jl 10, 1950–1955; Robert A. Spencer, Executive Editor and Donald F. Munro, Editor of Editorial Page N 1, 1955–Jl 1958; Robert Whittemore Jl 1, 1958–Mr 25, 1959; Charles A. King Mr 25, 1959–1960. *Format*: Six to sixty-two pages, varying sizes 10″ x 13″, 15″ x 21⅜″, 16½″ x 21⅜″, 17″ x 21″. *Price*: 25¢ per year (1914). *Comment*: *The Bulletin* was first published as a weekly and became a semi-weekly May 17, 1919. It was a daily from October 4, 1937 until its merger with the *Binghamton Sun* September 1, 1960. *The Bulletin* was published from several addresses in Endicott: 80 Broad Street, 113 Washington Avenue, 911 East Main Street. *Loc*: NBiHi: O 21, 1955 (93:37); Ag 20–23, 1956 (97:23–26). NEn: Ag 20, 1914–Ja 1, 1960 (1:1–100:1).

THE DAILY IRIS see *SUN-BULLETIN*

DAILY LEADER see *BINGHAMTON LEADER*

DELAWARE COUNTY COURIER (w) Deposit. Ja 26, 1855–?
(1:1–?). *Pub and Ed*: C. E. Wright. *Pol*: Republican. *Format*: Four
pages 15½" x 22". *Comment*: This seems to be the paper to which
Henry P. Smith refers in an item on the *Deposit Courier* when he
states "In 1856 [*sic*] Mr. C. E. Wright started a paper under patronage of an association; but its life was short." (*History of Broome
County*, p. 318.) *Loc*: NDeP: Mr 1855 (1:6).

DELAWARE COURIER see *THE DEPOSIT COURIER*

DEMOCRATIC LEADER see *DEMOCRATIC WEEKLY LEADER*

DEMOCRATIC WEEKLY LEADER (w) Binghamton. S 10, 1869–
1905// (?) (1:1–?). *Title changes*: *The Democratic Leader* 1869–?;
Democratic Weekly Leader ?–1905. *Pub and Ed*: Abram W. Carl
and Edward H. Freeman S 10, 1869–Jl 14, 1871; Abram W. Carl and
Fred M. Abbot Jl 14, 1871–D 22, 1871; Abram W. Carl D 22, 1871–?
and Ag 22, 1873–?; Abram W. Carl and Charles A. Hull Ja 10,
1873–?; Abram W. Carl 1888; Leader Publishing Co. 1893. *Pol*:
Democrat. *Format*: Four to eight pages, varying sizes 13" x 19½",
14½" x 21½". *Comment*: Listed at 3, 63, 65, 68 Court Street until
April 1875 when the newspaper moved to Water Street where it was
listed at several numbers, 93, 163, 110, etc. The final date of the
paper cannot be ascertained from issues in hand. However, Seward
states ". . . Mr. Carl continued the paper until his death in 1888. In
March, 1878 he issued the first number of the *Daily Leader,* one of
the strongest Democratic papers in Southern New York. After Mr.
Carl's death, his widow continued the papers until December, 1892,
when George F. O'Neil purchased the plant and continued the papers
under a Democratic political policy. During Mr. O'Neil's regime the
papers were carried on with success until the time they were acquired
by Jonas M. Kilmer and Willis Sharpe Kilmer in 1904, when *The
Binghamton Press* was established." (Seward, *Binghamton and Broome
County*, p. 280.) *Loc*: NBi: microfilm [S 10, 1869–Ag 19, 1887 (1:1–
18:52); Ap 24, 1891–Je 29, 1905 (21:33–?)]. NBiHi: Ja 13, My 19,
1871 (2:19, 37); S 6, 1872–Ag 29, 1873 (4:1–52).

THE DEPOSIT COURIER (w) Deposit My 31, 1848 to date (1:1
to date). *Title changes*: *Deposit Courier* 1848–1862; *Delaware Courier*
1862–1867; *Deposit Courier* 1867–1905; *Deposit Courier-Journal*
1905–?; *Deposit Courier* ?–1970; *The Deposit Courier* S 1970 to date.
Pub: M. R. Hulce, (Proprietor) 1848; C. E. Wright 1848–1855; Sylvester D. Hulce 1855–?; Allen and Carpenter 1862; Lucius P. Allen
1863–1868; Ambrose Blunt and Joshua Smith 1868; Charles N. Stow
1869–1872; Adrian L. Watson and Charles N. Stow 1872–?; Charles
N. Stow and Sons ?–1902; J. Daniel Kellogg 1905–1930; Deposit-
Courier Co. (William C. Stow, President) 1930–1937; John J. Stein
1938, then G. S. Van Ryper 1938; William Ryan 1967–1970; Hilton
Evans Ag 30, 1970 to date. *Ed*: C. E. Wright 1848–?; Lucius P.
Allen 1862; Allen and Carpenter 1863–?; Charles N. Stow 1869–1902;
John B. Stow 1902–1903; Charles N. Stow's Sons 1905; J. Daniel
Kellogg 1905–1930; J. D. and A. B. Kellogg 1919–1920; J. D. and A.

B. Kellogg and MacDonald 1921–?; C. H. and J. B. Stow 1935–?; George S. Van Ryper 1938–?; William C. Stow ? 1948–?; Robert S. Gulian 1955–? James F. Minehan 1955; George R. Venizelos 1955–1957; John O'Dell 1957–?. *Pol*: Republican although campaigned for Cass and Butler (Democrats) in 1848 and also advocated Free Soil. *Format*: Four to eight pages, varying sizes 13″ x 18¾″, 11¾″ x 16⅝″, 15½″ x 22¼″, 17½″ x 24″, 12⅞″ x 19″, 17½″ x 22″. *Price*: $1.50 per year (1866); $4.00 per year (1968). *Circ*: 1,730. *Comment*: On September 6, 1862 when Sylvester Hulce who was publisher and editor of the *Deposit Union Democrat* merged the latter paper with *The Courier*, he changed the title of both papers to the *Delaware Courier* and renumbered the paper volume 1, number 1 of the *Courier* and volume 10 of the *Deposit Union Democrat*. The newspaper has gone through a series of numbering changes. Published at 138 Front Street in Deposit. *Loc*: NBiHi: Mr 23, 1849 (1:49); Je 30, 1877 (15:44); My 31, 1879 (17:40); Mr 6, 1880 (18:28); [Ja 1, 1881–Mr 2, 1888 (19:19–26:29)]; D 26, 1901 (54:19); Ja 2, 1902 (54:20). NDeP: [Je 28, 1848–N 13, 1852 (1:5–5:4)]; [S 6, 1862–Jl 27, 1872 (n.s. 1:1–10:47)]; Ag 8, D 12, 1874; N 24, 1877 (16:13); [My 31, 1879–F 11, 1920 (17:38–?)]; Ja 3, N 6, 1929; [Ja 3, 1935 to date]. NIC/RHA: O 18, 1862 (1:7); [Ja 10, 1863–Ap 15, 1864 (1:19–2:33)]; F 24, 1865 (3:26); O 23, 1868 (7:7); Jl 9, S 11, 1869 (7:44; 8:1); D 9, 1871 (10:14); Ag 25, 1883 (22:1); O 23, N 13, 1885 (24:10, 13); S 15, 1892 (31:5); N 19, 1896 (35:13); O 15, 1903 (56:9); Mr 27, Ap 3, 1929 (n.s. 26: 21, 22); N 6, 1930 (83:22); N 17, 24, D 15, 1938 (91: 25, 26, 29); [Ja 14–O 21, 1943 (95: 34–96:22)]. *

DEPOSIT COURIER-JOURNAL see *THE DEPOSIT COURIER*

DEPOSIT JOURNAL (w) Deposit. Mr 3, 1887–N 29, 1905// (1:1–19:48). *Title changes*: *Tri-County Journal* Mr 3, 1887–Je 1892; *Deposit Journal* Je 1892–N 29,1905. *Pub*: A. D. Hitchcock 1887; Journal Publishing Co. 1888–1892; Babcock and Oakley Je 1892; O. S. Wadleigh 1895; Will L. Hough 1895–1899; A. W. Cook O 1899–?; J. Daniel Kellogg and MacDonald 1903–1905; MacDonald 1905. *Ed*: O. S. Wadleigh 1895; Will L. Hough 1895–1899; A. W. Cook O 1899–?; Kellogg and MacDonald 1903–?; MacDonald 1905. *Format*: Eight pages 19⅝″ x 25½″. *Comment*: Published in the Oquaga Block on Front Street (1888-1893). On December 6, 1905 the *Deposit Journal* merged with *The Deposit Courier*. *Loc*: NDeP: Mr 3, 31, Ap 28, My 19, S 1, N 17, 1887 (1:1–?); F 9, S 27, 1888 (2:?, 83); [Ap 4, 1889–S 11, 1890 (3:4–4:27)]; [Mr 5–Je 4, 1891 (4:52–5:13)]; Ja 12, My 11, Je 8, 1892 (5:41; 6:9, 13); Je 12, D 11, 1895 (9:15, 41); S 16, 30, N 2, D 16, 1896; Mr 31, Ag 11, 1897 (11:13); [Ja 6, 1898–O 18, 1899 (12:1–13:42)]; [My 13, 1903–N 29, 1905 (17:19–19:48)].

DEPOSIT UNION DEMOCRAT (w) Deposit. S 1853–Ag 30, 1862// (1:1–9:52). *Pub*: Sylvester D. Hulce 1853–1862. *Ed*: Sylvester D. Hulce 1853–?; Lucius P. Allen 1861. *Pol*: Union Democrat. *Format*: Four pages 17¾″ x 23⅝″. *Price*: $1.50 per year. *Comment*: Published from the corner of Broad and Water Streets opposite the Dela-

See also pp. 143, 285

ware House in Deposit. On September 6, 1862 the *Deposit Union Democrat* merged with the *Delaware Courier* which became *The Deposit Courier* in 1867 (q.v.). *Loc*: NDeP: D 15, 1854 (2:14); O 27, 1855 (3:7) My 10, Jl 19, N 1, 1856 (3:35, 45, 4:8); [Ja 1–D 24, 1859 (6:17–7:16)]; Ag 17, 1861 (8:50); Ja 4, Ap 12, 1862 (9:18, 32).

THE ENDICOTT BULLETIN see *THE DAILY BULLETIN*

ENDICOTT DAILY BULLETIN see *THE DAILY BULLETIN*

THE ENDICOTT TIMES (w) Endicott. 1851–My 1940// (1:1–?). *Title changes*: *The Union News* 1851–?; *The Union Weekly News* ?–My 30, 1874; *The Union News* Je 6, 1874–1910; *Union-Endicott News* 1910–Ja 1919; *News-Dispatch* F 1, 1919–N 27, 1930; *The Endicott Times* D 4, 1930–My 1940. *Pub*: Alfred E. Quinlan 1851–D 2, 1854; Ransom Bostwick 1854–?; Cephas Benedict; E. C. and G. W. Mersereau; Moses B. Robbins 1867–Mr 27, 1875; William F. Gilchrist 1875–?; Cephas Benedict and L. D. Cafferty 1880–1881; Cephas Benedict and Co. 1881–?; Cephas Benedict and Jesse E. Le Barron 1889–?; Jesse E. Le Barron 1898–1910; Charles Le Baron [*sic*] Goeller My 11, 1910–1919; Vivian W. Bradbury F 1, 1919–1931; E. J. Lloyd 1931–?; The Times Publishing Co., Inc. Ag 8, 1935–1938; Orlo M. Brees 1938–1940. *Ed*: Alfred E. Quinlan 1851–D 2, 1854; Cephas Benedict; Moses B. Robbins; William F. Gilchrist; Charles Le Baron Goeller My 11, 1910–?; Vivian W. Bradbury 1920–1928; Bruce Copeland Mr 14–My 1929; Lysander Smith My 1929; Norval B. Levy; Theodore H. P. Morse D 4, 1930–?; Orlo M. Brees F 1933–? *Pol*: Independent. *Format*: Four to twelve pages, varying sizes 15¾ " x 21¾", 16½" x 22", 17" x 23¼", 18" x 24", 17½" x 23½", 15" x 21"½, 12" x 17¼". *Circ*: 675 (1881). *Comment*: The paper was published from a number of addresses: News Building, Union, N. Y. (1899); 128 Main Street (1910); 130 to 136 Main Street (1915–1916); 124 Nanticoke Avenue (1930). On June 1, 1940, *The Endicott Times* was sold to *The Daily Bulletin* (q.v.). On December 31, 1931 the numbering changed from volume 79 to volume 39. *Loc*: NBiHi: D 21, 1853 (3:34); Ja 29–F 26, Mr 12–26, Ap 9–My 7, 1857 (6:34–38, 40–42, 44–48); Je 1, 1865 (14:51); Je 1, 29, 1877 (27:1, 5); S 20, O 4– 25, D 6, 27, 1878 (28:17, 19–22, 28, 31); Ja 17, 1879 (28:35); Ag 14, 1889 (38:15); Jl 11, 1894 (43:11). NEn: [My 27, 1868–Mr 27, 1875 (7:51–24:43)]; My 11, 1910–Ja 27, 1915 (58:15–62: 52); [Je 19, 1918–D 1935 (66:?–43:?)].

EVENING HERALD (d) Binghamton. F 28, 1889–Je 29, 1912// *Title changes*: *Binghamton Evening Herald* F 28, 1889–F 25, 1901; *Evening Herald* F 26, 1901–Je 29, 1912. *Pub*: J. B. Briggs and Edward H. Bogert 1889; Herald Publishing Co. S 2, 1889–?; Evening Herald Co. 1893–?; Southern Tier Publishing Co. D 3, 1910–Je 29, 1912. *Ed*: J. B. Briggs and Edward H. Bogert; Charles H. Turner; G. W. Beardsley; George Gilbert and H. G. More O 3, 1910–D 1910; George Gilbert D 1910–? *Pol*: Independent. *Format*: Eight to sixteen pages, 17⅜ " x 22¾". *Price*: $3.00 per year, 1¢ per copy. *Circ*:

8,100–8,400. *Comment*: On July 1, 1912 the *Evening Herald* suspended publication, combined with the *Binghamton Republican* (q.v.) and was issued as a morning paper. The *Binghamton Republican* changed its name to the *Binghamton Republican-Herald* (q.v.). This newspaper is currently the *Sun-Bulletin*. It was published at 217 Washington Street, the Herald Building, until March, 1903 then moved to the Strong Block on the corner of State and Henry Streets. *Loc*: NBi: F 28, 1889–Ap 1, 1890; D 9, 1893–Je 29, 1912. NBiHi: F 28, D 3, 1889; Mr 11, 13, 1890; F 12, 1897; Je 26, S 5, 6, 1901; O 9, 1904; S 15, N 4, 1906. NIC/MMN: S 18, 1906.

THE EVENING PRESS (d) Binghamton. Ap 11, 1904 to date (1:1 to date). *Title changes*: *Binghamton Press* Ap 11, 1904–S 11, 1905; *Binghamton Press and Leader* S 18, 1905–Ag 17, 1927; *Binghamton Press* Ag 24, 1927–S 16, 1960; *Evening Press and Sunday Press* S 23, 1960–?; *The Evening Press*. *Pub*: Willis Sharpe Kilmer Ap 1904–?; Jerome B. Hadsell N 12, 1912–? Fred Stein 1961–Je 1970; Orb C. Reeder Je 14, 1970 to date. *Ed*: James Bronson 1904–1905; Fred W. Stein 1941–1970; Erwin C. Cronk Je 14, 1970 to date. *Pol*: Independent. *Format*: Forty-four pages, varying sizes 17″ x 22″, 18⅜″ x 22⅝″. *Circ*: 15,000. *Comment*: First issued from offices located in the Kilmer Building at the corner of Chenango and Lewis Streets. Then moved to new twelve story Press Building on Chenango Street. July 6, 1965 moved to Vestal Parkway East. In September, 1905 when the *Binghamton Leader* (q.v.) merged with the *Binghamton Press*, which had then been publishing for a year and a half, the *Press* continued the numbering of the *Leader* and changed to volume 28. *The Evening Press* joined the Gannett Newspaper Group in 1943. *Loc*: NBi: Ap 11, 1904–Ap 11, 1954 (1:1–?). NBiHi: Ap 11, 1904 (1:1); S 6, 1906 (29:125); Mr 9, 1921 (43:278); Ap 14, 1924; S 25, 1925; S 6, 1933 (55:125); Ag 14, 1945 (Extra); Ap 11, 1954. NBi/Press: Ap 11, 1904 to date. NIC/MMN: S 6, 1906 (29:125); N 10, 11, 1926.

EVENING PRESS AND SUNDAY PRESS see *EVENING PRESS*

HARPURSVILLE BUDGET (w) Harpursville. My 26, 1886–? (1:1–?). *Title changes*: *Harpersville Budget* My 26–Ag 24, 1886; *Harpursville Budget* Ag 25, 1886–?. *Pub*: Emerson Demeree 1886–1921; C. H. Christian 1921–? *Ed*: Emerson Demeree 1886–1920; Edward E. Hotckiss [*sic*]; Charles H. Christian 1921–? *Pol*: Independent Republican. *Format*: Four to eight pages, varying sizes 9½″ x 13″, 15″ x 22″, 15½″ x 24″, 13″ x 20″. *Price*: 50¢ per year (1886); $1.00 per year (1894); $2.00 per year (1920). *Comment*: The spelling of the town of Harpersville was changed to Harpursville by the Postmaster General in 1886. Merged with Afton Enterprise, Chenango County, about 1927. *Loc*: NAft/Mrs. John Delsole; D 26, 1894 (9:33); F 12, Ap 8, 22, My 27, Ag 12, 1920 (34:41, 49, 51; 35:4, 15); D 9, 15, 1921 (36:32, 33). NBiHi: S 28, 1916–Jl 1, 1920 (31:21–35:9). NWi: [My 26, 1886–My 18, 1887 (1:1–52)]. *See also* p. 286

HARPURSVILLE-NINEVEH STANDARD (w) Windsor. Je 8, 1928–N 18, 1932// (1:1–5:18). *Pub and Ed*: Otis H. Chidester 1928–1931; Otis H. and Harmon O. Chidester 1931; John C. Packard Ja 8–Jl 1932; John C. and William L. Packard Ag 1932; John C. Packard O 21–N 1932. *Format*: Eight pages 13" x 20". *Price*: $1.50 per year. *Comment*: Published and edited in the office of the *Windsor Standard*. *Loc*: NWi/Standard Office: Je 8, 1928–N 18, 1932 (1:1–5:18).

THE ILLUSTRATED POST (w) Binghamton. D 1, 1894–? (1:1–?). *Pub and Ed*: Charles H. Turner and F. D. Van Amburgh D 1, 1894–Ag 10, 1895; G. C. Kinsley and F. D. Van Amburgh Ag 10, 1895–? *Format*: Eight to twelve pages 17" x 22". *Comment*: Published from 142-144 State Street, Binghamton. *Loc*: NBiHi: [D 1, 1894–Ag 10, 1895 (1:1–37)].

THE INDEPENDENT (w) Binghamton. Ja 1894–? (1:1–?). *Pub*: The Independent Publishing Co. *Ed*: Fred E. Kennedy. *Format*: Sixteen pages 11" x 14¾". *Comment*: Published at 149 State Street. *Loc*: NIC/RHA: Ja 10, 1901 (8:2).

THE INQUIRER (w?) Binghamton. 1907–? (1:1–?). *Format*: Eight pages 17½" x 21¾". *Price*: 5¢ per copy. *Circ*: 25,000. *Loc*: NIC/MMN: S 29, 1907 (1:7).

THE IRIS (semi-m then w) Binghamton. Je 4, 1842–O 21, 1853// (1:1–12:31). *Pub*: Charles P. Cooke 1842–?; R. Andrews 1844; Edwin T. Evans 1844–1853; William Stuart and Edwin T. Evans 1851–1853. *Ed*: C. P. Cooke; Joseph Boughton; N. S. Davis 1843; Edwin T. Evans; William Stuart 1851–1853. *Pol*: Independent then Republican (Whig). *Format*: Four to eight pages, varying sizes 9½" x 12", 15⅞" x 21¾", 13" x 19¾". *Price*: $1.00 per issue or $5.00 for six copies; $10.00 for 13 copies. *Comment*: The first issue states that the newspaper was issued as "A semi-monthly journal devoted to miscellany, moral and sentimental anecdotes, poetry and polite literature generally." By 1846, it was issued weekly. An announcement appeared in *The Iris,* October 21, 1853, stating that "arrangements have been made by which the *Iris* is to be discontinued and merged into a new and larger paper to be called the *Susquehanna Journal* (q.v.)." Originally published at Franklin Street about four doors south of Cary and Company's store and moved to Court Street opposite the American Hotel about 1851. *Loc*: NBi: microfilm Je 17, 1843–Jl 6, 1844 (2:1–?); Mr 28, 1851–Mr 19, 1852 (10:1–52). NBiHi: Je 4, 1842–Je 3, 1843 (1:1–?: 26); Je 15, 1849 (8:12); S 12, 1851 (10:25); [Mr 28, 1846–F 9, 1849 (4:38–7:32)]; F 6, 1852–O 21, 1853 (10:46–12:31).

JOHNSON CITY-ENDICOTT RECORD see *THE RECORD*

JOHNSON CITY RECORD see *THE RECORD*

JOHNSON CITY JOURNAL (w) Johnson City. 1927–O 4, 1962//

(1:1–34:16). *Pub*: Harry Morgan 1927–?; Johnson City Journal, Inc. (Harold J. Granger, Pres.) 1942–1962. *Ed*: Harry Morgan 1927–?; Jack Bartlett 1943–?; Al Lamb 1953–1962. *Format*: Ten to fourteen pages 17½" x 22". *Comment*: Published at 52 Broad Street, Johnson City. Information on the opening and closing dates was supplied by Mr. Harold J. Granger. Copies of the first and last issues have not been located. *Loc*: NJoh: O 12, 1955 (26:39); Mr 13, 1958 (28:49); [F 1–S 20, 1962 (33:34–34:14)].

LATEST MORNING NEWS (d) Binghamton. Mr 16, 1882–Mr 5, 1884// (no. 1–?) *Pub and Ed*: Ira L. Wales and Frank A. Mantz. *Format*: Four pages 17" x 21¾". *Price*: 50¢ per month. *Comment*: Published at Hotel Bennett Building. "The *Latest Morning News* was started by Wales and Mantz, March 16, 1882, and was discontinued March 5, 1884. It was a sprightly venture in the way of news, both local and telegraphic, and a member of the associated press, independent in politics." (H. P. Smith, *History of Broome County*, p. 225.) *Loc*: NBiHi: Jl 1, 1882 (no. 93).

LESTERSHIRE-ENDICOTT RECORD see *THE RECORD*

LESTER-SHIRE NEWS (w) Lestershire (Johnson City). 1890–? (1:1–?). *Pub*: Lester-Shire News Co. *Format*: 24½" x 27". *Comment*: Only the front page of this newspaper has been located. *Loc*: NBiHi: Ap 11, 1891 (2:16).

LESTERSHIRE RECORD see *THE RECORD*

LISLE GLEANER AND NEW ERA (w) Lisle. My 1871–D 1928// (1:1–56:11). *Title changes*: *The Lisle Gleaner* 1871–1916; *Lisle Gleaner and New Era* 1916–1928. *Pub*: Gilbert A. Dodge 1871–?; Eugene Davis 1871–?; Clinton J. Peacock 1911–?; William M. Storrs 1915– Je 1925; Vernon Leslie Spencer Je 1925–S 1927; Fred White S 1927– D 1928. *Ed*: Eugene Davis My 1871–? Cyrus Davis early 1900s; Alfred and Byron Livermore; Clinton J. Peacock 1911; William Storrs 1915–?; F. E. Terwilliger Je 2, 1921–Je 1925; Vernon Leslie Spencer Je 1925–1927; Fred White S 27, 1927–D 1928. *Pol*: Independent. *Format*: Four to eight pages, varying sizes 15⅝" x 22", 17½" x 24", 15" x 22". *Price*: $1.00 per year (1871); $1.50 per year (1917). *Comment*: Motto: "We Glean for the People of Northern Broome. We Labor for the Interests of Lisle and Our Pocket Book." Published at Main Street, near the depot in Lisle. *Loc*: NBiHi: Ja 10, Ap 11, My 2, O 10, 24, D 12, 1877 (6:36, 48, 51; 7:22, 24, 31); My 1, 1878 (7:51); Mr 16, 1881 (10:45). NIC/RHA: My 30, 1891 (21:5); [Ja 2, 1892–Ja 14, 1893 (21:36–22:38)]. NLi: Mr 1, 1873 (2:44); My 5, 1875 (4:51); Ag 1, 1887 (17: 18); O 4, 1890 (20:23); O 11, 26, 1911 (40:20, 22); Ja 4–D 27, 1917 (45:14–46:11); Ja 1, 1920– Jl 1, 1926 (47:32–54:5); S 14, 1927–D 28, 1928 (55:1–56:11). *]

MORNING STAR AND BINGHAMTON CHRONICLE see *BINGHAMTON CHRONICLE*

MORNING SUN see *SUN-BULLETIN*

*See also p. 287

MORNING SUN AND RECORD see *THE SUNDAY SUN AND RECORD*

NEWS-DISPATCH see *THE ENDICOTT TIMES*

NIOGA REPORTER see *CHENANGO AMERICAN AND WHIT-NEY POINT REPORTER*

THE PHOENIX see *BINGHAMTON PHOENIX*

THE RADICAL DEMOCRAT (w) Windsor. O 22, 1846–? (1:1–?). *Pub and Ed*: Frederick G. Wheeler. *Pol*: Radical Democrat. *Format*: Four pages 16½" x 23". *Loc*: NBiHi: O 22, 1846 (1:1).

THE RECHABITE (m) Binghamton. *Pub*: Parlor City Tent #129, Order of Rechabites. *Pol*: Temperance. *Format*: Four pages 10" x 13". *Loc*: NBiHi: Mr 1890.

THE RECORD (w) Johnson City. 1896–N 19, 1921// (1:1–25:35). *Title changes*: *Lestershire-Endicott Record* 1896–1898; 1900–1915; *Lestershire Record* 1899; *Johnson City-Endicott Record* S 4, 1915–Ap 1917; *The Record* My 5, 1917–N 19, 1921. *Pub*: Z. A. Stegmuller 1899; William H. Hill 1900; The Lestershire-Endicott Publishing Co. (William H. Hill, President) 1912–1916; Johnson City Publishing Co. (William H. Hill, Proprietor) 1916–1921(?). *Ed*: Z. A. Stegmuller 1899; William H. Hill 1900; George H. Lyon 1917–Jl 1919; Ernest E. Noonan Jl 19, 1919–N 19, 1921. *Pol*: Independent then Republican. *Format*: Eight to forty pages, varying sizes 15" x 22", 17" x 22". *Comment*: From the issues in hand we cannot establish the exact date of the title change from the *Lestershire-Endicott Record* to the *Lestershire Record* and then back again. The date of change to the *Johnson City-Endicott Record,* etc. was established. Lestershire was renamed Johnson City in 1915. The paper was published in the Publishing House on Arch Street. On November 26, 1921, *The Record* merged with the *Binghamton Morning Sun* and became the *Sunday Sun and Record* (q.v.). *Loc*: NBiHi: N 3, 1899 (3:168); S 21 1900 (4:214); My 25, 1912 (16:801, special Memorial Day Issue); Ag 31, 1912 (no. 815). NEn: [Ja 30, 1915–N 19, 1921 (19:931–25:35)]. NIC/RHA: [Ja 4–D 27, 1901 (5:229–280)]; Ja 3–Je 26, 1920 (23:47–24:20).

REPUBLICAN AND STANDARD see *BROOME REPUBLICAN*

REPUBLICAN HERALD (w) Binghamton. 1818–1823// (1:1–?). *Pub*: Abraham Burrell 1818–1822(?); Peter Robinson F 12, 1822–1823. *Ed*: Abraham Burrell 1818–1822(?); Peter Robinson F 22, 1822–? *Pol*: Republican. *Format*: Four pages 11½" x 18¼". *Comment*: According to Smith's *History of Broome County,* Abraham Burrell started the *Republican Herald* in opposition to *The Phoenix* (q.v.). In 1820, Dorephus Abbey purchased Burrell's interest and continued the paper for a few years and then sold out to an association of citizens. *Loc*: NBiHi: Je 1821–F 25, 1823 (3:1–4:37); Mr 11, 1823 (4:39).

SATURDAY CALL see *BINGHAMTON CHRONICLE*

SATURDAY SENTINEL (w) Binghamton. 1885–? (1:1–?). *Pub and Ed*: Mahon and Will S. Secor. *Format*: Four pages 15″ x 22″. *Comment*: Published at 179 Water Street. *Loc*: NBiHi: Jl 4, 1885 (1:?).

THE SUN see *SUN-BULLETIN*

THE SUN-BULLETIN (d) Binghamton. F 23, 1849 to date (1:1 to date). *Title changes*: *The Daily Iris* F 23, 1849–My 1, 1849; *Binghamton Daily Republican* My 2, 1849–Ja 21, 1878; *Binghamton Republican and Morning Times* Ja 22, 1878–Jl 8, 1878; *Binghamton Morning Republican* Jl 9, 1878–Je 4, 1879; *Binghamton Daily Republican* Je 5, 1879–Ap 1, 1889; *Binghamton Republican* Ap 1889–My 3, 1889; *Binghamton Morning Republican* My 4, 1889–Ja 2, 1890; *Binghamton Republican* Ja 3, 1870–Je 30, 1912; *Binghamton Republican-Herald* Jl 1, 1912–Ag 17, 1919; *The Morning Sun* Ag 18, 1919–S 4, 1924; *The Sun* S 5, 1919–Ja 22, 1927; *The Binghamton Sun* Ja 23, 1927–Ag 31, 1960; *Binghamton Sun and Daily Bulletin* S 1–O 16, 1960; *The Sun-Bulletin* O 17, 1960 to date. *Pub*: Edwin T. Evans F 23, 1849–?; William Stuart Ag 20, 1853; Carl Brothers and Taylor 1861; William Stuart and James S. Cary 1863; George J. Reid 1867; Binghamton Republican Assoc. (George J. Reid, President) F 1875–?; Republican Printing Co. 1878; Binghamton Publishing Co. O 5, 1878–N 19, 1910; Southern Tier Publishing Co. (Owner of the Binghamton Publishing Co.) 1910–1920; George F. Johnson 1920; William H. Hill 1921; The Binghamton Publishing Co. (William H. Hill, President) O 1, 1923–Ja 1, 1924; The Morning Sun, Inc. (William H. Hill, President) Ja 2, 1924–1945; The Binghamton Sun, Inc. 1945–1960; David Bernstein and Harry S. Milligan 1960–1964; Sun Bulletin, Inc. 1964 to date. *Ed*: William Stuart 1849–Jl 18, 1866; George J. Reid and James Malette 1867–1868; James Malette 1868–1874; Frederick G. Mather 1874–1877; Charles M. Dickinson 1878–? George Gilbert N 21, 1910; Charles W. Baldwin Je 23, 1911; George H. Lyon 1919; Walter H. Lyon 1921; William H. Hill O 5, 1921–1960; David Bernstein 1960 to date. *Pol*: Independent at first, then Republican. Currently Independent. *Format*: Four to twenty-four pages, varying sizes 16″ x 21½″, 17½″ x 24″, 17¼″ x 22″, 18½″ x 25½″, 21″ x 28″, 23½″ x 29″. *Price*: $7.50 per year (1885); $3.00 per year (1906); $9.00 per year (1936); $26.00 per year (current). *Comment*: Published over the Post Office, 11 Franklin Street (1849); from third floor over Fish and Squires', opposite the American Hotel, Court Street (1851); 27-29 Court Street, opposite the American Hotel (1863); 71 Court Street, opposite the Post Office (1864); Corner of Court and Exchange Streets(1865); then temporarily in the Morgan Block, Water Street; then on May 5, 1870 into the Republican Building at 98 Water Street where it remained until 1919 when it moved to State and Henry; then to 60 Henry Street. The change in volume numbers during the second decade of the twentieth century suddenly claiming 97 years of existence can be explained by the fact that the *Sun-Bulletin* claims the *Broome Republican* which began in 1822 as its predecessor. *Loc*: NBi: microfilm F 23, 1849 to date (1:1 to date).

NBiHi: F 23, 1849 (1:1); Ag 18, 1855 (7:153); S 11, 1856 (8:?); Mr 19, 1858 (10:23); O 11, 1862 (14:199); Ap 15, 25, My 17, N 8, 1865 (17:46), 55, 73, 223); Ap 14–17, N 24, 1866 (18:46, 43 [sic], 47, 48, 239); Ap 27, 1867 (19:55); Je 22, 23, S 22, 24, 1869 (21:102, 103, 181, 183); Ja 12, 1871 (22:274); Ja 6, 7, 9, 1873 (24: 269, 270, 272); Ap 4, 1874 (26:36); D 15, 1875 (27:254); Mr 20, 1876 (28:24); Mr 2, 1877 (29:8); Ja 31, F 20, Jl 6, Ag 30, D 12, 31, 1878 (no numbers printed); My 19, 21, 1879; S 9, O 5, 1880; Mr 17, 18, S 20, 1881; Mr 27, Jl 25, O 30, D 13, 1882; My 23, Ag 23, D 3, 1883; Jl 4, 1885 (fragments); My 17, 1886; Jl 29, Ag 15, 1887; Ag 2, 1895; S 6, 1933 (?:202); Mr 19, 1936, (114:44). NBi/Sun-Bulletin: microfilm Ja 1948 to date. NIC/MMN: O 29, 31, N 7, 12, 1853 (5:214, 215, 221, 226); My 25, 1861 (16:71); O 31, 1863 (15:216 [sic]); Ja 4, 7, 1873 (24:268, 270); Jl 21, Ag 18, 1919 (97: 104, 218); Je 19, 1943 (121:219). NWhP: Jl 4, 1906 (no volume or number). *See also* p. 287

SUNDAY MESSAGE (w) Binghamton. 1893–? This newspaper founded by O. J. Coughlin is probably the Sunday edition of the *Binghamton Message* (q.v.). Unfortunately, no issues have been located, but the historical comments and the dates seem to indicate a strong relationship.

THE SUNDAY MORNING REPUBLICAN (w) Binghamton. Ap 13–Ag 3, 1884// (1:1–17). *Pub*: Binghamton Publishing Co. *Pol*: Republican. *Format*: Eight pages 17½″ x 24″. *Comment*: Published at 166 Water Street. *Loc*: NBi: microfilm Ap 13, 1884–Ag 3, 1884 (1:1–17); NIC/MMN: Jl 13, 1884 (1:14).

SUNDAY MORNING STAR AND BINGHAMTON CHRONICLE see *BINGHAMTON CHRONICLE*

THE SUNDAY PRESS see *THE EVENING PRESS*

THE SUNDAY SUN AND RECORD (w) Binghamton. N 27, 1921–Ap 30, 1922// *Pub and Ed*: William H. Hill. *Pol*: Republican. *Format*: 17¼″ x 22″. *Comment*: This paper was the Sunday edition of the *Morning Sun* with which *The Record* (q.v.) had been merged. High overhead cost and a depleted circulation caused the paper to lose money and the paper was suspended April 30, 1922. *Loc*: NBi: N 27, 1921–Ap 30, 1922.

SUSQUEHANNA JOURNAL (w) Binghamton. O 28, 1853–1855// (?) (1:1–?). *Pub and Ed*: Reverend W. H. Pearne. *Format*: Four pages 18″ x 26″. *Comment*: In the October 21, 1853 issue of *The Iris* the following statement appeared: "Arrangements have been made by which the *Iris* is to be discontinued or merged into a new and larger paper to be called *The Susquehanna Journal* of which the Reverend William H. Pearne is to be the editor. It will be printed in the office of the *Broome Republican*. The first number will probably appear October 28, 1853." Smith's *History of Broome County* states that the

Susquehanna Journal merged with the *Broome Republican* in 1855. *Loc*: NBiHi: Mr 10, 1854 (1:20).

THE TINKLE (w) Binghamton. S 23, 1876–? (1:1–?). *Pub*: William McDiarmid. *Ed*: Oliver Chalktree (pseud). *Pol*: Republican. *Format*: Four pages 18" x 24". *Comment*: Published at Court St. in Phelps Hardware Block. The newspaper's sub-title read "A campaign and family newspaper." Campaigned strongly for Rutherford B. Hayes. The motto of the paper was "Call a spade a spade." Its contributors, like its editor, published under the pseudonyms: "Hon. Tintorette Tawkooky, Pliny O. Skatz, A.M., Miss Clara Tattle, Miss Adelaide Louise Calyx." *Loc*: NBiHi: S 23, 1876 (1:1).

TRI-COUNTY JOURNAL see *DEPOSIT JOURNAL*

THE UNION-ENDICOTT NEWS see *THE ENDICOTT TIMES*

THE UNION NEWS see *THE ENDICOTT TIMES*

THE UNION WEEKLY NEWS see *THE ENDICOTT TIMES*

THE VESTAL NEWS (w) Vestal. N 20, 1947 to date (1:1 to date). *Pub*: Stephen C. Hambalek and Robert R. Eckert 1947–1952; Robert R. Eckert D 1952–1954; James W. Trevitt O 6, 1954–My 1957; George R. Hill Je 6, 1957 to date. *Ed*: Stephen C. Hambalek and Robert R. Eckert 1947–1952; Robert R. Eckert 1952–O 6, 1954; James W. Trevitt O 1954–Je 1957; George R. Hill Je 6, 1957 to date. *Pol*: Independent. *Format*: Six to forty pages, varying sizes 11" x 17", 14" x 21½", 17" x 22¼", 18" x 22¼", 11½" x 16". *Price*: $2.00 per year (1947); $2.50 per year (1952); $3.50 per year (1959); $5.00 per year (1970). *Comment*: When Stephen C. Hambalek and Robert R. Eckert founded the paper they called themselves the Vestal News and Printing Company. In 1952 when Robert R. Eckert bought the controlling interest, he changed the name of the company to Southern Tier Publications, Inc., although the old name Vestal News and Printing Company still appeared in the paper that year. Stephen C. Hambalek also purchased the *Spencer Needle* in Tioga County. *Loc*: NVes: Latest issues only. NVes/News Office: N 20, 1947 to date (1:1 to date).

WHITNEY POINT REPORTER see *CHENANGO AMERICAN AND WHITNEY POINT REPORTER* and p. 287

WHITNEY'S POINT REPORTER see *CHENANGO AMERICAN AND WHITNEY POINT REPORTER*

WINDSOR STANDARD (w) Windsor. My 11, 1878 to date (1:1 to date). *Title changes*: Windsor Standard 1913–Je 12, 1924; The Windsor Standard Je 19, 1924–1968; Deposit Courier and Windsor Standard Ja 18, 1968–Je 1968; Windsor Standard Je 9, 1968 to date. *Pub and Ed*: C. E. Babcock My 11, 1878–My 18, 1894; William D. Osgood 1894–?; Ernest R. Chaffee 1907(?)–1914; Brainard W. Russell Ap 16–Ag 25, 1924; Otis H. Chidester Ag 25, 1924–Ap 16, 1931; Otis

H. and H. O. Chidester Ap 16 1931–Ja 1932; John C. Packard Ja 7, 1932–Ap 1, 1933; Otis H. and H. O. Chidester Ap 1933–My 4, 1933; Marvin H. Mallery My 4, 1933–My 18, 1967; Lawrence J. Coleman My 18, 1967–F 1969; Marvin H. Mallery Mr 1, 1969–S 1969; David E. Baker S 1969; Minerva J. Smith 1968 to date. *Format*: Four to ten pages, varying sizes 14⅜ " x 20¾ ", 17½ " x 24½", 16¾ " x 22½ ", 11¼ " x 16½ ". *Price*: $1.00 per year (1890); $4.00 per year (1970). *Comment*: Published over Wooster's store on the North Block, Windsor. *Loc*: NWi: Je 8, 1878 (1:4); My 20, 1882 (5:2); My 10, 1895– My 6, 1898 (18:1–20:52); My 12, 1899–My 2, 1902 (22:1–24:52); Ja 1, 1903–Ap 25, 1907 (25:35–29:52); Ag 17, 1916 (39:18); Ja 9, 1919 (41:39); Ja 13, 1920 (43 [*sic*]:40); N 11, 1920 (43:31); D 2, 1920 (43:34); Ja 12, 1922 (44:40); Ja 10, 1924 (46:40). NWi/Standard Office: My 11, 1878–My 8, 1880 (1:1–2:52); My 11, 1894– My 3, 1895 (17:1–52); [Ja 1, 1911 to date].

THE WINDSOR TIMES (w) Windsor. Ag 2, 1873–? (1:1–?) *Pub*: W. D. Haley Ag 9, 1873–S 6, 1873; A. E. Benedict S 1873–N 29, 1873; W. D. Haley D 1873–?. *Ed*: W. D. Haley Ag 9, 1873–N 29, 1873; A. E. Benedict D 1873–? *Pol*: Independent. "An independent Paper, Upholding the Views of No Political Party, but giving Unbiased Opinions on Public Matters and Advocating Local Interests and Social Welfare." *Format*: Four pages, varying sizes 15" x 22¼ ", 17‴ x 23". *Loc*: NBiHi: Ag 9, 1873–Jl 5, 1874 (1:2–49).

THE ADVERTISER-JOURNAL (d) Auburn. Mr 2, 1846–My 31, 1931// (1:1–no vol. no.). *Title changes*: *Auburn Daily Advertiser* Mr 2, 1846–Mr 7, 1861; *Auburn Daily Advertiser & Auburn Union* Mr 8, 1861–Ja 27, 1863; *Auburn Daily Advertiser & Union* F 3, 1863–Ag 15, 1867; *Auburn Daily Advertiser* Ag 22, 1867–N 28, 1913; The *Advertiser-Journal* N 29, 1913–My 31, 1931. *Pub*: Henry Oliphant Mr 2–S 14, 1846; Henry Montgomery S 15, 1846–My 25, 1848; Charles T. Ferris My 26, 1848–1849; Oscar F. Knapp and George W. Peck 1849–1877; Oscar F. and Horace J. Knapp, George R. and Henry D. Peck 1877–1883; Oscar F. and Horace J. Knapp, George R. and Henry D. Peck, and Edward H. Thomson Ja 2, 1883–S 2, 1913 (sometime before 1907 Oscar F. Knapp's name was dropped); Auburn Advertiser Publishing Co. (George W. Benham, Pres., Herbert J. Fowler, Secy-Treas., William E. Keeler, George W. Bowen, and D. E. French) 1913–1915; Advertiser-Journal, Inc. (Herbert J. Fowler, Pres.) F 24, 1915–1923; The Auburn Publishing Co. O 4, 1923–1931. *Ed*: Henry Oliphant Mr 2–S 14, 1846; Henry Montgomery S 15, 1846–My 25, 1848; Henry Montgomery and George W. Peck 1848–1849; George W. Peck 1849–1877; George R. and Henry D. Peck 1877–1888; George R. Peck 1888–?; Herbert J. Fowler S 2, 1913–1923; Victor J. Callahan and Rudolph W. Chamberlain 1923–1931. *Pol*: Whig; later Republican. *Format*: Four to sixteen pages, varying sizes, 13″ x 19″, 15½″ x 23″, 20″ x 27″. *Price*: $4.00 per year in advance, otherwise $4.50 (1846); $5.00 per year, 2¢ per copy (1850); $5.50 per year, 2¢ per copy (1859); $8.50 per year, 5¢ per copy (1872); $6.00 per year, 3¢ per copy (1893–1907); $6.00 per year, 2¢ per copy (1907). *Circ*: 4000 (1861–63); 4317 (1913). *Comment*: Originally published at 96 Genesee St.; at the corner of Genesee and State Sts. from December 1, 1846 until 1853; at the New Building adjacent to the Bank of Auburn in 1853; in 1856 at 118 Genesee St. Benjamin F. Hall, Henry Hall, and Charles A. Caulkin were editors in the 1850s and 1860s with George W. Peck (Elliot G. Storke, "History of the Press," *The Auburn Bulletin*, Dec. 13, 1877.) In 1931 the Auburn Publishing Co. which had been publishing the *Auburn Citizen* simultaneously with the *Advertiser-Journal* merged

Auburn Daily Bulletin.

VOLUME 2.   *AUBURN, N. Y., WEDNESDAY, MARCH 29, 1871*   NUMBER 342

the two newspapers and issued the *Citizen-Advertiser* (q.v.). *Loc*:
NAub: [Ap 1903–My 31, 1931]. NAubHi: Mr 28, Je 4, 1846 (1:24,
108); [My 25, 1848–My 31, 1931 (3:75–no vol. no.)]. NAuW: Jl 12,
1870 (25:101); Mr 24, 1875; My 28, 1877; My 21, 1881; Ag 13, 18,
1884; D 30, 1886. NIC/MMN: microfilm S 15, 1846–My 31, 1931
(1:169–no vol. no.). NIC/RHA: My 27, 1846 (1:75); S 15, 1846–
D 31, 1847 (1:169–2:260); D 27, 1848 (3:258); Ap 15, S 18, 1865
(20:40, 166); Ja 22, 23, 1867 (21:277, 278); O 11, 14, 1872 (17
[*sic*]: 216, 268); O 21, 22, 1881; 1895 (Anniversary Edition); D
1906 (Holiday Edition); Ja 14, 1911 (68th Year). NRU: [Mr 2,
1846–D 29, 1854 (1:1–9:255)]; O 14, 1872 (17 [*sic*]:219).

ADVOCATE OF THE PEOPLE (w) Auburn. S 18, 1816–Mr 11,
1818// (1:1–2:78). *Pub*: Henry C. Southwick. *Pol*: Democratic-
Republican. *Format*: Four pages 13″ x 20½″. *Comment*: Motto:
"Where liberty dwells there is my country—Franklin." Like many
other newspapers in Cayuga County, the *Advocate* died because the
county was not large enough to support several papers published
simultaneously. Southwick stated, "Cayuga County cannot support
three presses . . . the two denominated Republican, necessarily under
such a state of things divide . . . business between them, which is but
miserable compensation for either, but if joined together might perhaps sustain one press." *Loc*: NAubHi: [O 2, 1816–Mr 11, 1818
(1:3–2:78)].

AUBURN (w) Auburn. N 1887–F 16, 1889// (1:1–2:14). *Pub and
Ed*: William P. Allen. *Format*: Eight pages 11″ x 14¼″. *Price*: $2.00
per year in advance, 5¢ per copy. *Comment*: Motto: "Learning, Let-
ters and Laughter." Published at 101 Genesee St. Allen announced
that the February 16, 1889 issue of the newspaper would be the last.
He stated that he could hardly restrain a tear at seeing its departure
to "that other world where deceased journalistic ventures attain the
harp and crown and are forever released from skurrying [*sic*] about
for advertisements." Only 14 copies of the last issue were printed.
Loc: NIC/RHA: F 16, 1889 (2:14). *See also* p. 287

AUBURN AMERICAN see *AUBURN DAILY UNION* and *AU-
BURN WEEKLY UNION*

THE AUBURN ARGUS (w) Auburn. Ja 2, 1891–D 31, 1897//
(1:1–7:52). *Pub and Ed*: Jno. N. Bailey. *Pol*: Democrat. *Format*:
Eight pages 14½″ x 21½″. *Price*: $1.00 per year in advance. *Com-
ment*: Published at 24 State St.; on August 1, 1893 moved to 3 State
St. Bailey stated that he started *The Auburn Argus* "to supply an ap-
parent demand. It comes into being not to aid in any one man's ambi-
tion. The Democratic Party, much bigger than any dozen men in it,
is engaged in a powerful struggle with corporate greed, wealthy tariff
and monopoly loving plutocrats. . . . It [the *Argus*] will be against all
public evils and abuses. . . ." After 1897 the *Argus* merged with the
Weekly News and Democrat and was issued under a new title, the
Auburn Democrat-Argus (q.v.). *Loc*: NIC/MMN: Ja 2, 1891–D 31,
1897 (1:1–7:52).

AUBURN BANNER (w) Auburn. 1832–?. *Comment*: Listed in Winifred Gregory, *Union List of Serials*, p. 441. No issues located.

THE AUBURN BANNER AND GENESEE, ONEIDA AND BLACK RIVER CONFERENCE RECORD (w) Auburn. Ja 5, 1837–? (1:1–?). *Title changes*: *The Auburn Banner and Genesee, Oneida and Black River Conference Record* 1837–1838(?); *Conference and Family Recorder* 1839; *The Auburn Banner and Genesee, Oneida and Black River Conference Record* 1839–?. *Pub*: Joint Publishing Committee (Loring Grant, Jonathan Huestis, Israel Chamberlayne, George Peck, Zechariah Paddock, James Richardson, Charles Giles, Luther Lee and Albert D. Peck 1837; Loring Grant, Jonathan Huestis, George Peck, Zechariah Paddock, James Richardson, Luther Lee, Albert D. Peck, Manly Tester, Horace Agard and Isaac Stone 1838); Committee of Nine Ministers 1839. *Ed*: Israel Chamberlayne. *Format*: Four pages 17" x 23¾". *Price*: $2.00 per year in advance, $2.50 per year after 6 months; $3.00 per year after one year. *Comment*: Published at No. 8 and 11 Exchange Buildings. The newspaper was an organ of the Methodist Episcopal Church. *Loc*: NAubHi: Ja 3–D 26, 1838 (2:1–53). NIC/MMN: Ap 17, 1839 (3:15). NIC/RHA: Ja 5, 1837 (1:1); Mr 14, 28, 1838 (2:11, 13).

THE AUBURN BULLETIN (d) Auburn. F 16, 1870–S 30, 1905// (1:1–85:79327). *Title changes*: *Auburn Daily Bulletin* F 16, 1870–Je 1, 1879; *Auburn News and Bulletin* Je 2, 1879–Ja 2, 1885; *News-Bulletin-Auburnian* Ja 3–D 31, 1885; *The Auburn Bulletin* Ja 2, 1886–S 30, 1905. *Pub and Ed*: K. Vail & Co. (Kendrick Vail and William J. Moses) 1870–1879; William J. Moses 1879–? *Pol*: Independent. *Format*: Four to eight pages, varying sizes, 17" x 23½", 15¼" x 22". *Price*: $5.00 per year in advance, 3¢ per copy (1871–1872); $6.00 per year in advance, 15¢ per week (1872–1905). *Comment*: Published from the corner of Clark and Green Sts. Founded to fill "The want of a low priced daily paper within the means of the poor as well as the rich, independent of all cliques, devoted to the welfare of the taxpayer, the mechanics, the laboring man and the rights and interests of all classes. . . ." In the 1890s Moses is cited as the founder of the newspaper, but his name is not listed as a member of K. Vail & Co. before June 2, 1879. In the 1880s and in the twentieth century no publishers or editors are listed. However, according to Charles F. Rattigan (*History of Cayuga County, New York*, pp. 122-123) Edward M. Allen was editor for several years until 1893 when he was succeeded by Charles F. Rattigan who remained in that position until 1905. The *Auburn Morning News* (q.v.) merged with the *Daily Bulletin* June 2, 1879. From that date until June 7, 1882 double numbering appeared on the banner of the *Auburn News and Bulletin*. When the *Evening Auburnian* (q.v.) merged with the *Auburn News and Bulletin* on January 3, 1885, its title was carried on the banner for one year, then the newspaper reverted to its original title, *The Auburn Bulletin*, dropping the "Daily." On September 30, 1905 the editor anounced that the *Bulletin* would cease as such and would be issued as the *Auburn Citizen* (q.v.). *Loc*: NAub: Ja 3, 1871–D 31, 1878 (1:270–18:2651); Je 2, 1879–Je 30, 1881 (20:1–22:4848); S 20, 1881 (24:4917); Ja 2, 1903–S 30, 1905 (87:7119 [*sic*]–85:79327 [*sic*]). NAubHi: [F 16, 1870–D 31, 1879 (1:1–21: 2980); Ja 2, 1880–Je 30, 1881 (21:181–22:4848)]; S 20, 1881 (24: 4917); N 27, 1885 (29:6192); O 5, 1892 (50:7071); F 8, 1893 (51:7176); F 6, 1897 (58:8377). NIC/MMN: F 16, 1870–S 30, 1905 (1:1–85:79327 [*sic*]). NIC/RHA: D 16, 1873 (7:1181); Ag 1, 1874 (9:1293); S 20, O 18, 26, 1881 (24:4917, 4941, 4948).

AUBURN CAYUGA CHIEF see *CAYUGA CHIEF*

AUBURN CITIZEN (d) Auburn. O 2, 1905–Ap 1931// (1:1 [85: 79328]–?). *Pub*: Thomas Mott Osborne and Charles F. Rattigan 1905–1921; Auburn Publishing Co. 1921–1931. *Ed*: Charles F. Rattigan 1905–? *Pol*: Independent with Democratic leanings. *Format*: Ten to thirty-two pages, varying sizes, 11″ x 16¾″, 16¾″ x 21¾″. *Price*: 2¢ per copy. *Comment*: In 1905 Thomas Mott Osborne and Charles F. Rattigan, former *Bulletin* editor, formed a stock company, bought out *The Auburn Bulletin* (q.v.) and published a new paper, the *Auburn Citizen*, into which the *Bulletin* was merged. The numbering for *The Auburn Bulletin* appeared sporadically on the banner along with that of the *Citizen*. The Auburn Publishing Co. also published *The Advertiser-Journal* (q.v.) as a separate paper. The company finally decided to merge the *Auburn Citizen* with *The Advertiser-Journal* in 1931, and the *Citizen-Advertiser* (q.v.) emerged. The *Auburn Citizen* was published at 34-36 Dill St. throughout its twenty-six years as a separate paper. *Loc*: NAub: O 2, 1905–D 31, 1913 (1:1 [85:79328]–8:2339). NAubC: microfilm Ja 1920–D 1930. NAubHi: O 2, 1905 (1:1 [85:79328]); Mr 20, 1910 (fragment); NIC/MMN: O 2, 1905–Ap 30, 1909 (1:1 [85:79328]–4:1103 [88:80429]); My 1, 1928–Ag 31, 1928 (22:6931 [53:17938]–22:7033 [53:18040]). NIC/ RHA: My 1, 1909–D 31, 1919 (4:1104–15:1371).

AUBURN CITY NEWS (m) Auburn. Ap 1860–? (1:1–?). *Pub*: Lewis M. Dean. *Format*: Two pages 10″ x 13¼″. *Price*: 25¢ per year. *Circ*: 6,000. *Comment*: Motto: "A monthly newspaper devoted to the interests of the people." Published at the Advocate Building, 16 Clark Street. *Loc*: NAubHi: Ja 1861 (1:10).

AUBURN COMMERCIAL REVIEW Auburn. Ja 1, 1898–? (1:1–?). *Format*: Eight pages 15½″ x 21½″. *Comment*: Listed as an "historical, descriptive and commercial review," this first issue cited neither publisher nor editor nor frequency of publication. It listed jobbing, manufacturing and mercantile houses. *Loc*: NAubHi: Ja 1, 1898 (1:1).

AUBURN DAILY ADVERTISER see *THE ADVERTISER-JOURNAL*

AUBURN DAILY ADVERTISER AND AUBURN UNION see *THE ADVERTISER-JOURNAL*

AUBURN DAILY ADVERTISER AND UNION see *THE AD-VERTISER-JOURNAL*

AUBURN DAILY AMERICAN see *AUBURN DAILY UNION*

AUBURN DAILY BULLETIN see *THE AUBURN BULLETIN*

AUBURN DAILY ITEM see *THE EVENING AUBURNIAN*

AUBURN DAILY NEWS (d) Auburn. My 14–Ag 31, 1838// (?) (1:1–51). *Pol*: Non-Partisan: "We shall meddle with no one's politics or religion." *Format*: Four pages 8⅝ " x 11¾ ". *Price*: 50¢ per month, 2¢ per copy. *Comment*: Published at the Auburn Job Printing Office, No. 3 Centre Buildings. Neither publisher nor editor is listed. On June 8 the editor stated that there was no profit in the daily, and asked his subscribers to let him know if they wanted to have the paper continued. No newspapers have been located after August 31, 1838. *Loc*: NAubHi: [My 14–Ag 31, 1838 (1:1–51)].

AUBURN DAILY UNION (d) Auburn. F 1, 1855–Mr 7, 1861// (1:1–6:1884). *Title changes*: *Auburn Daily American* F 1, 1855–Je 18, 1859; *Auburn Daily Union* Je 20, 1859–Mr 7, 1861. *Pub*: William J. Moses 1855–1859; William J. Moses and Kendrick Vail 1859–1861. *Ed*: J. Stanley Smith 1855–1858; William J. Moses 1858–1859; Benjamin F. Hall and William J. Moses 1859–1861. *Pol*: American Party 1855–1859; Republican 1859–1861; Anti-Slavery and Temperance 1855–1861. *Format*: Four pages 16½ " x 24½ ". *Price*: $5.00 per year, 10¢ per week, 2¢ per copy. *Comment*: Motto: "Let us dare to do our duty" (Lincoln). Published every evening from the corner of Genesee and State Sts. An editorial in the *Albany Evening Journal,* July 23, 1860, stated that the newspaper was started as a distinctive "American" organ in New York State by J. Stanley Smith. "As the voters have wisely come to support Republican principles, so has the *Union* since it has been under the editorial wing of Honorable B. F. Hall." The newspaper was the official paper of the city and contains the official canvass for 1885 (N 21, 1855) and 1856 (D 9, 1856). In March 1861, the newspaper was sold to Knapp and Peck of the *Auburn Daily Advertiser* and was published as the *Auburn Daily Advertiser and Auburn Union* from March 8, 1861 until 1863 and then as the *Auburn Daily Advertiser and Union* until 1867. *Loc*: NAubHi: D 9, 1856 (Extra), D 18, 19, 1856 (2:580, 581); [Ja 10–Mr 28, D 9, 1857 (2:598–664, 3:870)]; Ap 23, Je 15, 1859 (4:1306, 1351); Ag 16, N 21, 1859 (4:1403–1486); Jl 2, 1860–Mr 7, 1861 (6:1677–1884). NIC/MMN: F 1, 1885–Mr 7, 1861 (1:1–6:1884).

AUBURN DEMOCRAT see *AUBURN DEMOCRAT-ARGUS*

AUBURN DEMOCRAT-ARGUS (w, semi-w) Auburn. S 17, 1868–? (1:1–?). *Title changes*: *The Auburn Democrat* S 17, 1868–D 1873; *Auburn Weekly News and Democrat* D 18–25, 1873; *Weekly News and Democrat* Ja 1, 1874–D 29, 1897; *Auburn Democrat-Argus* 1898 (?)–? *Pub and Ed*: Durston & Co. (Charles F. Durston, Esq.

and William J .Moses) 1868–1869; Jno. N. Bailey 1869–1873; Auburn Printing Co. (William J. Moses and H. Laurens Storke, Pres. and Secy-Treas.) D 18, 1873–1897; William J. Moses, 1898 (?)–?. *Pol*: Democrat. *Format*: Four to sixteen pages, varying sizes, 17" x 24½", 19¾" x 26½", 14¾" x 21¾", 16½" x 21". *Price*: $2.00 per year in advance, 50¢ quarterly (1868–1878); $1.50 per year in advance (1878–1886); $1.00 per year (1887–?). *Circ*: 1,600 (1872). *Comment*: During the campaign of 1868, Durston and Moses began the publication with the hope that they would "successfully expose the high handed wickedness that actuates the Jacobin Republicans in their cruel and unjust war upon the rights and liberties of the people of the country and especially of the laboring classes." In 1873 Moses started the *Auburn Weekly News* (q.v.) in order to fill subscribers' demands for a weekly news of the same politics as the *Auburn Morning News* (q.v.). The *Weekly News* continued for only a year and half and then was merged with the *Auburn Democrat* and was issued as the *Auburn Weekly News and Democrat* with continuous numbering of both the *News* and the *Democrat* until September 9, 1886. Publisher and editor are not listed on the masthead. The newspaper regularly published the official election canvass. Published at 16 Clark St.; then, 1883–1905, from William J. Moses' Book Bindery at 27–29 Clark Street; 34–36 Dill Street from 1905. *Loc*: NIC/ MMN: S 17, 1868–S 9, 1869 (1:1–52); D 18, 1873–D 26, 1889 (2:51 & 16:15–22:52); Ja 6, 1892–D 29, 1897 (25:1–26:53); Ja 2, 1900–D 30, 1913 (29:1–41:104).

AUBURN EVENING DISPATCH see *EVENING DISPATCH*

AUBURN FREE PRESS (w) Auburn. Je 2, 1824–My 15, 1833// (1:1–9:52). *Title changes*: *Free Press* Je 24, 1824–My 19, 1830; *Auburn Free Press* My 26, 1830–My 15, 1833. *Pub*: Richard Oliphant 1824–Jl 15, 1829; Henry Oliphant Jl 22, 1829–?. *Pol*: Democratic-Republican. *Format*: Four pages, varying sizes, 12¾" x 20", 15" x 20¼". *Price*: $1.50 to $2.00 per year. *Comment*: Motto: "The tyrant's foe; the people's friend." Published from the west corner of South and Genesee Sts. until April 14, 1830; then from the east corner of Hotel and Genesee Sts. In 1833 Oliphant merged the paper with the *Cayuga Republican* (q.v.) to form the *Auburn Journal* (q.v.). *Loc*: NAubHi: Ja 1, 1825–Mr 1, 1826 (1:32–2:40); My 31, 1826–My 21, 1828 (3:1–4:52). NRU/Rare: Je 2, 1824–My 24, 1825 (1:1–52); Ja 4, 1826–My 15, 1833 (2:32–9:52).

AUBURN GAZETTE (w) Auburn. Je 12, 1816–Mr 17, 1819// (1:1–3:41). *Pub and Ed*: Thomas M. Skinner and William S. Crosby Je 12–D 31, 1816; Thomas M. Skinner Ja 1817–Je 26, 1819. *Pol*: Independent. *Format*: Four pages 13" x 20⅓". *Price*: $2.00 per year. *Comment*: Published at the Printing Office and Book Store of Skinner and Crosby. William Crosby died, age 22, December 27, 1817. On June 23, 1819, Skinner sold the paper to Frederick Prince, but did not sever his connection. Skinner stated that he had started the *Gazette* because he felt that the federal government was in a terrible state, but since the government in 1819 was so much improved, he no longer felt the need to publish and sold the paper to Frederick Prince. Prince published the newspaper the following week under a new title, the *Cayuga Republican* (q.v.). *Loc*: NAubHi: Je 12, 1816– Mr 17, 1819 (1:1–3:41). NIC/RHA: [My 27, 1818–Mr 10, 1819 (2:103–3:40)].

AUBURN HERALD (semi-w) Auburn. 1865–? (1:1–?). *Pub and Ed*: N. T. Hackstaff and G. E. Bostwick. *Pol*: Democrat. *Format*: Four pages 15¾" x 22". *Price*: $4.00 per year delivered, $3.00 by mail. *Comment*: Published at the corner of State and Genesee Sts. Storke says this paper continued for only six months. (*History of Cayuga County*, p. 53). *Loc*: NMor: O 20, 1865 (1:8).

THE AUBURN IDEA (m?) Auburn. 1890(?)–? (1:1–?). *Format*: Eight pages 17½" x 22½". *Price*: 2¢ per copy. *Loc*: NAubHi: N 1894 (5:2).

AUBURN JOURNAL (w, semi-w) Auburn. My 22, 1833–? (1:1–?). *Title changes*: *Auburn Journal* My 22, 1833–My 21, 1834; *Auburn Journal and Advertiser* My 28, 1834–1846; *Auburn Journal* 1846–?; *Auburn Weekly Journal* 1848–?; *Auburn Journal and Weekly Union* Mr 1861–?; *Auburn Semi-Weekly Journal* 1906–?; *Auburn Journal*. *Pub*: Thomas Skinner and Henry Oliphant My 22, 1833–D 30, 1840; Henry Oliphant Ja 6, 1841–S 16, 1846; Henry Montgomery S 23, 1846–1848; Charles T. Ferris 1848–1849; Oscar F. Knapp and George W. Peck 1849–1877; Oscar F. and Horace J. Knapp, George R. and Henry D. Peck 1877–1883; Oscar F. and Horace J. Knapp, George R. and Henry D. Peck and Edward H. Thomson 1883–? *Ed*: Henry Oliphant 1833–1846; Henry Montgomery 1846–1848; George W. Peck 1849–1877; George R. Peck 1877–? *Pol*: Whig, Temperance; Republican. *Format*: Four to eight pages, varying sizes, 15¼" x 21¼", 17½" x 23½", 21" x 27¾", 23¾" x 29". *Price*: $2.00 per year delivered; $1.50 at the office; 4¢ per copy (1833–?); $5.00 per year, $4.00 per year in advance (1852–1856); $6.00 per year, 3¢ per copy (1906–?). *Comment*: In May 1833, Henry Oliphant merged the *Auburn Free Press* (q.v.) with the *Cayuga Republican* (q.v.), edited by Thomas Skinner, to form the *Auburn Journal*. In the first issue, the editor said he aimed "to instruct, amuse my patrons as far as is in my power—to place before them weekly a choice, rich and delicate journal of whatever may be interesting in news, instructive in knowledge or beautiful in poesy." On politics: "It is deemed only necessary to say that its course will be marked by unwavering attachment to the cause of genuine Republicanism . . . yet it will ever be our aim to keep its columns free from that servile devotion to a name which disgraces far too many of our public journals . . . we trust with confidence upon an enlightened public opinion . . . not on the spoils of party to sustain us." In March 1861, Knapp & Peck purchased the *Auburn Weekly Union* (q.v.) from William J. Moses and merged it and the *Journal* to form the *Auburn Journal and Weekly Union,* later the *Auburn Journal*. Published at the East corner of Genesee and

Hotel Sts. until 1835; then from Messers Carpenter and Bodley's stone
building; later from No. 1 Exchange Building. The official canvass
for Cayuga County is published in 1840. Loc: NAub: [My 31, 1837–
D 30, 1840 (5:3–8:34)]; [Ja 3, 1844–N 30, 1846 (11:35–14:35)].
NAubHi: My 22, 1833–My 21, 1834 (1:1–53); O 13, 1834 (Extra);
My 20, N 18, 1840 (8:2, 28); Ap 6, 1842 (9:48); Mr 8, Je 28, 1843
(10:44, 11:8); F 12, 19, Jl 16–30, 1845 (12:41, 42; 13:11–13); Mr
18, D 16, 1846 (13:46; 14: 33); Je 14, 28, S 13, 1848 (16:7, 9, 20);
Jl 14, 1852 (20:12); Ja 11, 1854 (21:36); Mr 16, 1859 (27:46); Jl
18, Ag 15, 29, O 3–17, 1860 (29:12, 16, 18, 23–25); My 2, Je 3, Jl
10, 1861 (30:1, 10, 15); F 19, Ap 2, 30, My 9, 30, 1862 (30:42,
48, 49, 52); Ja 31, 1866 (36:48); My 30, Je 20, 1877 (51:7 [sic], 7);
Mr 20, 1879 (52:55). NIC/MMN: S 23, 1846–D 29, 1847 (14:21–
15:35); N 20, 1850 (18:30); My 5, 1852–D 31, 1856 (20:2–23:87,
whole no. 1231); Ap 17, 1861 (29:50 fragment); Ja 3, 1877–D 26,
1877 (50:50–vol. 51); Ja 2–Je 29, 1906 (78th year); Ja 1, 1907–D
29, 1908 (80–81st year); Je 3, 1910–Je 27, 1913 (82–83rd year).
NRU: [My 22, 1833–Ap 28, 1847 (1:1–14:52)]; [Ja 4, 1877–D 1878
(vol. 51)].

AUBURN   JOURNAL   AND   ADVERTISER   see   *AUBURN
JOURNAL*

AUBURN   JOURNAL   AND   WEEKLY   UNION   see   *AUBURN
JOURNAL*

AUBURN LABOR WEEKLY (w) Auburn. N 4, 1910–? (1:1–?).
Pub: T. C. Shandley and J. F. Stevens N 11, 1910–1911; Cayuga
County News Co. (J. Charles Dayton, Pres.) Ja 13, 1911–? *Ed*:
James C. Caroll (also business agent) of the Central Labor Union.
Format: Four to eight pages, varying sizes, 16¼ " x 21¾ ", 18" x
21½ ". *Price*: 50¢ per year. *Circ*: 2,000. *Comment*: "Published by
and for the Central Labor Union by and for the Auburn People." It
was organized labor's official newspaper. In 1910 it was published at
39 Market Street; January 13, 1911 in rooms 32 and 33 Cady Block,
Smith Street; on July 12, 1912, room 85, Genesee St. The Printing
Office was on Owasco Rd. Although the dates of issues on each newspaper are reliable, the numbering is not. As many as eight issues are labeled
vol. 1 no. 39; many other single issues are completely out of consecutive order. *Loc*: NAubHi: N 4, 1910–D 27, 1912 (1:1–2:52).

AUBURN MISCELLANY Auburn. 1835–1839. *Comment*: No issues
located. Mentioned in Storke, *History of Cayuga County*, p. 51.
Started by Frederick Prince after unsuccessful venture with the *Cayuga Democrat* (q.v.).

AUBURN MORNING DISPATCH (d) Auburn. Jl 1, 1885–?
(1:1–?). *Pub*: Morning Dispatch Association. *Pol*: Independent.
Format: Eight pages (16 page anniversary edition) 15¼ " x 21½ ".
Price: $6.00 per year. *Comment*: A daily, weekly and Sunday edition
of the *Dispatch* was published each with its own volume and series
numbering and each starting in a different year, but all published

from 24 Dill St. The paper referred to itself as "The Brightest and Best Newspaper in Central New York." *Loc*: NAubHi: My 25, Jl 7, 10–12, 1886 (2:74; 3:6, 9–11); Ap 27, My 2, 1887 (3:256, 260). NIC/MMN: [Je 1–D 30, 1886 (2:106 [*sic* 3:1]–3:156)]; Jl 16, 18, 1887 (5:14, 17). NStV/Cooper: O 30, 1886 (3:104).

AUBURN MORNING NEWS (d) Auburn. Jl 6, 1868–Ja 27, 1871// (1:1–6:22). *Pub*: Dennis Brothers & Co. (David M. Osborne, J. Fred and Roland R. Dennis) 1868–1869; J. Fred and Roland R. Dennis and Charles E. Thorne Jl 2, 1869–1871. *Ed*: W. H. Barnes 1868–1869; Dennis brothers and Charles E. Thorne 1869–1871. *Pol*: Republican. *Format*: Four pages 19½ " x 26¾ ". *Price*: $8.00 per year in advance. *Comment*: Official paper of the City and County of Auburn. Published from the corner of Genesee and Mechanic Sts. This newspaper stated that it began "at an auspicious moment . . . when the telegraph bridged the Atlantic and united our eastern and western coasts. . . ." It expected to bring to its readers "What is freshest in the way of intelligence from all parts of the world." *Loc*: NAubHi: [Jl 6, 1868–Ja 27, 1871 (1:1–6:22)]. NIC/MMN: My 28, 1870 (4:584).

AUBURN MORNING NEWS (d) Auburn. Jl 16, 1872–My 31, 1879// (1:1–14:2121). *Pub*: Auburn Printing Co. (William J. Moses, Bus. Mgr. 1872–1873; Pres. 1873–1879; H. Laurens Storke, Secy-Treas. 1873–1879). *Ed*: William J. Moses 1872–1879; E. Houser 1872–1879. *Pol*: Democrat. *Format*: Four pages 17½ " x 23¼ ". *Price*: $9.00 per year in advance, $1.00 per month (1872); $8.00 per year in advance (1873–1878); $6.00 per year (1878–1879). *Comment*: Published at 16 Clark St. Official paper of the county; published the official canvass. On May 31, 1879 Moses announced that the *Morning News* would merge with the *Auburn Daily Bulletin*. This was issued June 2, 1879 as the *Auburn News and Bulletin* (q.v.). The *Cayuga County Independent* (Je 5, 1879) stated: "Mr. Moses doubtless strove hard to make the *News* a success but the odds were too strongly against him. After a struggle of almost 7 years it succumbed to the fate of its predecessor. . . . It is with deep regret that we observe a disposition on the part of our evening contemporaries to speak with levity of the death of the *Morning News* and to make the fact of its death an occasion for proclaiming their own many virtues. . . . Death is at all times a solemn event, and especially so is the death of a good newspaper, for as Milton quaintly observes, 'as good almost kill a man as kill a good newspaper; who kills a man kills a reasonable creature, but he who destroys a good newspaper kills reason itself. . . .'" *Loc*: NAubHi: Ja 1, 1878–My 31, 1879 (12:1684–14:2121). NIC/MMN: Jl 16, 1872–My 31, 1879 (1:1–14:2121).

AUBURN NEWS AND BULLETIN see *THE AUBURN BULLETIN*

AUBURN PATRIOT (w) Auburn. D 3, 1892–? (1:1–?). *Pub*: Louis Schewe. *Format*: Eight pages 15¾ " x 21¾ ". *Comment*: Published at

49 Market Street, the *Patriot* contained stories, Bible readings, sermons, recipes. It appeared to be written for women. *Loc*: NAubHi: D 10, 1892 (1:2).

AUBURN SEMI-WEEKLY JOURNAL see *AUBURN JOURNAL*

AUBURN SUNDAY DISPATCH (w) Auburn. Jl 1881–? (1:1–?). *Pub*: Morning Dispatch Association 1885–?. *Format*: Four pages 20¼" x 28¼". *Price*: $2.00 per year. *Circ*: 2,800 (1882). *Comment*: Published at 123 Genesee St.; then in 1883, 24 Dill St. The *Auburn Sunday Dispatch* was advertised in the *Evening Dispatch* and was probably printed as the Sunday edition of that paper. It was associated with the *Auburn Morning Dispatch* as of 1885. *Loc*: NAubHi: Jl 15, 1883 (3:2). NIC/MMN: [Jl 4, 1886–D 26, 1886 (3 [*sic*]:1–28)]. NIC/RHA: O 16, 1881 (1:15).

AUBURN TRUE PRESS (w) Auburn. 1872–F 18, 1876// (1:1–5:6). *Title changes*: The *Weekly True Press* 1872–D 31, 1875; *Auburn True Press* Ja 7–F 18, 1876. *Pub and Ed*: Uri Mulford. *Pol*: Democrat, temperance—aligned with Prohibition Party, 1875. *Price*: $1.25 per year in advance, 5¢ per copy; $1.50 per year (Jl 1875). *Format*: Four pages 20" x 26". *Comment*: Published at no. 2 State St., 1875; then no. 1 Exchange St. *Loc*: NAuW: F 18, 1876 (5:6, whole no. 206). NShw/Cleaveland: [Ap 15, 1875–Ja 14, 1876 (4:15–5:2)].

AUBURN WEEKLY AMERICAN see *AUBURN WEEKLY UNION*

AUBURN WEEKLY BULLETIN (w, semi-w) Auburn. Ja 1883–? (1:1–?). *Title changes*: The *Weekly Auburnian* Ja 1883–Mr 1, 1894; *Auburn Weekly Bulletin* Mr 8, 1894–? *Pub*: William J. Moses. *Ed*: Edward M. Allen Ja 9, 1885–1894; Charles F. Rattigan 1894–?. *Pol*: "Impressively independent, bound to no party and tied up with no clique." *Format*: Four to sixteen pages, varying sizes, 17" x 23¼", 16½" x 21½", 14¾" x 22". *Price*: $1.00 per year. *Comment*: The title of the newspaper was changed from the *Weekly Auburnian* to the *Auburn Weekly Bulletin* in response to requests from subscribers, probably to reflect the newspaper's association with the *Auburn Daily Bulletin* (q.v.). The paper was published from 27-29 Clark St. *Loc*: NIC/MMN: Ja 9, 1885–D 30, 1897 (3:2, whole no. 109–16:52, whole no. 5283); Ja 2, 1900–D 30, 1913 (19:1, whole no. 9998–42:104, whole no. 888933 [*sic*]).

AUBURN WEEKLY DISPATCH (w) Auburn. Mr 24(?), 1885–? (1:1–?). *Pub*: Morning Dispatch Association. *Format*: Eight pages 14½" x 21". *Price*: $1.00 per year in advance. *Loc*: NIC/MMN: [Jl 7–D 29, 1886 (2:17–3:38)].

AUBURN WEEKLY JOURNAL see *AUBURN JOURNAL*

AUBURN WEEKLY NEWS (w) Auburn. Ag 12, 1872–D 11, 1873// (1:1–2:50). *Pub*: Auburn Printing Co. (William J. Moses, Bus. Mgr. 1872–1873; William J. Moses, Pres., H. Laurens Storke,

Secy-Treas., Ap 17, 1873–D 11, 1873). *Ed*: William J. Moses and E. Houser. *Pol*: Democrat. *Format*: Four pages, varying sizes, 17″ x 23½″, 19¼″ x 26¼″. *Price*: $1.25 per year in advance (1872); $2.00 per year (1873). *Comment*: Published from 16 Clark Street. Printed the official canvass. In 1873 the Auburn Printing Co. purchased the *Auburn Democrat*, merged it with the *Auburn Weekly News*, and issued the *Auburn Weekly News and Democrat* on December 18, 1873. The numbering for both papers was retained. William J. Moses continued as the editor of that paper, which was subsequently merged with the *Auburn Argus* to form the *Auburn Democrat-Argus* (q.v.). Loc: NIC/MMN: Ag 12, 1872–D 11, 1873 (1:1–2:50).

AUBURN WEEKLY NEWS AND DEMOCRAT see *AUBURN DEMOCRAT-ARGUS*

AUBURN WEEKLY UNION (w) Auburn. F 7, 1855–Mr 6, 1861// (1:1–7:5). *Title changes*: *Auburn Weekly American* F 7, 1855–Je 15, 1859; *Auburn Weekly Union* Je 22, 1859–Mr 6, 1861. *Pub*: William J. Moses 1855–1859; William J. Moses and Kendrick Vail 1859–1861. *Ed*: James Stanley Smith 1855–1858; William J. Moses 1858–1859; William J. Moses and Benjamin F. Hall 1859–1861. *Pol*: American Party 1855–1859; Republican 1859–1861. *Format*: Four to eight pages, varying sizes, 20½″ x 26½″, 15″ x 22″. *Price*: $1.50 per year in advance. *Comment*: Published at the corner of Genesee and State Streets. The *Auburn Daily American* was published at the same time and became the *Auburn Daily Union* (q.v.) and subsequently the *Auburn Daily Advertiser and Auburn Union* (q.v.). The *Auburn Weekly Union* was merged with the *Auburn Journal* 1861 and formed *The Auburn Journal and Weekly Union*. *Loc*: NIC/MMN: F 2, 1859–Mr 6, 1861 (5:1–7:5). NIC/RHA: [F 7, 1855–Ja 26, 1859 (1:1–4:52)].

THE AUBURNIAN (w) Auburn. S 8, 1848–? (1:1–?). *Pub and Ed*: Andrew Shuman. *Format*: Four pages 6¾″ x 10⅝″. *Price*: 6¼¢ per month, 2¢ per issue. *Comment*: Motto: "Tall oaks from little acorns grow." Shuman planned to enlarge this newspaper when he had 500 subscribers. Probably short lived. In 1849, Andrew Shuman was co-publisher and editor of the *Cayuga Chief* (q.v.). *Loc*: NAubHi: S 22, 1848 (1:3).

THE AUBURNIAN 1877–1884 see *THE EVENING AUBURNIAN*

THE AURORA GAZETTE (w) Aurora. Je 19, 1805–1808// (1:1–?). *Pub and Ed*: Henry Pace. *Format*: Four pages, varying sizes, 10″ x 17½″, 17″ x 19″. *Price*: $2.00 per year. *Comment*: Storke states that the paper was owned and edited by Henry and James Pace (James' name does not appear in issues located) and that it continued less than two years (*History of Cayuga County*, p. 51). In May 1809 Pace moved to Auburn and issued the first number of the *Western Federalist* (q.v.). *Loc*: NAuW: framed F 12, 1806 (1:35); My 6, 1807 (2:99); Je 17, 1808 (3:146). NRU: Ja 14, 1807 (2:83).

THE AURORA GAZETTE (w) Aurora. Jl 18, 1868–? (1:1–?). *Pub and Ed*: James B. Hoff. *Format*: Four pages 12″ x 17¼″. *Price*: $2.00 per year or $1.50 per year in advance. *Comment*: This newspaper regarded itself as related to the earlier *Gazette* and put "Est. 1799" on the masthead. Hoff also published the *Union Springs Advertiser* (q.v.). *Loc*: NUS/Stryker: Jl 25, 1868 (1:2).

BURRITT NEWS (w) Weedsport. 1935–? (1:1–?) *Pub*: Burritt Press. *Format*: Four to eight pages, 9½″ x 12½″, 12″ x 18″. *Price*: $1.20 per year. *Comment*: Published at 42–46 South Seneca St. *Loc*: NWee/Finley: Mr 1, 1935–Ja 24, 1936.

CASKET OF GEMS. Union Springs. According to the *Union Springs Advertiser* (Je 12, 1919) this was a small literary paper published for a short time. No issues located.

THE CASTIGATOR (w) Auburn, Ithaca. Ja 1, 1823–S 26, 1829// (1–?). *Title changes*: *The Castigator* 1823–1828; *Old Hickory or the Castigator* F 1823–My 1828; *The Castigator* My 23–S 26, 1829. *Pub*: James M. Miller who published under pseudonym, Captain Caleb Cudgel & Co. and also Major Club. *Ed*: James M. Miller. *Pol*: Democrat. *Format*: Four pages 8″ x 9¼″ and 8⅝″ x 10¼″. *Comment*: Moved from Auburn to Tourtellot's store, Ithaca. May 7, 1828, the office was moved to the corner opposite Mr. Atwater's tavern on Aurora Street in Ithaca. *Loc*: NIDeW: Ja 1–Mr 29, 1823 (Fifth series 1–13); Je 1, Jl 22, 15 (misdated), Ag 5, 12, 19, 1828 (nos. 17, 20, 21, 24, 25, 26); My 23–S 26, 1829 (nos. 1–13). NIC/MMN: Ja 25, F 8, Mr 1, 1823 (Fifth series 4, 6, 9); My 9, 1828 (1:13). NIC/RHA: Ja 1–Mr 29, 1823 (Fifth series 1–13).

THE CATO CITIZEN (w) Cato. 1893 to date (1:1 to date). *Pub*: F. Howard Hosmer 1939–Ag 11, 1960; Theodore L. Miller Ag 25, 1960–Mr 4, 1965; F. Howard Hosmer Mr–Jl 1965; Angelo G. Palermo 1965 to date. *Ed*: F. Howard Hosmer 1939–1960; Theodore L. Miller 1960–1966; Louis F. Ryan 1966–Ag 1967; Angelo G. Palermo 1967–1971; June M. Welling 1971 to date. *Pol*: Republican. *Format*: Eight to twenty-four pages, varying sizes, 15½″ x 21¾″, 11½″ x 17½″. *Price*: $2.50 per year in advance, 5¢ per copy (1948–1951); $3.00 per year in advance, 7¢ per copy (F 1, 1951–1961); $3.00 per year, 10¢ per copy (1961–1966); $4.00 per year in advance, 10¢ per copy (1967–1971); $5.00 per year in advance, 15¢ per copy (1972). *Comment*: According to the *Cayuga Chief-Chronicle* (Jl 9, 1959) Jim Hunter was an early publisher of the *Citizen*. The newspaper includes Cayuga County election canvasses. *Loc*: NRC/Wayuga: [Ja 8, 1948–D 29, 1955 (55:9–63:8)]; Ja 3, 1957 to date (64:9 to date).

CAYUGA CHIEF (w) Auburn. Ja 4, 1849–? (1:1–?). *Pub and Ed*: Thurlow W. Brown Ja 1849; Thurlow W. Brown and W. Hooker Ja 18–Ap 11, 1849; Thurlow W. Brown and Andrew Shuman Ap 1849–Je 1850; Thurlow W. Brown Jl 1850–1851; Thurlow W. and Emma Brown Ja 13, 1852–1855. *Pol*: Independent in everything, neutral in nothing. Temperance, anti-slavery. *Format*: Four pages, varying sizes, 16″ x 22¼ ″, 18″ x 23¼ ″. *Price*: $1.00 per year in advance; $1.50 per year for Canada. *Comment*: Motto: "Governed by no faction—confined to no particular subject"; "The Wigwam—Speak the Truth and God defend the right"; "Excelsior" (1852); "Right on!" (1854). Published from the corner of 74 Genesee St. and South St. over the Post Office; then from the Exchange Building, corner Genesee and South Sts.; in 1854 from the Markham Block on North St. "It [the *Cayuga Chief*] was an original, vigorous and outspoken temperance journal, continued here [Auburn] for eight years when it was removed to Wisconsin, and there continued under the same ownership." (Storke, *History of Cayuga County*, p. 53) *Loc*: NAub: Ja 4, 1849–D 26, 1854 (1:1–6:52); D 25, 1855 (7:52 fragment). NAubHi: D 18, 1849 (1:51); Ja 1, My 7, 21, 28, Je 18, 1850 (2:1, 19, 21, 22, 25); F 10, Mr 30, 1852 (4:7, 14); Je 6, Ag 22–S 26, 1854 (6:23, 34–39). NAuW: Ag 24, S 21, 1852 (4:35, 39 fragments). NIC/ MMN: Mr 1, 22, My 24, 1853 (5:9, 12, 21). NIC/RHA: Ag 13, 1850 (2:33 fragment); Mr 4, 1851 (3:10); Ja 6, F 2, 1852 (4:2, 10); Jl 11, 1854 (6:28); O 9, 1855 (7:41). NUS/Stryker: D 26, 1854 (6:52 whole no. 312); N 13, 1855 (7:46 whole no. 358).

CAYUGA CHIEF (w) Weedsport, Red Creek, Weedsport. Je 16, 1877–Jl 2, 1959// (1:1–83:1). *Pub and Ed*: H. D. Brown & Co. (Dr. Ira D. and Harry Durwood Brown) 1877–1899; Harry Durwood Brown 1899–O 2, 1915; Harry D. Brown Estate O–D 1915; The Cayuga Chief Publishing Co. (George G. Valentine 1916–1939; George G., pub., and Elfred C. Valentine, ed., 1939–1944; George G. Valentine 1944–1946; George G. and Elfred C. Valentine 1946– 1956); F. Howard Hosmer 1957–1959. *Pol*: Independent Republican. *Format*: Four to eight pages 15¼″ x 21¼″. *Price*: $1.00 per year, 5¢ per copy (1877–1919); $1.50 per year (1919–1942); $2.00 per year, 5¢ per copy (1942–1951); $2.50 per year, 7¢ per copy (1951–1952); $3.00 per year, 7¢ per copy (1952–?). *Circ*: 1,800 (1871); 925 (1900s). *Comment*: The *Cayuga Chief* claimed it abhorred "neutral" papers. It declared its intention to be independent without being partisan. Motto: "Pledged to no party's arbitrary sway, we follow truth where'er she leads the way." Published in the Odd Fellows Building at the corner of Seneca and Brutus Sts., then 62 N. Seneca St. It contained the city's official canvass. The *Cayuga Chief* purchased the *Weedsport Sentinel* (q.v.) from George Nash's widow Katherine in December 1933, and merged with the *Port Byron Chronicle* in 1959 to form the *Cayuga Chief-Chronicle* (q.v.). *Loc*: NIC/MMN: microfilm Je 16, 1877–D 31, 1953 (1:1–77:26). NRC/Wayuga: Ja 7, 1954–Jl 2, 1959 (77:27–83:1). NWee/Finley: [Je 16, 1877–Jl 2, 1859 (1:1–83:1)].

CAYUGA CHIEF-CHRONICLE (w) Port Byron, Weedsport. O 1871 to date (1:1 to date). *Title changes*: *Port Byron Chronicle* O 1871–1921; *Port Byron Chronicle and Cayuga County News* N 19, 1921–1959; *Weedsport Cayuga Chief-Port Byron Chronicle* Jl 9,

1959–1966; *Cayuga Chief-Chronicle* 1967 to date. *Pub*: Charles E. Johnson 1873(?)–1882; Lasuvious Harrison King 1882–1923 (died Ap 27, 1923); Carrie King, owner, and Richard King 1923–1938; G. Welton Fickeisen Ag 27, 1938–1946; Robert and Frances Fox My 3, 1946–1947; Cayuga Chief Publishing Co., Inc. (George G. Valentine, Pub.) Jl 24, 1947–1956; F. H. Hosmer 1957–1960; Theodore L. Miller 1961–1965; F. H. Hosmer F–Jl 1965; Angelo G. Palmero Ag 1965 to date. *Ed*: Lasuvious Harrison King 1881–1923; Lois V. King 1923–1924; Richard King 1924–1938; G. Welton Fickeisen Ag 27, 1938–1946; Elfred C. Valentine 1947–1956; F. H. Hosmer 1957–1960; Theodore L. Miller 1961–1965; Louis F. Ryan 1966–1967; Angelo G. Palermo 1968–1971; June M. Welling 1971 to date. *Pol*: Republican. *Format*: Four to twenty-four pages, varying sizes, 18″ x 24″, 20¼″ x 26″, 16¼″ x 22″, 11½″ x 17½″. *Price*: $2.00 per year; $1.00 per year in advance, 5¢ per copy (1900–1917); $1.50 per year in advance, 5¢ per copy (1917–1943); $2.00 per year, 5¢ per copy (1943–1946); $2.50 per year, 7¢ per copy (1946–1952); $3.00 per year, 7¢ per copy (1952–1960); $3.00 per year, 10¢ per copy (1961–1966); $4.00 per year, 10¢ per copy (1967–1971); $5.00 per year, 15¢ per copy (1972). *Circ*: 1,200 (1915); 650 (1971). *Comment*: Motto: "Bright, spicy, clean and Republican. A paper for all the people with all the news of the day." "To be accurate, to be clear, to be good natured, to be alive, to be first in the field we have chosen for our own is the motto of this publication." (1904) First published in the Chronicle Building. According to Storke, the *Port Byron Chronicle* was started by Charles T. White who sold to Edward Clarke, who in turn sold to Ransom & Johnson in 1873 ("History of the Press," in *The Auburn Bulletin,* D 13, 1877). The Kings maintained control for almost sixty years when G. Welton Fickeisen, nephew to Lasuvious H. King, became publisher and editor. The *Chronicle* purchased the *Cayuga County News* (q.v.) in 1921 and merged with the *Weedsport Cayuga Chief* in 1959. *Loc*: NAubHi: N 26, 1881–Ja 14, 1882 (11:4–11); Je 29, 1907 (36:28); S 16, 1933 (10:37); Ag 4, 1934 (60 [*sic*] :31); Ja 8, 1938 (64:2). NIC/MMN: microfilm [Ja 5, 1900–D 31, 1953 (29:52–78:52)]. NRC/Wayuga: Ja 7, 1954 to date (79:1 to date). NWee/Finley: [Jl 9, 1959 to date (83:2 to date)].

CAYUGA COUNTY COURIER (w) Moravia. O 14, 1863–1871(?)// (1:1–?). *Pub*: Abner Osborne Hicks O 14–D 1863; Mrs. A. O. Hicks and Andrew J. Hicks D 1863–1864; Andrew J. Hicks and W. W. Nichols 1864–?; W. W. Nichols 1865(?)–Mr 1867; Andrew J. Hicks and A. H. Livingston 1867; A. H. Livingston 1867–1871. *Ed*: Abner Osborne Hicks O–D 1863; Andrew J. Hicks D 23, 1863–? *Pol*: Non-partisan. *Format*: Four pages, 17″ x 23″. *Price*: $1.50 per year in advance, 4¢ per copy (1863–1864); $2.00 per year in advance, 5¢ per copy (O 1, 1864–?). *Comment*: Motto: "National Integrity Must be Held Paramount to Party Advantage." Published on Main Street in Smith's Block, upstairs. Abner Osborne Hicks died on December 11, 1863 shortly after he established the newspaper. Although his wife was announced as co-publisher on December 23, 1863, only A. J. Hicks' name appears on the masthead thereafter. The newspaper considered itself non-partisan in politics, but it was loyal to the Union and condemned the Confederacy stating "We hold the Confederate rebellion to be the most wicked and unjustifiable revolt against liberty and law that ever disgraced history." The *Moravia Republican-Register* considers the *Cayuga County Courier* its forerunner and 1863 its founding date. No final issues located, but when Manville E. Kenyon bought the paper in 1871, he named it the *Moravia Valley Register,* enlarged it to 24" x 36" and numbered the first issue vol. 1 no. 1. *Loc*: NMor: O 14, 1863–O 5, 1864 (1:1–52).*

CAYUGA COUNTY INDEPENDENT see *CAYUGA COUNTY NEWS*

CAYUGA COUNTY NEWS (w) Auburn. F 8, 1874–N 1921// (1:1–?). *Title changes: Cayuga County Independent* F 8, 1874–D 31, 1909; *Cayuga County News* Ja 7, 1910–N 1921. *Pub and Ed*: John N. Bailey 1874–1878; D. C. McKay 1878–F 3, 1881; Julius A. Johnson F 10, 1881–1898; William B. Chisholm 1898–1907; James J. Hosmer 1907–1908; Cayuga County Independent Co. (J. Charles Dayton, Pres., Danforth R. Lewis, Vice Pres., Arthur J. Lewis, Secy, M. B. Underwood, Mgr.) 1908–1913; Cayuga County News Co. (Danforth R. Lewis, ed., and Lucinda Lewis, 1914; Robert E. Fenton, ed., and Arthur F. Smith, contributing ed. Je 5, 1914–1921). *Pol*: "Not neutral, but independent." *Format*: Four to sixteen pages, varying sizes, 20¼" x 27¼", 15" x 21", 17" x 22", 19" x 23". *Price*: $1.50 per year in advance, $1.75 out of county (1879–1883); $1.00 per year in advance (1883). *Circ*: 2,740 (1909); 2,660 (1910); 4,000 (1912). *Comment*: Published at 1 State St., second floor, 1879–1889; in May 1889 moved to Nos. 2 and 4 Genesee St.; later published at 32-33 Cady block, South St.; in 1914 moved to 85 Genesee St., then to 22 North St. and in 1919 to 5-9 Water St. Although no issues of this newspaper have been located for 1921, the *Port Byron Chronicle* announced its merger with the *News* on November 19, 1921. The paper contains official county canvasses and election returns. *Loc*: NAubHi: F 20, 1879–Ja 26, 1882 (6:3–8:52); F 9, 1882–Ja 16, 1890 (9:2–16:52); N 12, 1908–D 20, 1912 (35:46–39:51); [Ja 2, 1914–D 30, 1920 (41:1–47:52)].

CAYUGA DEMOCRAT (w) Auburn. D 4, 1833–Mr 25, 1835// (1:1–2:69). *Pub and Ed*: Frederick Prince. *Pol*: Democratic-Republican. *Format*: Four pages 15¾" x 20¾". *Comment*: Published at no. 3 Centre Buildings. *Loc*: NAubHi: D 4, 1833–Mr 25, 1835 (1:1–2:69).

CAYUGA DEMOCRAT (w) Union Springs. 1848//(1:1–?). *Pub*: William Clarke. No issues located. The *Union Springs Advertiser* (Je 12, 1919) indicates this was published for the Cass campaign.

CAYUGA LAKE HERALD (w) Union Springs. O 15, 1859–? (1:1–?). *Title changes: Union Springs Herald* 1859–N 30, 1861;

*See also p. 287

Cayuga Lake Herald D 13, 1861–? *Pub and Ed*: J. B. Clarke 1859–1863; B. G. Gibbs 1861–1862; Clarke Bros. 1862; Emerson B. Williams 1863–O 1863(?). *Pol*: Independent. *Format*: Four pages, varying sizes, 14¾″ x 20¾″, 16″ x 21¾″. *Price*: $1.50 per year in advance, 3¢ per copy. *Comment*: When the *Union Springs Herald* office was burned in 1861 the paper moved from the north side of Seminary St. to the South End of the Brick Block, merged with the *Cayuga Lake Recorder* and was issued as the *Cayuga Lake Herald* (*Union Springs Advertiser*, Je 12, 1919). *Loc*: NIC/RHA: N 28, 1862 (4:10). NUS/Stryker: O 15, 1859–O 5, 1860 (1:1–52).

CAYUGA LAKE RECORD (w) Union Springs. Ja 7–S 1864// (1:1–?). *Pub and Ed*: Jno. W. Stanton. *Format*: Four pages 15¼″ x 21″. *Price*: $1.50 per year. *Comment*: The numbering suggests that this paper considered itself the direct descendant of the *Cayuga Lake Recorder* (q.v.). *Loc*: NUS/Stryker: Je 2 [*sic*], 1864 (the inside date My 26, 1864 is probably correct) (5:9 New Series 1:22).

CAYUGA LAKE RECORDER (w) Union Springs. 1859–D 13, 1861// (1:1–?). *Pub and Ed*: I. O. Crissy and T. E. Hitchcock 1859; I. O. Crissy 1859–1861. *Comment*: The *Union Springs Advertiser* (Je 12, 1919) stated that in 1861 this paper merged with the *Union Springs Herald* to form the *Cayuga Lake Herald* (q.v.). No issues located.

THE CAYUGA NEW ERA (w) Auburn. Je 22, 1847–1857// (1:1–?). *Pub and Ed*: William L. Finn and Hollett 1851; William L. Finn 1852. *Pol*: Democrat. *Format*: Four pages 20½″ x 28″. *Price*: $1.00 per year in advance. *Comment*: Motto: "A Journal of Politics, Literature, Miscellany, Foreign and Local Intelligence." Published every Wednesday from the corner of 111 and 113 Genesee and State Sts. over the post office. According to Storke the newspaper was "formed in 1847 by the consolidation of the *Patriot* (q.v.) and *Tocsin* (q.v.) the two Democratic rivals [and] was designed to heal the old divisions in that party on the subject of slavery extension. . . . This journal was published for nearly ten years first by Merrill [*sic*], Stone & Co. . . . [then] by Stone, Hawes & Co., Finn & Hollett, and William L. Finn and discontinued in 1857." (*History of Cayuga County*, p. 52) *Loc*: NAubHi: Jl 9, 1851 (5:3 whole no. 211). NIC/MMN: O 20, 27, 1852 (1:16, 19).

CAYUGA PATRIOT (w) Auburn. O 19, 1814–Mr 3, 1847// (1:1–33:52). *Title changes*: The *Cayuga Patriot* 1814–Jl 14, 1824; *Cayuga Patriot* Jl 21, 1824–Mr 3, 1847. *Pub and Ed*: James G. Hathaway 1814; Samuel R. Brown 1814(?)–1815; James Beardslee 1816–1819; David Rumsey 1818–1819; Ulysses F. Doubleday 1819–1827; Ulysses F. Doubleday and Isaac S. Allen 1827–1831; Isaac S. Allen 1831–1833; Isaac S. Allen and Willett Lounsbury 1834–Je 1843 (Lounsbury died Je 5, 1843); Isaac S. Allen Je 1843–O 22, 1845); Ulysses F. Doubleday O 22 ,1845–N 1846; Henry A. Hawes and Henry M. Stone N 11, 1846–Mr 3, 1847. *Pol*: Anti-Federalist, Democratic-Republican. *Format*: Eight to four pages, varying sizes, 8¼″ x 10½″, 13″ x 20″,

15½″ x 20½″, 18″ x 24″½. *Price*: $2.25 per year, $2.00 per year half in advance, $1.75 per year in advance (1814); $2.00 per year or $1.50 per year in advance. *Comment*: Motto: "Pro Patria." Launched 1814 from the Wagon Shop on Lumber Lane (now Osborne St.); 1826–1846 published from the corner of Genessee [*sic*] and South Sts.; 109 Genesee St., 1846–1847. Doubleday became a Congressman in 1831 and gave up the publication for a short time. March 3, 1847 was the last issue of the *Patriot*. It merged with the *Tocsin* and became *The Cayuga New Era* (q.v.). *Loc*: NAub: Je 22, 1825–S 29, 1826 (11:11–12:24); Ap 1, 1829–Mr 3, 1847 (16:1–33:52). NAubHi: Ap 2, S 3, 1817 (3:129, 151); S 1, 1819 (5:255); Ag 2, S 6–13, 27, O 18–N 15, D 13–27, 1820 (6:303, 308, 309, 311; 7:314–318, 322–324); Ja 3–17, 31, F 7–14, 28, Ap 4–18, My 30, Je 6–20, Jl 25, Ag 8, O 3–17, D 13, 1821 (7:325–327, 329–331, 333, 338–340, 346–349, 354, 356, 364; 8:365, 366, 374); Ja 9–23, F 6, 20, Je 19–Jl 3, Ag 7, 21, S 4, O 16 ,1822 (8:378–380, 382, 384, 401–403, 408, 410, 412, 418); [O 22, 1823–Je 22, 1825 (10:471–11:558)]; N 17, D 8, 15, 1830 (17:34, 37, 38); Jl 9, 1834 (21:16); Je 17, 1835 (22:13); F 15, 1837 (23:48); Jl 5, 1837 (24:16); Ap 11, 1838 (25:4). NRU: [My 16, 1821–O 1, 1823 (7:344–9:468)]; Jl 23, 1845 (32:20). NUS/Stryker: N 9–D 14, 1814 (1:4 fragment, 1:5–9).

CAYUGA REPUBLICAN (w) Auburn. Mr 24, 1819–My 15, 1833// (1:1–15:739). *Pub*: Frederick Prince Mr 24, 1819–1821; Thomas M. Skinner 1822–1833. *Ed*: Augustus Buckingham 1819; Thomas M. Skinner 1819–Je 16, 1824; R. L. Smith Je 23, 1824–Ja 19, 1825; G. A. Gamage Ja 26–D 14, 1825; Thomas M. Skinner 1825–1833. *Pol*: Democratic Republican, Anti-Masonic. *Format*: Four pages, varying sizes, 12¼″ x 19¼″, 14¼″ x 21¼″, 10½″ x 15″. *Price*: $2.00 per year in advance or $2.50 per year. *Comment*: Motto: "Be just and fear not" (1819–1824); "A day—an hour of virtuous liberty is worth a whole eternity of bondage" (1824–1825); "Reason is man's distinguishing attribute . . . the freedom of speech his inalienable birthright . . . the liberty of the press his impregnable safeguard" (1825). This motto, which appeared under the new banner in January 1826, was dropped and, thereafter, various sayings relating to liberty of the press appeared on each week's edition. This newspaper follows the *Auburn Gazette* (q.v.) last issued March 17, 1819. Although Thomas Skinner was listed as printer, he was in fact the owner even though Frederick Prince was listed as publisher until October, 1821. On May 15, 1833 Skinner stated that he would publish a paper with Henry Oliphant of the *Free Press* (q.v.). On May 22, 1833, they issued the first number of the *Auburn Journal* (q.v.). *Loc*: NAubHi: [Mr 24, 1819–My 15, 1833 (1:1–15:739)]. NIC/ MMN: [Ap 21, 1819–Mr 29, 1820 (1:5–54)]. Jl 4–D 5, 1827 (9:433–455). NRU: N 23, 1831 (1 page extra).

CAYUGA REPUBLICAN (Weedsport) see *THE WEEDSPORT REPUBLICAN*

CAYUGA SPIRIT OF THE TIMES (w) Auburn. Ag 1862–

1863//(?) (1:1–?). *Pub and Ed*: William S. Hawley. *Format*: Four to eight pages, varying sizes, 20⅞ " x 28⅛ ", 15¾ " x 21¾ ". *Price*: $1.50 in advance, otherwise $2.00 per year. *Comment*: Published at the corner of Genesee and Exchange Sts. According to Charles Rattigan this newspaper lasted only a year and a half. William Hawley also issued one number of a daily of this title, but "this enterprise failing to receive proper encouragement was abandoned." ("The Press," *History of Cayuga County New York*, p. 121) *Loc*: NAubHi: Ap 29, My 27, Je 24, Jl 22, 29, Ag 19, S 2, 30, O 21, 1863 (1:43, 47, 51; 2:3, 4, 7, 9, 13, 16).

THE CAYUGA STANDARD (m) Auburn. Mr 1894–? (1:1–?). *Pub*: County Executive Committee. *Pol*: Prohibition Party. *Format*: Four pages 10¾ " x 15½ ". *Price*: 25¢ per year. *Comment:* Published at 23 Genesee St., and "devoted to the interests of the Prohibition Party and kindred organizations. . . . This paper goes to thousands of voters who are tired of seeing this country RUN BY THE GIN MILLS. . . . [The] saloon forces run the primaries of one or both old parties; the primaries run the parties; the parties run the government." In its first issue the county chairman of the Prohibition Party, H. L. Hoyt asked the "Republicans and Democrats to meet each other halfway in a new party, on a new platform, for warfare on a tremendous evil." *Loc*: NAubHi: Mr 1894 (1:1).

CAYUGA TELEGRAPH (w) Union Springs. Je 5, 1848–1872//(?) (1:1–?). *Pub and Ed*: William Clarke. *Format*: Four pages 15" x 22". *Price*: $1.50 per year in advance to village subscribers, $1.25 per year to office subscribers, $1.00 per year by mail. *Loc*: NUS/Stryker: Ag 15, 1849 (2:62).

CAYUGA TOCSIN (w) Auburn. Ap 5, 1839–1847// (1:1–9:?). *Pub*: Miller & Gelem Hine; Miller & Stowe; John C. Merrell & Hollett. *Ed*: Thomas Y. How, Jr. *Format*: Four pages, varying sizes, 18" x 24", 19¼ " x 26½ ". *Pol*: Democratic-Republican. *Price*: $1.50 per year in advance; $2.50 per year at end of year. *Comment*: Published at No. 1 Beach's Building, Genesee St. The *Cayuga Tocsin* and the *Cayuga Patriot* merged in 1847 and formed the *Cayuga New Era* (q.v.). *Loc*: NIC/RHA: Ap 1, 1840–Mr 24, 1841 (2:53–104). NRU: Ag 27, 1845 (7:23).

THE CAYUGA TOCSIN (w) Union Springs, Auburn. Ja 2, 1812–1813// (1:1–?). *Pub*: Royall T. Chamberlain. *Format*: Four pages 11" x 18¾ ". *Price*: $2.00 per year. *Comment*: Moved to Auburn between April 15 and June 2, 1813 (Brigham, *Newspaper Bibliography*, p. 748). *Loc*: NAubHi: O 15, 1812 (1:42).

CENTRAL NEW YORKER (w) Union Springs. Ap–D 1865// *Pub*: F. F. De Wolfe. No issues located. Mentioned in Storke, *History of Cayuga County*, p. 54 and *Union Springs Advertiser* (Je 12, 1919).

CENTRAL NEW YORKER (w) Auburn. 1878–? No issues located. Storke said this was an organ of the National Party (*History of Cayuga County*, p. 54).

THE CENTURY PLANT Auburn. Je 8, 1876// (1:1). *Pub*: The Auburn Centennial Association. *Ed*: D. E. Clapp, Ed., B. B. Snow, Miss Cox, H. L. Storke, H. J. Knapp, Mrs. D. R. Alward, C. J. Reed, Associate Editors. *Price*: 10¢. *Loc*: NAubHi: Je 8, 1876 (1:1).

THE CHRISTIAN AMBASSADOR (w) Auburn and New York City. 1851–? (1:1–?). *Pub*: Universalist Paper and Book Establishment (Rev. Henry Lyon, Business agent, New York City; Rev. H. H. Harter, Business agent, Auburn; Henry M. Stone, printer) 1859–?. *Ed*: John M. Austin 1851–? *Pol*: Independent, anti-slavery. *Format*: Four pages 18″ x 24½″. *Price*: $2.00 per year to mail subscribers, $2.50 by carrier. *Circ*: 8,000. *Comment*: Motto: "We are ambassadors for Christ." Although primarily a religious newspaper, the *Ambassador* contained articles of local and national interest. John M. Austin outlined the goal of the paper as follows: "To explain the scriptures, to proclaim the good tidings of the Gospel, to carry light . . . to maintain liberty for all mankind, both civil and religious . . . to aid in extinguishing the law of capital punishment and other unjustifiable statutes and in so perfecting the treatment of criminals that while a just penalty should be inflicted, its administration shall be in such a manner and spirit as to aid in the reformation of the guilty." On January 1, 1859, beginning with Vol. 9, No. 1, *The Christian Ambassador* began a new series. A joint stock company called the Universalist Paper and Book Establishment with a capital of $7,000 was established to purchase all the Universalist papers published in different sections of the state and to publish one journal for all. The newspaper was also to become the organ of the State Convention. Offices were located in both Auburn and New York City. The newspaper is continuously paged and indexed. *Loc*: NAubHi: Ja 1, 1859–D 28, 1861 (9:1–11:52).

CHRISTIAN UNION (w) Union Springs. Ja 22, 1859–?. *Pub*: J. B. Clarke. No issues located. According to the *Union Springs Advertiser* (Je 12, 1919) moved to New York October 15, 1859.

THE CHRONICLES (irr.) Auburn. Ag 10, 1838–? (1:1–?). *Pub*: Ezra the Scribe. *Format*: Eight pages. *Comment*: An unusual paper written in biblical style. Ezra signs himself "the translator" and reports current events in the manner of the Bible. He entitled page 1, "the First book of Chronicles." Sample: "Now it came to pass in the reign of James, surnamed Monroe, that the people built a strong place in the western part of DeWitt's Province for confining or reforming evil doers. . . ." Ezra stated that he would publish periodically, but "whether monthly or at shorter periods, is not yet determined. Circumstance must hereafter settle that question. Neither am I now able to say precisely how many numbers will be necessary to contain the whole." The identity of Ezra the Scribe was not revealed until October 1907 with the death of Reverend Silas E. Shepard. The biographical notice of his death revealed that Shepherd, editor of the *Primitive Christian,* also edited *The Chronicles* exposing the atrocities existing in Auburn Prison. *Loc*: NIC/MMN: microfilm Ag 10, 1838 (1:1).

CITIZEN-ADVERTISER (d) Auburn. Je 1, 1931 to date (1:1 to date). *Pub*: Auburn Publishing Co. (Lithgow Osborne, Director) 1931 to date. *Pol*: "Editorially independent, impartial and non-partisan." *Format*: Eight to sixteen pages, varying sizes, 15¾" x 21", 17" x 22". *Price*: 3¢ to 10¢ per copy. *Comment*: The Auburn Publishing Company, which had been publishing the *Auburn Citizen* and the *Advertiser Journal* simultaneously for about ten years, merged the two newspapers and on June 1, 1931 issued the *Citizen-Advertiser*. Volume and issue numbers for the three papers appeared in the August 28th issue. The masthead also reflects the fact that the *Citizen-Advertiser* included the *Auburn Bulletin*. In 1931, the *Citizen-Advertiser* was one of the few small local newspapers in the United States carrying both Associated and United Press wire services. The paper was first published at 34-36 Dill St. but in 1971 was moved to a new building at the northeast corner of State and Dill. *Loc*: NAub: Je 1, 1931 to date (1:1 to date). NAubHi: Je 1, 1931–D 1945; Ja 1950–D 1954. NAubC: Je 1, 1931 to date (1:1 to date). NIC/MMN: Mr 21, 1942.

CONFERENCE AND FAMILY RECORDER see *THE AUBURN BANNER AND GENESEE, ONEIDA AND BLACK RIVER CONFERENCE RECORD*

THE CORRECTOR (semi-m) Auburn. My 1, 1839–? (1:1–?). *Format*: Four pages 11½" x 16½". *Price*: "Terms: Made easy to all who deserve to arrive at the truth." *Comment*: Printed at the Auburn Job Printing Office. Probably an organ of the Auburn State Prison. *Loc*: NAub: My 1, 1839 (1:1). NRU: My 1, 1839 (1:1).

DAILY CAYUGA TOCSIN (d) Auburn. F 16, 1846–? (1:1–?) *Pub*: John C. Merrell & Co. *Ed*: Thomas Y. How, Jr. *Pol*: Democrat. *Format*: 14" x 18¾". *Price*: $4.50 per year in advance, $3.50 in advance by mail, 2¢ per copy. *Comment*: Published from the corner of Genesee and State Sts. *Loc*: NAubHi: Mr 11, 1846 (1:22); Jl 25, 1846 (1:139).

THE DAILY ITEM see *THE EVENING AUBURNIAN*

THE DIAMOND 1830. No issues located. Mentioned in Storke, *History of Cayuga County*, p. 51.

THE EVANGELICAL RECORDER Auburn. Ja–D 1818//. Edited by Rev. Dirck C. Lansing and printed by Thomas Skinner (Charles F. Rattigan, "The Press," in *History of Cayuga County New York*, p. 111). No issues located.

THE EVENING AUBURNIAN (d) Auburn. Je 25, 1877–Ja 2, 1885// (1:1–16:306). *Title changes*: *Auburn Daily Item* Je 25–N 1877; *The Evening Auburnian* 1877–1885. *Pub*: Urban S. Benton & Co. (Martin S. Webster, G. H. Wheeler, William H. Sanford, Rollin

L. Sarr) Je 25–N 1877; The Auburnian Printing Assoc. (Homer Lockwood, Urban S. Benton, M. C. Cuykendall) N 1877–1885. *Ed*: F. W. Mack 1883–1885. *Pol*: Independent. *Format*: Four pages, varying sizes, 15″ x 22½″, 18½″ x 24¼″. *Price*: $4.50 per year, 40¢ per month, 2¢ per copy (1877–1878); $5.00 per year in advance, 45¢ per month, 3¢ per copy (1879–1883). *Circ*: 2,160–2,500 (1877–1882). *Comment*: Referred to as the "Organ of the Workingman." Printed at Benton & Reynold's Steam Job Printing House, 1 Exchange St.; moved to 2 Exchange St. about 1880. In 1885 purchased by William J. Moses and merged with *The Auburn Bulletin* (q.v.). *Loc*: NAubHi: O 1–3, 1877 (1:84–86); [Ja 2, 1878–D 30, 1880 (2:161–7:158)]; Jl 14, Ag 9, 11, S 30, 1882 (11:11, 33, 35, 69); [Ja 3–D 31, 1883 (12:2–13:154)]; Ja 5, My 31, 1884 (14:4, 125). NIC/MMN: [N 8, 1878–My 7, 1881 (3:111–8:109)]; Jl 1, 1884–Ja 2, 1885 (14:150–16:306). NIC/RHA: S 20, O 14, 1881 (9:69, 90); Ja 18, 1883 (12:15).

THE EVENING DISPATCH (d) Auburn. Jl 1882–1885(?) (1:1–?). *Pub and Ed*: None listed. *Pol*: Republican. *Format*: Four pages 17″ x 23½″. *Price*: $4.50 per year, 40¢ per month, 2¢ per copy. *Comment*: Published at 24 Dill St. This paper was probably discontinued in 1885 when the *Auburn Morning Dispatch* (q.v.) was first issued. *Loc*: NAubHi: [Ja 2–D 31, 1884 (4:6–5:134)]. NAuW: Ag, 1884 (5:45).

THE FAIR HAVEN GRAPHIC (w) Fair Haven. O 1880–? (1:1–?). *Pub and Ed*: Fred H. Gee. *Format*: Four pages 17½″ x 24″. *Price*: $1.50 per year. *Circ*: 500. *Comment*: Issued every Friday at the rooms over O. F. Miller's store. *Loc*: NStV/Cooper: N 17, 1882 (2:5); Ja 5, 1883 (2:12).

FAIR HAVEN REGISTER (w) Fair Haven. Mr 20, 1890 to date. (1:1 to date). *Title changes*: *The Register* Mr 20, 1890–?; *The Fair Haven Register* ?–1927; *Fair Haven Register* 1928 to date. *Pub*: Will E. Bennett Mr 1890–1901; E. C. Smith D 2, 1901–?; C. M. Delling ?–?; W. G. Phippin ?–1939; F. Howard Hosmer 1939–1960; Theodore L. Miller 1961–1965; F. Howard Hosmer Mr–Jl 1965; Angelo G. Palermo 1965 to date. *Ed*: Will E. Bennett 1890–1901; E. C. Smith 1901–?; C. M. Delling; W. G. Phippin ?–1939; F. Howard Hosmer 1939–1960; Theodore L. Miller 1961–1966; Louis F. Ryan 1966–Ag 1967; Angelo G. Palermo 1967–1971; June M. Welling 1971 to date. *Pol*: "Independent in politics, upholding no party, but endeavoring always to uphold the right and ready at any time to rectify any injustice." *Format*: Four to twenty-four pages, varying sizes, 17½″ x 24½″, 15½″ x 22″, 11½″ x 17½″. *Price*: $1.25 per year in advance (1890–1900); $1.00 per year in advance (1900–?); $1.25 per year in advance (1921–1937); $1.50 per year in advance (1937–?); $2.50 per year in advance, 5¢ per copy (1947–1951); $3.00 per year in advance, 7¢ per copy (F 1, 1951–1961); $3.00 per year, 10¢ per copy (1961–1966); $4.00 per year in advance, 10¢ per copy (1967–1971); $5.00 per year in advance, 15¢ per copy (1972). *Circ*: Over 1,200. *Comment*: On January 29, 1948, fire destroyed the plant and main offices of the *Fair Haven Register*. Issues of early newspapers are difficult to locate and often in poor condition. Published every Thursday afternoon from the corner of Main and Richmond Sts., 1890–? *Loc*: NRC/Wayuga: [Ja 3, 1929 to date (39:49 to date)]. NStV/Cooper: [Mr 20, 1890–S 1902 (1:1–13:28)]; Ag 3–31, 1911 (22:25–29); Je 6–20, Ag 1, 29, N 28, 1912 (23:17–19, 25, 29, 42); My 29, Ag 7, 14, 1913 (24:16, 26, 27); F 17, Ag 14, 1921 (32:1, 27); S 22, 1927 (38:34); [Ja 12, 1928–My 22, 1941 (38:50–52:18) extremely broken run].

FREE PRESS see *AUBURN FREE PRESS*

THE GENOA HERALD see *THE WEEKLY HERALD*

THE GENOA SPY (w) Genoa Village. Ap 26, 1838–1839//(?) (1:1–?). *Pub and Ed*: Gelem Hine and McKenney. *Pol*: Democratic-Republican. *Format*: Four pages 13½″ x 19¼″. *Price*: $1.00 per year in advance or $1.50. *Comment*: A note found with the newspaper in the Cornell University Libraries written by Auburn genealogist, Clara Skilton, states: "It seems to have been a fiery little sheet, with a sharp stinger until the election of Mr. Seward over Governor Marcy. It was born in the vortex of intense politics and faded away following defeat." Since Gelem Hine was also publisher of the *Cayuga Tocsin* (q.v.), it is quite possible that *The Genoa Spy* was merged with the *Tocsin* and discontinued as a separate paper in 1839. *Loc*: NIC/RHA: O 4, 1838 (1:24).

THE GENOA TRIBUNE see *SOUTHERN CAYUGA TRIBUNE AND THE UNION SPRINGS NEWS*

THE GLEANER (semi-m) Poplar Ridge. N 1886–? (1:1–?). *Pub*: D. Wheeler & Son. *Ed*: W. C. Wheeler. *Pol*: Temperance. *Format*: Eight pages 11″ x 16″. *Price*: 75¢ per year, 40¢ for six months. *Loc*: NAuW: Ja 15, 1887 (1:6).

THE GOSPEL ADVOCATE AND IMPARTIAL INVESTIGATOR (semi-m) Auburn. *Pub*: Ulysses F. Doubleday, Doubleday & Allen, Printers. *Ed*: Orestes A. Brownson. *Format*: Sixteen pages 6¾″ x 10½″. *Price*: $1.50 per year in advance. *Loc*: NIC/RHA: Ag 22, 1829 (7:17).

GOSPEL MESSENGER AND CHURCH RECORD OF WESTERN NEW YORK (w) Auburn, Geneva, Utica. 1827–? (1:1–?). *Title changes*: *Gospel Messenger* 1827–?; *Gospel Messenger and Church Record of Western New York* by 1841–? *Pub*: The Society for Promoting Christian Knowledge. *Ed*: John Churchill Rudd 1827–N 15, 1848. *Format*: Four pages 10″ x 14½″. *Price*: $1.50 per year in advance, otherwise $1.75. *Comment*: An Episcopal newspaper widely circulated in New York, Pennsylvania, Connecticut, Georgia and Canada. Each volume is completely indexed. *Loc*: NAubHi: F 9, 1833–Ja 31, 1835 (7:1–8:52 whole numbers 313–416). NAuW: O 23, 1841–Ja 12, 1849 (15:39–22:52).

HOME AND HEALTH (m) Union Springs. Ja 1887–? (1:1–?). *Pub and Ed*: F. D. Pierce, M.D. *Format*: Four pages 15″ x 22¾″. *Price*: 25¢ per year. "We will receive stamps in payment for subscriptions, but we much prefer cash." *Comment*: *Home and Health*, "An Illustrated Family Journal," was published from the Sanitarium, Union Springs, and concerned itself with "household matters, hygiene, current events, general literature, and rural affairs." *Loc*: NUS/Stryker: Ja 1887 (1:1); Mr 1887 (1:3).

THE ILLUSTRATED SATURDAY RECORD (w) Auburn. Mr 19, 1910–? (1:1–?). *Pub*: Springsteen Publishing Co. *Ed*: A. M. York. *Format*: Eight pages 17″ x 22″. *Price*: $1.50 per year, 5¢ per copy. *Comment*: Policy: "To conserve and advance the interests of Auburn and Cayuga County . . . to reflect the business, industrial, social, political, and religious life in the area, briefly and entertainingly described and freely illustrated." *Loc*: NAubHi: Mr 19, 1910 (1:1).

THE ITEM see *THE EVENING AUBURNIAN*

LAWTON TALK Auburn. 1894–? (1:1–?). *Pub*: A. W. Lawton. *Format*: Four pages 10¾″ x 14″. *Comment*: The one issue located was entitled "Who is Lawton? Holiday edition." Published from offices at the west corner of Genesee and State Sts. *Loc*: N/ubHi: Ja 1895 (2:2).

LEVANA [*sic*] *GAZETTE; OR, ONONDAGA ADVERTISER* (w) Scipio (Levanna). Je 20, 1798–? (1:1–?). *Pub*: Roger Delano 1798–? *Format*: Four pages, varying sizes, 10½″ x 17¼″, 9¾″ x 15″. *Price*: $2.00 per year. *Loc*: NAubHi: N 21, 1798 (1:23). NRU: Ag 8, 1798 (1:8).

LIVING QUESTION (q) Auburn. *Pub*: Ministers Association of Auburn. *Ed*: Rev. W. H. Hubbard. *Price*: 2 copies for one year 10¢, 50 copies $1.00. *Loc*: NAubHi: Fragment.

MERIDIAN ADVERTISER Meridian. 1855–1856//. No issues located. Mentioned by Elliot G. Storke, *History of Cayuga County*, p. 54.

MERIDIAN SUN Meridian. Je 1854–1855//. No issues located. Mentioned by Elliot G. Storke, *History of Cayuga County*, p. 54, and by Winifred Gregory, *Union List of Newspapers*, p. 458.

MORAVIA CITIZEN see *MORAVIA REPUBLICAN*

MORAVIA REPUBLICAN (w) Jl 3, 1876–Mr 1, 1901// (1:1–25:51). *Title changes*: *Moravia Citizen* Jl 3, 1876–N 4, 1880; *Moravia Republican* N 11, 1880–Mr 1, 1901. *Pub and Ed*: Rev. Charles Ray Jl 1876–N 4, 1880; J. J. Pease and Byron A. King 1880–F 10, 1881; J.J. Pease F 17, 1881–O 1893; J. J. Pease and H. A. Stanton N 1893–1894; Stanton and Ballard Ap 20, 1894–N 1894; H. A. Stanton N 23, 1894–F 1896; P. M. Rathbun F 21, 1896–1901 (local editor from 1893). *Pol*: Independent; Temperance; Republican. *Format*: Four to eight pages, varying sizes, 18″ x 24″, 20″ x 26″. *Price*: $1.50 per year, $1.25 cash at subscription, $1.00 to ministers (1876); $1.50 per year in advance, $1.00 cash at subscription (1877–1883); $1.50 per year in advance, $1.25 cash at subscription, $1.00 to ministers (1884–1891); $1.25 per year, 3¢ per copy (1892–1897); $1.00 per year in advance, 3¢ per copy (1898–1901). *Comment*: Published from the corner of Main and Cayuga Streets, 1876–1877, then from the Steam Printing Office on Mill St. 1878–1894; Railroad St. near Main, S 21, 1894–1897; 6 Central St., 1897–1901. July 19, 1879, the *Moravia Citizen* was adopted as the organ of the South Cayuga District Temperance Union. On Nov. 4, 1880 Rev. Ray wrote that he was selling the paper in order to devote full time to ministerial work and to give Moravia, which already had a Democratic newspaper, a Republican organ. He therefore sold his paper to two staunch Republicans, J. J. Pease and Byron King, who changed the title to the *Moravia Republican*. Stated policy: "To give a brief summary of the current ideas of each week from all over the world and furnish at the same time a competent weekly discussion of the uniform Bible lessons now used by all denominations. . . . Few families can afford the expense of a local, metropolitan and religious newspaper. It is our aim to furnish these immeasurably in one." In 1901, the *Republican* was merged with the *Moravia Valley Register* and was issued thereafter as the *Moravia Republican-Register* (q.v.). *Loc*: NAubHi: F 24, 1881 (5:33); Mr 20, 1884 (8:37). NIC/MMN: microfilm Jl 13, 1876–Je 28, 1877 (1:1–52); [Jl 18, 1878–D 30, 1880 (3:2–5:25)]; [Ja 6, 1881–D 31, 1885 (5:26–10:26)]. NMor/MoR: [Jl 13, 1876–Mr 1, 1901 (1:1–25:51)].

MORAVIA REPUBLICAN-REGISTER (w) Moravia. F 10, 1871 to date (1:1 to date). *Title changes*: Moravia Valley Register F 10, 1871–1901; Moravia Republican-Register Mr 1901 to date. *Pub*: Manville E. Kenyon F 10, 1871–Je 1883; Manville E. Kenyon and W. A. Huntington Jl 1883–Jl 4, 1884; Manville E. Kenyon Jl 11, 1884–Ap 1898; Eugene A. Beach Ap 1898–1900; P. M. Rathbun 1901–Jl 13, 1934; Mabel Shove Rathbun Jl 20–Ag 10, 1934; Pearl M. Rathbun Ag 17–N 9, 1934; Charles H. Long N 16, 1934–Ap 23, 1937; Katherine G. Long 1937–1942; George W. Fickiesen Je 3, 1943–1961; G. W. Fickiesen and W. J. Newhart 1961–1962; Bernard F. McGuerty Ap 5, 1962–1966; Inter-County Publishers (Bernard F. McGuerty, A. K. Fletcher 1966–1970; Bernard F. McGuerty, Edward Lauckern and Clyde Chilson 1970 to date). *Ed*: Manville E. Kenyon 1871–1894; Manville E. Kenyon and Son 1894–1896; Manville E. Kenyon 1896–1899; Eugene A. Beach 1899–1900; P. M. Rathbun 1901–1934; Mabel Rathbun Ag 17–N 1934; Charles H. Long N 16, 1934–Ap 23, 1937; Katherine G. Long 1940; G. W. Fickiesen Je 3, 1943–?; Florence Weeks, News Editor, Je 3–Ag 5, 1943; F. Helen McLean, News Ed., Ag 12, 1943–?; Bernard F. McGuerty 1962 to date. *Pol*: Republican. *Format*: Four to twenty-four pages, varying sizes, 24″ x 36″, 18″ x 24″, 20″ x 26¼″, 15″ x 22″, 16¼″ x 22⅛″. *Price*: $1.50 per year in advance, $2.00 otherwise (1871–Ja 15, 1886); $1.25 per year (Ja 22,

1886–Ja 7, 1888); $1.00 per year in advance, $1.25 otherwise (Ja 13, 1888–1918); $1.25 per year in advance (1918–1920); $1.50 per year in advance, 5¢ per copy (1920–1943); $2.00 per year in advance, 5¢ per copy (1943–1947); $3.00 per year, 7¢ per copy (1947–1959); $3.00 per year, 10¢ per copy (1959 to date). *Circ*: 750 (1873), 7,500 (1963). *Comment*: The *Moravia Republican-Register* is a consolidation of two distinct newspapers, the *Moravia Valley Register*, established 1871, and the *Moravia Republican*, established July 3, 1876, but its masthead dates its antecedents back to the *Cayuga Courier* (q.v.) established in October 1863. However, when M. E. Kenyon purchased the *Courier* he renamed it the *Moravia Valley Register*, enlarged the format to 24″ x 36″ and numbered the first edition vol. 1, no. 1. The *Moravia Valley Register* merged with the *Moravia Republican* (q.v.) in March 1901 and has appeared as the *Moravia Republican-Register* since that date. The *Moravia Valley Register* was first published from an office on Main St.; moved to Mill St., 1874; to Main St. in Perry's new brick block, 1877; to Andrew's new block, 1886; to the office over Alley's Drug Store, 1891; to Railroad St., 1893; to the Union Block, 1897; finally to 6 Central St. where it is still being published. *Loc*: NAubHi: O 5, 1900 (30: 40). NCortHi: Jl 17, 1885 (15:26). NIC/RHA: O 10, 1963 (Anniversary edition). NMor: [F 10, 1871–D 31, 1897 (1:1–27:52)]; Ja 6–D 29, 1905 (29:44 & 33:44–30:43 & 34:43); [Ja 4, 1907–D 1970 (31:44 & 35:44–?)]. NMor/MoR: [Mr 8, 1901 to date (25:52 & 35:10 to date)].

MORAVIA VALLEY REGISTER see *MORAVIA REPUBLICAN-REGISTER*

MORNING DISPATCH see *AUBURN MORNING DISPATCH*

THE NEW KIRBY ADVERTISER (m) Auburn. F 1868–? (1:1–?). *Pub and Ed*: David Munson Osborne & Co. 1868–?; Knapp and Peck by 1875–? *Format*: Eight to twenty pages, varying sizes, 11¾″ x 15½″, 13¾″ x 20″. *Price*: March 1868, gratuitous; sometimes thereafter $1.00 per year in advance. *Comment*: Devoted to the interests of farmers, manufacturers, and merchants. Originally intended "to issue as many copies of the *Advertiser* as we can advantageously dispose of to manufacturers, merchants and farmers throughout the United States." Contained advertising and articles about the Kirby harvester made by D. M. Osborne & Co. *Loc*: NAubHi: Mr 1868 (1:2); Ap 16, 1875 (no vol. no.). NCortHi: Ap 16, 1875 (no vol. no.).

NEWS-BULLETIN-AUBURNIAN see *THE AUBURN BULLETIN*

NORTH CAYUGA TIMES (w) Port Byron. No issues located. See comment under *Port Byron Gazette*.

NORTHERN ADVOCATE see *NORTHERN CHRISTIAN ADVOCATE*

NORTHERN CHRISTIAN ADVOCATE (w) Auburn, Syracuse. Mr 12, 1841–? (1:1–?). *Title changes*: *Northern Advocate* Mr 12, 1841– 1844; *Northern Christian Advocate* 1844–? *Pub*: Published by a Committee of Six Ministers of the Genesee, Oneida and Black River Conference for the Methodist Episcopal Church. *Ed*: Nelson Rounds 1844–1848; William Hosmer 1848–1856; F. G. Hibbard 1856–1860; Rev. Isaac S. Bingham 1860–1864; Rev. D. D. Lore 1864–? *Format*: Four to eight pages, varying sizes, 18½ " x 25½ ", 14¾ " x 21", 20¾ " x 26½ ". *Price*: $2.00 per year in advance (?–1848); $1.00 per year in advance (1848–?); $1.50 per year in advance; $2.00 per year in advance (1866). *Comment*: Published at 84 Genesee St.; in the basement rooms of the Methodist Episcopal Church, 1845; 16 Clark St., about 1860. Moved to Syracuse about 1872. This paper contained regular news items as well as religious notes. William J. Moses printed the newspaper. The *Northern Advocate* "was first started by Rev. John E. Robie, in April, 1841, with Revs. F. G. Hibbard and William Hosmer, editors." (Elliot G. Storke, *History of Cayuga County*, p. 52) In 1844 the paper was purchased by the Methodist General Conference and the name changed to the *Northern Christian Advocate*. *Loc*: NAubHi: My 3, 1854 (14:18); Je 11, 1862 (22:24). NCortHi: Jl 6, 1853 (13:27); O 18, 1854 (14:42); S 30, 1863 (23:39); Ja 10, 1866 (31:2). NIC/RHA: Ap 2, 1845–D 31, 1856 (5:1–16:53); Mr 17, O 6, 1858 (18:11, 40); Mr 16, My 11, Ag 3, 1859 (19:11, 19, 31); S 19, D 19, 1860; (20:38, 51); Ja 9, 16, F 6, 1861 (21:2, 3, 6); [Ja 29–D 31, 1862 (22:5–53)]; Ja 7, 14, 28, 1863 (23:1, 2, 4); D 25, 1867 (27:52); Ja 2, 1868 (28:1).

THE NORTHERN INDEPENDENT (w) Auburn. Jl 31, 1856– 1865//(?) (1:1–?). *Pub*: Central New York Publishing Association. *Ed*: Rev. William Hosmer 1856–1865. *Pol*: Anti-Slavery, Temperance. *Format*: Four pages 18½ " x 25¾ ". *Price*: $1.00 per year in advance (1856); $1.50 in advance (1865). *Circ*: 9,840 (1857); 10,000 (1859). *Comment*: Motto: "No compromise with sin, no silent submission to wrong in church or state, a bold advocacy of all the moral issues of the age and especially of an uncompromising Christianity." Although a Methodist Episcopal newspaper, its aim was to establish a religious weekly which was not governed by any Conference. It was established when the *Northern Christian Advocate* was forced to temper its stand against slavery by the Southern Methodists. Published at 113 W. Genesee St. *Loc*: NAubHi: D 11, 1856 (1:18); Je 6, 1861 (5:44); Jl 19, 1866 (10:51). NBel/William C. Green: My 5, 12, 1864 (8:40, 41). NCortHi: Ap 9, 1857 (1:35); Ap 5, 1860 (4:35); D 24, 1863 (8:21). NIC/MMN: S 17, 1857 (2:6); Ap 5, S 9, 23, O 7, N 18, 1858 (2:36; 3:5, 7, 9, 15); My 12, 19, 1859 (3:40, 41); N 8, 15, 29, 1860 (5:14, 15, 17); F 6, 1862 (6:27). NIC/RHA: [Jl 31, 1856–Ag 5, 1858 (1:1–2:52)]; O 20, 1859 (4:11); Ap 20, 1865 (9:38).

NORTHERN PHOENIX Weedsport. 1830. No issues located. Mentioned by Elliot G. Storke in *History of Cayuga County*, p. 54. See comment under *Weedsport Advertiser*.

ONONDAGA ADVERTISER see *LEVANA GAZETTE; OR, ON-ONDAGA ADVERTISER.*

ORPHAN'S FRIEND (m) Auburn. Ag 1857–? (1:1–?). *Pub*: Cayuga Asylum for Destitute Children. *Ed*: Mrs. J. W. Haight. *Format*: Eight pages, varying sizes, 9½ " x 12½ ", 14" x 19⅜ ". *Comment*: Published at 24 Grover St. A single issue and a supplement have been the only items located. It may have been a house organ. *Loc*: NCortHi: My 1882 (25:5). NIC/RHA: Je 1893 (supplement).

THE OSBORNE MONTHLY (m) Auburn. *Pub*: David Munson Osborne & Co. *Format*: Four pages 17¾ " x 23½ ". *Price*: Free. *Comment*: Non-political newspaper "devoted to agricultural and manufacturing interests." *Loc*: NCortHi: My 1, 1882.

THE PATRIOT (Auburn) see *CAYUGA PATRIOT*

PORT BYRON CHRONICLE (1844) see *PORT BYRON HERALD*

PORT BYRON CHRONICLE (1871) see *CAYUGA CHIEF-CHRONICLE*

PORT BYRON CHRONICLE AND CAYUGA COUNTY NEWS see *CAYUGA CHIEF-CHRONICLE*

PORT BYRON GAZETTE (w) Port Byron. 1851–? (1:1–?). *Pub and Ed*: A. White and Co. 1854–?. *Pol*: Independent *Format*: Four pages 18½ " x 25¼ ". *Price*: $1.50 per year in advance, otherwise $2.00 per year. *Comment*: Motto: "Give me the liberty to know, to think, to believe and to utter freely according to conscience above all other liberties (Milton)." According to Hamilton Child "It was established in 1851, by Oliver T. Baird. . . . In 1860 it passed into the hands of Benj. Thompson, who sold to William Hosford in 1861. In 1862 it was bought by [Cyrus] Marsh and its title changed to the *North Cayuga Times*." (*Gazetteer and Business Directory of Cayuga County New York for 1867-1868*, Syracuse, 1868, p. 25) *Loc*: NAubHi: Mr 23, 1854 (3:30).

PORT BYRON HERALD (w) Port Byron. O 8, 1844–F 3, 1846//(?) (1:1–2:18). *Title changes*: Port Byron Chronicle O 1844–?; Port Byron Herald ?–1846. *Pub*: Frederick Prince 1844–1846. *Pol*: Independent. *Format*: Four pages, varying sizes, 10¾ " x 15¼ ", 11⅜ " x 16¾ ". *Price*: $1.00 per year in advance, 2¢ per copy. "If a person can't afford $1.00 per year we will take of any of our farmer subscriber's flour, beef, pork, butter, cheese or lard for the *Herald;* or money to purchase such articles will be equally acceptable." *Comment*: On February 3, 1846 the following notice appeared: "The limited patronage extended to our paper in consequence of the smallness of the size induces us to contemplate the suspension of the *Herald* and make an effort to establish one more respectable in dimensions. Should this meet the views of the community in this section of the country, they will of course make it manifest. The community in this region need a paper of more extended circulation. One that can be liberally patronized might live." The first issues of the paper may have been called the *Port Byron Chronicle.* According to Storke such a newspaper did exist in 1844 and was started by Frederick Prince. (*History of Cayuga County,* p. 54). *Loc*: NAubiHi: [N 12, 1844–F 3, 1846 (1:6–2:18)]. NRU: S 30, 1845 (1:52).

PORT BYRON TIMES (w) Port Byron. 1851–1870//(?). No issues located. Listed by Winifred Gregory, *Union List of Newspapers,* p. 486.

PRIMITIVE CHRISTIAN Auburn. 1835–1841. *Pub*: Silas E. Shepard. No issues located. Mentioned in Elliot G. Storke, *History of Cayuga County,* p. 51.

RUNDSHAU Auburn. German language newspaper. No issues located. Mentioned in Ayer's *Newspaper Directory,* 1880.

SOUTHERN CAYUGA TRIBUNE see *SOUTHERN CAYUGA TRIBUNE AND THE UNION SPRINGS NEWS*

SOUTHERN CAYUGA TRIBUNE AND THE GENOA TRIBUNE see *SOUTHERN CAYUGA TRIBUNE AND THE UNION SPRINGS NEWS*

SOUTHERN CAYUGA TRIBUNE AND THE UNION SPRINGS NEWS (w) Genoa, King Ferry. My 1891 to date (1:1 to date). *Title changes*: *Genoa Tribune* 1891–1931; *Southern Cayuga Tribune and the Genoa Tribune* 1931–1959; *Southern Cayuga Tribune and the Union Springs News* 1959 to date. *Pub and Ed*: Lynn E. Kirtland 1891–1895; Clarence A. and Frank W. Ames 1895–1900; Clarence A. Ames 1900–1907; Will Mosher 1907; Emma A. Waldo 1907–1924; Mary H. Waldo 1925–1928; Charles H. Long 1928–Ag 1935; Eva L. Winne 1935–1941; Henry Bradley 1941–F 1943; Alfred L. Field F 1943–Jl 1953; Cameron C. Peterman 1953–Jl 1955; Donald and Ruth Alvord Jl 1955–1966; Inter-County Publishers (Bernard McGuerty, Pres.) D 1966 to date. *Pol*: Temperance; Republican. *Format*: Eight to twenty-eight pages, varying sizes, 15″ x 22″, 12½″ x 19½″. *Price*: $1.50 per year, 5¢ per copy; $4.00 per year, 10¢ per copy (1970). *Comment*: Published in the Tribune Building, Genoa; moved to King Ferry, 1931. Masthead reads "established 1890." *Loc*: NGeno/Cummings: Ja 1898–D 27, 1966 (7:33–?). NIC/RHA: [F 17–D 22, 1922 (32:31–33:23)]; Ag 22, 1924 (35:6); Jl 19, 1929 (39:54). NMor: Mr 18, 1932 (42:37).

SWAMP ANGEL (irr.) Fair Haven. My 1876–? (1:1–?) *Pub*: Charles H. Possons. *Format*: Four pages 8½″ x 14″. *Price*: 50¢ per year. *Comment*: "Published now and then at Little Sodus Bay." From editorial in May 1876 issue, "Well, here is the first issue of a Fair Haven paper, although not as large as we intended to publish it, it is as large as we can afford. . . . The object of our present issue is merely to advertise and to give a few local happenings. But it is our intent to publish a small paper monthly, as long as we can do so and not lose money. Our monthly will be called *The Gazette* and will be an eight page sheet and double the size of this sheet and will have a subscription price of 50¢ per year in advance." *Loc*: NStV/Cooper: facsimile My 1876 (1:1).

TEMPERANCE UNION (m) Union Springs 1866–?. *Pub*: Park and Sheal. *Comment*: No issues located. Moved to Jordan and published as the *Pearly Fountain,* May 1866. (*Union Springs Advertiser,* Je 12, 1919).

THE UNION NEWS (w) Auburn. Ag–O 28, 1910// (1:1–1:7). *Pub*: Union News Publishing Co. (P. J. Burke, General Manager). *Format*: Four to eight pages 14½ " x 21½ ". *Price*: $1.00 per year, 3¢ per copy. *Comment*: Published under the direction of the Auburn Central Union at 39 Market St. Its mission "To assist in securing hours, wages and conditions demanded by union labor in all branches of industry." Probably only a few issues of *The Union News* were published since the first issue of the *Auburn Labor Weekly* (q.v.) also published by the Auburn Central Union appeared November 4, 1910. *Loc*: NAubHi: S, O 21, 28, 1910 (1:4, 6, 7).

UNION SPRINGS ADVERTISER (w) Union Springs. Je 14, 1866– Jl 30, 1942// (1:1–77:9). *Pub and Ed*: James B. Hoff 1866–1909 (died My 30, 1909, but listed as pub. and ed. until Ag 18, 1910); Charles D. Anderson 1910–1918; M. T. Collins F 1918–Ap 1, 1919; Edward Clark Cowles 1919–Ap 27, 1935; Harold E. and Bessie Cowles Stryker 1935–Ag 1942. *Pol*: Temperance; Republican. *Format*: Four to ten pages, varying sizes, 17½ " x 23¾ ", 19½ " x 21", 13" x 20". *Price*: $1.50 per year in advance, otherwise $2.00 per year. *Comment*: In January 1880 the *Advertiser* office moved into "the rooms over Roger's drug store, second door at head first flight of stairs." For most of its life the newspaper was published from Cayuga St. During World War II the paper was reduced to four pages and in 1942 it was discontinued "because of the effect of war conditions, the decrease in advertising revenue, plus the lack of local advertising support." *Loc*: NAubHi: Ag 9, O 25, 1877 (12:11, 22); Je 27, Jl 4, 18, S 12, D 12, 1878 (13:5, 6, 8, 16, 29); My 20, 1886 (21:1); F 28, 1895 (29:43). NUS/Stryker: [Ja 20, 1879–Jl 30, 1942 (12:36– 77:9)].

UNION SPRINGS HERALD see *CAYUGA LAKE HERALD*

UNION SPRINGS LEDGER (w) Union Springs. 1850// *Pub*: William Clarke and C. C. Williams. Mentioned in *Union Springs Advertiser* (Je 12, 1919).

UNION SPRINGS NEWS (w) Union Springs. Ja 8, 1943–Ag 27, 1959//(?) (1:1–16:30). *Title changes*: The Union Springs News Ja 8–O 8, 1943; Union Springs News O 15, 1943–1959. *Pub and Ed*: Alfred L. Field, ed. and pub., and Ada E. Hazzard, assoc. ed., Ja 8, 1943–D 22, 1944; Alfred L. Field D 29, 1944–Je 25, 1953; Cameron C. Peterman Jl 2, 1953– D 10, 1953; Cameron C. Peterman and Har-

riet I. Peterman D 17, 1953–Ap 14, 1955; Alfred L. Field Ap 21–
Jl 7, 1955; Donald W. Alvord Jl 14, 1955–Jl 12, 1956; Donald W.
and Ruth S. Alvord Jl 19, 1956–Ag 27, 1959. *Pol*: Republican. *Format*: Eight to twelve pages 14″ x 21½″. *Price*: $2.00 per year in ad-
vance, 5¢ per copy (1943–1947); $2.50 per year in advance, 6¢ per
copy (1947–1956); $3.00 per year in advance, 7¢ per copy (1957–
1959). *Comment*: Published in Union Springs January 8 through
January 29, 1943 and then in King Ferry with the *Southern Cayuga
Tribune and the Genoa Tribune*. In 1959 the *News* was merged with
the *Tribune* to form the *Southern Cayuga Tribune and Union Springs
News* (q.v.). *Loc*: NUS: [Ja 15, 1943–Ag 27, 1959 (1:2–16:30)].

WEEDSPORT ADVERTISER (w) Weedsport. 1827–1830// (1:1–?).
Pub: Frederick Prince 1827–?. *Format*: Four pages 12½″ x 20″.
Comment: Storke states that this newspaper became the *Northern
Phoenix* in 1830. (*History of Cayuga County*, p. 54) *Loc*: NWee/
Finley: Ap 16, 1828 (1:42).

WEEDSPORT ADVERTISER (w) Weedsport. 1850–? (1:1–?). *Pub*:
P. J. Becker. *Format*: Eight pages, 10½″ x 15½″. *Loc*: NWee/Fin-
ley: S 8–D 15, 1853 (4:38–52).

WEEDSPORT CAYUGA CHIEF see *CAYUGA CHIEF*

WEEDSPORT CAYUGA CHIEF-PORT BYRON CHRONICLE
   see *CAYUGA CHIEF-CHRONICLE*

WEEDSPORT MONITOR (w) Weedsport. 1860?–1862//(?) (1:1–?).
Pub: Smith & D. C. Van Allen. *Format*: Four pages, 16″ x 22″.
Comment: Published from Hamilton's Building, lower floor, corner of
Brutus and South Sts. *Loc*: NWee/Finley: F 14, S 19, 1861 (1:16,
47).

THE WEEDSPORT REPUBLICAN (w) Weedsport. O 1891–?
(1:1–?). *Title changes*: *Cayuga Republican* 1891–?; *The Weedsport
Republican* ?–? *Pub and Ed*: W. E. Churchill; W. E. Churchill & Son.
Format: Eight pages, varying sizes, 15″ x 22″, 18″ x 24″. *Price*: $1.00
per year. *Loc*: NWee/Finley: Ap 26, 1892 (1:32); Ja 24, 1899 (8:22
whole no. 368).

WEEDSPORT SENTINEL (w) Weedsport. F 1867–N 16, 1933//
(1:1–56:13). *Pub and Ed*: John and B. G. Gibb F 1867–1871; S. D.
Lee 1871; S. D. Lee and Bro. 1872; George R. Nash 1872–1933. *Pol*:
Republican. *Format*: Eight to four pages, varying sizes, 12″ x 18″,
20″ x 26″. *Price*: $1.25 per year in advance, otherwise $1.50. *Comment*: After George Nash's death his widow, Katherine Nash, sold
the newspaper to the Weedsport *Cayuga Chief* (q.v.) and the *Sentinel*
was merged into that paper as of December 1, 1933. *Loc*: NAubHi:
Ag 9, 1894 (18 [*sic*] :42). NWee/Finley: N 22, 1867 (1:41); O 8,
1869 (3:35); Mr 9, Ap 16, 1871 (5:48); Ag 15, S 12, 1872 (6:27,
31); [N 1, 1877–Jl 29, 1880 (12:3–14:44)]; [Mr 11, 1886–D 17,
1891 (11:11–16:8 [*sic*])]; Ja 25–Ap 26, 1893 (18:14–27); F 10, 1910
(32:20); Ap 24, 1912 (35:31); O 26, 1917 (40:7); O 26, N 23, 1922
(45:6, 11); D 11, 1930 (53:16); Ag 17, 31, O 5, 12, N 2, 16, 1933
(55:52; 56:2, 7, 8, 11, 13).

WEEDSPORT TIMES (w) Weedsport. F 2, 1854–? (1:1–?). *Pub*: Charles T. White. *Price*: $1.00 per year. *Comment*: No issues located. Mentioned by Lazelle R. Hopkins, *Facts Regarding Weedsport*, p. 7.

THE WEEKLY AUBURNIAN see *AUBURN WEEKLY BULLETIN*

THE WEEKLY HERALD (w) Genoa. Ag 1885–1890//(?) (1:1–?). *Title changes*: *The Genoa Herald*, 1885–1886(?); *The Weekly Herald*, 1886(?)–1890. *Pub and Ed*: Smith Murphy. *Format*: Four to eight pages, varying sizes, 14½″ x 21″, 16″ x 22″. *Price*: $1.00 per year in advance. *Comment*: When the A. & W. Railroad abandoned Genoa as a stop station in 1890, Publisher Smith Murphy moved to Auburn. Genoa was without a newspaper until Lynn E. Kirtland founded the *Genoa Tribune* (q.v.) May 1891. (*Biographical Review*, Boston, 1894, p. 344.) *Loc*: NAubHi: Je 1, 1889 (4:44). NGeno/ Cummings: Ap 17, 1886 (1:37).

WEEKLY NEWS AND DEMOCRAT see *AUBURN DEMOCRAT-ARGUS*

THE WEEKLY TRUE PRESS see *AUBURN TRUE PRESS*

WEEKLY UNION see *AUBURN WEEKLY UNION*

THE WESTERN BANNER (w) Auburn. O 1835(?)–? (1:1–?). *Ed*: Francis S. Wiggins 1835; Ezekiel Paddock 1836–? *Format*: Four pages 16″ x 22½″. *Comment*: Probably predecessor to the *Auburn Banner and Genesee, Oneida and Black-River Conference Record* (q.v.). Although a Methodist newspaper, it contained items of local interest. Published at No. 8 Exchange Building, second story directly over Mr. Norman Bennet's store. *Loc*: NIC/MMN: Ag 11, 1836 (1:42 fragment).

WESTERN FEDERALIST (w) Auburn. Je 7, 1809–? (1:1–?). *Pub*: Henry and James Pace. *Format*: Four pages, varying sizes, 10¾″ x 18″, 12¼″ x 20¼″. *Price*: $2.00 per year. *Comment*: Motto: "The Freedom of the Press is the Bulwark of Liberty." *Loc*: NAubHi: Ja 31, 1810 (1:35); Jl 11, 1810 (2:58); [Je 5, 1811–My 26, 1813 (3:105–4:208)]. NRU: D 20, 1809 (1:29); Ap 19, 1815 (6:307).

WESTERN LUMINARY (w) Watkins' Settlement (Scipioville). Mr 31, 1801–? (1:1–?). *Pub and Ed*: Ebenezer Eaton for Eaton & Co. *Format*: Four pages, varying sizes, 10½″ x 17½″, 12″ x 18¾″. *Loc*: NAubHi: Jl 21, 1801 (1:17). NIC/RARE: Je 16, 1801 (1:12).

CHEMUNG COUNTY

ADVERTISER see *ELMIRA ADVERTISER* and *WEEKLY AD-VERTISER*

THE AFTERNOON ADVERTISER see *ELMIRA ADVERTISER* (Afternoon Edition)

AMERICAN'S OWN (w) Elmira. c. 1856// No issues located. This was a Know-Nothing paper published for only a few months by the proprietors of the *Elmira Republican* (q.v.). See C. G. Fairman, "The Press of Chemung County," in Henry B. Peirce, *History of Tioga, Chemung, Tompkins, and Schuyler Counties, New York* (Philadelphia, 1879), p. 245, and Ausburn Towner, *Our County and Its People: A History of the Valley and County of Chemung* (Syracuse, 1892), p. 401.

AQUAE GLORIA (bi-m) Elmira. F 1, 1874–? No issues located. It was published by Dr. Wales Of the Water Cure and had a national circulation. (Fairman, "The Press," p. 245).

BAZOO (d) Elmira. 1880–? No issues located. This was a Greenback paper published by Hugh Coyle. (Towner, *Our County*, p. 399).

THE BAZOO (1877) see *ELMIRA DAILY BAZOO*

THE BUDGET see *ELMIRA BUDGET*

CHEMUNG COUNTY DEMOCRAT see *CHEMUNG DEMOCRAT*

CHEMUNG COUNTY GREENBACKER see *THE HORSEHEADS JOURNAL*

CHEMUNG COUNTY JOURNAL (w) Elmira. Ap 8, 1875–? (1:1–?). *Pub and Ed*: Frederick Wagner. *Format*: Four pages 19″ x 26″. *Comment*: Published at 4 Opera House Block in the German language. *Loc*: NEmHi: Ap 8, 1875 (1:1).

CHEMUNG COUNTY PATRIOT AND CENTRAL ADVOCATE Horseheads. c. 1836// No issues located. This paper was published briefly by J. Taylor Brodt to urge the selection of Horseheads as Chemung County Seat. (Fairman, "The Press," p. 244).

CHEMUNG COUNTY REPUBLICAN (w) Horseheads. Ag 1856–1858// (1:1–?). *Ed*: Florus B. Plimpton. *Format*: Four pages 17″ x 24″. *Price*: $1.50 per year. *Comment*: Motto: "A Weekly Newspaper devoted to the Useful and the Beautiful and to the dissemination of the Principles of Freedom." The *Republican* was published by William I. Hastings and "the chief motive for its establishment was to answer . . . the attacks of the *Philosopher* (q.v.) . . . that was loaded and primed for the hot canvass of 1856 by Samuel C. Taber." It was discontinued in 1858 and consolidated with the *Weekly Advertiser* (q.v.). (Towner, *Our County*, p. 400) *Loc*: NEmHi: F 20, 1857 (1:29).

THE CHEMUNG DEMOCRAT (w) Elmira. 1847–? (1:1–?). *Title changes*: Chemung Democrat 1847–?; The Chemung Democrat Mr 1848–? *Pub and Ed*: L. J. Bush. *Pol*: Democrat (Hunker). *Format*: Four pages 19″ x 24″. *Price*: $1.50 per year in advance. *Comment*: Motto: "The Constitution–The Cornerstone of the Democratic Party." Published at 53 Water St., opposite the Eagle Tavern. According to Fairman, "Mr. Bush remained with the paper perhaps a year, when David Fairchild took it, and it was for some time in the hands of that gentleman and his son, F. Orville Fairchild. It then became the property of Julius Taylor, who, in 1851, issued a daily edition," and the name of the paper was subsequently changed to the *Daily Karlon* (q.v.) (Fairman, "The Press," p. 242). *Loc*: NEmHi: My 2, N 9, 1848 (2:16, 43 whole no. 95). NIC/MMN: 0 5, D 7, 1847 (1:38, 47); Mr 7, 21, 1848 (2:8, 10).

THE CHEMUNG PATRIOT see *CHEMUNG COUNTY PATRIOT AND CENTRAL ADVOCATE*

CHEMUNG VALLEY REPORTER (w) Horseheads. 1864(?) to date (1:1 to date). *Pub and Ed*: George L. Mulford and J. Leroy Nixon ?–S 20, 1894; George L. Mulford S 27, 1894–?; Chemung Valley Reporter Co., Inc. (R. J. Cook, Pres., ?–Ja 5, 1933; J. Maxwell Beers, Pres., Ja 12, 1933–?; O. Stephen Popovich, ed. and pub., by Ja 12, 1942–Ja 28, 1943; Walter Impert, Pres., Ja 11, 1945–O 26, 1950; Joseph H. Lynch, ed. and pub., F 4, 1943–My 22, 1958; Peter P. Jankowski Je 1958–Je 1967; Thomas W. Mailey Jl 1967–Ag 1969; Thomas W. Mailey and Dan Driscoll Ag 1969 to date). *Pol*: Temperance; Independent; Democrat. *Format*: Four to twenty-four pages, varying sizes, 20½″ x 26½″, 15″ x 22½″, 16″ x 23″, 18″ x 23″, 17″ x 21″, 11″ x 16½″. *Price*: $1.00 per year in advance; $2.00 per year, 5¢ per copy (by 1930–1952); $2.50 per year, 6¢ per copy (1952–1963); 10¢ per copy (1964 to date). *Comment*: In 1893 the newspaper office was located in the Bennett Block. It had moved to 190 Franklin St. by the 1930s and remained there until 1967 when it moved to 209 S. Main St. The office was moved to 118 John St. in 1968, and to 205 S. Main St., its present location, in 1969. See "Comment" under *Horseheads Journal. Loc*: NEmHi: [Je 4, 1959–D 7, 1961 (101:7–103:34)]; N 3, 1966 (108:30); [F 16, 1967–My 4, 1967 (108:45–109:4)]; [My 23, 1968–D 3, 1970 (110:6–12:34)].

NHrC: O 19, 1893–Jl 30, 1896 (29:28–32:17); Mr 30–Ap 20, 1905 (40:49–52); [fragments Ja 1907–Je 28, 1911 (43:?–48:10)]; Ja 16, 1930–D 12, 1940 (45[sic]:41–76:38); Ja 1, 1942 to date (77:41 to date). NIC/RHA: Ja 2, 1969 to date (110:38 to date). NSpnHi: [Mr 29–Jl 5, 1951 (103:50–104:12)].

CITIZEN PRESS (w) Elmira. N 24, 1970 to date (1:1 to date). *Title changes*: The Citizen Press N 24, 1970–Ja 26, 1971; *Citizen Press* F 2, 1971 to date. *Pub*: John M. Anderson. *Format*: Twelve pages 11¼ " x 17". *Price*: $5.00 per year, 10¢ per copy. *Comment*: Published at 316 Morrowfield Ave. *Loc*: NEm: [N 24, 1970 to date (1:1 to date)].

THE CLARION see *INTER-STATE ADVOCATE*

THE DAILY BAZOO see *ELMIRA DAILY BAZOO*

THE DAILY BULLETIN (d) Elmira. F 24, 1880–? No issues located. This was a "workingman's paper . . . published by Hugh Coyle at 423 Carroll Street, in the Opera House block." William H. Arnold, "Newspapers of Elmira and Chemung County" (typescript in Steele Memorial Library, Elmira), p. 19.

DAILY DEMOCRAT see *DAILY KARLON* and *THE CHEMUNG DEMOCRAT*

DAILY HERALD see *ELMIRA MORNING HERALD*

DAILY KARLON (d) Elmira. 1851// No issues located. This newspaper was originally titled the *Daily Democrat* and was the daily edition of *The Chemung Democrat* (q.v.). The paper was published by Julius Taylor and the title changed when C. Chauncey, Herman and Celia Burr became the editors. The paper died by the end of 1851. (Fairman, "The Press," p. 242).

THE DEFENDER Elmira. No issues located. A temperance paper published from the Opera House block. (Arnold, "Newspapers," p. 21).

ELMIRA ADVERTISER (d) Elmira. F 8, 1854–Ja 31, 1963// (1:1–113:58). *Title changes*: Elmira Advertiser 1854–?; *Elmira Daily Advertiser* by 1862–1896; *The Elmira Daily Advertiser* 1897–1899; *The Elmira Advertiser* 1900–O 10, 1926; *Elmira Advertiser* O 11, 1926–Ja 31, 1963. *Pub*: Fairman Bros. 1854–1855; S. B. Fairman & Co. 1856–?; S. B. Fairman ?–Jl 12, 1864; Charles G. Fairman, Luther Caldwell Jl 13–Ag 31, 1864; Charles G. and Seymour B. Fairman, Luther Caldwell S 1, 1864–1868; Charles G. Fairman, Luther Caldwell, James S. Thurston Jl 1868–Ap 7, 1869; C. G. Fairman and James S. Thurston Ap 1869–O 18, 1870; *Advertiser Association* 1870–1889 (C. G. Fairman, Pres., 1870–1882(?); S. C. Taber, Secy, N 1870–1872; Robert R. R. Dumars, Secy., 1872–1874; Ausburn Towner, Secy., 1875–?; F. A. DeVoe, Treas., N 1870–1874); *Elmira Advertising Association* 1890–? (Clay W. Holmes, Bus. Mgr., 1890–?,

Pres., 1900–1906; Milo Shanks, Gen. Mgr., 1908–1913, Pres., S 1913–1918; John Beman, Bus. Mgr., 1903–1905, Pres., 1906–1908); Elmira Star Gazette, Inc. 1923–1963 (Herman Suter, Pres. & Gen. Mgr., 1923; Ralph V. Govin, Jr., Vice-Pres., 1923; Woodford J. Copeland, Pres. & Treas., 1924; Frank E. Gannett, Vice-Pres., Ja 1924, Pres. Ja 16, 1924–Ap 1957; Frank E. Tripp, Vice-Pres., Secy., Mgr., Treas., 1924–1957, Pres., Ap 1957–1963; Harry Thayer, Secy., 1923–1924; John E. Calkins, Bus. Mgr., 1926–F 1941; Thomas V. Taft, Bus. & Gen. Mgr., Ap 1941–1961; Lynn Bitner, Asst. Pub., Ap 1941–1945, Secy. & Gen. Mgr., 1946–Ja 31, 1951; Robert Eckert, Gen. Mgr., 1962–1963). *Ed*: Fairman Bros., 1854; C. G. and S. B. Fairman, M. Ells 1855–1856; S. B. Fairman and R. R. R. Dumars by 1857–?; S. ˙B. Fairman by 1860–Jl 1864; editors not generally listed until Frank E. Gannett, Editor-in-Chief, Ja 16, 1924–1936; Roy D. Wald 1925–1937; W. Charles Barber 1938–1948; Thomas E. Byrne 1949–1953; Covey C. Hoover 1954–1958; Jan Morse 1959–?; James E. Waters, Managing ed., 1962–1963. *City ed*: Robert J. Clark 1949–1953; Hillard Gordon 1954–1957; Burt Blazar 1958–1959; James Morse 1959; Edwin Collins 1960; James M. Milliken 1961–1963. *News ed*: Leo Kuss 1956–1959; James E. Waters 1960–1963; *Pol*: Republican; also Union, Prohibition. *Format*: Four pages plus, varying sizes, 11½″ x 17½″, 16″ x 21″, 17″ x 22″. *Price*: $4.00 per year, 10¢ per week; $5.00 per year, 10¢ per week (by 1862); $6.00 per year, 12½¢ per week, then $7.00 per year, 15¢ per week (1864); $9.00 per year, 20¢ per week, 5¢ per copy (1865–1888); $8.00 per year, 17¢ per week (1888–1889); $7.00 per year, 15¢ per week (1889–1890); $8.00 per year, 18¢ per week (1890); $6.00 per year, 3¢ per copy (1891–1904); $6.00 per year, 2¢ per copy (1905–1909); 2¢ per copy (1910–1919); 3¢ per copy (1920–1942); 4¢ per copy (1943–1947); 5¢ per copy (1948–1957); 7¢ per copy (1957–1963). *Comment*: In 1882, Sloat Fassett purchased the *Advertiser* from Fairman, but his name did not appear as owner on issues located. He disposed of his holdings during World War I (*Star-Gazette*, Jl 3, 1953, p. 22). Published in Dunn's Building corner of Lake and Water Sts. (1854), then from the Hathaway House, corner of Lake and Market Sts.; Advertiser Building, 100–102 Lake St. On January 31, 1963, the *Advertiser* consolidated with the *Elmira Star-Gazette* to form the *Star-Gazette* (q.v.). *Loc*: NCortHi: Mr 1, 6, 7, 1876 (23:50, 54, 55); N 27, 1885 (32:284); S 17, 1901 (48:75). NEm: microfilm [Je 4, 1855–F 16, 1856 (2:55–2:283)]; Ja 3, Je 30, 1862 (8:240–9:81); Jl 1, 1864–D 1920 (11:50–68:?); Ap 1923–Ja 31, 1963 (70:79–113:58). NEmHi: F 8–Jl 7, D 12, 1854 (1:1–?, 261); F 26, 1855 (1:284); D 1, 1856 (3:213); F 17, 1857 (3:277); Mr 17, S 20, 1858 (4:302, 5:152); My 2, 1860–S 25, 1865 (7:31–12:83); Je 8, S 12, 1868 (15:134, 215); [Jl 5–30, 1869 (16:157–178)]; My 28, 1870 (17:126); Jl 3, 4, O 11, 1871 (18:156, 157, 239); [Mr 7–D 5, 1872 (19:57–298 scattered issues)]; Ag 28, S 15, 1874 (21:202, 216); F 20, 27, O 20, 28, 1875 (22:43, 49, 248, 255); Ja 3, Je 21, Jl 4, 6, D 30, 1876 (23:1, 144, 155, 156, 306); F 26, Mr 24, 1877 (24:48, 71); F 26, 1877–Jl 15, 1898 (24:58–45:168);

Mr 3, 1902 (49:53); S 14, 1903 (50:219); Ja 17, N 4, 1918 (55:14, 264); Jl 8–10, 1935 (83:159–161); Je 28, 1939 (87:156); My 8, 9, Ag 15, 1945 (38[*sic*]:264, 265; 87[*sic*]:364 Extra edition for Japanese surrender). NEmS: microfilm [Je 4, 1855–F 16, 1856 (2:55–2:282)]; Ja 3, Je 30, 1862 (8:240–9:81); Jl 1, 1864–D 1920 (11:50–68:?); Ap 1923–Ja 31, 1963 (101:50–113:58). NIC/RHA: microfilm Je 4, 1855–F 16, 1856 (2:55–283); Ja 3–Je 28, 1862 (8:24–9:80); Ja 3–D 30, 1865 (11:187–12:164).

THE ELMIRA ADVERTISER (Afternoon Edition) (d) Elmira. Ap 13–Ag 17, 1898// (1:1–45:196). *Title changes*: *The Afternoon Advertiser* Ap 13–16, 1898; *The Elmira Advertiser* Ap 18–Ag 17, 1898. *Pol*: Republican. *Format*: Eight to twelve pages 17″ x 22½″. *Price*: $3.00 per year, 1¢ per copy. *Circ*: 4,780–9,155. *Comment*: The afternoon edition of the *Elmira Advertiser* (q.v.) was started as a separate publication numbered volume 1 numbers 1 through 3[*sic*] through April 16, 1898. On April 18, 1898, it picked up the numbering of the morning edition, volume 45, number 92. Through July 15, 1898 the newspaper's running title was *The Afternoon Advertiser,* then it became the *Elmira Evening Advertiser.* Published primarily to report on the war, it ceased August 17, 1898. *Loc*: NEmHi: Ap 13–Ag 17, 1898 (1:1–45:196).

THE ELMIRA BOOSTER (m) Elmira. Ap 1921–? (1:1–?). *Pub*: Elmira Chamber of Commerce. *Format*: Four pages 9½″ x 12½″. *Loc*: NEmHi: Je 21, 1921 (1:3).

ELMIRA BUDGET (w) Elmira. F 26, 1893–? (1:1–?). *Pub*: James Hill F 26, 1893–? *Pol*: Independent. "No one to fear and no one to favor." *Format*: Sixteen pages 17″ x 22¼″. *Price*: $2.00 per year, 5¢ per copy. *Comment*: Motto: "Paper for the masses and not for the classes." Published in the Budget Building, corner Third and Magee Sts., and Railroad Ave. *Loc*: NEm: microfilm F 26, 1893–F 18, 1894 (1:1–52). NEmHi: My 28, 1893 (1:14).

ELMIRA DAILY BAZOO (d) Elmira. Jl 2, 1877–1879(?)// (1:1–?). *Pub*: E. C. George & Co. *Ed*: E. C. George Jl 2, 1877–D 8, 1878. *Pol*: Greenback. *Format*: Two to four pages, varying sizes, 10″ x 13¾″, 5½″ x 9¼″. *Price*: 1¢ per copy charge beginning Ag 20, 1877. *Circ*: 10,000 weekly. *Comment*: Published at 136 E. Water St. Numbering started with July 4, 1877 issue, 1:3. On August 20, 1877 the paper was designated the "official organ of the workingmen of Elmira and Chemung County," and on October 23, 1877 the "official organ of the Greenback Labor Reform Party of Elmira, Chemung County and the twenty-seventh Senatorial District." On December 8, 1878 the editor announced "We will not issue another paper until our enlarged issue comes out." Fairman says the title of the paper was subsequently changed to the *Evening Herald* and the newspaper was discontinued shortly thereafter (Fairman, "The Press," p. 245). Contains official canvass. Loc: NEm: microfilm Jl 2, 1877–D 8, 1878

(1:1–2:61). NEmHi: Jl 5, 1877–D 8, 1878 (1:4–2:61). NEmS: microfilm Jl 2, 1877–D 8, 1878 (1:1–2:61).

ELMIRA DAILY FREE PRESS (d) Elmira. D 1878–1884(?)// *Pub*: The Free Press Co. (Trustees: S. T. Arnot, J. McGuire, R. T. Turner, S. C. Taber, H. W. Rathbone, Austin Lathrop, Jr., H. E. Purdy, C. C. B. Walker, Geo. F. Magee, E. F. Babcock, John Arnot, Jr., J. J. O'Connor, S. T. Reynolds) by 1879–? *Pol*: "Politically, the *Daily Free Press* will be Democratic. It will favor honest money, honest officials, honest candidates and honest men. It will oppose dishonest money, corrupt officials, improper candidates and nincompoops generally." *Format*. Four to twelve pages, varying sizes, 15½ " x 20½ ", 17¾ " x 25", 20" x 25". *Price*: $6 per year, 50¢ per month, 3¢ per copy (masthead), 5¢ per copy (banner). *Comment*: Published from the Free Press Building, 326 Carroll St. According to Towner, this paper merged with *Elmira Gazette* in 1884 to form the *Elmira Gazette and Free Press* (q.v.) (Towner, *Our County*, p. 400). *Loc*: NEmHardeman: Ag 25, 29, 1879 (1:202, 206). NEmHi: Mr 17, S 10, 1879 (1:65, 2:16); Ja 22, 1880 (2:18). NIC/MMN: S 23, 1881 (3:238). NRU: Mr 11, 1880 (2:60). NSpnHi: Ap 17, 1879 (1:92).

ELMIRA DAILY GAZETTE see *ELMIRA GAZETTE AND FREE PRESS*

ELMIRA DAILY HERALD see *THE ELMIRA HERALD* and *ELMIRA MORNING HERALD*

ELMIRA DAILY NEWS (d) Elmira. c. 1879. No issues located. Published about two weeks. (*Elmira Star-Gazette,* Jl 3, 1953, p. 26.)

ELMIRA DAILY PRESS (d) Elmira. 1859–? (1:1–?). *Pub*: Robert R. R. Dumars, 1859–?; Thayer and Whitley, by 1863. *Ed*: Robert R. R. Dumars, 1859–?; Thayer and Whitley, George S. Melville, Assoc. ed. by 1863. *Format*: Four pages 16½ " x 23". *Price*: 10¢ per week. *Comment*: "Official paper of the village." Published over Ayers' Jewelry store southeast corner of Lake and Water Sts. *Loc*: NEmHi: F 11, O 21, 1861 (2:216, 3:121); Jl 1, 1863 (4:990).

ELMIRA DAILY REPUBLICAN (d) Elmira. Je 1–Ag 5(?), 1846// (1:1–?). *Pub and Ed*: Seymour B. and Charles G. Fairman. *Format*: Four pages 13" x 23½ ". *Price*: $3.50 per year, 2¢ per copy. *Comment*: According to Fairman, this paper was "the outgrowth of a mania which existed in those days for daily papers. . . ." He states that it was discontinued on August 5, 1846 (Fairman, "The Press," p. 241). *Loc*: NIC/MMN: Je 19, 1846 (1:17).

ELMIRA DAILY REPUBLICAN (d) Elmira. S 1851–1857(?)// (1:1–?). *Pub*: Charles G. Fairman and Lathrop Baldwin, Jr. ?–Ja 4, 1853; Lathrop Baldwin, Jr. Ja 10, 1853–?; Lathrop Baldwin, Jr. and R. R. R. Dumars by My 1853–Ag 31, 1854; Lathrop Baldwin, Jr. and Hovey E. Lowman S 1854–? *Ed*: Charles G. Fairman ?–Mr 1853; Mason 1853; O. R. Burdick Je 1853–My 1854; L. Baldwin and R. R. R. Dumars My 1853(?)–?; Florus B. Plimpton, Assoc. Ed. and

then Ed., My 1854–? *Pol*: Whig; Know-Nothing. *Format*: Four pages.
Price: $5.00 per year in advance, 10¢ per week, 2¢ per copy (1852);
$4.00 per year in advance, 10¢ per week, 2¢ per copy (1853). *Circ*:
600 (1854). *Comment*: Published at Ayers' Building, corner of Lake
and Water Sts. (1853). According to Towner, Hovey Lowman ran the
paper alone after Baldwin retired and then sold the paper to Andrew
J. Calhoun & Son in 1856. It then became a "rampant Know-Nothing
organ." (Towner, *Our County*, p. 180) *Loc*: NEm: microfilm [S 8,
1852–D 15, 1854 (2:17–4:76)]. NEmS: microfilm [S 8, 1852–D 15,
1854 (2:17–4:76)].

THE ELMIRA ENTERPRISE (m) Elmira. Ja 1874–? (1:1–?). No
issues located. This newspaper was started by Miss Libbie Adams,
aged fifteen, who performed all the work, even the distribution to
subscribers. (Fairman, "The Press," p. 245)

ELMIRA EVENING ARGUS Elmira. Ag 1882//(?) No issues
located. Published by Parker & Co., 233 West Water St. Sold for a
penny. (Arnold, "Newspapers," p. 20)

ELMIRA EVENING NEWS (d) Elmira. Ag 25, 1894–? (1:1–?).
Pub: Elmira Evening News Publishing Co. *Pol*: Independent but with
Democratic and Labor leanings. *Format*: Four to eight pages, varying
sizes, 18″ x 23½″, 15½″ x 22½″. *Price*: $1.00 per year, 1¢ per copy.
Comment: "A Newspaper in all that the word implies. Published for
laboring men by laboring men." Published at 112 Lake St. and then
on October 27, 1894 from the Gazette Building. Its business office at
205 Market St. is often cited as place of publication. By 1907 it
merged into the *Elmira Star-Gazette* (q.v.). *Loc*: NEm: microfilm S
24–D 31, 1894 (1:24–107). NEmHi: Ag 25, [S 24–D 31, 1894 (1:1,
24–107)]; My 27, 1895 (?). NEmS: microfilm S 24–D 31, 1894
(1:24–107).

ELMIRA EVENING STAR (d) Elmira. My 24, 1888–Je 1907//
(1:1–?). *Title changes*: *The Evening Star* (1888–?); *Elmira Evening
Star*. *Pub and Ed*: Isaac Seymour Copeland and James F. Woodford;
Edson C. George (by 1895–?). *Pol*: Independent. *Format*: Four to
eight pages, varying sizes, 12½″ x 20″, 16″ x 22″, 17½″ x 23½″,
19½″ x 22″. *Price*: $2.50 per year in advance, 1¢ per copy. *Com-
ment*: Published at no. 215 W. Water St., 1888, then at the corner
of Nicks St. and Exchange Place. Noted as a penny evening paper.
Combined with the *Elmira Gazette, The Elmira Free Press* and the
Elmira Evening News July 1, 1907 and became the *Elmira Star-
Gazette* (q.v.). *Loc*: NEmHi: S 8, 1888 (1:88); [My 30–D 14, 1889
(2:6–169)]; Ja 16, 30, 31, F 1, Mr 27, Ap 1–5, 1890 (2:195–260);
O 29, N 4, 28, 1891 (4: 133, 137, 157); My 27, 1895 (8:3); Je 23,
1897 (10:27); F 17, My 2, 1898 (10:223, 276). NIC/MMN: Jl 8,
1899 (12:7); S 14, 16, 19, 1901 (14: 96, 97, 100). NIDeW: [My
3–Je 15, 1898 (10:277–11:20)].

ELMIRA EVENING UNION (w) Elmira. F 2–? 1882// *Comment*:
This newspaper was "started by the strikers of the *Gazette and Free*

Press with headquarters in the Opera House Block. It was printed in a one-story building on the north side of Carroll St. . . . It suspended publication the same year." (Arnold, "Newspapers," p. 19)

ELMIRA GAZETTE AND FREE PRESS (d) Elmira. 1858–Je 29, 1907// (1:1–63[sic]:337). *Title changes*: *Elmira Daily Gazette* 1858–?; *Elmira Gazette and Free Press* by 1891–1907. *Pub*: Louis A. and Charles Hazard 1866–N 1870; The Gazette Company 1870–1907. For company officers see *Elmira Gazette and Free Press* (w). *Pol*: Democrat. *Format*: Four to eight pages, varying sizes, 20½ " x 27", 17" x 22". *Price*: $8.00 per year, $2.00 per quarter, 15¢ per week (1872); $6.00 per year, 2¢ per copy (1891–1900); $3.00 per year, 1¢ per copy (1901–1906); 10¢ per week (O 1906–1907). *Comment*: Published at 104–106 Lake St. On June 29, 1907 announced consolidation with the *Evening Star* (q.v.) and became the *Elmira Star-Gazette* (q.v.). *Loc*: NEm: microfilm Ap 1, 1891–Je 29, 1907 (67:77–63[sic]:337). NEmHardeman: Ag 26, 1872 (14:100); Ja 3, 1878 (19:201); My 23, 1900 (77:122). NEmHi: [Jl 2, 1885–Je 29, 1907 (58:156–63[sic]:337)]. NEmS: microfilm Ap 1, 1891–Je 29, 1907 (67:77–63[sic]:337). NIC/MMN: Ag 22, 1886 (8:100); My 4, 1867 (9:5).

ELMIRA GAZETTE AND FREE PRESS (w) Elmira. Ag 1828–Je 1907// (1:1–?). *Title changes*: *Elmira Gazette* ?–O 30, 1845; *The Elmira Gazette* N 6, 1845–?; *Elmira Gazette* by 1849–?; *Elmira Weekly Gazette* by 1858–?; *Elmira Gazette and Free Press* by 1888. *Pub*: Brinton Paine 1831–1837; Brinton Paine and Cyrus Pratt S 30, 1837–Je 30, 1838; Cyrus Pratt Jl 7, 1838–Je 22, 1839; Cyrus Pratt and Irad L. Beardsley Je 29, 1839–N 9, 1839; I. L. Beardsley & Co. N 16, 1839–Mr 14, 1840; Cyrus Pratt and Beardsley Mr 21, 1840; Cyrus Pratt Mr 28, 1840–My 29, 1841; George Mason and William C. Rhodes O 7, 1841–Mr 30, 1848; George W. Mason Ap 6, 1848–1855; Samuel C. Taber and Philo B. Dailey ?–Jl 12, 1858; Samuel C. Taber Jl 22, 1858–S 23, 1858; Frederick A. DeVoe S 30, 1858–Jl 1864; Frederick A. DeVoe and Charles Hazard Jl 19, 1864–Jl 1866; Louis and Charles Hazard Jl 5, 1866–N 17, 1870; The Gazette Co. (David B. Hill, Pres., Royal R. Soper, Bus. Mgr.) N 24, 1870–1906; Frank E. Gannett and Erwin R. Davenport Je 6, 1906–Je 29, 1907. *Ed*: Thomas Maxwell 1831–?; George W. Mason Ap 6, 1848–1855; Samuel C. Taber and William C. Rhodes 1858(?)–?; Charles Hazard 1864–1879; Louis A. Hazard 1876–?; Frank E. Gannett 1906–1907. *Pol*: Democrat. *Format*: Four to eight pages 21" x 27". *Price*: $2.00 per year in advance (1835); $1.75 per year in advance, $2.50 otherwise (1844); $1.50 per year in advance (1850). *Circ*: 400 (1836); 2,200 (1858). *Comment*: According to Fairman, Job A. Smith preceded Brinton Paine as the proprietor of the *Gazette* from 1828 to 1831 (Fairman, "The Press," p. 240). On July 25, 1835 the Gazette Office moved to the east room of the basement in the building formerly called "The Mansion House" opposite the store of Messers Wickham & Tuthill and Gillett & Cone. Then in 1837 Payne & Pratt's offices were listed directly opposite the Eagle Tavern; by the 1840s at 1 E. Main St., then by the 1850s the offices were located at the corner of Water and Lake Streets, and by 1869 in the Opera House Block on Carroll St. The newspaper published the official canvass of Chemung County. There was a feud between the *Gazette* and the *Telegram* that led the editor of the latter paper to write, "The Elmira *Gazette* which is edited by a blackguard of the tramp species and mismanaged by a man who once run [*sic*] a one-house brewery and failed, on Wednesday last devoted a column or less of its so called editorial page to a bitter personal attack upon the *Telegram* and its proprietors . . . R. R. Soper should first clear his own skirts ere he seeks to smirch the garments of others." (*The Sunday Morning Telegram,* D 31, 1882) According to Towner, the Elmira *Gazette* merged with the *Elmira Weekly Free Press* in 1884 (Towner, *Our County,* p. 400). In July 1907, the *Elmira Gazette and Free Press* was consolidated with the *Elmira Evening Star* (q.v.) and issued as the *Elmira Star-Gazette* (q.v.). *Loc*: NEm: microfilm Jl 25, 1835–My 24, 1855 (7:363–27:52); Ja 11–D 26, 1872 (44:27–45:25); Ja 5–D 29, 1888 (51:1–52). NEmHi: Jl 25, 1835–S 27, 1849 (7:363–22:16 whole no. 1101); Je 2, 1853–My 24, 1855 (26:1–27:52); Ja 11, 1872–D 26, 1872 (44:27–45:25); Ja 5–D 29, 1888 (51:1–52). NEmS: microfilm Jl 25, 1835–My 24, 1855 (7:363–27:52); Ja 11–D 26, 1872 (44:27–45:25); Ja 5–D 29, 1888 (51:1–52). NHrC: Jl 15, 1858–D 27, 1860 (31:7–33:31); Ja 4, 1866–D 29, 1870 (38:26–43:28). NIC/MMN: Je 6, 1850 (22:1 whole no. 1145); Ag 5, 1880 (52:47); Ag 12, 1891 (67:160); S 13, 1901 (77:182). NIC/RHA: microfilm [Jl 25, 1835–My 25, 1855 (7:363–28:52)]; Ja 11–D 20, 1872 (44:27–45:25). NSpnHi: S 4, 1879 (51:49).

THE ELMIRA HEIGHTS COURIER Elmira Heights. c. 1896–1900. No issues located. Published by William H. and Claude R. Snyder (Arnold, "Newspapers," p. 22).

ELMIRA HEIGHTS REVIEW Elmira Heights. 1946–1950. No issues located. Mentioned in *Star-Gazette,* Jl 3, 1953, p. 26.

THE ELMIRA HERALD (d) Elmira. O 11, 1913–My 22, 1920(?)// (1:1–?). *Pub*: Elmira Herald Publishing Co., Inc.; The Herald Publishing Co., (F. W. Ross, Mgr. and Secy-Treas.) Mr 7, 1918–1920. *Ed*: Thomas Wrigley by 1918–? *Pol*: Democrat. *Format*: Eight to fourteen pages. *Price*: $3.00 per year, 6¢ per week delivered, 1¢ per copy; $4.00 per year, 10¢ per week, 2¢ per copy (Ap 16, 1917–?); $6.00 per year, 3¢ per copy (O 14, 1918–My 1919); $4.00 per year, 2¢ per copy (My 14, 1919–1920). *Comment*: Motto: "The News the day it happens." Published in the Richardson Building 1913–1917; the Herald Building 1918–1920. Contains city and county canvass. *Loc*: NEm: microfilm O 11, 1913–Mr 31, 1920 (1:1–7:145). NEmS: microfilm O 11, 1913–Mr 31, 1920 (1:1–7:145).

ELMIRA MORNING HERALD (d) Elmira. Jl 16–18, 1883//(?) (1:1–3). *Pub*: Charles G. Fairman and Whittet. *Price*: $5.00 per year in advance, 2¢ per copy. *Comment*: Sometimes referred to as the

Daily Herald. Published at 103 Baldwin St. *Loc*: Jl 17, 18, 1883 (1: 2, 3 fragments).

ELMIRA MORNING SUN (d) Elmira. Ja 14, 1895–? (1:1–?). *Pub*: Elmira Morning Sun Printing House. *Ed*: James H. Callahan, Managing Ed., J. LeRoy Nixon, Assoc. Ed. *Pol*: Democrat. *Format*: Six pages 18″ x 23½″. *Price*: $3.60 per year. *Comment*: Motto: "There's always room at the top." *Loc*: NEmHi: Ja 14 ,1895 (1:1).

ELMIRA MORNING TELEGRAM see *SUNDAY TELEGRAM*

ELMIRA MORNING TIDINGS see *SATURDAY TIDINGS*

ELMIRA RECORD (w) Elmira. 1932–? (1:1–?). *Pub*: Harold Gill. *Pol*: Independent. *Format*: Eight pages 9½″ x 12¼″. *Comment*: Published at 309 Washington St. *Loc*: NEmHi: D 7, 1934 (3:6).

THE ELMIRA REPUBLICAN (w) Elmira. My 4–D 30, 1831// (1:1–35). *Title changes*: Elmira Republican, and political and literary Register; The Elmira Republican. *Pub*: John Duffey. *Pol*: Whig. *Format*: Four pages 14½″ x 20″. *Loc*: NEmHi: My 4, 11, D 30, 1831 (1:1, 2, 35).

ELMIRA REPUBLICAN (w) Elmira. F 25, 1832–? 1857// (1:1–?). *Title changes*: The Elmira Republican F 25, 1832–F 1833; The Elmira Republican and General Advertiser Mr 2, 1833–?; The Elmira Republican by 1847–?; Elmira Republican 1855; Elmira Weekly Republican 1855–1856; Elmira Republican 1856(?)–1857. *Pub*: Ransom Birdsall Mr 12, 1831–1840; Ransom Birdsall and Elias S. Huntley 1832–1836; William Polleys and Carter 1840–1843; D. M. Cook 1843; William Polleys and Co. 1844–1846; Charles G. Fairman 1846–?; Charles G. Fairman & L. Baldwin, Jr. Ja 18–Jl 19, 1850; L. Baldwin, Jr. S 1850–?; Charles G. Fairman & L. Baldwin, Jr. 1851–?; Lathrop Baldwin, Jr. and H. E. Lowman ?–Je 1855; E. S. Lowman 1856–1857. *Ed*: Ransom Birdsall; Polleys and Carter 1842–1843; D. M. Cook 1843–1844; R. W. Wells 1843–1844; Elias S. Huntley 1844–1845; Seymour B. and Charles G. Fairman 1846; L. Baldwin, Jr. 1850; Charles G. Fairman and L. Baldwin 1851; L. Baldwin, Jr. 1853; E. S. Lowman and Florus Plimpton by 1855; E. S. Lowman 1856–? *Pol*: Whig, then Know-Nothing. *Format*: Four to six pages, varying sizes, 15″ x 24″, 18″ x 24″, 21″ x 26″. *Price*: $1.75 in advance, otherwise $2.00 per year (1844–?); $1.00 per year in advance, otherwise $2.00 per year (1846); $1.50 per year in advance (after N 22, 1850). *Circ*: 1,000 (1854). *Comment*: Published at 63 Water St. 1846–? Brick Building, corner Bridge, Water and Lake Sts. D 27, 1850–? *Loc*: NEm: microfilm [S 8, 1848–Jl 16, 1852 (n.s. 3:43–7:34)]. NEmHi: Mr 3–F 16, 1833 (1:2–52); [Mr 2, 1833–F 11, 1837 (2:2–5:52)]; Ap 11, 1840 (9:9 whole no. 504); Ja 1, 1842 (1:6 whole no. 594); Ja 8, Ap 16, 1847 (n.s. 2:8, 22); Jl 12, 1850 (5:35); Je 13, Ag 31, 1855 (4:126; 10:37); Mr 7, 1856 (11:19). NEmS: microfilm [S 8, 1848–Jl 16, 1852 (n.s. 3:43–7:34)]. NIC/MMN: D 6, 1834 (3:42 whole no. 225); F 6, Ag 28, 1841

(9:52, 10:29 whole no. 547, 576); F 5, 1842 (n.s. 1:11 whole no. 599); S 9, 16, D 23, 1843 (2:42, 43 n.s. whole no. 682, 683; 3:5 whole no. 697); My 25, S 21, O 19, D 7, 1844 (3:27, 44, 48 whole nos. 719, 736, 747; 4:3); O 18, 1845 (4:48 whole no. 792); Jl 17, 1846 (n.s. 1:35 whole no. 831); Ja 29, Ap 9, Jl 2, O 15, 1847 (n.s. 2:11, 21, 33, 48 whole nos. 859, 869, 881, 896); Ja 14, F 4, Mr 10, Ap 7, My 26, Je 16, Jl 14, 1848 (n.s. 3:9, 12, 17, 21, 28, 31, 35 whole nos. 909, 912, 917, 921, 928, 931, 935). NIC/RHA: O 9, 1844 (n.s. 3:48 whole no. 740); Jl 1, Ag 7, 1846 (n.s. 1:36, 37 whole nos. 833, 834); S 3, N 26, D 17, 1847 (n.s. 2:42; 3:26 whole nos. 890, 902, 905); Ap 7, 14, 1848 (n.s. 3:21, 22 whole nos. 921, 922); Ja 26, Jl 20, 1849 (n.s. 4:11, 36 whole nos. 963, 968); Ag 22, 1851 (n.s. 6:40 whole no. 1097); Ap 22, 1853 (n.s. 8:24 whole no. 1183).

ELMIRA REPUBLICAN AND CANAL ADVERTISER (w) Elmira. Ag 10, 1830–Ap 26, 1831// (1:1–38). *Pub*: William Murphy. *Ed*: Chauncey Morgan. *Pol*: Neutral. "Our government is Republican . . . our political feelings and principles are Republican . . . but we will pursue a Neutral course!" *Format*: Four pages 14½ " x 20". *Price*: $2.00 per year in advance. *Loc*: NEmHi: Ag 10, 1830–Ap 26, 1831 (1:1–38).

ELMIRA SENTINEL Elmira. c. 1880s. No issues located. Mentioned by Arnold, "Newspapers," p. 20.

ELMIRA STAR-GAZETTE (d) Elmira. Jl 1, 1907–Ja 31, 1963// (1:1–56:149). *Pub*: Star-Gazette Co. (I. Seymour Copeland, Pres., 1907–My 22, 1919; Erwin R. Davenport, Treas. and Mgr. 1907–1918, Vice-Pres. 1919–1925; Frank E. Gannett, Vice-Pres. 1907–1925, Pres. 1926–Ap 1957; Woodford J. Copeland, Pres., Treas., Mgr., My 23, 1919–1925; Frank E. Tripp, Secy., Adv. Dir. 1923–1925, Secy-Treas. 1926–1941, Vice-Pres. 1941–1957, Pres. and Pub. Ap 12, 1957–1963; James Woodford, Secy., 1907–1922; John J. Calkins, Bus. Mgr., 1926– F 1941; Thomas V. Taft, Bus. and Gen. Mgr., Ap 1941–1961; Lynn N. Bitner, Ass't Pub., Ap 1941–1957; Robert Eckert, Gen. Mgr., 1962–? *Ed*: Woodford J. Copeland and Frank E. Gannett 1907–1919; Woodford J. Copeland 1919–1922; Frank E. Gannett, Ed.-in-Chief, 1924–1936; George S. Crandall 1923–1959; George E. McCann, Managing Ed., 1941–1959; John J. Calkins, Vicinity Ed. 1921, City Ed. 1922; Donald Seeley, City Ed., Ag 12, 1942–1951; Covey C. Hoover, News Ed. then Managing Editor., 1957–1963; Frederick W. Box, City Ed., 1947–1959; Burton H. Blazar, City Ed., 1959–1963. *Pol*: Independent with Democratic leanings 1907–1914; then completely Independent N 7, 1914. "The *Star-Gazette* will not support any candidate merely because he is a Democrat or merely because he is a Republican. It will support only those it considers best fitted for the office and most entitled to endorsement regardless of party affiliations or party loyalty. So today the *Star-Gazette* dedicates itself anew as an independent and fearless journal, free from all outside influences of every name and nature, devoted solely to the best interests of the city and county, state and nation, regardless of all other considerations." *Format*: Variable pagination. *Price*: $3.00 per year, 25¢ per month, 10¢ per week (1907–1917); $4.00 per year in advance, $1.00 for 3 months, 50¢ per month, 2¢ per copy (1918–1919); $6.00 per year in advance, 50¢ per month, 15¢ per week, 3¢ per copy (1919–1923); $5.00 per year in advance, 50¢ per month, 15¢ per week, 3¢ per copy (1924–1942); $6.00 per year in advance, $1.75 for 3 months, 22¢ per week, 4¢ per copy (1942–1948); $9.00 per year, $1.00 per month, 30¢ per week, 5¢ per copy (1949–1957); $12.00 per year, $6.50 for 6 months, $3.50 for 3 months, $1.25 per month, 5¢ per copy (1957); $12.00 per year, $6.50 for 6 months, $3.50 for 3 months, 40¢ per week, 7¢ per copy (1957–1963). *Circ*: 18,940–39,811 (1912–1963). *Comment*: Consolidation of the "*Elmira Evening Star* founded 1888, *Elmira Gazette* founded 1828, *Elmira Free Press* founded 1878, *Elmira Evening News* founded 1894." Creed: "Bigger, Better, Busier Elmira!" Published at 104–106 Lake St. Official paper of the city of Elmira. On February 1, 1963, the *Elmira Advertiser* and the *Elmira Star-Gazette* combined into an all day newspaper currently called the *Star-Gazette* (q.v.). *Loc*: NEm: microfilm Jl 1, 1907–Ja 31, 1963 (1:1–56:149). NEmHi: Jl 1, 1907–Ja 31, 1963 (1:1–56:149). NEmS: microfilm Jl 1, 1907–Ja 31, 1963 (1:1–56:149). NIC/MMN: Ag 31, 1912 (fragment); N 11, 1918 (12:113); Ag 7, 1923 (17:32).

ELMIRA SUNDAY HERALD (w) Horseheads, Elmira. 1872 (?)–1878(?)// No issues located. It was first issued in Horseheads about 1870, brought to Elmira in 1872, and discontinued about 1878 (Arnold, "Newspapers," p. 20).

ELMIRA SUNDAY MORNING EXAMINER (w) Elmira. c. 1892. No issues located. Mentioned in *Star-Gazette*, Jl 3, 1953, p. 26.

ELMIRA SUNDAY MORNING PRESS (w) Elmira. 1863–1864// (?) (1:1–?). *Pub and Ed*: G. D. A. Brigman and J. A. Paine. *Pol*: Independent. *Format*: Four pages 18″ x 23½″. *Price*: $1.50 per year in advance. *Comment*: Official paper of the city. Published over Ayers' Jewelry Store southeast corner Lake and Water Sts. *Loc*: NEmHi: Je 19, 1864 (1:50).

ELMIRA TELEGRAM see *SUNDAY TELEGRAM*

ELMIRA TIDINGS see *SATURDAY TIDINGS*

ELMIRA UNION see *ELMIRA EVENING UNION*

ELMIRA WEEKLY ADVERTISER see *THE WEEKLY ADVERTISER*

ELMIRA WEEKLY ADVERTISER AND CHEMUNG COUNTY REPUBLICAN see *THE WEEKLY ADVERTISER*

ELMIRA WEEKLY FREE PRESS (w) Horseheads, Elmira. 1873–1884// No issues located. The *Horseheads Free Press* was started in 1873 by Horace E. Purdy and was moved to Elmira January 1, 1878

(Fairman, "The Press," p. 244). This newspaper, cited by Towner as the *Weekly Free Press,* was consolidated with the *Gazette* in 1884 to form the *Elmira Gazette and Free Press* (q.v.) (Towner, *Our County,* pp. 399–400). See also the *Elmira Daily Free Press.*

ELMIRA WEEKLY GAZETTE see *ELMIRA GAZETTE AND FREE PRESS*

THE ELMIRA WHIG (w?) Elmira. 1828–1829//(?) (1:1–?). *Pub:* James Durham, printer. *Pol:* Whig. *Format:* Four pages 13½ " x 21". *Price:* $1.75 per year in advance, otherwise $2.25. *Loc:* NEmHi: Jl 2, 1829 (fragment).

EVENING HERALD see *ELMIRA DAILY BAZOO*

EVENING NEWS see *ELMIRA EVENING NEWS*

EVENING REVIEW see *SATURDAY EVENING REVIEW*

THE EVENING STAR see *ELMIRA EVENING STAR*

EVENING UNION see *ELMIRA EVENING UNION*

THE FACTS (w) Elmira. 1895–? (1:1–?). *Pub:* The Facts Printing Co. *Pol:* Prohibition. *Format:* Four pages. *Price:* $1.00 per year. *Comment:* Published in the Advertiser Building, Market St. *Loc:* NEmHi: F 18, 1898 (3:41 fragments). *See also* p. 288

FAIRMAN'S DAILY ADVERTISER (d) Elmira. N 3, 1853–F 1, 1854// (1:1–1:74). *Pub:* Fairman Brothers. *Format:* Four pages 7¼ " x 11". *Circ:* 1,000. *Comment:* Published at first as an advertising medium with local and general news, the Fairman Brothers announced less than a year after the beginning of publication that they would double the size of the paper and call it the *Elmira Daily Advertiser* (q.v.). *Loc:* NEmHi: N 3, 1853–F 1, 1854 (1:1–1:74).

THE FAVORITE (semi-m) Elmira. Ja 15, 1856–? (1:1–?). *Pub:* Robinson & Co. *Ed:* J. T. Dudley and W. H. Robinson. *Format:* Four pages 10" x 14½ ". *Price:* 15¢ per quarter in advance. *Comment:* Motto: "Young America Forever." "Independent in everything; neutral in nothing. . . . Ardent advocate of Young America and right, unflinching opponent of old fogyism and wrong." Published on Lake St., first door south of the Haight House. *Loc:* NEmHi: Ja 15, 1856 (1:1).

FORT HENDERSON MEDDLAR (irr) Elmira. 1831. No issues located. Issued by Alexander S. Diven and Benedict Saterlee (Towner, *Our County,* pp. 183–184).

FREE PRESS see *ELMIRA WEEKLY FREE PRESS* and *ELMIRA GAZETTE AND FREE PRESS*

HORSEHEADS FREE PRESS see *ELMIRA WEEKLY FREE PRESS*

HORSEHEADS INDEPENDENT (w) Horseheads. c. 1880// No issues located. Appeared briefly. Mentioned in Arnold, "Newspapers," p. 19; also *Star-Gazette*, Jl 3, 1953, p. 26.

THE HORSEHEADS JOURNAL (w) Horseheads. 1858(?)–? (1:1–?). *Title changes: The Horseheads Journal* 1858(?)–?; *Southern Tier Greenbacker and Horseheads Journal* 1878(?)–?; *The Horseheads Journal* by 1886–? *Pub and Ed*: Thomas J. Taylor by 1874–1886(?). *Pol*: Republican, then Greenback. *Format*: Four pages 18″ x 24″. *Price*: $1.50 per year in advance (1874); $1.00 per year in advance (1882–1886). *Comment*: Devoted to Literature, News, Arts, and Politics. According to Towner, "The Horseheads *Journal* was first printed on April 16, 1858, by W. E. & H. A. Giles, and was continued by them for a little over a year. It lay dormant until April, 1866, when it was resurrected by S. C. Clisbe and Charles Hinton. Mr. Clisbe . . . retired and Mr. Hinton continued it irregularly for three years, when it came into the possession of Thomas Jefferson Taylor. Until 1877 it was Republican . . . but that year it espoused the Greenback theories and in 1878 it was removed to Elmira, its name . . . changed to the *Chemung County Greenbacker*. It was removed back to Horseheads and on April 14, 1887, its name again changed to the *Chemung Valley Reporter* (q.v.), under which designation it is now [1892] published by a company, its editor, Leroy Nixon, making it one of the brightest and most sparkling of country newspapers." (Towner, *Our County,* p. 400. See also Fairman, "The Press," p. 244.) *Loc*: NEmHi: Ag 12, 1874 (9:10 whole no. 426). NIC/RHA: Mr 1, 1882 (12:22 whole no. 826); My 1, 1886 (20:4 whole no. 1042).

THE HORSEHEADS POST see *THE POST*

HORSEHEADS WEEKLY FREE PRESS see *ELMIRA WEEKLY FREE PRESS*

THE HUSBANDMAN (w) Elmira. Ag 26, 1874–Ag 16, 1893// (1:1–19:899). *Pub*: The Husbandman Association (Charles Heller, Pres., 1874–F 12, 1879, O 29, 1879–F 1881; George W. Hoffman, Pres., F 19–O 22, 1879; no listing after 1881). *Ed*: William A. Armstrong Ag 1874–Mr 8, 1876; William A. Armstrong and Jonas S. Van Duzer Mr 15, 1876–Ap 2, 1879; none listed thereafter. *Pol*: New York State Grange. "We wouldn't give ten cents for the Republicans nor a dime for the Democrats." *Format*: Eight pages 15″ x 21″. *Price*: $1.50 per year (1874–Ag 6, 1879); $1.00 per year (1879–1893). *Circ*: 8,000. *Comment*: The newspaper had offices at Barney & Baldwin, 117 Baldwin St. (1877–1878), the corner of Water and Baldwin Sts. (1878), and the Old Savings Bank, Carroll St. (D 1878–1881); with Gridley & Underhill, corner State and Nick Sts. (1881–1882); and with Fitch, Billings & Co. (later Hosmer H. Billings), 112 Baldwin St. (1882–1891). On December 2, 1891 the office moved to The Husbandman Building, Chestnut St., Binghamton. *Loc*: NAuW: N 4, 1885 (12:585); Ja 20, S 1, 8, 1886 (12:596; 13:628, 629). NCortHi: Ap 5, 1882 (8:398). NEmHi: S 28, O 1, 1875 (no vol nos.); Ag 15, 1877 (3:156); Ag 21, 1878–Ag 13, 1879 (5:209–260). NIC/Mann: Ag 26, 1874–Ag 16, 1893 (1:1–19:899). NWhP: My 27, 1891 (17:872). *See also* p. 288

THE INDEPENDENT REPUBLICAN (w) Elmira. c. 1911. *Format*: 15″ x 20″. *Loc*: NIC/MMN: My 26, 1911 (fragment).

INTER-STATE ADVOCATE (w) Elmira. 1890–? (1:1–?). *Title changes*: *The Clarion* 1890–My 15, 1891; *Inter-State Advocate* My 22, 1891–? *Pub*: F. B. Shaw ?–1891 (?). *Pol*: Prohibition. *Format*: Four to eight pages, varying sizes, 13″ x 20″, 15″ x 18″. *Price*: 50¢ per year prior to Mr 27, 1891, then $1.00 per year. *Comment*: Published at 125 West Water St. *Loc*: NIC/MMN: F 27, Mr 27–Jl 17, 1891 (1:24, 27–42).

THE INVESTIGATOR (w) Newtown (now Elmira). Ja 1, 1820–? (1:1–?) *Pub*: Job A. Smith (also printer). *Pol*: Bucktail. *Format*: Four pages 12″ x 20½″. *Price*: $2.25 at end of year, $2.00 paid quarterly, $1.75 in advance. *Loc*: NEmHi: D 1, 1821 (2:101); Mr 16, Ap 27, Ag 3, N 16, 1822 (3:116, 122, 136, 150); My 29, 1823 (4:169).

THE KIRMESSITE (d) Elmira. My 21–25, 1888// (1:1–5). *Format*: Four pages 12″ x 14″. *Price*: 2¢ per copy. *Comment*: "Kirmessite" is a corruption of the German word *kirchmesse* which means church fair. This small publication was devoted to news of the fair held at the New York State Armory in Elmira in 1888. *Loc*: NEmHi: My 21–25, 1888 (1:1–5).

THE KIRMESSONIAN (d) Elmira. My 1891// (1:1–?). *Ed*: Mrs. Charles D. Metzger. *Format*: Four pages 14″ x 16″. *Comment*: Devoted to social news and news of the New York State Fair. *Loc*: NEmHi: My 28, 29, 1891 (1:4, 5).

THE LEADER see *SOUTHERN TIER LEADER*

MIDDAY SUN Elmira. 1879(?)// No issues located. It was published briefly in 1879 in the interest of the Greenbackers and edited by Thomas Jefferson Taylor (Towner, *Our County,* p. 399).

THE MILLPORT NEWS (w) Millport. Ap 17, 1867–? (1:1–?). *Pub*: S. C. Clizbe. *Format*: Four pages 13″ x 19¼″. *Price*: $1.50 per year. *Comment*: Publisher's office in the Crawfords Building, south of the Hotel. *Loc*: NMill: My 8, 1867 (1:4).

NEWTOWN TELEGRAPH (w) Newtown Village (now Elmira). N 1815–? (1:1–?). *Title changes*: *The Telegraph* 1815–1818(?); *Newtown Telegraph* by 1819. *Pub*: William Murphy 1815–? *Format*: Four pages 11½″ x 18″. *Comment*: According to Brigham, William Brindle and William Murphy established *The Telegraph* in 1815; then Murphy became sole proprietor until 1818 when he sold to Abner and Edson Harkness who finally sold to Erastus Shepard in 1819. Clarence S. Brigham, *History and Bibliography of American News-*

papers, 1690–1820 (Worcester, Mass, 1947), p. 710. *Loc*: NEmHi: O 15, 1816 (vol. and no. indistinct). *See also* p. 288

THE PHILOSOPHER (w) Horseheads. Ap 7, 1855–? (1:1–?). *Pub and Ed*: Samuel C. Taber and F. Orville Fairchild Ap–My 5, 1855; Samuel C. Taber My 12, 1855–? *Pol*: Know-Nothing (1855), then supported Buchanan, a Democrat. *Format*: Four pages 18″ x 24″. *Price*: $1.50 per year in advance. *Comment*: Motto: "An Independent Family Journal: Neutral in Nothing." Printed in the Brick Block. Published text of village ordinances. According to Fairman, the *Philosopher* was consolidated with the *Elmira Gazette* (q.v.) in 1857 and Samuel C. Taber became manager of the *Gazette* (Fairman, "The Press," p. 244). *Loc*: NEm: microfilm Ap 7, 1855–Mr 29, 1856 (1:1–52). NEmHi: Ap 7, 1855–Mr 29, 1856 (1:1–52). NEmS: microfilm Ap 7, 1855–Mr 29, 1856 (1:1–52). NHrC: Ap 28, 1855–Mr 29, 1856 (1:4–52).

THE POST (w) Horseheads. My 20, 1964–? (1:1–?). *Title changes*: *The Horseheads Post* My 20, 1964–?; *The Post* by Ja 20, 1965–? *Pub*: Robert G. Finley, Jr. *Ed*: Jean Finley. *Pol*: Non-partisan. *Format*: Six to twelve pages, varying sizes, 16¼″ x 22½″, 11″ x 17″. *Price*: 10¢ per copy (1964); 5¢ per copy (1965). *Circ*: 8,500. *Comment*: Published at 211 N. Main St. *Loc*: NEmHi: [My 20, 1964–Je 23, 1965 (1:1–2:6)].

SATURDAY EVENING REVIEW (w) Elmira. Mr 13, 1869–1871// (1:1–?). *Pub and Ed*: Orrin H. Wheeler and Robert M. Watts Mr–O 1869; Orrin H. Wheeler N 6, 1869–? *Format*: Eight pages 14″ x 20″. *Price*: $3.00 per year in advance. *Comment*: Motto: "A family paper, pleasing in variety, sound in morals, independent in politics, and choice in story and miscellany." Published at 28 Lake St. 1869–1871. *Loc*: NEm: microfilm Mr 13, 1869–Mr 4, 1871 (1:1–2:52). NEmHi: Ag 28, 1869 (1:25); Je 11, Ag 13, S 10, 17, 1870 (2:14, 23, 27, 28); [O 1–D 31, 1870 (2:30–43)]; Ja 28, F 25, Mr 4, 1871 (2:47, 51, 52). NEmS: microfilm Mr 13, 1869–Mr 4, 1871 (1:1–2:52). NIC/MMN: Ag 14, 1869 (1:23).

SATURDAY TIDINGS (w) Elmira. N 6, 1881–? (1:1–?). *Title changes*: *Sunday Morning Tidings* N 6, 1881–F 15, 1885; *The Elmira Tidings* F 22, 1885–?; *Elmira Sunday Tidings* by 1887; *Elmira Tidings* 1887(?)–Mr 17, 1888; *Saturday Tidings* Mr 24, 1888–? *Pub*: John B. Briggs and Isaac Seymour Copeland 1881(?)–?; Mark Bennett Ag 15, 1888–? *Pol*: Independent. *Format*: Eight pages, varying sizes, 15½″ x 22¼″, 17¼″ x 23″. *Price*: $2.00 per year, $1.50 per year in clubs of five, 5¢ per copy. *Comment*: Seemingly printed by the press of the *Advertiser* which was destroyed by fire on February 15, 1888 and then by the *Gazette* which had a fire on March 10 of the same year. About 1889 the *Tidings* was removed to Buffalo and was issued as *The Buffalo Illustrated Saturday Tidings*. *Loc*: NEm: microfilm [Ja 6, 1884–D 27, 1885 (3:9–5:9)] Ja 1–D 29, 1888 (7:10–8:6). NEmHi: D 11, 1881 (1:6); Jl 2, D 31, 1882 (1:35, 2:9); O 21, 1883 (2:50); Ja 13, Ap 27, D 21, 1884 (3:10, 25; 4:7); Jl 5, 1885

(4:35); Ap 18, S 5, 1886 (5:25, 45); Je 19, 1887 (6:34); Mr 10, 1888 (7:20). NEmS: microfilm [Ja 6, 1884–D 27, 1885 (3:9–5:9)]; Ja 1–D 29, 1888 (7:10–8:6). NIC/MMN: Ja 25, 1885 (4:1). NSpnHi: Ja 8, 1882 (1:10).

THE SATURDAY WORLD (w) Elmira. 1889//(?). No issues located. Mentioned by Arnold, "Newspapers," p. 20.

THE SEARCHLIGHT Elmira. c. 1920. No issues located. Labor newspaper published by Miles Hemingway (Arnold, "Newspapers," p. 22 and *Star-Gazette,* Jl 3, 1953, p. 26).

SOUTHERN TIER GREENBACKER AND HORSEHEADS JOURNAL see *THE HORSEHEADS JOURNAL*

THE SOUTHERN TIER LEADER (w) Elmira. F 28, 1874–? (1:1–?). *Pub*: The Leader Association (Trustees: James S. Thurston, Pres., P. C. Van Gelder, Treas., Horace A. Brooks, Secy). *Ed*: W. A. Armstrong. *Pol*: ". . . while Republican in its convictions and sympathies, the *Leader* is entirely independent of partisan control." Temperance (by 1875). *Format*: Eight pages 13″ x 20″. *Price*: $2.00 per year delivered in the city, $1.50 per year in advance by mail, $1.00 to clergymen. *Circ*: 1,000–3,000 (1874); 4,000 (1875). *Comment*: Published at 31 Lake St.; 153 Lake St. April 4, 1874–January 1876; 326 Carroll St. February 12, 1876–? Antagonistic to the *Daily Advertiser*. *Loc*: NEm: microfilm F 28, 1874–F 19, 1876 (1:1–2:52). NEmHi: F 28, 1874–F 19, 1876 (1:1–2:52). NEmS: microfilm F 28, 1874–F 19, 1876 (1:1–2:52). *See also* p. 288

STAR-GAZETTE (d) Elmira. F 1, 1963 to date (1:1 to date). *Title changes*: Star-Gazette and Advertiser F 1, 1963–Ja 21, 1967; Star-Gazette Ja 23, 1967 to date. *Pub*: Elmira Star-Gazette, Inc. (Frank E. Tripp, Pres. and Pub., F 1963–Ap 1964; Robert R. Eckert, Gen. Mgr., F 1963–1964; Paul Miller, Pres. and Pub., My 1964–?; Covey C. Hoover, Gen. Mgr. 1965–1967, Pub. Ja 1, 1968–F 27, 1971; Robert L. Collson, Pub., Mr 1971 to date.) *Ed*: Covey C. Hoover, Managing Ed., F 1963–1964; Burton H. Blazar, Managing Ed. 1965–1971 then Ed. 1972 to date; W. Charles Barber, Ed. of the Editorial Page, F 1, 1963–1967; Robert J. Clark, Ed. of Editorial Page, Ja 1, 1968 to date; William F. Mungo, Jr., Managing Ed., 1972 to date; Scott T. Donaldson, City Ed., 1970–? *Pol*: Independent. *Format*: Variable pagination 16″ x 23″. *Price*: 7¢ per copy (1963–1967); 10¢ per copy (1967–1970); 15¢ per copy (1971 to date). *Comment*: Consolidation of the *Elmira Star-Gazette* (1907), *The Elmira Advertiser* (est. 1853), *The Elmira Evening Star* (founded 1888), *The Elmira Gazette* (1828). Published at 201 Baldwin St. *Loc*: NEm: microfilm F 1, 1963 to date (1:1 to date). NEmS: microfilm F 1, 1963 to date (1:1 to date).

STAR-GAZETTE AND ADVERTISER (w) Elmira. Jl 22, 1961– Ja 26, 1963// (53:18 and 111:215–2:31). *Pub*: Frank E. Tripp; Robert R. Eckert, Gen. Mgr., 1961–1963. *Ed*: Covey C. Hoover,

Managing Ed., 1961–1963; Frederick W. Box, News Ed., 1961–?; Robert J. Clark, Ass't News Ed., 1961–?; James M. Milliken, City Ed., 1961–? *Format*: Variable pagination. *Price*: 7¢ per copy. *Comment*: The *Elmira Star-Gazette* (q.v.) and the *Elmira Advertiser* (q.v.) issued a combined Saturday edition beginning with 53:18 of the *Star-Gazette* and 111:215 of the *Advertiser*. Thereafter New Years and holiday editions were combined. On January 1, 1962, the combined edition was numbered vol. 1 no. 29 and the last combined weekly edition was 2:31. *Loc*: NEm: microfilm Jl 22, 1961–Ja 26, 1963 (53:18 and 111:215–2:31). NEmS: microfilm Jl 22, 1961–Ja 26, 1963 (53:18 and 111:215–2:31).

STAR-GAZETTE AND ADVERTISER see also *STAR-GAZETTE*

THE SUMMARY (w) Elmira. 1875–? (1:1–?). *Pub*: New York State Reformatory in Elmira. *Format*: Eight pages 10" x 14". *Loc*: NEmHi: Mr 3, 1895 (20:9 whole no. 570); O 21, 1916 (34:43).

SUNDAY MORNING TELEGRAM see *SUNDAY TELEGRAM*

SUNDAY MORNING TIDINGS see *SATURDAY TIDINGS*

SUNDAY PRESS see *ELMIRA SUNDAY MORNING PRESS*

SUNDAY REPUBLICAN (w) Elmira. c. 1881/1882. No issues located. Established by Luther Caldwell and Samuel C. Taber. Issued for a short time. Mentioned in Towner, *Our County,* p. 401, and *Star-Gazette,* Jl 3, 1953, p. 26.

SUNDAY TELEGRAM (w) Elmira. Ap 31, 1879 to date (1:1 to date). *Title changes*: *Sunday Telegram* 1879–?; *Sunday Morning Telegram* by Je 1882; *Elmira Morning Telegram* c. 1885–F 26, 1888; *Elmira Telegram* Mr 4, 1888–?; *Sunday Telegram* c. 1921–?; *The Sunday Telegram* 1928–F 27, 1967; *Sunday Telegram* Mr 5, 1967 to date. *Pub*: James Hill 1879–?; The Telegram Co. 1890–1893 (Harry S. Brooks, Mgr., 1890–?; Messers Hazard and Hill, other proprietors); Telegram Publishing Co. 1894–? (H. S. Brooks, Pres., 1894–?; A. Frank Richardson, Vice-Pres., by 1898–?); Elmira Star-Gazette, Inc. 1924 to date (Frank E. Gannett, Pres., Ja 16, 1924–Ap 1957; Frank E. Tripp, Vice-Pres. (also Secy, Treas., Mgr.) 1924–1957, Pres. Ap 1957–1964; Paul Miller, Pres., 1965–1968; Covey C. Hoover, Gen. Mgr. 1965–1967, Pub. 1968–1971; Robert L. Collson, Pub., 1971 to date; John Calkins, Gen. Mgr. and Bus. Mgr., by 1931–F 1941; Lynn N. Bitner, Ass't Pub. 1941–1945; Secy and Gen. Mgr. 1946–1951. *Ed*: James Hill 1879–?; Frank E. Trusdell, Managing Ed., ?–Ja 10, 1892; John Moore 1894–1919; Frank E. Gannett, Ed.-in-Chief, Ja 16, 1924–1936; M. D. Richardson, Ed., by 1924–N 20, 1932; E. C. Van Dyke N 27, 1932–Ja 6, 1946; Donald A. Seeley D 3, 1933–My 7, 1939; George S. Crandall, Exec. Ed., My 5, 1935–My 2, 1943; George McCann, Exec. Ed., My 9, 1943–1958; Thomas E. Byrne, Managing Ed. Ja 13, 1946–1954, Sunday Ed. 1961–1968; Thomas J. McCarthy, City Ed., My 1946–1961; Covey C. Hoover, Managing Ed., 1956–1959, 1961–1964; Alan J. Gould, Managing Ed., 1960; Robert J.

Clark, News Ed., 1956–1958; Burton H. Blazar, Managing Ed., 1965 to date; Gordon C. Allen, Sunday Ed., 1969–?; William F. Mungo, Jr., Managing Ed., 1972 to date. *Pol*: Non-partisan. "The *Telegram* is non-partisan and defies man, woman or child to put a finger on a letter that commits it to any party or a line that advocates the claims of any politician." (Ag 15, 1880) *Format*: Issued in sections, varying sizes, 15″ x 22″, 17″ x 22″, 18″ x 24″. *Price*: $2.00 per year, 5¢ per copy (1880–1888); $1.50 per year by mail, $1.00 for six months, 5¢ per copy (1889–1920s); $4.00 per year, 10¢ per copy (1924–1944); $5.00 per year, 10¢ per copy (D 1944–1955); $7.00 per year, 15¢ per copy (1955–1964); 20¢ per copy (1965–1968); 25¢ per copy (1969–1970); 30¢ per copy (1971 to date). *Circ*: 130,000 (1888); 178,013 (1892); 33,200 (1945); 45,439 (1950). *Comment*: Motto: "Pluck, Perseverance, Progress and Patriotism." "The People's Paper Pleases Everyone." Published from the Erie Building, 321 Carroll St. 1880–?; 201 Baldwin St. *Loc*: NCortHi: My 24, 1891 (Memorial Day issue). NEm: microfilm [My 16, 1880 to date (2:2 to date)]. NEmHi: Ja 8, Mr 5, 1882 (3:36, 44); Je 11, 1882–Ap 29, 1883 (4:6–52); Ja 13, 1884 (5:37); [My 10, 1885–Ap 19, 1891 (7:2–12:52)]; Ap 23, 1893 (Fiftieth Anniversary issue); My 5, 1895–Ap 30, 1899 (17:1–20:53); [My 22, 1904–Ap 24, 1921 (26:2–42:52)]; S 29, 1929 (52:22); N 27, 1932 (54:31); Jl 14, 1935 (57:11); Ja 4–F 22, 1943 (63:35–42); Je 13, 1954 (76:3). NEmS: microfilm [My 16, 1880 to date (2:2 to date)]. NIC/MMN: D 7, 1879 (1:31); D 19, 1880 (2:33); S 9, O 14, D 9, 1883 (5:19, 24, 32); F 3, My 24, Je 28, O 25, 1884 (5:40; 6:4, 9, 26); N 29, 1885 (7:31); Je 24, 1888 (10:9); N 2, D 14, 28, 1890 (12:28, 34, 36); N 10, 1912 (34:28); S 27, 1914 (35:22). NWat: Ag 24, 1879 (1:16). *

SUNDAY TIDINGS see *SATURDAY TIDINGS*

THE SUNDAY TIMES (w) Elmira. 1878// No issues located. Published for about a year by D. T. Daly (Towner, *Our County*, p. 401; *Star-Gazette*, Jl 3, 1953, p. 26).

THE TELEGRAPH (1815) see *NEWTOWN TELEGRAPH*

THE TELEGRAPH (1854) see *THE YOUNG AMERICAN*

TIOGA REGISTER (w) Newtown (Elmira). Ja 1824–? (1:1–?). *Pub*: Job A. Smith. *Format*: Four pages 12″ x 19″. *Comment*: Supported Adams and Clay. This was a predecessor of the *Elmira Gazette* (Fairman, "The Press," p. 239). Followed the *Investigator* (q.v.). *Loc*: NEmHi: Mr 4, 1826 (3:114). NIC/MMN: Mr 27, 1824 (1:13).

THE VALLEY BREEZE (w) Van Etten. 1890–? (1:1–?). *Pub and Ed*: D. W. Murray; L. S. Green by 1911. *Format*: Four to six pages, varying sizes, 15″ x 21¾″, 13″ x 19½″. *Price*: 50¢ per year, 2¢ per copy; $1.00 per year in advance, 3¢ per copy (by 1911). *Comment*: Published in the Breeze Building, 38 & 41 Main St. and then by 1911 from the Rochford Building. *Loc*: NIC/MMN: F 17, 24, Je 20, O

*See also p. 288

20, N 3, 1898 (7:21, 22, 40; 8:5, 7); Je 9, S 29, 1911 (21:30, 44); Je 14, 1912 (22:28). NIC/RHA: Ag 31, 1899 (8:49).

THE VEDETTE (w) Newtown (Elmira). Jl 4, 1818–? (1:1–?). *Pub*: William Murphy (printer). *Format*: Four pages 12″ x 19½″. *Comment*: Motto: "Vigilance, Fidelity, and Courage." When Erastus Shepard bought *The [Newtown] Telegraph* (q.v.) from the Harkness Brothers, William Murphy "purchased a press and type from Simon Kinney, Esq. of Towanda . . . and commenced *The Vedette*. Up to this time the *Telegraph* had been conducted upon principles of strict neutrality. But now it came out what was called in that day a Bucktail Paper. And you may be sure that *The Telegraph* and *The Vedette* did not live upon terms of the most perfect amity and good neighborhood. On the other hand, as soon as *The Vedette* had taken its position, armed and equipped, the war began and ceased only when the sinews of war were all exhausted, when they both, at once, ceased to live and fight . . . Under the editorial management of James Robinson, it became the efficient advocate of the Chemung Canal. . . ." (Arnold, "Newspapers," p. 3) *Loc*: NEmHi: photo plates D 5, 1818 (1:23); S 4, 1819 (1:62).

THE WEEKLY ADVERTISER (w, semi-w, w) Elmira. 1854–D 31, 1914//(?) (1:1–61:52). *Title changes*: Elmira Weekly Advertiser 1854(?)–1858(?); Elmira Weekly Advertiser and Chemung County Republican 1858–?; Elmira Weekly Advertiser by 1867; The Elmira Weekly Advertiser F 1869–?; The Elmira Advertiser by 1898–Ap 6, 1899; The Elmira Advertiser Weekly Edition Ap 13–My 25, 1899; The Elmira Weekly Advertiser Je 1, 1899–Ag 13, 1901; The Semi-Weekly Advertiser Ag 20, 1901–1902; The Weekly Advertiser Ja 2, 1903–D 31, 1914. *Pub and Ed*: Listed irregularly. For complete listing see *Elmira Advertiser*. *Pol*: Republican; also Union and Prohibition. *Format*: Eight to twelve pages 14″ x 21″. *Price*: $1.50 per year in advance or $2.00 (1859–?); $2.00 per year in advance, otherwise $2.50 (1867–?); $1.00 per year in advance (1889–Ag 20, 1901); $1.50 per year or $1.00 in advance (1901–1914). *Comment*: Published from 4, 6, 8, 10 Lake St. (1854–1862), Baldwin and Carroll Sts. (1867–?), 100-102 Lake St. (1898–1914). Contains official canvass of Chemung County. On February 15, 1888 the Advertiser Building was destroyed by fire. *Loc*: NEm: microfilm Ja 7, 1860–D 20, 1862 (6:15–9:13); Ja 5, 1867–D 18, 1869 (12:52–15:51); F 6–D 31, 1880 (27:6–52); Ja 4–D 26, 1884 (31:1–52); Mr 9, 1888–D 25, 1896 (35:10–43:52); Ja 6, 1898–D 31, 1914 (45:1–61:52). NEmHi: S 3, 1859 (5:49); F 18, 1860 (6:21); Je 15, Ag 3, 1861 (7:38, 45); O 3, 1863 (9:49); Je 18, 1864 (10:29); Je 28, F 4, Mr 4, 1865 (11:4, 5, 12); O 14, 21, 1871 (17:41, 42). NEmS: microfilm Ja 7, 1860–D 20, 1862 (6:15–9:13); Ja 5, 1867–D 18, 1869 (12:52–15:51); F 6–D 31, 1880 (27:6–52); Ja 4–D 26, 1884 (31:1–52); Mr 9, 1888–D 25, 1896 (35:10–43:52); Ja 6, 1898–D 31, 1914 (45:1–61:52). NIC/MMN: Jl 28, 1866 (12:31); O 12, N 23, 1867 (13:40, 46); O 14, 1892 (29:43). NWel: Ja 1–D 31, 1875 (22:1–52).

THE WEEKLY BULLETIN (w) Horseheads. c. 1871/1872. No issues located. Published by J. Reuben Drake and Edwin B. Foster (Arnold, "Newspapers," p. 16).

WEEKLY FREE PRESS see *ELMIRA WEEKLY FREE PRESS*

WEEKLY TELEGRAPH see *THE YOUNG AMERICAN*

THE YOUNG AMERICAN (w) Elmira. 1854–1855// No issues located. Published by James H. Paine and William S. Heggie (Towner, *Our County,* p. 183). Originally called the *Weekly Telegraph* (Arnold, "Newspapers," p. 14) and may be cited as *The Telegraph* (*Star-Gazette,* Jl 3, 1953, p. 26).

THE AFTON ENTERPRISE

and HARPURSVILLE BUDGET

AFTON, CHENANGO COUNTY, N. Y. THURSDAY, JULY 20, 1939

CHENANGO COUNTY

AFTON EAGLE (w) Afton. F–N 1875//. No issues located. Started by G. E. Bradt who published it until November 1875 and then sold to Jacob B. Kirkhuff who issued one number and then abandoned it. (James H. Smith, *History of Chenango and Madison Counties, New York: With Illustrations and Biographical Sketches of Some of Its Prominent Men and Pioneers,* [Syracuse: D. Mason & Co., 1880], p. 110.)

THE AFTON ENTERPRISE (w) Afton. 1878–F 13, 1969// (1:1–90:51). *Title changes*: *Afton Weekly Enterprise* by 1882–?; *The Afton Enterprise* by 1902–?; *The Afton Enterprise and Harpursville Budget* 192?–?; *The Afton Enterprise* ?–1969. *Pub and Ed*: N. E. Barton 1878–?; Frank M. Spooner by 1898–1902(?); A. L. Sherman by 1904–?; J. H. Crain by 1909–?; R. G. Hill by 1911–?; Charles D. Pendell by 1917–Jl 21, 1921; Emerson Demeree Jl 28, 1921–1931; Howard Adamy 1931–1958; Theodore M. Tracy N 6, 1958–F 13, 1969. *Pol*: Independent; Republican. *Format*: Four to ten pages, varying sizes, 18″ x 24″, 15″ x 22″, 17¼″ x 28″. *Price*: $1.00 per year (by 1889–?); $1.50 per year (by 1909–?); $3.00 per year. *Circ*: 1,200 (1912); 900 (1969). *Comment*: Motto: "Push, Energy, Pluck." Published over C. Hill & Son's Store by 1882; sometime after 1886, the Enterprise Block. During the 1920's the *Harpursville Budget* (Broome County) merged with the *Enterprise*. In 1969 the *Enterprise* merged into *The Tri-Town News* in Sidney (Delaware County). *Loc*: NIC/MMN: Jl 6, 1882 (2:38); F 19, 26, 1886 (6:18, 19). NIC/RHA: [Je 21, 1917–Ag 24, 1922 (40:42–44:52). NNoHi: Ja 17, 24, 1889 (9:12, 13); F 19, 1891; N 30, 1898 (19:8); Ja 9, 1902 (22:14); Ja 21, Ap 7, 1904 (24:16, 27); N 16, 1911 (32:8). NTu/Jacob: [D 9, 1909–F 13, 1969 (30:11–90:51)].

THE AFTON ENTERPRISE AND HARPURSVILLE BUDGET see *THE AFTON ENTERPRISE*

AFTON SENTINEL Afton. ca. 1878. No issues located. Mentioned in the *Windsor Standard,* May 11, 1878.

THE AFTON WEEKLY ENTERPRISE see *THE AFTON ENTERPRISE*

THE AGRICULTURIST see *THE REPUBLICAN AGRICUL-TURIST*

THE AMERICAN FREEMAN see *THE BAINBRIDGE FREEMAN*

THE ANTI-MASONIC TELEGRAPH see *THE CHENANGO TELEGRAPH*

BAINBRIDGE EAGLE Bainbridge. 1843–1846//(?). No issues located. ". . . started in 1843, by J. Hunt, Jr. In 1846, its name was changed to *The Bainbridge Freeman* (q.v.); and in 1849, it was merged in *The Chenango Free Democrat* (q.v.). . . ." (Smith, *Chenango,* p. 108.) We were unable to verify the connection between the *Eagle* and *The Bainbridge Freeman.*

BAINBRIDGE EXPRESS Bainbridge. ca. 1901. No issues located. Mentioned in the *Oxford Press,* December 27, 1901.

THE BAINBRIDGE FREEMAN (w) Bainbridge. My 21, 1846–1849//(?) (1:1–?). *Title changes*: *The American Freeman* by Ag 1846–?; *The Bainbridge Freeman* by N 1847–1849(?). *Pub and Ed*: E. S. Jennings Ag 1846–?; G. N. Carhart by N 1847–? *Format*: Four pages 18″ x 24″. *Price*: $1.50 per year (1846–?); $2.00 per year (by N 1847–1849); $1.50 per year (Jl 1849). *Comment*: Possibly succeeded the *Bainbridge Eagle* (q.v.). Merged in the *Chenango Free Democrat* (q.v.) "which was commenced at Norwich, January 1, 1849, by Alfred G. Lawyer." (Smith, *Chenango,* p. 108.) *Loc*: NIC/ MMN: N 18, 1847 (2:27); Mr 23, 1848 (2:45); Mr 2, 9, Ap 20, My 11, 1849 (3:41, 42, 48, 51). NNo: My 25, 1849 (4:1 whole no. 157). NNoHi: Ag 6, S 17, 1846 (1:12, 18); Ja 7, S 23, 1847 (1:34; 2:19); Jl 13, 1849 (4:8 whole no. 164).

THE BAINBRIDGE LEDGER (w?) Bainbridge. Ag 23, 1867–? (1:1–?). *Pub and Ed*: G. A. Dodge. *Pol*: Independent. *Format*: Four pages 17¾″ x 24″. *Price*: $1.50 per year. *Comment*: "*The Chenango Ledger* was started at Bainbridge August 23, 1867 by G. A. Dodge, and its name was changed the following week to *The Bainbridge Ledger,* at the request of many of the citizens of Bainbridge, who were desirous of seeing the name of the village at its head. The name was afterwards . . . changed to *The Saturday Review* (q.v.)." (Smith, *Chenango,* p. 109.) *Loc*: NIC/MMN: N 27, 1868 (2:15). NNoHi: S 27, 1867 (1:6).

THE BAINBRIDGE NEWS (w) Bainbridge, Deposit [Delaware County]. ?–1959// (?–?). *Title changes*: *The Bainbridge News and the Bainbridge Republican* 1934–?; *The Bainbridge News* by 1950– 1959. *Pub*: The Bainbridge News Co. by 1934–?; The Deposit Courier Co. (Edward J. Russell, Pres.). *Ed*: John B. Stow 1935–1959; Charles H. Peckham, Asst. Ed., Ap 30, 1935–? Claire Clark Knight ?–Ag 8, 1957; Charles D. Cook Ag 1957–S 1958; Roger H. Bard S 18, 1958–?; Louella Nelson, Managing Ed., F 1959; Edward J. Russell, Editorial Director, 1957–? *Format*: Eight pages 16″ x 22″. *Circ*: 1,300 (1934). *Comment*: Published at 20 North Main St., Bainbridge ?–1943(?);

The Deposit Courier Co., 138 Front St., Deposit by 1945–?. In 1959 the *News* merged with the *Sidney Record* and was issued as *The Sidney Record and Bainbridge News* in Sidney, Delaware County, and it is now a part of *The Tri-Town News* in Sidney. *Loc*: NSiT: [Ja 3, 1935–D 31, 1936 (68:1–69:53)]; [Ja 6–D 29, 1938 (71:1–52)]; Ja 4, 1940–D 30, 1943 (73:1–79:1); [Ja 4, 1945–D 30, 1948 (78:2–82:2)]; Ja 5–D 28, 1950 (88:3–89:2 [*sic* 83:3–84:2]); [Ja 3, 1952–F 12, 1959 (85:3–112:10)].

THE BAINBRIDGE NEWS AND THE BAINBRIDGE REPUB-LICAN see *THE BAINBRIDGE NEWS*

THE BAINBRIDGE PRESS (w) Bainbridge. 1938–? (1:1–?). *Pub and Ed*: M. B. MacLeod. *Pol*: Republican. *Format*: Eight pages 16½ " x 21¾ ". *Price*: $1.00 per year. *Circ*: 897 (1939). *Comment*: Published in the Clark Block. *Loc*: NIC/RHA: Ap 20, 1939 (1:21).

THE BAINBRIDGE REPUBLICAN (w) Bainbridge. 1871–1933// (1:1–?). *Title changes*: *The Bainbridge Republican* 1871–?; *The Bainbridge Republican and Express* by 1905–My 6, 1920; *Bainbridge Republican* My 13, 1920–?; *The Bainbridge Republican* by 1932–? *Pub and Ed*: Harvey Ireland by 1877–1887; G. L. Babcock and Son by Ag 1887–?; E. A. Clark by 1913–Je 27, 1918; A. Clark Jl 4, 1918–?; George C. and Charles H. Clark Ag 25, 1932–? *Pol*: Republican; Independent (under Babcocks 1887–?); Republican. *Format*: Four to eight pages, varying sizes, 17" x 24", 15" x 21". *Price*: $1.50 per year (1877); $1.00 per year (1882–?); $1.50 per year (1913–1932). *Comment*: Published at West Main St. three doors above the railroad station. Sometime in 1933 *The Bainbridge Republican* was issued as *The Bainbridge News and Republican,* later titled *The Bainbridge News* (q.v.). Original title may have been the *Monday Review* (q.v.). *Loc*: NIC/MMN: S 23, 1881 (11:11); S 8, 1882 (12:9). NIC/RHA: [Ap 5, 1917–F 3, 1921 (40:14–49:5)]. NNoHi: My 31, Je 14, 1877 (6:46, 48); D 1, 1882 (12:21); Ap 20, 1883 (12:41); D 26, 1884 (14:25); F 4, Ag 19, 1887 (16:31; 17:7). NSiT: Ja 19–D 28, 1905 (35:3–52); S 11, 1913–D 31, 1914 (43:1–44:1); Ja 6–D 28, 1916 (45:1–52); Ja 2, 1919–D 30, 1920 (47:1–48:52); Ja 7–D 31, 1932 (55:2–56:1).

THE BAINBRIDGE REPUBLICAN AND EXPRESS see *THE BAINBRIDGE REPUBLICAN*

THE CHENANGO AMERICAN AND WHITNEY POINT RE-PORTER (w) Greene. S 20, 1855 to date. *Title changes*: *The Chenango American* S 20, 1855–S 1960; *The Chenango American and Whitney Point Reporter* O 6, 1960 to date. *Pub and Ed*: Jared D. Denison and Frank B. Fisher S 20, 1855– Ag 2, 1866; Jared D. Denison Ag 1866–Ap 1868; Jared D. Denison and George C. Roberts My 7, 1868–My 1909; Jared D. Denison and Son My 27, 1909–My 1915; J. Fred Denison and Fred L. Ames My 1915–N 21, 1918; J. Fred Denison N 28, 1918–F 28, 1929; Norman O. Westcott Mr 7, 1929–My 31, 1945; Oscar H. Swenson Je 7, 1945–Jl 3, 1958; William

Marsland Jl 10, 1958–1961; Twin Valley Publishers, Inc. Ja 1962 to date (William D. Marsland, Pres.). *Pol*: American (1855); People's Union (1860); Union (1863); Republican (1866–1954); Independent. Format: Four to sixteen pages, varying sizes, 15″ x 21¾″, 18″ x 24″, 17½″ x 22″. *Price*: $1.25 per year (1855–?); $1.50 per year (1868); $1.00 per year (1900–?); $1.50 per year (?–1930); $2.00 per year (1930–1945); $3.00 per year (1946–1963); $3.50 per year (1963–1968); $4.00 per year, 10¢ per copy (1968 to date). *Circ*: 50 (1855); 1,382 (1856). *Comment*: Motto: "The Constitution of the United States—It is all that gives us a national character." Currently published from 12 South Chenango St. On May 6, 1915 *The Chenango American* announced that it had taken over the business of the *Broome County Herald*. The *American* merged with the *Whitney Point Reporter* (Broome County) in 1960. *Loc*: NGr: microfilm S 20, 1855 to date (1:1 to date). NIC/RHA: [Mr 5, 1917–Je 19, 1924 (63:40–70:52)]; [Je 19, 1947–D 29, 1955 (93:4–100:33)]. NNo: My 20, 27, 1970 (115:4, 5); [Ag 5, 1970 to date (115:15 to date)]. NNoHi: N 16, 1914 (60:21); Mr 11, 1915 (60:36); Jl 11, 1935 (81:5); Ag 29, 1940 (86:13).

CHENANGO CHRONICLE (w) Norwich. Ag 1864–N 1865// (1:1–2:13). *Pub and Ed*: George C. Rice and Elizur H. Prindle. *Pol*: Republican. *Format*: Four pages 18½″ x 26″. *Price*: $1.50 per year. *Comment*: Published over Goodrich's store. Merged with *The Chenango Telegraph* (q.v.) to become *The Chenango Telegraph and Chronicle* on November 15, 1865 (volume 37 number 36 of the *Telegraph*, volume 2 number 14 of the *Chronicle*) when Prindle bought out Rice's interest and arranged with B. Gage Berry and Lewis Kingsley of the *Telegraph* to merge the two papers. *Loc*: NNoHi: Je 16, 1865 (1:44).

CHENANGO COUNTY DEMOCRAT (w) Oxford. N 19, 1863–? (1:1–?). *Pub and Ed*: LaFayette Briggs. *Pol*: Democrat. *Format*: Four pages 18″ x 23⅝″. *Comment*: Published in Navy Island over H. S. Read's Drug Store. *Loc*: NIC/MMN: Ja 14, F 25, Mr 10, 1864 (1:9, 15, 17).

THE CHENANGO COUNTY FARM BUREAU NEWS (m) Norwich. 1915(?)–? (1:1–?). *Pub*: Chenango County Farm Bureau Association. *Ed*: Edwin P. Smith. *Format*: Ten pages 9″ x 12½″. *Price*: $1.00 per year. *Comment*: Published in the Hill Block corner Broad and West Main Sts. *Loc*: NNoHi: Ja 1919 (5:1).

THE CHENANGO DEMOCRAT Greene. ca. 1830. No issues located. Succeeded *The Chenango Patriot* (q.v.) published about 1830. Published by Joseph M. Farr. It was short lived. (Smith, *Chenango*, p. 108).

CHENANGO DEMOCRAT (w) Oxford. ca. Je 1868. No issues located. Published by E. S. Watson for a short time in the interest of the Democratic Party (Smith, *Chenango*, p. 109).

CHENANGO FREE DEMOCRAT (w) Norwich, Bainbridge. 1849–?
(1:1–?). *Pub*: J. D. Lawyer 1849–?; J. D. and Alfred G. Lawyer by
1850. *Ed*: J. D. Lawyer 1849–? *Pol*: Anti-Slavery, Democrat. *Format*: Four pages 18″ x 23″. *Price*: $1.50 per year. *Comment*: Motto:
"Free Soil, Free Labor, Free Speech, Free Men." "No More Slave
States—No Slave Territory." Published from the Stone Block, corner
of South Main St., upstairs, Norwich; by 1850 in Charles Row, West
St., a few doors above McCollom's Store, in Bainbridge. The newspaper was subsequently moved to Cobleskill, Schoharie County (Smith,
Chenango, p. 108). *Loc*: NIC/MMN: Ag 24, D 6, 1850 (2:34, 49);
Ap 25–My 16, 1851 (3:17–20). NNoHi: D 15, 1849 (1:50).

THE CHENANGO LEDGER see *THE BAINBRIDGE LEDGER*

THE CHENANGO NEWS Greene. 1850–? No issues located.
". . . Commenced at Greene in 1850 by A. T. Boynton. J. M. Haight
soon after became interested in its publication and subsequently its
sole proprietor. He moved the press to Norwich and . . . commenced
the publication of *The Temperance Advocate* (q.v.) in 1855. . . ."
(Smith, *Chenango*, pp. 108–109.)

THE CHENANGO PATRIOT Greene. 1830–? No issues located.
"*The Chenango Patriot* was commenced at Greene, in 1830, by Na-
than Randall. It subsequently passed into the hands of Joseph M.
Farr, who changed its name to *The Chenango Democrat* (q.v.). . . ."
(Smith, *Chenango*, p. 108.)

CHENANGO PATRIOT (w) Oxford. Ap 1809–1813// (1:1–?).
Pub and Ed: John B. Johnson. *Format*: Four pages 13¼″ x 21¼″.
Price: $1.50 per year at the office, otherwise, $2.00. "Wheat, corn,
oats, wool and flax will be received in payment for papers from those
who prefer paying in advance." *Comment*: The final date of publication of this newspaper is based on an item in the *Oxford Gazette*
(q.v.), December 7, 1813, which announced that the editor of the
Chenango Patriot had "relinquished his management" and that the
future conduct of the paper was to go to Chauncey Morgan who
would issue the paper under the title of *Oxford Gazette*. *Loc*: NIC/
RHA: S 11, 1811 (3:128). NOx: S 11, 1810.

THE CHENANGO PRESS (w) Guilford. F 13, 1879–? (1:1–?).
Title changes: *The Guilford Wave* F 13–Jl 1879; *The News and Wave*
Ag 6–N 1879; *The Chenango Press* by N 19, 1879–? *Pub*: Brown
Brothers (C. C. and C. O. Brown) F 1879–? *Ed*: Charles O. Brown
F–Ag 1879; C. C. and C. O. Brown 1879–? *Format*: Four
pages 15½″ x 22″. *Price*: $1.00 per year in advance. *Circ*: 1,000 to
1,300. *Comment*: Motto: "Devoted to Home Enterprise" (F–Jl
1879); "A Wide Awake News Sheet" (Ag–N 1879); "A Wide Awake
Sheet Devoted to Home Interests" (N 1879–?). *Loc*: NNo: [F 20–
N 26, 1879 (1:2–44)].

*CHENANGO REPUBLICAN. OR, OXFORD GAZETTE AND
PEOPLE'S ADVOCATE* (w) Oxford. Je 1826–1831//(?) (1:1–?).

Pub: William Hyer Je–S 1826; Benjamin Corey S 1826–D 1828; Daniel Mack and William E. Chapman Ja 7, 1829–S 1830; Daniel Mack S 29, 1830–? *Pol*: Neutral: "Unpledged and Unshackled" (1828); Independent, but with Anti-Masonic and Jacksonian leanings (1830). *Format*: Four pages 12¾ " x 19½ ". *Price*: $2.00 per year delivered, $1.50 per year at the office. *Comment*: It is possible that the *Chenango Republican* was succeeded by *The Oxford Republican* (q.v.). According to Smith, William E. Chapman and T. T. Flagler began a new series March 31, 1831 and "soon after changed its name to *The Oxford Republican.*" (Smith, *Chenango*, p. 108.) Since we found no issues of either paper between November 1830 and October 1834, we could not verify the connection. *Loc*: NIC/ RHA: S 8, 1826 (1:11). NOx: Ag 20, D 10–31, 1828 (3:9, n.s. 3:1–4); Ja 7, 1829–N 10, 1830 (3:5 whole no. 133–2 [*sic*]: 49 whole no. 229).

THE CHENANGO TELEGRAPH (w, semi-w, w) Norwich. Ap 8, 1829–Mr 16, 1951// (1:1–122:11). *Title changes*: *Anti-Masonic Telegraph* Ap 8, 1829–Mr 25, 1835; *Chenango Telegraph* Ap 1, 1835– Ap 7, 1847; *The Chenango Telegraph* Ap 14, 1847–?; *Chenango Telegraph* late 1862; *The Chenango Telegraph* by Mr 18, 1863–N 8, 1865; *The Chenango Telegraph and Chronicle* N 15–29, 1865; *The Telegraph and Chronicle* D 6, 1865–Mr 3, 1869; *The Chenango Telegraph* Mr 10, 1869–D 28, 1876; *The Chenango Semi-Weekly Telegraph* Ja 1, 1877–F 6, 1889; *Chenango Semi-Weekly Telegraph* F 9, 1889–?; *The Chenango Telegraph* by 1904–Mr 16, 1951. *Pub*: Elias P. Pellet and B. T. Cooke Ap 8, 1829–Mr 25, 1835; Elias P. Pellet Ap 1, 1835–Ja 15, 1840; Nelson Pellet Ja 1840–?; George C. Rice and Cyrus B. Martin by 1856–Mr 1861; George C. Rice Mr 6–D 4, 1861; George C. Rice and B. Gage Berry D 11, 1861–My 18, 1864; B. Gage Berry My 25–Ag 17, 1864; B. Gage Berry and Lewis Kingsley Ag 24, 1864–N 1865; B. Gage Berry, Lewis Kingsley and Elizur H. Prindle N 15, 1865–O 8, 1866; Kingsley & Co. (B. Gage Berry and Lewis Kingsley) O 8, 1866–Ja 12, 1870; Samuel P. Allen and B. Gage Berry Ja 1870–Ap 1874; B. Gage Berry Ap 1874–1875; B. Gage Berry & Co. (B. Gage Berry and E. W. Capron) Mr 11, 1875–1890; Charles A. Berry Ja 3–N 1891; Charles B. Crombie D 9, 1891–Mr 4, 1896; C. E. Merritt 1896–1903; Norwich Publishing Co. S 2, 1903–Mr 16, 1951 (Pres: William H. Clark 1903–Mr 13, 1928 [died Mr 12]; Edward H. Clark My 29, 1928–Mr 16, 1951). *Pol*: Anti-Mason; Whig; Independent with Republican leanings (1860); Union Republican; Republican. *Format*: Four to eight pages, varying sizes, 12½ " x 19", 15½ " x 20½ ", 16½ " x 22", 21½ " x 27", 18" x 23", 23" x 29". *Price*: $2.00 per year (1829–1840); $1.50 per year in advance (1841–?); $1.75 per year in advance (by 1859–1865); $2.00 per year (1866–?); $1.50 per year (by 1896–?); $1.50 per year in advance, otherwise $2.00 (1904–1918); $2.00 per year in advance, 3¢ per copy (1919–1951). *Circ*: 3,000 (1865). *Comment*: Motto: "Truth Without Fear." "An Independent Journal Devoted to the Diffusion of General Intelligence and the Discussion of Questions of Public Interest." The

Anti-Masonic Telegraph was published "one door north of the Bank of Chenango" (1829), then one door east of General H. DeForest's Eagle Tavern, north side of the public square; by 1834 moved to the new brick buildings four doors north of the Bank, upstairs—entrance from the main street. By 1840 office in the brick building above the bank; then by 1849 in the Milner Block on North Main St.; then from 1867–1868 in the Brick Block opposite the Eagle Hotel; the Stone Block directly opposite the Eagle Hotel until March 2, 1870, then in the new Brick Telegraph Block, Lock St., one block east of Eagle Hotel. Published weekly through December 1876, then published semi-weekly on Wednesday and Saturday until September 22, 1942, when it was again issued weekly. Official Republican newspaper. *Loc*: NCooHi: O 31, 1866 (38:34 and 8:12); S 18, 1867 (39:28); Jl 4, 1895 (Woman's Edition). NCortHi: Je 12, 1873 (45:15). NIC/ MMN: Ap 3, 1833 (5:1 fragment); microfilm [Ap 1, 1835–Mr 23, 1842 (7:1–13:52)]; [Mr 27, 1844–Mr 29, 1848 (16:1–19:52)]; D 31, 1851 (23:40); Mr 23, 1859–Mr 12, 1862 (31:1–33:52); Mr 18, 1863–D 27, 1871 (35:1–43:43); Ja 30, Jl 6, 1876 (47:46; 48:18); F 28, 1877 (49:17); My 3, 1884 (56:36). NNo: microfilm and bound vols. [Ap 8, 1829–Mr 23, 1842 (1:1–13:52)]; [Mr 27, 1844– Mr 29, 1848 (16:1–19:52)]; Ag 11, 25, 1858 (30:21, 23 fragments); Mr 23, 1859–Mr 12, 1862 (31:1–33:52); Mr 18, 1863–D 28, 1894 (35:1–66:104); [Jl 4, 1895–Mr 23, 1904 (67:3394–76:34)]; unbound Jl 2, 1904–Mr 16, 1951 (76:52–122:11). NNoHi: My 28, 1845 (17:8); My 28, 1851 (23:9); F 18, 1852 (23:45); Ja 19, 1853 (24:43); Jl 24, 1856 (28:18); Ja 27, 1858 (29:45); Ap 12, 1865 (37:5); S 19, 1866 (38:28); Mr 31, 1869 (41:4); Ja 31–My 22, 1872 (43:48–44:2); Ja 8, S 17, 1874 (45:45; 46:29); Ja 28, 1876 (fragment); O 8, 11, 1879 (51:81, 82); S 24, 1881 (53:77); N 7, 1885 (57:88); Mr 6, 1886 (58:19); N 5, 1907; Ja 12, 1909 (30:4).

THE CHENANGO TRIBUNE (w) Smyrna. Mr 1, 1881–? (1:1–?). *Title changes*: *Chenango Tribune* Mr 1881–Mr 1882; *The Chenango Tribune* Mr 11, 1882–? *Pub and Ed*: Frank J. Stanton. *Pol*: Republican. *Format*: Four to eight pages, varying sizes, 10½″ x 14¾″, 14½″ x 21″. *Price*: $1.00 per year, 5¢ per copy. *Comment*: Motto: "Right, Equity, Justice!" Published at the Old Stone Building, March to May, 1881; then over Brigg's store, May 21, 1881–? *Loc*: NNo: microfilm Mr 1, 1881–Mr 3, 1883 (1:1–4:104).

THE CHENANGO UNION (w) Oxford and Norwich. O 27, 1847 to date (1:1 to date). *Title changes*: *Chenango Union* 1847–1866; *The Chenango Union* O 1886 to date. *Pub and Ed*: LaFayette Leal and James H. Sinclair O 27, 1847–1853; Hubbard and Sinclair 1854– 1859; Harvey Hubbard 1859–1862; John F. Hubbard, Jr. 1863–Je 24, 1868; Gilbert H. Manning Jl 1, 1868–Ja 1, 1891; Gilbert H. Manning and Edward S. Moore Ja 8, 1891–D 1895; Edward S. Moore D 1895–1915; Edward S. Moore and George T. Tanner (ed.) 1915– 1918(?); Edward S. Moore 1918–Mr 29, 1945; Lewis W. Phelps Ap 5, 1945 to date. *Pol*: Democrat. *Format*: Four to eight pages, varying sizes, 21″ x 27″, 18″ x 23¾″, 23″ x 28″, 14″ x 21″. *Price*: $1.25 per year (1847–?); $1.50 per year (by 1858–1865); $2.00 per year (1865–ca. 1891); $1.50 per year (ca. 1891–1952); $2.00 per year (1952–1967); $3.00 per year (1967–1969); $4.00 per year (D 1969 to date). *Comment*: During 1847 and 1848 the *Union* maintained an office in W. B. Chapman's Bookstore in Oxford. In Norwich the office was in the Stone Block, South Main St., from 1847 through 1855; by 1863 in the Union Block, South Main St.; in the Union Block, 23 South Main St., 1873; Union Block, 170 Broad St., 1875; Sumner Block, 171 Broad St., 1876; the Union Building, 141 South Broad St., 1896; 171 South Broad St., 1908 to 1916; Colonia Place, 1916 to ca. 1961; and it is now located at 15 American Ave. The *Chenango Union* was formed when LaFayette Leal and James H. Sinclair of the *Oxford Republican* (q.v.) purchased the *Norwich Journal* (q.v.) from John F. Hubbard and consolidated the papers in 1847. (*Oxford Republican,* O 13, 1847.) A 44-page "industrial edition," March 24, 1910, contains many photographs and items of historical interest. *Loc*: NCooHi: Je 21, N 21, 1848 (1:35; 2:2); Ja 17, 31, Mr 14, Ap 4, My 10, Je 20, Jl 12, N 14, 1849 (2:13, 15, 21, 24, 30, 35, 47; 3:4); Je 19, 1850 (3:35); F 5, Ap 30, Je 4, Jl 23, N 12, 1851 (4:16, 28, 33, 40; 5:4); Ja 14, Mr 3, 31, Je 16, 23, Jl 14, Ag 25, N 17, D 8, 15, 1852 (5:13, 20, 24, 35, 36, 39, 45; 6:5, 8, 9); Ja 12, 26, Mr 16, 23, Je 8, 22, Ag 17, 1853 (6:13, 15, 22, 23, 34, 36, 44); [F 8–N 25, 1854 (7:17–8:6)]; Jl 18, Ag 29, 1855 (8:40, 46); D 30, 1857 (11:12); Je 27, Ap 14, Jl 14, S 29, 1858 (11:16, 27, 40, 51); Ja 19, My 25, 1859 (12:15, 33); [Ja 16, 1863–Ag 17, 1864 (16:16–17:46)]; Mr 29, 1865 (18:26); Mr 23, Jl 28, 1869 (22:23, 44). NCortHi: Ag 12, 1875 (28:47). NIC/RHA: My 31, Ag 30, 1848 (1:32, 45); Ja 10, F 21, Je 27, 1849 (2:12, 18, 30 fragments); Ja 9, Ap 3, 1850 (3:12, 24 fragments); Mr 12, S 17, O 15, 1851 (4:21, 48, 52); My 26, 1852 (5:32 fragment); Mr 22, 1854 (7:23); Jl 4, 1855 (8:38); Mr 26, Je 25, Ag 13, 1856 (9:24, 37, 44 fragments); Mr 4, S 30, 1857 (10:21, 51 fragment); Mr 17, 1858 (11:23 fragment); Ja 5, Ag 3, N 23, 1859 (12:13, 43; 3:7 fragments); Ap 25, 1860; Ja 29, 1862 (15:17); D 30, 1863 (17:13); Je 15, 22, 1864 (17:37, 38); My 2, Je 27, S 26, O 31, N 7, D 5, 26, 1866 (19:31, 39, 52; 20:5, 6, 10, 13); Ja 2–23, N 13, 1867 (20:14–17; 21:7); F 26, Mr 18, Ap 8, My 20, 1868 (21:22, 25, 28, 34); F 24, S 8, 15, D 8, 22, 1869 (22:22, 50, 51; 23:11, 13); Ja 19–F 9, Mr 9, 16, 30, Ap 20, S 7, 1870 (23:17–20, 24, 25, 27, 30, 50); My 31, D 13–27, 1871 (24:36; 25:12–14); Ja 10, F 14, 28, Mr 6, 20, N 28–D 19, 1872 (25:16, 21, 23, 24, 26; 26:10–13); Ja 16, 1873 (26:17); N 18, 1875 (29:9 fragment); Jl 27, S 14, 1876 (29:45, 52); Mr 14, 1878 (31:26); S 7–D 28, 1893 (47:2–18); Ja 19, 1899 (52:22); D 19, 26, 1901 (55:18, 19); [F 13–Ag 21, 1902 (55:26–56:1)]; Jl 9–23, O 22, N 5, 1903 (56:47–49; 57:10, 12); N 3, 10, D 1, 8, 1904 (58:13, 14, 17, 18); [Ja 5–Je 15, 1905 (58:22–44)]; [Ja 25, 1906–Jl 4, 1912 (59:24–65:45)]; [Ap 19, 1917–Ag 9, 1923 (70:35–76:52)]; Je 19, 1947–D 29, 1955 (100:48–109:23). NNb: Jl 4, 1849 (2:37); Jl 8, 1875 (28:42); S 2, 1909 (63:4). NNo: microfilm [Ja 1, 1862–Ag 9, 1906

(15:13–59:52)]; Ja 2, 1969 to date (122:26 to date). NNoHi: N 4, 1847 (1:4); My 24, Ag 30, 1848 (1:31, 45); S 19, D 12, 1849 (2:48; 3:8); [O 1, 1851–D 21, 1853 (4:50–7:10)]; N 11, 1854 (8:4); My 14, 1856 (9:31); Ag 18, 1858 (11:45); Ag 3, O 5, 1859 (12:43, 52); Ja 4, 1860–D 18, 1861 (13:13–15:11). NNoUn: Ja 2, 1879–D 30, 1880 (32:18–34:16); S 8, 1887–Ag 28, 1889 (41:1–42:52); S 13, 1894–Ap 4, 1895 (48:3–32); [Ag 18, 1904 to date (58:1 to date)].

CHENANGO WEEKLY ADVERTISER (w) Norwich. Ja 25, 1811–1812//(?) (1:1–2:75). *Pub*: John F. Fairchild. *Format*: Four pages 11″ x 18″. *Comment*: The probable date for last year of publication of the *Advertiser* is based on a statement in the June 25, 1812 issue in which "the publisher refers to the lack of advertising patronage and a possible discontinuance of his paper." (Clarence S. Brigham, *History and Bibliography of American Newspapers, 1690-1820* [Worcester, Mass.: American Antiquarian Society, 1947] p. 711.) *Loc*: NNo: Ja 9, 1812 (1:51).

CHENANGO WHIG AND MISCELLANEOUS JOURNAL (w) Oxford. 1834–? (1:1–?). *Pub and Ed*: Denison Smith Clark 1834–? *Pol*: Whig. *Format*: Four pages 16″ x 22½″. *Price*: $1.50 per year. *Comment*: The *Anti-Masonic Telegraph* mentioned the *Chenango Whig* in its July 9, 1834 issue and listed D. S. Clark as publisher. Clark also published *The Miniature* (q.v.). *Loc*: NOx: Mr 6, 1835 (1:34).

COLUMBIAN TELEGRAPH (1812) see *THE TELEGRAPH*

THE DAILY REPORTER (d) Norwich. ca. 1857–1858. No issues located. Published by G. H. Smith in 1857; purchased by Rice and Martin in 1858 and soon after discontinued (Smith, *Chenango*, p. 109).

THE EVENING SUN (d) Norwich. Mr 16, 1891 to date (1:1 to date). *Title changes*: *The Morning Sun* Mr 16, 1891–Mr 6, 1904; *The Norwich Sun* Mr 7, 1904–Jl 1961; *The Evening Sun* Ag 1, 1961 to date. *Pub*: Reed Campbell 1891–1899 (died); George H. Smith My 6, 1891–?; The Sun Publishing Co. D 9, 1895–Ag 29, 1903; The Norwich Publishing Co. Ag 31, 1903–1966 (Pres: William H. Clark Ag 31, 1903–Mr 15, 1928 [died Mr 12]; Edward H. Clark 1928–1961; Robert C. Roberts 1961–1966; Peter Imolenski 1966); The Norwich Sun, Inc. 1967 to date (Thomas J. McMahon, Pub. and General Mgr.). *Ed*: Reed Campbell 1891–1899; M. M. Campbell 1899–?; William H. Clark 1903(?)–?; P. L. Clark 1910–1950; Perry Browne 1950–1951; Robert J. Jones 1951–1961; John D. DeBiase Je 1, 1961–Ja 10, 1964; Ronald L. Tarwater 1964; Robert E. Whitmore 1965; Marjorie B. Chase, Managing Ed., 1966–1968; Joseph M. Quinn Ap 1968 to date. *Pol*: Independent. *Format*: Four to ten pages 17½″ x 23″. *Price*: $4.00 per year, 10¢ per week, 2¢ per copy (1891–?); 12¢ per week (by 1918–?); $9.00 per year delivered, $5.00 per year by mail (1933–?); $12.00 per year, 24¢ per week delivered, $6.00 per year by mail (by 1946–1947); $15.00 per year, 30¢ per week, 5¢ per copy delivered, $6.00 per year by mail (1947–1953);

$15.00 per year delivered, $9.00 per year by mail (1953–1959); $21.00 per year, 42¢ per week, 7¢ per copy delivered, $9.00 per year by mail (1959–1963); $20 per year, 40¢ per week, 8¢ per copy delivered, $13.00 per year by mail (1963–1968); 45¢ per week, 10¢ per copy delivered, $15.00 per year by mail (1968 to date). *Circ*: 700 (1891); 4,000 (1904); 4,200 (1967). *Comment*: Creed: "This paper will be the Friend of Government, of Morals and of Truth—Independent of Politics and Religion" (1913). Published at 27 Mechanic St. 1891–1904; The Telegraph Building, 11 Lackawanna Ave. F 1904–?; 7 Lackawanna Ave. by 1946–1971; 45-47 Hale St. 1971 to date. Reed Campbell founded the *Sun,* took George H. Smith as a partner, and formed the Sun stock company with Willie B. Leach; Smith was an editor of the *Sun* until 1910 (*The Norwich Sun,* Je 1, 1961). On March 7, 1904 when the name of the newspaper changed to *The Norwich Sun* the paper changed from a morning to an afternoon paper; it became an evening paper in 1928. The Norwich Publishing Co. also purchased *The Chenango Telegraph* from the estate of Mrs. C. E. Merritt in 1903, and William Clark was editor and manager of both newspapers. *The Chenango Telegraph* was the semi-weekly edition of *The Norwich Sun.* The *Sun* is the official city paper. On September 19, 1891 the newspaper began publishing a special edition known as *The Saturday Sun* for "farmers and others who reside at such a distance from the railroads and post office that they cannot receive a daily paper regularly." *The Saturday Sun,* which sold for $1.00 per year, was subsequently discontinued. *Loc*: NNo: Mr 16, My 6–15, 1891 (1:1, 45–53); microfilm My 16, 1891 to date (1:54 to date). NNoHi: Ja 1, 1895 (4:252); Ja 9, 1896 (5:257); O 24, 25, 1900 (10:190, 192 [*sic*]); Ja 11, Jl 16, O 24, 1906 (16:? fragment, 103, 229); O 25, 1907 (17:189); O 2, 1908 (18:170); Ja 11, 1909 (18: 253); O 12, 1915; Ja 14, 18, Mr 17, My 13, 1916 (24:255, 258, ?, ?); Mr 29, 1917 (26:11); N 11, 1918 (27:202); Je 7, 1919; O 25, N 1, 1924; S 2, 5, 1933 (43:144, 145); My 8, 945 (53:46).

FREE DEMOCRAT see *CHENANGO FREE DEMOCRAT*

THE GUILFORD MAIL (m) Guilford. 1888–? (1:1–?). *Pub and Ed*: Adrian Tisdale Robinson. *Format*: Four pages, varying sizes, 8½″ x 10″, 10″ x 12½″, 10″ x 15″. *Price*: 15¢ per year (1891–1893); 25¢ per year (1894–?). *Comment*: Published on Depot St. *Loc*: NNo: [Ap 1891–O 1892 (4:2–5:8)]; My 1863 (6:3); My, Jl, O 1894 (7:3, 5, 8); F, O 1895 (7:12; 8:8); Mr 1897 (10:1)]; [F 1899–Je 1904 (11:12–17:4)]; S 1906 (19:7); [Ja–Ag 1919 (31:11–32:6)]. NNoHi: S 1896 (9:9); My 1911 (24:3); S 1918 (31:7).

THE GUILFORD NEWS (w) Guilford. Ap 3, 1930–? (1:1–?). *Pub*: H. C. Colwell Ap 3–Je 27, 1930; E. E. Hotchkiss Jl 16, 1930–? Not listed thereafter. *Ed*: H. C. Colwell Ap 3–Je 27, 1930; Marion Marsh Jl 16, 1930–? *Pol*: Independent. *Format*: Twelve to four pages, varying sizes, 8″ x 10½″, 15″ x 22″. *Price*: $1.00 per year (Ap 3–My 16, 1930); $1.50 per year, 5¢ per copy (My 1930–?). *Comment*: Motto: "Tell all of the Truth and be really Kind." On July 16, 1930 an editorial entitled "The New *Guilford News*" may account for a gap in issues between June 27 and July 16: ". . . This paper is going to rise from the wreck of the old *Guilford News*. We have taken over the subscription list. We have an entirely new management and have a definite aim TO MAKE GUILFORD A CLEAN PLACE IN WHICH TO LIVE." Numbering so erratic it elicited an apology from the editor, March 11, 1931. *Loc*: NNo: [Ap 3, 1930–Mr 25, 1931 (1:1–52)]. NNoHi: Je 17, 1931 (2:12).

THE GUILFORD WAVE see *THE CHENANGO PRESS*

THE HOME NEWS see *THE SHERBURNE NEWS*

THE HOME NEWS OR WEEKLY ADVERTISER see *THE SHERBURNE NEWS*

THE HOME SENTINEL (w) Afton. Ap 8, 1876–? No issues located. ". . . commenced at Afton, April 8, 1876, by John F. Seaman, who has since been its editor and publisher. It was originally an independent paper, but was changed in 1878, becoming . . . Greenback party; though it is still conducted with an independence which makes it free from slavish subserviency to party. In size it is twenty-four by thirty-six inches; and has a circulation of about twelve hundred." (Smith, *Chenango*, p. 110).

THE JUNIPER see *THE QUILL AND PRESS*

THE LITERARY INDEPENDENT Norwich. 1858. No issues located. Published about four months "by a company of gentlemen connected with the Academy." (Smith, *Chenango*, p. 109.)

THE MINIATURE (m?) Oxford. F 7, 1835–? (1:1–?). *Pub and Ed*: Denison Smith Clark. *Format*: Four pages 11" x 16". *Price*: 25¢ for three months (1835). *Comment*: Published in the Fort Hill Building. Clark also published the *Chenango Whig and Miscellaneous Journal* (q.v.) *Loc*: NNo: F 14, 1835 (1:2).

MONDAY REVIEW (w) Bainbridge. Jl 10, 1871–? No issues located. ". . . started . . . July 10, 1871, by E. H. Orwen and Henry A. Clark, who sold about a year afterwards to the present proprietor, Harvey Ireland, who changed the name to the *Bainbridge Republican* (q.v.)." (Smith, *Chenango*, p. 109.)

THE MORNING STAR (w) Sherburne. Mr 27–My 8, 1810// No issues located. "In the prospectus of the *Republican Messenger* of May 22, 1810, it was stated that the junior editor, James Percival, 'has recently been employed in printing a Federal newspaper entitled *The Morning Star*, in this village; but . . . has thought proper to embark in an undertaking which promises fairer results.' The advertisements of *The Morning Star* were evidently continued in the *Republican Messenger* (q.v.), and judging from the dates of these advertisements, the former paper was established Mar. 27, and discontinued May 8, 1810." (Brigham, *Newspapers*, p. 741.)

MORNING SUN see *THE EVENING SUN*

THE NEW BERLIN GAZETTE New Berlin. 1850–? No issues located. "The New Berlin Gazette was established in 1850, by Joseph K. Fox and Moses E. Dunham, who published it in company a little less than a year, when Mr. Fox bought his partner's interest and changed the name to *The Saturday Visitor* (q.v.)." Smith, *Chenango,* p. 108.)

THE NEW BERLIN GAZETTE (w) New Berlin. F 19, 1859 to date (1:1 to date). *Title changes*: *New Berlin Pioneer* F 19, 1859–?; *The New Berlin Gazette* by 1873–1898; *New Berlin Gazette* 1899–?; *The New Berlin Gazette* by 1920 to date. *Pub and Ed*: Orlando Squires (ed.) and Joseph K. Fox 1859–?; Joseph K. Fox by 1873–?; R. Stillman by 1889–?; Joseph K. Fox and George H. Willard 1895–?; George H. Willard 1898–?; Lillie Willard; Christopher Burke, Jr. and Ray Willard 1947–?; Christopher Burke, Jr. ? to date. *Pol*: "Independent—not Neutral." *Format*: Four to eight pages, varying sizes, 13⅝" x 19", 18¾" x 26", 15" x 22". *Price*: $1.00 per year (1859–?). "Almost any kind of produce or provisions suitable for family use will be received of our agricultural subscribers in payment for the paper"; $1.50 per year (by 1873–1892); $1.25 per year (1892–?); $1.00 per year (1894–1917); $1.25 per year (1917–1920); $1.50 per year (1920–?); $5.00 per year (? to date). *Circ*: 10,000 (1879). *Comment*: Motto: "To Speak His Thoughts Is Every Freeman's Right." In 1895 published in the Jacobs Block; in 1876 over George Matteson's Wagon Shop on West St., first block above Cady Hall. *Loc*: NCooHi: F 8, 1873 (13:40 n.s. 2:49); My 26, S 22, D 1, 1877 (17:52; 18:17, 27 n.s. 7:10, 27, 37); F 23, 1895 (n.s. 25:56). NIC/ MMN: O 20, 1883 (n.s. 13:33). NIC/RHA: [Ap 7, 1917–D 30, 1922 (57:14–62:52)]. NNb: Ap 26, Je 28, 1873 (13:51; 14:8 n.s. 3:8, 17); Jl 17, 31, S 18, 1875 (16:8, 10, 17 n.s. 5:17, 19, 27); [Jl 15, 1876–S 22, 1877 (17:7–18:17 n.s. 6:17–7:26)]; Je 8, 15, Ag 3, O 19–N 2, 1878 (19:2, 3, 10, 21–23 n.s. 8:12, 13, 20, 31–33); Ja 11, Jl 5, 26–Ag 9, 1879 (19:33; 20:7, 10–12 n.s. 8:43; 9:20–22); Jl 24, 31, 1880 (21:10, 11 n.s. 10:20, 21); S 24, O 8, N 12, 19, 1881 (22:19, 21, 26, 27 n.s. 11:29, 31, 36, 37); My 20, Je 17, Jl 1, Ag 26, D 16, 1882 (23:1, 5, 7, 15, 31 n.s. 12:11, 15, 17, 25, 41); Ja 20, Je 9, Jl 14, 1883 (23:36; 24:2, 7 n.s. 12:46; 13:14, 19); D 27, 1884 (27:33 n.s. 14:44); Jl 18, 1885 (29:10); Ja 16, 30, My 8, 1886 (29:36, 38, 52); D 3, 1887 (31:29); Jl 18, Ag 8, N 28, 1889 (32:7, 10, 26 n.s. 19:17, 20, 36); Ja 23, F 27, D 27, 1890 (32:34, 39 n.s. 19:44, 49; 20:38); Ja 9, 30, Mr 5, N 24, 1892 (n.s. 22:39, 50; 23:? fragments); O 13, 1894; Mr 16, Je 1, 8, Ag 17, 24, 1895 (n.s. 25:49; 26:8, 9, 19, 20); Ag 6, 1898 (n.s. 29:19); Mr 11, D 16, 1899 (49:10, 50); Ap 7, 1900 (50:14); Je 29, 1901 (51:26); S 9, 1905 (55:36); Ag 22, 1908 (58:34); Ap 13, 1912 (62:15); Ag 16, 1913 (63:33); F 14, 1920 (60:7); Ja 1, 1921 to date (61:1 to date). NNbG: Ja 1, 1921 to date (61:1 to date) and scattered issues previous to 1921.

NEW BERLIN HERALD (w) New Berlin. 1832(?)–? (1:1–?).

Pub: Samuel L. Hatch 1833; Isaac Sheldon (printer) 1834–?; J. W. Marble by D 1836. *Ed*: Samuel C. Randall 1834–1835; Isaac C. Sheldon by My 1835; J. W. Marble by D 1836. *Pol*: Democrat (1834–?). *Format*: Four pages 13½" x 20". *Price*: $2.00 per year delivered, $1.50 per year at the office. *Comment*: Published in the southwest room of Welch's General Store. "*The New Berlin Herald* was commenced in 1831, by Samuel L. Hatch. In 1834, it was published by Randall & Hatch. It soon after passed into the hands of Isaac Sheldon, and subsequently into those of Hiram Ostrander, who changed its name to *The New Berlin Sentinel* (q.v.). It was discontinued about 1840." (Smith, *Chenango*, p. 108.) Loc: NNb: Je 12, 1833 (1:37); S 3, N 19, 1834 (2:100; [3:112]); My 20, 1835 (3:138); D 14, 21, 1836 (5:221, 222).

NEW BERLIN PIONEER see *THE NEW BERLIN GAZETTE* (1859 to date)

THE NEW BERLIN SENTINEL (w) New Berlin. ?–1840//. No issues located. Mentioned by Smith as a title change for the *New Berlin Herald* (q.v.) when that paper was purchased by Hiram Ostrander. It was discontinued about 1840. (Smith, *Chenango*, p. 108).

NEW BERLIN STAR (w) New Berlin. 1887–My 9, 1888 (1:1–1:27). *Pub and Ed*: McFarlane Bros. *Format*: Eight pages 11" x 16". *Price*: $1.00 per year. *Comment*: Issued briefly. The publisher made arrangements to issue a paper in Southern Florida to be called the *Progress* (My 9, 1888). *Loc*: NNoHi: My 9, 1888 (1:27).

THE NEWS AND WAVE see *THE CHENANGO PRESS*

THE NORWICH EVENING TELEGRAPH (d) Norwich. Mr 26, 1879–? (1:1–?). *Pub and Ed*: B. Gage Berry & Co. *Pol*: Republican. *Format*: Four pages 17½" x 24½". *Comment*: Published in the Telegraph Block, Lock St., one door north of the Eagle Hotel. It is possible that this newspaper did not last beyond 1879 and was an attempt by B. Gage Berry to start an evening edition of the *Telegraph*. In the issue for March 30, the numbering appeared as vol. 51 no. 26 coinciding with that of the *Semi-Weekly Telegraph* for March 29. *Loc*: Mr 26–30, N 14–20, 1879 (1:1–4 [*sic* 51:26], 6–11).

THE NORWICH JOURNAL (w) N 14, 1816–O 1847// (1:1–?). *Title changes*: The Norwich Journal N 14, 1816–Ap 12, 1817; *Norwich Journal* Ap 19, 1817–?; *The Norwich Journal* by 1827–1847. *Pub and Ed*: John F. Hubbard (also printer) 1816–?; John F. Hubbard and Ralph Johnson by 1828–1836; John F. Hubbard by 1838–?; John F. and W. B. Hubbard by 1841–1843; John F. Hubbard 1843–1847. *Pol*: Democratic-Republican. *Format*: Four pages, varying sizes, 12¾" x 19½", 11½" x 18", 13½" x 22½", 15½" x 20". *Price*: $2.00 per year delivered, $1.50 at the office. *Comment*: Motto: "Intelligence is the Life of Liberty." Published one door north of Mr. Steere's Tavern nearly opposite Garlic's Hotel (1817–1828); south of P. Fryer's Military Store (1828); south of D. Griffing's Hat Store

(1830–?). On February 5, 1817 J. F. Hubbard announced that he had bought and absorbed *The Volunteer* (q.v.). Publication of the paper was suspended from December 1818 to January 1819. Hubbard temporarily withdrew from the "editorial department" in 1828 to engage in politics (O 22, 1828); the partnership between Hubbard and Johnson was dissolved in 1836 and Johnson "withdrew from the establishment." (*Chenango Telegraph,* Ja 6, 1836.) Hubbard sold the *Journal* in October, 1847 to LaFayette Leal and J. H. Sinclair who merged the *Journal* with the *Oxford Republican* (q.v.) to form the *Chenango Union* (q.v.). (*Oxford Republican,* O 13, 1847.) *Loc*: NIC/MMN: Ag 28, 1834 (17:921); Je 14, 1838 (20:8); Jl 3, 1845 (29:1464 n.s. 8:12); Je 17, 1847 (30:1561 n.s. 10:9). NNo: microfilm [N 14, 1816–D 17, 1823 (1:1–7:364)]; N 14, 1827 (11:568); S 3, 1828–S 1, 1830 (12:610–14:713). NNoHi: Ag 5, 1829 (13:657); Ap 3, 1833 (16:848); N 18, 1841 (26:1330 n.s. 4:31); Ap 7, 13, 1842 (26:1349, 1350 n.s. 4:51, 52); My 18, 1843 (28:1419 n.s. 6:5); Ja 22, F 19, Ap 9, 1846 (29:1489, 1490, 1493 n.s. 8:41, 45, 52); Ap 29, 1847 (30:1554 n.s. 10:2). NOx: F 3, 1830 (13:683). NRU: Ap 16, 1817 (1:22); Ap 16, D 3, 1818 (2:74 fragment); F 25, Ap 29, 1819 (3:114, 123); Ja 4, Jl 19, 1820 (4:159, 186).

NORWICH NEWS Norwich. 1889. No issues located. A campaign paper calling itself "Independent Republican," but regarded as a Democratic organ by *The Chenango Semi-Weekly Telegraph.* Volume 1 number 4 appeared on October 19, 1889. It was published by the News Publishing Company with "no avowed editor." (*The Chenango Semi-Weekly Telegraph,* O 23, 1889.)

THE NORWICH POST (w) Norwich. N 11, 1881–? (1:1–?). *Pub*: John R. Blair 1881–? *Ed*: John R. Blair, George A. Thomas, Assoc. Ed., 1881–? *Pol*: Republican. *Format*: Four pages 18″ x 24″. *Price*: $1.00 per year. *Loc*: NIC/RHA: N 11, 1881–F 29, 1884 (1:1–3:17). NNo: My 18, Je 22, 1883 (2:38, 33).

NORWICH SENTINEL (w) Norwich. ca. 1878. No issues located. ". . . established in 1878 by a company of whom William W. Peters and Jasper L. Griffing were the principal ones, and was published in the interests of the Greenback party till the fall of that year, when it was discontinued." (Smith, *Chenango,* p. 110.)

THE NORWICH SUN see *THE EVENING SUN*

THE OLIVE BRANCH (w) Sherburne, Norwich. My 21, 1806–N 13, 1809// (1:1–4:182). *Pub*: Elihu Phinney and John F. Fairchild. *Format*: Four pages 10″ x 17″. *Price*: $2.00 per year or tuppence per copy. *Comment*: "Established . . . with the title of *Olive-Branch.* With the issue of June 11, 1806, the title was altered to *Olive Branch.* With the issue of May 20, 1807, John F. Fairchild became sole publisher, changed with the issue of Jan. 9, 1808 to John F. Fairchild & Co. The last issue at Sherburne was that of Feb. 6, 1808, vol. 2, no. 90, after which the paper was removed to Norwich, without change of title or volume numbering." (Brigham, *Newspapers,* p. 741.) "With the issue of Apr. 2, 1808, the paper was enlarged in size and the title altered to *The Olive-Branch.* With the issue of July 17, 1808, John F. Fairchild became sole publisher. The paper was discontinued with the issue of Nov. 13, 1809. . . ." (Brigham, *Newspapers,* p. 711.) *Loc:* NShe: N 5, 1806 (1:25).

THE ORACLE see *THE WESTERN ORACLE*

THE OTSELIC VALLEY NEWS (w?) South Otselic. 1905–? (1:1–?). *Pub and Ed:* Harry H. Hobart. *Format:* Four pages 13″ x 19″. *Loc:* NNoHi: D 28, 1905 (1:43).

OTSELIC VALLEY REGISTER (w) Pitcher, Cincinnatus [Cortland County]. 1874–1890(?) (1:1–?). *Pub and Ed:* John Henry Graves ca. 1874–1878(?); Will O. Greene by S 1881–?; Will Bennett by Je 1888–? *Pol:* Independent. *Format:* Four pages, varying sizes, 15½″ x 22½″, 17½″ x 23½″. *Price:* $1.50 per year in advance. *Circ:* 500. *Comment:* Motto: "The General Good." "This paper was established at Pitcher . . . on the 18th of April, 1874, by J. E. Lyons, who, after publishing it about four months, suddenly disappeared and has never since been heard from. The paper was then taken in hand by a stock company and was conducted by Eneas Fenton for a period of about four months, and then disposed of to John Henry Graves [who] removed the establishment to Cincinnatus, where he shortly afterward sold it to D. V. Joyner. He enlarged the sheet . . . and on the 3rd day of November, 1879, sold out to Will O. Greene, who immediately began making improvement both in the paper and the methods of carrying on the business. . . ." (H. P. Smith, ed., *History of Cortland County* [Syracuse, N. Y.: D. Mason & Co., 1885], p. 131.) The *Register* was moved to Cincinnatus as of May 23, 1877. Will Bennett, who purchased the paper from Greene in 1886, located the newspaper office in the Post Office block, then in the old Peck Tailor shop in Cincinnatus, and moved the paper to Fair Haven, N. Y. in 1890 (*The Homer Post,* Mr 31, 1933, p. 11). *Loc:* NCortHi: Je 13, 20, Ag 22, 1888 (15:11, 12, 21); Mr 13, 1889 (15:50). NIC/MMN: My 23, 1877 (4:7). NNoHi: Ja 16, 1878 (4:40); S 28, 1881 (8:25).

THE OXFORD GAZETTE (w) Oxford. D 7, 1813–1826//(?) (1:1–?). *Pub and Ed:* Chauncey Morgan D 7, 1813–? *Pol:* Independent; Republican (1817). *Format:* Four pages, varying sizes, 12¼″ x 20″, 11½″ x 18½″, 13¾″ x 20¾″. *Price:* $1.50 per year at the office, otherwise $2.00. *Comment:* Successor to the *Chenango Patriot,* Oxford, (q.v.). "The editor of the *Chenango Patriot* having relinquished his management of its concerns, the future conduct of the press will devolve upon the subscriber [Chauncey Morgan], who will issue the paper on the same terms as heretofore under the title of *Oxford Gazette.* . . . The printing office will be removed this week to the building formerly occupied by Isaac Sherwood, Esq. on the west side of the river." (*Oxford Gazette,* D 7, 1813.) *The Norwich Journal* mentioned S. G. Troop as editor of the *Gazette,* January 15, 1817; Mr. Morgan, April 10, 1822; and indicated that the *Gazette* had been sold to George Hunt, March 12, 1823. March 5, 1823 ". . . George Hunt became proprietor. June 23, 1824, Ebenezer Noyes became associated with Mr. Hunt in its publication. In February, 1825, it was sold to Howard & Carlisle, and shortly after Mr. Morgan again became proprietor, who sold to William G. Hyer, in 1826." (Henry Judson Galpin, *Annals of Oxford* [Oxford, N. Y.: The Oxford Times], p. 406.) It is possible that when William Hyer bought the *Oxford Gazette* he changed the title to the *Chenango Republican. or, Oxford Gazette and People's Advocate* (q.v.), but we have not located the issues necessary to verify the change. *Loc*: NIC/RHA: Ja 21, 1815 (2:8); My 17, 1826 (13:27). NOx: D 7, 1813–N 26, 1814 (1:1–52); Mr 6, 1816; N 27, 1816–N 19, 1817; N 24, 1819–D 27, 1820. NRU: S 5, 1821 (8:42).

OXFORD PRESS (w) Oxford. N 24, 1899–1906//(?) (1:1–?). *Pub and Ed*: Wellington Alexander ?–O 14, 1904; Wellington Alexander and Thomas L. Coventry O 14, 1904–? *Pol*: Independent. *Format*: Eight pages 14½" x 21½". *Price*: $1.00 per year. *Circ*: "Rapidly nearing the 900" (1900). *Comment*: Published at South Canal St. opposite the Bank Building. Probably discontinued by 1906 according to an editorial which appeared in the July 4, 1906 *Oxford Times* stating that Galpin and C. Edward Snell came into possession of the *Oxford Press* on July 1 and merged it with the *Oxford Times* to become the *Oxford Times and Press*. This title never appeared on the *Times* banner. *Loc*: NOx: N 24, 1899–O 14, 1904 (1:1–5:48).

THE OXFORD REPUBLICAN (w) Oxford. 1831(?)–O 13, 1847// (1:1–17:864). *Pub and Ed*: William E. Chapman and T. T. Flagler by 1834–?; William E. Chapman by 1838–?; R. A. Leal by 1842–?; Charles E. Chamberlin and R. A. Leal 1843–S 1843; R. A. Leal S 1843–1844; none listed F 15–My 23, 1844; LaFayette Leal My 30, 1884–O 13, 1847. *Pol*: Democrat. *Format*: Four pages 16" x 22". *Price*: $1.50 per year at the office, $2.00 per year by mail. *Comment*: Motto: "Progress in Literature, the Arts and Politics." This paper may have succeeded the *Chenango Republican. or, Oxford Gazette and People's Advocate* (q.v.) (Smith, *Chenango*, p. 108). In October 1847 LaFayette Leal and his partner, James H. Sinclair, purchased the *Norwich Journal* and merged the two papers to form the *Chenango Union* (q.v.). William E. Lewis was the printer as of September 7, 1843. In 1845 the address of the newspaper was given as Canal Square above W. E. Chapman's Bookstore. *Loc*: NIC/RHA: [Ag 15, 1844–O 13, 1847 (14:23 whole no. 699–17:864)]. NNo: D 19, 1838 (8:41 whole no. 405); F 8, 1844– My 22, 1845 (14:6 whole no. 672–14:52 whole no. 739). NNoHi: F 8, 1844 (14:6 whole no. 672). NOx: O 15, 1834 (4:32 whole no. 487); F 4, 1842–D 18, 1845 (12:5 whole no. 567–15:769).

OXFORD REPUBLICAN AND CHENANGO COUNTY DEMOCRAT (w) Oxford. 1841–? (1:1–?). *Pub and Ed*: Benjamin J. Welch, Jr. *Pol*: Democrat. *Format*: Four pages 15¾" x 22". *Loc*: NOx: Mr 5, 1841 (1:8).

THE OXFORD REVIEW see *THE REVIEW-TIMES*

THE OXFORD REVIEW-TIMES see *THE REVIEW TIMES*

THE OXFORD TIMES (w) Oxford. O 1838–Ja 1, 1915// (1:1–?). *Title changes*: *The Times* by 1839–? *The Oxford Times* by My 20, 1840–?; *Oxford Times* 1841–Ag 1868; *The Oxford Times* S 2, 1868–1915. *Pub and Ed*: Andrew F. Lee D 1838–? Andrew F. Lee and N. Pellet by Ap 7, 1839–?; Andrew F. Lee by 1840–?; Edward H. Purdy by 1841–O 6, 1841; E. H. Purdy and Charles D. Brigham O 13, 1841–S 28, 1842; E. H. Purdy O 1842–Ap 1843; H. H. Cooke My 1843–?; Waldo M. Potter My 1844–?; Waldo M. Potter (ed.) and Judson Galpin (pub.) by 1847–D 20, 1848; Judson B. Galpin D 1848–F 1893; Theodore B. Galpin F 1893–Ja 2, 1894; Theodore B. Galpin and Wellington Alexander Ja 9, 1894–S 5, 1899; Theodore B. Galpin S 12, 1899–Je 1906; Theodore B. Galpin and C. Edward Snell Jl 4, 1906–Ag 4, 1909; The Times Publishing Co. (C. Edward Snell, Pres.) 1909–1913; Jared C. Estelow (pub.) Jl 1913–1915. *Pol*: Whig; Republican. *Format*: Four to eight pages, varying sizes, 15¼" x 21½", 16½" x 22½", 18¾" x 23¼", 17½" x 22½". *Price*: $1.50 per year at the office, $2.00 per year by mail or delivered (by 1839–?); $1.25 per year at the office, $1.50 per year by mail or delivered (1844–?); $1.50 per year by 1867–?; $1.50 per year (1908–?); $1.00 per year (1913–?). *Circ*: 2,925 (1907); 2,750 (1908); 2,450 (1909). *Comment*: Motto: "A Free and Moral Press is the Palladium of our Liberty" (1839–1841); "A Protective Tariff, Land Distribution, Internal Improvements and Henry Clay" (1844–1845); "The Intelligence of the People is the only Safeguard of Liberty" (1845–?). Published at Navy Island, first door west of the river bridge, 1855, and first door west of the Post Office 1869. By 1894 published in the Galpin Block, entrance from the bookstore, and in 1906 from the *Times* block. The beginning date of the Times is mentioned in the *Chenango Telegraph*, October 17, 1838, announcing publication of the *Times* and citing Andrew F. Lee as editor and publisher. On January 1, 1915, *The Oxford Review* announced that George L. Stafford had purchased the *Oxford Times* plant and that by January 8, the two papers would be issued as the *Oxford Review-Times* (q.v.). *Loc*: NCooHi: O 18, 1854 (17:5); Ap 4, 1855 (17:29). NIC/MMN: F 19, 1846 (8:21). NIC/RHA: D 15, 1841 (4:11); Ja 18, Mr 1, 1843 (5:16, 22); O 24, N 21, D 5, 1844 (7:4, 8, 10); Mr 13, D 11, 1845 (7:24; 8:11); Ja 12, Mr 19, My 28, Ag 20, S 17, N 5, 1846 (8:17, 25, 35, 47, 51; 9:6); Ja 27, F 17, 1847 (9:18, 21); Mr 23, 1864 (26:29); S 25, 1867 (30:4). NNo: My 22, 1839 (1:33); My 20, 1840 (2:32); Jl 28, 1841 (3:43); Jl 13, 1842 (4:41); Ja 25, 1844 (6:17); My 2, 1844–S 25, 1845 (6:31–7:52); N 24, 1847 (10:9); N 2, 1853 (16:7); My 6, 1868 (30:36). NOx: Ap 17, 1839 (1:28); [Mr 18, 1840–Jl 17, 1900 (2:24–62:52)]; [Jl 6, 1904–Jl 1, 1914 (67:1–76:52)].

OXFORD TRANSCRIPT Oxford. 1853// No issues located. Commenced in 1853 by George N. Carhart and published about six months (Galpin, *Annals*, p. 409.)

PEOPLE'S ADVOCATE (w) Norwich. 1824(?)–1826//(?) (1:1–?). *Pub*: H. P. W. Brainard. *Format*: Four pages 12″ x 20″. *Price*: $2.00 per year, $1.50 at the office (1825). *Comment*: "A Day, an Hour of Virtuous Liberty, is Worth a Whole Eternity in Bondage—Addison." A reference from the scrapbook of Charles Johnson in the Guernsey Memorial Library indicates that the *People's Advocate* was established "1825 or thereabouts" by T. G. C. [*sic*] Brainard and William G. Hyer on East Green near the Eagle Tavern. (Charles Johnson, Scrapbook, v. 3, p. 72.) Smith states that Brainard started the *Advocate* at Norwich and . . . it subsequently passed into the hands of William G. Hyer (Smith, *Chenango*, p. 108). This paper is probably connected with the *Chenango Republican. or, Oxford Gazette and People's Advocate* (q.v.) published by Hyer in Oxford in 1826. *Loc*: NNo: My 18, 1825 (2:46 fragment).

THE PIONEER see *THE WEEKLY PIONEER*

THE PRESIDENT (w) Oxford. F 27,1808–? No issues located. Published in 1898 by Theophelus Eaton (Smith, *Chenango*, p. 108).

PRUNING HOOK (w) Norwich. Ag 14–?, 1840// (1:1–?). *Pub*: John F. Hubbard. *Pol*: Democrat. *Format*: Four pages 10½″ x 15½″. *Comment*: Campaign newspaper. "Van Buren and Johnson— The People's Candidates" appeared under the banner. *Loc*: NCooHi: Ag 28, S 25, O 1, 23, 1840 (1:3, 7, 8, 11).

QUILL AND PRESS (w) North Pharsalia. Ja 1879–? (1:1–?). *Pub*: Joseph C. White by 1881–? *Ed*: Joseph C. White by 1881–?; H. L. Barnes by 1884–? *Pol*: Independent. *Format*: Four to six pages 13″ x 20″. *Price*: $1.00 per year, 3¢ per copy. *Comment*: ". . . established in June, 1878 . . . by Joseph C. White . . . as *The Juniper,* an amateur weekly; with No. 10 of Vol. II the name was changed to *White's American Greenbacker,* advocating the principles and doctrine of that party. It is at present issued as the *Quill and Press.* . . ." (Smith, *Chenango*, p. 110). *Loc*: NNo: microfilm [Je 28, 1881–Je 14, 1883 (3:1–4:52)]. NNoHi: Jl 17, 1884 (6:4); F 12, 1885 (6:34).

THE REPUBLICAN AGRICULTURIST (w) Norwich. D 10, 1818– 1821//(?) (1:1–?). *Pub and Ed*: Thurlow Weed D 10, 1818–? *Pol*: Democratic-Republican (Pro DeWitt Clinton). *Format*: Four pages 11⅝″ x 19″. *Price*: $2.00 per year delivered or by mail, $1.50 per year at the office. *Comment*: Motto: "Where Liberty Dwells—There Is My Country." "He who causes but one spear of grass to grow where it does not, is more of a real service to the community, than the most splendid victories of Alexander the Conqueror." Thurlow Weed was owner and publisher and apparently editor from the first issue, December 10, 1818, through the issue of September 14, 1820. Actual sale by Weed was September 7, 1820, but the last issue was on the 14th. The new owner was Samuel Curtis, Jr. and the new editor James Birdsall. (*Norwich Journal, S* 13, 1820.) "The *Agriculturalist* [*sic*] retired from the field in 1821." (*Norwich Journal, Je* 6, 1821). *Loc*:

NNo: D 17, 1818 (1:2); Mr 18, 1819 (1:15). NRU: D 10, 1818–
D 2, 1819 (1:1–52).

REPUBLICAN MESSENGER (w) Sherburne. My 22, 1810–?
(1:1–?). No issues located. "Established May 22, 1810, by Pettit &
Percival [Jonathan Pettit and James Percival], with the title of *Republican Messenger.* The paper succeeded *The Morning Star* and
continued its advertisements. It was discontinued at Sherburne with
the issue of Jan. 1, 1811, vol. 1, no. 33, when the proprietors stated
that they proposed to remove the establishment 'a short distance to
the Westward.' Percival established the *Cortland Courier* at Homer,
about forty miles west of Sherburne, in March 1811." (Brigham,
Newspapers, p. 741.)

THE REVIEW-TIMES (w) Oxford, Greene. 1909 to date (1:1 to
date). *Title changes: The Oxford Review* 1909–Ja 1, 1915; *The Ox-
ford Review-Times* Ja 8, 1915–My 1, 1958; *The Review-Times* My
8, 1958 to date. *Pub:* George L. Stafford by 1910–Mr 9, 1928; George
L. and Clara M. Stafford Mr 1928–Mr 13, 1946; Clara M. Stafford
My 2, 1946–Ap 10, 1947; The Oxford Review-Times, Inc. 1947–1955;
Chenango Publications, Inc. (John Van Kleeck) N 10, 1955–1961; Twin
Valley Publishers, Inc. Ja 2, 1962 to date (William D. Marsland, Pres.,
1962 to date; John Van Kleeck, Vice Pres., 1962–?). *Ed:* Henry J. Galpin
?–S 1917; George L. Stafford 1917–My 1921; Samuel S. Hale My 6,
1921–F 10, 1928; George L. Stafford Mr 1928; Vernon L. Spencer Mr
23, 1928–My 21, 1942; Mary H. Jenks My 28, 1942–Mr 18, 1943; none
listed Mr 25, 1943–Ap 1944; Grace Slabey Roys My 4–O 5, 1944, Ap
12–S 20, 1945, S 1954–F 10, 1955; Vernon L. Spencer My 2, 1946–O 8,
1950; Ralph U. Jeffords O 15, 1950–S 1954; Grace S. Roys, Louise Tan-
ney, Gertrude Whitney, Assoc. Eds., Ap 6–S 1954; Fayne Adams, Ed.,
F 10–N 3, 1955, Assoc. Ed., N 10, 1955–N 1, 1956; John Van
Kleek N 10, 1955–1961; none listed thereafter. *Pol:* Republican. *Format:*
Eight to sixteen pages, varying sizes, 15″ x 21″, 10¾″ x 16½″, 18″ x
23″. *Price:* $1.00 per year (by 1910–1917); $1.50 per year (1918–
1946); $2.00 per year (Je 6, 1946–1947); $2.50 (Ap 17, 1947–?);
$3.00 per year (by 1958); $4.00 per year, 10¢ per copy (by 1970 to
date). *Comment:* By 1928 published at 2½ Main St., then moved to
Canal St. After fire at Canal St. in 1947, moved temporarily to the
second floor of the Bank Building; in 1948 moved to the Review-
Times Block, 6 Washington Ave. All of the above offices were in Oxford. Since 1962 its offices have been located at 12 South Chenango
St., Greene. Twin Valley Publishers, Inc. is a merger of Chenango
American and Chenango Publications, Inc. *Loc:* NIC/MMN: My 27,
1937 (28:34). NIC/RHA: Ap 6, D 28, 1917 (8:23; 9:9); [Ja 4,
1918–O 20, 1922 (9:10–13:52)]; Je 19, 1947–D 29, 1955 (37:39–
46:10). NNo: Ja 7, 1970 to date (65:16 to date). NNoHi: Mr 5,
1915 (6:18); Ja 31, Mr 28, 1919 (10:14, 22); Je 2, 1941–D 26, 1957
(32:37–47:16). NOx: N 11, 1910–N 3, 1911 (2:1–52); N 8, 1912–
Ja 1, 1915 (4:1–6:9); N 5, 1915 to date (7:1 to date).

SATURDAY REVIEW (w) Bainbridge. ca. Ja 24, 1872–S 4, 1875//.
No issues located. This newspaper succeeded *The Bainbridge Ledger*
(q.v.) and was merged in *The Bainbridge Republican* (q.v.) on September 4, 1875 when purchased by Harvey Ireland (Smith, *Chenango*,
p. 109).

THE SATURDAY SUN see *THE EVENING SUN*

THE SATURDAY VISITOR New Berlin. 1851–? No issues located.
Established as the *New Berlin Gazette* (1850–?) (q.v.). When Joseph
K. Fox became the sole owner the paper's name was changed to *The
Saturday Visitor*. "It was continued under that name two or three
years, when it was changed to *The New Berlin Pioneer,* and . . . again
changed to *The New Berlin Gazette* [1859 to date] (q.v.). . . ."
(Smith, *Chenango*, p. 108.)

SHERBURNE HOME NEWS see *THE SHERBURNE NEWS*

THE SHERBURNE NEWS (w) Sherburne. Mr 2, 1864 to date (1:1
to date). *Title changes*: *The Home News or Weekly Advertiser* Mr 2,
1864–?; *The Home News* ?–F 23, 1865; *Sherburne Home News* Ap
20, 1865–Ap 9, 1868; *The Sherburne News* Ap 16, 1868 to date.
Pub and Ed: Simeon B. Marsh 1864–O 11, 1866; LaMonte Gardiner
Raymond O 18, 1866–O 7, 1869; George and Frank D. Matteson O
15, 1869–Ap 16, 1870; Frank D. Matteson Ap 21, 1870–Ag 1871;
Frank D. Matteson and Peters S 1871–Ja 4, 1872; Frank D. Matteson
Ja 11–25, 1872; Thomas Randall F 3, 1872–D 3, 1881; John H.
O'Brian D 10, 1881–Ap 1909; John H. O'Brian and Harry J. Mc-
Daniel Ap 24, 1909–My 1911; Harry J. McDaniel and Ray V. Howard Je 3, 1911–Je 1918; Harry J. McDaniel Je 20, 1918–D 1919; Harry
J. McDaniel and Charles A. P. Kimball Ja 1, 1920–D 16, 1920; Harry
J. McDaniel D 23, 1920–Ap 1942; Harry J. McDaniel and Sons Ap
16, 1942–D 1958; John M. McDaniel Ja 1, 1959 to date. *Pol*: Independent. *Format*: two to twelve pages, varying sizes, 3" x 8½", 5½" x
9", 8¼" x 11", 12½" x 18½", 15½" x 21", 17" x 23", 19" x 25½",
13¾" x 21½". *Price*: $1.00 per year, 10¢ per month (1864); $1.25 per
year in advance (1865–?); $1.50 per year (1871–1947); $2.00 per year
(1947–?); $2.50 per year (by 1964–?); $3.00 per year (by 1969–?);
$4.00 per year. *Comment*: Motto: "An independent journal of home
interests and general intelligence." Published in the third story over
Colwell's shoe store 1864; then in the Brick Block, second door from
the National Bank by 1865–1868; Hiller Block, North Main St. 1868–
1870; then Smith Block, North Main St. 1870, but by May 1871 in the
Hiller and Merchant Block on State St.; over T. A. Fuller's Store, H.
& W. Affrey's Store, Hebbard and Amsden Store, and J. H. Shepard &
Co.'s Store, all on North Main St., between 1875 and January 30,
1904 when the newspaper office was moved to its present location in
the News Building, East State St. Publication was suspended February
23, 1865 because "the receipts of the *News* in its advertising patronage is not sufficient to warrent its further publication. . . . Some think
it would do better if enlarged—may reappear in a few weeks." (Edi-

torial F 23, 1865.) Publication was resumed on April 20, 1865. *Loc*: NIC/MMN: D 17, 1887 (24:38); Ja 21, 1888 (24:43); Ag 18, 1906 (43:24). NIC/RHA: Ap 5, 1917–D 27, 1923 (54:7–60:46); F 19, 1947–F 11, 1954 (83:8–90:8). NNoHi: Mr 23, 1864 (1:4). NShe: [Mr 2, 1864 to date (1:1 to date)].

SHERBURNE PALLADIUM Sherburne Village. 1836–? No issues located. ". . . commenced by . . . J. Worden Marble, who was afterwards interested in the publication of the *Broome County Courier*, at Binghamton to which place the *Palladium* was removed in 1839." (Smith, *Chenango*, p. 108).

SHERBURNE TRANSCRIPT (w) Sherburne. Jl 27, 1855–? (1:1–?). *Pub and Ed*: James M. Scarritt. *Format*: Four pages 15½ " x 22". *Price*: $1.00 per year (1855). *Loc*: NShe: [S 28, 1855–Jl 17, 1857 (1:10–2:52)].

THE SMYRNA CITIZEN (w) Smyrna. O 30, 1875–N 25, 1876// (1:1–3:5). *Pub and Ed*: George A. Munson. *Pol*: Neutral. "Neutral in Politics—We work by the Golden Rule." *Format*: Four to eight pages 10½ " x 15". *Price*: $1.00 per year, 5¢ per copy. *Comment*: "We have met with many difficulties and been censured for nearly everything we have done. Our paper was too small for some, too neutral for others and contained too much political matter for those who were on the 'other' side. We sell our paper to Frank W. Godfrey, the foremen of the *Sherburne News,* who next will start a weekly paper at Earlville." (Editorial, N 25, 1876). *Loc*: NNo: O 30, 1875–N 25, 1876 (1:1–3:5).

THE SMYRNA PRESS (w) Smyrna. 1897(?)–? (1:1–?). *Pub and Ed*: Albert G. Ladd by 1917–?. *Format*: Eight pages 17½ " x 21½ ". *Price*: $1.50 per year. *Loc*: NIC/RHA: Ap 5, 1917–Je 27, 1918 (21:17–22:29).

THE SOCIAL VISITOR New Berlin. ca. 1852. No issues located. ". . . An ephemeral publication of this period." (Smith, *Chenango*, p. 109.)

SOUTH NEW BERLIN BEE (w) South New Berlin, Gilbertsville [Otsego County]. Ja 2, 1897–S 30, 1965// (1:1–68:39). *Pub and Ed*: A. J. Payne 1897–Je 1946; Wilbur D. Hall Jl 1, 1946–1948; Fay Faulkner ?–O 29, 1948; Wilbur D. Hall N 5, 1948–Ja 1950; J. C. Barber Ja 16–N 1950; Alan D. Bruckheimer N 3, 1950–Mr 1, 1954; John A. Bacon Mr 1954–S 30, 1965. *Pol*: Independent. *Format*: Four to twelve pages, varying sizes, 13" x 19¼ ", 14" x 20½ ", 15" x 22", 10" x 14½ ". *Price*: $1.00 per year (1897–?); $1.25 per year (by 1917–?); $1.50 per year (by 1920–?); $2.00 per year (by 1946–?); $2.50 per year (by 1952–?); $3.00 per year. *Comment*: Published in the Bee Block or Bee Building, South New Berlin, from 1897 until 1950 when the paper was moved to Gilbertsville, Otsego County. On October 7, 1965, the *South New Berlin Bee* consolidated with the *Otsego Journal* of Gilbertsville and *The Morris Chronicle* into one paper called the *Otsego-Chenango Bee-Journal-Chronicle* published in Gilbertsville. *Loc*: NIC/RHA: Jl 21, 1917–Ja 26, 1924 (21:29–27:52); [Je 13, 1947–D 30, 1955 (50:24–58:52)]. NSnb: [Ja 2, 1897–D 29, 1908 (1:1–10:52)]; [Ja 2, 1916–S 30, 1965 (20:?–68:35)].

THE SOUTH OTSELIC GAZETTE (w) South Otselic. 1891–? (1:1–?). *Pub and Ed*: W. M. Reynolds. *Pol*: Independent. *Format*: Eight pages 14½" x 22". *Price*: $1.00 per year. *Loc*: NNoHi: My 7, 1903 (12:1).

THE SPIRIT OF THE AGE (w) Norwich. S 1852–? (1:1–?). *Pub: and Ed*: J. D. Lawyer by Jl 1853. *Pol*: Independent. *Format*: Four pages 16" x 21". *Price*: $1.00 per year. *Comment*: Motto: *"Salus Populi Suprema Lex."* "Devoted to Free Soil Principles, Temperance, Morality, Reform, Education and General Intelligence." Located at the Norwich Variety Store, Brick Block, North Main St. ". . . Commenced at New Berlin in 1852 by J. K. Fox, with J. D. Lawyer as editor. It was published only a short time." (Smith, *Chenango*, p. 109.) *Loc*: NNoHi: Jl 2, 23–Ag 6, 1853 (1:40, 43–45).

SUNDAY TIMES (w) Norwich. 1874//. No issues located. Published by W. L. Griffing (Smith, *Chenango*, p. 110).

THE TELEGRAPH (w) Norwich. Ag 19, 1812–1814//(?) (1:1–?). *Title changes*: Columbian Telegraph by D 9, 1812–?; *The Telegraph* by Mr 6, 1813–? *Pub*: James M. Miller. *Format*: Four pages 11" x 17". *Price*: $2.00 per year. *Comment*: Miller was still publishing *The Telegraph* in 1814 (Brigham, *Newspapers*, p. 712). He subsequently printed *The Volunteer* (q.v.). *Loc*: NIC/MMN: D 9, 1812 (1:17). NNo: Mr 6, N 27, 1813 (1:29; 2:67).

TEMPERANCE ADVOCATE (w) Norwich. 1855–? (1:1–?). *Pub*: J. M. Haight and Hitchcock. *Ed*: Augustus P. Nixon. *Pol*: Against "Hindoo and Democrat and Know-Nothing-Rum Party." *Format*: Four pages 18" x 24". *Comment*: Published over John Hammond's shoe store, No. 5 South Main St. *Loc*: NIC/MMN: N 16, 1855 (1:31).

THE TIMES see *THE OXFORD TIMES*

THE VOLUNTEER (w) Norwich. O 4, 1814–1817//(?) (1:1–?). *Pub and Ed*: John Burgess Johnson by 1816–? *Format*: Four pages 12" x 19½". *Comment*: "Established Oct. 4, 1814, with the title of *The Volunteer*, printed by James M. Miller, for Lot Clark. . . . The *Norwich Journal* of Feb. 5, 1817, announced that the *Volunteer* establishment had been transferred to the Editor [John F. Hubbard] of the *Journal*." (Brigham, *Newspapers*, p. 712). Possible successor to *The Telegraph* (q.v.). *Loc*: NCooHi: S 24, 1816 (2:104).

THE WEEKLY PIONEER (d, w) Norwich. 1872(?)–? ([1:1]–?). *Title changes*: *The Young Pioneer* by My 21, 1873–?; *The Weekly Pioneer* 1874–? *Ed*: W. M. Dietz. *Pol*: Republican. *Format*: Four pages 5½″ x 7″. *Price*: $1.00 per year, 3¢ per copy. *Comment*: Motto: "Industry, Perseverance, Economy." The running title was *The Pioneer*. It was published weekly beginning September 19, 1874. *Loc*: NNo: My 21, 23, 1873 (no vol. or no.); O 10, 1874 (3:4). NNoHi: S 19, 1874 (3:1).

THE WESTERN ORACLE AND CHENANGO WEEKLY MAG-AZINE (w) Sherburne. Ap 5, 1804–1806// (1:1–?). *Pub*: Abraham Romyen. *Format*: Sixteen pages 5½″ x 9″. *Price*: Not listed. "Publisher will accept agricultural produce and rags in settlement of money owed by subscribers for the *Oracle*." (S 13, 1804) *Comment*: "The first newspaper published in Chenango county . . . established at Sherburne Four Corners in 1803, by Abraham Romeyn[*sic*], from Johnstown, assisted by his brother Nicholas, and . . . printed in the front part of the building now occupied by Milton Bentley. It was a single octavo sheet, at first of bluish paper, and contained very few advertisements and but little local news. . . . Its pages were chiefly occupied by *foreign intelligence*. . . . It was probably discontinued as early as 1806." (Smith, *Chenango*, p. 107.) *Loc*: NNo: Ag 9–O 18, 1804 (1:19–29). NShe: My 3–Jl 12, 1804 (1:5–15).

WHITE'S AMERICAN GREENBACKER see *QUILL AND PRESS*

THE YOUNG PIONEER see *THE WEEKLY PIONEER*

THE ADVERTISER AND FREE PRESS (w) Cortland. Ag 1896(?)–? (1:1–?). *Pub*: The Advertiser and Free Press Publishing Co. *Format*: Four pages 8″ x 11″. *Circ*: 2,000. *Comment*: Published at 13 North Main St. Primary purpose was advertising. *Loc*: NCortHi: S 11, 1896 (1:3).

ANTI-MASONIC REPUBLICAN see *THE CORTLAND COUNTY WHIG*

THE BLUE RIBBON (w?) Cortland. Ja 24, 1879–? (1:1–?). *Pol*: Temperance. *Format*: Four pages 9¼″ x 11¾″. *Loc*: NHom: F 14, 1879 (1:4).

BUELL'S SATURDAY REVIEW (w) Cortland. Je 8, 1895–? (1:1–?). *Pub and Ed*: Clayton H. Buell. *Pol*: Republican. *Format*: Sixteen pages 15″ x 22¼″. *Price*: $2.00 per year (1895). *Comment*: Published from the corner of Main and Tompkins Sts. *Loc*: NCortHi: D 14, 21, 1895 (1:28, 29); Mr 7, 21, 1896 (1:40, 42).

CAMPAIGN DAILY (d) Cortland. 1859–? *Pub and Ed*: E. D. Van Slyck and S. G. Hitchcock 1859. *Pol*: Republican. *Format*: Four pages 9¼″ x 12¼″. *Comment*: Possibly issued by the *Republican Banner* (q.v.) since publishers and date coincide. *Loc*: NCortHi: N 1, 1859 (no issue numbers).

CENTRAL REFORMER (w) McGrawville. ?–1858// (1:1–?). *Pub*: Abram Pryne. *Ed*: Abram Pryne and L. G. Calkins. *Pol*: Independent. "A religious, literary and anti-slavery journal, independent of party and sect." *Format*: Eight pages 12″ x 18″. *Price*: $1.50 per year. *Comment*: Motto: "The truth shall make you free." This press was purchased by Van Slyck and Bateson who started the *Republican Banner* (q.v.) (H. P. Smith ed., *History of Cortland County* [Syracuse, N. Y.: D. Mason & Co., 1885], p. 125). *Loc*: NCortHi: My 5, 1858 (3:41, n.s. 1:10).

THE CHRISTIAN CONTRIBUTOR McGrawville. ca. 1848–1850. No issues located. Edited by President Grosvenor of New York Central College (*Cortland County Express,* O 11, 1849).

THE CINCINNATUS JOURNAL Cincinnatus. ca. 1878. No issues located. Published for a short time by John Henry White (*The Homer Post,* Mr 31, 1933).

THE CINCINNATUS REVIEW (w) Cincinnatus. N 20, 1930–Jl 24, 1931// (1:1–26). *Pub*: Norman O. Westcott N 20–D 18, 1930; Adrian W. Hicks D 25, 1930–Jl 24, 1931. *Ed*: Adrian W. Hicks N 20, 1930–Jl 24, 1931. *Format*: Four pages 15″ x 23″. *Comment*: Motto: "The only newspaper devoted to the interests of the Otselic Valley." *Loc*: NCortHi: Ap 9–23, My 7–Jl 24, 1931 (1:17–19, 21–26).

THE CINCINNATUS STAR (w) Cincinnatus. My 12, 1939–? (1:1–?). *Pub and Ed*: Velma Churchill Jones and Paul Augustus Jones 1939–? *Pol*: Independent. *Format*: Four to eight pages, varying sizes, 14″ x 22″, 16½″ x 22″, 11½″ x 16¼″, 14″ x 20″. *Price*: $1.00 per year in advance. *Comment*: Published at the *Star* Building, South Main St. The official newspaper of the town of Cincinnatus. Sub-title varies: "An informative interpretive weekly newspaper for the Otselic Valley communities" (1940); "Reaching the rural and village homes throughout the Otselic Valley" (1941). *Loc*: NCortHi: [Ag 11–D 22, 1939 (1:14–33)]; [Ja 5–Ap 19, 1940 (2:1–16)]; Jl 25–Ag 8, 22, 1941 (3:30–32, 34).

THE CINCINNATUS TIMES (w) Cincinnatus. Je 9, 1898–S 10, 1925// (1:1–28:17). *Pub and Ed*: Levi D. Blanchard 1898–1925. *Format*: Four to fourteen pages, varying sizes, 15″ x 22″, 17¾″ x 24″. *Price*: $1.00 per year (by 1910–1918); $1.25 per year (1919–?); $1.50 per year (by 1924–1925). *Comment*: Motto: "A newspaper for the home." *Loc*: NCin: Ag 4, 1898 (1:9); O 29, 1903 (6:21); Ja 5, F 16, 1911 (13:32, 38); F 15, 1912 (14:38); Ja 9, 1913 (15:33); Ap 23, Je 18, 1914 (16:48; 17:4); My 2, 1918 (20:49); Ag 28, 1919 (22:14); Ja 6, Mr 3, Ag 18, 1921 (23:33, 41; 24:13); S 14, 28, 1922 (25:17, 19); O 4, 1923 (26:20); Je 12, 1924 (27:4); Ag 14, 27, S 10, 1925 (28:13, 15, 17). NCortHi: [My 24, 1900–Mr 5, 1925 (2:51–27:42)]. NIC/MMN: microfilm [Ag 4, 1899–S 10, 1925 (1:9–28:17)].

THE CINCINNATUS TIMES (w) Cincinnatus. Je 16, 1950–? (1:1–?). *Pub*: Bruce E. and George S. Whitehead. *Ed*: Bruce E. Whitehead. *Pol*: Independent. *Format*: Four pages 15″ x 21½″. *Price*: $1.50 per year, $1.00 for six months, 60¢ for three months payable in advance. *Loc*: NCortHi: F 23, Mr 2, 1951 (1:37, 38).

COMMUNITY NEWS REVIEW (m) Homer. Ap 1942–? (1:1–?). *Pub and Ed*: R. Curtis Harris 1942–1951. *Pol*: Non-Partisan. *Format*: One to twelve pages, varying sizes, 8½″ x 14″, 7″ x 8¾″. *Circ*: 350. *Comment*: Published monthly for men in the armed forces. Volume 5 number 2 is undated and was issued semi-monthly. Published at 81 North Main St. *Loc*: NCortHi: My 16, S 16, D 16, 1942 (1:2, 6, 9);

F 16, 1943 (1:11); My 16–O 16, D 16, 1943 (2:2–7, 9); Ja 16, Mr 16–My 16, S 16, N 16, D 16, 1944 (2:10, 12; 3:2, 5, 6, 8, 9); F 16–S 16, 1945 (3:11–4:6); 1951 (5:2).

THE CORTLAND ADVERTISER (q) Cortland Village. My 1860–? (1:1–?). *Pub and Ed*: John R. Beden My 1860–? *Format*: Four pages 9½ " x 12". *Comment*: Devoted primarily to advertising with some local news. *Loc*: NCortHi: My 1860 (1:1).

CORTLAND ADVERTISER (w) Cortland. 1895–? (1:1–?). *Pub*: E. V. Bowker 1898–? *Format*: Four pages 11" x 14". *Comment*: Published at 5 Clinton Ave. Devoted primarily to advertising with some local news. *Loc*: NCortHi: Ap 17, 1898 (3:47).

CORTLAND ADVERTISER (w) Cortland. Jl 31, 1913–? (1:1–?). *Pub*: N. E. Bugbee. *Format*: Four pages 15" x 22". *Price*: Free. *Circ*: 4,000. *Comment*: Published at 21 Groton Ave. Devoted primarily to advertising with some local news. *Loc*: NIC/RHA: N 20, 1913 (1:17).

CORTLAND ADVOCATE (w) Cortland Village. O 7, 1831–? (1:1–?). *Pub*: Charles W. Gill O 7, 1831–My 17, 1833; C. W. Mason My 24, 1833–Ag 29, 1833; Henry S. Randall S 5, 1833–D 1836(?); Randall and Sheldon by D 29, 1836–?; David Fairchild by S 1837–?. *Ed*: Charles W. Gill O 7, 1831–My 17, 1833; Henry S. Randall My 24, 1833–?; David Fairchild by S 1837–? *Pol*: Democratic-Republican. *Format*: Four pages 16" x 21". *Price*: $2.00 per year. *Circ*: 500. *Comment*: Published directly opposite the Eagle Store in Cortland Village. ". . . as early as 1838, [David Fairchild] removed it [the *Advocate*] to Ovid, N. Y. [Seneca County], where he started the *Ovid Bee*." (Smith, *Cortland County*, p. 123.) The *Advocate* contains the county canvass (November 1833). *Loc*: NCort: My 29, 1834 (3:35); Ag 4, 11, 25, S 29, D 29, 1836 (5:45, 46, 48; 6:1, 14). NCortHi: S 21, 1837 (6:52). NCortSt: O 7, 1831–S 25, 1834 (1:1–3:52). NIC/MMN: microfilm O 7, 1831–S 25, 1834 (1:1–3:52); Ag 4, 11, 25, S 29, D 29, 1836 (5:45, 46, 48; 6:1, 14); S 21, 1837 (6:21).

CORTLAND AMERICAN (w) Cortland. Ag 23, 1855–Ag 1857// (1:1–?). *Pub and Ed*: Edwin F. Gould 1855–1857. *Pol*: Know-Nothing. *Format*: Four pages 18¼ " x 23½ ". *Price*: $1.25 per year in advance. *Comment*: Published in the Dixon Block, third story. Dates are from Smith, *Cortland County*, p. 125. See "Comment" under *Cortland Democrat* (1849–1855). *Loc*: NCortHi: N 15, 1855 (1:13).

CORTLAND CHRONICLE (w) Cortland Village. Ap 18(?), 1828–? (1:1–?). *Pub*: Rufus A. Reed and S. M. Osgood 1828–? *Pol*: Whig. *Format*: Four pages 13" x 19". *Price*: $2.00 per year by mail or delivered, $1.75 per year at the office. *Comment*: This may have been a predecessor to the *Cortland County Whig* (Smith, *Cortland County*, p. 121). *Loc*: NCortHi: Ag 22, 1828 (1:19).

CORTLAND CITIZEN (w) Cortland. O 12, 1906–? (1:1–?). *Pub*: Citizen Publishing Co. *Pol*: Democratic and Independence League.

Format: Eight to four pages, varying sizes, 17½ " x 22", 15¼ " x 22". *Circ*: 5,000. *Comment*: Motto: "The Citizen—the best advertising medium in Central New York." Before December, 1906 carried no news not related to the Cortland mayoral campaign. *Loc*: NCortHi: O 12–N 9, D 13, 20, 1906 (1:1–5, 10, 11).

CORTLAND COMMERCIAL REVIEW Cortland. ca. 1882. *Pub*: Fred C. Atwood and John P. Loucks. *Format*: Four pages 11" x 16". *Loc*: NCortHi: 1882 (one issue only undated).

CORTLAND COUNTY ADVERTISER (w) Homer. 1940–1941// (?) (1:1–?). *Pub*: Sanford H. Atwater and Phillip LeRoy Loomis. *Ed*: Phillip LeRoy Loomis. *Pol*: Independent. *Format*: Four pages 16" x 21¾". *Price*: $1.50 per year. *Comment*: Motto: "A modern weekly newspaper striving for Truth and Accuracy in Chronicling the News and Views of Cortland County and Outlying Communities." Published in the *Advertiser* Building. An article in the *Homer Independent*, My 31, 1960, states: "In 1940 for a short period prior to World War II . . . the *Cortland County Advertiser* set up shop in the old fire station on James Street, but the editor, Phillip LeRoy Loomis, went off to war and that was that." *Loc*: NCortHi: My 29, Jl 31, 1941 (2:3, 12).

CORTLAND COUNTY DEMOCRAT see *THE CORTLAND DEMOCRAT* (1864 to date)

CORTLAND COUNTY EXPRESS (w) McGrawville. Ag 12, 1847– D. 26, 1850// (1:1–4:20). *Title changes*: *McGrawville Express* Ag 12, 1847–Mr 1, 1849; *Cortland County Express* Mr 9, 1849–D 26, 1850. *Pub*: Samuel C. Clisbe and A. T. Boynton Ag 12, 1847–F 17, 1848; Almon H. Benedict and A. T. Boynton F 24, 1848–Jl 18, 1850. *Ed*: Samuel C. Clisbe Ag 12, 1847–F 17, 1848; Almon H. Benedict F 24, 1848–Jl 18, 1850; A. T. Boynton Jl 25–D 26, 1850. *Pol*: Neutral (1847–1848); Independent (1849–1850). The original subhead was "A Family Newspaper—Neutral in Politics." On August 17, 1848 Almon H. Benedict asserted his intention to "occasionally expose the rascally manoeuvering of parties—but, in general, . . . not to deviate from a course in harmony with [Clisbe's] object of making this a literary and family newspaper." *Format*: Four pages 16" x 21". *Price*: $1.00–$1.75 per year. *Comment*: On July 18, 1850, Almon H. Benedict explained his reasons for joining and leaving the newspaper: He had been promised a lot of printing by New York Central College; the *Christian Contributor* would be printed by the *Express;* local citizens would give monetary aid; and private remuneration was promised. However, the income from the paper did not warrant joint ownership and Benedict therefore withdrew. On December 26, 1850, A. T. Boynton stated in the final issue of the paper that he was moving type and press from its location over O. H. Salisbury's store to Chenango County. *Loc*: NCortD: Mr 2, 1848–Jl 18, 1850 (1:30–3:49). NCortHi: S 7, 1848 (2:5); My 17, 1849 (2:41). NCort/Kenyon: Ag 12, 1847–D 26, 1850 (1:1–4:20). NHom: Ap 19, D 20, 1849 (2:37;

3:19). NIC/MMN: Ja 25, 1849 (2:25). NOwHi: [O 21, 1847–O 11, 1849 (1:11–3:9)].

CORTLAND COUNTY NEWS (w) Cortland. N 1902–? (1:1–?). *Pub and Ed*: H. J. Barnum and N. E. Bugbee by 1903–? *Format*: Eight pages 15¼ ʺ x 22ʺ. *Price*: 75¢ per year. *Comment*: Published at 12 North Main St. *Loc*: NCortHi: S 10, N 5, 1903 (1:44, 52).

CORTLAND COUNTY REPUBLICAN (1855–1877) see *HOMER REPUBLICAN*

CORTLAND COUNTY REPUBLICAN (1897–1898) see *CORTLAND REPUBLICAN*

CORTLAND COUNTY REPUBLICAN AND AMERICAN see *CORTLAND REPUBLICAN*

CORTLAND COUNTY SENTINEL (w) McGrawville, Cortland. Je 5, 1878–? (1:1–?). *Title changes: The McGrawville Sentinel* Je 5, 1878– S1, 1887; *Cortland County Sentinel* S 8, 1887–S 3, 1896; *Cortland County Sentinel and McGrawville News* S 10, 1896–?; *Cortland County Sentinel* ?–? *Pub*: William A. Huntington 1878–1883; William A. Huntington and Fayette S. Berggren by Ap–S 1879; Fayette S. and Fred J. Berggren by Ap 1885–?; Fred J. Berggren 1889–?; The Cortland Standard Publishing Co. 1885–ca. D 1896; The Sentinel Co. 1897–? *Ed*: William A. Huntington 1878–?; Elmer F. Norcott ?–?; Fayette S. and Fred J. Berggren F 9, 1885– My 19, 1887; Fayette S. Berggren My 26, 1887–? *Pol*: Independent. *Format*: Four to eight pages, varying sizes, 13ʺ x 20ʺ, 15½ ʺ x 22ʺ, 18ʺ x 24ʺ, 20ʺ x 25½ ʺ, 17ʺ x 22ʺ. *Price*: $1.25 per year in advance (1878); $1.00 per year in advance, 5¢ per copy (1879–?). The aim of the paper was "to stay in the field as a poor man's paper, an honest man's paper and a newspaper"—at $1.00 a year. *Circ*: 300 (1885); 1,600 (1887). *Comment*: Motto: "For the Public Good." Published in McGrawville from June 5, 1878 until January 10, 1895. It was purchased by the *Cortland Standard* and its presses and material were moved to Cortland. On January 17, 1895, the paper began to be issued from the *Standard* office under its original name, but as a weekly edition of the *Standard*. Its name was later changed to the *Cortland Journal,* and it was finally merged in the *Semi-Weekly Standard*. (*Cortland Standard,* S 20, 1910.) No issues of the *Cortland Journal* have been located. The date of merger into the *Standard* cannot be determined from the issues in hand. *Loc*: NCort: Ja 7, D 30, 1897 (19:32; 20:31); My 8, 1902 (24:50). NCortHi: Je 5, D 18, 25, 1878 (1:1, 29, 30); My 28, Ag 6, 1879 (1:52; 2:10); Ag 10, S 28, 1881 (4:11, 18); O 5, 1882 (5:19); Ja 31, Ag 7, 1885 (7:32; 8:7); O 20, 1887 (10:18); Ag 29, 1889 (12:13); Mr 12, My 21, 1891 (13:41, 51); Ap 14, 1892 (14:46); D 10, 1896 (1928). NCortSt: S 8, 1887–D 25, 1902 (10:12–26 [*sic* 25]:31). NHom: Ja 2, 1896–D 27, 1900 (18:32–23:31). NIC/MMN: Ap 30, 1879 (1:48 fragment). NIC/RHA: Je 5, S 4, 1878 (1:1, 14); Je 25, S 10, O 1, D 10, 24, 1879 (2:4), 15, 18, 28, 30); O 6, 13, N 17, 1880 (3:19, 20, 25); Ag 30, 1883 (1:13); Jl 26,

1884 (7:8); Ag 27, 1885 (8:10); N 28, 1889 (12:26). NMac: F 12, 1885–S 1, 1887 (7:34–10:11); My 30, 1889 (11:50); F 13, Ag 14, S 11, 18, D 11, 1890 (12:37; 13:11, 15, 16, 28).

CORTLAND COUNTY SENTINEL AND MCGRAWVILLE NEWS see *CORTLAND COUNTY SENTINEL*

THE CORTLAND COUNTY STANDARD see *CORTLAND STANDARD*

THE CORTLAND COUNTY WHIG (w) Cortland and Homer. 1831–Ag 23, 1855//(?) (1:1–n.s. 16:14). *Title changes: Anti-Masonic Republican* 1831–1832; *Cortland Republican* 1832(?)–My 10, 1836; *Republican and Eagle* My 17, 1836–1840; *Cortland County Whig* 1840–My 1848; *The Cortland County Whig* My 18, 1848–Ag 23, 1855. *Pub*: Rufus A. Reed 1831–Je 28, 1836; Rufus A. Reed and Asa Bennett Jl 5, 1836–Ja 17, 1837; Rufus A. Reed Ja 24–D 12, 1837; Rufus A. Reed and Marvin Blodgett D 19, 1837–Ag 14, 1838; Rufus A. Reed Ag 21–O 16, 1838; Rufus A. Reed and Co. O 23, 1838–D 1841; Rufus A. Reed 1842–Ag 1844; Rufus A. Reed and J. S. Walker Ag 1844–Mr 20, 1845; Rufus A. Reed Mr 27, 1845–Ap 29, 1852; Rufus A. Reed and Cornelius B. Gould My 6–N 18, 1852; Cornelius B. Gould N 25, 1852–Mr 1854; E. F. and Cornelius B. Gould Mr–D 1854; Joseph R. Dixon and Cornelius B. Gould D 14, 1854–ca. Je 1855; Joseph R. Dixon and Case by Je 21, 1855–Ag 23, 1855. *Ed*: Rufus A. Reed 1831(?)–My 24, 1841; Ap 3, 1845–N 18, 1852; H. S. Conger and T. G. Turner Je 1–O 1841; H. S. Conger O 1841–Ag 8, 1844; J. S. Walker Ag 8, 1844–Mr 20, 1845; Cornelius B. Gouid N 25, 1852–Mr 9, 1854; E. F. and Cornelius B. Gould Mr–D 1854; Joseph R. Dixon D 1854–Ag 23, 1855. *Pol*: Whig. *Format*: Four pages, varying sizes, 16″ x 20″, 17″ x 22″, 18½″ x 24″. *Price*: $1.50 per year in advance, otherwise $2.00 per year by mail or delivered, $1.75 per year at the office. *Comment*: Motto: "The Constitution—Cornerstone of the Whig Party." No address given for publication office of newspaper until May 9, 1837 when it was published from C. Bishop's new brick building, third story, at the corner of Main and Port Watson Sts., Cortland. In Homer Village, its address was Mechanics Hall directly over Short and Wheadon's Shop. From 1841 to January 2, 1845, it was published in Cortland over Elder and Pomeroy's store nearly opposite the Clerk's office; in Homer from the grocery store of B. H. Coburn in 1842, then in the grocery store of George S. Stevens, and from 1844 to 1855 in the "second building south of William Sherman and Son's Store," later defined as Main St., 9 Sherman's Building. *Loc*: NCort: Ap 10, 1833–My 26, 1840 (2:33–9:41); My 11, 1841 (n.s. 1:50); [Mr 14, 1844–My 13, 1852 (13:31–21:41 or n.s. 4:42–12:52)]. NCortHi: N 4, 1834 (4:11); Ap 26, 1836 (5:36); Ag 8, 1834 (Extra—Broadside-Whig County Convention); Mr 21, 1837 (6:31); Ap 17, 1838 (7:35); Ap 13, Ag 10, O 5, D 21, 1841 (n.s. 1:46; 2:11, 19, 30); D 13, 1842 (12:18); F 7, O 10, 1843 (12:26; 13:9); My 23, 1844 (13:41); Ag 19, O 14, 1847 (17:2, 10);

My 4, S 7, D 21, 1848 (17:39; 18:5, 20); Ap 4, 18, Jl 11, 1850 (19:35, 37, 49); Ag 21, 1851 (21:3); S 9, 1852 (22:6). NCortUC: Ja 11, 1849 (18:23); Mr 2, D 14, 1854 (24:31; 30:19); Je 14–28, Jl 11, 26, Ag 9, 23, 1855 (30:45–47, 49, 51; 31:1, 3). NHom: Ja 5, 1832 (1:20); Ap 23, 1833 (2:35); Ja 28, 1834 (3:23); Ja 20, Mr 3, My 5, 19, Je 2, Jl 7, Ag 4, 1835 (4:22, 28, 37, 39, 41, 46, 50); Mr 1, Ag 9, 1836 (5:28, 51); Ja 3, F 14, Jl 11, 18, D 19, 1837 (6:20, 26, 47, 48; 7:18); Ag 21, 1838 (8:1); F 26, 1839 (8:28); F 25, 1840 (9:?); [Ag 25, 1840–F 8, 1844 (n.s. 1:13–4:37)]; [O 2, 1845–Ag 23, 1855 (n.s. 6:19–16:14)]. NIC/MMN: O 24, 1850 (20:12 n.s. 11:23); microfilm Ja 11, 1849 (18:23 n.s. 9:34); Mr 2, D 14, 1854 (n.s. 14:42; 15:30); Je 14–28, Jl 12, 26–Ag 9, 23, 1855 (n.s. 16:4–6, 8, 10–12, 14); NIC/RHA: D 6, 1836 (6:16); Ag 22, 1837 (7:1); Je 2, 1839 (8:46); Ja 12, S 28, 1841 (10:22 n.s. 1:33; n.s. 2:18); My 3, O 18, 1842 (n.s. 2:49; 12:10 n.s. 3:21); Ja 24, 1843 (12:24 n.s. 3:35); Je 4, 25, Jl 2, 1846 (15:43, 46, 47 or n.s. 7:2, 5, 6); N 8, 15, 1849 (19:14, 15 n.s. 10:25, 26).

CORTLAND COURIER (w) Homer Village. Mr 1811–1812//(?) (1:1–?). *Pub. and Ed*: James Percival. *Format*: Four pages 11¼" x 18". *Price*: $2.00 per year. *Comment*: The first issue probably appeared about March 20, 1811. R. Curtis Harris in the *Homer Independent,* May 31, 1960, states that "In 1812 the *Courier* was transferred to H. R. Bender and R. Washburne who published under the name of the *Farmer's Journal* for a short time, until it passed into the hands of Dr. Jesse Searl in 1813. He christened it the *Cortland Repository* [q.v.]. . . ." Also discussed in Smith, *Cortland County,* pp. 119–120. Percival had previously edited the *Republican Messenger* in Sherburne (Chenango County). *Loc*: NHom: Je 26, 1811 (1:15).

CORTLAND DAILY JOURNAL (d) Cortland. F 4, 1889–Jl 1892// (no. 1–?). *Title changes*: *Cortland Daily Message* F 4, 1889–?; *Cortland Daily Journal* ?–1892. *Pub*: Daniel S. Jones F 4, 1889–?; Daily Message Co. ca. 1889–?; Charles W. Smith 1891–1892. *Ed*: Daniel S. Jones F 4, 1889–? *Format*: Four to six pages 15" x 22". *Price*: $3.00 per year delivered by carrier. *Comment*: First published at 20 Port Watson St., then 12 West Court St. The official newspaper of Cortland County. Purchased by *The Cortland Standard* (q.v.) July 12, 1892 and continued under the title *Cortland Standard and Cortland Daily Journal* (*Cortland Standard,* S 20, 1919, p. 46). *Loc*: NCortHi: Jl 2, 1891 (3:125); Mr 15, Je 16, 17, 1892 (4:65, 145, 146). NHom: F 4, 1889 (no. 1).

CORTLAND DAILY MESSAGE see *CORTLAND DAILY JOURNAL*

CORTLAND DEMOCRAT (w) Cortland Village. My 12, 1840–D 1848// (1:1–9:?). *Title changes*: *The Cortland Democrat* My 12, 1840–?; *Cortland Democrat* by 1844–1848. *Pub*: Seth Haight and Henry W. DePuy My 12, 1840–My 4, 1841; Seth Haight My 12, 1841–? *Ed*: Henry W. DePuy My 12, 1840–?; Henry S. Randall

1841–? *Pol*: Jeffersonian Democrat. *Format*: Four pages 16½ " x 21¼". *Price*: $1.75 per year at office, $2.00 per year by mail or carrier (1840–1846); $1.50 per year in advance or $1.75 paid half-yearly by carrier, $1.25 per year in advance at the office or by mail (1846). *Comment*: ". . . Located over a hat store then kept by Canfield Marsh, on or near the site of the Union Hall Block." (Smith, *Cortland Co.*, p. 124.) In 1841 moved to an office in the Brick Building opposite the Eagle Tavern. "The division of the Democratic party in 1848 was disastrous to Mr. Haight and the *Democrat;* the paper supported Cass . . . the *Democrat* lost much of its influence and prosperity and Haight finally sold it to James S. Leach. . . ." (Smith, *Cortland County*, pp. 124–125). *Loc*: NCort: My 12, 1840–My 4, 1842 (1:1–2:52); [My 8, 1844–D 16, 1848 (5:1–932)]. NCortUC: microfilm My 12, 1840–My 4, 1842 (1:1–2:52); [My 8, 1844–D 16, 1848 (5:1–9:32)]. NHom: Je 30, Jl 13, O 13, 1840 (1:8, 10, 23); F 23, Mr 9, 16, Jl 7, 1841 (1:42, 44, 45; 2:9); D 21, 1842; My 29, 1844 (5:4); Ja 8, Mr 12, 1845 (5:36, 45); Mr 25, 1846 (6:47); Ap 19, N 11, 1848 (8:51; 9:27). NIC/MMN: microfilm: My 12, 1840–My 4, 1842 (1:1–2:52); [My 8, 1844–D 16, 1848 (5:1–9:32)]. NRU: S 11, O 23, 1844 (5:19, 25).

THE CORTLAND DEMOCRAT (w) Cortland. Ja 4, 1849–Ag 1855// (1:1 or 10:1–?). *Pub*: James S. Leach Ja 4–D 27, 1849; Quimby and Hyatt 1850–?; I. S. and G. W. Hyatt ca. Ag 1850– 1851/ 52(?); Henry G. Crouch 1851/52(?)–1855; Edwin F. Gould ca. 1855. *Pol*: Free Soil; American. *Format*: Four pages, varying sizes, 16¾ " x 23½"; 18½ " x 25½". *Price*: $1.00 per year (1854). *Comment*: "At about the time when Mr. Crouch sold the *Democrat* [*i.e.* 1855] the Know-Nothing excitement was at its height, and Mr. Gould soon changed the name of the paper to the *Cortland American* (q.v.), and devoted it to the interests of the new party." (Smith, *Cortland Co.*, p. 125.) *Loc*: NCort: Ja 4–D 27, 1849 (1:1–52 or 10:1–52). NCortUC: Ja 4–D 27, 1849 (1:1–52 or 10:1–52). NHom: Ag 9, 1849 (1:32 or 10:32); [Ja 17, 1850–My 31, 1855 (2:3–7:? or 11:3–16:20)]. NIC/ RHA: Ja 26, 1854 (6:3).

THE CORTLAND DEMOCRAT (w) Cortland. Mr 1, 1864 to date (1:1 to date). *Title changes*: The Cortland Democrat ?–N 20, 1868; *The Cortland County Democrat* N 27, 1868–Jl 1877; *The Cortland Democrat* Jl 1877 to date. *Pub*: H. G. Crouch and M. P. Callender 1864–1866; C. A. Kohler ca. 1866–1867; Lucien S. Crandall by 1867–1868; Benton B. Jones Ja 31, 1868–1873; Robert, Lamont and David Tallmadge by My 1, 1874–1875 (only D. Tallmadge, Ed. and Prop. appeared on papers); Benton B. Jones Ag 1875–D 1896; Benton B. Jones Estate 1896–F 24, 1899; Fay C. Parsons Mr 3, 1899–Ag 9, 1946; Fay C. Parsons Estate Ag 16, 1946–My 30, 1947; W. Lawrence and Reginald H. Harrington (later Harrington Brothers, Inc.) Je 6, 1947 to date. *Ed*: M. P. Callender 1864–1866; Benton B. Jones ca. 1866–1873; David Tallmadge 1874–1875; Benton B. Jones by 1875–D 20, 1896; Frank W. Collins D 27, 1896–D 31, 1897; Fay C. Parsons 1898–1946; W. Lawrence and Reginald Harrington Je 6,

1947–Je 5, 1959; Donn W. Elliott Je 12, 1959–My 21, 1964; W. Lawrence Harrington, Managing Ed., ca. My 1964 to date. *Pol*: Democrat. *Format*: Four to ten pages, varying sizes, 16″ x 22″, 22″ x 28″, 13½″ x 19″, 14¼″ x 21½″. *Price*: $2.00 per year (by 1884); $4.00 per year, 10¢ per copy (1970); $5.00 per year, 10¢ per copy (1972). *Comment*: Official paper of the city and county. Published in the Squires Block ca. 1864–1868; Keator Block (Main and Port Watson Sts.) ca. 1868–1871; Squires Building 1871–ca. 1876; 12 West Court St. 1877–ca. January 1, 1890; and 12 Railroad St. (now Central Ave.) ca. January 1, 1890 to date. *Loc*: NCort: microfilm Ja 31, 1868–Ap 14, 1871 (4:41–7:52); Ag 13, 1875 to date (12:18 to date). NCortD: ca. 1952 to date. NCortHi: My 12, 1865 (2:3); Ja 31, 1868–Ap 14, 1871 (4:41–7:52); Jl 11, 1873 (10:13); O 23, 1874 (11:28); [Ag 13, 1875–D 30, 1960 (12:18–96:45)]; D 30, 1964 to date (99:46 to date). NCortUC: microfilm Ja 31, 1868–Ap 14, 1871 (4:41–7:52); [Ag 13, 1875 to date (12:18 to date)]. NHom: Jl 15, 1864 (1:12); F 18, 1870 (6:44); N 8, D 6, 1872 (9:30, 34); Ja 29, 1875 (12:42); Ag 25, 1876 (13:20); F 21, 1879 (15:46); F 21, 1890 (26:48); Ap 11, 1890 (27:3). NIC/MMN: microfilm Ja 31, 1868–Ap 14, 1871 (4:41–7:52); My 2, 1879–D 29, 1966 (16:4–101:46). NIC/RHA: My 17, Je 14, 1867 (4:4, 8); Ja 15, N 29, 1869 (5:39; 6:28); D 6, 1872 (9:34); F 5, 1875 (12:43); Mr 31, Je 30, Jl 7, D 29, 1876 (12:51; 13:12, 13, 38); [Ja 19, 1877–N 2, 1883 (13:41–20:31)]; Mr 13, Ap 17, O 23, 30, 1885 (21:50; 22:3, 30, 31); Ag 5, 1904 (41:22); O 9, 1908 (45:32).

CORTLAND EVENING DEMOCRAT (d) Cortland. My 1875–? (1:1–?). *Pub*: David Tallmadge. *Pol*: Democrat. *Format*: Four pages 13″ x 19″. *Price*: 12¢ per week, 3¢ per copy. *Loc*: NCortHi: Je 12, 1875 (1:13). NIC/RHA: Je 11, 1875 (1:12).

CORTLAND EVENING STANDARD see *CORTLAND STANDARD*

CORTLAND FREE PRESS Cortland. ca. 1902–ca. 1912. No issues located. H. J. Barnum was the proprietor and the offices were located at 12½ N. Main St., then 6 Tompkins, 2 Tompkins, and 110 Main St. (George Hanford, *Directory of Cortland County, New York* [Elmira, 1902]; M. P. Goodhue, *Cortland, Homer and McGrawville Directory* [Elmira, 1912].)

THE CORTLAND GAZETTE (w) Cortland Village. 1857–1861// (1:1–?). *Pub and Ed*: Charles P. Cole. *Pol*: Democrat. *Format*: Four pages 18″ x 24″. *Price*: $1.00 per year in advance. *Comment*: In 1857 J. D. Robinson purchased the material of the defunct *Cortland American* (q.v.) and established the *Cortland Gazette*. In 1858 he sold it to John R. Beden. A few months later it passed into the hands of C. P. Cole, who had gained editorial experience with the *Syracuse Courier*. He improved the paper, added to the job printing, increased the circulation of the *Gazette* to about 1,000 copies and for a time had a good paying business (Smith, *Cortland County*, p. 125). About 1861 this paper combined with the *Republican Banner* and formed the *Gazette and Banner* (q.v.). *Loc*: NIC/RHA: Ag 12, S 30, 1858 (2:9, 16).

CORTLAND-HOMER PENNYSAVER (w) Cortland. Ap 9, 1964–? (1:1–?). *Pub and Ed*: Les Carr. *Format*: Twenty-four pages 7¼" x 10". *Price*: Free. *Comment*: Primarily an advertising newspaper with local news. *Loc*: NCortHi: Ap 9, 1964 (1:1).

CORTLAND JOURNAL (w) Cortland Village. 1825(?)–?. *Pub and Ed*: D. Smith and Tourtellot by Ap 12, 1826; D. Smith by Ag 31, 1826–? *Format*: Four pages 14½" x 19½". *Loc*: NHom: Ap 13, 1826 (?:78); Ag 31, 1826 (2:98).

CORTLAND JOURNAL see *CORTLAND COUNTY SENTINEL* and *CORTLAND WEEKLY JOURNAL*

CORTLAND LIBERTY HERALD see *THE LIBERTY HERALD*

CORTLAND MIDLANDER (m, q) Cortland. Ag 1933–? (1:1–?). *Pub and Ed*: Cortland Trust Co. Ag 1933–1936. *Pol*: Non-Partisan. *Format*: Four pages 8½" x 11". *Comment*: Sub-Title: "Here and there in Cortland County." Items of interest, non-controversial in nature, about business activities in Cortland County. *Loc*: NCortHi: Ag 1933–D 1934 (1:1–2:5); Mr 31–D 31, 1935 (3:1–4); Je 30, 1936 (mid-summer no.).

CORTLAND NEWS (w) Cortland. Je 25, 1880–? (1:1–?). *Pub and Ed*: Clayton H. Buell 1880–1882; F. G. Kinney 1882–1884(?); S. H. Strowbridge by 1884–? *Pol*: Independent. *Format*: Four pages 19" x 26". *Price*: $1.50 per year. *Comment*: Published at 13 North Main St. *Loc*: NCortHi: O 29, 1880 (1:10); Ja 14, 1881 (1:30); O 21, 1881 (2:18); Ap 28, 1882 (2:45); [Jl 7, 1882–Mr 11, 1887 (3:3–7:39)].

CORTLAND OBSERVER (w) Homer Village. S 28, 1825–1835// (1:1–?). *Pub and Ed*: Milton A. Kinney S 28, 1825–? *Pol*: Whig; Anti-Mason. *Format*: Four pages 13" x 20". *Price*: $2.00 per year delivered, $1.75 per year at the office. *Comment*: Its predecessor, the *Cortland Repository* (q.v.), was purchased in 1825 by Milton A. Kinney who named it the *Cortland Observer*. (H. C. Goodwin, "Impressions of Homer, No. 4," in Cortland County Historical Society's *Bulletin*, vol. 24, no. 3, Je 1970.) Kinney continued publication until 1833; then Simon S. Bradford ran it for three years. A Mr. Holmes took it about the year 1836, and sold it to Rufus A. Reed in 1837. Holmes changed its name to the *Homer Eagle* (q.v.). (Smith, *Cortland County*, p. 121.) *Loc*: NCort: S 28, 1825–S 14, 1832 (1:1–7:52). NCortHi: O 25 ,1826 (2:5); O 31, 1828 (4:6); F 19, 1830 (5:22); Ap 6, 1832 (7:29). NHom: S 28–D 25, 1825 (1:1–13); Ag 2, 1826 (1:45); Jl 25, 1828 (3:44).

THE CORTLAND PENNYSAVER (w) Cortland. N 18, 1971 to date (1:1 to date). *Pub*: No publisher listed N 18, 1971–F 29, 1972; David Narby and John Fattaruso Mr 7, 1972 to date. *Ed*: B. S. and

B. J. N 18, 1971–F 29, 1972; David Narby and John Fattaruso Mr 7, 1972 to date. *Format*: Eight to sixteen pages, varying sizes, 8¾ " x 11½ ", 11½ " x 17½ ". *Price*: Free. *Circ*: 12,000. *Comment*: Published from 18A Pendleton St., November 18, 1971 to January 12, 1972, and from 71 Clinton Ave., January 18, 1972 to date. *Loc*: NCortHi: N 18, 1971–Mr 7, 1972 (1:1–14); Ap 11, 1972 to date (1:19 to date).

CORTLAND REPOSITORY (w) Homer Village. D 8, 1813–S 15, 1825// (1:1–12:25). *Pub*: Dr. Jesse Searl and John W. Osborn by Jl 21, 1814–1820; Dr. Jesse Searl and Benjamin B. Drake Ja 14, 1820–D 1821; Dr. Jesse Searl Ja 1822–1825. *Ed*: Dr. Jesse Searl 1813–1825. *Pol*: Independent. *Format*: Four pages, varying sizes, 11" x 18½ ", 12½ " x 21". *Price*: $2.00 per year delivered, $1.75 at the office (1814–1819); $2.25 per year delivered, $2.00 at the office (1820–1825). *Comment*: Motto: "National virtue, the basis of political freedom." Successor to the *Farmer's Journal* (q.v.), predecessor of the *Cortland Observer* (q.v.). "Ample room is given in its columns to foreign news, but for many consecutive numbers not a line of what might, by the most liberal construction, be termed local news is found in its columns." (Smith, *Cortland County*, p. 120.) *Loc*: NCortHi: Jl 21, S 15, O 20, 1814 (1:33, 41, 46); Ja 14, 1820 (6:41); Ag 18, N 24, 1820 (7:20, 34); N 20, 27, Ja 29, 1822 (8:34, 35, 44); N 19, 1822 (9:34); S 17, O 29, N 12, 19, D 17, 1823 (10:25, 31, 33, 34, 38); Mr 24, My 5, N 12, 1824 (10:52; 11:6, 33); My 5, S 15, 1825 (12:6, 25). NHom: F 14, 1825 (11:42).

CORTLAND REPUBLICAN (w) Cortland Village. Je 30, 1815–1821// (1:1–?). *Pub and Ed*: James Percival Je 30–S 30, 1815; John W. Osborn and David Campbell O 7, 1815–Ag 9, 1816; John W. Osborn and Obadiah Boies Ag 16–D 6, 1816; John W. Osborn and David Campbell D 13, 1816–Ja 31, 1817; Benjamin S. and David Campbell F 7, 1817–Ap 17, 1819; David Campbell Ap 22, 1819–My 1821. *Pol*: Democratic-Republican. *Format*: Four pages, varying sizes, 13" x 18", 11" x 19", 13" x 19". *Price*: $2.00 per year payable quarterly (1815–1817). The January 24, 1819 issue carried the following notice: "Those who are indebted to this office, and expect to pay grain, are requested to deliver it by the first of February next; and those who have contracted to pay wood, are invited to improve the present favorable time, and all who owe money, are informed, that it cannot be paid too soon." An editorial in the May 16, 1821 newspaper lamented that there was a great "rage for establishing newspapers . . . nearly every village in the state had one, many two." In Cortland County three papers were published weekly with patronage "barely sufficient for one." As of May 26, 1821, David Campbell stated that he would "reduce the size of the paper so that receipts and expenditures [would] be more in balance. Times are hard, money scarce. Subscription price will be ½ of old price. . . ." *Loc*: NCort: Je 30, 1815–My 16, 1821 (1:1–6:47). NCortHi: O 18, 1820 (6:18). NHom: Mr 22, 1816 (1:39); Ap 25, 1818 (3:44); Ag 29, 1818 (4:10).

CORTLAND REPUBLICAN (1832–My 10, 1836) see *CORTLAND COUNTY WHIG*

CORTLAND REPUBLICAN (1855–1877) see *HOMER REPUBLICAN*

CORTLAND REPUBLICAN (w) Cortland. S 23, 1897–? (1:1–?). *Title changes*: *Cortland County Republican* S 23, 1897–Ja 14, 1898; *Cortland County Republican and American* Ja 21, 1898–?; *Cortland Republican* by Ag 1898–? *Pub*: The Republican Publishing Co. 1897–1898; H. J. Barnum and N. E. Bugbee 1898–? *Pol*: Republican. *Format*: Four to eight pages 15″ x 22″. *Price*: $1.00 per year in advance, 10¢ per month (1897–1898); 75¢ per year (1898–?). *Comment*: Motto: "Honest politics; Honest primaries." Published at the Churchill Building, 19 North Main St. *Loc*: NCortHi: O 7–29, 1897 (1:3–7); Ja 14, 21, F 4, 11, Ag 12, 1898 (1:18, 19, 21, 22, 48).

CORTLAND STANDARD (w, semi-w, w) Cortland. Je 25, 1867–D 1922// (1:1–?). *Title changes*: *The Cortland County Standard* Je 25, 1867–Ap 30, 1872; *Cortland Standard and Journal* My 7, 1872–Ap 26, 1877; *The Cortland Standard* My 3, 1877–S 17, 1885; *Cortland Standard* S 24, 1885–Mr 1919; *Cortland Standard and Homer Republican* Mr 1919–Ap 1921; *Cortland Standard* Ap 1921–D 1922. *Pub and Ed*: F. G. Kinney Je 25, 1867–Ap 30, 1872; Wesley Hooker My 7, 1872–Mr 28, 1876; William H. Clark Ap 3, 1876–ca. Ap 28, 1892; William H. Clark and Edward D. Blodgett Mr 8, 1892–Ag 12, 1893; Cortland Standard Printing Co. Ag 1893–D 1922 (William H. Clark, Pres.). *Pol*: Republican. *Format*: Four to ten pages, varying sizes, 20¾″ x 27¼″, 22″ x 28″, 18″ x 23″, 15″ x 22½″. *Price*: $2.00 per year (by 1871–1922), 5¢ per copy (1892), 2¢ per copy (1919). *Circ*: 1,000 (1867); 1,300 (1876). *Comment*: Motto: "Let all the ends thou aim'st at be thy Country's, thy God's, and Truth's" (1867). Published from Garrison Block over C. W. Collin's Grocery Store, June 1867–September 29, 1868; Moore's Brick Block, 3rd floor October 6, 1868–February 6, 1879; Mahan Block, Court St. February 13, 1879–February 1883; *Standard* Building, corner of Main and Tompkins Sts., March 1, 1883 to 1922. The *Standard* was published weekly until May 5, 1892, semi-weekly May 10, 1892–September 29, 1917, and weekly October 1917–1922. A daily *Cortland Standard* (q.v.) was also published after 1892. In 1872 Wesley Hooker merged the *Standard* with the *Cortland Weekly Journal* and the *Homer Herald* (Smith, *Cortland Co.*, p. 126). Volume 1 number 1 was dated July 25, 1867 on the masthead, but July 29, 1867 on the inner pages. *Loc*: NCort: Mr 21, 1876–Jl 5, 1892 (9:47–n.s. 347). NCortHi: [Ag 24, 1869–Mr 3, 1905]. NCort/Mullen: D 26, 1871 (5:26). NCortSt: Je 25, 1867–D 1922 (1:1–?). NCortUC: D 26, 1871 (5:26); D 7, 1875 (n.s. 4:32); Jl 4, 1919 (no. 25). NHom: D 26, 1871 (5:26); D 7, 1875 (n.s. 4:32); Jl 9, 1885 (18:948); Jl 15, Ag 5, 1886; F 13, 1890; Ja 7, 1892–D 29, 1903; Jl 4, 1919 (no. 25). NIC/MMN: D 26, 1871 (5:26); D 7, 1875 (n.s. 4:32); Jl 4, 1919 (no. 25). NIC/RHA: Jl 1, 1873 (n.s. 2:9); [My 2, 1876–S 6, 1883 (10:1–17:852)]; [Mr 12–O 22, 1885

(18:931–19:963)]. NIDeW: Je 29, 1900 (n.s. no. 79). NMara: O 19, 1882 (16:806).

CORTLAND STANDARD (d) Cortland. Mr 8, 1892 to date (no. 1 to date). *Title changes*: *Cortland Standard* Mr–Jl 12, 1892; *Cortland Standard and Cortland Daily Journal* Jl 13, 1892–Ja 18, 1893; *Cortland Standard* Ja 19, 1893–Mr 5, 1919; *Cortland Standard and Homer Republican* Mr 6, 1919–Ap 2, 1921; *Cortland Standard* Ap 4, 1921 to date. *Pub*: William H. Clark and Edward D. Blodgett 1892–Ag 12, 1893; Cortland Standard Printing Co. Ag 14, 1893 to date (Pres: William H. Clark 1893–Ap 12, 1928; Edward H. Clark Ap 13, 1928 to date). *Ed*: William H. Clark 1892–Ap 12, 1928; Edward H. Clark Ap 13, 1928 to date. *Pol*: Republican. *Format*: Four to thirty-two pages, varying sizes, 22″ x 28″, 18″ x 23″, 15″ x 22½″. *Price*: 10¢ per week, 3¢ per copy (1901); $7.50 per year, 15¢ per week (1919); $30.00 per year, 60¢ per week, 10¢ per copy (1969); $39.00 per year, 75¢ per week, 15¢ per copy delivered, $28.00 per year by mail (1970 to date). *Circ*: 3,000 (1892); 5,000 (1916); 5,400 (1934); 8,530 (1956); 8,924 (1957); 10,047 (1962); 11,000 (1967). *Comment*: Published from the *Standard* Building, corner of Main and Tompkins Sts. The running title was *Cortland Evening Standard*, Jl 6, 1892–?. In 1925 the *Standard* purchased the *Cincinnatus Times* (1898–1925) (q.v.). William H. Clark died March 12, 1928, but his name remained on the masthead until mid-April. Special editions: Woman's Edition, F 22, 1895, 16 pages; Industrial number, D 1895, 46 pages; Hudson-Fulton celebration number 1609–1909, S 25, 1909, 24 pages; Historical-Industrial edition, S 20, 1910, 72 pages; Old Home Week edition, Je 11, 1928, 96 pages; Cortland Fair Centennial edition, Ag 10, 1938, 48 pages; Cortland County Sesquicentennial, Jl 16, 1958, 16 pages. *Loc*: NCort: Jl 1, 1913 to date. NCortHi: Mr 8, 1892–D 31, 1966 (no. 1–no. 307). NCort/Mullen: D 1895 (Industrial no.); S 20, 1910 (Historical-Industrial edition); Je 11, 1928 (Old Home Week edition); S 18, 1967; Je 24, S 8, 1969. NCortSt: Mr 8, 1892 to date (no. 1 to date). NCortUC: microfilm Jl 1, 1913 to date. NHom: Mr 8, 1892–D 30, 1905 (no. 1–?).

CORTLAND STANDARD AND CORTLAND DAILY JOURNAL see *CORTLAND STANDARD*

CORTLAND STANDARD AND HOMER REPUBLICAN see *CORTLAND STANDARD*

CORTLAND STANDARD AND JOURNAL see *CORTLAND STANDARD*

THE CORTLAND TRIBUNE (w) Cortland. D 13, 1948–O 5, 1950// (1:1–2:58). *Pub*: Cortland Tribune Publishing Co., Inc. D 23, 1948–O 5, 1950 (Gerald Mayer, Pres. and Treas., John T. Ryan, Exec. Vice-Pres. and Sec., D 1948–Mr 2, 1950; Ralph L. Reeder, Pub., Mr 9–Ap 20, 1950; John Troy Gilman, Pub., Je 22–Jl 27, 1950). *Ed*: Gerald Mayer and John T. Ryan D 23, 1948–Mr 2, 1950; Harry A. Mullen Mr 9–Je 15, 1950; Robert D. Van Auken Je 22–O 5, 1950.

Pol: Independent. *Format*: Twelve to sixteen pages 17″ x 22½ ″. *Price*: $2.00 per year, $3.00 per year outside of central New York. *Comment*: Published from 33 North Main St., D 1948–S 15, 1949; then from 11 Orchard St. The first issue stated that it was published "in response to a growing need of our community" and that its goals were to uphold the American way of life, to improve educational facilities, to cultivate respect for religious institutions, to encourage legitimate business enterprises and to promote and encourage the cultural life of the community. *Loc*: NCort: microfilm D 23, 1948–O 5, 1950 (1:1–2:58). NCortHi: D 23, 1948–O 5, 1950 (1:1–2:58). NCortUC: microfilm D 23, 1948–O 5, 1950 (1:1–2:58). NIC/MMN: microfilm D 23, 1948–O 5, 1950 (1:1–2:58).

CORTLAND TRI-WEEKLY DEMOCRAT (tri-w) Cortland. ca. Jl 1875–?. Only one issue of this paper located. It is undoubtedly connected with the *Cortland Democrat* (1864 to date) (q.v.) and the *Cortland Evening Democrat* (q.v.). It is possible that the *Cortland Evening Democrat* could not get enough subscribers so that publication was decreased to three times per week. It was also published by the office of the *Cortland Democrat*. *Loc*: NCortHi: Jl 6, 1875 (no vol. or no.).

CORTLAND WEEKLY JOURNAL (w) Cortland Village. My 20, 1869–My 18, 1872 (1:1–?). *Pub and Ed*: William H. Livermore 1869–1872. *Pol*: Independent. *Format*: Four pages 22″ x 28″. *Price*: $2.00 per year in advance. *Comment*: Dates of publication taken from William H. Livermore, "Reminiscences," *Cortland Standard* supplement, May 3, 1883. This newspaper was the successor to the *Gazette and Banner* (q.v.). In 1872, Livermore sold it to Edward and Emma Molloy who continued publication until May 18, 1872 and then sold it to Wesley Hooker who consolidated the *Journal* with *The Cortland Standard* (q.v.). (Smith, *Cortland County*, p. 126.) *Loc*: NCort: D 2, 1869 (1:28). NCortHi: Ag 25, 1870 (2:14).

CORTLAND WEEKLY MUSEUM (w) Homer. 1819(?)–?. No issues located. Mentioned in Clarence S. Brigham, *History and Bibliography of American Newspapers, 1690–1820*, (Worcester, Mass.: American Antiquarian Society, 1947) p. 582.

DAILY INDEPENDENT (d) Marathon. Jl 19–21, 1877//. No issues located. Edgar L. Adams said he started the *Daily Independent* but had to discontinue it after three days because a railroad strike prevented the delivery of paper (*The Marathon Independent*, Jl 22, 1903).

THE ENTERPRISE (m?) Truxton. 1896(?)–? *Pub and Ed*: Enterprise Publishing Co. *Format*: Eight pages 11″ x 15″. *Price*: 25¢ per year. *Loc*: NCortHi: D 1903 (7:9).

FARMER'S JOURNAL (w?) Cortland. 1812–1813. No issues located. H. R. Bender and R. Washburne purchased the *Cortland Courier* (q.v.) from James Percival and changed its name to the

Farmer's Journal. "This firm paid more particular attention to the agricultural interests of the county, but evidently without attaining such a measure of success as to justify their continuance in the profession; so they sold to Dr. Jesse Searl, in the year 1813." (Smith, *Cortland County,* p. 120.)

THE FIRE BELL Cortland. 1883–? (1:1–?). Pub and Ed: Not listed. *Format*: Four pages 11¾ " x 18". *Circ*: 5,000. *Loc*: NCortHi: Ap 1, 1885 (3:1).

THE GAZETTE AND BANNER (w) Cortland. O 3, 1861–Ap 1869// (1:1–8:?). *Pub and Ed*: Charles Parley Cole 1861–1869. *Pol*: Union Republican. *Format*: Four to eight pages, varying sizes, 17¾ " x 22½ ", 18¼ " x 24", 13½ " x 19¼ ". *Price*: $1.50 to $2.00 per year. *Comment*: Motto: "Eternal Vigilance is the Price of Liberty." Charles Parley Cole died about April 1, 1869. After his death the newspaper "passed through the hands" of J. V. P. Gardner of Utica, his uncle, and was sold to W. H. Livermore who changed the name to *Cortland Weekly Journal* (q.v.). (Livermore, "Reminiscences.") By June, 1867 the newspaper was located at the "corner of Main and Court Streets, directly opposite Messenger Bank and adjoining the Messenger Hall Block." *Loc*: NCort: S 18, 1862 (1:50); F 20, 1869 (8:21). NCort/Heppel: My 8, 15, 1862 (1:32, 33); Jl 16, Ag 13, O 29, 1863 (2:41, 45; 3:4); Ja 14, Mr 24, 1864 (3:15, 25). NCortHi: D 12, 26, 1861 (1:11, 13); Ap 10, Ag 14, 28, S 18, O 2, D 18, 1862 (1:28, 45, 47, 50, 52; 2:11); Ja 1, Je 18–Jl 2, Ag 27, 1863 (2:13, 37–39, 47); My 11, Je 1–15, N 2, 1865 (4:32, 35–37; 5:5); S 27, 1866 (5:52); S 14, 21, N 16–30, 1867 (6:50, 51; 7:7–9); F 1, Mr 7, 1868 (7:18, 23). NHom: D 25, 1862 (2:12); Je 18, Jl 9, N 26, 1863 (2:37, 40; 3:8); Ja 31, 1867 (6:16). NIC/RHA: Je 14, 1867 (6:37).

THE GLOBE (m) Cortland. S–D 18, 1933// (1:[1]–3). *Pub and Ed*: Richard Ames and Robert Hitchcock S–N 1933; Richard Ames D 1933. *Pol*: Independent. *Format*: Eight pages 5" x 8½ ". *Price*: 3¢ per copy. *Comment*: In a personal interview Mr. Richard Ames stated that the newspaper was printed on a Kelsey hand press. Number one was not given an issue number and date since there was no thought of continuing the publication. However, he did number and date issues two and three. The paper was published at 9 Arthur Ave. *Loc*: NCortHi: S 1933 (1:[1]).

HOMER EAGLE (w) Homer. Ag 1835–My 10, 1836// (1:1–?). *Pub and Ed*: Albert L. Holmes and Carr S. Huntington. *Pol*: Republican. *Format*: Four pages. *Price*: $2.00 per year delivered, $1.75 per year at the office. *Comment*: On May 17, 1836 the *Eagle* was combined with the *Cortland Republican* and issued as the *Republican and Eagle* which was finally titled the *Cortland County Whig* (q.v.). *Loc*: NCortUC: microfilm D 1, 1835 (1:15). NHom: microfilm D 1, 1835 (1:15). NIC/MMN: microfilm D 1, 1835 (1:15).

HOMER HERALD (w) Cortland. Jl 7, 1871–ca. Ja 1872// No issues located. Published by William H. Livermore in the offices of the *Cortland Weekly Journal* (q.v.), "but devoted to the interests of the town of Homer." It was discontinued when Livermore sold both papers to Edward and Emma Molloy (Smith, *Cortland County,* p. 126).

THE HOMER INDEPENDENT (w) Homer. N 19, 1959–D 27, 1962// (1:1–4:7). *Pub*: Walter W. Grunfeld N 19, 1959–D 27, 1962. On Ja 11, 1962, the masthead changed to read "Published by the independent newspapers of Homer, Marathon and Tully. Walter W. Grunfeld, editor and publisher." *Ed*: Robert Haskell N 19, 1959–Ja 29, 1960; Walter W. Grunfeld F 5, 1960–D 27, 1962. *Pol*: Independent. *Format*: Six to eight pages 17" x 22". Special Christmas issue annually, twelve to sixteen pages 10¾" x 17¾". *Price*: Free (N 19–D 31, 1959); $3.00 per year, 10¢ per copy (1960–1962). *Circ*: 2,200. *Comment*: Published from 35 South Main St. from November 19, 1959 to July 28, 1961, then moved to 10 Main St. From 1959 to 1960 subtitled "All People Belong in a Small Town—They are Only Guests in a Large City"; changed to "A Community Institution Devoted to the People it Serves." In addition to annual Christmas and New Year Greetings editions, the following special editions of the paper appeared: a jubilee issue, May 31, 1960; a bowling edition during the week of October 27, 1960; the 91st anniversary of the birth of Marathon and the opening of the new newspaper shop, November 24, 1960. The newspaper has won several journalism awards for its contents and special editions. *Loc*: NCort: N 19, 1959–D 27, 1962 (1:1–4:7). NCortHi: N 19, 1959–D 27, 1962 (1:1–4:7). NIC/MMN: microfilm N 19, 1959–D 27, 1962 (1:1–4:7). NMara/Grunfeld: N 19, 1959–D 27, 1962 (1:1–4:7).

THE HOMER POST (w, semi-w, w) Homer. O 23, 1931–My 15, 1936// (1:1–6:20). *Pub*: Don Goddard O 23, 1931–Ag 5, 1932; Grant H. Ames and Don Goddard Ag 12–D 23, 1932; Don Goddard D 30, 1932–My 15, 1936. *Ed*: Don Goddard O 23, 1931–My 15, 1936. *Pol*: Republican. *Format*: Eight to twenty-four pages, varying sizes, 15¼" x 22", 12" x 18", 17" x 22". *Price*: $2.00 per year (O 1931–Ja 1933); $1.00 per year (Ap 21–28, 1933); 50¢ per year (My 5–O 26, 1933); $1.00 per year, 5¢ per copy (O 13, 1933–My 15, 1936). *Circ*: 3,000. *Comment*: Motto: "Dependability, Fairness, Service." The newspaper went through a number of subtitle changes. From Ap 28, 1933–Ap 20, 1934 and then again from S 7, 1934–My 15, 1936 it was called "Central New York's Weekly News Magazine"; Ap 27–My 1, 1934 "Central New York Bi-Weekly News Magazine"; from My 4–Ag 31, 1934 "Central New York's Semi-Weekly News Magazine." My 1–Ag 31, 1934 it was issued on a semi-weekly basis (Tuesday and Friday) and then was again issued as a weekly. Several addresses were listed: South Main St. Ja 22–Ap 22, 1932; 6 Wall St. Ap 29, 1932–F 10, 1933; Homer Town Hall from F 17, 1933–My 15, 1936. Note that the address at 6 Wall St. constituted a part of the space occupied by the *Homer Republican* from about 1880 to 1897. Charles H. Stevens, former editor and publisher of the *Homer Repub-*

lican (q.v.) wrote a local history column for the *Post* in 1931 and became its editorial counselor. *Loc*: NCort: microfilm O 23, 1931–My 15, 1936 (1:1–6:20). NCortHi: O 23, 1931–My 15, 1936 (1:1–6:20) also on microfilm. NHom: O 23, 1931–My 15, 1936 (1:1–6:20). NIC/MMN: microfilm O 23, 1931–My 15, 1936 (1:1–6:20).

HOMER REPUBLICAN (w) Homer. Ag 30, 1855–Mr 6, 1919// (1:1–64:39). *Title changes*: *Cortland County Republican* Ag 30, 1855–Ag 30, 1877; *The Homer Republican* S 6, 1877–Je 10, 1909; *Homer Republican* Je 17, 1909–Mr 6, 1919. *Pub*: Joseph R. Dixon and W. H. Case by 1855; Joseph R. Dixon 1855–1876; William O. Bunn Jl 28, 1876–Je 5, 1884; Charles H. Stevens and Charles H. Danes Je 12, 1884–N 29, 1917; Charles H. Stevens D 6, 1917–Mr 14, 1918, Charles H. Stevens and Son Mr 21, 1918–Mr 6, 1919. *Ed*: Joseph R. Dixon 1855–1876; William O. Bunn S 6, 1876–Je 5, 1884; Charles H. Stevens Je 12, 1884–Mr 6, 1919. *Pol*: Republican. *Format*: Four to eight pages, varying sizes, 18″ x 26″, 16″ x 22″, 18″ x 24″, 22″ x 27½″. *Price*: $1.50 per year in advance (1855–1865); $2.00 per year in advance, $2.50 per year delivered (1866–?); $2.00 per year in advance, 5¢ per copy (1879–?). *Circ*: 1,908 (1878). *Comment*: Motto: "An Independent Family Paper—Devoted to Freedom, Temperance, News of the Day, and the Intellectual and Social Improvement of the People." Motto dropped in the early 1870s. Published at 8–10 Sherman Block S 1855–Mr 1859; Mechanics Hall, third story, Main St., 1859–Jl 1876; Wall St., Bank Block, first floor, Jl 28, 1876–Jl 5, 1894; Union Building, Main St., Jl 12, 1894–Mr 6, 1919. In March, 1919 the *Homer Republican* merged with the *Cortland Standard* (q.v.) and was published as the *Cortland Standard and Homer Republican* until April 12, 1921. In 1882 William Bunn "associated George Fisher in the editorial management of the paper. . . ." (Smith, *Cortland County,* p. 122.) *Loc*: NCort: Ap 2, 1857 (2:32); Jl 9, 1891–Je 23, 1898 (37:1–43:52); Je 29, 1899–Mr 6, 1919 (45:1–64:39). NCortHi: My 29–Ag 14, 1856 (1:40–51); F 11, Ap 15, 1858 (3:25, 34); Jl 21, 1859 (4:48); [Ja 26, 1860–D 27, 1866 (5:23–12:20)]; [O 22, 1868–F 24, 1876 (14:11–21:31)]; Jl 9, 1891–Je 23, 1898 (37:1–43:52); Je 29, 1899–Mr 6, 1919 (45:1–64:39). NCortUC: microfilm [S 6, 1855–Je 19, 1856 (1:2–43)]; Mr 24, 1859 (4:31); [Mr 7, 1861–Je 11, 1868 (6:29–13:44)]; N 4, 1869 (15:13); S 1, 1870 (16:4); Mr 2, Je 8, D 7, 1871 (16:30, 44; 17:19); [Ja 15, 1874–Jl 2, 1891 (19:25–36:52)]; Je 30, 1898–Je 22, 1899 (44:1–52). NHom: S 6, 1855–Je 19, O 30, 1856 (1:2–43; 2:10); [Mr 24, 1859–Je 11, 1868 (4:31–13:44)]; [N 4, 1869–Ag 30, 1876 (15:13–23:6)]; S 6, 1877–Mr 6, 1919 (23:7–64:39). NIC/MMN: microfilm [S 6, 1855–Je 19, 1856 (1:2–43)]; Mr 24, 1859 (4:31); [Mr 7, 1861–Je 11, 1868 (6:29–13:44)]; N 4, 1869 (15:13); S 1, 1870 (16:4); Mr 2, Je 8, D 7, 1871 (16:30, 44; 17:19); [Ja 15, 1874–F 24, 1876 (19:25–21:31)]; Jl 28, 1876–Mr 6, 1919 (22:1–64:39). NIC/RHA: Ja 2, 1879 (24:24); F 12, Je 3, 1880 (25:30, 46).

THE HOMER TIMES (w) Homer. 1890–? (1:1–?). *Pub and Ed*: A. E. Marvin. *Format*: Eight pages 13″ x 20″. *Price*: $1.50 per year.

Comment: Published over G. H. DeVany's shoe store, 6 North Main St. *Loc*: NCortHi: N 7, 1890 (1:17); Mr 18, 1896 (2:36).

THE INDEPENDENT see *THE MARATHON INDEPENDENT*

THE INDEPENDENT REPUBLICAN Cortland. 1882(?). *Pol*: Republican. *Format*: Two pages 21½ " x 27¾ ". *Comment*: Motto: "Vote for Fair Caucuses and Honest Conventions! Vote to Wipe Out the Slavery of the Ring." *Loc*: NCortHi: 0 31, 1882 (no. vol. or issue no.).

THE INDEPENDENT VILLAGER (m, w) Marathon. My 27, 1961 to date. (1:1 to date). *Title changes*: *The 7-Valley Villager* My 27, 1961–Ap 19, 1971; *The Independent Villager* My 24, 1971 to date. *Pub and Ed*: Walter E. Grunfeld (Independent Newspapers of Marathon and Tully) My 27, 1961 to date. *Pol*: Independent with Democratic leanings. *Format*: Sixteen to thirty-two pages 11½ " x 17½ ". *Price*: Free (My 1961–Ap 1963); $2.00 per year (My 1963–Ap 1971); Free (My 1971 to date). *Circ*: 12,873. *Comment*: Published at 10 East Main St. ". . . No other media published in central New York now reaches everyone. The *Villager* does with the exception of the city of Cortland. We intend to be primarily a rural publication. . . . Therefore, this paper is not circulated in the city of Cortland." (May 27, 1961). The *Villager* was last issued as a monthly Ap 19, 1971 (7:23), and became a weekly My 24, 1971. The issue numbers were continued in sequence, but the volume numbers were dropped. *Loc*: NCort: My 27, 1961 to date (1:1 to date). NCortHi: My 27, 1961–Jl 1963 (1:1–3:3); S 1963–N 1964 (3:5–4:7); [Ja 1965 to date (4:9 to date)]. NMara/Grunfeld: My 27, 1961 to date (1:1 to date).

THE JUDGE (irr) Cortland. ca. 1883. *Pol*: Independent. *Format*: Four pages 11" x 14". *Comment*: An independent political information sheet urging voters to remove judicial office from politics. *Loc*: NCortHi: O 31, 1883 (no. vol. or no.).

THE LIBERTY HERALD Cortland. 1846(?). No issues located. Anti-slavery newspaper published by James W. Eeles and Nathaniel Goodwin. Later published by Samuel R. Ward, Negro orator and preacher, who also published *The True American and Religious Examiner* (q.v.). (Smith, *Cortland County*, p. 132.)

THE McGRAWVILLE ADVERTISER. McGrawville. Jl 26, 1866–? (1:1–?). No issues located. Mentioned in Edgar L. Welch, *"Grip's" Historical Souvenir of Cortland* (Syracuse: Standard Press, 1899), p. 224.

McGRAWVILLE EXPRESS see *CORTLAND COUNTY EXPRESS*

McGRAWVILLE SENTINEL see *CORTLAND COUNTY SENTINEL*

THE MARATHON INDEPENDENT (w) Marathon. Jl 19, 1870 to date (1:1 to date). *Pub*: Wallace Kelley Jl 19, 1870–1876; Charles

A. Brooks and Andrew H. Day 1876–1878; Charles A. Brooks and Edgar Lyman Adams N 6, 1878–1880; Edgar L. Adams 1880–Ja 26, 1881; Charles A. Brooks and Fred H. Gee F 2–Mr 2, 1881; Edgar L. Adams and Fred H. Gee Mr 9–O 5, 1881; Edgar L. Adams O 12, 1881–1940; Ray C. Walter ca. 1940–1946; Bruce E. and George S. Whitehead 1946–Jl 14, 1955; Walter W. Grunfeld Jl 21, 1955 to date. *Ed*: Eliakin Weld; Wallace Kelley 1870–1876; Edgar L. Adams 1876– Ja 26, 1881; Charles A. Brooks and Fred H. Gee F 2–Mr 2, 1881; Edgar L. Adams Mr 9, 1881–1940; Ray C. Walter 1940–1946; Bruce E. and George S. Whitehead 1946–1947; Bruce E. Whitehead Ap 10, 1947–Jl 14, 1955; Walter W. Grunfeld Jl 21, 1955 to date. *Pol*: Independent. *Format*: Four to sixteen pages, varying sizes, 14½ " x 21", 17¼ " x 23¾ ", 11½ " x 16¼ ". *Price*: $1.50 per year (1875); $5.00 per year in advance in locality, $6.00 per year outside (1970). *Comment*: Motto: "A home paper devoted to local news." From 1870 to 1872 published over G. L. Swift's store; the Smith block My 1872–N 1878; then the Peck block N 6, 1878; the Mantanye block O 12, 1881. It is presently published at 10 East Main St. *Loc*: NCortHi: Jl 11, 1871 (1:52); O 7, 1873 (4:13); F 3, 1874 (4:30); My 24, 31, S 6, 20, 1876 (6:46, 47; 7:9, 11); N 6, 1878 (9:18); My 7, 14, 1879 (9:44, 45); Jl 14, 21, 1880 (11:2, 3); O 5, 12, 1881 (12:14, 15); Ap 7, 1886 (16:41); My 6, 1903 (33:42); Ja 8, 1908 (38:25); Jl 24, 1958 (Sesquicentennial 88:45); O 22, 1959 (90:6); Ag 31, 1961) (Centennial Issue: Marathon 91:52). NHom: D 22, 1875 (6:24). NIC/MMN: My 16, 1871 (1:44); Mr 3, S 15, D 29, 1880 (10:35; 11:11, 26); N 16, 1881 (12:20); O 24, 1883 (14:17); S 1, 1886 (17:10); Ja 5, 1887 (17:28); D 19, 1900 (31:22); N 5, 1902 (33:16); Jl 22, 1903 (34:1). NIC/RHA: [Ja 7, 1891–S 14, 1892 (21:28–23:10)]. NMara: F 7, 1871 (1:30); Ja 19, 1876 (6:28); F 27, Ap 3, 1878 (8:34, 39); My 26, 1880 (10:47); Ja 12, S 21, 28, 1881 (11:28; 12:12, 13); Jl 2, 1890 (21:1); S 10, 1902; (33:8); My 12, 1903 (33:43); Mr 16, O 5, 1921 (51:35; 52:12); F 22, 1922 (52:32); Jl 1, 1931 (61:52); [Ap 9, 1941–Jl 3, 1952 (71:38–82:47)]; [Mr 15, 1956–Ja 24, 1963 (86:26–93:21)]. NMara/Grunfeld: Jl 19, 1870–Jl 8, 1873 (1:1–3:52); Je 2, 1874 (4:47); Ja 5, 1881–D 26, 1888 (11:27–19:26); My 1, 1889 (19:44); Mr 12, 1902 (32:34); Ja 3, 1952 to date. NSpnHi: D 14, 1898.

THE MARATHON LEADER (w) Marathon. F 12, 1863–? (1:1–?). *Title changes*: *The Marathon Mirror* 1863–Mr 13, 1866; *The Marathon Leader* Mr 20, 1866–? *Pub and Ed*: G. A. Dodge 1863–?; Eliakim S. Weld 1864; B. F. Alleger 1865; P. D. and C. A. Van Vradenburg by 1866–? *Pol*: Independent. *Format*: Four pages, varying sizes, 12" x 14", 13" x 19", 16" x 21¾". *Price*: $1.25 per year in advance. *Comment*: Motto: "An Advocate of Truth, Temperance, Morality, Religion and Universal Liberty." The title was changed to *The Marathon Leader* on the grounds that the *"Leader"* was easier to say than the *"Mirror."* Ornamental lettering was substituted for the plain lettering of the *Mirror*. P. D. and C. A. Van Vradenburg "abandoned the paper" about 1866. In 1868 C. D. Smith revived it as *The Marathon News* (q.v.), and published it about a year. (Smith, *Cortland County*, p. 130.) *Loc*: NCortHi: F 26, 1863 (1:3); N 12, D 3, 24, 1864 (2:40, 43, 46); Je 17, Jl 1, 15, 1865 (3:18, 20, 21); Ja 23, F 6, Mr 6, 20–Ap 3, Ag 14, N 6, D 4, 18, 25, 1866 (3:47, 49; 4:1, 3–5, 23, 37, 41, 43, 44); Ja 1, 22, Ap 15, Je 18, 1867 (4:45, 48; 5:8, 17). NMara/ Grunfeld: Jl 2, S 24, 1863 (1:21, 33); Ap 22, 1865 (3:10); My 1, 8, 29, Ag 28, 1866 (4:8, 10, 13, 25).

THE MARATHON MIRROR see *THE MARATHON LEADER*

THE MARATHON NEWS (w) Cortland. 1868–1899//(?). *Title changes*: *The Marathon Weekly News* 1868(?)–1869; *The Marathon News* 1869–? *Pub and Ed*: C. Dwight Smith 1868(?)–?. *Pol*: Independent. *Format*: Four pages 15″ x 22″. *Price*: $1.25 per year in advance. *Comment*: The numbering of the *Marathon News* in 1869 appears to be a continuation of *The Marathon Leader* (q.v.). C. Dwight Smith revived that paper, changed the title, conducted it about a year and then "the establishment was purchased by Wallace Kelley who issued the first number of the [*Marathon*] *Independent* [q.v.]." (Smith, *Cortland County*, p. 130.) *Loc*: NCortHi: O 6, 1868 (6:19); Je 10, Ag 12, D 28, 1869 (7:1, 10, 30). NMara: Ja 14, 1869 (6:33); Jl 22, 1869 (7:7).

MARATHON TELEGRAPH (m) Marathon. My 1856–? (1:1–?). *Pub and Ed*: George Lucien Swift 1856–1857. *Format*: Two to four pages, varying sizes, 9″ x 11¾″, 10½″ x 15½″. *Price*: 25¢ per year. *Circ*: 300–400 (1856); 1,500 (1857). *Comment*: First newspaper published in Marathon village. It may have lasted for a year or two only. Although established by Mr. Swift to advertise his business, it had many items of local interest. *Loc*: NCortHi: Jl, O, D 1856 (1:3, 6, 7); My 1857 (1:12). NIC/RHA: Ap 1857 (1:11).

THE MARATHON WEEKLY NEWS see *THE MARATHON NEWS*

THE MONITOR (w) Cortland. Ag 4, 1886–? (1:1–?). *Pub*: The Monitor Printing Co. *Ed*: Rev. William Reddy by F 29, 1887–?; Levi S. Lewis by 1888–? *Pol*: Prohibition. *Format*: Four to eight pages, varying sizes, 22½″ x 28″, 15″ x 22″. *Price*: $1.50 per year, 5¢ per copy. *Comment*: Motto: "The extermination of the liquor traffic shall continue to be made an issue in national politics until the traffic is outlawed by the federal government." Published at 20 Port Watson St. *Loc*: NCort: N 1, 1888 (no. 118). NCortHi: Ag 4, 18, O 20, 1886 (1:1, 2, 11); F 29, Je 15, Ag 3, N 2, 1887 (1:27, 45, 52; 2:13); Ag 30, N 1, 1888 (nos. 109, 118); S 26, 1889 (no. 165). NHom: S 5, 1889 (no. 162).

THE MORNING STAR McGrawville. ca 1848–1850. No issues located. Mentioned in Hamilton Child, *Gazetteer and Business Directory of Cortland County, N.Y. for 1869*, p. 67 and Smith, *Cortland County*, p. 132. The newspaper was edited by E. J. Burnham (*Cortland County Express*, O 11, 1849).

THE NEW CORTLANDER (w?) Cortland. S 1, 1933–? (1:1–?). *Pub*: John Moore, Son and Co. *Ed*: John Moore. *Pol*: Independent. *Format*: Eight pages 12″ x 17½″. *Price*: $2.00 per year in advance. *Comment*: Motto: "Newest and only politically independent newspaper in Cortland County." Published at 6 Main St. *Loc*: NHom: S 1, 1933 (1:1).

OTSELIC VALLEY REGISTER (w) Pitcher [Chenango County], Cincinnatus. 1874–1890(?) (1:1–?). *Pub and Ed*: John Henry Graves ca. 1874–1878(?); Will O. Greene by S 1881–?; Will Bennett by Je 1888–? *Pol*: Independent. *Format*: Four pages, varying sizes, 15½″ x 22½″, 17½″ x 23½″. *Price*: $1.50 per year in advance. *Circ*: 500. *Comment*: Motto: "The General Good." "This paper was established at Pitcher . . . on the 8th of April, 1874, by J. E. Lyons, who, after publishing it about four months, suddenly disappeared and has never since been heard from. The paper was then taken in hand by a stock company and was conducted by Eneas Fenton for a period of about four months, and then disposed of to John Henry Graves [who] removed the establishment to Cincinnatus, where he shortly afterward sold it to D. V. Joyner. He enlarged the sheet . . . and on the 3d day of November, 1879, sold out to Will O. Greene, who immediately began making improvements both in the paper and the methods of carrying on the business. . . ." (Smith, *Cortland County*, p. 131.) The *Register* was first published in Cincinnatus on My 23, 1877. Will Bennett, who purchased the paper from Greene in 1886, located the newspaper office in the Post Office block, then in the old Peck Tailor shop, and moved the paper to Fair Haven, N. Y. in 1890. (*The Homer Post*, Mr 31, 1933.) *Loc*: NCortHi: Je 13, 20, Ag 22, 1888 (15:11, 12, 21); Mr 13, 1889 (15:50). NIC/MMN: My 23, 1877 (4:7). NNoHi: Ja 16, 1878 (4:40); S 28, 1881 (8:25).

PEOPLE'S JOURNAL (w) Marathon. Ja 10, 1861–? (1:1–?). *Pub and Ed*: John B. Beden and Eliakim S. Weld Ja 10, 1861–?; Eliakim S. Weld My 16, 1861–Ja 16, 1862; Eliakim S. Weld and George A. Chase Ja 23, 1862–? *Pol*: Independent. *Format*: Four pages, varying sizes, 18½″ x 24″, 15″ x 22″. *Price*: $1.00 per year. *Comment*: "The first printing office in Marathon was started by the late John B. Beden, who started the *Tioughniogian* and a few weeks later in conjunction with E. S. Weld, who was then principal of the Academy, changed it to the first number of the *People's Journal*. . . ." (Edgar L. Welch, *Grip's Historical Souvenir of Marathon* [Fayetteville: Bulletin Publishing Co., 1901], p. 81.) *Loc*: NCortHi: Ja 10, My 16, 1861 (1:1, 17). NIC/MMN: Ja 16, 1862 (1:52). NMara: Ja 23, 1862 (2:1).

POLITICAL FREE PRESS Homer. 1830–ca. Mr 1831// No issues located. Mentioned in Goodwin, "Impressions," p. 2.

THE PROTESTANT SENTINEL Homer. 1831–1833//(?). No issues located. Published by John Maxon. (Childe, *Gazetteer*, p. 67.)

REASON'S APPEAL Cortland. ca 1906// *Pub*: *Cortland Democrat*. *Pol*: Democratic and Independence League. *Format*: Four pages

12½ " x 18½ ". *Comment*: Campaign newspaper published from 12 Central Ave. *Loc*: NCortHi: One undated issue (no vol. or no.).

THE RECORD (irr) Cortland. O 22, 1958–? (1:1–?). *Pub*: Appears to be the Cortland County Democratic Committee. *Pol*: Democrat. *Format*: Four pages 15" x 21¾". *Comment*: Motto: "Facts not generally printed in Cortland." Published "every little while." *Loc*: NCortHi: O 22, 1958 (1:1).

REPUBLICAN see *CORTLAND COUNTY WHIG* and *HOMER REPUBLICAN*

REPUBLICAN AND EAGLE see *CORTLAND COUNTY WHIG*

THE REPUBLICAN BANNER (w) Cortland. S 1, 1858–S 1861// (1:1–4:?). *Pub*: Edward D. Van Slyck and P. H. Bateson S 1, 1858–Mr 16, 1859; Edward D. Van Slyck and S. G. Hitchcock Mr 23, 1859–Je 1860; Edward D. Van Slyck Je 20, 1860–Ap 10, 1861; Edward D. Van Slyck and A. M. Ford Ap 17, 1861–S 1861. *Ed*: Edward D. Van Slyck S 1, 1858–S 1861. *Pol*: Republican, Temperance. "We shall not allow the great question of Temperance to rest until the hydra-headed monster, Intemperance, shall be forever banished from our land." (S 1, 1858) *Format*: Four pages, varying sizes, 18½ " x 23¾ ", 19" x 25¼ ". *Price*: $1.00 per year. *Comment*: S 1, 1858–F 23, 1859 published in unfurnished room in Van Slyck's dwelling on Greenbush St., one door north of Railroad St. near the depot; then moved to an office in Barnard's block opposite the Cortland House on Main St. The newspaper combined with the *Cortland Gazette* (q.v.) to become *The Gazette and Banner* in 1861. *Loc*: NCort: S 1, 1858–S 18, 1861 (1:1–4:4). NHom: S 7, 1859 (2:2); Jl 24, 1861 (3:48).

THE SCORPION Solon. No issues located. An anonymous letter dated April 12, 1951 (photocopy in Cortland County Historical Society) says, "You asked about the old . . . papers, the names of them, my father and Harve Stone printed for the edification of the old Solonites. I imagine they had new titles with each edition. I have two of them, one is called *The Solon Bugle* and the other *The Scorpion*. As I've told you they are printed by hand and with illustrations. They are about falling to pieces, they are so worn and very tender. The *Bugle* was printed Jan. 20, 1849–*The Scorpion*, Feb. 20, 1852. . . ."

THE 7-VALLEY VILLAGER see *THE INDEPENDENT VILLAGER*

THE SOLON BUGLE see *THE SCORPION*

SOUTH CORTLAND LUMINARY AND REFORMED METHODIST INTELLIGENCER (w) South Cortland. Jl 18, 1837–? (1:1–?). *Pub*: Publishing Committee of the New York and New York Western Conference of the Reformed Methodist Church (C. Whiting, O. F. Brewer, I. Ketchum *et al.*). *Ed*: Wesley Bailey. *Format*: Four to eight pages, varying sizes, 10" x 14⅞ ", 14" x 19". *Price*: $1.50 per year in advance, otherwise $2.00. *Comment*: Moved to Fayetteville, Onondaga

County, by Wesley Bailey in 1839 where it was called the *Fayetteville Luminary*. *Loc*: NCooHi: Jl 18, 1837–F 28, 1839 (1:1–2:32).

THE SPECTATOR (w) Virgil Village. Je 10, 1833–? (1:1–1:9). *Pub and Ed*: W. Woodard. *Format*: Four pages 8½" x 9½". *Comment*: This was a manuscript newspaper. "Persevering to the last, we had no *press*, no *type;* but by procuring foolscap paper to be headed with the printed words in Roman capitals, "The Spectator" we weekly issued our closely written columns to an admiring public; and imitating the great essayist Addison, in the style of our articles and in the manners we reformed, as well as in our paper's name, for three long years we continued the faithful monitors of the public through the medium of the *press*, composed of the fists of Frank, myself, Hyde, and other worthy contributors." (W. O. Reynolds, in *Festal Gathering of the Early Settlers and Present Inhabitants of Virgil. . . . August 1853* [Dryden, N. Y.: A. M. Ford, 1878], p. 50.) *Loc*: NCortHi: Je 10–Ag 5, 1833 (1:1–9).

STANDARD AND JOURNAL, JUNIOR (irr) Cortland. Ap 21, 1874–? (1:1–?). *Pub*: Wesley Hooker. *Pol*: Republican. *Format*: Four pages, varying sizes, 5¾" x 9", 8¼" x 12". *Comment*: Published by the *Cortland Standard*. *Loc*: NCortSt: Ap 21, My 5, 1874 (1:1, 2).

THE SUBSOILER (irr) Homer. Ag 1862–? (1:1–?). *Pub and Ed*: Burnham and Pierce. *Format*: Four pages 9" x 13¼". *Comment*: Devoted primarily to agricultural news. *Loc*: NCortHi: Ag 1862 (1:1).

THE TELEPHONE (m?) McGrawville. F 1888–? (1:1–?). *Pub and Ed*: E. W. Hayes. *Format*: Four pages 13" x 20". *Price*: 25¢ per year. *Comment*: The only issue located is a sample copy. *Loc*: NCortHi: F 1888 (1:1).

TIOUGHNIOGIAN (w?) Marathon. ca. 1861//. No issues located. See "Comment" under *People's Journal*.

TOWN AND COUNTRY: Arctic Series Cortland. *Pub and Ed*: Squires and Co., Grocers, Dealers in Salt and Seed. *Format*: Four pages 9½" x 12½". *Price*: Free. *Comment*: Published at 23 South Main St. Only one issue has been located. *Loc*: NCortHi: 1882 (v. 14).

TOWN AND COUNTRY PENNYSAVER (w) Cincinnatus. 1955–? (1:1–?). *Pub and Ed*: Les Carr. *Format*: Twenty-six to thirty-two pages 8½" x 11". *Comment*: Motto: "A Free Newspaper, dedicated to Rural readers of Central New York." Published at West Main St. Although devoted primarily to advertising, it contained news items of local interest. *Loc*: NCortHi: O 27, 1960 (6:41); Ag 3–N 16, 1961 (7:30–44).

THE TOWN MEETING (m) Homer. *Pol*: Prohibition. *Format*: Four pages 7½" x 10½". *Price*: Free. *Comment*: No volume number listed on the only issue located. *Loc*: NCort F 1882.

TRI-COUNTY PENNYSAVER (w) Homer. S 15, 1969–? (1:1–?). *Pub and Ed*: Robert and Carol Sutton. *Format*: Sixteen pages, varying sizes, 8″ x 12″, 7¼″ x 10¼″. *Comment*: Primarily devoted to advertising but with some items of local interest. *Loc*: NCortHi: S 29–O 14, 1969 (1:3–5).

THE TRUE AMERICAN see *THE TRUE AMERICAN AND RELIGIOUS EXAMINER*

THE TRUE AMERICAN AND RELIGIOUS EXAMINER (w) Cortland. F 1845–? (1:1–?). *Title changes*: *The True American* by D 24, 1845–?; *The True American and Religious Examiner* by Mr 8, 1848–? *Pub and Ed*: Eeles and Goodwin by D 1845–?; Samuel R. Ward by Mr 1848–? *Pol*: Liberty Party, Anti-Slavery, Temperance. *Format*: Four pages 13½″ x 19½″. *Price*: $1.00 per year in advance, $1.25 per year after six months, otherwise $1.50 per year. *Comment*: Published over the store of H. C. Goodrich (1845). *The True American* was founded on February 5, 1845 by James W. Eeles and Nathaniel Goodwin. Stedman and Clisbe later published the paper from November 25, 1846–? (Robert E. Stilwell, *Records: Notebooks* [in Cortland County Historical Society], v. 9.) Samuel R. Ward published the paper from about August 1847 to August 1848 and the paper was suspended on August 28, 1848 (unpublished research of Catherine Hanchett, 6 Isabel Dr., Cortland). *Loc*: NHom: D 24, 1845 (1:47). NSyU: Mr 8, 1848 (4:6).

THE TRUE REFORMER (bi-w) Scott. N 3, 1869–? (1:1–?). *Pub and Ed*: James E. N. Backus 1869–? *Pol*: Temperance. *Format*: Four pages 16½″ x 22″. *Price*: $2.00 per year in advance delivered, $1.50 per year in advance by mail or at the office. *Comment*: Motto: "The True Reformer aims to remove all Influences which obstruct harmonious Human Growth." *Loc*: NCortHi: N 3, 1869 (1:1); S 21, 1870 (1:24).

THE TRUXTON COURIER (w) Truxton. Ap 1, 1885–? (1:1–?). *Pub and Ed*: Burr T. Burlingham and Elmer Frank Norcott Ap 1– My 13, 1885; Elmer Frank Norcott My 27, 1885–? *Format*: Four pages, varying sizes, 15″ x 22″, 11″ x 16″. *Price*: $1.00 per year. *Comment*: The editor initially stated, "We intend to publish a live, newsy, clean and sensible paper, devoted to the moral as well as business interests of town, county, state and nation." By August 26, 1885 the newspaper had to be diminished in size for "The *Courier* has met many hardships and trials during its short career and it has been with difficulty that the editor has kept the little craft afloat during that time . . . . In the future it will be entirely made up from local news and matter of home interest . . . ." *Loc*: NCortHi: Ap 1, 8, 22–My 13, 27, Je 7, Ag 26, S 9, 1885 (1:1, 2, 4–7, 9, 12, 18, 20).

THE VILLAGE MUSEUM (w) Cortland Village. O 9, 1820–? (1:1–?). *Pub*: T. J. Sutherland and D. Hills by O 16, 1820–? *Ed*: Genius and Co. by O 16, 1820–? *Format*: Four pages 7″ x 10¼″.

Price: 50¢ for twelve numbers. *Loc*: NCortHi: O 16–N 20, 1820 (1:2–6).

THE VILLAGE REPUBLICAN Cortland. F 1898–? (1:1–?). *Pub and Ed*: Republican Village Committee. *Pol*: Republican. *Format*: Four pages 11″ x 14″. *Loc*: NCortHi: Mr 5, 1898 (1:2).

THE WESTERN COURIER (w) Homer, Cortland. O 1820–? (1:1–?). *Pub and Ed*: Elijah J. Roberts and D. G. Hull. *Pol*: Republican. *Format*: Four pages 12½″ x 20¼″. *Price*: $2.00 per year to village and mail subscribers. *Comment*: Published nearly opposite the Presbyterian Meeting House in Homer Village. "After a very short time this establishment was removed to Cortland, and then began a wordy battle more bitter and persistant than the former one . . . between the new candidate for political fame and the *Republican* [*Cortland Republican* (q.v.)] . . . . *The Western Courier* was conducted as such until 1824, when its name was changed to the *Cortland Journal* (q.v.)." Loc: NCort/Mullen: Mr 6, 1821 (1:20).

THE ADVERTISER Hancock. No issues located. First issued January 9, 1901. (*Deposit Courier,* Ja 10, 1901.)

THE ANDES RECORDER (w) Andes. D 5, 1867–1892// (1:1–?). *Title changes*: *The Recorder* D 5, 1867–?; *The Andes Recorder* by 1880. *Pub*: A. D. Hitchcock D 5, 1867–Ja 9, 1868; A. D. Hitchcock and Bryson Bruce Ja 16, 1868–Jl 9, 1868; Bryson Bruce Jl 16, 1868–?; Frank G. Barkley by 1880–?; William Clark by 1881. *Pol*: Republican. *Format*: Four pages 13″ x 19″. *Price*: $1.00 per year in advance (1867–?). *Comment*: Motto: "Independent in all things—Neutral in nothing. 'Let every man be fully persuaded in his own mind' " 1867–? Published on Main St. over B. Conner's store 1867–?; by 1873 over Joshua K. Hood's store; in the *Recorder* Building one door below the First National Bank, Main St. by 1880. Editorials in the first six numbers were by Rev. James Bruce, then by Bryson Bruce. In August, 1871, the paper was sold to Rev. W. W. Shaw and F. G. Barkley, as Bruce became editor of the *Binghamton Daily Republican*. In September, 1872, Mr. Barkley became sole proprietor, and in 1877 A. S. Robinson was admitted as partner, and was connected with the paper until

Newspaper press room, early twentieth century. From the Ward Collection, New York State Historical Association, Cooperstown.

April, 1879. (*History of Delaware County, N. Y.: With Illustrations, Biographical Sketches and Portraits of Some Pioneers and Prominent Residents* [New York: W. W. Munsell & Co., 1880], p. 113.) The newspaper was moved to Stamford in April, 1892 by William Clark and issued as the *Stamford Recorder* (q.v.) (David Murray, ed., *Delaware County, New York: History of the Century, 1797–1897* [Delhi, N. Y.: William Clark, 1898], pp. 562, 602). No connecting issues have been located, but the numbering of the *Stamford Recorder* confirms the connection to the Andes paper. *Loc*: NAnd: D 5, 1867–N 26, 1868 (1:1–52). NCooHi: D 5, 1867–N 26, 1868 (1:1–52). NIC/RHA: S 23, 1880 (13:41).

THE ANDES RECORDER (w) Andes. April 21, 1892–1939//(?) (1:1–?). *Pub*: The Recorder Co. 1892–?; S. F. Adee and Lawson ?–F 1894; Miller and Crawford Mr 2, 1894–My 13, 1898 (Eds. and Props.); Thomas W. Miller My 20, 1898–1939(?). *Format*: Four pages 15″ x 21¼″. *Price*: $1.00 per year in advance, 3¢ per copy (1892). *Comment*: Published in the Murray Building. The paper was Republican, sold for $1.50 per year, and had a circulation of 800 in 1910 and 750 from 1914 to 1939. (*Ayer Directory of Publications* [Philadelphia, 1880 to date].) *Loc*: NCooHi: [Ap 28, 1892–S 2, 1938 (1:2–47:12)]. NIC/RHA: Je 10, 1892 (1:8).

ARENA ENTERPRISE Arena. 1889–ca. 1891. No issues located. Started in 1889 by H. D. Ellsworth, and published for about three years. (Murray, *Delaware County*, p. 603.) The village of Arena was sold at auction and the region flooded by the Pepacton reservoir in 1954 (*Catskill Mountain News*, Ag 15, 1963).

BLOOMVILLE MIRROR see *MIRROR-RECORDER*

CATSKILL MOUNTAIN NEWS (w) Margaretville. 1894 to date (1:1 to date). *Title changes*: *Margaretville Messenger* 1894–Je 1902; *Catskill Mountain News (and Margaretville Messenger)* Jl3–S 11, 1902; *Catskill Mountain News* S 18, 1902 to date. *Pub*: W. H. Eells Jl 3, 1902–Ap 29, 1904; Clarke Alair Sanford My 6, 1904–D 7, 1934; Sanford Chevrolet, Inc. D 14, 1934–Mr 31, 1939; Clarke Alair Sanford Ap 7, 1939–O 23, 1957; Clarke Alair and Roswell R. Sanford O 30, 1957–My 1964 (Clarke Alair Sanford died My 15, 1964); Catskill Mountain Publishing Corporation (Roswell R. Sanford, Pres. and Pub.) 1964 to date. *Ed*: W. H. Eells Jl 3, 1902–Ap 29, 1904; Clarke Alair Sanford My 6, 1904–F 14, 1919; Charles P. Elam F 21, 1919–Ja 20, 1922; James Lull Mr 24, 1922–Ja 19, 1923; M. B. Gilbert Ja 4, 1924–F 15, 1924; Le Roy Palmer N 7, 1924–Mr 12, 1926; Rowland A. Hill Ap 7, 1939–N 7, 1963; Alton M. Weiss Ap 2, 1970 to date. *Pol*: Republican. *Format*: Four to twelve pages, varying sizes, 17¼″ x 23¾″, 11½″ x 16¼″, 13″ x 18″, 17½″ x 22″. *Price*: $1.00 per year in advance (Jl 3, 1902–D 1919), 5¢ per copy, then 3¢ per copy (1903–1914); $1.50 per year in advance, 5¢ per copy (Ja 1, 1920–1943); $2.00 per year, $1.50 per year in the county, 5¢ per copy (1944–1950); $3.00 per year, 7¢ per copy (S 1, 1950–S 9, 1960); $4.00 per year, 10¢ per copy (S 16, 1960–Mr 25, 1965); $5.00 per year, 10¢ per copy (Ap 1, 1965–My 30, 1968); $6.00 per year 10¢ per copy (Je 6, 1968–F 11, 1971); $7.50 per year, 15¢ per copy (F 18, 1971 to date). *Circ*: 399 (Jl 3, 1902); 975 (1903); 1,100 (1904). *Comment*: The *Margaretville Messenger* was established in 1894, "owned by a stock company, with John Grant as editor and Dr. J. W. Telford as assistant." (Murray, *Delaware County*, p. 513.) It was sold to W. E. Eells in 1902. He renamed it the *Catskill Mountain News* and published it until his death in 1904. The *News* later purchased *The Utilitarian* and, in December 1927, altered the *News'* numbering and date of establishment (1863) to reflect the history of the earlier paper. The paper's numbering was erratic in 1913 and there were no volume or issue numbers from 1914 through 1919. The paper contains primarily local news of Margaretville and the surrounding communities of Andes, Fleischmanns, Pleasant Valley, Dunraven, Roxbury, Kelly Corners and others. "The plant was located in rooms over the Peoples National Bank. When the present Buick garage was erected in 1912–13 the plant was moved to the new location and larger Linotype added. When the garage business drove the *News* out of that building, it was moved to the street floor of the Masonic building. . . . A third move for the newspaper plant brought it to the Galli-Curci theatre, from where it is today published." (*Catskill Mountain News,* Ag 15, 1963.) The *News* is currently published from its own plant on Main St. *Loc*: NMargC: Jl 3, 1902–D 26, 1919 (8:30 whole no. 393–no vol. or no.); Ap 1, 1922–D 26, 1924 (26:9 whole no. 1361 [*sic*]–30:45 whole no. 1253); Ja 1, 1926 to date (30:46 whole no. 1306 to date).

CHARLOTTE VALLEY NEWS (w) East Davenport. D 27, 1877–? (1:1–?). *Pub and Ed*: Marcus M. Multer. *Price*: $1.00 per year in advance. *Comment*: "Near the close of the year 1877 Marcus M. Multer started the *Charlotte Valley News* . . . in the village of Davenport. In 1879 Edward O'Connor bought it and established it in town." (*History of Delaware*, p. 146.) *Loc*: NCooHi D 27, 1877–Ag 29, 1878 (1:1–36).

THE CHRONICLE-TIMES (w) Walton. 1901–1916//(?). No issues located. "The *Chronicle* and *Times* of Walton have combined forces and will be *The Chronicle-Times*." (*The Deposit Courier,* My 30, 1901.) The closing date is from Winifred Gregory, ed., *American Newspapers, 1821–1936* (New York: Wilson, 1937) p. 496.

THE CHURCH REVIEW Delhi. 1893//. No issues located. "Published . . . for nine months . . . by Adee & Lawson." (Murray, *Delaware County*, p. 603.)

THE CYCLONE see *THE PEOPLE'S PRESS*

DAILY DESPATCH (d) Sidney. 1894//. No issues located. Published by the Wier Brothers (Murray, *Delaware County*, p. 602).

THE DAILY MIRROR (d) Stamford. O 22–N 1, 1902//(?) (1:1–6). *Pub and Ed*: Clifford Champion. *Pol*: Democrat. *Format*: Two to four pages 11½ " x 18". *Comment*: Published as a campaign paper by Clifford Champion running as an anti-trust candidate. The first editorial states, *"The Daily Mirror* stands for honesty, decency and true Democracy. It is edited and printed and distributed in my own interests as a Democratic candidate of the People for Congress in the 24th Congressional District. . . ." *Loc*: NSt: O 22–N 1, 1902 (1:1–6).

THE DAILY REPORTER see *THE REPORTER*

DELAWARE CHIEF (w) Hobart. ca. 1867. No issues located. Published by George T. Foote (Murray, *Delaware County,* p. 602; *History of Delaware,* p. 298).

DELAWARE COUNTY DAIRYMAN (w) Franklin. Je 30, 1868– Mr 7, 1952// (1:1–no. vol. or no.). *Pub and Ed*: Joseph Eveland & Son by 1905–?; S. B. D. Belden by 1931–?; Jesse Palmeter by 1946– 1952. *Pol*: Republican. *Format*: Four to eight pages 15″ x 22″. *Price*: $1.00 per year (1905–?); $1.50 per year in Delaware and Chenango counties, $1.25 per year elsewhere (by 1919–?); $2.00 per year (by 1946–1952). *Comment*: The original title of the newspaper was the *Franklin Register;* the title was changed to the *Delaware County Dairyman* in 1883 (Murray, *Delaware County,* p. 602). "The *Franklin Register* was founded by Albert D. Hitchcock and Theodore Smith, June 30th 1868. It was a four page journal, 22 by 32 inches, and was filled with a choice selection of readable news. October 27th, Smith sold out his interest to Hitchcock, who remained sole editor and publisher until, in September, 1869, James Clearwater was associated with him as publisher, for a few months. February 22nd, 1870, J. K. P. Jackson purchased a half interest and was associated with Mr. Hitchcock until November 8th, 1870, when he bought Hitchcock's interest. December 26, 1871, Mr. Jackson sold the office to Smith & Hoyt, who continued to publish the paper until April 15th, 1873, when Smith purchased Hoyt's interest. He continued sole proprietor until November 22nd, 1877, when the paper was purchased by N. L. Lyon. From April 1st, 1877, to December 25th, 1877, L. F. Raymond acted as editor and publisher for Mr. Smith. Lyon changed the *Register* from an independent paper to a Republican organ, and sold it to Joseph Eveland & Co. . . . . [It is] published on Friday of each week, at the rate of $1.00 a year. It has a circulation of about 800 copies." (*History of Delaware,* p. 184). In an editorial on March 7, 1952 Jesse Palmeter announced the sale of the paper. "We have struggled against the lack of interest in their local paper by the village merchants shown through their indifference to advertising—which is the life blood of any newspaper . . . . The subscription list of the *Dairyman* will be taken over by the *Unadilla Times* [Otsego County] published by Lynn Earl." *Loc*: NFra: Ja 2, 1931–D 27, 1940 (59 [*sic*]: n.s. 2413 whole no. 3225– 73:n.s. 2061 whole no. 3743). NFra/Finch: D 13, 1946 (no. vol. or no.); Mr 7, 1952 (no vol. or no.). NIC/RHA: N 17, 1905 (38:1152 whole no. 1953); Ja 12, 1906 (38:1160 whole no. 1962); F 7, 1919 (49:1743 whole no. 2641).

DELAWARE COUNTY ENTERPRISE see *THE TRI-TOWN NEWS*

DELAWARE COUNTY NEWS see DELAWARE STANDARD

THE DELAWARE COURIER see THE DEPOSIT COURIER
(Broome County Bibliography).

THE DELAWARE EXPRESS (w) Delhi. Ja 1839–Jl 25, 1942//
(1:1–104:33). Title changes: Delaware Express by 1862–? The Delaware Express by D 1866. Pub: Norwood Bowne 1839–?; William
Clark by 1895–?; Arthur C. Wyer by 1913–?; Delaware Express Co.
by 1935–1942. Ed: Norwood Bowne 1839–?; William Clark by
1895–?; Arthur C. Wyer by 1913–Ap 7, 1939; C. D. Bonsted Ap 14–
S 15, 1939; George Van Ryper S 22, 1939–O 10, 1941; Edward L.
Stevens O 17, 1941–1942. Pol: Whig; Republican. Format: Four to
eight pages, varying sizes, 14¾ " x 22", 17½ " x 24", 16¼ " x 22".
Price: $1.50 per year (1875); $1.00 per year (by 1895–?); $2.00 per
year (by 1926–?). Comment: Motto: " 'The Natural Place of Virtue
Is Near Liberty' Montesquieu" (1840). "Independent but Never Neu-
tral—An Independent Republican Newspaper" (1935). "The Delaware
Express was issued in January, 1839, by Norwood Bowne, who re-
mained its editor and publisher until his death, January, 1890, a period
of fifty-one years. After his death the paper was published by his son,
Charles N., for a short period, when it was published by Bowne &
Gillies, then by P. M. Gillies, and he afterwards sold to Mr. S.
F[orman] Adee; Mr. Adee sold to William Clark . . . ." (Murray,
Delaware County, p. 349.) Clark published the paper from 1894 to
1905. (The Delaware Express, D 30, 1938.) On July 25, 1942 The
Delaware Express merged with The Delaware Republican and was
published under the title The Delaware Republican Express (q.v.)
Loc: NAnd: D 5, 1913 (74:49). NBov/Davidson: F 27, 1867 (29:10
whole no. 1463). NCooHi: N 3, 1841 (3:41); N 16, 1895 (57:50).
NDe: Ja 4, 1935–Jl 25, 1942 (97:1–104:30). NDeD: O 8, 1862
(24:? whole no. 1237); Ja 7, Mr 18, 1863 (24:51 whole no. 1250;
25:9 whole no. 1260); Ja 6, D 21, 1864 (25:51 whole no. 1302; 26:52
whole no. 1349); F 1, 1865 (27:6 whole no. 1355); D 26, 1866 (29:1
whole no. 1454); Ja 16–30, 1867 (29:4–6 whole nos. 1457–1459);
D 23, 30, 1868 (30:52; 31:1 whole nos. 1558, 1559); Je 15, 1870
(32:24 whole no. 1635); My 15, 1872 (34:20 whole no. 1735); S 13,
1877 (39:30 whole no. 2014); D 30, 1880 (whole no. 2186); Mr 26–
Ap 30, 1926 (94:13–18). NHan: Ag 19, S 9, N 11, 1840 (2:30, 33,
42); D 19, 1860 (22:48 whole no. 1143); D 2, 1875 (37:49 whole
no. 1921). NRU: Jl 24, 1844 (6:27).

THE DELAWARE GAZETTE (w) Delhi. N 18, 1819–N 3, 1915//
(1:1–?). Title changes: Delaware Gazette N 18, 1819–Je 23, 1824;
The Delaware Gazette Je 30, 1824–Ja 3, 1838; Delaware Gazette Ja
10, 1838–D 1845; The Delaware Gazette Ja 7, 1846–1864; Delaware
Gazette 1864–?; The Delaware Gazette by Ja 7, 1874–1915. Pub and
Ed: John J. Lappon N 18, 1819–Mr 27, 1822; David Johnson Ap 3,
1822–Mr 20, 1833; Anthony M. Paine and Jacob D. Clark Mr 27,
1833–My 8, 1839; Anthony M. Paine My 15, 1839–F 7, 1872; George

H. Paine and Ira B. Kerr F 14, 1872–O 12, 1881; George H. Paine and Sherrill E. Smith 1881–Ja 17, 1894; Sherrill E. Smith 1894–O 21, 1914; L. G. Smith O 21, 1914–N 11, 1914; H. R. Smith N 11, 1914–Je 30, 1915; Arthur C. Wyer Jl 7–S 22, 1915; Gazette Pub. Co. (William Clark, Ed.) S 29–N 3, 1915. *Pol*: Independent; Democratic-Republican; Democrat. *Format*: Four pages, varying sizes, 12″ x 19″, 15½″ x 22″, 18″ x 23″. *Price*: $1.50 per year (1819–1821); $2.00 per year delivered, $1.50 per year otherwise (1821–1864); $2.00 per year (1864–1871); $1.75 per year (1871–1872); $1.50 per year (1872–1896); $1.00 per year in advance (1896–N 3, 1915). *Comment*: "The first newspaper published in the county . . . and . . . the only one published prior to 1821." (Murray, *Delaware County*, p. 601.) Final date is from Gregory, *Newspapers*, p. 449. *Loc*: NCooHi: N 9, 1842 (24:4). NDe: N 18, 1819–N 3, 1915 (1:1–96:51). NHan: Ap 22, 1863 (44:31). NIC/MMN: Je 14, 1837 (18:34). NIC/RHA: Ja 7, F 18, 25, Ap 22, Jl 29, Ag 5–19, S 2, 9, 1874 (55:18, 24, 25, 33, 47–50, 52; 56:1). NRU: S 6, 1821 (2:43). NWaHi: Ag 24, N 16, 1859 (40:48; 41:8); Ja 4, Je 28, Jl 12, O 26, 1865 (46:16, 41, 43, 57).

DELAWARE JOURNAL Delhi. 1834–?. No issues located. ". . . issued April 16, 1834, by Whipple & Wright . . . published but a few years." (Murray, *Delaware County*, p. 349).

THE DELAWARE REPUBLICAN (w) Delhi. 1821–ca. 1825//. No issues located. "*The Delaware Republican* . . . was issued in June, 1821, Elijah J. Roberts publisher. H. H. Nash afterwards became its publisher, and it was discontinued in 1825 or thereabouts." (Murray, *Delaware County*, p. 349.)

THE DELAWARE REPUBLICAN (w) Delhi. S 1830–D 12, 1832//. *Pub*: J. McDonald and Norwood Bowne. *Format*: One page 11″ x 15¾″. *Comment*: Started by George Marvine in September, 1830 (Murray, *Delaware County*, p. 349). "This present Extra [D 12, 1832] is issued to inform our patrons that the publication of the *Delaware Republican* is to stop for a time." *Loc*: NCooHi: D 12, 1832 (Extra).

THE DELAWARE REPUBLICAN (1860) see *THE DELAWARE REPUBLICAN EXPRESS*

THE DELAWARE REPUBLICAN EXPRESS (w) Delhi. My 12, 1860 to date (1:1 to date). *Title changes*: *The Delaware Republican* My 12, 1860–O 10, 1863; *The Delaware Republican and Visitor* O 17, 1863–Mr 5, 1865; *The Delaware Republican* by Ap 1, 1865–Jl 23, 1942; *The Delaware Republican-Express* Jl 30, 1942–1953; *The Delaware Republican Express* 1953 to date. *Pub*: Alvin Sturtevant and Theophilus F. McIntosh My 12, 1860–F 1868; Theophilus F. McIntosh and Joseph Eveland F 8, 1868–D 25, 1869; Theophilus F. McIntosh Ja 1870–Ap 13, 1895; Theophilus F. McIntosh and Robert P. McIntosh Ap 20, 1895–O 1901; Robert P. McIntosh O 1901–My 2, 1937; Katherine McIntosh My 9, 1937–Ap 30, 1938; "The Delaware Republican" (Charles H. and John B. Stow, William Van Wagner My 1938–1948; Henry L. Hovemeyer Ja 1, 1949–S 29, 1970) My 1938–S

29, 1970; Stamford Publishing Co. O 15, 1970 to date (Charles L. Ryder, Pres.). *Ed*: Alvin Sturtevant, G. W. Reynolds, Corresponding Ed. by 1863–?; Theophilus F. McIntosh 1870–O 1901; Robert P. McIntosh O 1901–My 2, 1937; Katherine McIntosh My 9, 1937–Ap 30, 1938; John B. Stow 1938–1948; Henry L. Hovemeyer Ja 1, 1949–S 29, 1970; Charles L. Ryder O 15, 1970 to date. *Pol*: Republican. *Format*: Four to thirty-two pages, varying sizes, 18″ x 24″, 15½″ x 21½″, 17½″ x 22¼″. *Price*: $1.50 per year (1861); $1.00 per year (1863); $1.50 per year (1864–?); $2.50 per year (1949); $2.00 per year (1951); $4.00 per year, 10¢ per copy (1964–Je 30, 1972); $5.00 per year, 15¢ per copy (Jl 1, 1972 to date). *Comment*: Motto: "A Journal of News, Politics, and Literature." First published in the office over the post office, then in the building on Main St., by 1876 in the Brick Block. From 1938 to date it has been published at 2 Court St., west side of Public Square. In October 1863, Sturtevant and McIntosh purchased the *Franklin Visitor* (q.v.) from G. W. Reynolds and continued the *Republican* as *The Delaware Republican and Visitor*. In 1970 "the *Republican Express* became a member of the Ryder group of community newspapers, including the Stamford *Mirror Recorder* (q.v.); the *Windham Journal;* the *Cobleskill Times-Journal,* with Cherry Valley Gazette section; the *Worcester Times-Schenevus Monitor;* and a seasonal publication, *Ski News of the Catskills.*" (*The Evening Press,* Binghamton, S 30, 1970). Contains the official canvass. *Loc*: NBiHi: Ja 11–F 8, 1879 (19:975–979). NDe: Jl 30, 1942 to date (83:? to date). NDeD: My 12, 1860 to date (1:1 to date). NIC/MMN: Je 24, 1876 (17:842). NIC/RHA: My 15, 1935 (76:1). NHan: F 23, 1861 (1:42); [D 19, 1863–O 1, 1864 (4:189–230)]; D 22, 1866 (7:346 fragment). NWaHi: S 21, 1867 (8:385).

DELAWARE STANDARD. 1887–1893// No issues located. "A prohibition paper, was started in November 1887 by Rev. W. M. Howie. After several changes, Wm. S. Cole, the owner changed the name to the *Delaware County News* which suspended in 1893." (Murray, *Delaware County,* p. 603.)

DELAWARE TIMES see *THE ROXBURY TIMES*

THE DEMOCRAT Sidney. 1874. No issues located. Published by J. K. P. Jackson (Murray, *Delaware County,* p. 602).

THE DEPOSIT COURIER see Broome County Bibliography . Also: *Pub*: Edward J. Russell, Jr., 1955–1958. *Ed*: J. Daniel Kellogg 1941–1948; Ralph Lent 1958–Je 4, 1959; Raymond E. Ruegger Je 4, 1959–S 8, 1960; Charles D. Cook S 26, 1960–1965; George D. Brower 1965–1967; William Ryan 1967–Ag 29, 1970; Hilton Evans Ag 30, 1970 to date.

DEPOSIT TIMES see *DEPOSIT TIMES AND DEMOCRAT*

DEPOSIT TIMES AND DEMOCRAT Deposit. 1874–1876// No issues located. Founded by S. C. Clizbe, lasted about two years (*History of Delaware,* p. 319). Murray (*Delaware County,* p. 602) refers to this paper as the *Deposit Times.*

DOWNSVILLE HERALD (w) Hancock. O 16, 1947–? *Pub*: Hancock Herald O 1946–?. *Ed*: Louise Knapp, managing ed. *Pol*: Independent. *Format*: Four pages 17″ x 21½″. *Price*: $2.00 per year in advance, 5¢ per copy (D 1947–?). *Comment*: Downsville had been without a newspaper since April 25, 1946 when the Peck Brothers "suspended publication owing to their age, mechanical difficulties and general conditions throughout the country. . . ." The *Hancock Herald*'s plans to publish a paper for the Downsville area to supplant the old newspaper were completed by October 1947. (*Downsville Herald* O 16, 1947.) Possibly lasted only two years. *Loc*: NHanH: O 16, 1947–My 3, 1949 (1:1–2:30).

DOWNSVILLE NEWS (w) Downsville. 1875–Ap 25, 1946// (1:1–?) *Pub and Ed*: Peck Bros. by 1945. *Pol*: Independent. *Format*: Eight pages 20″ x 26″. *Price*: $1.50 per year (1945). *Circ*: 500 (1910–?). *Comment*: The *Downsville News* was started by A. E. Peck in 1875 (Murray, *Delaware County,* p. 602). The final date of publication has been taken from the *Downsville Herald* October 16, 1947. The circulation figure is from the *Ayer Directory. Loc*: NSiHi: S 27, 1945 (68:49).

FLEISCHMANNS HERALD see *THE GRIFFIN-FLEISCHMANN HERALD*

FLEISCHMANNS HERALD-NEWS see *THE GRIFFIN-FLEISCH-MANN HERALD*

FLEISCHMANNS NEWS (w) Griffin Corners. 1908–? No issues located. According to the *Ayer Directory* (1910, p. 585), the *News* was published by E. D. Gregory, edited by Wilson Bertrand, and sold for $1.00 per year in 1910. The *News* merged with the *Griffin-Fleischmann Herald* (q.v.) by 1914.

FLEISCHMANNS PRESS (w) Fleischmanns. Ag 1922–? (1:1–?). *Pub*: Rutherford H. Brown and Sydney Flisser. *Format*: Eight pages 11″ x 15″. *Price*: $1.50 per year. *Loc*: NFL/Kelly: S 22, 1922 (1:6).

FRANKLIN REGISTER see *DELAWARE COUNTY DAIRYMAN*

FRANKLIN VISITOR (w) Franklin. Ap 14, 1855–O 6, 1863 (1:1–?). *Pub and Ed*: G. W. Reynolds by 1857–?; Abell & Brown 1860; G. W. Reynolds 1861–1863. *Pol*: Anti-Slavery, Republican, Union. *Format*: Four pages, varying sizes, 19″ x 24″, 16½″ x 23″. *Price*: $1.50 per year (1857–?); $1.00 per year, 4¢ per copy (1858–?). *Circ*: 1,800 (1857). *Comment*: Motto: "'I also will shew mine opinion.'" Published on Main St. opposite the old church by 1857. "The *Weekly Visitor,* afterwards called the *Franklin Visitor,* was established by George W. Reynolds, March 28, 1855 and was a Republican organ." (*History of Delaware,* p. 184.) "In October, 1863, the *Franklin Visitor* was purchased of G. W. Reynolds by Messrs. Sturtevant and

McIntosh, and consolidated with the *Delaware Republican* [later the *Delaware Republican Express* (q.v.)]. . . ." (*History of Delaware,* p. 161.) *Loc*: NCooHi: Ja 8, 15, 1857 (2:38, 39 whole nos. 90, 91); Ap 3, 1861–Ap 8, 1862 (6:51 whole no. 311–7:52 whole no. 364). NFra/Finch: Ja 14–Mr 4, Mr 18–My 12, My 26, 1858 (3:39–46, 48–4:3, 5). NHan: My ?, 1860 (6:5 fragment); S 11, O 23, N 13, 1861 (7:22, 28, 31 whole nos. ?, 340, 343); [F 4, 1862–My 19, 1863 (7:43 whole no. 365–9:5); O 6, 1863 (9:28 whole no. 439). NIC/RHA: D 31, 1857 (3:37 whole no. 141).

GRIFFIN'S CORNERS HERALD see *THE GRIFFIN-FLEISCH-MANN HERALD*

THE GRIFFIN-FLEISCHMANN HERALD (w) Fleischmanns (Griffin Corners). O 1890–? (1:1–?). *Title changes: Griffin's Corners and Fleischmann's Herald* by 1893–?; *The Griffin-Fleischmann Herald* by 1907–? *Pub*: Wilson Bertrand by 1893–?; J. B. Gregory by 1907–? *Pol*: Republican. *Format*: Four pages, varying sizes, 13" x 20", 17½" x 24". *Price*: $1.00 per year (1907). *Comment*: *Ayer Directory* carried listings of this newspaper until 1920 under the following titles: *Griffin's Corners Herald* (1891); *Griffin-Fleischmann Herald* (1910, 1912); *Griffin-Fleischmann Herald-News* (1914–1916); and *Fleischmanns Herald* (1917–1920). Publishers and editors were listed as J. K. P. Jackson (1891); George B. Rich (1910); Theodore B. Seelman and Tompkins (1912); Theodore B. Seelman (1914–1916); A. H. Todd, publisher (1917–1920), B. D. Tompkins, editor (1917–1918), and Frank Greene, editor (1919–1920). *Loc*: NFl/Kelly: Ja 23, 1907 (18:16). NIC/RHA: Jl 29, 1893 (3:41).

GRIFFIN-FLEISCHMANN HERALD-NEWS see *THE GRIFFIN-FLEISCHMANN HERALD*

THE HANCOCK GUARDIAN (w) Hancock. F 4, 1870–? (1:1–?). *Pub and Ed*: A. B. Cornwell 1870–? *Format*: Four pages 16" x 23". *Price*: $1.50 per year. *Comment*: Motto: "Semper Fidelis." *Loc*: NHan: F 4, 18, Mr 4, 25, My 27, Je 17, Jl 1, 15, S 30, O 7, N 11, 18, 1870 (1:1, 3, 5, 8, 17, 20, 22, 24, 35, 36, 41, 42).

HANCOCK HERALD (w) Hancock. My 10, 1873 to date (1:1 to date). *Pub*: The Herald Association 1873–?; Benjamin Haines & Co. by F 2, 1877–My 1878; W. C. McNally My 24, 1878–S 29, 1887; Charles T. White O 6, 1887–Ag 10, 1893; Herbert W. Wagner Ag 17, 1893–Jl 1920; Herbert W. Wagner and Clayton G. Forester Ag 5, 1920–Ag 29, 1940; Clayton G. Forester S 5, 1940–S 1945; Clayton G. and Clayton C. Forester S 1945–D 1945; Hancock Herald Inc. Ja 3, 1946 to date. *Ed*: Benjamin F. Haines by Ag 1873–Ja 18, 1878; Peter E. Low by Ja 18–My 10, 1878; W. C. McNally My 1878–S 29, 1887; Charles T. White O 6, 1887–Ag 10, 1893; Herbert W. Wagner Ag 17, 1893–Jl 1920; Herbert W. Wagner and Clayton G. Forester Ag 5, 1920– Ag 1940 (Wagner died Mr 17, 1940); Clayton G. Forester S 5, 1941–S 1945; Stuart C. Curnock Ja 3, 1946–D 9, 1948; Charles T. White, Assoc. Ed. 1941–?; Clayton G. Forester and Paul J. Fagan,

Asst. Ed., Charles T. White, Assoc. Ed. D 16, 1948–1952; Paul J. Fagan Ap 24, 1952 to date. *Pol*: Independent. *Format*: Four to eight pages, varying sizes, 15¾ " x 21½ ", 18" x 25", 13" x19", 18" x 23". *Price*: $1.50 per year in advance (1873–?); $1.00 per year (by 1893–1917); $1.50 per year, 5¢ per copy (1918–1950); $2.50 per year, 7¢ per copy (N 1950–Mr 1964); $3.00 per year, 10¢ per copy (Ap 1964–1967); $3.50 per year, 10¢ per copy (Ap 1967–1968); $4.00 per year, 10¢ per copy (1968 to date). *Comment*: Motto: "Hew to the Line; Let the Chips Fall Where They May." "The Largest Circulation of any Independent Democratic Paper Published in Delaware County." (1961 to date.) Although the newspaper supported the position of the Ontario and Western Railroad and was considered its voice for many years, it regularly asserted that it "printed the news without bias and without playing favorites." (From an editorial, Ag 16, 1938.) In 1874, the paper was published in the Stoddard Building on Front St., then from October 1874 until 1878 it was published in the Allison Block, Front St., then in Ayres' New Building. It is currently published in the *Herald* Building, 14 E. Main St. *Loc*: NHan: [My 31, 1873–Mr 16, 1882 (1:4–9:45)]; S 20, 1883 (11:18); N 27, 1884 (12:29); [F 5–Jl 2, 1885 (12:38–13:8)]; F 10, Jl 14, 1887 (14:39, 15:9); [Ja 5, 1888–F 14, 1889 (15:34–16:40)]; Ap 12, 1900 (27:50); Ag 4, 1904 (32:16); My 10, 1906 (34:5); current issues. NHanH: [Ag 28, 1874 to date (21:16 to date)].

THE HANCOCK TIMES (w) Hancock. Mr 1870–1874// (1:1–?). *Title changes*: *The Hancock Weekly Times* Mr 1870(?)–?; *The Hancock Times* by Jl 16, 1870–1874. *Pub and Ed*: S. C. Clizbe 1870–1874. *Pol*: Republican. *Format*: Four pages 16" x 22". *Price*: $1.50 per year (1870); $2.00 per year (1872). *Circ*: Over 1,000 (1874). *Comment*: No issues of *The Hancock Times* later than 1874 have been located. Clizbe started a newspaper in Deposit, *Deposit Times and Democrat* (q.v.), in 1874. *Loc*: NHan: [My 22, 1870–My 15, 1874 (1:10–5:20)].

HANCOCK TRUE FLAG (w) Hancock. Ag 1872–? (1:1–?). *Pol*: Democrat. For Greeley Reform Ticket. *Format*: Four pages 14" x 20". *Price*: $1.00 per year. *Comment*: Motto: "The Union, the Constitution and the Laws." *Loc*: NHan: S 12, 1872 (1:6).

THE HANCOCK WEEKLY TIMES see *THE HANCOCK TIMES*

HOBART FREE PRESS (w) Hobart. 1866–? (1:1–?). No issues located. "This paper was started in 1866 by Charles H. Cleveland. It was soon stopped . . . ." (*History of Delaware*, p. 298).

HOBART HERALD (w) Hobart. 1912–1914//. No issues located. Democratic weekly established by A. A. Bernard. It was 13 pages 13¼ " x 19½ " and sold for $1.25 per year. (*Ayer Directory*, 1912–1914.) This was probably the original title of *The Hobart Times* (q.v.) which did not appear in the *Ayer Directory* until 1915 at which time its date of establishment was listed as 1912.

HOBART INDEPENDENT (w) Hobart. 1885–1913//(?). No issues

located. A four page, 13″ x 20″, Republican newspaper established in 1885 by Amasa J. Champion. Later edited and published by Edward A. Ackley (by 1910), and L. H. DeSilva (by 1912). (*Ayer Directory.*)

THE HOBART TIMES (w) Hobart. 1912(?)–1928// (1:1–?). *Pub and Ed*: R. G. Hill by 1918–? *Format*: Four pages 15″ x 22″. *Price*: $1.00 per year (1918). *Comment*: Original title may have been *Hobart Herald* (q.v.). The publisher was U. S. G. Morgan by 1915, Edward A. Ackley in 1916, and R. G. Hill 1917–1928. The paper sold for $1.50 per year 1925–1928 (*Ayer Directory*). *Loc*: NBiHi: D 28, 1918 (6:40).

THE MARGARETVILLE MESSENGER see *CATSKILL MOUNTAIN NEWS*

MARGARETVILLE STANDARD (w) Margaretville. ca. 1881. No issues located. The *Ayer Directory* for 1881 lists an independent four page, 22″ x 30″ newspaper called the *Standard* published in Margaretville in 1881. It is no longer listed by 1883.

THE MIDLAND TIMES (w) Sidney Plains. O 1872–? (1:1–?). *Pub and Ed*: C. T. Alverson O 1872–Ja 18, 1873; S. T. Morehouse Ja 25, 1873–?; John H. Graves by F 28, 1874–? *Pol*: Independent. *Format*: Four pages 12″ x 20″. *Price*: $1.00 per year in advance. *Comment*: Published from an office in Hodgkin's Block. An editorial in the January 25, 1873 issue stated that on that day C. T. Alverson was retiring and S. T. Morehouse was taking over. "The *Times* will continue in the same outspoken, independent plan regarding truth and justice. . . ." (*The Midland Times,* Ja 25, 1873). *Loc*: NSiHi: Ja 25, 1873 (1:14); F 28, 1874 (2:17).

THE MIRROR-INDEPENDENT (d) Stamford and Hobart. Je 3–20, 1902// (1:1–13). *Pub and Ed*: Clifford Champion and Edward A. Ackley. *Format*: Four pages 17½″ x 23″. *Price*: 3¢ per copy. *Comment*: Published by Clifford Champion of the *Stamford Mirror* (q.v.) and Edward A. Ackley of the *Hobart Independent* (q.v.) to report on the Montgomery murder trial. *Loc*: NSt: Je 3–19[*sic*] (1:1–13).

MIRROR RECORDER (w) Bloomville, Stamford. My 28, 1851 to date (1:1 to date). *Title changes*: *Bloomville Mirror* My 28, 1851–My 13, 1871; *Stamford and Bloomville Mirror* My 23, 1871–My 12, 1874; *Stamford Mirror* My 19, 1874–O 2, 1905; *Stamford Mirror and Recorder* O 16, 1905–?; *The Mirror-Recorder* by Ja 1, 1908–1917; *Stamford Mirror-Recorder* by Ja 2, 1918–Ag 17, 1950; *Mirror Recorder* Ag 24, 1950 to date. *Pub*: Simon B. Champion My 28, 1851–S 9, 1903 (died); Estate of Simon B. Champion S 15, 1903–O 2, 1905; Leo H. DeSilva O 9, 1905–?; Stamford Press, Inc. ?–?; Stamford Publishing Co. 1949 to date (John W. Nash, Pub., D 28, 1950–O 30, 1952; Charles L. Ryder N 6, 1952 to date). *Ed*: Simon B. Champion 1851–S 9, 1903; Simon B. Champion & Son Ja 20, 1880–Ja 22, 1884; Amasa J. Champion, Assoc. Ed., 1890–?; Clifford Champion, Assoc.

Ed., S 30, 1902–?; Leo H. DeSilva O 16, 1905–?; Robert A. West, Assoc., Ed., Je 1, 1920–Ja 1, 1953; John W. Nash, Managing Ed., Ja 6, 1949–O 30, 1952; Leonard E. Delmar Ag 24–S 13, 1950; Anna Elwynn S 20, 1950–Ag 6, 1953; Elsie A. Vermilya O 1953– Jl 1, 1954; Anna C. Laux Jl 15, 1954–1960; Charles Ryder, Jr., Ed. and Mgr. 1956–1968, Ed. and Co-pub. 1969 to date. *Pol*: National Democrat (1852–1855); American Party (1856–1859); Democrat (1860); Union (1861); Democrat (by 1863 to date). *Format*: One to twenty pages, varying sizes, 4" x 7⅛", 5½" x 8¾", 8¼" x 11½", 11" x 17½", 18" x 23", 16" x 23". *Price*: 25¢ per year (Je 1851–Mr 15, 1852); 50¢ per year in advance (Mr–D 22, 1863); 75¢ per year (D 29, 1863–Ag 23, 1864); $1.00 per year (Ag 30, 1864–?); $2.00 per year (by 1933–1948); $3.00 per year, 8¢ per copy (1949–1956); $3.50 per year, 10¢ per copy (1956–1966); $4.00 per year, 10¢ per copy (1967–1968); $5.00 per year, 10¢ per copy (1969–1971); $5.00 per year, 15¢ per copy (1971 to date). *Circ*: 516 (Mr 1852); 1,125 (Ap 1853); 1,900 (O 1854); 2,900 (Ap 1858); 3,000 (Ag 1858); 3,600 (1863); 2,000 (1891). *Comment*: Motto: " 'Approve where we can—censure where we must' " (1851); "The Greatest Good to the Greatest Number" (from D 22, 1851). Published in Bloomville 1851 to September 6, 1870; published in Stamford September 13, 1870 to date. Simon B. Champion was listed as " 'Champ,' Printer" through October 20, 1851. Early issues contain the official canvass. On October 9, 1905 the *Stamford Mirror* was sold to the Recorder Co. and on the same day both papers were sold by the Recorder Co. to Leo H. DeSilva of Grand Gorge, N. Y. The two papers were consolidated and were to be issued under the name *Stamford-Mirror-Recorder*. (*Stamford Mirror and Recorder,* O 16, 1905 editorial.) *Loc*: NCooHi: Je 17, 1851 (fragment); [Ag–D 29, 1851 (1:9–29)]; Ja 12, 19, F 2, 16, Mr 15, 22, 1852 (1:32, 33, 34, 36, 40, 41); D 27, 1853 (3:[29]); N 10, D 15, 1857 (7:23, 28); Ap 27, 1858 (7:47); Ja 1, 1861–D 30, 1862 (10:31–12:31); D 31, 1867 (17:32); D 6, 1870 (20:29); Ja 3, 1871 (20:33); O 6, 1903 (53:26). NHan: Je 3, 24, Jl 8, 29, Ag 5–19, S 30, O 14, N 4, D 30, 1862 (12:1, 4, 6, 9–12, 17, 20, 23, 31). NSt: My 28, 1851 (facsimile); Je 24, Jl 29, 1851 (1:4, 8); [Ag 18, 1851–Mr 29, 1852 (1:40[*sic*]–42)]; Ap 19, 1853–Ag 28, 1855 (2:45– 5:12); Jl 15, 1856–D 26, 1905 (6:6–55:38); Ja 5, 1933–Ja 2, 1947 (82:44–96:46); Ja 6, 1949 to date (98:47 to date). NStM: Ja 2, 1866–D 31, 1878 (15:32–28:34); Ja 5, 1904–O 9, 1905 (53:39– 55:27); Ja 1, 1908–D 27, 1916 (57:39–66:40); [Ja 2, 1918 to date (67:41 to date)]. NWaHi: N 2, 1858 (8:22); Je 30, D 22, 1863 (13:5, 30).

MONTHLY CROAKER (m) Delhi. 1887–1891// No issues located. "The *Monthly Croaker,* an amateur publication, was issued in July, 1887, by John F. Van Der Cook, Jr., a boy only twelve years old, and continued without intermission until November, 1891." (Murray, *Delaware County,* pp. 349–350.)

THE MORNING ECHO (w) Delhi. Jl 16, 1860–? (1:1–?). *Pub*: George P. Hill. *Price*: 25¢ for twenty issues, 3¢ per copy. *Comment*:

Motto: "Devoted to the Investigation of Passing Events. 'Watchman, tells us of the night.' " Printed by Sturtevant & McIntosh. *Loc*: NSt: Jl 16, 1860 (1:1).

THE NEWS AND WAVE Sidney. 1879. No issues located. Published in 1879 by C. C. & C. O. Brown (Murray, *Delaware County*, p. 602). The Brown Brothers also published a newspaper in Guilford, Chenango County, called *The News and Wave* and later *The Chenango Press* as late as November 1879.

THE PEOPLE'S PRESS (w) Walton. O 27, 1885–? (1:1–?). *Title changes*: *The Walton Cyclone* O 27, 1885–F 1886; *The Cyclone* Mr 2, 1886–?; *The People's Press* by Ag 24, 1886–? *Pub and Ed*: Frank B. Eels and Fred E. Low O 27, 1885–Je 1886; Frank B. Eels Je 15, 1886–?; A. F. Flummerfelt, ed., by Ag 24, 1886–? *Pol*: Democrat. *Format*: Four pages, varying sizes, 8¾ " x 12", 13" x 20". *Price*: $1.00 per year, 10¢ per month (1885–?). *Circ*: 500 (Mr 1886). *Comment*: F 2, 1886, the editors announced that "the enlargement of the Cyclone to its present size, has entailed considerable expense to the proprietors. In order that a Democratic paper may become prosperous in the village of Walton, it is absolutely necessary that the party that it represents should support it. . . ." "In 1886 [*The Walton Cyclone*] was changed to the *Peoples Press* and soon discontinued." (Murray, *Delaware County*, p. 603.) *Loc*: NWa: O 7–D 8, 22, 1885 (1:1–7, 9); Ja 12–Ag 10, 1886 (1:11–41). NWaHi: F 2, 1886 (1:14); Je 15, 1886 (1:33); Ag 24, 1886 (1:43).

THE RECORDER see *THE ANDES RECORDER* (1867–1892)

THE REPORTER (d) Walton. My 2–Je 30, 1898// (1:1–52). *Pub*: The Reporter Co. *Ed*: Paul Nichols and John P. White. *Pol*: Democrat. *Format*: Four pages 15" x 21". *Price*: 30¢ per month, 2¢ per copy. *Comment*: Published at the *Reporter* Building, 86 Delaware St. This edition was published by the *Walton Reporter* (q.v.) to report on the war, but it was discontinued after two months because Walton could not support a daily paper. *Loc*: NWa: My 2, 1898–Je 30, 1898 (1:1–52).

THE ROXBURY TIMES (w) Roxbury. Ja 1879–Je 16, 1951// (1:1–72:24). *Pub and Ed*: H. G. Cartwright ?–S 19, 1895; John H. Dudley and Co. (C. E. Follett) S 26, 1895–Ag 26, 1897; John H. Dudley S 2, 1897–Je 1, 1899; Fred L. Rose Je 8–D 29, 1899; John H. Dudley Ja 5, 1900–D 1908; Fred W. Lutz Ja 2, 1909–Je 16, 1951. *Pol*: Republican. *Format*: Four pages 18" x 24". *Price*: $1.00 per year in advance (1895–1924); $1.50 per year (1924–1951). *Comment*: Subtitle: "The Best Equipped Office Along the Ulster & Delaware Railroad" by 1903–?; "One of the Best Equipped Offices and Advertising Papers in the Catskill Mountains" by 1939. "The first newspaper in Roxbury was started January, 1879 by a man named McArthur, who printed an eight-page paper in an office on the second floor of the old hotel. He brought with him a man named Spencer who was also a photographer. Unfortunately neither man was noted for sobriety and after a few months the paper faced failure. However, the village had a number of enterprising citizens who wanted a newspaper so some twenty men of the town, among whom were Henry C. Soop, George W. Lauren, Richard B. Robinson, Burrett B. Bouton, Daniel D. Andries, James E. More, formed a stock company and instituted the *Delaware Times* as a Democratic paper. The second editor was J. C. Crowley. The next editor was Edward S. Tompkins. The oldest copy yet located is dated August 26, 1886. At this time Tompkins was editor. The name changed to *Roxbury Times* some time between 1886 and 1894. It became Republican in character about this time." (Caroline Evelyn More and Irma Mae Griffin, *History of the Town of Roxbury* [Walton: Walton Reporter Co., 1953], p. 72.) The publication was issued somewhat irregularly and was finally discontinued in 1951 owing to the ill health of the publisher. The paper stated that it had "A large circulation among an intelligent class of farmers and mechanics making it the best advertising medium." *Loc*: NRo: microfilm S 19, 1895–Je 16, 1951 (16:37–72:24).

THE RURAL TIMES Sidney. 1881. No issues located. Published by Mr. Jones (Murray, *Delaware County*, p. 602).

THE SIDNEY ADVOCATE Sidney. 1895–? No issues located. ". . . established in 1895 by Bolton & Stanton, and J. F. Andrews is now [1898] the editor and publisher." (Murray, *Delaware County*, p. 603.)

THE SIDNEY CENTER TRANSCRIPT Sidney. 1895–? No issues located. ". . . started in 1895 by W. J. Weyrauch, and Chas. H. Schutts is the present [1898] editor and publisher." (Murray, *Delaware County*, p. 603.)

SIDNEY ENTERPRISE see *THE TRI-TOWN NEWS*

THE SIDNEY HERALD (w) Sidney Plains. D 1874–? (1:1–?). *Pub*: M. W. D. Fenton. *Pol*: Independent. *Format*: Four pages 13″ x 20″. *Price*: $1.00 per year in advance. *Comment*: Office on Liberty St., first door from Main St. *Loc*: NSiHi: Je 12, 1875 (1:33).

SIDNEY RECORD (w) Sidney Plains, Sidney. D 7, 1882–My 6, 1948 (1:1–?). *Pub and Ed*: Arthur Bird D 7, 1882–1937; Estate of Arthur Bird 1937; C. E. Bird 1938–1944; W. H. Randall 1945–1948. *Format*: Six to eight pages, varying sizes, 12½″ x 19¼″, 15″ x 22″. *Price*: $1.50 per year (1882–1944); $1.75 per year (1945–1948). *Comment*: Published at Sidney Plains 1882–Jl 29, 1886, then Sidney from Ag 5, 1886–1948. Merged with the *Sidney Enterprise* in My 1948 and on My 13, 1948 was issued as the *Sidney Record-Enterprise,* later *The Tri-Town News* (q.v.). *Loc*: NSiHi: D 7, 1882–1948 (1:1–?).

THE SIDNEY RECORD AND BAINBRIDGE NEWS see *THE TRI-TOWN NEWS*

SIDNEY RECORD-ENTERPRISE see *THE TRI-TOWN NEWS*

STAMFORD AND BLOOMVILLE MIRROR see *MIRROR RE-CORDER*

STAMFORD MIRROR see *MIRROR RECORDER*

STAMFORD MIRROR AND RECORDER see *MIRROR RECORDER*

STAMFORD MIRROR-RECORDER see *MIRROR RECORDER*

STAMFORD RECORDER (w) Stamford. Ap 23, 1892–O 9, 1905// (n.s. 1:1–?). *Pub*: Stamford Printing and Publishing Co. by 1894–? The Recorder Co. (J. Giles Ford, Prop.) by Ap 9, 1904–O 9, 1905. *Ed*: William Clark, Ed. and Mgr., Ap 23, 1892–Ag 25, 1894; Edward A. Ackley S 1, 1894–?; J. Giles Ford ?–Mr 1905; Albert W. Terry Ap 1, 1905–?. *Pol*: Republican. *Format*: Eight pages, varying sizes, 15" x 22", 13" x 18¼". *Price*: $1.00 per year. *Comment*: Although the newspaper in 1894 said that it began in 1867, which was the date of the establishment of the *Andes Recorder,* it actually began in Stamford in 1892. "The *Stamford Recorder* was established in the village in April, 1892, by a company composed of representative Republicans who desired an exponent of their political faith. The name of the corporation is The Stamford Printing and Publishing Company, and the printing plant of the *Andes Recorder* was purchased by William Clark, who became editor and manager of the Stamford Recorder." (Murray, *Delaware County,* p. 562.) On October 9, 1905, the *Stamford Mirror* was sold to the Recorder Co. and on the same day, both papers were sold by the Recorder Co. to Leo H. DeSilva who merged them into the newspaper that was eventually published as the *Mirror Recorder* (q.v.). *Loc*: NDeD: [Ap 23, 1892–D 31–1898 (n.s. 1:1–7:38)]; Ap 9, 1904–Je 10, 1905. NSt: My 5, 1894–Ap 11, 1896 (27th year, n.s. 3:1–4:1).

STANDARD see *MARGARETVILLE STANDARD*

THE STAR Sidney. 1870. No issues located. "The Star—was the first paper published in Sidney, beginning in 1870, by Owen and Wright." (Murray, *Delaware County,* p. 602.)

THE STAR OF DELAWARE (w) Delhi. Jl 24, 1858–? (1:1–?). *Pub*: Charles B. Smyth Jl 24, 1858–Ap 9, 1859; Charles B. Smyth and Theophilus F. McIntosh Ap 16, 1859–?; Theophilus F. McIntosh by Ag 27, 1859–?; Charles B. Smyth by F 11, 1860–? *Ed*: Charles B. Smyth 1858–? *Pol*: Neutral. "Neutral in politics and unsectarian in religion." *Format*: Four pages, varying sizes, 13½" x 20", 14½" x 21½". *Price*: $1.00 per year (1858–?), 3¢ per copy (Jl–D 1858), 4¢ per copy (D 11, 1858–?). *Circ*: 2,500 (Jl 24, 1858). *Comment*: Motto: "Be Right; and Go Ahead." The office was directly opposite the Post Office on Main St. The paper was originally printed by Simon B. Champion on the press of the *Mirror,* later the *Mirror Recorder* (q.v.), until April 16, 1858 when Smyth and McIntosh went into partnership on their own job printing establishment. *The Star of Delaware* described itself as "a first class family newspaper . . . having for its object the advancement of religion, science, literature, agriculture, commerce and everything else that may commend itself to the wisdom of enlightened men." According to the *Delaware Republican Express* (Jl 1, 1971), it survived one year. *Loc*: NCooHi: N 6, 1858 (1:13). NDeD: Ag 27, 1859 (2:3). NHan: Jl 9, 1859 (1:48); F 11, 1860 (2:25). NSt: Jl 24, 1858–Jl 2, 1859 (1:1–47).

THE STUDENT Andes. 1866–1867// No issues located. "The first paper published in Andes was founded by Rev. Peter Smeallie who came to Andes in 1864 as principal of the Collegiate Institute. . . . The first number of *The Student* was issued September 5th, 1866. The publisher was Albert D. Hitchcock, a practical printer, then a student. . . . The first editors were Clark L. McCracken . . . and Edward McKee. . . . Mr. Smeallie died February 4th, 1867, and was succeeded by his brother Rev. James M. Smeallie, who enlarged the paper to a quarto. A press was subsequently purchased by A. D. Hitchcock, who enlarged it to a 19 x 26 folio weekly, and changed the name to the *Andes Recorder* [q.v., 1867 edition]." (*History of Delaware,* p. 113.)

THE TRI-TOWN NEWS (w) Sidney. 1895 to date (1:1 to date). *Title changes: Delaware County Enterprise* 1895–S 1912; *Sidney Enterprise* S 25, 1912–My 6, 1948; *Sidney Record-Enterprise* My 13, 1948–F 12, 1959; *The Sidney Record and Bainbridge News* F 19, 1959–D 1967; *The Tri-Town News* Ja 1, 1968 to date. *Pub*: The Delaware Publishing Co., Inc. ?–1912 (C. S. Hitchcock, Pres.); V. D. Keeler Ag 28, 1912–1945; John A. MacLachlan Ap 17, 1947–1961; James M. MacLachlan Ja 5, 1961–Ja 1, 1969; Twin Valley Publishers, Inc. Ja 1969 to date (William D. Marsland, Pub., Edward Roelle, Gen. Mgr.). *Ed*: C. S. Hitchcock ?–1912; V. D. Keeler Ag 28, 1912–1943(?); John A. MacLachlan Ap 17, 1947–1960; James M. MacLachlan Ja 5, 1961–1969; Doris Lawrence Mr 2, 1969 to date. *Format*: Eight to twenty-two pages, varying sizes, 15″ x 21¾″, 16½″ x 21¼″, 17¼″ x 21¾″. *Price*: $1.00 per year in advance (1912–?); $1.50 per year in advance (by 1921–1947); $2.00 per year, 6¢ per copy (1948–1950); $2.50 per year (1950–1951); $3.00 per year (1951–?); $3.50 per year, 10¢ per copy (by 1956–?); $4.00 per year, 10¢ per copy (1968–1971); $5.00 per year, 15¢ per copy (1972). *Circ*: 5,500 (1969 to date). *Comment*: Published in the People's National Bank Building until April 1, 1922, then from the corner of Grant and Division Sts.; 11 Division St. by 1948 to date. James MacLachlan purchased the *Unadilla Times* (Otsego County) from William and Mary Ryan in September 1967 but continued the name of the paper as the *Sidney Record and Bainbridge News* continuing the *Unadilla Times* through December 1967. On February 21, 1969 *The Tri-Town News* incorporated the *Afton Enterprise* (Chenango County). Its banner reads "*The Tri-Town News,* Sidney–Bainbridge–Unadilla, continuing the *Sidney Record* (q.v.), the *Bainbridge News* [Chenango County], the *Unadilla Times* and the *Afton Enterprise and Harpursville Budget.*" *Loc*: NBai: Ja 1, 1969 to date (114th year:41 to date).

NSi: [Ja 3, 1912 to date (16:33 to date)]. NSiHi: D 27, 1916 (22: 30); F 16, 1933 (39[sic]: 27); Jl 11, 1935 (39:27); Ag 3, 17, 1939 (45th year no nos.); My 25, Je 8, 15, Ag 17, O 26, 1944 (49th year); Ja 11, 25, F 1, 8, 22, Mr 8, 15, 29, Ap 5, 19, N 22, 1945 (49th[sic]– 51st year); Je 10–F 28, Ap 25, Je 6, 1946 (51st year). NSiT: Ja 7, 1970 (115th year:41 to date), they keep only three years on file.

THE UNAHANNA Sidney. ca. 1890. No issues located. Published by the Wier Bros. (Murray, *Delaware County,* p. 602).

THE UTILITARIAN (w) Margaretville. Jl 7, 1863–1918//(?) (1:1– ?). *Pub*: Dr. Orson M. Allaben. *Pol*: Democrat. *Format*: Four pages 12½″ x 20″. *Price*: $1.00 per year in advance, 3¢ per copy. *Comment*: Motto: "A Family Journal, Devoted to the Fireside, the Field, and the Forum." "The first newspaper in the town of Middletown, the *Utilitarian,* was printed and published July 7, 1863 by . . . Dr. Orson M. Allaben. . . . The paper was purchased in 1868 by A. R. Henderson and H. T. Becker. It was again sold in 1879 to Attorney J. K. P. Jackson." (*Catskill Mountain News,* Ag 15, 1963, section 2.) It was a Democratic paper (*History of Delaware,* p. 266). The final date is based on the last year *The Utilitarian* appeared in the *Ayer Directory. The Utilitarian* was eventually purchased by the *Catskill Mountain News* (q.v.). *Loc*: NMargC: Ap 28, 1864 (1:42).

VALLEY NEWS Sidney. 1879. No issues located. Published by Clayton Brown (Murray, *Delaware County,* p. 602).

VILLAGE RECORD (w) Hobart. No issues located. Published by George T. Foote (*History of Delaware,* p. 298).

VOICE OF THE PEOPLE Delhi. 1846–? No issues located. "The *Voice of the People,* (the organ of the anti-renters), was issued by William S. Hawley, in June, 1846, and a few years thereafter was discontinued." (Murray, *Delaware County,* p. 349.)

WALTON BLADE see *THE WALTON JOURNAL*

THE WALTON CHRONICLE (w) F 3, 1869–1901//(?) (1:1–?). *Title changes*: *The Walton Weekly Chronicle* F 3, 1869–F 1, 1871; *The Walton Chronicle* F 8, 1871–? *Pub*: Albert D. Hitchcock 1869– 1871; Albert D. Hitchcock and Bryson Bruce S 6, 1871–N 26, 1872; Bryson Bruce D 1872–My 1, 1873; William A. White My 8, 1873– 1882; William A. White and Son 1883–Ag 1891; The Chronicle Association Ag 20, 1891–?. *Ed*: Albert D. Hitchcock 1869–1871; Albert D. Hitchcock and E. P. Berray, Assoc. Local Ed., F 22–Ag 1871; Albert D. Hitchcock and Bryson Bruce S 6, 1871–N 26, 1872; Bryson Bruce D 1872–?; W. H. Eells, Managing Ed., 1891–1892; T. Sanderson Ap 7, 1892–Mr 29, 1894. *Pol*: Independent; Republican (by 1871); Liberal, supported Greeley (1872); Republican (1873). *Format*: Four pages, varying sizes, 18″ x 23″, 20″ x 26½″. *Price*: $1.50 per year in advance (1869–1888); $1.00 per year in advance, otherwise $1.25 (by 1891–?). *Comment*: Published from T. Guild's Building until 1871; over Guild & Child's Store, Delaware St., after September 6, 1871. According to an item in *The Deposit Courier*, May 30, 1901, the *Chronicle* merged with *The Walton Times* (q.v.) and became *The Chronicle-Times* (q.v.). *Loc*: NDeD: D 27, 1871 (3:151). NWa: F 3, 1869–D 27, 1888 (1:1–20:52 whole no. 1038); Ja 1, 1891–D 27, 1894 (23:1 whole no. 1143–26:49 whole no. 1349); Ja 7, 1896– D 29, 1898 (24:1 whole no. 1457–30:48 whole no. 1561). NWaHi: Ap 5, 1877 (9:10 whole no. 426); Ag 31, 1882 (14:31 whole no. 708); Ap 28, 1884 (16:36).

WALTON CHRONICLE-TIMES see *THE CHRONICLE-TIMES*

THE WALTON CYCLONE see *THE PEOPLE'S PRESS*

THE WALTON JOURNAL (w) Walton. My 19, 1856–? (1:1–?). *Title changes*: *The Walton Blade* My 19, 1856–My 13, 1857; *The Walton Journal* My 20, 1857–? *Pub and Ed*: Edward P. Berray My 19–S 2, 1856; Edward P. Berray and Charles E. Pine S 9, 1856–Jl 22, 1857; Edward P. Berray Jl 1857–? *Pol*: Independent; Republican (from S 30, 1858). *Format*: Four pages, varying sizes, 11" x 16¼", 11½" x 17½", 9" x 12". *Price*: 75¢ per year (1856–Ja 13, 1859); 40¢ per year (Ja 20, 1859–?). *Comment*: Motto: "Not bound to swear in the words of any man." "Independent in Everything—Neutral in Nothing." "Pledg'd but to Truth, to Liberty and Law; No favor sways us and no fear shall awe." Suspended publication October 28, 1857 until September 30, 1858. Published over N. Fitch's store, corner of Main and Mead Sts. (1857). This newspaper was probably discontinued in 1859. (*History of Delaware*, p. 334.) *Loc*: NWa: My 19, 1856–O 28, 1857 (1:1–2:23); S 30, 1858–Mr 18, 1859 (2:25–2:50). NWaHi: Mr 3, S 16, 1857 (1:42; 2:17).

WALTON REPORTER (w) Walton. 1881 to date (1:1 to date). *Title changes*: *The Walton Star* 1881–?; *The Walton Reporter* by My 17, 1883–Ag 13, 1904; *Walton Reporter* Ag 20, 1904 to date. *Pub*: James W. Bulkley and John Platt White 1881–S 3, 1887; John P. White S 17, 1887–F 1, 1890; The Reporter Co. F 22, 1890 to date (Paul Nichols 1890–1897; Paul Nichols and John P. White, Mgrs., Ja 23, 1897–Ag 21, 1915; Estate of Paul Nichols and John Platt White, owners, Ag 28, 1915–?; none listed (?–1965); George F. White, Pres., by S 16, 1965 to date, John R. Clark, Vice-Pres., by 1968 to date). *Ed*: S. T. Morehouse 1881–?; J. W. Bulkley and John P. White by 1883–S 3, 1887; John P. White S 10, 1887–F 1, 1890; Paul Nichols F 22, 1890–Ja 16, 1897; Paul Nichols and John P. White Ja 23, 1897–Ag 21, 1915 (Nichols died Jl 20, 1915); John P. and Edward S. White Ag 28, 1915–S 4, 1920; John P. (died Ja 6, 1927) and George F. White S 11, 1920–Ja 8, 1927; Edward S. White Ja 15–O 1, 1927; Edward S. and George F. White O 8, 1927–M 1947); Edward S. (died O 3, 1947) and George F. White and John Clark Ap 4–O 10, 1947; George F. White and John R. Clark O 17, 1947–S 9, 1965; John R. Clark and Albert L. Peake S 16, 1965 to date. *Pol*: Democrat. *Format*: Four to eighteen pages, varying sizes, 15½" x 21¾", 20" x 25½",

19″ x 25″, 14½″ x 21″, 17¼″ x 22¼″, 16½″ x 20¼″. *Price*: $1.50 per year (1883–1886); $1.00 per year in advance, otherwise $1.50 (1887–1920); $1.50 per year, 5¢ per copy (1920–1942); $2.00 per year, 5¢ per copy (1942–1949); $3.00 per year, 8¢ per copy (1949–1957); $4.00 per year, 10¢ per copy (1958–1970); $5.00 per year, 15¢ per copy (Ja 1, 1971 to date). *Circ*: 2,400 (1890); 4,500 (1895–1896); 6,000 (1900); 7,000 (1903); 7,980 (1906); 6,700 (1934). *Comment*: Published next to the Post Office, Gardiner Place (1881–1885). The combined title *The Reporter and Star* appeared on the masthead by May 17, 1883 until September 17, 1887. *Loc*: NHan: Je 13, 1885 (5:16 whole no. 223). NWa: [My 17, 1883–D 28, 1934 (3:2–52:52 whole no. 2814)] [Ja 5, 1940 to date (59:1 whole no. 3078 to date)]. NWaHi: O 21, 1881 (1:33); Ap 14, 1882 (2:6 whole no. 58). NWaR: Ja 4, 1935–D 29, 1939 (54:4 whole no. 2816–58:52 whole no. 3077).

THE WALTON STAR see *WALTON REPORTER*

THE WALTON TIMES (w) Walton. N 19, 1892–1901// (1:1–?). *Pub and Ed*: W. H. Eells 1892–?; E. P. Sweet, Ass't Ed., 1894–? *Format*: Eight pages 15″ x 22″. *Price*: $1.00 per year in advance. *Comment*: Published at 83 Delaware St. Combined with *The Walton Chronicle* (q.v.) in 1901 and issued as *The Chronicle-Times* (q.v.) (*The Deposit Courier*, My 30, 1901). *Loc*: NDeP: Ja 4, 1895 (3:8). NWaHi: [Mr 17–S 28, 1894 (2:18–46 whole nos. 70–98 incomplete issues)].

WALTON TRUE PRESS Walton. 1872. No issues located. Started by Harvey Ireland and subsequently merged into *The Walton Chronicle* (q.v.) (Murray, *Delaware County,* p. 602).

WEEKLY VISITOR see *FRANKLIN VISITOR*

YOUNG PATRIOT Delhi. 1860. No issues located. Listed in Murray, *Delaware County,* p. 602.

AMERICAN BANNER Cherry Valley. 1853–? No issues located. John B. King purchased the *Cherry Valley Gazette* (q.v.) in 1853 and issued that paper for one year as the *American Banner*. "King disposed of it to A. S. Botsford, by whom it was renamed *The Gazette*. It subsequently passed into the hands of J. L. Sawyer, its present able and efficient editor." (*History of Otsego County* [Philadelphia: 1878], p. 33.)

BUTTERNUT VALLEY NEWS (w) Garrattsville. 1891–? (1:1–?). *Pub and Ed*: Will Pope. *Format*: Eight pages 11" x 16". *Price*: $1.00 per year. *Loc*: NCooHi: Jl 13, 1893 (3:27).

THE CASTIGATOR (w) Cooperstown. F 6, 1841–? (1:1–?). *Pub*: Z. & X. Plunkett. *Ed*: Joel Bodkin. *Format*: Four pages 8¾" x 12¼". *Price*: 50¢ per quarter. "No subscriptions will be received for more than one quarter." *Comment*: Motto: "Tell the truth and shame the Devil." Printed by Benedict, Elmer & Co. The publisher and editor were both pseudonyms.   *Loc*: NCooHi: F 6–20, Mr 6–Ap 10, 1841 (1:1–3, 5–10).

CHERRY-VALLEY GAZETTE (w) Cherry Valley. O 8, 1818– 1832// (1:1–?). *Pub*: Lemuel and Bethel Todd O 8, 1818–My 29, 1821; B. Todd Je 5, 1821–F 4, 1823; "Printed for the Proprietors" F 11, 1823–1832. *Format*: Four pages 12" x 19". *Price*: $2.00 per year (1818–1832). *Loc*: NChe: O 8, 1818–S 13, 1831 (1:1–13:676). NCooHi: S 1824–S 20, 1825 (7:313–364); S 25, 1827–S 16, 1828 (10:469–520).

CHERRY VALLEY GAZETTE (w) Cherry Valley. Je 1832–1932//? (1:1–?). *Title changes*: *Cherry Valley Gazette* 1832–?; *The Cherry Valley Gazette* by 1873–?; *The Gazette* by 1917–?; *Cherry Valley Gazette and Richfield Times* by 1927–?; *Cherry Valley Gazette* by O 1928–? *Pub and Ed*: Charles M'Lean Je 1832–?; Amos S. Botsford by My 23, 1849–?; Charles McLean by O 9, 1850–?; Amos S. Botsford by Mr 7, 1855–? (died June 1875); Smith and John L. Sawyer by 1872–?; John L. Sawyer (Pub.) and F. LeVere Winne (Mgr.) by 1917–?; Charles L. Ryder Ag 13, 1925–? *Pol*: Independent. *Format*: Four to eight pages, varying sizes, 15" x 20", 18½" x 24", 16½" x 22¾", 15½" x 21½", 17" x 19". *Price*: $2.00 per year (1832); $1.00 per year (1849); $2.00 per year (1850); $1.50 per year (1859); $1.50 per year in advance, 3¢ per copy (by 1925); $1.50 per year in advance, 5¢ per copy (by 1926). *Comment*: Motto: "A Family Newspaper—Neutral in Politics—Devoted to Literature, Science, Agriculture, Education, Morals, Amusement, and General Intelligence." (1846) "An Independent Journal:—Devoted to Temperance, Morals, Literature, Wit and Poetry." (1849) "A Weekly Independent Family Journal Devoted to Agriculture, Miscellaney, Romance and General Intelligence." (1861) "Independent on all Subjects; Neutral on None."

(1863) "Best Weekly in Otsego Co.—Covers the Cherry Valley Turnpike District." (1926). "In 1853 [it] was sold to John B. King, and issued one year as the *American Banner* [q.v.]. King disposed of it to A. S. Botsford by whom it was renamed *The Gazette*." (*History of Otsego County,* p. 32.) New Series established in 1845; in 1851; in 1855; and 1871. Then between 1908 and 1917 the numbering was changed so that it appeared that the paper had been established in 1818. Published from the Chitter Block (1917); Genesee St. (1925); then published at the Gazette office on Alden St. (1926). *Loc*: NChe: Jl 10, 1831–Je 10, 1834 (1:4–2:52); Jl 24, 31, 1861 (35:1901; 1902 n.s. 7:31, 32); Je 4, 1862 (36:1844 n.s. 8:24); Ja 21, Mr 25, Je 10, Ag 26, S 2, 30, 1863 (37: 1877, 1886, 1897, 1908, 1909, 1913 n.s. 9:5, 14, 25, 36, 37, 41); My 17, Ag 23, 1865 (39:1998, 2010 n.s. 11:21, 35); O 10, 17, 1866 (12:13, 14); Ag 14, 1867 (13:5); F 1, 8, Ap 12, 1873 (2:40, 41, 50); O 31, 1874 (4:27); Jl 1, 1875 (5:10); S 27, 1877 (7:23); D 19, 1889 (19:37); S 2, 1897 (27:26). NCheHi: Ap 29, 1846 (25:1251 n.s. 2:3); My 23, 1849 (28:1410 n.s. 5:5); O 9, D 25, 1850 (29:1452, 1463 n.s. 1:28, 39); Mr 5, 1851 (29:1473 n.s. 1:49); Mr 7, 1855 (31: 1570 n.s. 1:10); S 8, 1859 (35:1805 n.s. 5:37); My 30, N 14, 1860 (36:1842, 1865 n.s. 6:23, 47); My 13, 1863 (37:1893 n.s. 9:21); Je 22, Jl 6, 20, 27, O 12, 26, N 2, 23, 30, D 7, 1872 (2:8, 10, 12, 13, 24, 26, 27, 30, 31, 32); [F 1–N 1, 1873 (2:40–3:27)]; Jl 6, 1876 (6:11); Ag 29, 1878 (8:19); Mr 10, 1881; (10:47); F 7, 1884 (13:43); Mr 18, 1886 (15:47); Ap 19, 1888 (17:2); Ap 3, 1890 (19:52); S 17, 1891 (21:24); O 6, 1892 (22:27); Mr 10, 1898 (28:2); Mr 3, Ap 7, 1904 (33:48; 34:1); N 21, 1907 (37:?); Ja 30, 1908 (37:45); Ja 18, 1917 (98:37); [Ap 9, 1925–D 28, 1928 (107th year:?–110th year:20)]; F 1, 1933 (115:26 frag.).

CHERRY VALLEY GAZETTE AND RICHFIELD TIMES see *CHERRY VALLEY GAZETTE* (1832–1932//?)

THE CHERRY VALLEY NEWS (w) Cherry Valley. O 13, 1932 to date (1:1 to date.) *Pub and Ed*: F. LeVere Winne O 13, 1932–?; Frederick F. Parshall, Jr. by Jl 14, 1966–? *Format*: Four to ten pages, varying sizes, 15″ x 22″, 11½″ x 16″. *Price*: $1.50 per year in advance (1932); $2.50 per year, 10¢ per copy (by 1952). *Comment*: Motto: "The Only Newspaper printed in Historic Cherry Valley—A Home Paper for the Home." (1932) "News of the People in the Towns of Cherry Valley, Roseboom, Middlefield, Springfield, Sharon Springs and Vicinity. Otsego County's Only Tabloid Newspaper." (1952) "Otsego County's First Tabloid Newspaper." (1966) Merged with the *Cobleskill Times-Journal* about 1970. *Loc*: NChe: O 13, 1932 (1:1). NCheHi: Je 5, Jl 24, S 4, 25, 1952 (20:39, 46, 52, ?); Je 4, 1953 (21:39); Ja 5, 1956 (24:18); Ag 7, 1958 (fragment); Mr 5, Ap 2, 1959 (27:27, fragment); F 11, 1960 (28:24); O 3, 1963 (33:52); Jl 14, 1966 (37:45); Jl 13, 1967 (fragment).

CHERRY VALLEY TEMPERANCE INVESTIGATOR see *TEMPERANCE INVESTIGATOR*

COOPERSTOWN FEDERALIST see *FREEMAN'S JOURNAL*

COOPERSTOWN JOURNAL Cooperstown. 1878(?)–? No issues located. Mentioned in a note in the *Binghamton Daily Leader* of July 1878 stating that it was connected with the *Republican* October 31, 1878 and its editors were Edmister, Brownson and Marcan.

DAVENPORT STANDARD see *SCHENEVUS FREE PRESS DAVENPORT STANDARD*

THE DRAFTED MEN'S ADVOCATE (m) Cooperstown and Albany. *Pub*: "The State Committee of Drafted Men." *Format*: Four pages 14½ " x 20". *Price*: $1.00 per year in advance (1897). *Comment*: Publishing address listed as Farmer Publishing Company Building, Cooperstown and 238 Lark St., Albany. *Loc*: NCooHi: Mr 1897 (11:9).

THE EDMESTON LOCAL (w) Edmeston. 1882(?)–D 28, 1961// (1:1–78:52). *Title changes*: The Edmeston Local by 1890–1920; Edmeston Local by 1923–?; The Edmeston Local by 1929–D 28, 1961. *Pub and Ed*: Sherwood and Payne by 1890–?; D. Stanley Cooke by My 5, 1917–Mr 31, 1923; D. Stanley Cooke and L. M. Cooke Ap 7, 1923–?; LeRoy Palmer by Ap 26, 1929–F 1937; LeRoy Palmer (Pub.) and Marie B. Palmer (Ed.) Mr 5, 1937–1945; Herman P. Bolstein and George F. Breler (with Mrs. LeRoy Palmer as Edmeston Ed.) by My 25–D 21, 1945; Herman P. Bolstein (with Mrs. Frederick W. Loomis as Edmeston Editor by S 28, 1945) Ja 1946–Ja 1949; Virginia and Alfred Leiserson by Ja 21–S 30, 1949; Allen D. Bruckheimer (Pub.) and Natalie and David Fowler (Eds.) O 7, 1949–F 26, 1954; John A. Bacon Mr 5, 1954–D 28, 1961. *Format*: Eight pages, varying sizes, 17½ " x 24", 15" x 22". *Price*: $1.00 per year (1890); $1.50 per year (1923); $2.00 per year (1929); $1.50 per year (1936); $2.00 per year, 7¢ per copy (1945–1954); $3.50 per year, 10¢ per copy (1961). *Comment*: Motto: "Business is Business, Go in and Win" (1890); "Devoted to the Progress and Interest of Edmeston and Otsego County." The banner claims that it was established in 1882. On December 28, 1961, *The Edmeston Local* merged with *The Morris Chronicle* (q.v.). *Loc*: NCooHi: Mr 15, My 24, 1899 (n.s. 2:41, 50). NEd: Mr 28, 1895 (12:42 Ladies Edition); [My 5, 1917–D 28, 1961 (34:47–78:52)].

THE EVENING NEWS (d) Oneonta. S 14, 1891–? (1:1–?). *Pub*: George H. Smith and Co. *Ed*: George H. Smith. *Pol*: Independent. *Format*: Four pages 18" x 23½ ". *Price*: $3.00 per year. *Comment*: Motto: "The Poor Man's Friend and the People's Protector." *Loc*: NOn: [S 14, 1891–Ag 15, 1892 (1:1–286)].

THE FOURTH Cooperstown. 1883–? (1:1–?). *Pub and Ed*: Russell and Clinton. *Format*: Four pages 11" x 15". *Comment*: Motto: "Let Joy and Mirth be Unconfined." Full of advertisements and announcements of events of the Fourth of July celebration. *Loc*: NCooHi: Jl 4, 1883 (1:1).

THE FREEMAN'S JOURNAL (w) Cooperstown. O 22, 1808 to date (1:1 to date). *Title changes: Impartial Observer* O 22, 1808–My 1809; *Cooperstown Federalist* Je 3, 1809–1817; *Freeman's Journal and Otsego County Advertiser* 1817–S 1819; *Freeman's Journal* 1819–?; *The Freeman's Journal with which is combined the Milford Tidings* My 28, 1919–Je 16, 1920; *The Freeman's Journal* (with *"and Oneonta Press"* appended in masthead but not in banner) Ja 11, 1922–Je 1, 1972; *The Freeman's Journal* Je 1, 1972 to date. *Pub*: William Andrews 1808–1809; John H. Prentiss 1809–?; John H. and H. Prentiss by O 1810–?; Samuel M. Shaw and Co. 1880–1902; George H. Carley 1902; The Freeman's Journal Co., Inc. 1909 to Mr 20, 1919; Augustus Paul Cooke Mr 20, 1919–Je 5, 1920; The Freeman's Journal Co. Je 5, 1920–Je 1, 1972; Robert and Stanley Lennon Je 1, 1972–Jl 10, 1972; Fred Lee Publishing Co. Jl 10, 1972 to date. *Ed*: John H. Prentiss 1809–1851; Samuel M. Shaw 1851–1902; George H. Carley Ja 1, 1903–1919; Augustus Paul Cooke Mr 26, 1919–Je 16, 1920; Rowan D. Spraker 1920–Ap 13, 1955; Rowan D. Spraker, Jr. Ap 13, 1955–Je 1, 1972; Greg Fieg Je 1, 1972–Ag 8, 1972; G. Ray Leavitt Ag 8, 1972 to date. *Pol*: Federalist; Democrat. *Format*: Four to twenty-four pages, varying sizes, 18¼ " x 24½ ", 12" x 20", 22" x 28½ ", 11½" x 16" (1972 to date). *Price*: $1.50 per year by 1861; $2.00 per year in advance (1870); $1.50 per year in advance (by 1897); $2.00 per year in advance (by 1926); $2.50 per year in advance (by 1949); $3.00 per year, 10¢ per copy (by 1957); $2.00 per year in New York State, $5.00 per year out of state, 10¢ per copy (1973). *Comment*: Motto: "What I know to be true, that I will declare;—and what I feel it to be my duty to represent, that I will have the boldness to publish." (1809) "Principles, not Men." "The Old Reliable Democratic Family Newspaper of Otsego County." (1973). First published on "commercial row"; then moved to the "iron clad" building (February, 1875), 90 Main Street (1910); the Leatherstocking Building on Main Street (by 1926); 32 Main Street (by 1929); Hotel Fenimore (1935); the corner of Main and Pioneer Streets (November, 1935–November, 1961); temporarily moved to the National Commercial Bank and Trust Company building (November 10, 1961–July 12, 1962); 62 Pioneer Street (July 12, 1962 to date). In 1924 the business and editorial offices of *The Freeman's Journal* and *The Otsego Farmer* (q.v.) were combined. Walter Littell became managing editor and part owner of *The Freeman's Journal* and editor of *The Otsego Farmer*. The former was Democratic and the latter Republican. Both papers were printed by the same press, and except for editorials the content of the two papers was the same. (W. R. Littell, *A History of Cooperstown* [Cooperstown, 1929]) (R. D. Spraker, F. C. Carpenter, *Supplement to A History of Cooperstown* [Cooperstown, 1963]). The masthead of *The Freeman's Journal* (1973) states, "Milford Tidings absorbed in 1920; Otsego Farmer absorbed in 1972; Richfield Springs Mercury absorbed in 1973; Weekly Pioneer absorbed in 1973." *Loc*: NChe: F 6, 1957 (149:48 whole no. 8338). NCooHi: O 22, 1808 to date (1:1 to date). NNorHi: My 3, 1861 (53:39). NRU: Je 17, 1809 (1:35); My 20, 1839 (31:37).

FREEMAN'S JOURNAL AND OTSEGO COUNTY ADVERTISER
see *THE FREEMAN'S JOURNAL*

THE GAZETTE see *AMERICAN BANNER* and also *CHERRY VALLEY GAZETTE*

GAZETTE AND EXAMINER Cherry Valley. ca. 1857. No issues located.

GILBERTSVILLE EAGLE AND TRUE DEMOCRATIC AND PATRIOTIC REFLECTOR see *GILBERTSVILLE EAGLE AND TRUE RELIGIOUS AND PATRIOTIC REFLECTOR*

GILBERTSVILLE EAGLE AND TRUE RELIGIOUS AND PA-TRIOTIC REFLECTOR (irr) Gilbertsville. 1896(?)–? (1:1–?). *Title changes*: *Gilbertsville Eagle and True Democratic and Patriotic Reflector* 1896(?)–1901; *Gilbertsville Eagle and True Religious and Patriotic Reflector* by 1901–? *Pub and Ed*: James Lakin Gilbert. *Format*: Six pages 12″ x 15¾″. *Comment*: An anti-Christian, pro-Satan vehicle which stated that it was published from "Satan's Hollyhawk Den in Gilbertsville," later called "Hollihock Den." The 1897 issue of the newspaper stated that it was the "Second Epistle of the son of his Satanic majesty's true creator or Devil (all one) to Jew, Christian, Mormon and all other Heathen sects." *Loc*: NCooHi: 1897 (2:2). NGil: 1897 (2:2); 1898 (3:3); 1901 (6:1).

THE GLIMMERGLASS (d, except Sunday during the season) Cooperstown. Jl 19, 1909–? (1:1–?). *Pub*: Freeman's Journal (George H. Carley) 1909–1919; John Wilcox Co., Inc. 1920–1921; The Freeman's Journal 1922–? *Format*: Four pages, varying sizes, 12½″ x 19½″, 15″ x 22″. *Price*: 50¢ per month, 2¢ per copy (1909–?); $1.00 per season in advance, 2¢ per copy (by 1914); 3¢ per copy by 1958–1967; 5¢ per copy 1968–? *Comment*: "Issued daily in the summertime from the office of The Freeman's Journal. Usually ran mid-June to end of August or mid-Sept." *Loc*: NCooHi: Jl 19, 1909–S 1, 1948 (1:1–40:40); Jl 7, 1958–Ag 30, 1968 (50:1–59:40).

THE GOLDEN RULE (m) Roseboom. 1872–? No issues located. "A small temperance newspaper . . . edited by H. D. Elwell and published monthly. The subscription price was ten cents for six months. This little paper was continued for about eighteen months, when on January 1, 1874 it was enlarged and its name changed to *The Temperance Canoe* [q.v.]. . . ." (*History of Otsego County*, p. 35.)

HARTWICK REPORTER (w) Hartwick. Ap 14, 1915–? (1:1–?). *Pub and Ed*: A. D. and C. S. Hitchcock Ap 14, 1915–Mr 20, 1918 (A. D. Hitchcock died Mr 24, 1918); C. S. Hitchcock Mr 27, 1918–Ag 26, 1925; Loren A. Mann S 2, 1925–Ag 25, 1926; C. S. Hitchcock by S 1, 1926–Ap 27, 1930 (C. S. Hitchcock died); Mrs. C. S. Hitchcock Ap 30–My 7, 1930; N. M. Hitchcock My 14–My 28, 1930; Frank E. Boyce Je 4, 1930–? *Pol*: Independent. *Format*: Four to eight pages, varying sizes, 17¾″ x 24½″, 17″ x 19½″. *Price*: $1.00 per year (1915); $1.25 per year (1918); $1.50 per year (1931). *Comment*: Motto: "An Independent Weekly Paper, Devoted to the Interests of Hartwick and Vicinity Towns." (1917–1926); "A Weekly Paper, Devoted to the Interests of Hartwick and Vicinity Towns." (1926–?). *Loc*: NCooHi: [Ap 14, 1915–O 21, 1942 (1:1–29:26)].

THE HARTWICK REVIEW (w) Hartwick. My 1902–? (1:1–?). *Pub*: W. D. Dyke and R. P. Stoddard. *Ed*: Glenn Jackson. *Format*: Four pages 18¼ " x 24". *Loc*: NCooHi: Jl 24, 1902 (1:12).

HARTWICK SEMINARY MONTHLY (m) Hartwick Seminary ca. 1880–? (1:1–?). *Title changes*: Hartwick Seminary Monthly ca. 1880; *Hartwick Seminary Monthly and Eastern Lutheran* ca. 1887; *The Monthly* ca. 1909; *Hartwick Seminary Monthly* ca. 1926. *Format*: Four to eight pages, varying sizes, 8½ " x 11", 7" x 9". *Comment*: The first few issues were hand written. *Loc*: NCooHi: [Jl 1880–Ap 1926 (1:7–22:187)]. *See also* p. 288

HARTWICK VISITOR (w) Hartwick. 1902–? No issues located. Mentioned in Bacon's history. (Edwin F. Bacon, *Otsego County, New York* [Oneonta, N. Y.: 1902], p. 40.)

THE HERALD see *THE OTSEGO HERALD, OR WESTERN ADVERTISER*

HERALD AND DEMOCRAT see *THE ONEONTA HERALD*

HOME AND ABROAD see *THE OTSEGO DEMOCRAT* (Oneonta)

THE HYDE PARK NEWS (m) Hartwick Seminary. 1895(?)–? (1:1–?). *Pub and Ed*: Samuel J. Petrie. *Pol*: Independent. *Format*: Four pages 7¼ " x 10½ ". *Price*: 20¢ per year. *Loc*: NCooHi: Ag 14, S 14, 1895 (1:2, 7).

THE IMPARTIAL OBSERVER see *FREEMAN'S JOURNAL*

THE LIVING ISSUE (w) Cooperstown. 1876(?)–? (1:1–?). *Pub and Ed*: George D. Scrambling and Jones by 1882. *Pol*: Temperance, (National Prohibition Advocate). *Format*: Four pages 15½ " x 22½ ". *Price*: $1.50 per year. *Comment*: Motto: "Let Acts Harmonize with Words." *Loc*: NCooHi: Je 22, 1882 (7:51).

THE MILFORD TIDINGS see *THE OTSEGO TIDINGS*

THE MONTHLY see *HARTWICK SEMINARY MONTHLY*

THE MORNING CALL Oneonta. 1871//(?) No issues located. Possibly started in 1871 and only lasted two issues.

THE MORRIS CHRONICLE (w) Morris. D 12, 1865–S 1965 (1:1–?). *Title changes*: The Otsego Chronicle D 12, 1865–?; *The Morris Chronicle* by 1869–? *Pub and Ed*: William A. Smith D 12, 1865–?; Leman P. Carpenter by 1869–Mr 3, 1875; Leman P. Carpenter & Son [Edwin E. Carpenter] 1877–Ap 7, 1920; B. Franklin Waite

Ap 14, 1920–?; Preston Wright by Ag 6, 1924–?; LeRoy Palmer ?–?; John A. Bacon by 1956–? *Pol*: Independent. *Format*: Four to sixteen pages, varying sizes, 14″ x 20″, 18″ x 24″. *Price*: $1.00 per year in advance (by 1903–?); $1.25 per year in advance (1920); $1.50 per year (1921–?); $2.50 per year, 7¢ per copy (1954–?); $3.00 per year, 10¢ per copy (by 1962). *Circ*: 1,000 (1890). *Comment*: "Devoted to the Interests and Progress of the Butternut Valley." (1901). "So far as we have been able to learn, the first home of the *Chronicle* was in the stone building built in 1845 by Jacob Lull for a shoe and leather shop and presently owned by Mrs. H. W. Naylor. The *Chronicle's* next home was in the building now owned by Warren Kinney and from there moved to the site of Sheldon's Auction Gallery. Following this, it made its home on South Broad Street in what is now the American Legion Building, and here it stayed for thirteen years until in 1900, it was moved into a building of its own on Main Street now the Naylor Company Office. Still later, it occupied the Library Building. The *Chronicle* always held a strong place in the affection of the people of Morris. . . ." (Joyce Foote, *Morris, New York, 1773–1923*, [Morris, N. Y.: 1970], p. 44.) The following Otsego County papers combined with the *Chronicle*: *The Otsego Valley News* of Hartwick (q.v.) by 1957 and the *Edmeston Local* (q.v.) by 1961. In 1965, the *Morris Chronicle* became part of the *Otsego-Chenango Bee Journal Chronicle* (q.v.). *Loc*: NCooHi: [D 12, 1865–F 4, 1868 (1:1–2:30)]; [My 26, 1869–Je 1938 (3:7–?)]. NMor: [Ag 10, 1898–Ap 8, 1925 (41:3–58:14)]; [Ap 2, 1954–Jl 11, 1963 (90:14–99:28)]. NSNB: 1899 (33:3).

NEW ERA (irr) Oneonta. S 13, 1877–? (1:1–?). *Pub*: An Association of Prohibitionists in Oneonta, George D. Scrambling, Business Manager. *Ed*: "The Editorial Staff is composed of gentlemen of undoubtable Prohibition Sentiments." *Pol*: Prohibition. *Format*: Four pages 22″ x 31″. *Price*: $1.50 per year (1877–1878). *Circ*: 1,000 (1877–1878). *Comment*: Motto: "Who is My Neighbor?" *Loc*: NCooHi: S 13, N 1, 1877 (1:1, 7); [Ap 12–N 1, 1878 (1:23–48)].

THE NEW YORK FARMER (w) Cooperstown. S 8, 1893–? (1:1–?). *Pub*: The Farmer Publishing Co. 1893–1901 (A. B. Crist, Henry Scott, C. H. Parshall). *Format*: Eight pages 17″ x 22″. *Price*: $1.50 per year (1893); $1.00 per year (1894). *Comment*: Motto: "A Farm and Home Paper." Published in the Farmer Blocks. *Loc*: NCooHi: [S 8, 1893–O 10, 1901 (1:1–7:52)].

THE NULLIFIER (w) Cooperstown. My 7, 1833–? (1:1–?). *Pub and Ed*: Anonymous. *Format*: Four pages 7½″ x 10½″. *Loc*: NCooHi: My 27, S 19, 1833 (1:4, 22).

ONEONTA COMMERCIAL Oneonta. No issues located.

ONEONTA DAILY LOCAL (d) Oneonta. My 2, 1887–? (1:1–?). *Pub*: The Local Publishing Co. *Format*: Four pages 11″ x 16″. *Price*: 10¢ per week, 2¢ per copy. *Comment*: Motto: "The Pioneer Daily of Otsego County." Published at No. 12 Broad St. *Loc*: NOnHC: My 2,

1887–F 19, 1888 (1:1–?). NOnHi: My 2, 18, O 12, 1887 (1:1, 15, 139).

ONEONTA DAILY NEWS (d) Oneonta. F 20, 1888–? (1:1–?). *Pub*: News Publishing Co. *Format*: Four pages 11" x 16". *Price*: $4.00 per year, 10¢ per week, 3¢ per copy (1891). *Comment*: Published at 1 Broad St., Oneonta; then 17 Chestnut St. in the News Cottage. *Loc*: NChe: Mr 30, 1891 (4:931). NCooHi: Ap 17, 1888 (1:50). NOn: N 12, 1888 (1:227); Ap 4, 1889 (2:348). NOnHC: F 20, 1888–Je 18, 1890 (1:1–?).

ONEONTA DAILY STAR see *ONEONTA STAR*

ONEONTA DAILY TIMES see *ONEONTA TIMES*

ONEONTA DISPATCHER (bi-m) Oneonta. 1880(?)–? (1:1–?). *Pub*: The Railway YMCA A. & S. Division, D. H. Canal Railroad. A. C. Holley, President; C. C. Swift, Railroad Secretary. *Price*: 10¢ per copy (1885); 25¢ per year 5¢ per copy (1886). *Loc*: NOnHI: N–D 1885 (6:5); Je–Jl 1886 (7:3).

ONEONTA GAZETTE Oneonta. 1840(?) No issues located. Dudley Campbell in a history published in 1906 refers to this paper. "The first newspaper here of which we have any record was the *Oneonta Gazette*." (Dudley Campbell, *A History of Oneonta From its Earliest Settlement to the Present Time*, [Oneonta, N. Y.: 1906], p. 93.)

THE ONEONTA HERALD Oneonta. 1838–1840//(?) (1:1–?). No issues located. According to Edwin Moore, an Oneonta newspaperman, *The Oneonta Herald* was founded in 1838 by Edward Graves. It lasted about a year and was sold to William J. Knapp in 1839 and the name changed to the *Oneonta Weekly Journal* (q.v.) which suspended publication about 1842. The *Oneonta Star* of September 28, 1950, p. 15-A, reported that the *Herald* once lamented that their weekly receipts amounted to only $2.00 and if customers wanted the newspaper to continue, they would have to settle up.

THE ONEONTA HERALD (w) Oneonta. F 9, 1853–Mr 10, 1947 (1:1–?). *Title changes*: Oneonta Herald F 9, 1853–S 22, 1869; *The Oneonta Herald* S 29, 1869–1873; *Oneonta Herald and Democrat* Ja 2, 1874–?; *Herald and Democrat* 1882–1883; *The Oneonta Herald* Ja 3, 1884–1947. *Pub*: Leman P. and J. B. Carpenter F 9–S 7, 1853; Leman P. Carpenter S 1853–D 12, 1866; George W. Reynolds D 1866–N 9, 1870; Charles S. Carpenter N 17, 1870–S 12, 1872; Charles S. and J. W. Carpenter S 19, 1872–D 1873; E. W. Capron and Edward M. Johnson Ja 2, 1874–Ja 1875; Edward M. Johnson by 1875–?; Edward M. Johnson and Willard E. Yager by 1882–?; Willard E. Yager and E. W. Fairchild 1883–?; G. W. Fairchild Ja 2, 1890–D 1900; G. W. Fairchild & Co. (A. B. Saxton, D. W. Peck) by Ja 3, 1901–?; Oneonta Herald Publishing Co. F 1907–? (G. W. Fairchild, Pres.; C. W. Peck, Vice-Pres.; A. B. Saxton, Sec. & Treas.); Otsego Publishing Co. My 2, 1912–? (H. W. Lee, Pres.); Oneonta Star Inc. 1945–1947 (James H. Ottoway, Pres.; Eugene J. Brown, Gen. Manager). *Ed*: Leman P. and

J. B. Carpenter F 9–S 7, 1853; Leman P. Carpenter S 1853–D 12, 1866; George W. Reynolds D 1866–N 9, 1870; Charles C. Carpenter 1870–?; E. W. Capron and Edward M. Johnson Ja 2, 1874–Ja 1875; Charles S. Carpenter 1875–?; Edward M. Johnson Je 1875–D 15, 1881; Andrew B. Saxton by 1901–? *Format*: Four to ten pages, varying sizes, 16″ x 21″, 15″ x 22½″, 16″ x 22″, 23½″ x 21½″. *Price*: $1.50 per year in advance (1853–?); $1.00 per year (1860); $1.50 per year (1868–?). *Comment*: Motto: "Pledged but to Truth, To Liberty, and Law." (1861). "Once in the Path of Duty, Never turn Back, or Falter for Difficulties. The Dawn will seem the Brighter if its Coming finds us Advancing." (1873) The paper was first called the *Oneonta Herald* in 1853; then merged with *The Otsego Democrat* (q.v.) in 1874; and finally resumed its original title in 1884 and was absorbed by the *Oneonta Star* Mr 17, 1947. In 1853 published one door south of E. R. Ford's, then on Main Street (by 1867). By 1868 listed at Blend's new building on Main Street over Tobey, Altman & Co.; then by 1873 in the Reynolds Block; then just listed as published from the corner of Main and Broad Streets. By 1906 the address was listed as 282 Main Street. By 1912, Broad Street appears as B. W. Fairchild's business address. *Loc*: NCooHi: Ap 14, 1858 (6:8); S 23, O 7, 1868 (16:31, 33); Ja 27, My 19, 1869 (16:49; 17:13); Jl 24, 1873 (20:25); Je 26, 1874 (n.s. 1:33); Je 18, Jl 9, 1880 (n.s. 7:31, 34); Jl 8, 1881 (n.s. 9:34); D 17, 1903 (51:5 n.s. 16:30); Mr 10, 1904 (51:17 n.s. 16:42); Ap 2, 1908 (55:20 n.s. 20:39). NIC/ MMN: Ag 12, 1943 (53:43). NOn: [F 9, 1853–D 26, 1946 (1:1– 64:31)]. NOnHi: D 19, 1860 (8:43); F 13, 1861 (8:51); My 21, 1862 (10:13); Je 26, 1867 (15:16); S 29, O 13, N 17, 24, 1869 (13:32, 34, 39, 40); Mr 9, 1870 (18:30); Ag 3, 1871 (19:22); Mr 29, S 11, N 14, 1873 (20:18, 31; n.s. 1:1); Je 26, 1874 (n.s. 1:33); Ja 8, 15, Mr 26, Ap 30, My 7, Je 23, 1875 (n.s. 2:9, 10, 20, 25, 26, 37); Ag 31, 1882 (n.s. 9:41); Mr 5, 1885 (32:16); Ap 3, 1890 (37:21 n.s. 2:46); Ap 30, N 26, D 24, 31, 1896 (43:25 n.s. 8:47; 44:2, 6, 7 n.s. 9:24, 28, 29); Ap 12, 1906 (53:15 n.s. 18:45). NOnHS: microfilm [F 9, 1853–D 26, 1946 (1:1–64:31)]. NOnSUCO: microfilm [F 9, 1853–D 26, 1946 (1:1–64:31)].

ONEONTA HERALD AND DEMOCRAT see *THE ONEONTA HERALD*

ONEONTA LEADER (semi-m) Oneonta. 1901–? (1:1–?). *Pub and Ed*: W. D. Van Dyke & Co. *Format*: Four pages 17½″ x 23½″. *Price*: 50¢ per year. *Comment*: Published at the Windsor Block, Chestnut St. *Loc*: NCooHi: O 1, D 14, 1901 (1:6; 2:1); My 10, 1902 (3:1).

ONEONTA PRESS see *THE FREEMAN'S JOURNAL AND ONEONTA PRESS*

THE ONEONTA PRESS see *ONEONTA PRESS AND OTSEGO COUNTY DEMOCRAT*

ONEONTA PRESS AND OTSEGO COUNTY DEMOCRAT (w)

Oneonta. 1876(?)–? (1:1–?). *Title changes*: *The Oneonta Press* 1876(?)–?; *Oneonta Press and Otsego County Democrat* by 1904–? *Pub and Ed*: Raymond and Smith (by 1884–?); Henry G. Bishop by 1904–? *Pol*: Democrat. *Price*: $1.25 per year (1882). *Comment*: Motto: "Democracy, Truth, Progress." "*The Oneonta Press* now in its first volumes, was established by G. W. Reynolds. Mr. Reynolds is a veteran newspaper editor and publisher, and the *Press* ranks among the best journals in this section." (*History of Otsego County*, p. 34.) According to Dudley Campbell, *The Oneonta Press* was established in 1876 by W. H. Jefferson. "It has been successively under the management of Raymond & Smith, Coates & Weed, S. W. Ferenbaugh, and is now under the management of Henry G. Bishop, who became proprietor in 1894." (Campbell, *A History of Oneonta*, pp. 93–94.) *Loc*: NIC/MMN: Mr 5, 1885 (8:44). NOnHi: Ag 31, 1882 (6:17); N 20, 1884 (8:29); Mr 5, 1885 (8:44); F 4, 1904 (30:36).

ONEONTA SPY (w) Oneonta. 1887–? (1:1–?). *Pub*: E. C. Reynolds and Albert D. Hitchcock ?–1895; Albert D. Hitchcock 1895–? *Format*: Four pages 21" x 26". *Price*: $1.00 per year in advance (1899). *Comment*: Motto: "Home and Vicinity News, Home Interests, General Intelligence, Literature and Opinion." (1899) "The *Oneonta Spy* was first published by George W. Reynolds, who was succeeded by E. C. Reynolds, and in 1895 it was purchased by Albert D. Hitchcock, who continued its management until its recent discontinuance." (Campbell, *A History of Oneonta*, p. 94.) *Loc*: NOnHi: F 20, O 2, 1894 (fragment, 8:28); D 26, 1899 (13:40).

THE ONEONTA STAR (d) Oneonta. Je 19, 1890 to date (1:1 to date). *Title changes*: *The Oneonta Star* Je 19, 1890–?; *Oneonta Daily Star* 1898–1940; *The Oneonta Star* Ag 1, 1940 to date. *Pub*: Harry W. Lee 1890–S 1908; Otsego Publishing Co. S 1908–Mr 1912 (Edward S. Clark, Pres. by 1910–?; Harry W. Lee, Pres. by 1915–?; Frances A. Lee, Pres. by Mr. 1936–N 1944); Oneonta Star Inc. Division of Ottaway Newspapers, (James H. Ottaway, Pres. D 1, 1944–?); Donald Clifford ? to date. *Ed*: Harry W. Lee 1890–1936; Frances A. Lee 1938–1947; Eugene J. Brown 1947–?; Andrew B. Saxton ?–?; Frank Perretta S 1966 to date. *Pol*: Independent. *Format*: Four to sixteen pages, varying sizes, 11" x 15", 16" x 22". *Price*: 10¢ per week, 3¢ per copy (1887–1940); $30.00 per year, 15¢ per copy (? to date) *Circ*: 3,000 (1913); 13,000 (1950). *Comment*: An editorial of June 19, 1890, stated that it was to be ". . . an independent newsy paper devoted to the interests of Oneonta and Susquehanna Valley. A daily full of local news and free from all vulgarities. . . . The *Star* will have no pets. We shall be true to our friends." Published from the Westcott Block, under W. H. Ives' Crockery Store (1889); then from the Wilber Block, Corner of Main and Front Sts. (June 19, 1890); News Cottage, 17 Chestnut St. (October 1, 1890); Niles Block on Broad St. (1890); 14 Broad St. (1901); 12-14 Broad St. (1935); and presently from 102 Chestnut St. The September 28, 1950 issue of *The Oneonta Star* claims that in 1912 Harry W. Lee bought *The Oneonta Herald* (q.v.), a weekly paper, owned by George W. Fairchild, to keep Fairchild from changing it to a daily paper and competing with the *Star*. On March 17, 1947, *The Oneonta Herald* was combined with the *Star*. *Loc*: NOnHC: [Je 19, 1890–O 31, 1948 (1:1–?)]. NOnStar: microfilm 1917–1967. NOnSUCO: microfilm 1966 to date.

ONEONTA TIMES (d) Oneonta. N 1, 1897–? (1:1–?). *Format*: Four pages 11″ x 16″. *Comment*: "The *Oneonta Times* sprang up during a controversy over the Oneonta Normal School. George I. Wilber, brother of David Forrest Wilber, was President of the Local Board of the Normal School, and had brought serious charges against the principal, Dr. James N. Milne, who finally was ousted. The *Star* published the Wilber charges and the new opposition paper [The *Times*] sided with Dr. Milne. When the controversy ended, the *Times* folded." (*Oneonta Star,* September 28, 1950, p. 15-A.) *Loc*: NCooHi: N 1, 1897 (1:1).

ONEONTA WEEKLY JOURNAL (w) Oneonta. S 17, 1840–? (1:1–?). *Pub*: William J. Knapp 1840–? *Format*: Four pages 20″ x 26″. *Comment*: "In 1840, a newspaper was established here which was hereafter conducted by Wm. J. Knapp for about two years when, owing to poor health, Mr. Knapp was compelled to discontinue its publication. It was the *Oneonta Weekly Journal*." (Dudley M. Campbell, *A Sketch of the History of Oneonta,* [Oneonta, New York: 1883], pp. 52–53). *Loc*: NOnHi: S 17, 1840 (1:1); N 18, 1841 (2:6).

THE OTEGO LITERARY RECORD (w) Otego. S 17, 1868–? (1:1–?). *Pub and Ed*: E. H. Orwen and Tompkins. *Format*: Four pages. *Price*: $1.50 per year. *Comment*: *The Otego Literary Record* was started at Otego in 1868. By 1872 it was called *The Otego Record* and was published by E. H. Orwen. (Hamilton Child, *Gazetteer and Business Directory of Otsego County, New York for 1872–3,* [Syracuse, N. Y.: 1872], p. 65.) On pages 9 and 262 of Child's *Gazetteer* Alpheus S. Foot is listed as editor and proprietor. Office located in Clark Block. No issues of the newspaper under the latter title have been located. *Loc*: NCooHi: S 17, 1868. NOnHi: D 24, 1869 (2:16).

THE OTEGO RECORD see *THE OTEGO LITERARY RECORD*

THE OTEGO TIMES (w) Otego. 1881–? (1:1–?). *Pub and Ed*: Vincent S. Fuller ("Editor Dan"). *Pol*: Neutral. *Format*: Four pages 20″ x 26″. *Price*: $1.25 per year in advance; otherwise $1.50. *Comment*: Published at River St. Probably changed title to the *Rural Times* (q.v.) whose publisher and editor was also Vincent S. Fuller, but we have been unable to locate issues to substantiate this premise. *Loc*: NOt: Jl 4, 1888.

OTEGO VALLEY NEWS (w) Laurens. D 29, 1898–? (1:1–?). *Pub and Ed*: V. F. and L. A. Dykeman. *Format*: Eight pages 13″ x 20″. *Price*: $1.00 per year in advance. *Comment*: Motto: "Representative Journal of Otego Valley." *Loc*: NCooHi: D 29, 1898 (1:1).

O-TE-SA-GA GAZETTE (annually) Cooperstown. 1957(?)–?
(1:1–?). *Pub*: H. J. Merrick, Jr. *Format*: Four to eight pages, varying sizes, 11″ x 17½″, 8½″ x 11″. *Price*: Free. *Comment*: Chiefly
a vehicle for advertising resorts and entertainment spots in Cooperstown. *Loc*: NCooHi: Je 1957 (1:1); 1960 (1:3).

THE OTSEGO-CHENANGO BEE JOURNAL CHRONICLE (w)
Gilbertsville. My 10, 1876 to date. *Title changes*: *The Otsego Journal*
My 10, 1876–S 30, 1965; *The Otsego-Chenango Bee Journal Chronicle*
O 7, 1965 to date. *Pub*: James E. Marble My 10, 1876–?; Will M.
Dietz by D 13, 1876–?; Oscar H. Swenson 1941–?; Journal Publish-
ing Co. (John A. Bacon, Pub & Ed. ?–Ja 1968; Ralph St. Denny F 2,
1968 to date). *Pol*: Republican. *Format*: Four to eight pages, varying
sizes, 10½″ x 14″, 15½″ x 20″, 19″ x 24″, 20″ x 26½″, 10″ x 14½″.
Price: 75¢ per year, otherwise $1.00 (1876–1879); $1.00 per year in
advance, then $1.25 per year (1879–?); 10¢ per copy (by 1965);
$3.00 per year in advance, 10¢ per copy (by 1967). *Circ*: 815
(1876–?); 1,480 (1892–1894); 1,485 (1895–?). *Comment*: Motto:
"A live local paper." (1871); "A Live, Independent Local Newspaper
Devoted to the Best Interests of the People of the Butternut Valley."
(1877–?). Published on Commercial Street. This newspaper combined
the *South New Berlin Bee, The Otsego Journal* of Gilbertsville, the
Morris Chronicle, The Otsego Observer, the *Otego Valley News* of
Hartwick and *The Edmeston Local,* and published news for Wyoming,
Sidney, Unadilla and Mount Upton. (See also *South New Berlin Bee*
in the Chenango County Bibliography, October 1972, *New York History*.) *Loc*: NCooHi: [1876–1878]; 1881; 1934. NGil: [My 10, 1876
to date]. NMor: [D 23, 1965–Je 29, 1967 (90:52–92: no issue no.)].

THE OTSEGO CHRONICLE see *THE MORRIS CHRONICLE*

THE OTSEGO COUNTY COURIER Louisville, in the town of Morris. 1845–1847// (1:1–?). No issues located. "*The Otsego County
Courier* was commenced at the village of Louisville, in the town of
Morris, by Wm. H. S. Wynans, in 1845." (Child, *Gazetteer*, p. 64.)
In the *History of Otsego County,* p. 33, there is mention that "the
first newspaper in Morris was established by W. H. Winans, in 1846,
and discontinued in 1847." The name of the newspaper is not mentioned but it probably is *The Otsego County Courier*.

THE OTSEGO COUNTY DEMOCRAT (w) Oneonta. ca. 1876(?)
Pub and Ed: H. G. Bishop. *Format*: Eight pages 15″ x 22″. *Price*:
$1.00 per year in advance. *Comment*: Motto: "Devoted to the Inter-
ests of the People and the Principles of the Democratic Party." Combined with the *Oneonta Press* to become the *Oneonta Press and Otsego
County Democrat* (q.v.) *Loc*: NOnHi: My 5, Jl 14, 1898 (22:49;
23:7).

OTSEGO COUNTY GRANGE NEWS (semi-m) Cooperstown.
1936–? (1:1–?). *Pub*: Printed by the Butler Press for the Otsego
County Grange. *Ed*: Anna K. Whipple. *Format*: Four pages 12½″ x

19". *Comment*: Published at 11 Delaware Street. *Loc*: NCooHi: Je 1, 1939 (4:11).

THE OTSEGO COUNTY LEADER Otego. 1873//. No issues located. "*The Otsego County Leader,* a new paper published at Otego has 'gone where the woodbine twineth.' After a feeble existence of only one short week, it has left us to be known no more on earth. We understood friend Carpenter of the *Herald,* did not get pay for the white paper on which it was printed." (*Delhi Gazette,* February 14, 1873.)

OTSEGO DEMOCRAT (w) Cooperstown. Mr 13, 1847–S 29, 1855// (1:1–9:31). *Pub*: James I. Hendryx 1847–1855. *Format*: Four pages 19" x 23". *Comment*: Combined with *The Otsego Republican* in 1855 and was thereafter issued as the *Republican and Democrat. Loc*: NCooHi: [Mr 13, 1847–S 29, 1855 (1:1–9:31)].

THE OTSEGO DEMOCRAT (w) Oneonta. 1869–1874// (1:1–?). *Title changes*: *Home and Abroad* 1869–1873; *The Otsego Democrat* 1873–1874. *Pub and Ed*: G. A. Dodge 1869–1873; W. H. Jefferson 1873–1874. *Pol*: Mason; Independent. *Format*: Four pages 15" x 22". *Price*: $2.00 per year (1869); $1.00 per year in advance (1873). *Comment*: Motto: "Devoted to Choice Literature, News, Agriculture, Masonic Intelligence, etc., etc." (1869) "An Independent Newspaper Devoted to the Best Interests of Society in General and of Oneonta in Particular." (1873) Child's *Gazetteer* states that the newspaper was first started as *The Susquehanna Independent* and published under that title until June 5, 1869, when the name was changed to *Home and Abroad.* (Child, *Gazetteer,* pp. 64–65.) There is no evidence to support this premise. *The Oneonta Herald and Democrat* (q.v.) was a consolidation of *The Otsego Democrat* and the *Oneonta Herald* in 1874. *Loc*: NOnHi: N 27, 1869 (1:26); Ag 5, 1871 (3:10); Ja 4, Je 11, 1873 (4:33, 5:6).

THE OTSEGO EXAMINER (w) Cooperstown. Ag 21, 1854–1857// (?) (1:1–?). *Pub*: Committee of two. *Pol*: Democrat (?). *Format*: Four pages 5" x 7". *Circ*: 128 (1854). *Comment*: Motto: "Men—not Principles." Seems to have been published as a facetious newspaper filled with political squibs. ". . . established in 1855 [*sic*] by Robert Shanklard. It subsequently passed into the hands of Mr. [B. W.] Burditt, and in 1857 was discontinued." (*History of Otsego County,* p. 35.) *Loc*: NCooHi: Ag 21, 31, 1854 (1:1, 2).

THE OTSEGO FARMER (w) Cooperstown. 1877 to Je 1, 1972 (1:1 to 86:36). *Title changes*: *The Otsego Farmer* 1877–D 1910; *The Otsego Farmer* (with "*and Otsego Republican*" appended to the banner but not to the masthead) Ja 6, 1911–Je 1, 1972. *Pub*: H. L. Russell 1885–O 17, 1891; H. L. Russell & A. H. Crist 1891–1892; The Farmer Publishing Co. 1893–S 2, 1904; A. H. Crist, Henry Scott, C. H. Parshall 1904–1906; Arthur H. Crist Co. 1907–O 1, 1920; Otsego Farmer, Inc. 1920–Je 1, 1972. *Ed*: H. L. Russell 1885–O 18, 1891; H. L. Russell & A. H. Crist 1891–?; Walter R. Littell O 8, 1920–

1922(?); Harry F. Davis by N 1923–Ap 18, 1924; Wm. T. Powell Ag 22, 1924–Je 19, 1925; Walter R. Littell Je 19, 1925–Ja 6, 1956; Frank R. Carpenter Ja 6, 1956–Je 1, 1972. *Pol*: Independent, then Republican. *Format*: Eight to fourteen pages, varying sizes, 15″ x 22″, 16⅞″ x 22″, 19½″ x 24″, 17½″ x 22½″, 19″ x 23″. *Price*: $1.50 per year (1886–1896); $2.00 per year (ca. 1920); $3.00 per year (ca. 1950). *Circ*: 3,200 (1898); 5,100 (1907). *Comment*: Published from the Crist Building 1911–1913; from the Cooperstown Press Building by 1921 until 1923; temporarily from 27 Main Street by 1923; Cooperstown Press Building from Ag 13, 1924. In 1924 publishing and editorial offices combined with those of *The Freeman's Journal* (q.v.). In June, 1972 Robert and Stanley Lennon purchased *The Freeman's Journal* and *The Otsego Farmer* and discontinued publication of the latter. The newspaper was renumbered as a new series July 21, 1888. *Loc*: NCooHi: [D 5, 1885–Je 1, 1972 (8:47–86:36)]. NHar: keeps the last five years on file. NOnHi: Ja 28, 1916 (30:9).

OTSEGO HERALD: OR, WESTERN ADVERTISER see *OTSEGO HERALD* , p. 289

THE OTSEGO JOURNAL see *THE OTSEGO-CHENANGO BEE JOURNAL CHRONICLE*

THE OTSEGO OBSERVER see *THE OTSEGO-CHENANGO BEE JOURNAL CHRONICLE*

OTSEGO REPUBLICAN (w) Cooperstown. Je 1(?), 1829–1855 (1:1–?). *Title changes*: *The Tocsin* ?–N 28, 1831; *Otsego Republican* D 5, 1831–1855. *Pub and Ed*: Chauncey E. Dutton & W. Hewes by Ja 1830–?; Chauncey E. Dutton ?–O 11, 1830; Chauncey E. Dutton and Henry W. Hopkins O 1830–Ap 1831; Henry W. Hopkins My 9, 1831–?; Henry W. Hopkins and A. W. Clark ?–?; A. W. Clark 1834–Jl 3, 1837; Andrew M. Barber Jl 10, 1837–Jl 20, 1840; I. K. Williams Ag 1840–Ja 31, 1842; William J. Clark F 1842–?; Andrew Barber by 1847–? *Pol*: Anti-Masonic 1829–? *Format*: Four pages, varying sizes, 15″ x 19½″; 16″ x 21″. *Price*: $2.00 per year in advance, $2.50 at end of year (1829–1831). *Comment*: Motto: "Be Just and Fear Not." "*The Tocsin* was commenced at Cooperstown in June 1829, by Dutton and Hewes. In 1839 its name was changed to *The Otsego Republican*." (Child, *Gazetteer*, p. 63.) In 1855 *The Otsego Republican* merged with *The Otsego Democrat* to become the *Republican and Democrat* (q.v.) and was issued as a new series newspaper which later changed its name back to *The Otsego Republican* (q.v.). *Loc*: NChe: My 31, 1847 (19:4). NCheHi: Ja 4, Jl 12, 1830 (1:32; 2:7); My 31, 1847 (19:4). NCooHi: [My 31, 1830–My 18, 1835 (2:1–6:52)]; [My 23, 1836–My 8, 1843 (8:1–14:52)]. NOnHi: Ja 4, Jl 12, 1830 (1:32; 2:7); D 28, 1835 (7:32); Ag 22, 1836 (8:14); My 22, 1843 (15:2).

THE OTSEGO REPUBLICAN (w) Cooperstown. O 6, 1855–1911// (?)

(n.s. 1:1–?). *Title changes*: *Republican and Democrat* O 6, 1855–Je 8, 1861; *The Otsego Republican* Je 15, 1861–D 25, 1869; *Republican and Democrat* Ja 1, 1870–D 27,1877; *Otsego Republican* Ja 3, 1878–? *Pub and Ed*: James I. Hendryx and Jerome B. Wood by Mr 14, 1857–?; James I. Hendryx by Ja 7, 1860–1872; James I. Hendryx and Charles F. Hendryx 1873–1874; Russell and Andrew Davidson 1874–Jl 9, 1884; Andrew Davidson Jl 16, 1884–1892; Andrew and Clarence W. Davidson 1893–N 12, 1902; Clarence W. Davidson N 19, 1902–1911. *Pol*: Republican. *Format*: Four pages, varying sizes, 17¾ " x 24", 23" x 29½ ". *Price*: $1.50 per year (1857); $2.00 per year (1881). *Comment*: Office on second floor in the Stone Building next East of Worthington (1847) then from Main and Pioneer Sts.; then Davis' Brick Block (1857). Office in the Republican Building (1870). The volume numbering of the newspaper changed radically in 1878 when its numbering from n.s. volume 24, no. 17 to volume 50, in order to date its ancestry back to *The Tocsin* (q.v.) published in 1829. Combined with the *Otsego Farmer* (q.v.) in 1911. *Loc*: NChe: Ja 3, O 25, D 6, 1847 (19:35 [*sic*], 25, 31); O 16, 1848 (20:24); Ag 20, 1849 (21:46); S 21, 1881 (54:4). NCooHi: [O 7, 1855–D 29, 1909 (n.s. 1:1–82:23)]. NOnHi: Mr 14, 1857 (*Republican* 28:45; *Democrat* 11:523); Ja 7, 1860 (n.s. 5:5; *Republican* 31:38; *Democrat* 13:46); Mr 9, 1861 (7:24; *Republican* 32:47; *Democrat* 15:1); Ja 8, 1870 (15:17); Je 8, N 11, 1871 (n.s. 16:43, 17:9).

OTSEGO REPUBLICAN PRESS (w) Cherry Valley. 1812–1813//. No issues located. "Established Aug. 14, 1812, by Clark & Crandal [Israel W. Clark and Edward B. Crandal], with the title of *Otsego Republican Press*. The paper was discontinued with the issue of Aug. 6, 1813, vol. 1, no. 52." (Brigham, *History and Bibliography,* pp. 566–567.)

OTSEGO SPY (w) Cooperstown. 1826–? (1:1–?). *Pub and Ed*: Butler and Rice by My 6, 1826; Doctor Noter by Jl 29, 1826; Tim Castigator, Esq. by S 9, 1826–? *Format*: Four pages 9" x 11". *Price*: 75¢ per quarter. *Comment*: Motto: "What in my secret soul is understood, My tongue shall utter, and my deeds make good." "Who dares think one thing and another tell, my soul detests him as the gates of hell. (Homer)" *Loc*: NCooHi: Ap 15, My 6, Jl 29, Ag 26, S 2, 9, 23, D 9, 1826 (1:4, 7, frag, 23, 24, 25, 27, 38).

THE OTSEGO TIDINGS (w) Milford. N 8, 1889–1919//(?) (1:1–?). *Title changes*: *The Milford Tidings* N 8, 1889–Ag 26, 1897; *The Otsego Tidings* S 1897–1919. *Pub*: D. H. Crowe 1889–?; John Wilcox by 1910–1915; the John Wilcox Estate 1916–1919. *Ed*: Frank C. Carpenter 1916–1919. *Format*: Four pages 18" x 24", 15½ " x 21¾ ". *Circ*: 586 (1891); 900 (by 1910); 1,000 (by 1915–1919). *Loc*: Milford Public Library: N 8, 1889–O 31, 1914 (1:1–25: ?); NCooHi: [F 2, 1899–S 5, 1918 (10:13–29:44)].

THE PASTORAL VISITOR (m) Fly Creek, Westford. 1882–? (1:1–?). *Ed*: Rev. Benjamin P. Ripley. *Format*: Eight to twelve pages

7½" x 10¼". *Price*: 25¢ per issue. *Comment*: Published in the interests of the Fly Creek charge of the M. E. Church, Otsego District, Wyoming Conference. *Loc*: NCooHi: Jl 1, S 6, N 8, D 9, 1882 (1:4, 6, 8, 9); [Ja–D 2, 1883 (2:10–12; 14:20)]; Ja, Mr & Ap, Je 1884 (3:9 whole nos. 21, 22, 25).

REPUBLICAN AND DEMOCRAT see *THE OTSEGO REPUBLICAN* O 7, 1855–?

RICHFIELD SPRINGS DAILY (w) Richfield Springs. 1888–1918(?) (1:1–?). *Pub*: Frank E. Mungor. *Ed*: Miss Ella Winne 1896–1909; Clarence E. Ackerly 1910–1918(?). *Comment*: Published during July and August for the tourists of Richfield Springs. The daily arrivals, "an imposing array of names of the country's prominent citizens," were listed in each issue. (Ella L. Winne and Greta G. Hughes, *The Town of Richfield, A Collection of Local History Articles* [Richfield Springs: 1961], p. 102.) *Loc*: NRS/Palmer: scattered issues.

RICHFIELD SPRINGS MERCURY (w) Richfield Springs. Jl 19, 1867–Jl 20, 1972 (1:1–104:52). *Pub and Ed*: Henry L. Brown Jl 19, 1867–O 1868; Cornelius Ackerman O 1868– Mr 1833; W. T. Coggeshall Mr 1883–Mr 21, 1885; Frank E. Mungor Mr 21, 1885–1887; Frank E. Mungor and Byron G. Seamons 1887–1895; Frank E. Mungor 1895–1910; Frank E. Mungor and Clarence E. Ackerly 1910–1926 (Frank E. Mungor died in 1926); Clarence E. Ackerly 1926–Jl 1, 1953; Mr. and Mrs. LeRoy Palmer and Son (Thomas Palmer) Jl 1, 1953–Jl 20, 1972. *Format*: Four pages, varying sizes, 18" x 24", 15" x 22", 11" x 17". *Price*: $1.50 per year payable in advance (1867–1953); $2.00 (1953–1968); $4.00 (1968–1972). *Comment*: Motto: "A Journal for the Social Circle and the Man of Business; Devoted to Agriculture, Mechanics and General Intelligence." (1867–?) The first issue was devoted entirely to the sulphur springs in Richfield Springs, the surrounding area, and advertisements. First printed on the Getman Block on Lake Street; then on the second floor of the Hinds and Allen Block on Main Street, now Buchanan Hardware Company Block (1868–Mr 31, 1887); and then on Center Street, on the Mercury Block (1887–Jl 20, 1972); *The Freeman's Journal*, which bought the *Mercury's* mailing list in 1972, maintains an office at the Mercury Block. *Loc*: NRS/Palmer: Jl 19, Ag 16, O 4, 1867 (1:1, 5, 12); Mr 13, 1869 (2:29); Mr 20, 24, 1871 (4:44, 45); Mr 4, 1876 (10:34); N 25, 1882 (17:21); Ja 13, Ap 28, 1883 (17:28, 40); Mr 14, Ag 13, 1885 (fragment, 20:8); D 30, 1886–Jl 20, 1972 (21:28–104:52); Mrs. Charles Hughes, 85 West Main Street, Richfield Springs, N. Y.: S 4, 25, O 2–23, N 6–27, D 4, 9, 1875; O 21, 1876; Mr 26, Je 16, 1877; F 16, Mr 30, My 4, Je 8, 15, Jl 13, 27, S 14, 28, N 2, 1878; Ap 5, 12, Mr 29, Je 14, Jl 5, 26, Ag 2–30, S 13–27, O 25, 1879; Mr 6, 27, My 15, Je 5, Jl 3–31, Ag 14, S 25, D 11, 1880; Ja 1, Mr 19, My 28, Je 4, 18, Jl 2, 23, 30, S 17, O 15, 29, 1881; F 25, My 20, 27, Je 3, Jl 8, 15, 29, S 2, O 7, 21, N 11, 25, D 6, 23, 1882; Ja 6, 13, 27, F 3, 24, Mr 10, 17, 31, Ap 7–28, My 5–26, Je 2–30,

Jl 7, 14, 28, Ag 25, S 15, 22, O 6, 20, N 3, 10, 24, 1883; F 9, 23, Ag 23, 30, S 6, 13, 27, O 4, 11, 25, N 1–29, D 6, 1884.

THE RURAL CRITIC (semi-m) Garrattsville. 1890(?)–? (1:1–?). *Pub*: H. A. Hubbard. *Format*: Four pages 11″ x 16″. *Price*: 25¢ per year in advance. *Comment*: Motto: "This paper gives more news in less space for less money than any other in this section. It is a letter from home." *Loc*: NCooHi: N 13, 1892 (3:10).

RURAL TIMES (w) Otego. 1881(?)–? (1:1–?). *Pub and Ed*: V [incent] S. Fuller ?–1924; Gerald S. Fuller by Ja 6, 1925–? *Format*: Four to eight pages, varying sizes, 13″ x 20″, 15″ x 22″, 20″ x 26″. *Price*: $1.25 per year in advance, 3¢ per copy; $1.50 per year in advance, otherwise $2.00, 5¢ per copy (by 1924). *Comment*: Motto: "Devoted to Local and Family Reading and to the Interest of Agriculture and Farm." (1892) "The only Agricultural Paper in the Second Assembly District of Otsego County." (by 1905) "The Mission of this paper is service to its Advertisers and Readers—Growing in Favor with Both." (by 1926) Published in the Times Block on River St. *Loc*: NCooHi: Ag 19, 1891 (10: n.s. 7, 8); My 27, 1896 (14: n.s. 45); N 9, 1898 (17: n.s. 18); Je 14, 1905 (23: n.s. 47); Ap 3, Jl 10, 1907 (26: n.s. 38; 52); Je 18, 1913 (32: n.s. 49); D 15, 22, 1926 (44: n.s. 19, 19 [*sic*]); Mr 8, 1929 (46: n.s. 31); Ag 29, S 19, 1930 (no vol. no.: 48, 51). NOnHi: Jl 27, 1910 (30: n.s. 3). NOt: [Ag 17, 1892– Mr 17, 1909 (11: n.s. 9–28: n.s. 36 whole nos. 652–1445)]; [Ap 11, 1917–D 31, 1919 (36: n.s. 39–39: n.s. 25 whole nos. 1840–1982)]; NOt/Connor: Ap 23, Je 11, N 26, 1926 (42: n.s. 41, 48; 43: n.s. 20 whole nos. 2056, 2063, 2087); [Ja 6–D 30, 1925 (44: n.s. 24 [*sic*]– 44: n.s. 23 whole nos. 2145 [*sic*]–2144)]; D 26, 1927 (45 n.s. 16 whole no. 1954).

SATURDAY CRITIC (w) Oneonta. Jl 2, 1894–1899(?) (1:1–?). *Pub*: Oneonta Trades and Labor Council. *Ed*: George A. Smith. *Format*: Four pages 15″ x 23″. *Price*: $1.00 per year. *Comment*: Motto: "The Workingman's Exponent." "Truth, Equality & Justice." "The Official Organ of the Oneonta Trade and Labor Council." *Loc*: NCooHi: Jl 11, 1896–Jl 3, 1897 (3:1–52). NOnHi: Jl 21, 1894 (1:1).

SAW-BUCK (m) Cherry Valley. No issues located. ". . . published at Cherry Valley by John Fea." (*History of Otsego County*, p. 35.)

SCHENEVUS FREE PRESS DAVENPORT STANDARD (w) Schenevus. 1897(?)–?. *Pub*: E. E. Brownell & Son by 1899–? *Format*: Eight pages 15″ x 22″. *Loc*: NCooHi: [D 13, 1899–My 29, 1901 (3:1–4:25 *Press*; 5:22–6:44 *Standard*)].

SCHENEVUS MONITOR (w) Schenevus. S 1864–? (1:1–?). *Pub and Ed*: Jacob J. Multer and Son ?–?; Jacob J. Multer N 1864–Ap 1876; S. J. Douglass by Je 1876–?; Orra L. Tipple by 1899; The Schenevus Publishing Co. 1951–?; The Dairy Man Press by 1952–?; Fred Smith, Ed. *Pol*: "Neutral . . . until the fall of 1868 during Grant's first presidential campaign. . . . espoused the cause of Democracy." (*History of Otsego County*, p. 35.) *Format*: Four to eight pages, varying sizes, 13⅓" x 18", 16" x 22", 21" x 26". *Price*: $1.25 per year in advance (1864–?); $1.50 per year (1941); $2.00 per year (1952). *Comment*: Motto: "First,—Have Something to Say; Second,—Say it." (under Multer) "A Journal for the Social Circle and the Man of Business Devoted to News and Knowledge." (under Douglass) "Published the general news of the counties of Otsego, Delaware and Schoharie, and in brief, the news of the world." (*History of Otsego County*, p. 35). *Loc*: NCooHi: S 27, O 25–N 8, 1864 (1:3, 7–9); Mr 8, 15, Ap 5, Je 7, O 4, 1865 (1:24, 25, 28, 37, 52); S 5, 1866 (2:46); N 24, 1869 (6:6); Ap 15, Je 24, 1876 (12:26, 36). NOnHi: Mr 9, 1899 (35:24); Fe 14, 1901 (37:21); [Ag 7–O 16, 1941 (n.s. 13:18–28)]; Je 26, 1941 (13:12); Ap 17, 1952 (24:1).

THE SUSQUEHANNA INDEPENDENT (w) Oneonta. Jl 13, 1868 (1:1–?). No issues located. ". . . started July 31, 1868 by G. A. Dodge, at Oneonta. It was published under this title until June 5, 1869, when the name was changed to *Home and Abroad* [q.v.]." (Child, *Gazetteer*, p. 64.)

THE SUSQUEHANNA NEWS Unadilla. 1840(?)–1848(?)// No issues located. "In August, 1840, the publication of *The Susquehanna News* was begun by Edward A. Groves, formerly of Cooperstown, N. Y. in the old Mechanics' Hall, terms two dollars and fifty cents at the end of the year. Its proclivities must have been Democratic, for under the heading of the paper was the Jacksonian motto, 'It is not in a splendid government supported by powerful monopolies and aristocratical establishments that the paper will find happiness or their liberties protection.' *The Susquehanna News* was continued about one year when in August, 1841, the name was changed to *The Unadilla News* [q.v.] and was published by George W. Nobel, of Unadilla, about eighteen weeks in the same place without any change in terms or politics." (*History of Otsego County*, p. 33.)

THE SUSQUEHANNA WAVE (w) Otego. 1881–? (1:1–?). *Pub and Ed*: Andrew F. Flummerfelt. *Format*: Four pages 17¾" x 23". *Price*: $1.50 per year in advance. *Comment*: Motto: "A Journal Devoted to Home Interests." *Loc*: NCooHi: N 25, 1885 (5:21). NOt: N 28, 1883 (3:21).

THE SWITCH Cooperstown. No issues located. ". . . was started March 11, 1809, at Cooperstown. It represented its editor's name as Anthony Switchem. It was short lived." (Child, *Gazetteer*, p. 63.)

THE TELEGRAPH (semi-m) Louisville. F 21, 1846–? (1:1–?). *Ed*: A. S. Avery. *Pol*: Temperance. *Format*: Four pages 5" x 10¾". *Price*: 25¢ in advance for six months. *Loc*: NCooHi: F 21, 1846 (1:1).

THE TEMPERANCE CANOE (m) Roseboom, Cherry Valley. 1874–? No issues located. ". . . on January 1, 1874, it [*The Golden*

Rule] was enlarged and its name changed to *The Temperance Canoe,* its editors being H. D. Elwell, of Roseboom, M. W. Russell, of Cooperstown, and B. K. Douglass of Edmeston. It was continued as a monthly publication, its terms being fifty cents a year. It was then made the official paper of the Good Templars in the County. Its motto was 'Fear God and Paddle your own Canoe.' In June, 1875, it was again enlarged, and published weekly; its publication office being moved to Cherry Valley. Its publishers were Elwell, Douglass & Co. the name was again changed to *The Temperance Investigator* [q.v.], its terms being made one dollar per year." (*History of Otsego County,* p. 35.)

TEMPERANCE INVESTIGATOR (w) Cherry Valley. 1875(?)–? (1:1–?). *Pub and Ed*: Elwell, Finch & Scrambling. *Pol*: Temperance. *Format*: Four pages 15½" x 21½". *Price*: $1.00 per year in advance (1881). *Comment*: Motto: "Fear God and Work for Temperance." Considered ". . . a change of title for *The Temperance Canoe*. Its publishers were Elwell, Douglass & Co. until 1877 when its management changed, and H. D. Elwell and John D. Finch became its editors. At the present time [1878] it is edited by them and printed at the office of *The Cherry Valley Gazette*." (*History of Otsego County,* p. 35.) *Loc*: NChe: Ja 13, 1881 (6:34).

THE TOCSIN see *THE OTSEGO REPUBLICAN* 1829–?

THE TOCSIN FOR THE TOURIST (w, during the tourist season) Laurens. Jl 4, 1968 to date (1:1 to date). *Format*: Eight pages 11½" x 16". *Price*: Free. *Comment*: Published during the summer season as a guide to events in the Cooperstown region by The Village Printer and Mid-State Recreation Publications, Inc. of Laurens. *Loc*: The Village Printer office in Laurens: Jl 4, 1968 to date (1:1 to date).

THE UNADILLA ADVERTISER Unadilla. No issues located. "The *Unadilla Advertiser* was published for a time." (Child, *Gazetteer,* p. 65.)

UNADILLA HERALD Unadilla. No issues located. "The publication of the *Unadilla Herald* was commenced by William S. Hawley, of Canajoharie, N. Y., in the former residence of the late Judge Page, and was continued about one year. For want of sufficient public patronage being given to the newspapers which had been started in Unadilla and been forced to suspend their publications, or for some other cause, there was no further effort made to publish a newspaper in this village for about nine and a half years." (*History of Otsego County,* p. 33.)

UNADILLA NEWS (w) Unadilla. 1841//(?) No issues located. "In August, 1841, the name [for *The Susquehanna News* (q.v.)] was changed to the *Unadilla News* and was published by George W. Noble, of Unadilla, about eighteen months in the same place without any change in terms or politics." (*History of Otsego County,* p. 33.)

THE UNADILLA TIMES (w) Unadilla. Je 1855–D 1967// (1:1–?).
Pub and Ed: George Downing Raitt ?–1909 (died Je 30, 1909); T.
R. Raitt 1909–?; T. R. Raitt and Lynn P. Earl by 1920–?; Lynn P.
Earl by 1927–1955; Arthur L. Ingalls 1955–1966; William Ryan O 2,
1966–1967. *Pol*: Democrat; Independent (1955–1966). *Format*: Eight
pages 13″ x 20″. *Price*: $1.00 per year (1900–1920); $1.50 per year
(by 1927–?). *Comment*: When William Ryan, publisher and editor
of the *Unadilla Times* bought the *Deposit Courier* October 2, 1967, he
sold the *Unadilla Times* to James MacLachlan of the *Sidney Record
and Bainbridge News* (see Delaware County bibliography). He continued publication only until December 1967 then incorporated the
Unadilla Times into the Sidney paper. Published at the Bailey and
Robinson Block by 1900; then from the Beardsley Block. *Loc*:
NNorHi: N 29, 1912 (58:28); F 7, 1913 (58:38). NSiT: [Ja 5,
1900–D 13, 1901 (46:31–47:28)]; [Ja 2, 1903–D 30, 1904 (48:31–
50:31)]; [Ja 2–Jl 31, 1914 (39:33–40:11)]; Ja 1–D 33 [*sic*], 1920
(55:34–56:25); [Ja 7–N 25, 1927 (72:37–73:31)]; [Ja 17–D 26, 1941
(85:40–86:36)]; Ja 4–D 31, 1951 (84:3–?).

THE VALLEY NEWS (w) Schenevus. 1868–? No issues located.
". . . in 1868, an opposition Republican paper, [to *The Schenevus
Monitor* (q.v.)] *The Valley News*, was started, with a capital of
$5,000; but owing to a split in the party in the county at the time,
that organ became weakened, and was defunct in about a year and a
half after its publication." (*History of Otsego County*, p. 35.)

THE WATCH-TOWER (w) Cherry Valley, Cooperstown. Ap 6,
1814–N 28, 1831(?)// (1:1–18:922). *Pub*: Israel W. Clark ?–My
29, 1817; E[dward] B. Crandal Je 5, 1817–S 1822; E. B. Crandal and
Nash S 1822–S 1823; E. B. Crandal 1823–N 28, 1831. *Format*: Four
pages 15″ x 19″. *Comment*: "*The Watch-Tower* was established in
Cherry Valley in 1813. It was removed to Cooperstown in 1814, and
published by Israel W. Clark until May 1817. . . ." "In May, 1817
. . ., Clark removed to Albany and the paper was published by
E[dward] B. Crandal . . . The paper was continued until after 1820."
(Brigham, *History and Bibliography*, p. 569.) *Loc*: NCooHi: [Ap 3,
1817–N 28, 1831 (4:157–18:922)]. NOnHi: Ap 8, 1822 (9:419);
Ja 26, 1829 (15:774).

WEEKLY COURIER Unadilla. F 1842(?)–1844(?)// No issues located. "In February, 1842, the *Weekly Courier* was started by Edson
S. Jennings, of Unadilla, who published it in the Baldwin House
about one and a half years. It was neutral in politics. T. S. Ames was
connected with the *Courier* for a short time, but the firm of Ames and
Jennings was dissolved and Mr. Jennings became the sole proprietor."
(*History of Otsego County*, p. 33.)

THE WEEKLY PIONEER (w) Cooperstown. *Pub*: Fred W. Lee.
Ed: G. Ray Leavitt. *Format*: Thirty-two pages 11½″ x 16½″. *Comment*: Motto: "The Largest Circulation in Otsego County." Published
at 195 Main St., Oneonta, N. Y. Distributed free of charge. News of

Burlington Flats, Colliersville, Edmeston, Fly Creek, Garrattsville, Hartwick, Hartwick Seminary, Laurens, Maryland, Mt. Vision, Middlefield, Milford, Oaksville, Oneonta, Otego, Portlandville, Schenevus, Toddsville, Unadilla, Wells Bridge, West Oneonta, West Burlington, West Edmeston, Westford. Absorbed by *The Freeman's Journal* in 1973.

WHARTON VALLEY ECHO Edmeston. See p. 289

WORCESTER TIMES (w) Worcester. S 1, 1875–1958//. (1:1–?). *Title changes*: *The Worcester Times* S 1, 1875–?; *Worcester Times* by D 1900–? *Pub and Ed*: M. W. D. Fenton S 1, 1875–Ap 27, 1876; Marcus M. Multer My 4, 1876–Jl 27, 1877; J. W. Bush Ag 3, 1877– Ja 21, 1881 (A. E. Smith, Ed. Ag 3, 1877–D 6, 1878); A. E. Smith D 29, 1879–?; Charles C. Wentzler by My 9, 1901–Ap 17, 1902; A. E. Babcock Ap 17, 1902–?; G. C. Shafer by 1930–? *Format*: Four to eight pages, varying sizes, 13½″ x 19½″, 15½″ x 21½″, 18″ x 23½″, 12½″ x 19″. *Price*: $1.00 per year in advance (1875–Ag 1876); $1.25 per year in advance (S 8, 1876–?); $1.00 per year in advance (by 1901); $1.50 per year in advance (by 1920–1947); $2.00 per year (1948–1950); $2.50 per year (1951–?). *Comment*: Motto: "An Independent Weekly Newspaper." (1891) *Loc*: NCooHi: [S 1, 1875–My 15, 1884 (1:1–9:37)]; [S 3, 1885–D 31, 1891 (9:1–17:18)]; [Ja 4–Je 16, O 6–D 1, 1892 (17:20–42; 18:6–14)]; Ja 26, Mr 2, My 11, 1893 (18:22, 27, 37); F 27, S 10, 1896 (21:27; 22:3); D 27, 1900–D 30, 1914 (26:17–40:19); Je 9, 1915 (40:42); N 16, 1920 (46:13); S 25, 1929 (55:8); D 28, 1938 (64:22); [My 7, 1941–Jl 15, 1942 (66:42–67:52 fragments)]; Mr 1, Jl 27, Ag 2, 1944 (69:27, 48, 49); [Ja 24, 1945–D 14, 1955 (69:22–80:17)]. NOnHi: O 22, 1891 (17:8).

THE WORCESTER TIMES AND SCHENEVUS MONITOR (w) Worcester. 1958 to date (1:1 to date). *Pub*: Charles L. Ryder. *Ed*: Milton V. Wright. *Format*: Eight pages 16⅝″ x 22⅛″. *Price*: $3.00 per year; $2.00 per six months, $1.00 per three months, 8¢ per copy. *Comment*: In 1958 the *Schenevus Moniter* (q.v.) and the *Worcester Times* (q.v.) were combined and became *The Worcester Times and Schenevus Monitor*. *Loc*: NCooHi: My 28, 1959 (85th year:29). NOnHi: S 30, 1965 (91st year:6).

BURDETT HOME RECORD (w) Burdett. 1899(?)–? (1:1–?). *Pub*: John Probes by F 1901; Charles P. Stowell by 1903. *Ed*: S. C. Cassidy by 1900–?; John Probes by 1901–?; Charles P. Stowell by 1903. *Format*: Four to eight pages 18″ x 24″. *Price*: 75¢ per year in advance, 3¢ per copy (1900–1901). *Comment*: Motto: "A Wholesome Family Newspaper." *Loc*: NIC/MMN: My 1, 1901 (3.27); D 28, 1903 (6:9). NMnHi: F 28, 1900 (2:?); F 27, 1901 (3:18).

BURDETT LOCAL VISITOR (w) Burdett. D 1867–Jl 13, 1870// (1:1–?). *Pub*: Montrose St. John 1867–1870. *Format*: Four pages 8⅞″ x 11⅞″. *Pol*: Democrat. *Comment*: The newspaper was started by Montrose St. John at age 15. He discontinued publication to concentrate on *Red Hot* (q.v.). *Loc*: NIC/MMN: Mr 4, 1869 (1:11).

THE CHEMUNG DEMOCRAT (w) Havana [now Montour Falls], Jefferson [now Watkins Glen]. ca. 1831. No issues located. In 1842 J. I. Hendrix [*sic*] brought *The Chemung Democrat* to Jefferson from Havana. Two years later he changed its name to the *Democratic Citizen* (q.v.). It was discontinued about six years later. (Frank W. Severne, "Annual Report of County Historian," in *Proceedings of the Board of Supervisors* [Watkins Glen, N. Y. 1953], p. 132.)

CHEMUNG WHIG (w) Havana. ca. 1843. No issues located. When Thomas J. Taylor purchased *The Havana Republican* (q.v.) from Barlow Nye in 1842, he changed the name to the *Chemung Whig*. (Severne, "Annual Report," p. 131.)

THE CORONA BOREALIS Jefferson. ca. 1851. No issues located. "A literary paper . . . published for a time during [1851] . . . ." (Henry B. Pierce, *History of Tioga, Chemung, Tompkins, and Schuyler Counties, N. Y.* [Philadelphia, 1879] p. 568.)

DEMOCRATIC CITIZEN (w) Jefferson [now Watkins Glen]. 1841–? (1:1–?). *Pub and Ed*: J. I. Hendryx. *Format*: Four pages 15″ x 22″. *Comment*: "The first newspaper published at Watkins was *The Chemung Democrat* [q.v.] which was moved from Horseheads to Havana [now Montour Falls] in the year 1840 and thence to Jefferson [now Watkins Glen] in 1842. Its name was soon after changed to the *Democratic Citizen* and it was issued by J. I. Hendryx [subsequently of the *Otsego Republican*] until the year 1850." (Pierce, *History of Tioga*, p. 568.) *Loc*: NMnHi: Ja 30, 1846 (5:13 fragment).

FAMILY VISITOR see *WATKINS FAMILY VISITOR*

FREE PRESS (w) Montour Falls. 1889–Mr 26, 1924// (1:1–34th year: 29 whole nos. 1–6431). *Title changes: Havana Free Press; The Havana Free Press* by N 1893–?; *Montour Falls Free Press* 1898–?; *Free Press* by 1908–?. *Pub*: C. B. Ball by 1891–1911; A. H. Stoddard and Teetsel O 5, 1911–1913; A. H. Stoddard 1913–1918; C. B. Cronk by 1919–1924. *Ed*: C. B. Ball and A. G. Ball, Asst. Ed., by 1891–?; A. G. Ball by 1898–?; C. B. Ball ?–1911; A. H. Stoddard O 5, 1911–?; C. B. Cronk 1919–1924. *Format*: Four to eight pages, varying sizes, 15″ x 22″, 17½″ x 23½″. *Price*: $1.00 per year strictly in advance, 5¢ per copy (by 1891–?). *Comment*: Motto: "A Weekly Paper Devoted to the Interests of the Village and County." Early papers carried a temperance column. Office in Decker Block over E. Weller's Store. Loc: NMn: Ja 14, 1904–Mr 26, 1924 (15:18–34:29) whole nos. 748–6431). NMnHi: Ja 8, O 15, D 31, 1891 (2:16; 3:4, 16 whole nos. 68, 108, 118); Je 16, 1892 (3:39 whole no. 142); N 2, 30, 1893 (5:7, 11 whole nos. 214, 218); N 8, D 6, 1894 (6:8, 12 whole nos. 268, 272); My 26, S 29, O 6, 1898 (9:38; 10:4, 5 whole nos. 454, 472, 473); Jl 12, S 20–27, N 22, D 13 ,1900 (11:45; 12:3, 4, 12, 15 whole nos. 565, 575, 576, 584, 587); F 7, 28, 1901 (12:23, 26 whole nos. 595, 598); Mr 6, 1902 (13:27 whole no. 651); Je 23, 1904 (15:41 whole no. 771); Ap 2, 9, O 29, 1908 (19:30, 31, fragment); Mr 5, 1924 (34:26 whole no. 6428).

THE GREENBACK LABOR ADVOCATE see *THE HAVANA DEMOCRAT 1877*

THE HAVANA DEMOCRAT (w) Havana. Ap 25, 1855–? No issues located. Published for a short time only by J. Ketchum Averill and Jesse Baxter. (Severne, "Annual Report," p. 132.)

THE HAVANA DEMOCRAT (w) Havana. ca. 1877–? No issues located. *The Havana Enterprise* (q.v.) was purchased from Mason Weed by S. H. Ferenbaugh, who changed its name to *The Havana Democrat*. During the Greenback Movement, *"The Havana Democrat* was changed to *The Greenback Labor Advocate* for one year and then the old name was resumed . . . . In November 1882 S. W. Ferrenbaugh [*sic*] brought *The Havana Democrat* to this village [Watkins] changing its name to *The Watkins Herald* [q.v.]." (Severne, "Annual Report," p. 132.)

THE HAVANA ENTERPRISE (m, then semi-m) Havana. S 1869–1877// (1:1–?). *Title changes*: *The Havana Enterprise* S 1869–My 1870; *Havana Enterprise* My 16, 1870–1872; *The Havana Enterprise* My 9, 1872–? *Pub*: J. M. and Mason N. Weed and C. M. Boyce Ja–O 1, 1870; Mason N. Weed O 15, 1870–1872; William Hibbard Page 1872–? *Ed*: C. M. Boyce S–N 1869; Mason N. Weed O 15, 1870–1872; William Hibbard Page 1872–? *Pol*: Republican. *Format*: Four pages, varying sizes, 11″ x 14″, 16″ x 22″, 17¼″ x 23½″. *Price*: Free (S 1869); 10¢ per year (N 1869–F 1870); 25¢ per year (Ap 1870–1871); $1.00 per year in advance (My 1872–?); $1.50 per year, 1¢ per copy (by 1875). *Circ*: 3,500 (1869–F 1870); 3,000 (1870–1871); 2,200 (Mr 1871–?). *Comment*: Motto: "A Paper for the People." "Official Paper of the Village." Published in the Weed's Block by 1872, then listed as office opposite the Montour House ("see the big sign") 1875, then in Langley Hall by 1875. According to Severne *The Havana Enterprise* was sold in 1877 to S. H. Ferenbaugh who changed the name to *The Havana Democrat* (q.v.). (Severne, "Annual Report," p. 132.) *Loc*: NIC/RHA: S 16, 1875 (7:20 whole no. 218). NMn: [S 1869–Ag 29, 1872 (1:1–4:18 whole nos. 1–60)]. NMnHi: S 16, D 23, 1875 (7:20, 34 whole nos. 218, 232); Ja 11, F 28, 1877 (8:37, 45 whole nos. 287, 294).

HAVANA FREE PRESS see *FREE PRESS*

HAVANA JOURNAL (w) Havana. S 1, 1849–Ap 1853// (1:1–?). *Pub and Ed*: Waldo M. Potter S 1, 1849–? *Pol*: Whig. *Format*: Four pages 17½″ x 23″. *Price*: $1.00 per year in advance, $1.50 after six months (1849–1851). *Comment*: Published "in the room where *The Chemung Whig* [q.v.] was formerly printed, directly west of the Canal Bridge, over the store of R. K. Eastman." In 1851 Waldo Potter sold the *Journal* to J. Wesley Smith (afterward editor of *The Albany Argus*) and Hamlin who, in turn, sold to John B. Look in 1853. (Severne, "Annual Report," p. 132.) *Loc*: NMn: S 1, 1849–O 24, 1851 (1:1–3:9).

HAVANA JOURNAL (w) Havana. Ap 16, 1853–S 9, 1865// (1:1–
13:17). *Pub and Ed*: John B. Look Ap 16, 1853–My 1864; John B.
Look and E. A. Hotchkiss My–N 26, 1864; John B. Look and A. E.
Fay D 3, 1864–S 9, 1865. *Pol*: Whig, Republican (Union Party).
Format: Four pages 15½" x 22". *Price*: $1.00 per year in advance,
$1.50 to village subscribers (1853–1864); $1.50 per year by mail or
at the office, $2.00 to village subscribers, 5¢ per copy (1864); $2.50
per year to village, $2.00 by mail (Ag 1864–1865). *Circ*: 250-1,500
(1853–1864). *Comment*: Motto: "The Strongest Plume in Wisdom's
Pinion is the Memory of Past Folly." Published in an office in Corwin's Block, Main St. John B. Look became ill sometime in 1864 and
Hotchkiss, who had done most of the editing although not always
listed, asked A. E. Fay of the *Olean Times* to join the newspaper.
Hotchkiss then resigned. In September 1865 Look sold out to Charles
Cook who then started a new edition of the *Journal* (q.v.). The December 19, 1863 edition contains a census of persons enrolled in several districts of Schuyler County. *Loc*: NIC/RHA: Ap 16, 1853–Ap
4, 1857 (1:1–4:52 whole nos. 1–208); D 19, 1863 (2:30 whole no.
550). NMn: Mr 14, 1857 (4:49 whole no. 205); Ap 11, 1857–Ap 2,
1859 (5:1–6:52 whole nos. 209–312); Ag 2, 1862–S 9, 1865 (10:10–
13:17 whole nos. 478–641). NMnHi: Ap 16, 1853–D 29, 1855 (1:1–
3:38 whole nos. 1–142); S 27, 1856 (4:24 whole no. 181); Ja 29, 1859
(6:43); Mr 15, 1862 (9:42 whole no. 458); My 7, 1864–S 9, 1865
(11:51–13:17 whole nos. 571–641).

HAVANA JOURNAL (w) Havana. S 16, 1865–? (1:1n.s.–?).
Pub and Ed: Charles Cook S 16, 1865–1866; Cook Estate from 1866–
F 1867; A. G. Ball F 16, 1867–Ja 1881; No publisher or editor listed
1881–?; Charles A. Thomas by 1901–? *Pol*: Republican. *Format*:
Four to eight pages, varying sizes, 19½" x 27", 21¼" x 27½". *Price*:
$1.50 per year in advance (1865–1868); $2.00 per year in advance
(by 1871–?). *Circ*: "This Paper has a Larger Circulation than Any Other
Paper in Schuyler County." *Comment*: Published in an office in Corwin's Block, Main St. 1865–1868; then office in Tracy Block, Rooms
7 and 8 over Second National Bank; from April 15, 1871 in Langley
Hall. The following statement will fill out some of the details of ownership. "After Mr. Cook's death in 1866, it was published for a time
by his estate and sold to A. B. [*sic*] Ball in February 1867, who continued its publication for more than thirty years, having as his business associate in the later years, Hull Fanton . . . . *The Havana Journal* was continued by Hull Fanton for about a year after the establishment of the *Montour Falls Free Press* [q.v.] [in 1898]." (Severne,
"Annual Report," p. 132.). *Loc*: NIC/RHA: S 1, 1866 (1:51 n.s.); Jl
17, 1869 (20:45 n.s. whole no. 201). NMn: S 16, 1865 (1:1 n.s.); F 1,
1868–S 4, 1869 (19:21–20:52 n.s. whole nos. 125–208); S 7, 1872–
Ag 26, 1876 (24:1–27:52 n.s. whole nos. 365–572); D 9, 1876
(38:15 n.s. whole no. 587); Ag 31, 1878–Ag 21, 1880 (30:1–31:52
n.s. whole nos. 677–780); Ja 3, 1885–D 25, 1886 (36:20–38:19 n.s.
whole nos. 1008–1112); Ja 7, 1888–D 30, 1893 (39:1165–45:2233).
NMnHi: S 16, 1865–F 16, 1867 (1:1–2:23 n.s. whole nos. 1–75); Ja

18, 1868 (19:19 n.s. whole no. 123); F 1, 1868–Ag 31, 1872 (19:21–23:52 n.s. whole nos. 125–364); Mr 27, 1875 (26:30 n.s. whole no. 498); S 2, 1876–Ag 17, 1878 (38:1–29:51 n.s. whole nos. 573–675); Ag 28, 1880–D 27, 1884 (32:1–36:19 n.s. whole nos. 981–1007); N 28, 1901 (46th year: 2275 n.s. whole no. 23).

THE HAVANA OBSERVER (w) Havana. 1829–? (1:1–?). *Format*: Four pages. *Price*: $2.00 per year in advance (by 1832). *Comment*: In 1830 F. W. Ritter purchased *The Tioga Patriot* (q.v.) which was begun at Havana in 1828 from L. B. and S. Butler. He then changed the name to *The Havana Observer* which was suspended and sold in 1835 to Nelson Colegrave who changed the name to *The Havana Republican* (q.v.). (Severne, "Annual Report," p. 131.) *Loc*: NMnHi: Ja 11, 1832 (3:32 whole no. 136).

THE HAVANA REPUBLICAN (w) Havana. Je 14, 1837–Mr 9, 1842// (n.s. 1:1–34). *Title changes*: The Havana Republican 1837–Ag 28, 1839; Havana Republican S 4, 1839–?; The Havana Republican ?–Mr 9, 1842. *Pub*: Nelson Colegrave 1837–1838; Barlow Nye by 1838–1842. *Pol*: Republican. *Format*: Four pages, varying sizes, 14″ x 21″, 14¾″ x 22″. *Price*: $2.00 per year in advance, otherwise $2.50 (1837–1842). *Comment*: Motto: "Where Liberty Dwells There Is My Country." On March 9, 1842 Nye stated in an editorial that "to continue the publication of this paper with its present support or such as it came into our hands four years ago would instead of benefiting us be the means of depriving those whom it owes of their just due. It will therefore be discontinued finally with its present number." "It was sold in 1841 or 42 to Thomas J. Taylor who changed the name to *The Chemung Whig* [q.v.]." (Severne, "Annual Report," p. 131.) *Loc*: NIC/RHA: Ag 2, 1837 (2:8 whole no. 60). NMn: Ag 16, 30, S 6, 20, 1837 (2:10, 12, 13, 15 whole nos. 62, 64, 65, 67); [Je 13, 1838–Je 10, 1840 (3:2–4:52 whole nos. 106–208)]; [Jl 24, 1841–Mr 9, 1842 (n.s. 1:1–34)]. NMnHi: 0 4, 1837 (2:17 whole no. 69); F 20, 1839 (3:37 whole no. 141).

THE HAVANA REPUBLICAN (w) Havana. 1845–? (1.1–?). *Pub*: William H. Ongley by 1846–?; Hamblin and Smith by 1851–? *Ed*: William H. Ongley by 1846–?; J. Wesley Smith by 1851–? *Pol*: Free and Independent (1846–1849). *Price*: $2.00 per year within the year, $1.50 per year in advance (by 1846). *Comment*: Published north side of Main St., two doors west of the Canal Bridge. "In 1847 Ongley changed the name of the paper to *Life in the Country and Havana Republican*. It was sold in 1848 to S. C. Cleveland who discontinued the publication and went to Penn Yan with *The Yates County Chronicle*." (Severne, "Annual Report," p. 131.) *Loc*: NMn: Ap 15, 1846 (2:9 whole no. 61); My 16, 1849 (?); F 28, 1851 (7:2 whole no. 314).

THE HAVANA REPUBLICAN (w) Havana. 1882–? (1:1–?). *Pub and Ed*: None listed. *Format*: Four pages 15″ x 20½″. *Comment*: Motto: "A Republican Family Newspaper chiefly devoted to the Dissemination of the Local News of Schuyler County." This newspaper was the successor to *The Itemizer* (q.v.) according to Severne and its name changed to *The Havana Republican*. (Severne, "Annual Report," p. 132.) *Loc*: NMn: Ja 7, 1886 (5:49 whole no. 257.)

HECTOR HERALD Burdett. ca. 1850. No issues located. Published for a time by Charles Stoll. (Severne, "Annual Report," p. 134.)

THE HOME VISITOR (m) Watkins. Ap 1875–? (1:1–?). *Pub and Ed*: Fred H. Gates. *Format*: Four pages 7¼ " x 9½ ". *Price*: 12¢ per year (1875). *Comment*: Printed at the Book and Job Printing Office of A. Allen, Trumansburg, N. Y. *Loc*: NMnHi: Ap 1875 (1:1).

INDEPENDENT FREEMAN. Jefferson. Je 15, 1850–? No issues located. "On the 15th of June of that year [1850], the *Independent Freeman* was started by W. B. Slawson and Co. In 1851 it was changed to the *Jefferson Eagle*, and continued under that its new name but a few months." (Pierce, *Tioga*, p. 568.) *See also* p. 289

THE ITEMIZER (w) Havana. ca. 1880–1882. No issues located. "In the early eighties a paper was published for a time in Havana. It was called *The Itemizer* and was edited for a time by Sam Payne and later by the Keyser Bros. On October 23, 1882 *The Itemizer* was purchased by the following well known Republicans and its name changed to *The Havana Republican* [q.v.]: Col. Charles W. Claugherty, Myron H. Weaver, Elbert P. Cook, Samuel C. Keeler, Baxter T. Smelzer, M.D. all of Havana; William H. Wait, Freemont Cole, Hon. Oliver P. Hurd, all of Watkins Glen. They employed Sam Payne as editor." (Severne, "Annual Report," p. 132.)

JEFFERSON EAGLE see *INDEPENDENT FREEMAN*

THE JEFFERSONIAN (w) Jefferson [Chemung, later Schuyler Co.] Mr 13, 1847–? (1:1–?). *Pub*: St. John and O. B. Turrell ?–N 6, 1847; O. B. Turrell N 13, 1847; O. B. Turrell and Hurd N 20, 1847–? *Pol*: Democrat. *Format*: Four pages 15½ " x 20". *Price*: $1.50 per year for those who call at the office, $1.00 per year by mail (1847–1848). *Comment*: Motto: "A Family Newspaper Devoted to General Intelligence, Agriculture, Morality, Politics, etc." *Loc*: NMnHi: [Je 26, 1847–Ja 8, 1848 (1:16–44)].

LIFE IN THE COUNTRY AND HAVANA REPUBLICAN see *HAVANA REPUBLICAN 1845*

MONTOUR FALLS FREE PRESS see *FREE PRESS*

ODESSA FREE BAPTIST (m) Odessa. S 1889–? (1:1–?). *Pub*: Free Baptist, Odessa. *Ed*: Rev. O. H. Denney. *Format*: Four pages 11½ " x 15½ ". *Comment*: Religious, not political. *Loc*: NIC/MMN: O 1889 (1:2).

THE OLD SCHOOL DEMOCRAT Jefferson. ca. 1840. No issues located. "In 1840, *The Old School Democrat,* a campaign paper, was published in Jefferson. It was discontinued after a few months." (Severne, "Annual Report," p. 132.)

THE ORACLE ADVERTISER (irr.) Watkins. 1901–? *Pub and Ed*: None listed. *Format*: Four pages 9½ " x 12½ ". *Comment*: Content is primarily local advertising. *Loc*: NMnHi: D 18, 19, 1901.

OUR TOWN (w) Montour Falls. D 12, 1924–? (1:1–?). *Pub*: Troop 1, Boy Scouts of America. *Format*: Eight to four pages, varying sizes, 8½ " x 11", 12½ " x 17½ ". *Comment*: "Published by Troop 1, Montour Falls, N. Y. Boy Scouts of America, in the Village Interest." *Loc*: NMnHi: D 12, 1924 (1:1); [Ja 2–Ag 14, 1925 (1:4–36)].

RED HOT (semi-m) Burdett. S 3–N 12, 1870// (1:1–11). *Pub and Ed*: Montrose St. John. *Pol*: Democrat. *Format*: Four pages 10" x 13". *Comment*: In the November 12, 1870 issue, the publisher stated that he would change the paper to a weekly, but changed his mind in the same issue and stated that he was suspending publication and would go elsewhere to publish a newspaper. *Loc*: NIC/MMN: N 12, 1870 (1:11).

THE REVIEW ADVERTISER (d) Watkins Glen. 1941(?)–? (1:1–?). *Pub*: Barton L. Piper. *Format*: Four pages 8½ " x 11". *Comment*: Motto: "The Paper with the News." Printed by the *Watkins Review*. *Loc*: NMnHi: O 17, 1941 (1:266); Mr 21, 22, 1944 (4:90, 91).

SCHUYLER COUNTY CHRONICLE (w) Watkins Glen. 1908–1919// (1:1–?). *Pub*: Schuyler County Chronicle Association. *Ed*: John Corbett 1908–1917; B. B. Weldy 1918–1919. *Format*: Eight pages 15" x 20". *Price*: $1.00 per year in advance (1909–?). *Comment*: Successor to the *Watkins Democrat* (q.v.). *Loc*: NIC/RHA: [Ja 7, 1909–D 25, 1913 (2:54–6:313)]. NMnHi: Ja 6–D 29, 1910 (3:106–157); Ap 20, Ag 31, 1911 (4:173, 192); Ag 22, S 12, 19, O 17, D 12, 1912 (5:243, 246, 247, 251, 259); Je 26, Jl 24, Ag 21, S 4, 18, O 22, N 6, 1913 (6:287, 291, 295–297, 299, 301, 306); Mr 19, Ap 16, My 7, 14, Je 25, Ag 20, O 22, N 5, 1914 (7:325, 329, 332, 333, 339, 347, 356, 358); [Ja 7–Je 24, 1915 (8:367–391)].

SCHUYLER COUNTY DEMOCRAT (w) Watkins. My 13, 1864–? (1:1–?). *Pub and Ed*: S. C. Clizbe. *Pol*: Democrat. *Format*: Four pages 17½ " x 23½ ". *Price*: $1.50 per year in advance. *Comment*: Motto: "The Union as It Was and the Constitution as It Is." Official paper of the village. "*The Schuyler County Democrat* was established in 1865 [?] by an association of Democrats, at the head of which was George J. Magee, as a Democratic organ, and placed in charge of S. C. Clizbe. He conducted it about fifteen months when it was transferred to the editorial control of M [orvaldon] Ells." (Pierce, *History of Tioga*, p. 569.) Clizbe then started *The Watkins Independent* (q.v.). *Loc*: NMn: Je 3, 1864 (1:4).

THE SCHUYLER COUNTY DEMOCRAT 1866 see *WATKINS DEMOCRAT*

THE SCHUYLER COUNTY PRESS (w) Watkins. D 21, 1859–? (1:1–?). *Pub*: S. Maxwell Taylor. *Pol*: "Republican—in the fullest sense!" *Format*: Four pages 13¼ " x 20½ ". *Price*: $1.00 per year in advance, otherwise $1.50. *Comment*: Motto: "Freedom is National; Slavery Sectional." *Loc*: NMn: D 21, 1859 (1:1); Ja 18, F 8, 15, Mr 7, 21, 1860 (1:5, 8, 9, 12, 14).

SCHUYLER COUNTY TIMES (w) Watkins. ca. 1873//. No issues located. "About the year 1873 a small weekly paper known as the *Schuyler County Times,* was started by Thomas and Gates (L. G. Thomas, editor), who continued it for about six months, when it suspended, and was the last paper attempted in Watkins." (Pierce, *History of Tioga,* p. 269.)

THE SCHUYLER COUNTY UNION (w) Montour Falls. My 1863–ca. 1864. No issues located. "In May, 1863, [*The Watkins Republican* (q.v.)] was sold to George D. A. Bridgeman who published it for about nine months under the name of *The Schuyler County Union.* It was then sold to L. M. Gano who began its publication January 28, 1864, under the name of *The Watkins Express.*" (Severne, "Annual Report," p. 133.) It is possible that Bridgeman changed the name of the paper sometime between May and August 1863 to the *Watkins Weekly Union* (q.v.).

THE SON OF TEMPERANCE AND SCHUYLER COUNTY UNION (w) Watkins. 1860–1862//(?) (1:1–?). *Pub and Ed*: A. C. Lumbard. *Format*: Four pages 16½ " x 23½ ". *Comment*: "In 1860, Azro C. Lambert [*sic*] now connected with the Millerton (Pa.) *Advocate,* started *The Son of Temperance,* which acquired quite a circulation outside as well as within the county, and was published about two years, when it was discontinued, and most of its material united with that of the *Republican* office." (Pierce, *History of Tioga,* p. 569.) *Loc*: NMn: F 14, Mr 14, 1862 (2:40, 44 whole nos. 92, 96).

THE TIOGA PATRIOT (w) Havana. 1828–1830//. No issues located. "The publication of *The Tioga Patriot* was begun in June 1828 at Havana, its editors being L. B. and S. Butler. It was sold in 1830 to F. W. Ritter who changed the name to *The Havana Observer* [q.v.] . . ." (Severne, "Annual Report," p. 131.)

WATKINS DAILY RECORD (d) Watkins. My 15, 1901–? (1:1–?). *Pub*: Watkins Printing Co. *Ed*: J. H. Thompson, Managing Ed. *Format*: Four pages 15" x 24¾ ". *Price*: 1¢ per copy (1905). *Loc*: NMn: My 15, 1905 (1:1).

WATKINS DEMOCRAT (w) Watkins. Mr 13, 1866–1908//(?) (1:1–?). *Title changes*: The Schuyler County Democrat Mr 13, 1866–?; *Watkins Democrat* 1876(?)–1908. *Pub*: Morvaldon Ells and Wm. A. Burritt 1866–?; William H. Baldwin by 1871–?; F. E. Wixson by 1905–?; Watkins Printing Co. by 1906–1908 (owned by Mrs. A. Thompson as of Jl 18, 1907–1908). *Ed*: Morvaldon Ells 1866–?; F. E. Wixson, Assoc. Ed. and J. H. Thompson, Managing Ed. Ja 4–Ag 23, 1906; J. H. Thompson, Ed. and Manager Ag 30, 1906–? *Pol*: Democrat. *Format*: Four pages, varying sizes, 18" x 24", 22" x 26", 20" x 26", 14" x 21". *Price*: $2.00 per year in advance (1866–?);

$1.00 per year in advance (by 1871–?); $1.50 per year in advance (by 1877–1900); $1.00 per year in advance (by 1904–?). *Comment*: Motto: "The Union and the Constitution." "A Square Deal for Everybody." Published at the Schuyler County Democrat Book and Job Printing Dept. over the clothing store of Charles Magee, corner of Franklin and Warren St., by 1905 in the Democrat Building, Watkins. *Loc*: NIC/MMN: Ag 3, 1870 (8:3 whole no. 332). NIC/RHA: D 4, 1878 (14:39 whole no. 767); F 5, 1879 (14:48 whole no. 776); S 7, 1881 (17:27 whole no. 911); F 1, Je 28, 1882 (17:47, 18:16 whole nos. 932, 953); Mr 24, 1886 (22:4 whole no. 1148); F 21, Mr 7–21, Ap 4–25, My 2, Jl 11, 1889 (24:50, 52; 25:1 2, 4–8, 18 whole nos. 1300, 1302–1304, 1306–1310, 1320); Ap 23, 1891 (27:6 whole no. 1414); Je 30, 1892 (28:6 whole no. 1476); Ja 4, Je 21, Jl 12, Ag 2, 9, N 22, 1894 (29:40; 30:44, 47, 50, 51; 33:14 [*sic*] whole nos. 1555, 1579, 1582, 1585, 1586, 1601); O 29, 1896 (35:14 whole no. 1702); F 1, Mr 3, 1900 (38:28, 41 whole nos. 1872, 1885); [Ja 4, 1906–D 19, 1907 (44:33–46:31 whole nos. 2180–2222)]. NMnHi: Mr 20, 1866 (1:2 n.s.); F 1, 1871 (6:46 whole no. 358); Ja 31, 1877 (12:47 whole no. 671); Ag 21, 1878 (14:24 whole no. 752); O 18, 1894 (33:9 whole no. 1596); Mr 8, 1900 (38:33 whole no. 1877); N 10, 1904 (43:26 whole no. 2121); Ag 3, 1905 (44:12 whole no. 2159).*

THE WATKINS EXPRESS (w) Watkins. 1854 to date (1:1 to date). *Pub and Ed*: Levi M. Gano Ja 1864–1876; Levi M. Gano and J. Brighan by Ja 1876–1877; Levi M. Gano 1877–N 26, 1885; Levi M. Gano and John Corbett D 31, 1885–Ag 27, 1891; Levi M. Gano 1891–1903; Marcus M. Cass 1903–1909; Schuyler County Printing and Publishing Co. Ap 1, 1909–1923(?) (Frank A. Frost, Pres., George J. Magee, Vice-Pres. Ap 1, 1909–1919); Frank W. Severne by 1924–1960(?); Fannie and Alfred W. Johnson 1961(?)–1964; Watkins Review, Inc. ca. 1964 to date. *Ed*: Levi M. Gano Ja 1864–1876; Levi M. Gano and J. Brighan by Ja 1876–1877; Levi M. Gano by Ap 5, 1877–N 26, 1885; Levi M. Gano and John Corbett by 1885–Ag 27, 1891; Levi M. Gano 1891–1903; Marcus M. Cass, Jr. 1904–1909; Albert M. Hall Ap 1–S 1, 1909; None listed S 8, 1909–Ag 17, 1910; Frank W. Severne, Ed. and Manager by 1910–1944; Frank W. Severne, Editor, Fannie M. Johnson, Assoc. Ed. 1945–1959; Fannie M. Johnson and Alfred W. Johnson 1960–Ja 1964; Malcolm Currie Ja 8, 1964 to date. *Pol*: Republican. *Format*: Four to sixteen pages, varying sizes, 15″ x 21″, 18″ x 22″, 20″ x 25″, 11½″ x 17¼″. *Circ*: 2,548 (1933); 1,118 (1972). *Price*: $2.00 per year in advance, $2.50 if not paid in 3 months (by 1866); $1.50 per year in advance (by 1875); $1.00 per year in advance (by 1909–1914); $1.50 per year, 5¢ per copy (by 1927–1944); $2.00 per year (1945–1956); $3.00 per year, 10¢ per copy (1957–1961); $4.00 per year, 10¢ per copy (1962–1967); $4.50 per year (1968 to date). *Comment*: Motto: "The Old Home Paper" (1927–?). The newspaper dates its history back to the establishment of *The Watkins Republican* (q.v.) in 1854 by J. Ketchum Averill, which later became the *Schuyler County Union* (q.v.). In January 1864 it was sold to Levi M. Gano

*See also p. 290

who continued the numbering of the newspaper when he changed
the title to *The Watkins Express. Loc*: NIC/RHA: D 28, 1865 (12:31
whole no. 603); N 11 ,1869 (16:24 whole no. 804); Jl 14, 28, Ag 18,
25, 1870 (17:7, 9, 12, 13 whole nos. 839, 841, 844, 845); [D 12,
1872–D 31, 1874 (19:29–21:? whole nos. 965– 1072)]; [Ja 13, 1876–
D 25, 1879 (22:34–26:32 whole no. 1126–1332)]; Ag 26–S 16, 1880
(27:15–18 whole nos. 1367–1370); S 22, 29, 1881 (28:19, 20 whole
nos. 1423, 1424); [Ja 12, 1882–O 20, 1892 (28:35–39:25 whole nos.
1439–2101)]; [Ja 11–D 12, 1894 (40:37–41:33 whole nos. 2065–
2165)]; F 13, 1895 (41:42 whole no. 2174); F 22, 1900 (41:45 whole
no. 2384); F 18, Jl 14, 21, D 29, 1904 (50:44; 51:13, 14, 37 whole
nos. 2592, 2613, 2614 fragment); Ja 7, 1909–Ap 23, 1919 (55:37–
64:47); [Ap 20, 1932–D 26, 1934 (77:44–79:21)]. NMnHi: Mr 22,
1866 (12:43 whole no. 615); D 24, 1868 (15:31 whole no. 759); Ja
28, 1875 (21:36 whole no. 1076); Jl 18, 1878 (25:9 whole no. 1257);
O 16, 1879 (26:22 whole no 1322); Jl 15, 1880 (27:9 whole no.
1361); S 27, 1883 (30:20 whole no. 1528); Jl 17, Ag 21, 1884
(31:10, 15 whole nos. 1570, 1575); Jl 12, 26, Ag 30, 1888 (35:10,
12, 17 whole nos. 1778, 1780, 1785); My 2, Je 27, 1889 (35:52;
36:8 whole nos. 1820, 1828); Ap 18, 1895 (41:51 whole no. 2131);
N 24, 1898 (45:32 whole no. 2319); Mr 8, 1900 (46:47 whole no.
2386); S 19, 1901 (48:23 whole no. 2466); Mr 26, 1913 (59:45
no whole no.); Ap 22, 1914 (60:43 no whole no.); [Je 8, 1927–Ja 1,
1969 (73:3–110:19)].

WATKINS FAMILY VISITOR (w) Watkins. N 1852–? (1:1–?).
Title changes: *The Family Visitor* 1852–?; *Watkins Family Visitor* by
Mr 1853–? *Pub and Ed*: D. M. Bishop and George Martin. *Pol*: Neutral. *Format*: Four pages 16¼ " x 22½ ". *Price*: $1.00 per year in ad-
vance. *Comment*: Motto: "A Weekly Repository of Literature, Science, and General Intelligence." *Loc*: NIC/RHA: Mr 23, 1853
(1:19). NMnHi: F 2, 1853 (1:12).

THE WATKINS HERALD (w) Havana, Watkins. ?–Mr 7, 1896
(1:1–?). *Pub*: S. H. and Louis W. Ferenbaugh ?–F 22, 1896; John
Corbett F 29–Mr 7, 1896. *Ed*: John Corbett F 29–Mr 7, 1896: *Format*: Four pages 15" x 18". *Price*: $1.00 per year in advance. *Com-
ment*: "In November 1882 S. H. Ferrenbaugh [*sic*] brought *The Havana Democrat* to this village, changing its name to *The Watkins
Herald*. In 1885, Lewis [*sic*] W. Ferenbaugh became associated with his
father in the publication of the *Herald*. In 1896, the *Herald* was sold
to John Corbett who with his brother, J. J. Corbett established the
Watkins Review [q.v.] . . ." (Severne, "Annual Report," p. 133.) Although the *Review* was renumbered, vol. 1, no. 1, it retained the
"whole numbering" of the *Herald. Loc*: NIC/MMN: Ja 11, F 22–
Mr 7, 1896 (18:35, 41–3 whole no. 973, 979–981).

THE WATKINS INDEPENDENT (w) Watkins. 1866–? (1:1–?).
Pub: S. C. Clizbe 1866–? *Format*: Four pages 18" x 24". *Price*: $2.00
per year. *Comment*: Motto: "Truth and Justice are Eternal." ". . . *The
Watkins Independent* was continued a year or two, when it was

abandoned, and the material moved out of the county." (Pierce, *History of Tioga*, p. 569.) *Loc*: NMn: N 23, 1866 (1:37).

THE WATKINS REPUBLICAN (w) Watkins. My 27, 1854–Ja 1864(?)// (1:1–?). *Pub and Ed*: J. Ketchum Averill 1854–1855; S. M. Taylor by N 2, 1855–1856; Morvaldon Ells by O 16, 1856–My 1863(?). *Pol*: Independent, then Republican. *Format*: Four pages 16½" x 23". *Price*: $1.50 per year to village subscribers calling at the office, $2.00 delivered (1854); $1.00 per year in advance, if not paid strictly in advance $2.00 will be charged invariably (1855). *Comment*: Motto: "A Family Newspaper—Independent in all Subjects" (1856); "The People are Sovereign—and the Will of the Majority is Law" (1859). In 1856 Morvaldon Ells became the editor and remained so for the next seven years. In May 1863, *The Republican* was sold to George D. A. Bridgeman who published it for about nine months under the name of *The Schuyler County Union* (q.v.). It was then sold to L. M. Gano who began its publication January 2, 1864 under the name of *The Watkins Express* (q.v.). (Severne, "Annual Report," p. 135.) Official paper of the County. *Loc*: NMn: Je 25, 1854 (1:5); N 2, 1855 (2:23 whole no. 75); O 16, 1856 (3:21 whole no. 125); My 12, 1859–S 19, 1861 (5:10–8:8 whole nos. 259– n.s 382).

WATKINS REVIEW (w) Watkins Glen. Mr 14, 1896 to date (1:1 to date). *Pub*: John Corbett and J. J. Corbett Mr 14, 1896–Mr 10, 1897; Barton L. Piper Mr 17, 1897–1938; B. L. Piper Estate ?–1940; Antoinette J. Piper 1941–1949; Hart Seely 1950–1952; Waverly Sun Recorder 1953–1954; Malcolm Currie 1955–1959; Watkins Review, Inc. 1960 to date. *Ed*: Barton L. Piper Mr 1897–?; Barton L. Piper and F. E. Wixson by Ja 6, 1909–O 16, 1912; Barton L. Piper O 23, 1912–1938; B. L. Piper, Jr. 1939–1950; Hart Seely 1951–1952; Walter Grunfeld by 1953; Hart I. Seely, Jr. 1954; Malcolm Currie 1955 to date. *Pol*: Independent 1896–Mr 1897; Democrat Mr 17, 1897 to date. *Format*: Eight to twelve pages, varying sizes, 15" x 22", 18" x 20½". *Price*: $1.00 per year (1896–1938); $1.50 per year (by 1940– 1944); $2.00 per year (1945–1954); $2.50 per year (1955); $3.00 per year (1956–1961); $4.00 per year (1961–1971); $5.00 per year (1972 to date). *Circ*: 1,650 (1972). *Comment*: Successor to *Watkins Herald* (q.v.). An editorial of March 17, 1897, states, "Time has demonstrated that the field for a local, independent newspaper is too limited to allow its publisher to achieve the success that untiring effort should compass, as it is distasteful to the present manager to make this paper a political publication, it has been accordingly sold to one who will direct the paper in that direction. Barton L. Piper is the new owner . . . [the] next issue will announce its political destinies to be . . . Democratic." Listing of editors and publishers from 1959 to date is based on information in Ayer's *Directory*. *Loc*: NIC/RHA: [Mr 28, 1896–Jl 10, 1901 (1:3–6:19)]; D 16, 1903 (8:42); N 9, D 7, 1904 (9:37, 41); Ja 3, 1906–D 25, 1907 (10:45–12:44); F 5, Ap 29–30, 1919 (23:52; 24:11, 12); D 7, 1921 (26:44); N 1, 1922 (27:39); Ja 10, 1923 (27:50); F 19, 1930 (25 [*sic* 35]: 2); My 14, 1941

(46:14); 1951 (3rd annual souvenir edition). NMn: S 29, 1897 (2:?); Ja 10, F 8, 1911 (15:47, 51); S 28, 1921 (26:34); O 27, 1926 (31:38); Ap 21, 1954 (59:4).

WATKINS WEEKLY UNION (w) Watkins. ?–Ja 1864//(?) (1:1–?). *Pub and Ed*: George D. A. Bridgeman. *Pol*: Democrat. *Format*: Four pages 18½" x 25". *Price*: $1.50 per year in advance. *Comment*: It can be assumed from the only issue located that Bridgeman changed the name of the *Schuyler County Union* (q.v.) to the *Watkins Weekly Union*. *Loc*: NMn: Ag 27, 1863 (n.s. 10:14 whole no. 481).

THE OVID GAZETTE

AND INDEPENDENT

OVID, NEW YORK, NOVEMBER 21, 1958   10c PER COPY — $3.50 PER YEAR —

SENECA COUNTY

THE AMERICAN REVEILLE see *SENECA FALLS-WATERLOO REVEILLE*

DAILY SENECA OBSERVER (d) Waterloo. Je 1846–? (1:1–?). *Pub*: Charles Sentell and Sylvester Pew. *Ed*: Charles Sentell. *Price*: $4.00 per year. *Comment*: Published from the office at Main Street. "This daily was established by the *Waterloo Observer* when telegraphic communication was established with Waterloo Village, but the paper was short-lived." (*History of Seneca County, New York with Illustrations* [Philadelphia, 1876], p. 54.) *Loc*: NWat: microfilm Je 27, 1846 (1:15).

THE FARMER AND SENECA FALLS ADVERTISER (w) Waterloo, Seneca Falls. Ag 6, 1823–? (1:1–?). *Title changes*: Seneca Farmer 1823–N 23, 1825; *The Seneca Farmer and Waterloo Advertiser* N 30, 1825–N 1829; *Seneca Farmer and Waterloo Advertiser* D 2, 1829–?; *Seneca Farmer and Seneca Falls Advertiser* 1831–1836; *The Farmer and Seneca Falls Advertiser* 1836–? *Pub and Ed*: William Child 1823–1827; G. H. Merrell and Co. S 19, 1827–Mr 1828; William Child Ap 2, 1828–1832; William Child and John H. Child (ed) D 6, 1832–? *Pol*: Republican; Anti-Masonic; Whig. *Format*: Four pages 15" x 22". *Price*: $2.00 per year (1823). *Comment*: Published opposite the Court House, Waterloo from 1823 to 1831, then published in the village of Seneca Falls a few rods west of the Seneca House. *Loc*: NIC/RHA: [N 24, 1830–Jl 27, 1831 (8:18–9:1)]; Je 6–Ag 29, 1832 (9:46–10:6); Ja 2, 1833 (10:24). NWat: microfilm S 22, 1824 (2:3); [Ja 12–D 21, 1825 (2:24–3:21)]; F 15, Mr 1–22, S 13–20, N 29, 1826 (3:29, 31–34; 4:7–8, 18); [Ja 17, 1827–F 16, 1837 (4:25–14:28)].

THE FARMER REVIEW see *THE INTERLAKEN REVIEW*

FARMER VILLAGE REVIEW see *THE INTERLAKEN REVIEW*

FREE SOIL UNION see *SENECA FREE SOIL UNION*

THE GAZETTE AND SENECA ADVERTISER (w) Waterloo. Ja 19, 1826–? (1:1–?). *Pub*: H. Gates and Voorhies. *Price*: $2.00 per

189

year if delivered, $1.50 otherwise (July 1826); $2.50 per year if delivered, $2.00 otherwise (October, 1826). *Loc*: NWat: microfilm Jl 26, O 18, 1826 (1:26, 40).

GLAD TIDINGS (w?) Seneca Falls. 1862(?)–? (1:1–?). *Format*: Four pages 7″ x 10″. *Comment*: The only issue located contains advertisements and personal testimonials. *Loc*: NWat: Ja 3, 1882 (22:1).

THE HORNET (irr.) Waterloo. Je 22, 1839–? (1:1–?). *Pub*: J. Strickland. *Pol*: Independent. "We must have a press conducted in the independent principle, and above and beyond the reach of faction of party." *Format*: Four pages. *Price*: $1.75 per year in advance. *Comment*: Motto: "No favor sways us and no fear shall awe." Published occasionally at 87 Wall Street. *Loc*: NWat: microfilm Je 22, 1839 (1:1).

THE INTERLAKEN REVIEW (w) Farmer [now Interlaken]. Jl 23, 1887 to date (1:1 to date). *Title changes*: *Saturday Morning Review* Jl 23, 1887–D 29, 1888; *Farmer Village Review* Ja 5, 1889–Je 25, 1892; *The Farmer Review* Jl 2, 1892–Je 24, 1904; *The Interlaken Review* Jl 1, 1904 to date. *Pub*: Thomas P. Hause Jl 23, 1887–Ja 25, 1929; No publisher listed F 1–Ag 2, 1929; The Interlaken Review, Inc. Ag 9, 1929–Jl 2, 1948; Weighous and Co. Jl 9, 1948–Je 29, 1956 (owned by the Interlaken Review, Inc.); Wanda M. and Duane C. Waid Jl 6, 1956–1965; I-T Publishing Corp. 1965 to date. *Ed*: Thomas P. Hause Jl 23, 1887–Ja 25, 1929; Fred W. Blauvelt F 1, 1929–D 31, 1946; Adrian C. Dickerson Ja 3, 1947–Jl 2, 1948; Anthony H. Weighous Jl 9, 1948–Je 29, 1956; Duane C. Waid Jl 6, 1956 to date. *Pol*: Neutral. *Format*: Four to eight pages, varying sizes, 16½″ x 23½″, 18″ x 23¾″, 19″ x 23¾″, 20″ x 25½″, 20″ x 24½″, 15″ x 22″, 12″ x 17½″, 13¾″ x 20¾″, 11¼″ x 17″. *Price*: $1.25 per year in advance, otherwise $1.50 (1887); $1.50 per year (1917); $2.00 per year (1920); $3.00 per year (1956); $3.50 per year (1958); $4.00 per year (1966). *Circ*: 724 (1889); 1,200 (1893); 1,172 (1968). *Comment*: Motto: "A newspaper with personality." (1933); "The only newspaper in the world that cares anything about Interlaken." (1939). Published opposite P. R. Shafer's Jewelry Store in 1888, then moved to the New Building on Railroad Street in 1893, and to the Carman Building next to Lowe's Mobil Station in 1966. *The Interlaken Review* is now published in Trumansburg, and is identical, except for its banner, to the *Ovid Gazette* (q.v.) and the *Trumansburg Free Press* (Tompkins County, q.v.). *Loc*: NIC/RHA: Je 22, 1895 (8:48); Je 16, 1900 (13:47); Mr 23, 1901 (14:35); Ja 9, D 4, 1903 (16:25; 17:20). NIn: Jl 23, 1887–Je 28, 1907 (1:1–20:52); Jl 3, 1908–Je 27, 1930 (22:1–43:52); Jl 17, 1931–Je 26, 1936 (45:3–49:52); Jl 2, 1937–Jl 28, 1944 (50:1–56:52); [Jl 5, 1946–Je 30, 1950 (60:1–63:53)]; Jl 1, 1955 to date (68:1 to date). NOv: N 28, 1919 (20:22).

THE LILY (m, then semi-m) Seneca Falls, New York; Mt. Vernon, Ohio; Richmond, Ind. Ag 1849–? (1:1–?). *Pub and Ed*: Amelia

Bloomer Ag 1849–D 1854; Mary B. Birdsall Ja 1855–? *Pol*: "Devoted
to the interests of women." "Devoted to the emancipation of women
from intemperance, injustice, prejudice and bigotry." *Format*: Four
to eight pages, varying sizes, 9½ " x 12½ ", 11½ " x 18½ ". *Price*: 50¢
per year in advance. *Comment*: Issued as a monthly until June 1,
1853 when it became semi-monthly. The August 1852 issue contains
an address by Ann Preston designed for adoption at the Women's
Rights Convention at Westchester, Pa. *Loc*: NSenHi: Ag, 1852 (4:8);
Je 1, 1853 (5:11); D 15, 1854 (6:23).

THE LODI CHRISTIAN ADVOCATE (m) Lodi. Jl 1904–? (1:1–?).
Pub and Ed: Hoyt F. Hill. *Format*: Four pages 9" x 12". *Loc*:
NIC/RHA: Jl–S 1904 (1:1–3); Ja–Ap, Jl, N 1905 (2:1–4, 6, 11).

THE MEMORIAL (m) Seneca Falls. 1838–? (no. 1–?). *Pub and Ed*:
Ansel Bascom. *Format*: Four pages, 12" x 18". *Price*: $1.00 per year
in advance. *Comment*: Motto: "Devoted to a reduction of the costs
attending legal proceedings in the collection of debts." *"The Memorial,*
a legal reform journal, was commenced at Seneca Falls in 1838 by
Ansel Bascom. It vigorously advocated reform in the codification of
laws and urged important amendments to the State Constitution. It
was printed at the Democrat Office and published monthly, until the
calling of the Constitutional Convention in 1846 of which body Mr.
Bascom was chosen a member. *The Memorial* is regarded as having
been the main agent in bringing about that legal reform in the code of
legal procedure that has superseded the old common law system of
pleading and practice, not alone in New York, but in other states and
in Great Britain." (*History of Seneca County*, p. 55.) *Loc*: NIC/
MMN: Jl 1839 (extra). NSenHi: O 19, 1839 (2:36 fragment).

THE OBSERVER AND UNION see *SENECA OBSERVER*

THE OVID BEE (w) Ovid. F 21, 1838–F 26, 1873// (1:1–37:9).
Pub: David Fairchild and Son F 21, 1838–1839; Corydon Fairchild
1839–F 1872; Oliver C. Cooper F 1872–1873. *Ed*: David Fairchild
1838; Corydon Fairchild. *Pol*: Independent with Democratic proclivities. *Format*: Four pages 15" x 20". *Price*: $2.00 per year in ad-
vance, otherwise $2.50. *Comment*: Motto: "A Family Journal—Fear-
less and Independent—Devoted to Literature, Agricultural Science
and General Intelligence." David Fairchild, publisher of the *Ovid Bee*
published the *Cortland Advocate* prior to moving to Ovid in 1838. In
the inaugural issue of the *Bee* David Fairchild expressed the neutral
position of the paper as follows:
> "The *Bee* will mingle in no party strife
> For banks, nor anti-banks, nor local broils,
>   But lead a social peaceful, busy life—
>   Unpledged to sects, unbribed by promised spoils."
>   (*History of Seneca County*, p. 55)
The Ovid Bee was published from an office located on East Main
Street, directly opposite the Court House Green, entrance upstairs
three doors east of W. Weaver's Saddlery Shop. Later moved to the
new Brick Block, west side of Academy Street (third story) over the

Boot and Shoe Store of John T. Cornell and directly opposite the Stone Block of A. Joy. In the 1850's located on Main Street opposite the Franklin House. The closing date of *The Ovid Bee* was established from the masthead of the *Ovid Gazette and Independent* which carried the statement *"The Ovid Gazette and Independent* is the outgrowth of *The Ovid Bee* established in 1838 which was discontinued February 26, 1873 and succeeded by *The Independent,* March 5, 1873." *Loc*: NCooHi: F 11, 1846 (9:1); Ja 4, 1854 (16:36). NIC/ MMN: Je 30, 1852 (fragment); D 22, 1858 (extra); Ja 4, 1860 (22:30). NIC/RHA: [F 20, 1839–N 27, 1861 (2:1–24:26)]; Ja 21– D 30, 1863 (25:34–26:32); Mr 15, 1865 (27:44); My 6, 1866 (29:3); Ja 9, 1867–Je 8, 1870 (30:2–33:23); Ja 8–F 26, 1873 (38:2– 9). NOv: D 5, 1838 (1:42); Ja 23, 1839 (1:49); My 21, 1845 (8:15); Ap 22, 1846 (9:11); Mr 17, Jl 28, 1847 (10:5, 24); Ja 17, Mr 14, My 16, Je 13, 20, Jl 25, O 24, D 19, 1849 (11:49; 12:5, 13, 17, 18, 23, 35, 43); Ag 21, 1850 (13:26); Ap 27, O 12, 1853 (16:3, 26); [Mr 28, 1855–D 3, 1856 (17:48–19:30)]; [Mr 23–D 28, 1859 (21:42–22:29)]; Ja 25, F 29, Mr 14, 1860 (22:33, 38, 40); [Ja 9– My 15, 1861 (23:32–50)]; S 4, 1867 (30:34); Ja 8, F 19, My 6, 1868 (31:3, 9, 20). NSenHi: N 15, 1843 (6:40); N 5, 1845 (8:39); N 11, 1863 (26:25).

THE OVID EMPORIUM (w) Ovid. 1832–? (1:1–?). *Pub and Ed*: Bishop Ovenshier. *Pol*: Republican. *Format*: Four pages 13½ " x 20". *Price*: $2.00 per year. *Loc*: NIC/RHA: Je 13, 1832 (1:35).

THE OVID GAZETTE (w?) Ovid. ca. 1817// No issues located. This was probably the title change from the *Seneca Patriot* (q.v.). George Lewis changed the name of the paper to *The Ovid Gazette* at the close of a single volume and when Elisha Williams secured the removal of the county seat to Waterloo, Lewis moved the press to that village and changed the name of the paper to *The Waterloo Gazette* (q.v.) (*History of Seneca County,* p. 54.)

THE OVID GAZETTE (w) Ovid. ca. 1818–? (1:1–?). *Pub and Ed*: Michael Hayes by 1821–? *Format*: Four pages, varying sizes, 11" x 18", 12" x 20", 21⅜ " x 17⅞ ". *Price*: $2.00 per year. Loc: NIC/ MMN: My 9, 1826 (9:30). NIC/RHA: Ja 31, F 7, Mr 7–D 20, 1821 (4:15, 16, 20–5:9).

THE OVID GAZETTE (w) Ovid. 1894 to date (1:1 to date). *Title changes*: *The Ovid Gazette* 1894–1901; *The Ovid Gazette and Independent* Ja 1901–?; *The Ovid Gazette* O 1, 1964 to date. *Pub and Ed*: Charles E. Garnett 1894–1913; J. W. Shaw 1914–1915; George M. Pashley 1915–1930; S. E. Mekeel 1930–S 1964; Inter-County Publishers Inc. O 4, 1964 to date (Duane C. Waid, ed.). *Pol*: Democrat. *Format*: Four to twelve pages, varying sizes, 15½ " x 21¾ ", 18" x 24", 16½ " x 24", 11" x 16½ ". *Price*: $1.25 per year (1902); $2.00 per year (1935); $3.00 per year (1951); $3.50 per year (1958); $4.00 per year, 10¢ per copy (1963–1970); $5.00 per year, 15¢ per copy (1971 to date). *Comment*: Motto: "Home, Her Institutions and Interests." In January 1901, *The Ovid Independent* (q.v.) was purchased by Charles E. Garnett, publisher of *The Ovid Gazette*. He consolidated the two papers under the name of *The Ovid Gazette and Independent*. No issues of *The Ovid Gazette* which was established in 1894 according to the mastheads of later issues of *The Ovid Gazette* and which was published separately until 1901 have been located. By 1902, the *Gazette and Independent* retained not only the numbering of the original papers, the *Independent* and the *Gazette*, but also had its own numbering, v. 1 no. 1. By 1905, the numbering of the original papers was discontinued. *Loc*: NCooHi: N 21, 1958 (143:47). NIC/RHA: Ja 9, 1901–D 7, 1902 (28:48, 7:4–30:52), 7:52 and 2:52); [Ja 4, 1905–D 11, 1907 (5:3–6:52)]; Ja 6, 1909–Ag 12, 1912 (8:4–11:35); Ja 13, 1916–D 28, 1923 (15:2–20:52); Ja 1, 1926–S 17, 1964 (25:1–149:38). NIn: O 1–D 31, 1964 (149:40–53). NOv: N 19, 1913 (12:46); Je 8, 1916 (15:23); Ag 30, 1917 (16:35); Ap 22, O 7, 1920 (17:17, 41); D 14, 1923 (20:50); Ja 11, 1929 (28:2); Ja 10, 1930 (29:2); Ja 4, 1935–S 24, 1964 (34:1–149:39); Ja 6, 1966 to date. NSenHi: Ap 23, 1902 (30:11).

THE OVID GAZETTE AND INDEPENDENT see *THE OVID GAZETTE* (1894 to date)

OVID GAZETTE AND SENECA COUNTY REGISTER (w) Ovid. 1830–? No issues located. In 1830, the title of the newspaper, the *Seneca Republican* (q.v.) was changed to the *Ovid Gazette and Seneca County Register* and published for a brief time under the charge of John Duffy. (*History of Seneca County*, p. 54.)

THE OVID INDEPENDENT (w) Ovid. Mr 1873–1901// (1:1–?). *Pub and Ed*: Oliver C. Cooper 1873–?; Robert Hydon and Robert D. Patterson by Mr 1896–Jl 1897; Robert D. Patterson Jl–N 1897; Patterson Bros. (Robert D. and Lester) N 1897–1901. *Pol*: Independent. *Format*: Four pages, varying sizes, 20″ x 25″; 21″ x 26″. *Price*: $1.50 per year in advance (by 1885); $1.00 per year in advance (by 1897). *Comment*: Motto: "Independent in Everything; Neutral in Nothing." When Cooper bought *The Ovid Bee* from Corydon Fairchild, he changed the name of the paper to *The Ovid Independent*. He published the paper with Nelson Hyatt "until the great fire of October 12, 1874, burned out the entire establishment. Mr. Hyatt then retired, and the junior member of the firm, Oliver C. Cooper re-established the paper." (*History of Seneca County*, p. 55.) In 1901, *The Ovid Independent* was purchased by Charles Garnett, publisher of *The Ovid Gazette* and consolidated with the latter paper under the name of *The Ovid Gazette and Independent* (q.v.). The numbering of the *Independent* was maintained along with that of the *Gazette* until 1902. Published in Van Nostrand Hall entrance on the north side of the building nearly opposite the Presbyterian Church. *Loc*: NIC/MMN: S 10, 1879 (fragment); Je 30, 1880 (fragment); O 25, 1887 (15:35). NIC/RHA: Jl 16, 1889 (17:20); [F 25, 1896– D 5, 1900 (24:1–28:43)]. NIDeW: S 21, 1881 (9:30). NOv: Je 12, 1888 (16:16); Ag 20, 1889 (17:25); S 6, 1899 (27:30). NSenHi: Ap 8, 1885 (13:6); O 25, 1887 (15:35).

THE POLK-WRIGHT (d?) Seneca Falls. ca. 1844//. No issues located. Josiah T. Miller, editor of the *Seneca Falls Democrat* (q.v.) in 1839 and later owner, "issued during a few months of the year 1844 a Democratic campaign sheet, under the title of *The Polk-Wright*" Miller being editor. (*History of Seneca County,* p. 55.)

THE REPUBLICAN (w) Ovid Village. F 9, 1820–? (1:1–?). *Pub and Ed*: George Lewis. *Pol*: Republican. *Format*: Four pages 11″ x 17″. *Price*: $2.00 per year. *Loc*: NIC/RHA: Mr 29, 1820 (1:8).

THE REPUBLICAN OBSERVER (w) Waterloo. F 20, 1828–? (1:1–?). *Pub and Ed*: Moses Severance. *Pol*: Democrat. *Format*: Four pages 13¼″ x 19½″. *Price*: $2.00 per year. *Comment*: Motto: "Pledged but to Truth." "The [*Waterloo*] *Gazette* [q.v.], which for the last two years has been published in this village, has been discontinued and the establishment has fallen into our hands. With that paper we had nothing to do . . . . All connection with that paper or its conductors we disavow. It shall be our object to make the *Observer* a paper of general intelligence, divested of those extremes of party strife, the tendency of which is to bias rather than instruct . . . ." (*The Republican Observer* F 20, 1828.) *Loc*: NIC/RHA: O 15, 1828 (1:35). NWat: F 20, 1828 (1:1).

REVEILLE see *SENECA FALLS-WATERLOO REVEILLE*

SATURDAY MORNING REVIEW see *THE INTERLAKEN REVIEW*

THE SENECA CHIEF (w) Waterloo. S 18, 1897–? (1:1–?). *Pub and Ed*: Oliver C. Cooper. *Pol*: Non-partisan. *Format*: Four pages. *Price*: $1.00 per year in advance. *Loc*: NWat: microfilm S 18, 1897 (1:1).

SENECA COUNTY COMMERCIAL (w) Seneca Falls. 1924–Je 1928// (1:1–?). *Pub and Ed*: E. D. Clark 1925. *Format*: Ten pages 17″ x 24″. *Comment*: "Devoted to Agricultural and Commercial interests of Seneca County Farmers." Merged with *The Seneca Falls Reveille* (q.v.) June 21, 1928. The inside running title, *Seneca Falls Reveille-Standard Commercial* reflected the merger. *Loc*: NSen/ Reveille Office: D 3, 1925 (2:16).

THE SENECA COUNTY COURIER Seneca Falls. ca. 1836–? No issues located. ". . . established in 1836 by Isaac Fuller & Co., O. H. Platt, then a leading lawyer, became its first editor. Platt was succeeded by Dexter C. Bloomer." (*History of Seneca County,* p. 54.)

THE SENECA COUNTY COURIER (w) Seneca Falls. Je 4, 1839– 1843// (1:1–?). *Title changes*: Seneca County Courier 1839–?; *The Seneca County Courier* by 1840–? *Pub and Ed*: Isaac Fuller and Dexter C. Bloomer 1839–?; Flavius Josephus Mills and Dexter C. Bloomer ?–Je 1841; Flavius Josephus Mills and John Jay Davis Je 30, 1841–? *Format*: Four pages 18¾″ x 24½″. *Price*: $2.00 per year in advance. *Comment*: Motto: "Principles—not men." *Loc*: NSenHi: [S 15–D

29, 1840 (2:16–31)]; Ja 5–My 26, 1841 (2:32–52). NWat: Ag 20, S 24, N 5, 1839 (1:12, 17, 23); Je 2, N 10, 24, 1840 (2:24, 26, 28); Ja 5, Ap 14, My 12, 26, Jl 7, Ag 18, S 1, 1840 (2:32, 40, 50, 52; 3:6, 12, 14); F 9, 1842 (3:37).

SENECA COUNTY COURIER (w) Seneca Falls. 1843–1845// (n.s. 1:1–?). *Pub*: John Jay Davis and Dexter C. Bloomer by 1844–1845. *Ed*: John Jay Davis by 1844–? *Pol*: Whig. *Format*: Four pages 18″ x 24¼″.*Comment*: An item appeared in the April 2, 1845 edition of the *Courier* advertising the sale of the newspaper to "any sound Whig." *Loc*: NRU: O 2, 1844 (n.s. 2:52). NSenHi: Ag 21, 1844 n.s. 2:46). NWat: microfilm S 25, N 6, 13, D 11, 1844 (n.s. 2:51; 3:5, 6, 10); Ja 15, Ap 2, 1845 (3:25, 26).

SENECA COUNTY COURIER (w, then semi-w) Seneca Falls. My 1845–1848// (n.s. 1:1–?). *Pub and Ed*: N. J. Milliken and Fuller 1845–1848; N. J. Milliken and Mumford My–S 1848. *Pol*: Whig. *Format*: Four pages 16″ x 20½″. *Price*: $1.50 per year in advance, otherwise $2.00 (1845). *Circ*: 1,000 (1848). *Comment*: Published at 3 Down's Block near the Post Office; then in 1846 moved to the Post Office. Semi-weekly by 1847. *Loc*: NRU: S 17, 1845 (n.s. 1:19). NSenHi: Jl 24, 1846 (2:21 whole no. 468); N 16, D 3, 1847 (n.s. 3:53, 58); [Mr 10–Ag 22, 1848 (3:86–4:29)].

THE SENECA COUNTY COURIER (w, semi-w) Seneca Falls. S 25, 1848–Ag 1902// (1:1–65:?). *Title changes*: *Seneca County Courier* S 25, 1848–?; *The Seneca County Courier* by 1866–?; *Seneca County Semi-Weekly Courier* Ja 13–N 26, 1880; *The Seneca County Courier* D 2, 1880–? *Pub*: W. H. Foster and O. G. Judd 1849–1850; Isaac Fuller and O. B. Judd 1850; Isaac Fuller O 10, 1850–1865; Sylvester Pew and Simeon Holton 1865–1871; Sylvester Pew 1871–1875; Horace W. Knight and Arthur S. Baker Ap 19, 1876–1878; Horace W. Knight Je 13, 1878–1879; A. H. Comstock 1879–My 4, 1882; The Courier Printing Co. My 11, 1882–? *Ed*: Dexter C. Bloomer 1849–1850; Isaac Fuller O 1850–1865; Simeon Holton 1865–?; Simeon Holton and Arthur Baker Ja 26, 1871–1872; Arthur S. Baker O 31, 1872–?; A. H. Comstock 1879–My 4, 1882. *Pol*: Whig; Republican. *Format*: Four to eight pages, varying sizes, 18¾″ x 24½″; 16″ x 20½″, 17″ x 22¾″, 20½″ x 27″. *Price*: $1.50 per year (1849); $2.00 per year (1864); $1.50 per year (1880). *Circ*: 1,000 (1848). *Comment*: Motto: "Freedom and right against slavery and wrong" (1860). In 1859, it was published in Seneca Falls next to Mr. Arnett's Mill, then in the Phoenix Company's new block on Fall Street. In 1890 after a fire, the publishing office was moved to the rear of the public telephone office over Golder's store, first door west of the Stanton House. In 1885 it referred to itself as the "Only Republican Paper in the County." The *Courier* merged with the *Seneca County Journal* (q.v.) on August 21, 1902. *Loc*: NIC/MMN: Je 5, 12, 1851 (3:41, 42); Ag 28, 1873 (38:3); Jl 6, 1880 (44:74). NIC/RHA: Ag 13, 1885 (50:3). NOv: Jl 16, 1857 (20:47); F 24, Je 30, Ag 4, 1859

(22:27, 45, 50); Ja 26, Mr 15, Ag 16, S 6, O 4, 1860 (22:23, 30, 52; 24:3, 7); F 20, Mr 6, Jl 17, O 2, N 13, D 4, 1862 (25: 27, 29, 48; 26:7, 13, 16); O 18, 1866 (30:13). NSenHi: S 21, 1849 (2:4); O 10, 1850 (3:7); Ap 10–Ag 7, 1851 (3:31–50); Ja 29–Ap 15, 1852 (15:23–34); F 3, Ag 25, S 22, O 27, 1853 (16:24; 17:1, 5, 10); Ag 2, N 22, 1855 (18:49; 19:3); [Ag 29, 1858–S 5, 1867 (21:36–31:4)]; [Je 16, 1870–Jl 7, 1887 (33:34–51:50)]; [Ja 2, 1890–D 28, 1893 (53:14–57:13)]; [N 12, 1896–Mr 15, 1900 (60:7–63:24)]. NWat: S 25, O 27, 1848 (n.s. 1:1, 9); Mr 29, Ap 19, My 3, 1850 (2:31, 34, 36); Ap 15, 1858 (21:34); Ap 20, O 5, 1865 (28:36; 29:8); Ap 11, 1867 (30:38); N 3, 1870 (34:13); O 16, 1873 (38:10); [My 8, 1879–D 29, 1887 (43:40–52:13)]; Je 26, Jl 31, 1890 (53:39, 44). Also on microfilm.

SENECA COUNTY COURIER-JOURNAL (w) Seneca Falls. F 26, 1885–D 21, 1944// (1:1–102:49). *Title changes*: *Seneca County Journal* F 26, 1885–Ag 13, 1902; *Seneca County Courier-Journal* Ag 21, 1902–D 21, 1944. *Pub*: The Journal Publishing Co. F 26, 1885–D 21, 1944. *Ed*: N. B. Stevens 1885–1886; William J. Pollard 1895–N 1910; Edwin F. Bussey D 1, 1910–S 7, 1911; Charles W. Combs S 1911–S 16, 1915; J. D. Pollard S 23, 1915–D 21, 1944. *Pol*: Republican. *Format*: Four to eight pages, varying sizes, 20″ x 26″, 20″ x 28″, 16″ x 22″. *Price*: $1.50 per year in advance (1885); $2.00 per year (1923). *Comment*: Motto: "Devoted to the Best Interests of the People in Church and State." The office was located in the Partridge Block until April 1917 when it moved to the Clary Block, where it remained until it ceased publication in 1944. *Loc*: NSenHi: F 26, 1885 (1:1); S 15, 1886 (2:29); N 2, 9, D 14, 1887 (3:36, 37, 42); Ja 3, 1888 (3:48); [Mr 13, 1889–O 19, 1892 (5:2–8:32)]; Ag 30, 1893 (9:26); [Mr 27, 1895–D 31, 1936 (11:1–94:46); Ja 4, 1940–D 21, 1944 (97:4–102:49).

SENECA COUNTY JOURNAL see *SENECA COUNTY COURIER-JOURNAL*

THE SENECA COUNTY NEWS (w) Waterloo, Seneca Falls. D 20, 1878–1964// (1:1–?). *Title changes*: *Seneca County News* D 20, 1878–Ap 1951; *The Seneca County News* My 3, 1951–1964(?). *Pub*: Albert L. Childs D 20, 1878–S 24, 1885; Elias Vair and James E. Medden S 25, 1885–1898; Elias Vair 1898–S 1928; No publisher listed 1928–1938; Seneca Press Publishing Co., Inc. Mr 10, 1938–1964(?) (N. G. Gould, Pres.). *Ed*: Albert L. Childs D 20, 1878–S 24, 1885; Elias Vair S 25, 1885–S 1928; George C. Starkey O 3, 1928–1936; Roscoe E. Haynes Ap 23, 1936–?; Mrs. Donald Huff O 9, 1947–Ap 20, 1961; Mrs. Marjorie Paddison Ap 27, 1961–?. *Pol*: Democrat (1878–1885). "Politically it will be Democratic. The agricultural as well as the business interests of the community will be recognized or consulted." Republican (1885–?). *Format*: Four to eight pages, varying sizes, 17¼″ x 23½″, 11¾″ x 17¼″. *Price*: Fluctuates between $1.50 to $2.00 per year from D 25, 1878 until 1956, then $3.00 per year. *Comment*: Published at the Academy of Music,

Waterloo 1878–1961; then 83 Fall Street, Seneca Falls 1962. *Loc*:
NIC/MMN: F 14, 1879 (2:9); Ja 23–F 6, 1880 (2:58–60); Je 23,
1881 (3:132); O 16, 23, D 25, 1883 (no series no.); Ja 8, 1884
(6:265). NWat: [D 20, 1878–D 29, 1914 (1:1–37:1879)]; [F 8,
1916–N 3, 1920 (38:1927–42:2172)]; Ja 4, 1922–D 27, 1962
(43:2253–79:52).

SENECA COUNTY NEWSLETTER (w) Geneva [Ontario County].
1877–? (1:1–?). *Pub*: James Malette. *Ed*: James Malette; James and
F. A. Malette 1897–? *Pol*: "Independent, not neutral." *Format*: Four
to twelve pages 14″ x 22″. *Price*: $1.00 per year (1887); $1.50 per
year (1894). *Circ*: 4,500 (1887); 9,000 (1889). *Comment*: Published in the Smith Block, Linden Street, Geneva. Although printed
in Geneva, County of Ontario, this newspaper was distributed throughout Seneca County. *Loc*: NWat: [Ja 22–D 31, 1887 (10:2–51)]; Ja
26, F 2, 1889 (12:3–4); O 13, 20, 1894; Ap 10, My 8, 1897 (fragments).

SENECA COUNTY PRESS (semi-w, then w) Seneca Falls. 1912–
1970(?)// (1:1–?). *Pub*: Seneca Press Publishing Co. 1915–? *Ed*:
R. W. Kellogg 1915–?; L. D. Stafford 1931–?; Mrs. William R. Paddison. *Format*: Four to sixteen pages, varying sizes, 17½″ x 22″,
17½″ x 24″. *Price*: $1.50 per year (1915); $2.00 per year (1931);
$3.00 per year (1962). *Comment*: Motto: "Leader in personal and
local news." The *Seneca County Press* was the official city newspaper.
It was published at the Arcade Building, 83 Fall Street February 11,
1931–July 4, 1951. The newspaper was published as a weekly from
February 11, 1931–? *Loc*: NIC/MMN: D 24, 1941 (30:22); Ja 3,
1962 (46:19). NOv: N 13, 1929 (18:14). NSenHi: Mr 19, 1915
(3:60); Ja 28, 1920 (8:26); F 11, 1931 (20:27); Ja 6, Jl 21, 1937
(25:23, 51); [Ja 5–Je 20, 1945 (32:24–33:48)]; Jl 4, O 24, 1951
(35:52; 36:16). NWat: Ja 6, 1937 (25:23); O 30, 1940 (29:14); Ja
3, 1962 (46:19).

SENECA COUNTY SENTINEL (w) Ovid, Farmer [now Interlaken].
Ja 19, 1860–Mr 1, 1866// (1:1–7:9). *Pub*: Arthur T. Williams 1860–
?; John M. Riley ?–O 26, 1865; Oscar M. Wilson N 1865–? *Ed*: T. R.
Lounsbury 1860–?; John M. Riley ?–O 26, 1865; Oscar M. Wilson N
1865–? *Pol*: Independent. "Purely Independent Course." *Format*:
Four pages, varying sizes, 18½″ x 25″, 15½″ x 21½″. *Price*: $1.50
per year. *Comment*: Motto: "Fearlessly to advocate truth and repre-
hend error." "The *Seneca County Sentinel* was commenced at Ovid,
January 19, 1860, by A. S. [*sic*] Williams, under Republican colors.
Mr. Williams sold to T. R. Lounsbury, a native of Ovid, and present
professor of English Literature at Yale College. During the same year,
1860, the paper was bought by S. M. Thompson, and by him conducted till 1861, when it passed into control of D. G. Caywood. Sale
was made to Riley and Baldwin; the latter disposed of his interest to
his partner, John Riley, who removed the office to Farmer Village . . . ." (*History of Seneca County*, p. 55.) In March of 1866 the
paper was moved to Trumansburg, Tompkins County, and was pub-

lished under its new name, *Tompkins County Sentinel* (see in *New York History,* April 1971). *Loc*: NIC/MMN: O 26, 1865–Mr 1, 1866 (6:13–7:9). NIC/RHA: Ja 19, 1860 (1:1).

SENECA COUNTY STANDARD see *SENECA FALLS-WATERLOO REVEILLE*

SENECA COUNTY WAR CHEST ASSOCIATION (?) Seneca Falls. 1918–? *Pub*: Seneca County Home Defense Committee, W. D. Pomeroy, Chairman. *Format*: Eight pages 17″ x 24″. *Loc*: NIC/RHA: Ag 19, 1918.

SENECA DEMOCRAT (semi-w) Waterloo Village. O 31, 1853–? No issues located. "It apparently was a short lived attempt to influence an election. It was opposed to the stand taken by the *Seneca Observer* in the matter of Democratic principles and policy." (John E. Becker, *A History of the Village of Waterloo, New York, and Thesaurus of Related Facts* [Waterloo, 1949], p. 164.)

SENECA EVENING JOURNAL (m) Farmer Village. ca. F 1867–? No issues located. Published as a monthly by Jacob Bergen at Farmer Village, Seneca County, New York, and devoted to Literature, Local News, etc. A twenty-four column paper. (From an add in Hamilton Child, *Gazetteer and Business Directory of Seneca County, New York for 1867–8* [Syracuse, 1867], p. 220.)

THE SENECA FALLS DEMOCRAT (w) Seneca Falls. O 3, 1839–? (1:1–?). *Title changes*: *The Seneca Falls Democrat* O 3, 1839–1842; *Seneca Falls Democrat* 1842–1846; *The Seneca Falls Democrat* F 27, 1846–? *Pub*: Published by an Association of Gentlemen O 3, 1839–S 29, 1842; Mortimer J. Smith and Sylvester Pew O 6, 1842–Mr 23, 1843; Sylvester Pew and Co. My 18, 1843–Ap 18, 1844; Flavius Joseph Mills Ap 25, 1844–? *Ed*: Josiah T. Miller O 3, 1839–? *Pol*: Democrat. *Format*: Four pages, varying sizes, 17½″ x 23½″, 18″ x 24½″. *Price*: $2.50 per year. *Comment*: Motto: "Be just and fear not, but persevere unto the end." *Loc*: NIC/RHA: Ap 30, 1840 (1:31). NSenHi: [O 3, 1839–Ap 17, 1846 (1:1–n.s. 2:51 whole nos. 1–341)].

SENECA FALLS JOURNAL (w) ca. 1829–? Seneca Falls. No issues located. In the summer of 1829, O. B. Clark issued a proposal to publish the *Seneca Falls Truth* which was to be "Anti-Masonic in sentiment and Anti-Jacksonian in politics. Mr. Clark found ready support in that village" and in 1829 issued a paper called the *Seneca Falls Journal,* "the pioneer publication of the village." William Clark purchased the *Journal* and issued it for a year. In 1832, Brown entered into partnership with William Child and merged his paper with *The Seneca Farmer.* It was thereafter issued as *The Seneca Farmer and Seneca Falls Advertiser* (q.v.). (*History of Seneca County,* p. 54.)

SENECA FALLS REGISTER Seneca Falls. ca. 1835–1837//. No issues located. After Joseph K. Brown sold his interest in the *Seneca Farmer and Seneca Falls Advertiser* to William Child, publisher of the *Farmer,* he started this paper. It lasted about two years. (*History of Seneca County,* p. 54.)

SENECA FALLS REVEILLE see *SENECA FALLS-WATERLOO REVEILLE*

SENECA FALLS-WATERLOO REVEILLE (w) Seneca Falls. Ja 13, 1855 to date (1:1 to date). *Title changes: The American Reveille* Ja 13, 1855–Je 16, 1860; *The Seneca Falls Reveille* Je 23, 1860–Ja 1948; *Seneca Falls Reveille* 1948–Ag 13, 1968; *Seneca Falls-Waterloo Reveille* Ag 14, 1968 to date. *Pub*: George A. Sherman and Arthur S. Baker 1855–1856; Gilbert Wilcoxen and Sylvester Pew Jc 12–Je 14, 1856; Gilbert Wilcoxen Je 15, 1856–D 31, 1858; Henry Stowell and Alanson P. Holly Ja 1, 1859–Ja 6, 1860; Henry Stowell Ja 7–Je 22, 1860; Henry Stowell and Mark Heath Je 23, 1860–My 16, 1862; Henry Stowell My 17, 1862–O 10, 1918; E. D. Clark O 11, 1918–F 11, 1926; Seneca Falls Reveille, Inc. F 12, 1926 to date (E. D. Clark, Pres. F 12, 1926–1948, Edward L. Bowman, Pub. F 12, 1926–1948; John B. Souhan, Pub. 1949–?; William A. Murphy, Pub. Ag 1953– Je 23, 1955; Michael D. Gustina, Pub. Je 30–O 27, 1955; James S. Kellogg, Pub. N 3, 1955–?; Robert J. Glessing, Pub. Ap 28, 1965–Jl 4, 1967; Thomas D. Williams, Pub. Jl 5, 1967–Jl 3, 1968; Joseph Burt, Pub. Jl 3–Ag 21, 1968; Joseph Burt and Howard Van Kirk, Pubs. Ag 28–O 25, 1968; Howard Van Kirk, Co-publisher, Roger Chapin, Pres. N 1, 1968 to date). *Ed*: Gilbert Wilcoxen Ja 13, 1855–D 25, 1858; Henry Stowell Ja 1, 1859–Je 16, 1860; Henry Stowell and Mark Heath Je 23, 1860–My 10, 1862; Henry Stowell My 17, 1862–O 5, 1918; E. D. Clark O 12, 1918–1946; Edward L. Bowman 1946–F 4, 1949; Fred Blauvelt F–Je 3, 1949; John B. Souhan Je 1949–?; William A. Murphy Ag 1953–S 8, 1955; Jeanette Rott S 15–29, 1955; Eric Landburg O 6–27, 1955; James S. Kellogg N 3, 1955–?; Robert J. Glessing Ap 1965–Ag 9, 1967; Richard B. Broyles Ag 1967–My 8, 1968; Howard Van Kirk My 1968 to date. *Pol*: American or Know-Nothing Party; Democrat; currently, Independent. When the paper was started it was dissatisfied with the lack of political honesty of the two parties. The *American Reveille* took the following stand, "The position, then, that we occupy as a publishing journalist, is upon the broad American Platform. Our aim will be to advance America and American interests, in the broadest sense of the term. We hold it our duty to stand aloof from no subject that involves our social, political, or moral welfare as a people." *Format*: Four to sixteen pages, varying sizes, 16¼" x 22½", 20" x 26½", 17" x 24", 11½" x 17". *Price*: $1.50 per year (1855–1864); $4.00 per year (1965); $5.50 per year (1969). *Circ*: 347 (1856); 1,966 (1972). *Comment*: Motto: "Our Country, Her Institutions, and Her Interests" (1860). In 1855 the newspaper was published one door east of the Post Office upstairs, then moved to Cayuga Street, two doors from Fall Street. In 1858 it was located in Partridge's new bank block, third floor, Fall Street. From 1860–1862, it was published in the first floor of the Holly Building and then moved to Mrs. Jackson's new building until May 16,

1863. It then moved again to the corner of Fall Street opposite Carr's Hotel and in September, 1866 to the Old Stone Mill on Fall Street nearly opposite Hoag's Hotel and remained there until August, 1890 when it moved to the Miller Building on Fall Street. It is now being published from the Reveille Building, 32 Fall Street. Several newspapers merged with the *Reveille. The Seneca County Standard* and the *Seneca Falls Reveille* consolidated November 3, 1922. The title of the newspaper remained the *Seneca Falls Reveille* but a running title was added inside the paper, *Seneca Falls Reveille and Seneca County Standard.* Prior to the consolidation, the *Standard* was published for about twelve years in Waterloo by Oscar J. Connell. It claimed to be non-partisan, but had Democratic leanings. On June 21, 1928 the *Seneca County Commercial* merged with the *Seneca Falls Reveille,* the inside running title became the *Seneca Falls Reveille-Standard and Commercial. Loc*: NIC/MMN: Mr 9, 1906 (52:12). NIC/RHA: My 3, 1857 (8:22); [Ap 2, 1864–S 25, 1868 (10:13–14:39)]; F 4, 1870 (16:5); [My 12, 1871–My 16, 1873 (17:19–19:20)] [Ap 6–O 12, 1888 (34:17–44)]; Ag 30, 1901 (47:36); F 13–27, 1903 (49:8–10); Mr 31, 1905 (51:15); Jl 31, Ag 7, 1908 (44:33–34); Jl 14, 1916 (63:31). NOv: 75th Anniversary issue, N 1929. NSen/Reveille Office: Ja 6–D 29, 1899 (45:2–46:1); Ja 11–D 27, 1901 (47:3–48:1); [Ja 2, 1919–D 28, 1923 (66:4–70:4)]; Ja 2–D 25, 1925 (71:5–72:4); Ja 4–D 27, 1929 (75:6–75:52); [Ja 4, 1935–D 27, 1950 (81:1–96:52)]; Ja 6–D 29, 1955 (101:1–51); Ja 4, 1967 to date (112:48 to date). NSenHi: [Ja 13, 1855–O 17, 1890 (1:1–36:43)]; S 2, 1892 (38:37); F 24, S 8, 1893 (39:10, 38); N 1, 1895 (41:45); [Ag 14, 1896–D 29, 1916 (42:33–64:3)]; Mr 15, Jl 26, O 11–18, 1918 (65:14, 33, 44–45); [Ja 16, 1920–S 15, 1922 (66:6–68:41)]; F 12, 1926 (72:11); O 28, 1927 (7:48); [Ja 25, 1929–N 2, 1934 (75:9–80:45)]; [Mr 20, 1936–F 25, 1938 (82:12–85:8)]; D 27, 1940 (87:52); [Ap 30, 1943–D 31, 1952 (90:18–99:53)]; [Ap 28, 1965 to date (111:15 to date)]. NWat: Ap 18, 1879 (25:17); N 13–27, 1885 (31:48–50); Ap 30, Jl 23, 1886 (32:20, 32); Jl 8, 1887 (33:30); F 15, 1895 (41:9); Jl 5, 1901 (47:28); F 20, Mr 13, 1903 (49:9, 12); Ap 1, 1904 (50:16); Mr 10, Ag 18, 1905 (51:12, 35); My 4, 1906 (52:20); D 25, 1908 (55:1); Ja 8, Mr 5, D 11, 1909 (55:3, 11, 50); F 3, 10, Ag 18, 25, 1911 (57:7, 8, 35, 36); Mr 7, 1913 (59:12); [My 7–D 24, 1915 (62:22–63:2)]; Ja 1, 1969 to date (114:48 to date).

SENECA FARMER see *THE FARMER AND SENECA FALLS ADVERTISER*

SENECA FARMER AND SENECA FALLS ADVERTISER see *THE FARMER AND SENECA FALLS ADVERTISER*

THE SENECA FARMER AND WATERLOO ADVERTISER see *THE FARMER AND SENECA FALLS ADVERTISER*

SENECA FREE SOIL UNION (w) Seneca Falls. S 5, 1848–S 1849// (1:1–?). *Pub and Ed*: N. J. Milliken. *Pol*: Free Soil Party. *Format*: Four pages 16¾″ x 22¾″. *Price*: $1.50 per year in advance (1848–

1849). *Comment*: The September 13, 1849 issue of the *Seneca Observer* (q.v.) carried an announcement by N. J. Milliken that the *Free Soil Union* would be merged with the *Observer* due to the financial situation of the *Union* and the fact that the question for which it stood had been resolved. *Loc*: NSenHi: [S 16, 1848–My 18, 1849 (1:4–37)].

THE SENECA LIVE OAK (m) Lodi. My 1864–? (1:1–?). *Pub*: J. M. and L. C. Galloup 1864–? *Ed*: E. S. Mattison 1864–? *Format*: Four pages, 10½ " x 15½ ". *Price*: 50¢ per year. *Comment*: Published in the interest of science and literature. *Loc*: NIC/RHA: Je 1, Ag 1, 1864 (1:2, 4).

SENECA OBSERVER Waterloo. 1824(?)–? No issues located. Becker states that there was a paper in Havana called the *Seneca Observer* which first made its appearance in 1824, edited and published by Charles Sentell. "For a short time it was issued as *The Observer and Union,* after which the original name was continued." (Becker, *Waterloo,* p. 95.) We have found only those issues of the *Seneca Observer* for 1832, volume 1, no. 1, edited and published by Charles Sentell (see also *Waterloo Observer* 1832).

SENECA OBSERVER AND UNION see *WATERLOO OBSERVER (1832)*

SENECA PATRIOT (w) Ovid. 1815–1817//. No issues located. "The pioneer printer of Seneca County was George Lewis, who in the year 1815, started in the village of Ovid a small sheet entitled the *Seneca Patriot.* The office of publication was located on Seneca Street, in the upper story of a building on whose site the engine house now stands . . . . At the close of a single volume, Mr. Lewis changed the name of the paper to *The Ovid Gazette* [1817 q.v.]." (*History of Seneca County,* p. 54.) "Established Aug. 25, 1815, by George Lewis & Co., with the title of *Seneca Patriot* . . . . Samuel R. Brown of Auburn established the paper, putting in George Lewis as printer . . . . Upon the removal of the county seat to Waterloo, Lewis went to that town, where he established the *Waterloo Gazette.*" (Clarence S. Brigham, *History and Bibliography of American Newspapers, 1690–1820* [Worcester, Mass., 1947], p. 715.)

SENECA REPUBLICAN (w) Ovid. ca. 1827. "The *Seneca Republican* was started at Ovid, in 1827. James Bogart already mentioned as a pioneer newspaper publisher in Geneva, was the proprietor, and Michael Hayes the superintendent and editor. This was originally published as the *Ovid Gazette* (1818 q.v.) and Mr. Hayes changed its title to the *Seneca Republican* when he became its owner. The *Republican* was known as a Clintonian advocate. (*History of Seneca County,* p. 54.)

SENECA SACHEM (m) Seneca Falls. ca. Ja 1–? 1863//. No issues located. "A monthly historical and local journal published for a few months . . . conducted by Francis M. Baker." (*History of Seneca County,* p. 55.)

THE WASP (irr.) Waterloo. Je 20, 1836–? (1:1–?). *Pub and Ed*: Hyder Ali Bill. *Format*: Four pages. *Price*: $1.00 per year. *Comment*: The following statements were made in the first issue. "The *Wasp* is published once in a while, as occasion may require at $1.00 per annum." "To Our Patrons: You will wish to know what objects we have in view . . . you will ask to what political party and to what religious party or sect do you belong to. With politics we shall not meddle in the least, nor shall we key our paper to support the doctrines . . . of any religious sect. Our principle and great object is to correct the manners and morals of the young men of our village. We write more particularly for the young." Below the banner was the statement "Here I comes mit a pees nest." It was printed and published by Hyder Ali Bill at the sign of the Bee's Nest, one door below the Observatory. *Loc*: NWat: microfilm Je 20, 1836 (1:1).

WATER BUCKET (w) Seneca Falls. F 25, 1842–? (1:1–?). *Pub*: Dexter C. Mills and Amelia Bloomer 1842–? *Pol*: Temperance. "Devoted exclusively to the cause of temperance." *Format*: Four pages 12" x 18". *Price*: $1.00 per year. *Loc*: NSenHi: F 25–Ag 19, 1842 (1:1–20).

WATERLOO ENTERPRISE (m) Waterloo. Ap 1871–? (1:1–?). *Pub and Ed*: Tall and Richardson. *Format*: Eight pages. *Comment*: "The publishing of the *Waterloo Enterprise* as an advertising medium was continued in 1874 by William H. Burton and J. A. Burton, a 20 column paper, neatly printed, with a claimed free distribution of 5,000 copies." (Becker, *Waterloo*, p. 208.) *Loc*: NWat: microfilm S 1871 (1:6).

WATERLOO ENUNCIATOR (w) Waterloo. Ja 2, 1822–? (1:1–?). *Pub and Ed*: B. B. Drake. *Pol*: Democrat. *Format*: Four pages. *Price*: $2.00 per year. *Comment*: B. B. Drake purchased the printing apparatus for the *Enunciator* from Hiram Leavenworth who had been publishing the *Waterloo Gazette* (q.v.). The prospectus of the paper stated that it would follow "a course of purest principle of Republicanism . . . Care will be taken to select such foreign and domestic intelligence deemed most interesting to patriot, politician and agriculturist. The general progress of religion, literature and the arts will occasionally be noted." The paper was printed and published every Friday, probably in the upper floor of Lester Weyburn's residence. *Loc*: NWat: microfilm Ja 2–Mr 20, 1822 (1:1–12).

WATERLOO EVENING REGISTER (d except Sunday) Waterloo. Mr 1–Je 7, 1875//. *Pub and Ed*: Register Printing Co. (Will R. Kennard, Ed. and Proprietor). *Format*: Four pages. *Price*: $5.00 per year, 2¢ per copy, 10¢ per week. *Comment*: Kennard stated on June 7, 1875: "This issues closes first and last volumes of the Evening Register. Have struggled 84 consecutive days and we now yield up the ghost." *Loc*: NWat: microfilm My 2–Je 7, 1875 (vol. 1, no issue nos.).

WATERLOO GAZETTE (w) Waterloo. My 1817–? (1:1–?). *Title*

changes: *Waterloo Gazette* My 28, 1817–1819; *The Waterloo Gazette* by Je 1819–N 1820; *Waterloo Gazette* N 1820–? *Pub and Ed*: George Lewis 1817; Hiram Leavenworth 1818–? *Format*: Four pages. *Price*: $2.00 per year delivered. *Comment*: The office of the newspaper was located in a small building just west of the Eagle Tavern and was printed in the Old Tavern Building of John Van Tuyl which was later moved back in the field north of the Hunt Homestead on Main Street. "The issue of October 1, 1817, contained an article in which the editor thanked his patrons for their support, but said 'He must relinquish his position; the great scarcity of money renders his business unprofitable.' " (Volume 1, number 30.) On December 17, 1817, it stated that it was printed and published by Hiram Leavenworth. (Becker, *Waterloo*, p. 79.) Moses Severance stated in volume 1, no. 1 of the *Republican Observer* (q.v.) on February 20, 1828, "The *Gazette*, which for the last two years has been published in this village, has been discontinued and the establishment has fallen into our hands." We have been unable to determine whether the *Gazette* mentioned is the same as that established in 1817.

WATERLOO OBSERVER (w) Waterloo. 1828(?)–1832// (1:1–?). *Pub and Ed*: Charles Sentell. *Format*: Four pages 15″ x 20″. *Price*: $2.00 per year in advance, otherwise $2.50. *Comment*: According to Becker this may be a title change for the *Republican Observer* (q.v.) when Sentell obtained the paper from Severance, but we have located no late issues of the *Republican Observer* or early issues of the *Waterloo Observer* to confirm this supposition. The volume numbering is a clue to the connection between the two papers. *Loc*: NIC/RHA: D 8, 1830 (3:147).

WATERLOO OBSERVER (w) Waterloo. 1832–? (1:1–?). *Title changes*: *Seneca Observer* 1832– S 6, 1849; *Seneca Observer and Union* S 13, 1849–?; *Seneca Observer* ?–1870; *Waterloo Observer* 1870–? *Pub*: Charles Sentell by 1832–?; James C. Wood 1834–1837; H. H. Riley 1837–1838; Loring Guild and Tobey 1839; H. H. Riley and Knox 1839; James C. Wood 1840–?; Charles Sentell 1841–?; Sylvester Pew and F. A. Marsh 1844–?; Sylvester Pew and Charles Sentell by 1846–1853; Edward W. Sentell 1866–?; Edward W. Sentell and Oliver C. Cooper 1867(?)–1869(?); N. Hyatt 1870–1872; William H. and William A. Burton 1873–1875; William H., William A. and John A. Burton 1875–1878; William H. Burton 1879–1884; William H. and William A. Burton 1884–1885; William H. Burton 1885–1889; The Observer Publishing and Printing Co. F 20, 1889–?; Albert L. Childs 1894–1900; S. H. and Louis W. Ferenbaugh 1900–O 1932; Rowland L. Hughey O 21, 1932–Ja 22, 1959; Waterloo Observer 1960–?. *Ed*: Charles Sentell 1832–1834; H. H. Riley 1837–1838; Knox and James C. Wood 1838–1841; Charles Sentell 1841–?; Edward Sentell and F. A. Marsh 1844–?; Edward W. Sentell and Oliver C. Cooper 1867(?)–1869(?); N. Hyatt 1870–1873; William H. and John A. Burton 1873–1878; William H. and John A. Burton 1878–1879; William H. Burton 1879–1884; Clinton M. Stahl F 20, 1889–Ap 4, 1894; Albert L. Childs Ap 11, 1894–1900; S. H. and Louis W.

Ferenbaugh 1900–O 1932; Rowland L. Hughey O 21, 1932–Ja 22, 1959. *Pol*: Democrat. *Format*: Four to ten pages, varying sizes, 13¼ " x 19½ ", 15" x 21", 18½ " x 24½ ", 17" x 23", 14½ " x 21¾ ", 12" x 17½ ". *Price*: $2.00 per year (1828); $2.50 per year delivered, $1.50 by mail or at office (1833–?); $3.00 per year (1948). *Comment*: Motto: "Pledged but to truth." There is considerable confusion regarding the beginning date of the second *Waterloo Observer*. The masthead dates its inception from 1826. In an 1880 issue of the *Waterloo Observer* a statement appears to the effect that Moses Severance purchased a *Gazette* from B. B. Drake in 1826. However, Severance claims that he purchased the *Gazette* in 1828 when he started the *Republican Observer*. The only paper we have located which was published at that time by Drake is the *Waterloo Republican* (q.v.). Perhaps by 1828 Drake had changed the name of the paper to the *Gazette*. It may be surmised that Sentell purchased the *Republican Observer* from Severance and changed the title to the *Waterloo Observer* in 1828 (q.v.). In the 1830's the paper was published in the lower story of No. 13 Central Buildings on Main Street. From 1856 to 1859 the office was listed in Hunt's Block, Main Street. Later, it was published at 39-41 Virginia Street. In September 1849 *The Seneca Free Soil Union* (q.v.). merged with the *Seneca Observer* and was published as *The Seneca Observer and Union*. Its title was changed to *Waterloo Observer* again in 1870 and it remained as such at least through 1961. *Loc*: NIC/RHA: My 8, 1833 (2:71); Ja 15, 29, 1834 (3:107, 109); My 15, 1838 (6:333); F 5, 1839 (7:372); O 12, 1848 (17:41); Ja 29, 1852 (21:5). NSenHi: Ja 10, 1856 (26:2); Ja 6–D 29, 1859 (29:1–52). NWat: [Ap 3, 1833–Je 17, 1835 (2:66–4:18)]; Mr 8, Ag 16, N 22, D 20, 1837 (6:272, 295, 309, 311); Mr 19, O 30–D 25, 1839 (7:378, 408–416); [Ja 1, 1840–N 27, 1844 (7:417–13:672)]; [N 4, 1846–D 27, 1849 (15:44–18:51)]; Ja 7–D 30, 1858 (28:2–52)]; Ja 6–D 29, 1869 (43:1–52); O 17, 1870 (44:41); My 10, 1871 (45:19); Je 5, 1872 (fragment); [Ja 1, 1873–D 30, 1904 (47:1–78:33)]; [Ja 4, 1907–D 30, 1910 (80:33–85:34)]; Ja 2–D 31, 1936 (110:33–111:35); Ja 5, 1940–D 27, 1946 (114:35–121:35); Ja 2, 1948–Mr 17, 1961 (122:36–140:16).

WATERLOO REGISTER (w) Waterloo. Je 30, 1874–? (1:1–?). *Pub*: Register Printing Co., Will R. Kennard 1874–? *Ed*: Will R. Kennard 1874–? *Format*: Four pages. *Price*: $1.50 per year. *Comment*: The offices of the newspaper were located in Rooms 1 through 5 of Gay's Commercial Building upstairs on Main and Virginia Streets. *Loc*: NWat: microfilm D 8, 1874 (1:24); Ja 12, Mr 2, My 18, 25, 1875 (1:29, 36, 47–48).

WATERLOO REPUBLICAN (w) Waterloo. Ja 4, 1823–? No issues located. "In 1822, the *Waterloo Republican*, under the management of B. B. Drake, made its entry upon public life, and the [*Waterloo*] *Gazette* [q.v.] was discontinued." (*History of Seneca County*, p. 54.) Becker establishes the date as January 4, 1823 from an issue he saw of volume 1, no. 1. He states that the last issue he found was July 15, 1823. (Becker, *Waterloo*, p. 91.)

WATERLOO REVEILLE (w) Seneca Falls. O 4, 1967–Ag 7, 1968//
(1:1–45). *Pub*: Reveille Publishing Co., Inc., Thomas D. Williams,
Pub. *Ed*: Richard B. Broyles. *Format*: Twelve pages, 17″ x 23″.
Comment: Published at 32 Fall Street, Seneca Falls. The newspaper
merged with the *Seneca Falls Reveille* on August 14, 1968; it has
since become the *Seneca Falls-Waterloo Reveille* (q.v.). *Loc*: NWat:
O 4, 1967–Ag 7, 1968 (1:1–45).

THE WESTERN TIMES Waterloo. ca. 1830. No issues located.
". . . a Waterloo publication, by Ebenezer P. Mason . . . ." (*History
of Seneca County*, p. 54.)

THE WREATH AND LADIES LITERARY REPOSITORY Water-
loo. ca. 1831. No issues located. ". . . issued by Edwin Wheeler, in
1831, from the Observer Office. It saw but a few numbers . . . ."
(*History of Seneca County*, p. 54.)

THE ADDISON ADVERTISER AND WOODHULL SENTINEL
(w) Addison. Mr 3, 1858–Ap 27, 1967// (1:1–109:17). *Title changes*: *The Addison Advertiser* Mr 3, 1858–N 1869; *Addison Advertiser* D 1, 1869–Je 1881; *The Addison Advertiser* Jl 7, 1881–O 11, 1883; *Addison Advertiser* O 18, 1883–Mr 28, 1905; *Addison Semi-Weekly Advertiser* Ap 4, 1905–Jl 29, 1907; *Addison Tri-Weekly Advertiser* Ag 5, 1907–Ja 9, 1912; *Addison Semi-Weekly Advertiser* Ja 16, 1912–Mr 24, 1921; *The Addison Advertiser* Mr 31, 1921–Jl 13, 1933;

Addison Advertiser Jl 20, 1933–Je 4, 1936; *The Addison Advertiser* Je 11, 1936–S 1, 1938; *The Addison Advertiser and the Woodhull Sentinel* S 8, 1938–My 7, 1959; *The Addison Advertiser and Woodhull Sentinel* My 14, 1959–Ap 27, 1967. *Pub*: E. M. Johnson & H. Baldwin Mr 10–S 8, 1858; E. M. Johnson S 15, 1858–Ag 28, 1867; E. M. Johnson, Henry S. Dow, and W. R. Bates 1865–1866; E. M. Johnson & Amos Roberts S 4, 1867–Ja 29, 1873; George H. Hollis F 5, 1873–Je 30, 1881; Amos Roberts Jl 7, 1881–Ja 1, 1904; Amos Roberts & Burrell Vastbinder Ja 7–D 31, 1904; Burrell Vastbinder Ja 1, 1905–F 24, 1921; Lyman J. Seely Mr 3–Mr 24, 1921; Steuben News Inc. Mr 31 1921–F 25, 1937 (Lyman J. Seely, Pres.); Maurice E. Miller Mr 4, 1937–O 9, 1963; Robert G. Aldrich and Sandra C. Aldrich O 16, 1963–Jl 29, 1966; Southern Tier News, Inc. Jl 27–S 28, 1966; Mildred Yongue and C. M. Yongue O 5, 1966–Ap 27, 1967. *Ed*: E. M. Johnson & H. Baldwin Mr 10–S 8, 1858; E. M. Johnson S 15, 1858–Ag 28, 1867; No editor listed S 4, 1867–Ap 28, 1869; E. M. Johnson and Amos Roberts My 5, 1869–Ja 29, 1873; George H. Hollis F 5, 1873–Je 30, 1881 (died My 20, 1881); Amos Roberts Jl 7, 1881–Ja 1, 1904; Amos Roberts and Burrell Vastbinder Ja 7–D 31, 1904; Burrell Vastbinder Ja 1, 1905–F 24, 1921; A. C. Baggerly Mr 3–Mr 24, 1921; Lyman J. Seely Mr 31, 1921–N 22, 1928; Maurice E. Miller N 29, 1928–My 7, 1959; William H. Wright, Jr. My 14, 1959–Ja 7, 1960; No editor listed Ja 14, 1960–S 12, 1962; Philip R. Elmes S 19, 1962–O 9, 1963; Robert G. Aldrich O 16, 1963–Jl 20, 1966; Maurice E. Miller and Virginia Miller Jl 27–S 28, 1966; Mildred Yongue and C. M. Yongue O 5, 1966–Ap 27, 1967. *Pol*: "Independent on all subjects in 1858 then Democratic on all subjects." (Millard F. Roberts, *Historical Gazetteer of Steuben County, New York* [Syracuse, N. Y.: 1891], p. 72.) Republican (?–1963); Nonpartisan (1963–1967). *Format*: Four to eight pages, varying sizes, 15½" x 21½", 16" x 22½", 18" x 22", 19" x 25", 13" x 19½", 14½" x 21", 15" x 22", 15½" x 21", 17" x 25". *Price*: $1.00 per year (1858–1860); $1.50 per year (1861–1864); $2.00 per year (1865–1877); $1.50 per year (F 8, 1877–1883); $1.00 per year (1884–D 25, 1919); $1.50 per year (Ja 1, 1920–D 29, 1927); $2.00 per year (Ja 5, 1928–D 1932); $1.50 per year (Ja 5, 1933–Jl 15, 1943); $2.00 per year (Jl 22, 1943–Je 16, 1949); $2.50 per year (Je 23, 1949–My 3, 1956); $2.50 per year, 10¢ per copy (My 10, 1956–D 26, 1957); $3.00 per year, 10¢ per copy (Ja 2, 1958–O 9, 1963); $3.50 per year (O 16–N 13, 1963); $4.00 per year, 10¢ per copy (N 20, 1963–Ap 27, 1967). *Comment*: Motto: "A Family Newspaper Devoted to the Interests of the Farmer and the Community in General and Independent on all Subjects." (1858). In 1859 the word "Independent" was changed to "Democratic", and then by October 1859, "Democratic" was again changed back to "Independent." Published over the Bakery, opposite the Addison Bank (Mr 10, 1858–1859); over New Engine Room on the south side of the river (1859–Ja 15, 1862); nearly opposite Curtis' Gristmill, northside of river (Ja 22, 1862–Ag 3, 1864); over Dr. Wagner's Drug Store, North side of the river, one door east of Bank (Ag 10, 1864–F 27, 1867); Tuscarora St. (Ja 5, 1893–D 30, 1897); Main St. (Ja 6, 1898–1928); no address listed but probably Main St. (1928–1964); then Main St. (Ja 1, 1964–Ap 27, 1967). *Loc*: NAdd: [Mr 10, 1858–Ap 27, 1967 (1:2–109:17)]. NCort/Mullen: Ap 12, 1865–F 28, 1866 (8:3–9:49). NCortHi: [Ap 14, 1858–D 7, 1859 (1:7–2:41)]; D 30, 1863 (6:43); Mr 16, 1864 (7:2); [Ap 12, 1865–Ag 15, 1866 (8:3–9:21)]; F 19, Ap 22, 1868 (10:48; 11:5); S 7, 1870 (13:25); Mr 8, S 20, 1871 (13:51; 14:27); S 10, 1873 (16:26); Ja 14, Ag 6, 1874 (16:44; 17:21); Ja 20, 1876 (18:45); Ap 10, 1879 (22:5); O 11, 1883 (26:41); Ap 6, 1885 (28:32); Ag 11, 1887 (30:32); Ap 30, 1891 (34:18); F 25, Mr 3, Je 9, D 15, 1892 (35:8, 9, 23, 50); D 28, 1933, 75th Diamond Jubilee Edition (74:52); Ja 4, 1940 (81:1). NIC/MMN: F 16, 1905 (48:7 whole no. 2396); Ag 26, 1907 (50:71 whole no. 2656).

ADDISON POST (w) Addison. Ag 9, 1967 to date (1:1 to date). *Pub*: Addison Post, Inc. Ag 9, 1967 to date. *Ed*: Oakley Hayes Ag 9, 1967 to date. *Format*: Sixteen to twenty-four pages, varying sizes, 7″ x 10″, 11″ x 17″. *Price*: Free to local residents by mail. *Circ*: 4,000 (1967–1968); 4,500 (1969 to date). *Comment*: Published at 42 Main St. *Loc*: NAdd/Addison Post, Inc.: Ag 9, 1967 to date (1:1 to date).

THE ADDISON RECORD (w) Addison. D 3(?), 1881–? (1:1–?). *Pub and Ed*: M. Kinne by 1883–? *Pol*: Democrat. *Format*: Four pages 15⅜″ x 21¾″. *Price*: $1.00 per year in advance. *Comment*: Published in the Westlake Block, second floor. "*The Addison Record* was established by O. B. Ireland, December 3, 1881. Mr. Ireland was succeeded by F. B. Orser and George Jones, who on March 25, 1882, were succeeded by M. Kinne. The paper has been conducted by the present proprietor, C. B. Mowers, since June 11, 1886. It is Democratic in politics." (Roberts, *Historical Gazetteer*, p. 78.) *Loc*: NIC/MMN: D 13, 1883 (3:3 whole no. 107).

THE ADDISON REPUBLICAN (w) Addison. 1840–? (1:1–?). *Pub*: E. Booth 1840–? *Ed*: W. Barnes 1840–? *Pol*: Whig Republican. *Format*: Four pages 15″ x 22″. *Price*: $2.00 per year, payable half yearly; if not paid within the year, $2.50. *Loc*: NCortHi: D 24, 1840 (1:13).

ADDISON SEMI-WEEKLY ADVERTISER see *THE ADDISON ADVERTISER AND WOODHULL SENTINEL*

ADDISON TRI-WEEKLY ADVERTISER see *THE ADDISON ADVERTISER AND WOODHULL SENTINEL*

ATLANTA NEWS see *COHOCTON VALLEY TIMES-INDEX*

THE AVOCA ADVANCE see *AVOCA ADVANCE PRESS*

AVOCA ADVANCE PRESS (w) Avoca. My 17, 1879(?)–? (1:1–?). *Pub*: The Avoca Publishing Co. by 1928 (C. H. Higby, Pub.). *Ed*: C. H. Higby by 1918; Mrs. George Conklin, local editor by 1928. *Format*: Four to eight pages 16⅛″ x 22¼″. *Comment*: "In the fall of 1878 W. E. Churchill opened a job printing office in the village of Avoca. In May, 1879, he sold the office to W. T. Coggeshall, who issued vol. 1, no. 1 of *The Avoca Advance,* a weekly paper, on the 17th of May 1879. Martin A. Hoadly purchased the *Advance* in 1883, and was the editor and proprietor until April, 1884, when he sold to Alvin Wood, who issued it until August, 1887, when the plant was sold to Fred C. Dean, who on account of sickness was unable to assume the duties and control and at once sold to W. T. Coggeshall and George C. Silsbee. In March, 1888, the co-partnership was dissolved, Mr. Coggeshall retiring. The paper has always been independent in politics. Since Mr. Silsbee has had control of the paper it has been enlarged. A new Howe cylinder press has taken the place of the hand-press and the office where the plant is now located has been built. It now has a circulation of nearly fifteen hundred." (Roberts, *Historical Gazetteer,* p. 78.) *Loc*: NIC/MMN: D 28, 1928 (49:12); Ja 4, 24, F 7, 1929 (49:13, 16, 18).

AVOCA HERALD (w) Avoca. Mr 20, 1931–1942//. No issues located. Mentioned in *Union List of Newspapers,* p. 441. Merged with *The Steuben Courier* (q.v.) of Bath, N. Y. on July 3, 1942.

THE BAND HERALD (irr) Prattsburgh. N 1–6, 1897// (No vol. or no.). *Pub*: Austin's Band, Prattsburgh. *Format*: Four pages 8″ x 10″. *Price*: Free, to be circulated at the Band Fair. *Comment*: A four page information newspaper on the Band Fair held in Prattsburgh containing ads, railroad information and some local news. Only one issue published. *Loc*: NIC/RHA: N 1–6, 1897.

BATH CLIPPER (w, then m) Bath. F 20, 1874–? (1:1–?). *Pub and Ed*: R. J. Davison & A. Ellas McCall F 20, 1874–?; A. Ellas McCall by Je 1874. *Format*: Four pages, varying sizes, 7″ x 8¾″,10″ x 12⅞″. *Price*: 30¢ for 6 months (F 1874–?); 25¢ for 6 months, 40¢ per year (Je 1874–?). *Loc*: NIC/MMN: F 20, 27, Mr 6–27, Je ?, 1874 (1:1, 2, 3–6, 9).

THE BATH ECHO (w) Bath. Ap 4, 1874–? (1:1–?). *Pub*: The Echo Printing Co. (Charles E. Clute). *Ed*: Charles E. Clute. *Format*: Four pages 9⅞″ x 12⅞″. *Comment*: Published at 4 Liberty St. ". . . was published by Clute and McCall for four or five months in 1874." (Roberts, *Historical Gazetteer,* p. 77.) *Loc*: NIC/MMN: My 16, 23, 1874 (1:7, 8).

BATH GAZETTE see *THE BATH GAZETTE AND GENESEE ADVERTISER*

THE BATH GAZETTE AND GENESEE ADVERTISER (w) Bath. D 21, 1796–1800//(?) (1:1–?). No issues located. "*The Bath Gazette and Genesee Advertiser* was unquestionably the first newspaper printed in Steuben County. It was published by William Kersey and James Edie [*sic* Eddie] . . . . In 1798 Colonel Williamson wrote: 'The printer of *The Ontario Gazette* dispenses weekly not less than one thousand papers and the printer of the *Bath Gazette* from four hundred to five hundred.' As near as can be ascertained from this late date, the *Bath*

Gazette lived some four years." (Roberts, *Historical Gazetteer,* p. 75.) "Established Dec. 21, 1796, judging from the date of the earliest issue located, that of Jan. 5, 1797, vol. 1, no. 3 . . . ." (Clarence S. Brigham, *History and Bibliography of American Newspapers, 1690–1820* [Worcester, Mass.: 1947], p. 552.)

THE BATH PLAINDEALER (w) Bath, Hammondsport. My 5, 1883–Ja 23, 1929// (1:1–?). *Pub*: McCall, Drew & Black My 5, 1883–My 3, 1884; The Plaindealer Co. My 10, 1884–S 28, 1912; A. Ellas McCall O 5, 1912–S 11, 1920; Lyman J. Seely S 18, 1920–?; Steuben News Co. by 1924 (Lyman J. Seely, Pres. 1924–?). *Ed*: Orson L. Drew and A. Ellas McCall My 5, 1883–My 3, 1884; A. Ellas McCall My 10, 1884–S 11, 1920; Lyman J. Seely, Managing Ed., A. Ellas McCall, Local Ed. S 18, 1920–?; Lyman J. Seely by Jl 1924. *Pol*: Independent. *Format*: Eight pages 18" x 21½". *Price*: $1.50 per year in advance, 5¢ per copy (1883–?); 99¢ per year in advance, 5¢ per copy, otherwise $1.50 (by Ja 1898–1920); $1.50 per year in advance (1920); $2.00 per year in advance, otherwise $2.50 (1921–?). *Comment*: In the September 11, 1920 editorial stating that he had sold the paper to Lyman J. Seely, publisher of *The Hammondsport Herald and Savona Review,* A. Ellas McCall gave this brief history of the *Plaindealer.* "The *Plaindealer* was started by myself, Orson Drew and William Black in 1883, thirty-seven and ½ years ago. Mr. Drew retired in almost a year and Mr. Black during the second year." The office was in the basement of the Opera House Block and then moved to the Ives Block. *The Bath Plaindealer* combined with *The Hammondsport Herald* (q.v.) January 23, 1929. *Loc*: NIC/MMN: microfilm My 5, 1883–Mr 5, 1921 (1:1–38:52); Jl 26, 1924 (42:21).

THE BATH SUNDAY NEWS (w) Bath. 1881–? (1:1–?). *Pub*: L. R. Smith & Co. *Ed*: A. Ellas McCall. *Format*: Four pages 9⅞" x 13". *Price*: 25¢ for 2 months, 3¢ per copy (1881). *Comment*: "The *Bath Sunday News* was published about six months by L. R. Smith and Co.,—A. E[llas] McCall editor—in the year 1881." (Roberts, *Historical Gazetteer,* p. 77.) *Loc*: NIC/MMN: Ap 3, 1881 (1:6).

BATH TRI-WEEKLY CONSERVATIVE (tri-w) Bath. 1868–? (1:1–?) *Pub and Ed*: Charles E. Clute. *Pol*: Democrat. *Format*: Four pages 7" x 10¼". *Price*: $2.00 per year in cash in advance, 2¢ per copy. *Comment*: "Charles Clute commenced the publication of this newspaper in August 1868 and continued it for about six months. It was a spicey little sheet." (Roberts, *Historical Gazetteer,* p. 77.) *Loc*: NIC/MMN: O 15, 1868 (1:26).

THE BREEZE (w) Prattsburgh, Cohocton. 1881(?)–? (1:1–?). *Pub and Ed*: G. W. Peck. *Format*: Four pages 17¼" x 24". *Loc*: NIC/RHA: Mr 15, 1887 (6:7).

CANISTEO CHRONICLE (w) Canisteo. 1900–? (1:1–?). *Pub and Ed*: Leon L. Hough. *Pol*: Independent. *Format*: Eight pages 15" x 22". *Price*: $1.00 per year. *Circ*: 2,000 (1903). *Comment*: Published at 11 Depot St., Blue Front Building, by October 14, 1903. *Loc*: NCortHi: O 14, 1903 (4:1).

CANISTEO REPUBLICAN (w) Canisteo. 1880(?)–? (1:1–?). *Pub and Ed*: Charles G. Harris by Mr 16, 1888–? *Pol*: Republican. *Format*: Eight pages 20″ x 26″. *Price*: $1.00 per year. *Loc*: NCani/ Latham: Mr 16, Je 15, Ag 10, D 7, 1888 (8:34, 48; 9:3, 20); [Ja 4– N 29, 1889 (9:24–10:20)].

THE CANISTEO TIMES (w) Canisteo, Addison. Ja 25, 1877–D 26, 1957// (1:1–91:52). *Title changes*: *Canisteo Times* by O 7, 1880– D 29, 1892; *The Canisteo Times* Ja 5, 1894–S 13, 1900; *The Times-Republican* S 20, 1900–Mr 25, 1908; *The Times* Ap 1, 1908–F 13, 1918; *The Canisteo Times* F 20, 1918–? *Pub*: A. H. Bunnell by O 7, 1880–Mr 25, 1886; Frank B. Smith Ap 1, 1886–Ap 14, 1892; Frank A. Fay Ap 21, 1892–Ja 4, 1900; J. Claude Latham Ja 11, 1900–Ja 8, 1948 (died Ja 9, 1948, name carried through O 1948); Joseph Latham, Jr. and Chilton Latham (Bros.) Ja 9, 1948–Ap 1, 1954; Frances Latham (Mrs. Joseph Latham, Jr.) and Chilton Latham Ap 8, 1954– S 26, 1957; Maurice E. Miller O 3, 1957–D 26, 1957. *Ed*: A. H. Bunnell by Mr 25, 1886; Frank B. Smith Ap 1, 1886–Ap 14, 1892; Frank A. Fay Ap 21, 1892–Ja 4, 1900; J. Claude Latham Ja 11, 1900–Ja 8, 1948; Chilton Latham O 14, 1948–S 26, 1957; Maurice E. Miller O 3–D 26, 1957. *Pol*: Independent (to Ja 1900); Republican (Ja 1900–1957). *Format*: Four to twelve pages, varying sizes, 20″ x 25″, 14″ x 22″, 18″ x 22″. *Price*: $1.50 per year, $1.00 per year in advance (1880–1899); $2.00 per year, $1.50 per year in advance (1919– 1936); $2.00 per year (1950–1956); $2.50 per year, 5¢ per copy (Ja 1956–D 26, 1957). *Circ*: 1,200 (1887); 1,250 (1900); 2,509 (1909). *Comment*: Motto: "An Independent Family Journal." ". . . a weekly newspaper started in the village of Canisteo January 25, 1877 by S. H. Jennings." (Roberts, *Historical Gazetteer*, p. 78.) Published in the Times Building, Depot Street from 1900–1957 in Canisteo and then moved to Addison, New York, October 3, 1957. *Loc*: NCani/ Latham: [O 7, 1880–D 26, 1957 (4:34–91:52)]. NCortHi: Ja 20, 27, D 29, 1881 (4:49; 5:1, 49); Jl 7, 1882 (6:24).

CANISTEO VALLEY JOURNAL see *THE CANISTEO VALLEY JOURNAL AND NATIONAL AMERICAN*

THE CANISTEO VALLEY JOURNAL AND NATIONAL AMERICAN (w) Hornellsville. F 13, 1856–1862//(?) (1:1–?). *Title changes*: *National American* 1856–?; *The Canisteo Valley Journal* ?–?; *The Canisteo Valley Journal and National American* ?–? *Pub and Ed*: D. C. Pruner & C. M. Harmon by 1858–?; Charles A. Kinney O 30, 1858–?; R. S. Lewis Ja 1861–? *Pol*: American Party, then Republican. *Format*: Four pages 17″ x 22½″. *Price*: $1.50 per year. *Comment*: Published in the Canisteo Block, Hornellsville. After the death of C. M. Harmon in 1868, "*The American* became the property of Charles A. Kinney in September 1858. He soon changed its name to *The Canisteo Valley Journal* and made of it a newsy local newspaper, independent in politics . . . . Mr. R. S. Lewis, who bought the newspaper in January 1861 from Kinney continued it as a Republican newspaper until August 1862, when it was discontinued."

(Roberts, *Historical Gazetteer,* p. 80.) *Loc*: NAlm/Reynolds: O 30, 1858–Ja 12, 1861 (n.s. 2–3:13 whole no. 117).

THE CANISTEO VALLEY TIMES see *HORNELL TIMES*

COHOCTON ADVERTISER (w) Cohocton. 1870–1871//. No issues located. H. B. Newell began publication of the *Advertiser* in April 1870. He sold out (1871) to James Hewitt who changed the name of the paper to the *Cohocton Tribune* (q.v.). (James Folts' letter to the South Central Research Library Council [SCRLC] April 9, 1972.)

COHOCTON HERALD (w) Cohocton. ca. 1872. No issues located. "The next paper [published in Cohocton after the *Cohocton Journal*] was a weekly published by H. B. Newell in 1872, called the *Cohocton Herald* and shortly afterward purchased by James C. Hewitt and changed to the *Cohocton Tribune* [q.v.]. In 1875 William A. Carpenter became the proprietor and changed the name to the *Cohocton Valley Times* [q.v.]." (Roberts, *Historical Gazetteer,* p. 78.)

COHOCTON JOURNAL Cohocton. ca. 1859. No issues located. "The first newspaper established in Cohocton was in 1859, by William Waite Warner, and was called the *Cohocton Journal.* It was only issued about two years when Mr. Warner moved West." (Roberts, *Historical Gazetteer,* p. 78.) Laura E. Weld was Assoc. Ed. There is some question about the beginning date. In a letter from James D. Folts, Cohocton, March 30, 1972 to SCRLC, the beginning date is listed as January 1861. He states that Warner went West after three months.

COHOCTON TIMES see *COHOCTON VALLEY TIMES-INDEX*

COHOCTON TIMES INDEX see *COHOCTON VALLEY TIMES-INDEX*

COHOCTON TRIBUNE (w) Cohocton. ca. 1873. No issues located. James C. Hewitt purchased the *Cohocton Herald* (q.v.) and the *Cohocton Advertiser* (q.v.) and changed the titles of the newspapers to the *Cohocton Tribune.*

COHOCTON VALLEY TIMES (w) North Cohocton. 1875–1902//. No issues located. "In 1875 William A. Carpenter became the proprietor [of the *Cohocton Tribune*] and changed the name to the *Cohocton Valley Times,* which name it still retains. Edgar A. Higgins succeeded Mr. Carpenter in 1878, who continued to own the paper until November 1889, when he sold out his interest. Since that time Stephen D. Shattuck has been the editor. The *Times* is non-partisan in politics." (Roberts, *Historical Gazetteer,* p. 78.) Mr. Shattuck remained editor until his death in 1901. During this time the paper was printed on the second floor of the present McKinley Block. (James Folts' letter to SCRLC March 1972.) Vincent Tripp purchased the *Cohocton Valley Times* from the heir of Stephen Shattuck in 1902 and combined it with the *Index* as the *Cohocton Valley Times-Index* (q.v.).

COHOCTON VALLEY TIMES-INDEX (w) Cohocton. 1892–Ag 7, 1963 (1:1–86:21). *Title changes*: *Atlanta News* ?–Jl 5, 1893; *Cohocton Index* Jl 12, 1893–1902; *Cohocton Times-Index* O 8, 1902–?; *Cohocton Valley Times-Index* by Ag 24, 1904–Ag 7, 1963. *Pub and Ed*: Vincent L. Tripp 1902–1942; Vincent L. Tripp Estate 1942–?; Edith L. Strobel by 1942–? *Pol*: Independent. *Format*: Eight pages, varying sizes, 15″ x 21½″, 11½″ x 17½″. *Price*: $3.00 per year. *Circ*: 800 (1886); 2,000 (1911); 1,500 (1917); 1,150 (1927); 750 (1962). *Comment*: "The first number of the *Atlanta News*, edited by H. C. Hatch, appeared June 29, 1892. Brothers Vincent L. and Milton R. Tripp bought this paper in June 1893 and moved it to Cohocton the next year renaming it the *Index*." Milton Tripp resigned as a partner in 1899 and went to Colorado for his health. The first location of the *Index* was in the West side of the Maichle Block (now Masonic Temple). The paper was moved to the *Times-Index* Building which was popularly known as the Bee-Hive. The building was demolished in 1969. Vincent Tripp purchased the *Cohocton Valley Times* from the heir of S. D. Shattuck in 1902 and renamed the paper *Cohocton Times-Index*. The *Times-Index* ceased publication on November 22, 1961 (87:38) and resumed publication with reduced page size and offset printing on December 5, 1962 (85:38). Note change in volume numbering. It ceased publication on August 7, 1963 because of declining advertising and revenue. *Loc*: NCoh/Folts: Ja 2–Ag 7, 1963 (85 [*sic*]:42–86:21). NCoh/Strobel: Je 28, 1893–Je 20, 1894 (2:1–52); Je 23, 1897–D 30, 1908 (6:1–28:33); Ja 4, 1911–D 26, 1945 (40:34–74:40). NCohCS: Ag 30, 1950–N 22, 1961 (76 [*sic*]:24–87:38). NIC/MMN: Jl 15, 1903 (12:8); F 16, 1921 (50:42); Mr 12, 19, Ap 2–My 7, Je 8, Jl 2, 9, 1924 (53:46, 47, 49–52; 54:1–2, 8, 10, 11).

THE CONSTITUTIONALIST (w) Bath. Ag 23, 1837–? (n.s. 1:1–?). *Pub*: Charles Adams Ag 23, 1837–F 10, 1841; M. F. Whittemore & Co. F 17, 1841–? *Ed*: Charles Adams Ag 23, 1837–F 10, 1841; R. B. Van Valkenburgh F 24, 1841–? *Pol*: Whig. *Format*: Four pages 15″ x 22″. *Price*: $2.00 per year in advance, or $2.50 at end of year (1837–1841). *Comment*: Published on Liberty St., 3rd story Brick Block. *Loc*: NAub: [Ag 21, 1839–Ja 6, 1841 (n.s. 3:1–4:21)]. NBa: Ag 23, 1837–Ag 14, 1839 (n.s. 1:1–2:52); Ja 20–Ag 11, 1841 (4:23–52). NIC/RHA: [Ag 23, 1837–F 16, 1842 (n.s. 1:1–5:27)].

CORNING AND BLOSSBURG ADVOCATE (w) Corning. Jl 21, 1840–? (1:1–?). *Pub*: Charles Adams Jl 31, 1840–Jl 30, 1841; Henry H. Hull and May Ag 4–S 8, 1841; Henry H. Hull S 8, 1842–? *Ed*: Charles Adams Jl 31, 1840–Jl 30, 1841; Henry H. Hull Ag 4, 1841–? *Pol*: Whig. *Format*: Four pages. *Price*: $2.00 per year, (1840–?). *Comment*: Published on Market St. *Loc*: NCor: microfilm [Ag 21, 1840–Ag 17, 1842 (1:4–3:3)]. NIC/MMN: microfilm [Ag 21, 1840–Ag 17, 1842 (1:4–3:3)].

CORNING DAILY DEMOCRAT see *THE CORNING LEADER*

CORNING DAILY JOURNAL (d) Corning. S 7, 1891–1920//
(1:1–?). *Pub*: George W. Pratt S 7, 1891–D 30, 1906; George E.
Ransom and Harry H. Pratt by Jl 12–D 3, 1907; Corning Journal
D 4, 1907–? *Ed*: George W. Pratt S 7, 1891–D 30, 1906; Harry H.
Pratt Ja 1907–1919; John L. Chalfield by 1920. [Chalfield cited in
Ayer's *Directory* 1920.] *Format*: Four to six pages. *Pol*: Republican.
Price: $3.00 per year, 1¢ per copy (1891–1895); $5.00 per year, 2¢
per copy (1895–1905); $3.00 per year, 1¢ per copy (1906–?). *Circ*:
1,900 (1893); 1,671 (1898); 1,985 (1899). *Comment*: Motto: "We
stand by our friends; our friends are those who stand by us." Pub-
lished at 37 E. Market St. According to the *Union List of Newspapers,*
the *Daily Journal* merged into the *Evening Leader* (q.v.) in 1920.
Loc: NCor: microfilm Ja 2, 1892–D 31, 1910 (2:1–19:311).
NCorCC: microfilm Ja 2, 1892–D 31, 1910 (2:1–19:311). NIC/
MMN: S 7, 1891–D 31, 1915 (1:1–24th year :309).

CORNING DEMOCRAT (w) Corning. Ap 22, 1857–? (1:1–?).
Pub: Charles R. Huston by Jl 1–N 4, 1857; Frank B. Brown N 11,
1857–Mr 26, 1868; Frank B. Brown & Co. Ap 2–Je 25, 1868; Frank
B. Brown and Dan E. DeVoe Jl 2–D 24, 1868; Dan E. DeVoe &
Rowland Ja 7–D 20, 1869; Frank B. Brown Ja 6, 1870–D 23, 1886;
Frank B. Brown & Son Ja 6, 1887–? *Ed*: Charles R. Huston by Jl
1–N 4, 1857; Frank B. Brown N 11, 1857–Je 25, 1868; Frank B.
Brown and Dan E. DeVoe Jl 2–D 24, 1868; Dan E. DeVoe Ja 7–D
30, 1869; Frank B. Brown Ja 6, 1870–? *Pol*: Democrat. *Format*: Two
to eight pages. *Prices*: $1.00 per year (1857); $1.50 per year (1860);
$1.00 per year (1891). *Comment*: Motto: "We go where Democratic
principles point the way, when they cease to lead, we cease to follow." Published from Dr. Graves' New Block second story 1857–1868,
then from January 1869 to December 1870 in the Arcade Block, then
opposite the post office January 1871 to 1887. On May 26, 1884 a
daily edition, the *Corning Daily Democrat* (q.v.) was published simultaneously with the weekly edition. *Loc*: NCor: microfilm [Jl 1, 1857–
Ap 7, 1864 (1:11–7:52)]; [Jl 5, 1866–Je 27, 1878 (11:1–22:52)]; Jl
5, 1882–N 29, 1884 (27:1–29:23); D 3, 1885–N 24, 1887 (31:23–
33:21). NCorCC: microfilm Jl 1, 1857–Ap 7, 1864 (1:1–7:52); [Jl
5, 1866–Je 27, 1878 (11:1–22:52)]; Jl 5, 1882–N 29, 1884 (27:1–
29:23); D 3, 1885–N 24, 1887 (31:23–33:21). NIC/MMN: microfilm [Ap 22, 1857–D 31, 1896 (1:1–41:51 whole nos. 1–2058)].

CORNING DEMOCRAT DAILY SERIES see *THE CORNING
LEADER*

CORNING EVENING LEADER see *THE CORNING LEADER*

CORNING INDEPENDENT (w) Corning. D 17, 1874–1879//(?)
(1:1–?). *Pub*: T. S. DeWolfe D 16, 1874–Ag 18, 1875; T. S. De-
Wolfe and H. S. Edson Ag 25, 1875–? *Ed*: T. S. DeWolfe D 16,
1874–? *Pol*: Independent. *Format*: Four pages. *Price*: $1.50 per year.
Comment: "DeWolfe sold it [the *Corning Independent*] to Dr. A. J.

Ingersol about two years afterward [after it started in 1874]. While Dr. Ingersoll owned that office the paper was published as a Greenback organ by Uri Mulford. The paper was discontinued in 1879." (Roberts, *Historical Gazetteer,* p. 79.) *Loc:* NCor: microfilm D 16, 1874–D 29, 1875 (1:1–55). NCorCC: D 16, 1874–D 29, 1875 (1:1–55).

CORNING JOURNAL (w) Corning. My 12, 1847–Je 28, 1905// (1:1–?). *Title changes: Corning Journal* My 12, 1847–Ja 27, 1854; *The Corning Journal* F 3, 1854–Ag 2, 1866; *Corning Journal* Ag 9, 1866–F 25, 1869; *The Corning Journal* My 4, 1869–My 19, 1870; *Corning Journal* My 26, 1870–Je 28, 1905. *Pub:* Thomas Messenger Jl 21, 1847–Jl 16, 1851; A. W. McDowell & Co. Jl 23, 1851–Ap 1, 1853; George W. Pratt Ap 8, 1853–Jl 8, 1869; George W. Pratt and T. S. DeWolfe Jl 15, 1869–N 12, 1874; George W. Pratt N 19, 1874–Je 28, 1905. *Ed:* Thomas Messenger Jl 21, 1847–Jl 16, 1851; George W. Pratt Jl 23, 1851–Je 28, 1905. *Pol:* Whig by 1849; Republican. *Format:* Four to eight pages. *Price:* $1.25 per year in advance, $1.50 if paid in 3 months, $2.00 at end of year (1847–1865); $2.50 per year in advance (1866); $2.00 per year in advance (1867); $1.00 per year (1880); $1.50 per year (1881–1891); $1.00 per year (1892). *Comment:* Motto: "Freedom of Speech, and Freedom of the Press, for the sake of Freedom" (F 3, 1854–?). "An Independent Family Newspaper—Free From Party Politics." "A Family Newspaper: Devoted to Politics, News, Agriculture, Literature, Science, the Markets, &tc." Published over P. H. Hubbell's Store, 29 Market St. *Loc:* NCor: microfilm Jl 21, S 22, D 8, 1847 (1:11, 20, 31); [Mr 22, 1848–D 28, 1892 (1:46–46:52)]; Ja 3–D 26, 1894 (48:1–52); Ja 5, 1898–D 27, 1899 (52:1–53:52); Ja 9, 1901–Je 28, 1905 (55:2–59:26). NCorCC: microfilm Ja 5, 1866–D 28, 1892 (20:1–46:52); Ja 3–D 26, 1894 (48:1–52); Ja 5, 1898–D 27, 1899 (52:1–53:52); Ja 9, 1901–Ja 28, 1905 (55:2–59:26). NIC/MMN: microfilm [Jl 21, 1847–D 28, 1865 (1:1–19:52)]. Not filmed: [Ap 1, 1853–D 26, 1900 (6:46–54:52)]. NIC/RHA: [Jl 28, 1851–Ap 8, 1853 (5:10–6:49)]; [My 21, 1851–D 26, 1900 (5:1–54:52)].

THE CORNING LEADER (d) Corning. ?–S 23, 1965//(?–119:224). *Title changes: Corning Democrat Daily Series* My 26–N 29, 1884; *The Corning Daily Democrat* D 1, 1884–?; *The Daily Democrat* by 1900–S 18, 1902; *The Evening Leader and Corning Daily Democrat* S 19, 1902–Ap 13, 1917; *The Evening Leader* Ap 14, 1917–D 31, 1953; *The Corning Leader* Ja 2, 1954–S 23, 1965. *Pub:* Frank B. Brown My 26, 1884–?; Frank B. Brown & Son by Ja 3, 1887–?; Edwin S. Underhill & Co. O 1, 1902–Jl 14, 1907; Edwin S. Underhill Jl 15, 1907–Mr 2, 1929; The Estate of Edwin S. Underhill Mr 4, 1929–Ja 2, 1930; W. A. & Edwin S. Underhill, Jr. Ja 3, 1930–D 31, 1946; Corning Leader Inc. Ja 2, 1947–S 23, 1965 (W. A. Underhill, Pres. Ja 2, 1947–O 4, 1961; Edwin S. Underhill, III, Pres., Matthew F. Carney, Jr. Co-Pub. O 1961–S 23, 1965). *Ed:* Frank B. Brown My 26, 1884–?; Edwin S. Underhill O 1, 1902–Mr 2, 1929; Edwin

S. Underhill, Jr. Mr 4, 1929–Ja 2, 1930; W. A. Underhill Ja 3, 1930–Ag 9, 1954; George H. Bevan Ag 10, 1954–S 23, 1965. *Pol*: Democrat; Independent (1917–1965). *Format*: Four to twenty-four pages 13″ x 20″. *Price*: $1.50 per year, 2¢ per copy (1884–?); $3.00 per year (1891); $2.00 per year, 1¢ per copy (1902–1917); $5.00 per year, 2¢ per copy (1910–1920); $5.00 per year, 3¢ per copy (1924–1946); $8.00 per year, 30¢ per week, 5¢ per copy (1947–1952); $10.00 per year, 7¢ per copy (1958); $15.00 per year, 7¢ per copy (1959–1965). *Circ*: 4,369 (1899); 4,064 (1902); 6,238 (1904); 6,820 (1907); 7,890 (1909); 8,636 (1912). *Comment*: Motto: "All the News the Day it is News." (1899); "We go where Democratic Principles point the way; when they cease to lead, we cease to follow." A daily edition was issued simultaneously with the weekly editon of the *Corning Democrat* (q.v.) beginning on May 26, 1884. Published at 31½ E. Market St., then on Cedar St. opposite City Hall. *The Corning Leader* is still being published as *The Leader* (q.v.) under the same publisher and editor, but was completely renumbered as vol. 1, no. 1 on September 24, 1965. It now appears as a separate entry in this bibliography under its new title. *Loc*: NCor: microfilm O 1, 1902–My 6, 1908 (35:232–41:108); D 23, 1946–S 23, 1965 (84:302–119:224). NCor/Museum of Glass Library: Je 22, 1951 (105:147 Corning Glass Works Centennial Edition). NCorL: microfilm O 1, 1902–S 23, 1965 (35:323–119:224). NIC/MMN: microfilm My 26–N 29, 1884 (28:48 Daily Series Pt. 1–29:23 Daily Series Pt. 160 whole nos. 1412–1439). Mr 11, 1924–Je 12, 1927 (47:60–60:140). NIC/RHA: My 27, 1884–Je 15, 1897 (28:48 [*sic*]–28:13); Ja 3, 1900–S 30, 1902 (32:179–35:231).

CORNING NEWS (w) Corning. 1939(?)–1956//(?) (1:1–?). *Pub*: Maurice E. Miller by Ja 12, 1949–1953; Southern Tier News Co. 1954–1956 (From Ayer's *Directory* 1950–55). *Ed*: Charles J. Chatfield ?–Ag 31, 1949; Hillard Gordon N 2, 1949–1953. *Pol*: Independent, then Republican. *Format*: Sixteen to twenty-four pages 11½″ x 15½″. *Price*: $2.00 per year, 5¢ per copy (by 1948–?). *Circ*: 1,650 (1956). *Comment*: Published at 133 Pine St., 1939(?)–1953. Ayer's starts to list the *News* in the 1950 *Directory* citing first issue in 1938. Then in later issues 1939 is given as date of establishment. It probably ceased publication in 1956 when Robert Corthell was editor and the Corning News, Inc. was the publisher. It was published at 10 Bridge St. *Loc*: NPP/Town of Erwin Museum: S 15, 1948 (9th year: 46); [N 24, 1948–S 27, 1951 (9th year:46–12th year:48)].

THE CORNING NEWS (w) Corning. Ap 3, 1955–? (1:1–?). *Title changes*: *Corning Sunday News* Ap 3–D 1, 1955; *The Corning News* D 8, 1955–? *Pub*: Maurice E. Miller Ap 3–Ag 28, 1955; Corning News, Inc. S 4, 1955–? *Ed*: George Ebbert (Managing Ed.) by Ap 3, 1955– Jl 24, 1955; Lance Nichols Jl 31, 1955–? *Format*: Twelve pages 16″ x 22½″. *Price*: $4.00 per year, 10¢ per copy (1955–?). *Comment*: Published at 30 Centerway, then from September 4, 1955 at 10 Bridge St. *Loc*: NAdd: Ap 3, 1955–Ja 26, 1956 (1:1–44).

CORNING SUNDAY NEWS see *THE CORNING NEWS* Ap 3, 1955.

THE DAILY ADVOCATE (irr) Bath. S 20–22(?), 1880//(?) (1:1–?). *Pub and Ed*: A. L. Underhill. *Format*: Four pages 18″ x 23⅝″. *Price*: 5¢ per copy. *Comment*: "Today for the first time in the history of the Steuben Agricultural society is issued a daily paper devoted exclusively to the interests of the great and growing enterprise. . . . devoted exclusively to the County Fair—descriptions of exhibits, personal notices, trials of speeches. . . . There will be a daily issue of 2,000 copies or more, if there should be demand. *The Daily Advocate* will be published Wednesday, Thursday and Friday." (*Daily Advocate,* p. 1, S 20, 1880.) *Loc*: NIC/MMN: S 20, 1880 (1:1).

THE DAILY DEMOCRAT see *THE CORNING LEADER*

THE DAILY NEWS (d) Hornellsville. ca. 1877–1878// No issues located. "The daily edition of the *Times* [see *Hornell Daily Times*] began with *The Daily News*—Hornellsville's first daily newspaper—a little two column folio established by Benzinger and Osincup October 22, 1877. They sold it to Tuttle and Brigham February 25, 1878, who enlarged it and continued its publication as the *Daily Times*." (Roberts, *Historical Gazetteer,* p. 81.)

THE DAILY PRESS (d) Hornellsville. ca. 1889–? No issues located. "*The Daily Press* was established March 9, 1899, by the Press Publishing Co. consisting of John Tolan and Leon Hough, and published from the Herald Office. In February, 1890, Mr. Tolan secured an independent office from which he has since published the *Press* as sole proprietor. It is an evening paper, independent in politics." (Roberts, *Historical Gazetteer,* p. 82.)

THE DAILY TIMES see *HORNELL DAILY TIMES*

DEMOCRATIC VIDETTE (w) Hornell. ca. S 1865–? No issues located. "*The Democratic Vidette* was established S 28, 1865, by Burdick Brothers, and was published successfully by Burdick & Cooper, John M. Riley & Co., A. J. Riley & Co., and William H. Baldwin. It was democratic in politics. . . . [Baldwin] sold the *Vidette* office to Thacher & Tuttle, who changed its name to *The Canisteo Valley Times* (q.v.) and made it Republican in politics, beginning with its publication January 10, 1867." (Roberts, *Historical Gazetteer,* p. 80.)

THE ECONOMIST (w) Hornellsville. ca. 1872. No issues located. "*The Economist,* the first number of which was issued March 8, 1872, was started as an advertising sheet published weekly, in the interest of M. A. Tuttle and other merchants. After running a year, it was sold to Graham and Dawson and issued as the *Hornellsville Herald*." (Roberts, *Historical Gazetteer,* p. 81.)

THE ENTERPRISE (w) Painted Post. Je 26, 1877–? (1:1–?). *Pub and Ed*: F. L. Covert Je 26, 1877–? *Format*: Four pages 13″ x 20½″. *Loc*: NPP/Town of Erwin Museum: Je 26, 1877 (1:1).

THE ERA Hornellsville. ca. 1887. No issues located. "*The Era* was established in 1887 by S. H. Jennings, in the interest of the Labor Party. After running about a year it was removed to Almond [Allegany County]." (Roberts, *Historical Gazetteer,* p. 82.)

THE EVENING CHRONICLE (d) Corning. ca. 1891. No issues located. "*The Evening Chronicle,* a daily newspaper neutral in politics, was started by Mr. Ed. Mott, May 4, 1891." (Roberts, *Historical Gazetteer,* p. 79.)

THE EVENING LEADER AND CORNING DAILY DEMOCRAT
see *THE CORNING LEADER*

THE EVENING PRESS (d) Hornellsville. Mr 9, 1889–? (1:1–?). *Pub*: Press Pub. Co. Mr 9, 1889; John Tolan Mr 22, 1890–? *Ed*: John Tolan Mr 22, 1890–? *Format*: Four pages, varying sizes, 12½ " x 17½ ", 15" x 19¼ ". *Price*: $3.00 per year, 1¢ per copy (1889–?). *Comment*: Published at 32 Seneca St., until January 2, 1890 then Rawson Building, Broad St. *Loc*: NHor: Mr 9, 1889–D 31, 1892 (1:1–4:248).

THE EVENING TRIBUNE (d) Hornellsville, Hornell. F 4, 1878 to date (1:1 to date). *Title changes*: *Hornellsville Evening Tribune* F 4, 1878–?; *The Evening Tribune* by 1888–D 30, 1890; *Evening Tribune* Ja 5–Mr 15, 1891; *The Evening Tribune* Mr 16, 1891–1908; *The Evening Tribune and Hornell Daily Times* by Jl 1, 1908–Ja 30, 1909; *The Evening Tribune-Times* F 1, 1909–N 10, 1934; *The Evening Tribune* N 11, 1934 to date. *Pub*: J. Greenhow & Son & Dawson F 4–O 15, 1878; J. Greenhow & Son O 17, 1878–?; W. H. Greenhow by F 13, 1888–D 31, 1908; The W. H. Greenhow Co. Ja 2, 1909 to date (W. H. Greenhow, Pres., Ja 2, 1909–F 8, 1920. Greenhow died D 1918, but his name was carried on as Pres. until 1920. H. M. S. Greenhow, Pres., F 8, 1920–Ja 7, 1924; Mrs. W. H. Greenhow, Pres. Ja 8, 1924–Mr 27, 1929; Mrs. Olive G. Buisch, Gen. Manager Ja 8, 1924–D 5, 1948; Mrs. Olive G. Buisch, Pres., Louis G. Buisch, Gen. Manager 1948–?). *Ed*: No editor listed F 4, 1878–?; W. H. Greenhow by F 13, 1888–Ap 2, 1918; No editor listed 1918–?; C. W. Newman, Managing Ed., by 1920; Miss S. Mabel Wombough S 23, 1924–D 4, 1948; Anthony F. J. Draille D 6, 1948–Mr 16, 1951; Louis G. Buisch Mr 17, 1951 to date. *Pol*: Democrat. *Format*: Four to thirty-six pages, varying sizes, 15" x 21½ ", 17" x 23", 15" x 22½ ", 11½ " x 15". *Price*: $5.00 per year, 10¢ per week (?–?); $5.00 per year, 3¢ per copy (1888–1890); $3.00 per year, 1¢ per copy (1891–1916); 40¢ per month, 2¢ per copy (1917–1920); 50¢ per month, 15¢ per week, 3¢ per copy (1921–Ap 4, 1942); 75¢ per month, 20¢ per week, 4¢ per copy (Ap 5, 1942–D 31, 1947); 75¢ per month, 30¢ per week, 5¢ per copy (Ja 2, 1948–F 2, 1957); $1.25 per month, 36¢ per week, 6¢ per copy (F 4, 1957–Ja 3, 1959); $1.75 per month, 42¢ per week, 7¢ per copy (Ja 5, 1961–F 2, 1963); $2.20 per month, 50¢ per week, 10¢ per copy (F 4, 1963–My 29, 1969); $3.25 per month, 75¢ per week, 15¢ per copy (Je 1, 1970 to date). *Comment*: Published at the

Tribune Building 57-59 Broad St., Hornellsville, then Tribune-Times
Building, 85 Canisteo St., Hornell, 1925 to date. Hornellsville became
Hornell in 1907. *Loc*: NHor: Jl 1, 1892–D 31, 1894 (v. 16, issues
not numbered); Ja 3, 1899 (v. 21); Ja 1–Je 30, 1904 (v. 22 [*sic*]–26);
Jl 1–D 31, 1908 (v. 29); Ja 3–D 31, 1910 (v. 30–31); Ap 1–Je 30,
1916 (v. 37); N 26, 1951 (v. 73). NHorT: F 4–D 30, 1878 (1:1–279);
[F 13, 1888 to date (12:304 to date)]; microfilm 1961 to date.

THE EVENING TRIBUNE AND HORNELL DAILY TIMES see
THE EVENING TRIBUNE

THE EVENING TRIBUNE AND HORNELL TIMES see *THE
EVENING TRIBUNE*

EVENING TRIBUNE-TIMES see *THE EVENING TRIBUNE*

FARMERS' ADVOCATE see *STEUBEN ADVOCATE COMBINED
WITH THE KEUKA GRAPE BELT AND THE PRATTS-
BURGH NEWS*

FARMERS' ADVOCATE AND STEUBEN ADVERTISER see
*STEUBEN ADVOCATE COMBINED WITH THE KEUKA
GRAPE BELT AND THE PRATTSBURGH NEWS*

FARMERS' GAZETTE (w) Bath. 1816–? No issues located. Published by David Rumsey. (Guy H. McMaster, *History of the Settlement of Steuben County, N. Y.* [Bath, New York: 1853], p. 167).

THE HAMMONDSPORT HERALD see *HAMMONDSPORT HER-
ALD AND BATH PLAINDEALER*

HAMMONDSPORT HERALD AND BATH PLAINDEALER (w)
Urbana, Hammondsport. Ag 28, 1874–1931//(?) (1:1–?). *Title changes*:
The Hammondsport Herald by 1882–?; *Hammondsport Herald* by
1890–Ap 24, 1896; *The Hammondsport Herald* My 6, 1896–?; *The
Hammondsport Herald and Bath Plaindealer* by 1928–F 14, 1929;
Hammondsport Herald and Bath Plaindealer F 21, 1929–? *Pub*: Mrs.
B. Bennitt and Mrs. E. B. Fairchild 1874–?; Lew H. Brown by 1882–
N 24, 1917; None listed D 1, 1917–Mr 27, 1918; Hammondsport
Herald, Inc. Ap 3, 1918–Mr 9, 1921 (L. B. Brown, Pres.); Steuben
News, Inc. Mr 16, 1921–D 26, 1928 (Lyman J. Seely, Pres. Mr 16,
1921–D 26, 1928; R. E. Castleman, Mgr. Ja 3–O 31, 1929); Maurice
E. Miller N 7, 1929–1931. *Ed*: Lew H. Brown and Reynolds by 1881;
Lew H. Brown by 1882–N 26, 1917; No editor listed D 1, 1917–Mr
27, 1918; Lyman J. Seely Ap 3, 1918–D 26, 1928; Maurice E. Miller
Ja 3–Ag 17, 1929; C. G. Higby Ag 22, 1929–Ja 2, 1930; Frank W.
Wood Ja 9–D 11, 1930; Edgar Miller D 18, 1930–1931. *Pol*: Independent. *Price*: $1.50 per year in advance (1874); $1.00 per year in advance, $1.50 outside of the county (My 3, 1882–Ja 14, 1920); $1.50
per year (Ja 21–Jl 7, 1920); $2.00 per year (Jl 14, 1920–Ap 16,
1931). *Comment*: Motto: "An Independent Local Newspaper"
(1881). "The *Hammondsport Herald* was established May 1, 1874
[in Urbana] by Mrs. B. Bennitt and Mrs. E. R. Fairchild. It is issued

weekly. May 1, 1875, the half "interest" owned by Mrs. Bennitt was sold to Mrs. Fairchild, the latter having charge of the paper until the fall of 1876 when Mr. L. H. Brown bought a half interest. The partnership existed for one year when Mr. Brown became sole proprietor and still continues to edit and publish the paper." (Roberts, *Historical Gazetteer,* p. 82.) By December 3, 1931 the *Hammondsport Herald and Bath Plaindealer* combined with the *Keuka Grape Belt* (q.v.). The latter paper adopted the numbering of the *Hammondsport Herald* and the two titles appeared on the masthead until February 29, 1940. By March 7, 1940 the *Hammondsport Herald* was dropped and the paper continued as the *Keuka Grape Belt. Loc*: NBa/Greenhow: My 3, 1882–Ap 30, 1884 (9:1–10:52); [My 7, 1890–Ap 23, 1924 (17:1–50:52)]; My 4, 1927–Ap 25, 1928 (55:1–52); Ap 25. 1929–Ap 16, 1931 (56:1–57:52). NCortHi: O 5, 1881 (8:23); D 5, 1883 (10:33). NHa: Ja 7, 1914–D 26, 1929 (41:30–56:36). NIC/MMN: [Ap 28, 1874–Ap 25, 1928 (1:1–60:52)]. NIC/RHA: My 18, 1881 (8:3); My 3, 1922–Ap 25, 1923 (49:1–52); [Ja 4, 1928–D 26, 1929 (55:36–56:36)]. NMn: D 16, 1874 (1:33).

HORNELL DAILY TIMES (d) Hornell. F 25(?), 1878–D 21, 1907// (1:1–29:307). *Title changes: Hornell Daily Times* ?–Ag 23, 1881; *The Hornell Daily Times* Ag 24, 1881–My 26, 1883; *The Daily Times* My 28–S 22, 1883; *The Morning Times* S 24, 1883–D 31, 1887; *Morning Times* Ja 2–Mr 10, 1888; *The Morning Times* Mr 12, 1888–?; *Hornellsville Morning Times* by 1893–Jl 30, 1904; *The Morning Times* Ag 1, 1904–N 13, 1907; *Hornell Daily Times* N 14–D 31, 1907. *Pub*: Johnson Brigham by Ja 2, 1879–Ja 3, 1881; Brigham & Co. Ja 4–My 17, 1881; H. S. Tomer, W. J. Jackman & Dolson My 17, 1881–Mr 3, 1882; H. S. Tomer & J. S. Dolson Mr 4–Je 30, 1882; H. S. Tomer, J. S. Dolson & J. W. Mack Jl 1, 1882–O 10, 1885; J. S. Dolson & J. W. Mack O 11–D 10, 1885; J. S. Dolson D 11, 1885–Ap 17, 1888; The Times Association Ap 17, 1888–Jl 30, 1898 (J. S. Dolson, Pres. Ap 17, 1888–Ap 17, 1889); Tuttle and Brunell Ag 1, 1898–Jl 30, 1904. *Ed*: Johnson Brigham by Ja 2, 1879–My 17, 1881; H. S. Tomer & W. J. Jackman My 17, 1881–Mr 3, 1882; H. S. Tomer Mr 4–Je 30, 1882; H. S. Tomer & J. W. Mack Jl 1, 1882–O 10, 1885; J. W. Mack O 11, 1885–O 6, 1886; G. B. Pelton O 7, 1886–N 17, 1887; No editor listed N 18, 1887–?; Wm. H. Reynolds & E. L. Dolson Ja 2–Ap 17, 1888; J. W. Mack Ap 18, 1888–Ap 17, 1889; No editor listed Ap 17, 1889–? *Format*: Four to eight pages, varying sizes, 13" x 18½", 14" x 21", 17" x 24", 19" x 24½", 21 x 27½", 17" x 22½". *Price*: $5.00 per year, 3¢ per copy (1880–1889); $5.00 per year, 2¢ per copy (1900–1904); $4.00 per year, 1¢ per copy (1904–1907). *Comment*: Published from the Times Building corner of Main & Church Sts., then Main St.; by 1904 from 50-52 Broad St. In 1908 combined with *The Evening Tribune* (q.v.) to become the *Evening Tribune-Times. Loc*: NHor: Ja 2–D 31, 1879 (2:60–3:58); Ja 3–Je 30, 1881 (4:974–1121). NHorT: Ja 2, 1879–D 31, 1889 (2:60–12:901); Jl 8, 1893–D 31, 1907 (15:162–29:307).

HORNELL EVENING TRIBUNE see *THE EVENING TRIBUNE*

HORNELL TIMES (semi-w) Hornellsville. Ja 10, 1867–? (1:1–?). *Title changes*: *The Canisteo Valley Times* 1867–?; *Hornell Times* ?–? *Pub and Ed*: R. M. Tuttle ?–S 5, 1877; R. M. Tuttle and Johnson Brigham S 8, 1877–? *Pol*: Republican. *Format*: Four pages 15″ x 21½″. *Price*: $1.50 per year. *Comment*: Published at Main St. *Canisteo Valley Times* appears as a subtitle on the 1877 issues located. *Loc*: NHorT: Ja 2–N 14, 1877 (11:1–91).

HORNELL WEEKLY TRIBUNE (w) Hornellsville. N 26, 1851–? (1:1–?). *Title changes*: *Hornellsville Tribune* N 26, 1851–N 17, 1859; *The Hornellsville Tribune* N 26, 1859–Ag 1873; *Hornellsville Tribune* S 25, 1873–Ag 1876; *The Hornellsville Tribune* S 1, 1876–Ja 5, 1877; *Hornellsville Tribune* Ja 1877–1879; *Hornellsville Weekly Tribune* Ja 2, 1880–Ap 27, 1906; *Hornell Weekly Tribune* My 7, 1906–1911. *Pub*: Edwin Hough D 3, 1851–S 18, 1853; Edwin Hough and Charles A. Kinney S 22, 1853–S 21, 1854; Edwin Hough S 28, 1854–My 20, 1858; Edwin Hough & Son (Edwin H. Hough) My 27, 1858–N 17, 1859; Edwin Hough & Co. (Edwin Hough, Edwin H. Hough, A. S. Baker) N 24, 1859–S 12, 1861; Edwin Hough & Son S 19, 1861–Ap 2, 1868; Edwin H. Hough & Charles M. Beecher Ap 9, 1868–Ja 28, 1869; Daniel R. Shafer F 4, 1869–Je 24, 1870; J. Greenhow & Son Jl 1870–Ja 1, 1880; J. Greenhow & Charles F. Peck Ja 2, 1880–?; W. H. Greenhow Ja 2, 1885–My 22, 1910; The W. H. Greenhow Co. My 27, 1910–? (W. H. Greenhow, Pres. My 27, 1910–?). *Ed*: Edwin Hough D 3, 1851–D 11, 1852; Edwin Hough and Charles A. Kinney D 18, 1852–S 21, 1854; Edwin Hough S 28, 1854–N 17, 1859; Arthur S. Baker N 26, 1859–S 12, 1861; Edwin Hough S 19, 1861–Ap 2, 1868; Charles M. Beecher Ap 9, 1868–Ja 28, 1869; Daniel R. Shafer and Charles M. Beecher F 4, 1868–O 7, 1869; Daniel R. Shafer O 14, 1869–Je 24, 1870; none listed Jl 1, 1870–Ja 1, 1880; Charles F. Peck Ja 2, 1880–D 26, 1884; W. H. Greenhow Ja 2, 1885–? *Pol*: "At first an Independent newspaper, it became Democratic for about two years, but espoused the Republican cause with the organization of that party and remained so until its sale in 1869 to D. R. Shafer. Since that time it has been Democratic." (Roberts, *Historical Gazetteer*, p. 79.) *Price*: $1.50 per year by mail, $2.00 by carrier (1851–1867); $2.00 per year by mail, $2.50 by carrier (1868–1870); $1.50 per year in advance (1871–1874); $1.00 per year (1875–1877); $1.50 per year (1878–1888); $1.00 per year, 3¢ per copy (1881–1907); 50¢ per year (1911). *Loc*: NHorT: microfilm D 3, 1851–D 29, 1899 (1:2–47:6); Ja 4, 1901–D 26, 1902 (49:6–51:5); Ja 1–D 30, 1904 (52:5–53:2); Ja 6, 1906–D 27, 1907 (54:3–57:2); Ja 7, 1910–D 22, 1911 (59:2–60:51).

HORNELLSVILLE EVENING TRIBUNE (tri-w) Hornell. S 2, 1873–? (1:1–?). *Pub and Ed*: Not listed. *Format*: Four pages 15″ x 21½″. *Price*: $2.50 per year. *Comment*: Published at Canisteo, Elm & Broad St. *Loc*: NHortT: [S 2, 1873–D 29, 1874 (1:1–2:50)].

HORNELLSVILLE EVENING TRIBUNE (1878) see *THE EVENING TRIBUNE*

HORNELLSVILLE MORNING TIMES see *HORNELL DAILY TIMES*

HORNELLSVILLE WEEKLY TRIBUNE see *HORNELL WEEKLY TRIBUNE*

THE INDIAN SPEAKS (irr) Painted Post. Ap 8, 1944–D 11, 1945// (1:1–2:6). *Pub*: Not listed. *Ed*: Harry Childs Ap 8, 1944– D 11, 1945. *Format*: Sixteen pages 4″ x 9″. *Price*: Free, mailed to Armed Forces and local residents. *Circ*: 950 (1944–1945). *Loc*: NPP/Town of Erwin Museum: Ap 8, 1944–D 11, 1945 (1:1–2:6).

KEUKA GRAPE BELT (w) Hammondsport. Ag 1, 1929–1942// (1:1–?). *Title changes*: *Keuka Grape Belt* Ag 1, 1929–N 26, 1931; *Keuka Grape Belt Combined with the Hammondsport Herald and Bath Plaindealer* D 3, 1931–F 29, 1940; *Keuka Grape Belt* Mr 7, 1940–? *Pub*: The Keuka Grape Belt Co. Ag 1, 1929–O 6, 1932 (Merritt M. Landon, Pres.); The Steuben Farmers' Advocate, Inc. O 13, 1932–Ap 1, 1937 (Merritt M. Landon, Pres.); Merritt M. Landon Ap 8, 1937–1942. *Ed*: Graham M. Burch Ag 1, 1929–Je 12, 1930; Laura L. Swarthout Je 19, 1930–D 28, 1939; Mrs. Mable Sandford Ja 4–Jl 18, 1940; John A. Southard Jl 25–Ag 29, 1940; Mrs. Archie Spangler S 5, 1940–? *Format*: Eight pages, varying sizes, 17″ x 22½″, 11″ x 17½″. *Price*: $2.00 per year, 5¢ per copy (1929–1942). *Comment*: The volume numbering of the *Keuka Grape Belt* changed from its original numbering of vol. 1, no. 1, to vol. 57 when it combined with the *Hammondsport Herald and the Bath Plaindealer* in 1931. The final date of publication is based on Ayer's *Directory* which does not list the newspaper after 1942. *Loc*: NBa: Ja 4, 1939–D 25, 1941 (70:1 [*sic*]–67:52). NBa/Greenhow: Ag 1, 1929–D 26, 1935 (1:1–61:52); Ja 4, 1939–Je 25, 1942 (65:1–68:26). NHa: Ag 1, 1929–D 30, 1939 (1:1–63:43). NIC/MMN: microfilm Ag 1929–D 31, 1936 (1:1–63:1); Not filmed Ag 1, 1929–D 24, 1936 (1:1– 62:52). NIC/RHA: Ja 2–D 24, 1936 (62:1–52).

KEUKA GRAPE BELT COMBINED WITH THE HAMMONDS- PORT HERALD AND BATH PLAINDEALER see *KEUKA GRAPE BELT*

THE LEADER (d) Corning. S 24, 1965 to date. (1:1 to date). *Pub*: Corning Leader, Inc. S 24, 1965 to date (E. S. Underhill, III, Pres. and Matthew F. Carney, Co-Pub S 27, 1965 to date). *Ed*: George H. Bevan S 24, 1965 to date. *Pol*: Independent. *Format*: Sixteen to twenty-four pages. *Price*: $15.00 per year, 7¢ per copy (1965–1967); $15.00 per year, 10¢ per copy (1968 to date). *Comment*: A continuation of *The Corning Leader* (q.v.). The numbering of that paper was changed September 24, 1965 and the newspaper was renumbered vol. 1, no. 1. *Loc*: NCor: S 24, 1965 to date (1:1 to date). NCorL: microfilm S 24, 1965 to date (1:1 to date). NCor/Museum of Glass Library: O 21, 1968 (4:249, special issue on Corning Glass Works).

THE LEADER see also *THE CORNING LEADER*

THE MORNING TIMES see *HORNELL DAILY TIMES*

NATIONAL AMERICAN see *THE CANISTEO VALLEY JOURNAL AND NATIONAL AMERICAN*

THE NORTH COHOCTON TIMES (w) Cohocton. My 1873–? (1:1–?). *Pub and Ed*: William A. Carpenter. *Format*: Four pages 16" x 21¾". *Comment*: "In May 1873, William A. Carpenter at the age of fourteen commenced publication of the *Cohocton Times* in N. Cohocton. He printed the paper on a hand press set up in a barn. The next year he purchased the *Cohocton Tribune* [q.v.] from James Hewitt, and moved to Liberty to establish the weekly *Cohocton Valley Times* [q.v.]." (Roberts, *Historical Gazetteer,* p. 78.) *Loc*: NIC/ MMN: Ja 22, Mr 26, 1874 (2:4, 13).

PAINTED POST TIMES (w) Painted Post. O 5, 1870–? (1:1–?). *Title changes*: *Painted Post Times* O 5, 1870–?; *The Painted Post Times* by 1873–?; *Painted Post Times* by 1876–? *Pub and Ed*: S. H. Ferenbaugh O 5, 1870–? *Pol*: Republican (1870–?). *Format*: Four pages, varying sizes, 21" x 28", 17½" x 23½". *Price*: $1.50 per year in advance, otherwise $2.00 per year (1870–?); $1.00 per year in advance (1876–?). *Comment*: Published in the second story of B. C. Woods Building 1870, then by 1873 in the Sash Factory Office, north side of Water Street. *Loc*: NCortHi: D 17, 1873 (4:12); D 29, 1876 (7:13). NPP/Town of Erwin Museum: O 5, 1870–S 25, 1872 (1:1–2:13).

PLEASANT VALLEY FRUIT AND WINE RECORDER (irr) Hammondsport. S 20, 1870–? *Pub and Ed*: A. L. Underhill S 20, 1870–? *Format*: Eight pages 11½" x 15". *Price*: $1.00 per year, 5¢ per issue. *Loc*: NBa: [S 20, 1870–S 1872 (1:1–no vol. or no.)].

THE POST (w) Painted Post. D 6, 1916–? (1:1–?). *Pub and Ed*: Francis A. Brown D 6, 1916–? *Format*: Sixteen pages 10" x 12½". *Price*: $1.50 per year (1916–1917). *Circ*: 2,000 (1916–1917). *Comment*: Published at the Odd Fellows Temple, Hamilton Street. *Loc*: NPP/Town of Erwin Museum: D 6, 1916–Ap 25, 1917 (1:1–14).

PRATTSBURGH ADVERTISER (semi-m) Prattsburgh. My 1867–? (1:1–?). *Pub and Ed*: E. V. Parker & Co. 1867–? *Price*: Free (1867); $1.50 per year in advance, or $2.00 if not paid within the month (by 1871). *Format*: Four pages, varying sizes, 9" x 11", 15½" x 21½". *Comment*: Motto: "A Semi-monthly Mercantile Journal, Devoted to the Advertising Public"; "A Semi-monthly Mercantile Journal, Devoted to Advertising Generally." In addition to advertisements, it carried all sorts of bits of information about the community, jokes, poetry, etc. Office first floor over P. C. Howe's Store in 1871. *Loc*: NIC/RHA: My, Je 1867 (1:1, 4).

PRATTSBURGH ADVERTISER (w) Prattsburgh. O 11, 1867–? (1:1–?). *Title changes*: *Prattsburg Advertiser* O 11–O 25, 1867; *Prattsburgh Advertiser* N 1, 1867–? *Pub and Ed*: Caleb B. Hoke O 11, 1867–?; Paul C. Howe by N 9, 1871–? *Pol*: Independent (on masthead for O 11, 1867–Jl 14, 1870). *Format*: Four pages 15½ " x 21½ ". *Price*: $1.50 per year in advance or $2.00 if not paid within one month (1871–?). *Comment*: Office first floor over E. V. Parker's store. Prattsburgh was spelled without the "H" in the title of the first three issues of the newspaper. Loc: NIC/RHA: [O 11, 1867–O 24, 1872 (1:1–5:5 whole nos. 1–250)].

PRATTSBURGH ADVERTISER (w) Prattsburgh. 1921–? (1:1–?). *Pub and Ed*: Leona Bancroft by 1923–? *Format*: Four pages 17¼ " x 23". *Price*: $2.00 per year. *Circ*: 800 (1924). *Loc*: NIC/RHA: My 11, 1923 (3:11); S 17, 24, N 19, D 3, 1926 (6:29, 30, 38, 40); Ag 19, D 9, 1927 (7:25, 41); Mr 2, 1928 (8:1); Jl 29, D 2, 1932 (12:22, 40).

THE PRATTSBURGH ARGUS (w) Prattsburgh. Ja 3, 1878–? (1:1–?). *Pub*: R. H. Stewart & Co. 1878–? *Format*: Four pages 16¼ " x 21¾ ". *Price*: $1.00 per year (1878). *Comment*: Motto: "Devoted to the Interests of Prattsburgh and Vicinity." *Loc*: NIC/ RHA: Mr 6, 13, 1878 (1:10, 11).

THE PRATTSBURGH NEWS (semi-m) Prattsburgh. Ap 1864–? (1:1–?). *Pub*: George E. Hayes & Co. by 1864–? *Format*: Four pages, varying sizes, 9¼ " x 12½ ", 17" x 23½ ". *Price*: 50¢ per year by 1864; $1.50 per year in advance by 1886. *Comment*: "Motto: "Devoted to Local News and General Intelligence." *Loc*: NIC/RHA: My 7, 1864 (1:2).

THE PRATTSBURGH NEWS (w) Prattsburgh. D 12, 1872–D 2, 1920// (1:1–48:53). *Pub and Ed*: Paul C. Howe O 11, 1872–Je 10, 1875; Paul C. Howe and Son, Proprietor Je 17, 1875–N 22, 1883; Paul C. Howe's Sons (Will L. and G. W. Howe) N 29, 1883–Mr 8, 1900 (Paul C. Howe died Mr 1886); Will L. Howe and Clara B. Chisholm Mr 15, 1900–Je 28, 1906; Will L. Howe & Co. (Will L. Howe & Charlotte W. Howe) Jl 1906–1920. *Pol*: Independent. *Format*: Four to eight pages, varying sizes, 15½ " x 21½ ", 17¼ " x23½ ", 21½ " x 27½ ". *Price*: $1.50 per year in advance, or $2.00 if payment delayed (1872–D 1887); $1.25 per year in advance, or $1.50 if payment delayed (1888–1892); $1.00 per year in advance, or $1.25 after 3 months (1892–1916); $1.25 per year in advance (1917–1920). *Comment*: Motto: "Devoted to Local News and General Intelligence." An editorial of December 12, 1872, stated, "The cause of education will be duly considered, and those practical hints given which are needed to improve the home training of the sons and daughters. . . . The thoughts and plans of successful education, science and morality will receive our most careful thought. . . . We shall devote every possible effort for the accomplishment of the desired rational facilities of Prattsburgh, Pulteney and the towns of the north. . . . In short, the news will become the oracle of the people. . . ." "We commence without a printing office or other resources. . . ." First issue printed in Bath by A. L. Underhill, publisher of the *Steuben Advocate* (Editorial of December 2, 1920.) On March 16, 1900, George W. Howe sold his half interest to Clara Chisholm. In this edition, the editor Will

Howe said that *Prattsburgh News* would be published in one page of the *Advocate* for Bath. *Loc*: NIC/RHA: D 12, 1872–D 2, 1920 (1:1–48:53).

THE PRATTSBURG PRESS (w) Prattsburg. Ja 26, 1928–? (1:1–?). *Pub and Ed*: Charles G. Higby 1928–? *Pol*: Democrat. *Format*: Four to eight pages. *Price*: $2.00 per year, 5¢ per copy. *Comment*: Motto: "Trade at Home." *Loc*: NIC/RHA: [Ja 26–S 20, 1928 (1:1–33)].

THE PRIMITIVE CHRISTIAN (m) Bath. No issues located. "*The Primitive Christian* was printed in the office of Richardson and Dowe in 1844. Rev. Jabez Chadwick was the editor and publisher. It was an octavo and issued monthly. It lived less than two years." (Roberts, *Historical Gazetteer*, p. 76.)

THE ROSE (semi-m) Bath. 1844–? (1:1–?). *Pub and Ed*: J. S. Vincent. *Format*: Eight pages 9" x 11⅞". *Price*: $1.00 per year in advance. *Comment*: Motto: "A Semi-Monthly Journal Devoted to Literature and the Arts, Embellished with Engravings." "*The Rose* a literary monthly was published in the office of George B. Richardson and Dowe for J. S. Vincent in 1844 and was discontinued when the editor enlisted as a soldier in the Mexican War." (Roberts, *Historical Gazetteer*, p. 76.) *Loc*: NIC/MMN: N 21, 1844 (1:9).

THE SATURDAY NEWS Bath. No issues located. ca. Ap 25, 1868//. "*The Saturday News* was established by Enos W. Barnes who issued the first number on April 25, 1868. It only lived some five or six months." (Roberts, *Historical Gazetteer*, p. 77.)

THE SAVONA RUSTLER (w) Bath. My 19, 1888–? No issues located. "*The Savona Rustler*, issued weekly, was established May 19, 1888, by T. L. Ward. It is Independent in politics." (Roberts, *Historical Gazetteer*, p. 77.)

STEUBEN ADVOCATE see *STEUBEN ADVOCATE COMBINED WITH THE KEUKA GRAPE BELT AND THE PRATTSBURGH NEWS* see also *STEUBEN COURIER-ADVOCATE*

STEUBEN ADVOCATE AND THE KEUKA GRAPE BELT see *STEUBEN ADVOCATE COMBINED WITH THE KEUKA GRAPE BELT AND THE PRATTSBURGH NEWS*

STEUBEN ADVOCATE COMBINED WITH THE KEUKA GRAPE BELT AND THE PRATTSBURGH NEWS (w, then d) Bath. Mr 1823–Je 1958// (1:1–?). *Title changes: Farmer's Advocate and Steuben Advertiser* by My 8, 1823–?; *Farmers' Advocate* by Ap 10, 1828–?; *Farmers' Advocate, and Steuben Advertiser* by Ag 28, 1828–?; *Farmers' Advocate* by Ja 28, 1830–?; *Steuben Farmers' Advocate* by Ja 7, 1835–D 8, 1920; *Steuben Farmers' Advocate and the Prattsburgh News* D 15, 1920–D 27, 1935; *Steuben Advocate* Ja 3, 1936–Jl 17, 1942; *Steuben Advocate and the Keuka Grape Belt* Jl 27, 1942–Je 1, 1951; *Steuben Advocate With Which is Combined the Keuka Grape Belt* Je 8, 1951–F 1, 1952; *Steuben Advocate Combined with the Keuka Grape Belt and the Prattsburgh News* F 4, 1952–Je 1958. *Pub*: Henry D. Smead by My 8, 1823–Ap 4, 1849; W. C. Rhodes Ap 11, 1849–Ja 1, 1851; W. C. Rhodes and W. A. McDowell Ja 8–Jl 16, 1851; W. C. Rhodes Jl 23, 1851–My 6, 1857; P. S. Donahe My 13, 1857–Ag 1, 1860; A. L. Underhill Ag 1, 1860–Ja 1, 1868; A. L. Underhill and T. S. De Wolfe Ja 8, 1868–D 29, 1869; A. L. Underhill Ja 8, 1870–D 25, 1883; A. L. Underhill & Son Ja 2, 1884–D 26, 1888; Edwin S. Underhill Ja 2, 1889–S 25, 1895; The Steuben Farmers' Advocate O 2, 1895–D 30, 1935 (A. L. Underhill, Edwin S. Underhill, John Underhill, Directors O 2, 1895–D 31, 1902; Edwin S. Underhill, Secy. Ja 7, 1903–Jl 31, 1907; C. Underhill, Pres. Jl 10, 1907–Jl 7, 1915; Edwin S. Underhill, Sec-Treas. Jl 14, 1915–Ap 2, 1924; J. F. Palmer, Pres. Ap 9, 1924–D 28, 1927; Merritt M. Landon, Pres. Ja 4, 1928–D 30, 1935); Merritt M. Landon, Ja 3, 1936–Jl 19, 1946; C. Lambert Fay Jl 26, 1946–D 28, 1951; Steuben Advocate, Inc. Ja 4, 1952–1958 (Louis G. Buisch, Pres. Ja 4, 1952–1958). *Ed*: Benjamin F. Smead by My 8, 1823–Ap 4, 1849; W. C. Rhodes Ap 11, 1849–My 6, 1857; A. J. McCall My 3, 1857–D 28, 1859; No editor listed Ja 4–Jl 25, 1860; A. L. Underhill Ag 1, 1860–Ja 1, 1868; A. L. Underhill and T. S. DeWolfe Ja 8, 1868–Ja 1, 1870; A. L. Underhill Ja 8, 1870–D 26, 1888; Edwin S. Underhill Ja 2, 1889–Mr 18, 1925; Merritt M. Landon Mr 25, 1925–D 28, 1927; No editor listed Ja 4, 1927–D 20, 1935; Merritt M. Landon Ja 3, 1936–Jl 19, 1946; No editor listed Jl 26, 1946–My 2, 1947; C. Thurston Carlson My 9, 1947–Mr 2, 1951; Merritt M. Landon Mr 9, 1951–1958. *Pol*: Democrat. *Format*: Four to twenty pages, varying sizes, 14½ " x 19½ ", 18½ " x 23¾ ", 24" x 30", 16½ " x 22½ ". *Price*: $2.25 per year, half-yearly in advance (1823); $2.50 per year (Ja 5, 1831–Ap 4, 1849); $1.50 per year (Ap 9, 1849–D 29, 1871); $2.00 per year (Ja 4, 1872–D 26, 1873); $1.00 per year (Ja 2, 1874–D 27, 1916); $1.00 per year in Steuben Co., $1.50 elsewhere (Ja 3, 1917–D 31, 1919); $1.50 per year (Ja 7–Jl 16, 1920); $2.00 per year (Jl 21, 1920–D 6, 1946); $2.50 per year (D 13, 1946–F 1, 1951); $6.00 per year, 30¢ per week, 5¢ per copy (F 4, 1951–1958). *Comment*: Published at Poulteney Square, by January 1, 1831; then 19 Liberty St., January 3, 1849–December 28, 1887; 42 Liberty St., from January 4, 1888; then from the Barton Building, corner of Wilkes and Advocate Avenues November 16, 1951; and 42 Liberty St. February 4, 1942. Combined with *The Steuben Courier* (q.v.) June 18, 1958 which subsequently became *The Steuben Courier-Advocate* on July 25, 1968. *Loc*: NAng: My 20, 1830 (14:373 n.s. no. 20). NAub: N 28, 1838 (16:49). NBa: Ja 5, 1831–D 26, 1832 (9:1–10:42); Ja 1, 1835–D 27, 1899 (22:1–84:52); Ja 1, 1902–Mr 31, 1958 (87:1–143rd year: 76). NBa/Greenhow: D 22, 1841–D 14, 1842 (26:1–52); D 20, 1843–D 25, 1844 (28:1–29:2); [My 13, 1856–Mr 31, 1958 (43:1–143rd year:76)]. NIC/MMN: microfilm: My 8, 1823 (1:7); S 2, 1824 (2:24); My 19, 1825 (3:9 whole no. 113); Ag 31, 1826 (4:24 whole no. 180); [Ja 4, 1827–N 1, 1946 (4:41–131:44)].

STEUBEN ADVOCATE WITH WHICH IS COMBINED THE

KEUKA GRAPE BELT see STEUBEN ADVOCATE COM-
BINED WITH THE KEUKA GRAPE BELT AND THE
PRATTSBURGH NEWS

THE STEUBEN AMERICAN (w) Bath. Ja 1855–My 6, 1857//
(1:1–3:19). Pub and Ed: A. L. Underhill by Ja 2, 1856–My 7, 1857.
Format: Four pages 17½ " x 23". Price: $1.50 per year. Comment:
Published at New Brick Block. "The Steuben American was started
in Bath January 1, 1856 . . . and published until the summer of 1857,
when it was sold to P. S. Donahe. The printing office was used thereafter to publish the Steuben Farmers' Advocate [q.v.] which had a
few weeks before been destroyed by fire." (Roberts, Historical Gazetteer, p. 76.) Loc: NBa: Ja 2, 1856–My 6, 1857 (2:1–3:19). NIC/
RHA: Ja 2, 1856–My 6, 1857 (2:1–3:19).

STEUBEN AND ALLEGANY PATRIOT, AND SPIRIT OF AGRI-
CULTURE AND MANUFACTURES (w) Bath. N 26, 1816–?
(1:1–?). Title changes: Steuben Patriot and Spirit of Agriculture and
Manufactures by 1822; Steuben and Allegany Patriot, and Spirit of
Agriculture and Manufactures by F 1823. Pub and Ed: Benjamin
Smead. Format: Four pages 13⅛ " x 20". Price: $2.00 per year in
advance, or $2.50 due at the close of 6 months, or $3.00 if not paid
till the year expires (1822). Comment: Published on the corner of
Morris St. and Pine Alley. "In 1816, Mr. David Rumsey published
at Bath the Farmers' Gazette [q.v.] and Captain Benjamin Smead
started at the same place the Steuben and Allegany Patriot. This sheet
is the most unquestionable antiquity which the county has produced."
(McMaster, History of the Settlement of Steuben County, N. Y., p.
167.) "The Patriot under different names remained in the Smead
family up to the fourth of April, 1849, when it passed into the hands
of William C. Rhodes who continued its publication as the Steuben
Farmers' Advocate up to January 30, 1857, when the office took fire
and the establishment was entirely consumed. Mr. Rhodes sold the
goodwill of the concern to P. S. Donahe, who, on the 31st of May,
1857, resumed the publication of the Steuben Farmers' Advocate,
[q.v.], A. J. McCall, Ed." (Roberts, Historical Gazetteer, p. 75.) Loc:
NIC/MMN: F 7, Ap 11, 1822 (4:11; 6 [sic]:20 whole nos. 271,
280); F 27, 1823 (7:14 whole no. 326.)

STEUBEN COUNTY DEMOCRAT (w) Bath. N 14, 1843–? (1:1–?).
Title changes: Steuben Democrat N 14, 1843–Mr 20, 1844; Steuben
County Democrat Ap 10, 1844–? Pub and Ed: G. B. Richardson and
John Dow N 15, 1843–? Price: $2.00 per year in advance. Pol: Dem-
ocrat. Comment: Motto: "Unity of Feeling, Unity of Purpose and
Freedom of Principle." Published at East side at Liberty St., third
story center south Brick Block. According to historian Millard Roberts, this newspaper was a continuation of The Constitutionalist, carried on by George B. Robinson and John Dowe. Its publication was
suspended in 1844. In 1848 the paper was revived by J. L. Bush as
the Steuben Democrat (q.v.) (Roberts, Historical Gazetteer, p. 76.)

Loc: NIC/RHA: [N 15, 1843–Mr 20, 1844 (1:1–1:18)]; Ap 10–My 22, 1844 (1:21–27).

STEUBEN COURIER see *STEUBEN COURIER-ADVOCATE*

THE STEUBEN COURIER-ADVOCATE (w) Bath. S 20, 1843 to date (1:1 to date). *Title changes*: *Steuben Courier* S 20, 1843–F 16, 1853; *The Steuben Courier* F 23, 1853–F 12, 1892; *Steuben Courier* F 19, 1892–Ag 7, 1896; *The Steuben Courier* Ag 14, 1896–Je 26, 1942; *The Steuben Courier and the Avoca Herald* Jl 3, 1942–My 24, 1946; *The Steuben Courier* My 31, 1946–Je 12, 1958; *The Steuben Courier and the Steuben Advocate* Je 19, 1958–Jl 18, 1968; *The Steuben Courier-Advocate* Jl 25, 1968 to date. *Pub*: Henry H. Hull and Whittemore S 20, 1843–S 10, 1845; Henry H. Hull S 17, 1845–F 27, 1856; Henry H. Hull and C. G. Fairman Mr 5–D 17, 1856; Henry H. Hull D 26, 1856–D 30, 1863; Henry H. Hull and Barnes Ja 7, 1864–Je 30, 1875; Henry H. Hull & Son Jl 7, 1875–Je 28, 1876; H. S. Hull Jl 5, 1876–Ag 14, 1890; C. W. Hull et al. Ag 25, 1890—F 13, 1891; The Courier Co., Ltd. F 20, 1891–Ja 6, 1899; The Courier Co., Ltd. D 1, 1899–Ap 4, 1968 (Cassie Hull Kasson, Pres. D 1, 1899–Jl 1, 1916; H. O. Elkins, Pres. Jl 28, 1916–S 2, 1921; W. W. Babcock, Pres. S 9, 1921–D 28, 1928; Henry O. Elkins, Pres. Ja 4, 1929–Ja 4, 1946; Robert E. Cole, Pres. Ja 11, 1946–Ap 2, 1948; Chilton Latham, Pres. Ap 9, 1948–Ap 4, 1968); Greenhow Newspapers, Inc. Ap 12, 1968 to date (Louis G. Bligh, Jr., Pres.). *Ed*: Henry H. Hull S 20, 1843–F 27, 1856; Henry H. Hull and C. G. Fairman Mr 5–D 17, 1856; Henry H. Hull D 26, 1856–D 30, 1863; Henry H. Hull and Barnes Ja 6, 1864–Je 30, 1875; Henry H. Hull Jl 7, 1875–Je 28, 1876; H. S. Hull Jl 7, 1876–Jl 11, 1890; John F. Parkhurst Jl 18, 1890–F 23, 1906; H. O. Elkins Mr 2, 1906–Ja 4, 1946; Doris Shilling Ja 11–F 15, 1946; Charles Mathew, Managing Ed., F 15, 1946–Ja 26, 1947; S. Charles Force, Managing Ed. Ja 31–O 31, 1947; No editor listed N 7, 1947–Mr 9, 1951; C. Thurston Carlson Mr 17, 1951–O 19, 1956; Marion B. Latham O 26, 1956–F 19, 1959; Sylvia K. Bonlayer F 26–Ag 13, 1959; No editor listed Ag 30, 1959–Ap 28, 1960; Robert N. Rolfe My 5, 1960–D 23, 1965; Helena L'Hommedieu D 30, 1965–Ag 16, 1966; No editor listed Ag 25–O 22, 1966; James C. Malone O 27, 1966–D 28, 1967; Peter Young Ja 4–Mr 7, 1968; Marion B. Latham Mr 14–Ap 4, 1968; Bert L. Jarnagin Ap 11–S 19, 1968; Marion B. Latham S 26, 1968–?; Jared Kreste ? to date. *Pol*: Whig; Republican by 1854. *Format*: Four to thirty pages, varying sizes, 15½ " x 20½ ", 22" x 27½ ", 24" x 30", 17" x 23", 15" x 22". *Price*: $2.00 per year (S 20, 1843–Ja 24, 1844); $1.50 per year (Ja 31, 1844–S 21, 1864); $2.00 per year (S 28, 1864–D 29, 1870); $1.50 per year (Ja 4, 1871–Je 30, 1875); $1.00 per year in Steuben Co., $1.50 elsewhere (Jl 7, 1875–D 5, 1919); $1.50 per year (D 12, 1919–D 5, 1920); $2.00 per year (D 12, 1920–N 29, 1946); $2.50 per year (D 6, 1946–Ja 20, 1956); $3.00 per year (Ja 27, 1956–Jl 4, 1968); $3.50 per year (Jl 11, 1968–?); $4.50 per year (My 20–Jl 1971); $4.25 per year (Jl 29, 1971–?); $6.00 per year, 15¢ per copy (? to date). *Comment*:

Published in the Brick Block, Liberty St., September 20, 1843–August 26, 1857; Steuben St., as of September 2, 1857; then Liberty St., by August 7, 1861; Buel St., Courier Building, by August 17, 1883; Smith Block, 9 East William St., by July 28. 1916 to date. *Loc*: NAlmHi: Jl 16, 1943 (94:29). NBa: Ja 7, 1874–D 31, 1880 (31:18–38:18). NBa/Greenhow: S 20, 1843 to date (1:1 to date). NCooHi: Ap 17, 24, 1879 (36:33, 34). NIC/RHA: S 3, 1845 (2:51); Ap 23, 1856 (13:35 whole no. 659); Mr 18, 1857–Ag 3, 1859 (14:30–16:48 whole nos. 706–832); O 26, 1859–Jl 30, 1862 (17:8–19:48); D 17, 1873 (31:15 supplement); S 27, 1876 (34:4); Mr 21, 1877 (34:29); Mr 31, 1893 (50:33); Mr 1, 1912 (67:28); Je 6, Ag 22, 1913 (70:42; 70 [*sic*]:1); F 23, N 30, D 7, 1923 (80 [*sic*]:25; 80:13, 14); Mr 28, Ap 25, My 2, 9, 1924 (80:30, 34, 35, 36); Jl 16, 1943 (99:49 Centennial edition); Ap 13, 1956 to date (111:15 to date).

STEUBEN DEMOCRAT (w) Bath. Je 14, 1848–? (1:1–?). *Pub*: L. J. Bush & Messenger Je–O 18, 1848; L. J. Bush O 25, 1848–Mr 1849; C. W. Hudson Ap 4, 1849–? *Ed*: L. J. Bush Je 1848–Mr 1849. *Pol*: Democrat. *Format*: Four pages 14" x 20½". *Price*: $1.00 per year in advance, $2.00 at end of year (1848). *Comment*: Motto: "The Constitution—The Cornerstone of the Democratic Party." Published East side of Liberty St. third story center Red Block November 15, 1843–? Office on north end of Merchant's Exchange, Liberty St., 1848–1849. According to Roberts this newspaper was a continuation of *The Constitutionalist*. George B. Richardson and John Dowe continued *The Constitutionalist* as the *Steuben County Democrat* (q.v.) "till sometime in 1844 when its publication was suspended. In 1848 the *Democrat* was revived by J. L. Bush and in 1849 it passed into the hands of George H. Bidwell by whom it was continued till 1852." (Roberts, *Historical Gazetteer*, p. 76.) *Loc*: NIC/RHA: Je 14, 1848–Je 13, 1849 (1:1–52).

STEUBEN FARMERS' ADVOCATE see *STEUBEN ADVOCATE COMBINED WITH THE KEUKA GRAPE BELT AND THE PRATTSBURGH NEWS*

STEUBEN FARMERS' ADVOCATE AND THE PRATTSBURGH NEWS see *STEUBEN ADVOCATE COMBINED WITH THE KEUKA GRAPE BELT AND THE PRATTSBURGH NEWS*

THE STEUBEN MESSENGER (w) Bath. Ap 17, 1828–1844//. No issues located. "*The Steuben Messenger* was commenced in Bath by David Rumsey, the first number of which was issued on the 17th day of April, 1828. On the second day of December, 1830, Mr. Rumsey sold out to S. M. Eddy who continued its publication for a time and sold out to W. P. Angel. When Mr. Angel got control of the paper he changed the name to *The Constitutionalist* [q.v.] and continued its publication till some time in 1834 when it passed into the hands of Charles Adams. On the tenth day of February 1841, Mr. Adams sold to R. L. Underhill and the paper was continued in the name of M. F. Whittemore and Co., till the spring of 1843 when it passed into the hands of George B. Richardson and John Dowe who continued it as the *Steuben Democrat* till sometime in 1844 when its publication was suspended." (Roberts, *Historical Gazetteer,* p. 76.)

STEUBEN PATRIOT see *STEUBEN AND ALLEGANY PATRIOT*

STEUBEN PATRIOT AND SPIRIT OF AGRICULTURE AND MANUFACTURES see *STEUBEN AND ALLEGANY PATRIOT AND SPIRIT OF AGRICULTURE AND MANUFACTURES*

STEUBEN REPUBLICAN (w) Bath. Ag 15, 1822–1823//(?) (1:1–?). *Pub and Ed*: Erastus Shepard. *Pol*: Republican. *Format*: Eight pages 9″ x 10½″. *Price*: 50¢ per quarter, 2¢ per copy in advance or 3¢ per copy at office; $2.00 per year by mail (1822). *Comment*: Succeeded the *Western Republican* (q.v.). In the first issue, Shepard stated, "the object of the publisher in discontinuing the *Western Republican* and substituting the paper now proposed, is first to get a new subscription list, with the names of as few who are unable to pay as circumstances will permit, and second to adopt a title less assuming and more appropriate to the section of the country from which the paper will probably derive its principal support." *Loc*: NIC/MMN: Ag 15, N 7, 14, 1822 (1:1, 11, 12).

STEUBEN SENTINEL (w) Woodhull. 1880–? (1:1–?). *Pub and Ed*: R. C. Park by 1881–? *Pol*: Independent. *Format*: Four pages 15¾″ x 22″. *Price*: $1.00 per year invariably in advance. *Comment*: Motto: "Discretion of Speech is Superior to Eloquence." Roberts states that the paper was founded in 1879 by R. C. Park . . . "and commenced publication at Troupsburg, N. Y., and continued the same for a period of one year, after which it was removed to Woodhull and took up quarters in a small room in the Hopkins brick building, soon after removing to more commodious quarters in the same building. . . . The paper has proved a success and maintains a steady growth. It is independent in politics." (Roberts, *Historical Gazetteer,* pp. 82–83.) *Loc*: NCortHi: Ag 25, 1881 (2:23).

STEUBEN SIGNAL (w) Hornellsville. Ap 4, 1883–Ap 4, 1888// (1:1–5:52). *Pub*: Signal Publishing Co. 1883–1888 (M. A. Tuttle, F. M. Sheldon, J. L. Stanton, Executive Commitee). *Ed*: None listed. *Pol*: Prohibition. *Format*: Four pages, varying sizes, 17″ x 23″, 20″ x 25″. *Price*: $1.00 per year. *Comment*: Published at 28 Seneca St. *Loc*: NHorT: Ap 4, 1883–Ap 4, 1888 (1:1–5:52).

STEUBEN TIMES (w) Atlanta. July 30, 1897–? No issues located. Benjamin A. Osborne started the *Steuben Times* at Atlanta on July 30, 1897. The 29th number appeared February 11, 1898. A few days after the printing office was burned, and Vincent Tripp "Purchased the goodwill and list. . . ." (James Folts' Letter of April 9, 1972 to SCRLC office.)

THE STEUBEN WHIG (w) Bath. 1828(?)–? *Pub and Ed*: Printed by William H. Swaine. *Pol*: Whig. "Devoted to the cause of the present general administration." *Format*: Eight pages 6½″ x 10″. *Comment*: *The Steuben Whig* was published at Bath during the political campaign of 1828 by Wm. H. Swaine, the founder of the *Philadelphia Ledger*. *Loc*: NIC/MMN: O 20, 1828 (1:12).

THE TEMPERANCE GEM Bath. No issues located. "*The Temperance Gem* was printed in the Advocate office for Jennie and Caroline Rumsey in 1854. It was afterwards printed in Elmira." (Roberts, *Historical Gazetteer*, p. 76.)

THE TIMES see *THE CANISTEO TIMES*

THE TIMES-REPUBLICAN see *THE CANISTEO TIMES*

THE TRI-WEEKLY CONSERVATIVE see *BATH TRI-WEEKLY CONSERVATIVE*

TRIBUNE see *HORNELL WEEKLY TRIBUNE*

THE UNION ADVERTISER Wayland. ca. 1863. No issues located. "*The Union Advertiser* was established by H. B. Newell in the fall of 1863. It is a weekly paper, neutral in politics, and devoted to general news and literature. About 1889 C. F. Newell was admitted and the firm name changed to Newell Brothers." (Roberts, *Historical Gazetteer*, p. 82.)

THE VOICE OF THE NATION (w) Addison. Ja 3–D 19, 1855// (1:1–51). *Pub*: Charles L. Phelps Ja 3–F 28, 1855; A. L. Underhill Mr 7–D 19, 1855. *Ed*: Charles L. Phelps and A. L. Underhill Ja 3– F 28, 1855; A. L. Underhill Mr 7–D 19, 1855. *Format*: Four pages 17½ " x 23". *Price*: $1.50 per year. *Comment*: Published in the Delemater Block. *Loc*: NBa: Ja 10–D 19, 1855 (1:2–51).

THE WAYLAND REGISTER (w) Wayland. ca. 1889. No issues located. "*The Wayland Register* was started at Wayland, N. Y., May 1, 1889, by C. F. Dean, its present proprietor. It is published weekly and is non-partisan. It is an eight page, five column newspaper, 26 x 40 inches." (Roberts, *Historical Gazetteer*, p. 82.)

WEEKLY MONITOR (w) Painted Post. 1891–? (1:1–?). *Pub and Ed*: C. C. and S. C. Redfield N 29, 1895–? *Format*: Four pages 17½ " x 23½ ". *Loc*: NPP/Town of Erwin Museum: N 29, 1895 (4:1); Ap 24, 1896 (4:22).

THE WESTERN REPUBLICAN (w) Bath. O 6, 1819–1822// (1:1–?). *Pub and Ed*: Erastus Shepard. *Pol*: Republican. *Format*: Four pages 12½ " x 20". *Price*: 50¢ per quarter. *Comment*: "In November 1822, the name was changed to the *Steuben Republican* [q.v.] and in February 1823, its publication was suspended." (Roberts, *Historical Gazetteer*, p. 75.) Contains the Steuben County Census for 1820. *Loc*: NIC/MMN: Ap 18, 1821 (2:80); Ap 27, 1822 (3:119, pt. 2 fragment).

WOODHULL SENTINEL see *THE ADDISON ADVERTISER AND WOODHULL SENTINEL*

TIOGA COUNTY

THE ADVOCATE see *WAVERLY ADVOCATE*

THE AHWAGA CHIEF (w) Owego. F 23–D 28, 1872// (1:1–38). *Pub and Ed*: Horace A. Brooks. *Pol*: Liberal Republican. *Format*: Four pages 20¼ " x 26¾". *Comment*: Motto: "Honor, Truth, and Justice; Union, Liberty, and Progress." "At the conclusion of the presidential campaign of 1872, in which *The Ahwaga Chief* supported Horace Greeley, the paper was discontinued having proved a losing venture. Mr. Brooks removed the establishment to Elmira in January, 1873, where in company with Colonel James S. Thurston and P[hineas] C. Van Gelder he subsequently began the publication of a Republican Methodist temperance weekly called the *Southern Tier Leader*." (Leroy Wilson Kingman, *Our County and Its People. A Memorial History of Tioga County, N. Y.* [Elmira: W. A. Ferguson, 1897], p. 210.) *Loc*: NOwHi: F 23–D 28, 1872 (1:1–38). *See also* p. 290

THE AMERICAN CONSTELLATION (w) Union, Chenango. N 22, 1800–1803//(1:1–?). *Pub and Ed*: Daniel Cruger, Jr. N 1800–Ag 1803. *Format*: Four pages 10¼ " x 18". *Price*: $2.00 per year. For subscribers "who cannot pay in cash, merchantable winter wheat will be received in payment." *Comment*: Although the *Constellation* was dated "Union, Tioga County, New York" it was actually printed at Chenango Village, Tioga County, about one mile above the newer city of Binghamton. It was dated "Union" for that was the only post office in the area. Cruger moved the publication from Union to Owego, Tioga County in 1801. In 1803, he sold the paper to Henry Steward and

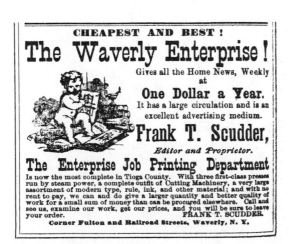

Stephen Mack who changed the name of the newspaper to the *American Farmer* which later became the *American Farmer and Owego Advertiser* (q.v.). *Loc*: NOwHi: S 12, 1801 (1:43).

AMERICAN FARMER see *AMERICAN FARMER AND OWEGO ADVERTISER*

AMERICAN FARMER AND OWEGO ADVERTISER (w) Owego Village. Ag 1803–1814 (1:1–?). *Title changes*: *American Farmer* Ag 1803–?; *American Farmer and Owego Advertiser* ?–1814. *Pub and Ed*: Stephen Mack and Henry Steward Ag 1803–F 1804; Stephen Mack F 1804–? *Pol*: Republican. *Format*: Four pages, varying sizes, 11″ x 18¼″, 13″ x 21″, 11″ x 17½″. *Comment*: Stephen Mack and Henry Steward bought the *American Constellation* newspaper and printing office from Daniel Cruger in 1803. "Some time previous to 1811, the name *American Farmer* was changed to *American Farmer and Owego Advertiser,* which name it bore until Judge Mack's death, in 1814." (Leroy Kingman, *Our County and its People,* p. 197.) Stephen Mack, publisher and editor was not a printer, but town supervisor and county judge. He died April 16, 1814. The newspaper office was located on the second floor of Stephen Mack's home on Front Street. The house was torn down in 1826. *Loc*: NBiHi: Ap 20, O 17, N 2, 16, 1808 (5:36, 6:10, 12, 14); D 18, 1811 (9:19); Ja 1, 1812 (9:21). NOwHi: Jl 23, 1806 (3:49); Mr 8, Jl 29, Ag 12, 1807 (4:31, 50, 52); F 8, 1809 (4[*sic*]:26); O 9, 1811 (9:9).

THE BLADE see *OWEGO WEEKLY BLADE*

CANDOR COURIER (w) Candor. Jl 20, 1899–S 29, 1966// (1:1–68:18). *Pub*: Hiram J. Beebe Jl 20, 1899–Ja 21, 1906; Ephraim A. & Will L. Beebe 1907; Will L. Beebe Ja 28, 1906–1934; C. Arthur Beebe 1935–1952; Robert Fox 1952–1956; William A. Muir 1956–S 29, 1966. *Ed*: Will L. Beebe Jl 20, 1899–1934; C. Arthur Beebe 1935–O 30, 1952; Frances Fox 1952–1956; William A. Muir N 8, 1956–S 29, 1966. *Pol*: Republican (1899–1952); Democrat (1952–1966). *Format*: Four to eight pages, varying sizes, 19¾″ x 26″, 15″ x 22″, 18″ x 24″, 20″ x 26½″, 12½″ x 17⅜″, 15″ x 24″, 8″ x 11½″. *Price*: $1.50 per year. *Comment*: Unable to compete with rising costs, the *Courier* folded on September 29, 1966 after 70 years of publication. William Muir stated "The country weekly is an anachronism, it doesn't have a place anymore." The *Courier* was sold to the Tioga Publishing Company and was incorporated into the *Tioga County Courier-Gazette* (q.v.). *Loc*: NCand: Jl 20, 1899–F 22, 1900 (1:1–32); My 12, 1900 (1:39); Mr 20, 1902 (3:36); [Jl 17, 1902–S 29, 1966 (4:1–68:18)]. NIC/RHA: Ja 27, 1920 (31:37); N 5, 1925 (27:20); [Ja 7, 1926–D 29, 1927 (27:29–29:29)]; N 1, D 13–27, 1928 (30:19, 26–28); Ja 3–Je 27, 1929 (30:29–31:4); Ag 7, 1941 (43:10).

CANDOR FREE PRESS (w) Candor. ?–Ap 8, 1873// (1:1–?) No issues located: "The first newspaper in Candor was established in 1867, and called the Candor *Press* [q.v.]. . . . The paper was subsequently sold to Benj. B. F. Graves, who changed its name to the Candor

Free Press. The office was burned in the night of April 8, 1873. Nothing was saved from the flames except a paper cutter." (Leroy Kingman, *Our County and Its People,* p. 217.)

CANDOR INDEPENDENT (w) Candor. O 7, 1876–D 1879// (1:1–?). No issues located. "The Candor *Independent* was founded by T. H. Pride. The first number appeared October 7, 1876. One side was printed in New York and the other in Candor. The paper was sold to W. H. Young, who published it until December, 1879, when he closed the office and removed the material to Owego, where he joined John McCormick in publishing the Owego *Blade.*" (Leroy Kingman, *Our County and Its People,* p. 217.)

CANDOR PRESS (w) Candor. O 9, 1867–? No issues located. "The first newspaper in Candor was established in 1867, and called the Candor *Press,* the first number being issued October 9. The proprietors were Samuel C. Clisbe and another printer named Manchester, the firm name being S. C. Clisbe & Co. The paper was subsequently sold to Benj. B. F. Graves, who changed its name to the Candor *Free Press* [q.v]." (Leroy Kingman, *Our County and Its People,* p. 217.)

CANDOR REVIEW (w) Candor. Mr 19, 1874–D 18, 1875// (1:1–?). No issues located. ". . . James D. Cameron and Ira L. Wales came from Owego and began the publication of the Candor *Review. . . .* The first number of the *Review* was issued March 19, 1874. Mr. Cameron withdrew from the paper in June, 1874. . . . The office was burned in the night of December 18, 1875, and as Wales was uninsured the paper was suspended indefinitely." (Leroy Kingman, *Our County and Its People,* p. 218.)

CANDOR STANDARD (w) Candor. Ja 22, 1885–Ag 1887// (1:1–?). No issues located. "John R. Beden issued the first number of the Candor *Standard* January 22, 1885, but publication was discontinued in August, 1887, for want of sufficient support." (Leroy Kingman, *Our County and Its People,* p. 217.)

DAILY FREE PRESS AND OWEGO DAILY RECORD (d, except Sunday) Owego, Waverly. D 20, 1886–Ja 19, 1911//(1:1–n.s. 2:279). *Title changes*: *Owego Daily Record* D 20, 1886–F 21, 1909; *Daily Free Press and Owego Daily Record* F 22, 1909–Ja 19, 1911. *Pub*: Clayton S. Scott and Odell J. Watros D 20, 1886–1907; Byram L. Winters 1907–Ja 19, 1911. *Ed*: Clayton S. Scott and Odell J. Watros 1886–1907; Odell J. Watros and Fred B. Appleget Je 24, 1907–Ap 2, 1908; G. E. and Ivan C. Purple and Fred B. Appleget Ap 9, 1908–1910; joined by Joseph B. Duff in 1909; G. E. and Ivan C. Purple D 7, 1910–Ja 19, 1911. *Pol*: Independent then Republican (1906–1911). *Format*: Four to twelve pages, varying sizes, 17″ x 21¾″, 15″ x 21″, 22″ x 27½″, 13½″ x 19½″, 19″ x 23½″. *Price*: $4.50 per year, 10¢ per week (1887); $3 per year (1908). *Circ*: 2,000 (1888); 4,000 (1911). *Comment*: Motto: "With Malice Toward None and the News for All." First published at Lake Street, Owego, then moved to Waverly at which time the title was changed to the *Daily Free Press and*

Owego Daily Record. This newspaper was the daily edition of *The Waverly Free Press and Tioga County Record* (q.v.). A *Daily Free Press* never existed as a separate newspaper title. *Loc*: NIC/MMN: [D 20, 1886–Ag 31, 1910 (1:1–n.s. 2:162)]. NOwHi: Jl 25, 1887 (1:182); F 4, 1888 (4:39); Ap 30, My 5, 1894 (8:110, 115); O 22, 1903 (17:257); N 15, 1904 (18:279); Ap 10, 1905 (19:94); Ag 2–6, 1909 (n.s. 1:137–141); Jl 5–6, 1910 (n.s. 2:113–114). NWav: [Jl 1, 1887–D 31, 1897 (1:103–12:10)]; S 1, 1910–Ja 19, 1911 (n.s. 2:163–279).

DAILY GAZETTE see *OWEGO DAILY GAZETTE*

DAILY NEWS AND ADVERTISER (d) Owego. O 1847–? (1:1–?). *Pub and Ed*: Andrew H. Calhoun. *Format*: Four pages 9¼" x 12¼". *Loc*: NOwHi: O 23, 26, 1847 (1:5, 7).

DAILY OWEGOAN (d) Owego. Ag 7–O 7, 1879 (1:1–?). No issues located. "The next attempt to found a daily newspaper in Owego was made by Dorsey B. Gibson. . . . His paper made its appearance August 7, 1879. It was called the *Daily Owegoan*. It was a poor thing and expired with its issue of Oct. 7, 1879." (Leroy Kingman, *Our County and Its People*, p. 212.)

THE ECHO (d) Waverly. N 18–D 1876//(1:1–?). No issues located. "The first attempt to establish a daily newspaper in Waverly was made by Ira L. Wales, who was publishing the weekly *Review*. The paper was called *The Echo*, and appeared November 18, 1876. Its publication ceased in December for want of support, after an existence of a little over two weeks." (Leroy Kingman, *Our County and Its People*, p. 217.)

EVENING JOURNAL see *WAVERLY ADVOCATE*

THE FAMILY JOURNAL AND TEMPERANCE ADVOCATE (w) Owego. Ja 18–F 15, 1879// (1:1–5). No issues located. "B. B. F. Graves . . . issued the first number of a temperance organ called *The Family Journal and Temperance Advocate*, Jan. 18, 1879. Only five numbers were published, the last one being issued Feb. 15, 1879." (Leroy Kingman, *Our County and Its People*, p. 211.)

THE GLEANER (w) Candor. Ag 11, 1892–? (1:1–?). *Pub and Ed*: Blackman and Co. (Rev. Arthur G. Bloomfield and Arthur Blackman) 1892–1893; Arthur G. Bloomfield 1893–1897; Arthur G. Bloomfield and Son 1897–?; Arthur R. Bloomfield. *Pol*: Temperance. *Format*: Four pages, varying sizes, 11" x 16", 18¼" x 24½", 13" x 20½". *Price*: $1.00 per year. *Loc*: NCand: My 11–Je 1, 1893 (1:40–43); Ag 23, 1894 (3:2); [Ja 2–D 24, 1896 (4:21–5:20)]; Ap 8, Je 24, S 2, 9, O 14, 1897 (5:35, 45; 6:3, 4, 9). NOwHi: Ag 18, 1892 (1:2).

THE HERALD (NEWARK VALLEY) see *TIOGA COUNTY HERALD*

THE LUMINARY see *WAVERLY LUMINARY*

NEWARK VALLEY HERALD see *TIOGA COUNTY HERALD*

NICHOLS NEWS (w) Nichols. S 4, 1890–F 19, 1891// (1:1–?). *Pub and Ed*: N. R. Teeple. *Format*: Four pages 14¾″ x 22″. *Price*: $1.25 per year. *Comment*: The town of Nichols and Mr. Teeple, a young New York lawyer, were apparently ill suited to each other. In his second number, September 11, 1890, Teeple tells his public: ". . . it is not your duty to kill the editor if the the paper is not liked, rather, an indignation meeting should be called." In its last issue, dated February 19, 1891, Mr. Teeple said he was "completely disgusted with the town" because of the "lack of public spirit" and that "he would shortly remove to a larger town . . . and he did." (Leroy Kingman, *Our County and Its People*, p. 219.) *Loc*: NNich/Burtis Everett: S 11, O 23, 1890 (1:2, 8).

THE NICHOLS RECORDER (w) Nichols. D 27, 1901–1908// (1:1–6:?). *Title changes*: *The Nichols Recorder* D 27, 1901–D 12, 1907; *Nichols Recorder and Agricultural Times* D 19, 1907; *The Nichols Recorder* D 26, 1907–1908. *Pub and Ed*: Frank H. Ross D 27, 1901–F 1907; Nichols Band and Hose Co. F 1907–?; J. Byron Dixon Ag 8, 1907–1908. *Pol*: Non-partisan. *Format*: Four pages, varying sizes, 11″ x 16″, 14¾″ x 22″, 17½″ x 24¼″. *Price*: $1.00 per year. *Circ*: 500 (1907). *Comment*: The December 19, 1907 issue, a special Christmas edition was titled the *Nichols Recorder and Agricultural Times*. It contained local history and biography. In it Editor Dixon explained that after Frank Ross left, the paper needed an editor and the Nichols Band needed someone to play some certain instrument. They advertised, and got J. Byron Dixon, who offered both talents. The *Recorder* merged with the *Waverly Sun* (q.v.) in 1908. *Loc*: NNich/John Edsall: D 19, 1907 (6:28). NNich/Burtis Everett: D 27, 1901 (1:1); Ja 24, Mr 7, N 21, 1902 (1:5, 11, 48); F 1, 1906 (5:7); F 20, D 19, 1907 (6:7, 28); F 6, 1908 (6:35).

NICHOLS RECORDER AND AGRICULTURAL TIMES see *THE NICHOLS RECORDER*

OLD HOME WEEK DAILY (d) Owego. Ag 2–7, 1909// (no series numbers). *Pub and Ed*: Betts and Brockway. *Format*: Four pages 12½″ x 19½″. *Comment*: Published at 210 Front Street. *Loc*: NOwHi: Ag 2–7, 1909 (no series numbers).

THE OWEGO ADVERTISER see *TIOGA COUNTY SUN-TIMES AND HERALD*

OWEGO AMERICAN (w) Owego. Ag 23–N, 1855// (1:1–?). No issues located. "Upon the outbreak of 'know Nothingism,' in 1855, Andrew H. Calhoun, who had been seventeen years editor of the Owego *Advertiser,* began the publication of a weekly newspaper in support of the new American party. It was called the Owego *American,* and its first number was issued August 23, 1855. . . . In the fall election this year Mr. Calhoun was the Know Nothing candidate for state senator and was defeated. After the election publication of the

American was discontinued." (Leroy Kingman, *Our County and Its People,* p. 207.)

THE OWEGO AND TIOGA COUNTY GAZETTE see *TIOGA COUNTY COURIER-GAZETTE*

THE OWEGO BLADE see *OWEGO WEEKLY BLADE*

OWEGO DAILY BLADE (d) Owego. N 4, 1882–Ap 23, 1887// (1:1–5:145). *Title changes*: *Owego Daily Blade* N 4, 1882–Mr 19, 1884; *Owego Evening Blade* Mr 20, 1884–Ja 7, 1885; *Owego Daily Blade* Ja 8, 1885–Ap 23, 1887. *Pub and Ed*: Eugene B. Gere N 4, 1882–Ap 23, 1887. *Pol*: Republican. *Format*: Four pages, varying sizes, 12¼ " x 19¼ ", 17½ " x 22½ ". *Loc*: NOwHi: [N 4, 1882–Ap 23, 1887 (1:1–5:145)].

THE OWEGO DAILY GAZETTE (d) Owego. My 27, 1861–O 1862// (1:1–2:140(?)). *Pub and Ed*: Hiram A. Beebe. *Pol*: Union Party. *Format*: Four pages 13" x 19". *Comment*: This was Beebe's third attempt at establishing a daily edition of the *Owego Gazette* (q.v.). "He believed that the anxiety of the people to obtain the latest news from the war between the north and the south, would create a demand for a daily paper sufficient to ensure its success. The news from the seat of war gave the paper a fair circulation, but it did not receive sufficient advertising patronage to make its publication profitable, and it was accordingly discontinued during the last week in October, 1861 [*sic*]." (Leroy Kingman, *Our County and Its People,* p. 212.) *Loc*: NIC/RHA: O 21, 1862 (2:140). NOwHi: Jl 16, 1861 (1:44).

OWEGO DAILY NEWS AND ADVERTISER see *DAILY NEWS AND ADVERTISER*

OWEGO DAILY PRESS (d) Owego. D 3, 1896–Ap 17, 1897// (1:1–?). No issues located. "The first number of the Owego *Daily Press* was issued December 3, 1896. Its publication was begun by C. E. Greenwood, R. P. Hogan, W. H. Smullen and C. N. Forsyth. It was discontinued with its issue of April 17, 1897." (Leroy Kingman, *Our County and Its People,* p. 213.)

OWEGO DAILY RECORD see *DAILY FREE PRESS AND OWEGO DAILY RECORD*

OWEGO EVENING BLADE see *OWEGO DAILY BLADE*

OWEGO FREE PRESS (w) Owego. S 2, 1828–? (1:1–?). *Pub and Ed*: Stephen S. Chatterton. *Pol*: Republican (Whig). *Format*: Four pages 21" x 25". *Comment*: Stephen Chatterton, publisher of the *Republican Chronicle* in Ithaca, started this paper in Owego in order to support Whig Candidates John Quincy Adams and Richard Rush for the presidency and vice-presidency. He published the *Gazette* in Ithaca at the *Republican and Chronicle* offices. The newspaper was discontinued shortly after the election but we cannot ascertain the exact date from the issues in hand. *Loc*: NOwHi: S 9, 23, 30, D 3, 10, 1828; Ja 14, 1829 (1:2, 5, 6, 16, 17, 21).

THE OWEGO GAZETTE 1814 see *TIOGA COUNTY COURIER-GAZETTE*

OWEGO GAZETTE (w) Owego. 1843–? (no series numbers). *Pub*: Thomas Woods. *Ed*: Gideon O. Chase. *Pol*: Democrat ("Barnburner" faction). *Format*: Four pages 16″ x 24″. *Comment*: This paper was one of two competing *Owego Gazettes* published simultaneously in 1843. At this time, the local Democratic party split into two factions, "Hunkers" and "Barnburners." To gain control of the *Gazette*, which was published by Hiram Beebe, a "Hunker," the Barnburners convinced Thomas Woods to foreclose the mortgage he held on the *Gazette* establishment. Beebe, however, had arranged to continue publishing from Calhoun's *Advertiser* office, so that for a period of weeks two *Owego Gazettes*, distinguished locally as "Wood's Gazette," and "Poor House Gazette," were published. Both papers claimed payment for the same legal advertising, and when the verdict of the courts awarded payment to Beebe, Woods discontinued publication and moved his presses to New Berlin. (Leroy Kingman, *Our County and Its People*, pp. 202 ff.) *Loc*: NOwHi: O 20, N 17, D 15, 1843 (no series numbers).

OWEGO PRESS (m) Owego. S 1886–Ag 1887// (1:1–12). *Pub*: Charles R. Burnette. *Format*: Four pages, varying sizes, 8″ x 10½″, 10″ x 13½″. *Comment*: Published at the Post Office Block, 34 Lake Street. "The first issue of the *Owego Press*, a small monthly newspaper, devoted to the interest of free schools, was published by Charles R. Burnette, the proprietor of a job printing office. It appeared September 1, 1886, and expired with its twelfth number." (Leroy Kingman, *Our County and Its People*, p. 211.) *Loc*: NOwHi: O 1886, My 1887 (1:2, 9).

OWEGO REPUBLICAN (w) Owego. S 19–N 1832// (1:1–?). *Pub and Ed*: Stephen S. Chatterton and C. O. Flynn. *Pol*: Whig. *Comment*: ". . . in the campaign of 1832, S. S. Chatterton and C. O. Flynn, who were publishers at Ithaca of the *Tompkins American*, to which name the *Republican and Chronicle* had been changed, established in Owego the *Owego Republican*, the first number of which was issued September 19, 1832. The *Republican* supported Henry Clay, the Whig candidate for president. This paper was printed in Ithaca, and its publication was suspended after election." (Leroy Kingman, *Our County and Its People*, p. 199.) *Loc*: NOwHi: O 17, 1832 (1:5).

OWEGO SOUTHERN TIER TIMES see *TIOGA COUNTY SUN-TIMES AND HERALD*

OWEGO TIMES see *TIOGA COUNTY SUN-TIMES AND HERALD*

THE OWEGO TIMES-TIOGA COUNTY HERALD see *TIOGA COUNTY SUN-TIMES AND HERALD*

OWEGO TRADE REPORTER Owego. 1868(?)–1871// (1:1–?). *Pub and Ed*: Charles H. Keeler. *Format*: Four pages, 11″ x 15½″.

Price: Free. *Comment*: Charles H. Keeler, who had been conducting a job printing office in Owego, published the *Owego Trade Reporter* as a small advertising sheet for free circulation. He converted the paper into a weekly newspaper, called the *Tioga County Herald* (q.v.) in 1871. *Loc*: NOwHi: Ag 1, 1869 (2:8).

OWEGO WEEKLY BLADE (w) Owego. Ja 1, 1880–Ap 22, 1887// (1:1–8:7). *Title changes*: *Owego Weekly Blade* Ja 1, 1880–F 10, 1882; *The Owego Blade* F 17, 1882–D 26, 1884; *Owego Blade* Ja 2, 1885–F 26, 1886; *Owego Weekly Blade* Mr 5, 1886–Ap 22, 1887. *Pub*: William H. Young and John McCormick Ja 1–D 1880; John McCormick D 1880–N 11, 1881; Eugene B. Gere and John McCormick N 18, 1881–1882; The Owego Blade Company (Eugene B. Gere, Pub.) F 17, 1882–Ap 22, 1887. *Ed*: William H. Young and John McCormick Ja 1, 1880–D 1880; John McCormick D 31, 1880–N 11, 1881; Eugene B. Gere N 18, 1881–Ap 22, 1887. *Pol*: Republican. *Format*: Four pages, varying sizes, 17" x 23½"; 19¾" x 25½", 15" x 21¾". *Comment*: "John McCormick who had been formerly in the *Times* office had obtained possession of the old *Workingman* plant. William H. Young, who had discontinued the publication of the *Independent* at Candor, removed his printing material to Owego and with two plants McCormick and Young launched their venture on the sea of journalism." (Leroy Kingman, *Our County and Its People*, p. 211.) No issues of the *Workingman* which first appeared in November 1877 or of the Candor *Independent* have been located in Tioga County. *Loc*: NOwHi [Ja 1, 1880–Ap 22, 1887 (1:1–8:7)].

OWEGO WEEKLY NEWS (w) Owego. Je 5, 1888–? (1:1–?). *Ed*: W. A. Bandler, George M. Dutcher, E. S. Johnson, Benjamin Powell. *Format*: Four pages 8½" x 12". *Comment*: Published at the *Owego Record* Office. *Loc*: NOwHi: Je 5–Jl 10, 1888 (1:1–6).

THE O-WE-GO-IN Owego. Mr 4, 1919–? (1:1–?). *Pub*: Citizens' Committee for the Organization of a Chamber of Commerce for Owego and Vicinity. *Format*: Four pages 8" x 12½". *Comment*: The *O-We-Go-In* was printed by the Job Department of the *Owego Gazette*. *Loc*: NOwHi: Mr 4, 1919 (1:1).

PROGRESS (m) Spencer. N 1886–?// (1:1–?). No issues located. "Vol. 1, No. 1, of *Progress*, a monthly journal devoted to schools, appeared at Spencer in November, 1886. William W. Abbott was 'editor-in-chief.' It was short lived." (Leroy Kingman, *Our County and Its People*, p. 219.)

THE RESOLUTE (w) Owego. Ap 12, 1879–N 8, 1879// (1:1–?). No issues located. "*The Resolute*, another temperance organ, followed the *Advocate*. It was published by a company of which John L. Matson, John J. Hooker, and Van Ness Russell were the trustees. The company purchased the old *Workingman* plant. The first issue was dated April 12, 1879. It expired peacefully with its issue of Nov. 8, 1879. G. M. Jordan was at first its editor, and afterward it was published by Jordan and G. W. Tyson." (Leroy Kingman, *Our County and Its People,* p. 211.)

SOUTHERN TIER TIMES see *TIOGA COUNTY SUN-TIMES AND HERALD*

SPENCER HERALD see *SPENCER TOWN NEWS*

SPENCER NEEDLE (w) Spencer. Ja 5, 1888 to date (1:1–to date). *Pub and Ed*: William R. Swartout Ja 5, 1888–D 8, 1892; George M. Pashley D 15, 1892–Ap 1, 1899; John A. Bell Ap 8, 1899–Ja 8, 1903; Jesse R. Hart Ja 15, 1903–Mr 19, 1943; Hart I. Seely Mr 26, 1943–1945; Spencer Needle, Inc. (L. Cleone Horton, Ed. 1951–Ja 3, 1952) Mr 1945–1952; Alice B. Pope Ja 10–S 18, 1952; Robert R. Eckert S 25, 1952–Mr 1953; Harold Wilcox Mr 1953–Mr 4, 1954; Peter P. Jankowski Mr 11, 1954 to date. *Pol*: Independent, then Republican (1943), then Independent (1954). *Format*: Four to ten pages, varying sizes, 14½" x 21½", 17½" x 23", 13" x 19½", 12½" x 18½", 17½" x 22", 12" x 18". *Price*: $1.00 per year (1888–1917); $1.50 per year (1917); $2.00 per year (1944); $2.50 per year (1954). *Circ*: 2,250 (1969). *Comment*: The *Needle* was first published in the rear lot of Charles A. Seely's residence (1888–1892), then at the Post Building, Corner of Main and Tioga Streets (December 29, 1892), then the Day Building, Corner of Main and Tioga Streets (January 11, 1894), the Needle Building, between Fisher's Store and the E. C. and N. Depot (August 22, 1895), and finally, the Emmon's Block, 13 Main Street, South, its present address. *Loc*: NIC/RHA: S 6, 1923 (36:35); [Ap 26–Ja 31, 1946 (58:17–59:5)]; [Ap 26–D 27, 1945 (58:17–52)]; Ja 3, 17–31, 1946 (59:1, 3–5). NSpe: Ja 3, 1889–D 29, 1921 (2:1–34:52); Ja 6, 1927–D 25, 1941 (40:1–54:52); Ja 7, 1943–D 26, 1946 (56:1–59:52); Ja 1–D 30, 1948 (61:1–53); Ja 5, 1950–Ja 25, 1951 (63:1–64:4); Ja 7, 1954–D 25, 1969 (67:1–81:52). NSpe/Theresa Cortright: Ag 2, 1888 (1:31); Jl 24, 1890 (3:30); Jl 26, 1900 (13:30); Je 28, 1906 (19:26); F 6, 1908 (22:6); Je 11, 1942 (55:24); Mr 18, 25, 1943 (56:11, 12). NSpe/Payne Museum: [O 16–D 25, 1902 (15:42–52)]; [Ja 1–D 24, 1914 (27:1–36 [*sic*]:52)]; Jl 13, 1922 (35:28); My 10, 1923 (36:19); Ap 10, 1924 (37:14); O 14, D 9, 1926 (39:41, 48); F 2, 1928 (41:2); Mr 24, Je 2, 1949 (62:12, 22); Ja 18–F 1, Ap 26, N 29, D 13, 1951 (64:3–5, 17, 48, 50); Ja 10, N 27, D 18, 24, 1952 (65:2, 47, 50–51); F 6, 1953–D 30, 1954 (66:6–67:52); Ap 5, 1962 (74:14); [Mr 11–O 14, 1965 (77:10–41)]. NSpe/Alice B. Pope: [Ja 10–S 25, 1952 (65:2–38)].

SPENCER NEWS (w) Spencer. F 27, 1947–Ja 2, 1952// (1:1–5:44). *Pub*: Frank Masters 1947–1948; Raymond S. Schoonover 1948–1949; Louis D. Riker 1949–Jl 19, 1951; Alice B. Pope Jl 26, 1951–Ja 2, 1952. *Ed*: Frank Masters 1947–1948; Louis D. Riker 1948–Ja 11, 1951; Alice B. Pope Ja 18, 1951–Ja 2, 1952. *Pol*: Independent "but admit to slight list to the Republican side of things" (*Spencer News,* Jl 26, 1951). *Format*: Four to eight pages, varying sizes, 13" x 20", 12¾" x 18½". *Price*: $1.00 per year. *Comment*: "In January of 1952, the Popes (Alice and Theodore) purchased the *Spencer Needle* subscription list and name from the Seely family in Waverly and, as 'Oddie' Pope wrote in the columns of the newly merged paper, the *'Spencer Needle* came home in a physical sense—home to the plant which the late J. R. Hart helped to build with his own hands and which he himself edited for 47 years.' 'With the merger, the Popes returned to the old name, *"Spencer Needle,"* and the paper was indeed "home again!" ' " (*Spencer Needle,* Jan. 1952). *Loc*: NOwHi: F 27, Mr 6, 1947 (1:1, 2). NSpe/Payne Museum: [Mr 3–D 1, 1949 (3:2–41)]; Ja 25, Ap 26, 1951 (4:47; 5:8). NSpe/Alice B. Pope; [Ja 18, 1951–Ja 2, 1952 (4:46–5:44)].

SPENCER TOWN NEWS (w) Spencer. Ag 22, 1878–N 1894// (1:1–?). *Title changes*: *The Spencer Herald* Ag 22, 1878–1894; *Spencer Town News* 1894–N 1894. *Pub and Ed*: F. H. Pride and F. E. Foote Ag 22–N 1878; F. E. Foote N 1878–1880; J. Leroy Nixon 1880–1887; Phineas C. Van Gelder 1887–?; Phineas C. Van Gelder and Son (F. C. Van Gelder, ed.) 1888–1890; W. W. Wisegarver 1890–1891; Phineas C. Van Gelder 1891; Dr. Paul W. Burge 1891–N 1894. *Format*: Four pages, varying sizes, 17" x 23", 13" x 20". *Price*: $1.25 per year. *Comment*: Published at the Emmon's Block over the furniture store. Since only two issues have been located information on publishers and editors, and on changes in title have been taken from an article in the *Spencer Needle* January 9, 1959. *Loc*: NOwHi: Ja 2, 1879 (1:20). NSpe/Payne Museum: D 13, 1888 (10:50).

TIMES-HERALD see *THE TIOGA COUNTY SUN-TIMES AND HERALD*

TIOGA AND BRADFORD DEMOCRAT (w) Waverly. Ja 7, 1863–? (1:1–?). *Pub*: Francis H. Baldwin Ja 7, 1863–O 6, 1864; John McCormick O 13, 1864–?. *Ed*: Francis H. Baldwin Ja 7, 1863–? *Pol*: Democrat. *Format*: Four pages 18" x 23". *Price*: $1.50 per year (1863); $2.00 per year (1864). *Comment*: Published at the corner of Broad and Fulton Streets. The October 13, 1864 issue of the *Democrat* announced the sale of the paper to John McCormick. However, Baldwin's name remained on the masthead as editor and proprietor while John McCormick was listed as publisher. *Loc*: NWav: [Ja 7, 1863–D 22, 1864 (1:1–2:41)].

TIOGA COUNTY COURIER-GAZETTE see *TIOGA COUNTY GAZETTE & TIMES*

TIOGA COUNTY GAZETTE & TIMES (w) Owego. Je 15, 1814 to date. (1:1 to date). *Title changes*: *The Owego Gazette* Je 14, 1814–F 3, 1839; *The Owego and Tioga County Gazette* F–N 1, 1839; *The Owego Gazette* N 7, 1839–Ag 23, 1967; *Tioga County Courier-Gazette* Ag 28, 1967–Ag 25, 1971; *Tioga County Gazette & Times* S 1, 1971 to date. *Pub*: Stephen B. Leonard Je 15, 1814–O 1827, 1829–1831, 1831–1833; Stephen B. Leonard and Jonas B. Shurtleff O 1827–O 13, 1829; Stephen B. Leonard and Cook 1831; Stephen B. Leonard and John J. C. Cantine 1833–1835; Jonas B. Shurtleff and

Bull 1835–1836; Jonas B. Shurtleff 1836; Jonas B. Shurtleff and John Frank 1837–1838; Jonas B. Shurtleff 1838–1839; Edward P. Marble 1839–1841; Charles C. Thomas (Alanson Munger, Ed.) Jl 15–D 1842; Hiram A. Beebe Ja 1843–Jl 13, 1845; Thomas Pearsall Jl 26, 1845–1846; Stephen B. Leonard until Mr 27, 1846; David Wallis and E. F. Wallis Mr 28, 1846–O 22, 1847; Hiram A. Beebe O 29, 1847–1868; Hiram A. Beebe and Bolton 1868–1869; Hiram A. Beebe 1869–Ag 17, 1871; Hiram A. Beebe O 29, 1847–1868; Hiram A. Beebe and Bolton (Hiram A. Beebe, Ed.) 1868–1869; Hiram A. Beebe 1869–Ag 17, 1871; Hiram A. Beebe and Leroy W. Kingman Ag 24, 1871–Ag 25, 1880; Leroy W. Kingman (also shown as the Gazette Co., Leroy Kingman, Pres.) S 23, 1880–D 18, 1947; The Owego Gazette, Inc. (Dana S. Johnston, Pres., M. L. Whittenberger, Vice-Pres. and Gen. Mgr.) 1948–Jl 3, 1968; Tioga County Publishing Co., Inc. (owned by the Owego Gazette Inc., Dana S. Johnston, Pres. 1968 to date; John A. Mehaffey, Vice-Pres. and Pub. Jl 10, 1968–Ag 13, 1969; Lewis P. Fons, General Mgr. Ag 20 1969–Mr 25, 1970; Duane O. Short, General Mgr. D 29, 1971 to date) Ag 7, 1968 to date. *Ed*: Same as publishers until 1948, then Henry E. Kingman. Ja 8–N 25, 1948; Thomas Y. Funston D 2, 1942–N 10, 1949; L. Neil Brown N 17, 1949–Ag 31, 1950; James R. Raftis S 7, 1950–?; Jack Beisner Jl 2, 1958–Jl 1966; William Muir Jl 1966–Jl 25, 1967; M. L. Whittenberger Ag 1, 1967–Jl 3, 1968; John A. Mehaffey Jl 10, 1968–Ag 13, 1969; Lewis P. Fons Ag 20–S 3, 1969; Cynthia E. Hathaway S 10–D 10, 1969; Cynthia E. Kourt D 17, 1969–Mr 4, 1970; Clifford R. Towner Ap 1, 1970–S 1, 1971; Lewis P. Fons S 8–D 22, 1971; Clifford R. Towner D 29, 1971 to date. *Pol*: Democrat (1814–1967); Independent Republican (1971 to date). *Format*: Four to sixteen pages, varying sizes, 19″ x 22″, 12″ x 21″, 15½″ x 23½″, 22″ x 28″, 20″ x 26½″, 10″ x 14½″, 17″ x 23″. *Price*: $2.00 per year (1877); $1.50 per year (1892); $2.00 per year (1951); $5.00 per year, 10¢ per copy (1967); $6.00 per year, 15¢ per copy (1971 to date). *Circ*: 3,700 (1971). *Comment*: Motto: "An Independent Democratic Newspaper" (1967); "An Independent Newspaper" (1971); "An Independent Republican Newspaper" (S 22, 1971). "Official Newspaper of Tioga County, the Town of Tioga, Town and Village of Candor." Stephen Leonard who had purchased half an interest in the *American Farmer* in 1813 did not work on this paper, but returned to Albany in 1813 or 1814. When he read of Judge Mack's death in 1814, returned to Owego, purchased the paper and changed the name of the paper immediately to the *Owego Gazette*. The newspaper was first published in 1814 at the Pumpelly Block, second story, over John Hollenback's store. Then, in 1821, the paper was published on Front Street. In the 1830s it was moved to an office on the third story of the Exchange Block. In 1836 the newspaper moved to the second story of a building in which Mr. Shurtleff had a general country store on the first floor. This building was deliberately burned down in 1837, and the *Gazette* was wiped out. Edward Marble revived the press and re-established the *Gazette* at the second story of the Rollin Block on Lake and Front Streets. In 1841, Charles Thomas moved the office to the third story of Carmichael's new brick building in 1843. In 1849 fire destroyed the *Gazette* again and then Beebe moved it to the red brick building in the northeast corner of Lake and Front Streets. The office moved several times until Beebe built the Gazette block on the east side of Lake Street to which the office was moved in 1867 and where it is still located. The Tioga Publishing Co. purchased the *Candor Courier* (q.v.) in 1966, incorporated it into *The Owego Gazette* and issued both papers as the *Tioga County Courier-Gazette*. In September 1971 the *Tioga County Courier-Gazette* and the *Tioga County Sun-Times and Herald* (q.v.) were merged and the consolidation called the *Tioga County Gazette & Times*. *Loc*: NIC/RHA: Ja 21, 1817 (3:33); [Ja 7–D 29, 1864 (51:22–52:21)]; [D 10, 1931–S 23, 1937 (no series nos.)]; N 4, 1970–Mr 17, 1971 (170:49–171:14). NOwHi: D 14, 1814–Je 6, 1815 (1:27–52); [Ja 19, 1819–O 8, 1829 (5:33–27:10)]; F 9, My 18, D 13, 1830 (27:27, 40; 28:1); Mr 2, 9, 1831 (28:28, 29); D 30, 1836 (24 [sic]: 14); [Ja 18, 1837 to date (25:17 to date)]. NSpe/Payne Museum: N 29, D 20, 1877 (65:19, 20); Ja 3, 1878 (65:24); Ja 2, 1879 (66:24).

TIOGA COUNTY GREENBACKER Owego. Ag 22, 1878// (1:1). No issues located. "George F. Cameron, who was proprietor of a news office in Lake Street, published one number of the *Tioga County Greenbacker*. It appeared Aug. 22, 1878." (Leroy Kingman, *Our County and Its People*, p. 211.)

TIOGA COUNTY HERALD (w, semi-w, w) Newark Valley. Mr 4, 1876–Ag 1966// (1:1–?). *Pub and Ed*: Charles L. Noble 1879–?; S. P. More and G. E. Purple 1890; Ivan C. Purple 1896–1897, 1905–1931; G. E. Purple 1897, 1901–1904, 1907; A. L. Sherman and L. A. Worden 1909–1910; Grace B. Allen 1944–1945; Grace B. and Lloyd C. Allen 1946–1957. *Pol*: Independent Republican. *Format*: Four to eight pages, varying sizes, 15″ x 22″, 18″ x 23½″. *Comment*: Published from an office in the Hess Block (1881). The *Tioga County Herald* merged with the *Owego Times* (q.v.) on September 2, 1966, and became the *Times-Herald* (q.v.). This newspaper, according to Kingman, constituted "The first attempt to establish a newspaper at Newark Valley. . . . March 4, 1876, George M. Jordan, a harness maker who had dabbled in journalism in Owego, removed to Newark Valley, and in company with George Riley, Jr., a practical printer, issued the first number of the Newark Valley *Herald*. . . . In May, 1876, Riley sold his interest to Henry A. LeBarron, of Union. August 25, 1877, Charles L. Noble purchased LeBarron's interest, and January 1, 1878, became sole proprietor. *Loc*: NCortHi: O 8, 1887 (12: 32). NIC/MMN: S 24, 1881 (6:30); Jl 8, 1882 (7:19); Mr 8, 1890 (15:1); F 28, 1902 (26:52); N 20, 1903 (28:38). NIC/RHA: D 20, 1901 (26:42); F 8, 1907 (31:50); Jl 13, 1909 (34:30); Jl 15, 1910 (35:40); [My 16, 1924–F 27, 1925 (56:11–53 [sic]:52)]; Mr 5, 1926 (58:1); Ag 11–S 1, S 15–29, 1944 (74:23–26, 23–30); My 1, 1953 (83:9). NOwHi: Jl 5, 1879 (4:19); S 30, 1882 (7:31); S 4, 1896 (21:26); D 17, 1897 (22:42); S 8, 1905 (30:27); S 14, 1928 (60:29); My 1, 8, 22, 1931 (63:9, 10, 12); Ja 18, 1946 (75:46); D 20, 1949 (79:44); My 25, 1955 (85:4); Ja 4, 1957 (86:44).

TIOGA COUNTY RECORD (w) Owego. Mr 18, 1871–Ja 17, 1907//
(1:1–34:46). *Pub and Ed*: Charles H. Keeler 1871–1885; Clayton S.
Scott and Odell J. Watros 1885–? *Pol*: Neutral. *Format*: Four pages,
varying sizes, 20″ x 26″, 22″ x 27″. *Price*: $1.00 per year in advance,
$1.50 per year otherwise. *Circ*: 500 (1871); 1,500 (1879). *Comment*:
The newspaper was published in the Record Block in 1881. The
Tioga County Record merged with the *Waverly Free Press* on January
25, 1907 to become *The Waverly Free Press and Tioga County Rec-*
ord (q.v.) *Loc*: NIC/MMN: Ag 8, 1885–Ja 17, 1907 (15:22–36:46).
NIC/RHA: Je 11, 1881 (11:13); Jl 11, 1889 (19:20). NOwHi: My
10, 1888 (18:10). NWav: [Mr 8, 1888–Mr 4, 1897 (18:1–26:52)].

TIOGA COUNTY SUN-TIMES AND HERALD (w) Owego. Mr 17,
1836–Ag 27, 1971// (1:1–136:17). *Title changes: The Owego Ad-*
vertiser Mr 17, 1836–My 1853; *Southern Tier Times* Je 2, 1853–Ap
5, 1854; *Owego Southern Tier Times* Ap 12, 1854–My 31, 1855;
Owego Times Je 7, 1855–Ag 26, 1966; *Owego Times-Tioga County*
Herald S 2, 1966–Ag 25, 1967; *Tioga County Times-Herald* S 1,
1967–O 30, 1970; *Tioga County Sun-Times and Herald* N 6, 1970–
Ag 27, 1971. *Pub*: Andrew Hamilton Calhoun Mr 17, 1836–ca. 1849;
Andrew Hamilton Calhoun and son 1849–1852; Myron S. Barnes
1853–?; William Smyth 1854–1872; William Smyth and Son Ja 1873–
My 1899; William Smyth My 1899–S 1919; Stuart Worthington Smyth
S 1919–S 1941; Owego Times, Inc. O 2, 1941–D 15, 1953; Tioga Pub-
lishing Co. D 22, 1953 to date. *Ed*: Same as publishers until O 2,
1941, then: Jack Bartlett O 2, 1941–Mr 15, 1945; Paul L. Hooper Mr
22, 1945–Ja 24, 1946; Laverne N. English F 21, 1946–Ja 30, 1947;
Charles Mathews F 6, 1947–F 23, 1950; Alan J. Tucker, Jr. Ag 10,
1950–F 25, 1956; Jack Bartlett Mr 1956–Ap 8, 1966; Jack Beisner
Ap 15, 1966–1968?; John A. Mehaffey Ag 9, 1958–Ag 15, 1969; Cynthia E. Hathaway S 19–D 12, 1969; Cynthia E. Kourt D 19, 1969–
D 1970; Clifford R. Towner Mr 27–D 1970; Lewis P. Fons Ja 1, 1971
to date. *Pol*: Whig, then Republican. *Format*: Four to fourteen pages,
varying sizes, 18½″ x 23½″, 19½″ x 24½″, 15″ x 21″, 20½″ x 27″,
19½″ x 26″, 22½″ x 29½″, 17½″ x 23″. *Price*: $1.00 per year
(1863); $1.50 per year (1864); $5.00 per year, 10¢ per copy (1968);
$6.00 per year (1970). *Comment*: Motto: "Officially designated Re-
publican newspaper for Tioga County." Prior to the establishment of
the *Owego Advertiser,* two other Whig papers had appeared in Owego,
namely the *Owego Free Press* (q.v.) and the *Owego Republican* (q.v.)
both of which supported Whig candidates for the presidency and were
discontinued after the election. Andrew Hamilton Calhoun was another Whig supporter. He first published the *Advertiser* from the second floor of Jonathan Platt and Ely's Brick Building, directly opposite
the Post Office. About 1847 the office moved to the Rollin Block, Lake
Street. Their office burned in 1849 and they moved to the third story
of the Village Hall, number 853. In 1855 they were in the third story
of Chatfield's Brick Building on the corner of Main and Ithaca Streets,
which building was later known as Thurston's Brick Block. In 1864,
it was moved to Taylor's Brick Block at the northeast corner of Main

and North Avenues, then to the Times Block in 1902, and to the Times Building in 1904. It is currently published at 28 Lake Street. Between 1855 and 1856 the newspaper could not settle on a name and was called the *Owego Weekly Times, Owego Times,* etc. "Two newspapers published in Owego as competetors for 135 years have been merged into one which will be published every Wednesday starting next week [September 1, 1971] the 135 year-old *Owego Times* and the 171 year-old *Owego Gazette* will combine to be published as the *Tioga County Gazette & Times* starting next week. The two separate newspapers had, in recent years, both been published by The Tioga Publishing Co., Inc. which will continue to publish the combined newspaper. The newspapers are among the four oldest newspapers in New York state being published today. . . ." (Ag 27, 1971, *Tioga County Sun-Times and Herald,* p. 1.) *Loc*: NIC/MMN: S 9, 1858; Je 9, Jl 21, 1859; S 22, 1881; Ja 15, 1891; Ag 3, 1926; Ap 26, 1927; [N 1, 1927–N 3, 1936 (4:33–84:34)]; N 6, 1970–Mr 19, 1971 (135: 27–46). NOwHi: [Mr 17, 1836–Mr 30, 1837 (1:1–2:2)]; [Ja 5, 1843– N 9, 1848 (7:44–13:37)]; [Ap 11, 1850–D 30, 1852 (15:2–17:4)]; [Je 8, 1854–Ag 27, 1971 (2 [*sic*]–136:17)]. NSpe/Payne Museum: O 29, N 5, 1863 (11:21, 22); F 11, Ag 25, 1864 (11:36; 12:12); O 28, 1908 (56:28); F 23, 1911 (58:16); S 3, 1917 (62:21); D 2, 23, 1920 (68:35, 38).

THE TIOGA FREEMAN (w) Owego. My 1848–S 1850//. *Pub*: John Dow. *Ed*: Gideon O'Lima Chase. *Pol*: "Free Soil" faction of the Democratic Party. *Format*: Four pages 17½ " x 23". Motto: "Here shall the Press the people's rights maintain, unawed by influence and unbribed by gain." "In the spring of 1848, there was another division in the democratic party of this state, which resulted in the establishment in Owego of the *Tioga Freeman,* the organ of the "Free Soil" faction of the party, the first number of which appeared May 2. It was owned by a stock company, composed of Judge C. P. Avery, Judge Thomas Farrington, John J. Sackett, Gideon O. Chase, and others, many of whom had been members of the "Barnburner" faction in 1843. John Dow was publisher and Mr. Chase the editor . . . through lack of business ability on the part of the management the paper proved unprofitable . . . [and] in September, 1850, publication was discontinued . . ." (Leroy Kingman, *Our County and Its People,* p. 208.) The paper was first published over Charles Pumpelly's store, a wooden building, until a fire in 1849. *The Tioga Freeman* was then moved to Front Street and then to Main Street over Fay's Drug Store. *Loc*: NOwHi: Jl 19, S 13, N 22, 1848 (1:11, 19, 29).

THE WAVERLY ADVOCATE (w) Waverly. S 17, 1852–D 31, 1901// (1:1–?). *Pub*: Francis H. Baldwin S 17, 1852–1853; M. H. Bailey 1853; Francis H. Baldwin and William Polleys 1854(?)–N 30, 1850; William H. Polleys and Oliver Hazard Perry Kinney D 7, 1860– Mr 7, 1884; E. M. Fenner and Co. O 2, 1884–Je 1885(?); Wellar and Shear(?) Je 1885–N 1885(?); E. H. Vincent(?) N 1885–1888; Francis M. Perley 1888–N 1894(?); Charles E. Currie and Harry W. Romer(?) N 1894–1896; Charles E. Currie(?) 1896–?; Dickinson and Gaudy ca. 1898–? *Ed*: Francis H. Baldwin S 17, 1852–?; Baldwin and Polleys 1854(?)–N 30, 1860; Oliver Hazard Perry Kinney D 7, 1860–Ja 25, 1884; George D. Genung F 1, 1884–Ag 1884; E. M. Fenner Ag 1884–?; Dickinson and Gaudy ca. 1898. *Pol*: Originally Independent then Republican by 1858. *Format*: Four pages, varying sizes, 17½" x 22¾", 19¾" x 25", 20½" x 26½", 14" x 21". *Price*: $1.50 per year (1852); $1.00 per year (1879); 50¢ per year (1898). *Circ*: 1,200 (1879). *Comment*: Motto: "One Constitution, One Country, One Destiny." The newspaper was published at Spalding's Block, South Side of Broad Street (1852); Empire Block, Broad Street, opposite Davis' Hall (1858); Davis Block, under Davis Hall (1864); S. E. Corner, Broad and Clark Streets (September 1, 1865); Van Duzer's Block, Broad Street (March 13, 1868); Advocate Block, Broad Street (April 1870); Post Office Block, Fulton Street (November 20, 1874). The early issues of 1898 carried neither volume nor issue numbers. According to an editorial in the *Waverly Free Press* of January 4, 1902, *The Advocate* "suspended publication last Tuesday [the end of December 1901]. The paper was sold to Harry E. Green of New York, who did not intend to continue publishing." *Loc*: NIC/MMN: S 17, 1852–S 9, 1853 (1:1–52); [Ja 8, 1858–D 25, 1868 (6:17–17:21)]. NIC/RHA: Ag 19, 1881 (29:34). NOwHi: N 20, 1857 (6:10); [Ap 16, 1858–S 5, 1862 (6:31–10:51)]; Ap 8, Ag 26, 1870 (18:33, 52); My 19, 1876 (24:30); Mr 14, 1891 (extra edition). NWav: [Ja 8, 1869–O 2, 1884 (17:23–33:29)]; Ja 4–D 30, 1898 (no series no.–50:4).

WAVERLY ADVOCATE Waverly. S 1895–My 29, 1897// (1:1–?). No issues located. "The first number of the Waverly *Evening Journal* was issued August 1, 1895, by a combination of the forces of the *Advocate* and *Tribune*. C. E. Currie, of the *Advocate*, was business manager. . . . Mr. Alvord sold his interest to his partners in September, 1895, and the name of the paper was changed to the *Advocate*. Its publication was discontinued May 29, 1897." (Leroy Kingman, *Our County and Its People*, p. 217.)

WAVERLY AND ATHENS DEMOCRAT Waverly. 1867–1870// (1:1–?). No issues located. "The publication of the *Waverly and Athens Democrat* was begun at Waverly by David P. Schultz in the winter of 1867. A year afterward Samuel C. Clisbe became his partner, but remained only a few months. The paper died a natural death in 1870, and the printing material was sold to the *Advocate*." (Leroy Kingman, *Our County and Its People*, p. 215.)

WAVERLY DAILY REVIEW (d) Waverly. Ap 4–16, 1881// (1:1–12). *Pub and Ed*: Ira L. Wales. *Format*: Four pages 14½" x 21¼". *Comment*: Ira L. Wales, publisher of the *Waverly Review* (q.v.) announced that this would be a two weeks daily to "cover the sessions of the Wyoming conference." (*Waverly Daily Review*, Ap 16, 1881) *Loc*: NWav: Ap 4–16, 1881 (1:1–12).

WAVERLY DEMOCRAT (w) Waverly. Jl 4–N 1892// (1:1–?).

No issues located. ". . . Mr. Campbell had purchased in New York on credit a new press and materials and had made arrangements to print a new democratic paper in Waverly. The new venture was called the Waverly *Democrat*. The first number appeared July 4, 1894. Its existence under the circumstances was naturally brief. It was published four months, until the close of the fall campaign, when the bills for material, etc., became due. Its suspension was announced the week before the election in November." (Leroy Kingman, *Our County and Its People,* pp. 216–217.)

THE WAVERLY ENTERPRISE (m, semi-m, w) Waverly. O 15, 1867–O 5, 1876// (1:1–9:?). *Pub and Ed*: Frank T. Scudder 1867–1875; Phineas C. Van Gelder 1875–1876; Phineas C. Van Gelder and Amos Roberts 1876; Amos Roberts and J. A. Fraser Jl–O 5, 1876. *Pol*: Neutral. *Format*: Four pages 13" x 19¼". *Price*: $1.00 per year. *Comment*: "At first the *Enterprise* was a monthly paper, but December 15, 1869, was changed to a semi-monthly. January 1, 1871 it was again changed to a weekly . . . October 5, 1876 the office was burned. The presses and materials were insured for $5,000, which about covered the loss. After the destruction of the *Enterprise* office, its former foreman, James B. Bray, who had been conducting a job printing office in Waverly, purchased the subscription list and good will of the concern and began printing a new independent republican weekly called the *Waverly Free Press* (q.v.)." (Leroy Kingman, *Our County and Its People,* pp. 215–216.) The newspaper was published at the Exchange Block over Sawyer's Bank; then at Scudder's Steam Printing House at Fulton and Railroad Streets. *Loc*: NOwHi: O 14, 1871 (4:40). NWav: Ja 7, 1871–My 11, 1872 (4:1–5:19).

WAVERLY EVENING JOURNAL Waverly. Ag 1–S 1895// (1:1–?) No issues located. "The first number of the Waverly *Evening Journal* was issued August 1, 1895, by a combination of the forces of the *Advocate* and *Tribune*. C. E. Currie, of the *Advocate,* was business manager. It was a four page, six column folio. Mr. Alvord sold his interest to his partners in September, 1895, and the name of the paper was changed to the *Advocate* [q.v.]." (Leroy Kingman, *Our County and Its People,* p. 217.)

THE WAVERLY FREE PRESS see *THE WAVERLY FREE PRESS AND TIOGA COUNTY RECORD*

THE WAVERLY FREE PRESS AND TIOGA COUNTY RECORD (w) Waverly. N 22, 1876–Jl 1915// (1:1–no series no. 9:27). *Title changes*: *The Waverly Free Press* 1876–Ja 18, 1907; *The Waverly Free Press and Tioga County Record* Ja 25, 1907–? *Pub*: James B. Bray N 22, 1876–D 19, 1877, Ja 1878–N 1, 1890; Cyrus W. Marsh D 1877–Ja 1878 (2 weeks only); Free Press Publishing Co. N 8, 1890–F 27, 1892; Bernard Gordon and George G. Pendell Mr 5–Ap 2, 1892; George G. Pendell Ap 1892–O 20, 1896; George D. Genung and Clayton Smith O 27, 1896–O 5, 1906; Fred B. Appleget O 12, 1906–Je 14, 1907; Byram L. Winters Je 21, 1907–? *Ed*: James B.

Bray N 22, 1876–Ja 1890; James B. Bray and Bernard Gordon Ja 1890–F 27, 1892; Bernard Gordon and George G. Pendell Mr 5–Ap 2, 1892; Charles D. Pendell Ap 9, 1892–Jl 14, 1894; George D. Genung Jl 21, 1894–O 5, 1906; Fred B. Appleget O 12, 1906–D 20, 1907; Byram L. Winters D 27, 1907–? *Pol*: Republican. *Format*: Four to twelve pages, varying sizes, 14″ x 21″, 10¾″ x 15¾″, 12½″ x 19¾″, 15″ x 22″. *Price*: $1.00 per year (1876); 35¢ per year (1879); 40¢ per year (1889); 50¢ per year (1882); 75¢ per year (1904); $1.00 per year (1907); $1.25 per year (1909); $1.50 per year (1911). *Circ*: 1,900 (1891); 2,330 (1896); 3,000 (1899); 5,100 (1907). *Comment*: Motto: "Independent—Not a Clam by any Means." The paper was published from the corner of Fulton and Elizabeth Streets (1877), then the Weatherly Block, over Unger's Tobacco Store on North Side of Broad Street (August 31, 1878). It then moved to 70 North Broad Street over Van Velsor and Co.'s Clothing Store in 1882 and then to the Free Press Building, 15 Fulton Street just above the Post Office opposite Tioga Hotel (1884); "opposite Opera House" in 1895. In 1901 the newspaper was listed at 29 Fulton Street and in 1907 at the Manoca Temple, on the Corner of Fulton and Elizabeth Streets. Two major changes in numbering sequence occurred: the first in 1880 when James Bray, who had purchased the *Waverly Enterprise* subscription list in 1876, adopted the *Enterprise* as predecessor, along with its heritage of years, so that Vol. 4 became Vol. 15; the second in 1907, when Fred Appleget abandoned his double numbering (one each for the *Waverly Free Press* and the *Tioga County Record*), and started a new series for the consolidated paper (March 29, 1907, 1:10) with the tenth number of Vol. 1. *The Free Press* consolidated with the *Tioga County Record* on January 25, 1907. The plant was advertised for sale on May 28th, 1915, and the last issue was probably that of July 2, 1915. *Loc*: NIC/MMN: [Mr 6–D 25, 1886 (19:10–51)]; [Ja 7, 1888–D 29, 1905 (21:1–38:52)]; Ja 4, 1907–D 31, 1909 (40:1–3:49); Ja 6, 1911–D 25, 1914 (4[*sic*]:1–7:52). NOwHi: My 3, 1879 (3:21); My 16, 1891 (24:20); S 7, 14, 1901 (34:36, 37). NWav: [N 22, 1876–1879 (1:1–?)]; [My 6, 1882–D 30, 1893 (15:18–26:51)]; Ja 4–D 26, 1896 (29:1–52); Ja 7, 1899–Jl 2, 1915 (32:1–9:29).

WAVERLY LUMINARY (w) Waverly. O 3, 1851–Ag 1852// (1:1–?). No issues located. "The first paper printed in Waverly was the Waverly *Luminary,* established October 3, 1851, by Thomas Messenger, with an office on the second floor of the Spaulding block. After an existence of ten months the *Luminary* ceased to illuminate." (Leroy Kingman, *Our County and Its People,* p. 213.) "The *Waverly Advocate* is the lineal successor of the *Waverly Luminary,* which rose upon the world of newspaperdom on the 3d of October, 1851, Thomas Messenger being the prime mover to that end. . . . The *Luminary* shone but about ten months, when it was eclipsed by the departure of its publisher . . ." (Henry B. Pierce, *History of Tioga, Chemung, Tompkins, and Schuyler Counties, New York* [Philadelphia: Everts and Ensign, 1879], p. 107.)

WAVERLY REVIEW (w) Waverly. F 4, 1876–Ap 4, 1882// (1:1–?). *Title changes*: *The Waverly Review* (1876–?); *Waverly Review*. *Pub and Ed*: Ira Wales. *Pol*: Democrat. *Format*: Four pages 19½ " x 26". *Comment*: The paper was published at the Campbell Block, Corner of Broad and Fulton Streets. "Ira L. Wales, who had published the *Review* at Candor, and whose office had been burned, removed to Waverly the material that had been saved from the fire, and established the *Review,* a democratic weekly paper, the first issue of which appeared February 4, 1876. The paper was published under various adverse circumstances until April 4, 1882, when Mr. Wales discontinued it and removed the material to Binghamton, where he founded the *Latest Morning News*. This, too, was a short-lived and unprofitable journal." (Leroy Kingman, *Our County and Its People,* p. 216.) *Loc*: NOwHi: My 19, 1876 (1:15); O 30, 1880 (5:42).

THE WAVERLY SUN, NICHOLS RECORDER AND VALLEY NEWS (w) Waverly. 1908–O 28, 1970// (1:1–63:42). *Title changes*: *The Waverly Sun* 1908; *The Waverly Sun and Nichols Recorder* 1908–My 4, 1966; *The Waverly Sun, Nichols Recorder and Valley News* My 11, 1966–O 28, 1970. *Pub*: Genung-Scureman Publishing Co. ?–ca. 1922; The McEwen Press, Inc. ca. 1923–D 1935; Waverly Sun, Inc. (Hart I. Seely, Pres. 1936–1951; Marguerite Seely, pub., 1951–1970) Ja 2, 1936–O 28, 1970. *Ed*: Ray McEwen ?–ca. 1932; Harry Bacon F–Ag 24, 1933; L. Robert Oaks Ag 31, 1933–Je 4, 1936; Frank Dean Je 11–O 22, 1936; V. L. Spencer O 29, 1936–Mr 25, 1937; G. W. Tetherly Ap 1, 1937–Mr 10, 1938; V. S. Pultz Mr 17–D 29, 1938; William F. Tait Ja 5–Ap 22, 1939; Rodgers Hale Ap 29, 1939–O 8, 1942; Gilbert Stinger O 14, 1942–Ag 19, 1943; Constance Lane Ag 26–N 25, 1943; Constance Lane and Robert Oaks D 2, 1943–F 1, 1945; Constance Lane and Lucille Lunger F 8–Jl 19, 1945; Lucille Lunger Jl 26, 1945–My 16, 1946; Dent L. Green My 23, 1946–S 8, 1949; Charles J. Chatfield S 15, 1949–Ja 19, 1950; Bert Miller Mr 2–N 23, 1950; David H. Fowler N 30, 1950–Ag 30, 1951; Jerome O. Colley S 6–N 15, 1951; Walter W. Grunfeld D 13, 1951–ca. 1955; Lowell Leake ca. 1955–1960; Hart I. Seeley, Jr. 1960–O 28, 1970. *Pol*: Republican. *Format*: Four to eight pages 17½ " x 23". *Price*: $1.00 per year (1919); $2.00 per year (1946); $2.50 per year (1956); $3.00 per year (1959); $3.50 per year (1956); $6.00 per year (1970). *Comment*: The paper was published at the N.P.L. Building in Waverly. In October 1970, the newspaper was purchased by the *Times-Herald* (q.v.). *Loc*: NIC/RHA: Ap 25, 1946 (39:17); Ap 5, 1956–O 28, 1970 (48:14–63:42). NOwHi: Je 4, 1915 (8:13); Je 28, 1923 (16:24); Jl 19, 1935 (28:22); My 5, 1938 (31:2); O 2, 9, 1941 (34:18, 19); My 27, 1943 (suppl.); My 31, 1945 (suppl.).

WAVERLY TRIBUNE (w) Waverly. Ap 27, 1882–1896?// (1:1–?). *Pub*: William H. Noble and A. G. Reynolds Ap–My 1882; William H. and Albert C. Noble 1882–1894; William H. Campbell 1894–? *Pol*: Independent. *Format*: Eight pages 12¾ " x 19". *Comment*: According to Leroy Kingman (*Our County and Its People,* p. 216), William

H. Campbell defaulted on his payments to the Noble brothers, and the paper reverted to them in May of 1894. They sold it to Currie and Romer in January of 1895, who discontinued the paper by 1896. *Loc*: NWav: Ap 27, 1882–Ap 19, 1883 (1:1–52).

THE WORKINGMAN (w) Owego. N 1877–F 28, 1879// (1:1–?). No issues located. "At the time of the Greenback agitation, in 1877, Merritt E. Webster, a former employee of the *Gazette,* who was conducting a small job printing office, formed a partnership with Benjamin B. F. Graves and began publication of a weekly paper called the *Workingman.* Its first number appeared November 1, 1877. August 9, 1878, George M. Jordan became editor and publisher. The paper died a natural death with its issue of February 28, 1879." (Leroy Kingman, *Our County and Its People,* p. 211.) "*The Working Man* was established in Owego, Nov. 2, 1877, by M. E. Webster and B. B. F. Graves, in the interest of the 'Greenback' party, for the fall campaign." (Pierce, *History of Tioga, Chemung, Tompkins, and Schuyler Counties, New York,* p. 107.)

THE ADVANCE (w) Trumansburg. N 1873(?)–? (1:1–?). *Pub*: A. F. Allen. *Format*: Four pages 11" x 16½". *Loc*: NIDeW Ja 31, F 21, 1874 (1:7, 10).

THE AMERICAN CITIZEN (w) Ithaca. 1855–F 25, 1863// 1:1–?). *Title changes*: *The American Citizen* 1855–1859; *American Citizen and Old Ithaca Chronicle* 1859–Mr 6, 1861; *The American Citizen* 1861–1863. *Pub*: A. E. Barnaby & Co. 1855–1857; A. Spencer Ap 22, 1857. *Ed*: A. E. Barnaby 1855–1857; A. Spencer Ap 22, 1857. *Pol*: American or Know Nothing Party. "In 1860 it supported the Breckenridge–Douglas and Bell ticket and the party of the Constitutional Union. In 1861 it went in for the Union having voted for the disunion ticket the week before." (*Ithaca Journal*, September 14, 1864). *Format*: Four pages 19½" x 26½". *Comment*: The *American Citizen* began where the *Ithaca Chronicle* (q.v.) left off on July 11, 1855. The following item appeared in the *Templar and Watchman* (q.v.) on July 18, 1855: "This paper [the *Ithaca Chronicle*] which was established nearly 26 years ago breathed its last on Wednesday. It could not die, however, without giving the Maine law a kick. Poor windbroken, jaded nag, peace to thy ashes. Over the grave of the *Chronicle* is to appear the *American Citizen*, an advocate of Hindoism [sic] and free trade in 'niggers'." G. Whitfield Farnham's *Directory of the Village of Ithaca* dates the last issue February 25, 1863. *Loc*: NIC/MMN: [Ja 21, 1857–D 3, 1862 (28:2–33:45)]. NIDeW: O 31, N 14, 1855 (1:16, 18); D 28, 1859 (30:51); Mr 19, My 21, Je 25, Jl 2, 23, 1862 (33:8, 17, 22, 23, 26).

THE
ITHACA DEMOCRAT!

A WEEKLY DEMOCRATIC NEWSPAPER,

IS PUBLISHED EVERY THURSDAY MORNING BY

SPENCER & WILLIAMS.

THE AMERICAN CITIZEN AND OLD ITHACA CHRONICLE
see *THE AMERICAN CITIZEN*

AMERICAN JOURNAL see *ITHACA JOURNAL* (w)

ANTI-MASONIC SENTINEL (w) Trumansburg. F 5, 1829–? (1:1–?). *Pub and Ed*: R. St. John. *Pol*: Anti-Masonic. *Format*: Four pages 12″ x 20¼″. *Comment*: Second paper published in Trumansburg. It was preceded by the *Lake Light* (q.v.), also anti-Masonic in character. *Loc*: NIDeW: [F 5–Mr 5, 1829 (1:1, 3–4)].

THE BRIDGE BUILDER (m) Groton. My 1, 1883–? (1:1–?). *Pub*: Groton Iron Bridge Company. Printer: *Groton and Lansing Journal*. *Format*: Four pages 19½″ x 25½″. *Comment*: Object was to advance the interest taken in the care of highways and bridges. *Loc*: NGr/ Town Clerk's Office: My 1–S 1, 1883 (1:1–5).

THE BUCKEYE (w) Ithaca. 1836(?)–? *Pol*: Whig campaign paper backing Harrison for President. *Format*: Four pages 8½″ x 11½″. *Comment*: No record of first or final issues found in Tompkins County. Printed by D. D. and A. Spencer "four doors West of the hotel, Owego Street." *Loc*: NIDeW: Ag 6, S 3, 10, 1836 (nos. 13, 17, 18).

THE CASTIGATOR (w) Ithaca. Ja 1, 1823–S 26, 1829// (1–?). *Title changes*: The Castigator 1823–1828; Old Hickory or the Castigator F 1828–My 1828; *The Castigator* My 23–S 26, 1829. *Pub*: James M. Miller who published under pseudonym, Captain Caleb Cudgel & Co. and also Major Club. *Ed*: James M. Miller. *Pol*: Democrat. *Format*: Four pages 8″ x 9¼″ and 8⅝″ x 10¼″. *Comment*: *The Castigator* was published in Auburn before it was published from J. Tourtellot's store in Ithaca. On May 7, 1828, the office was moved to the corner opposite Mr. Atwater's tavern on Aurora Street in Ithaca. *Loc*: NIDeW: Ja 1–Mr 29, 1823 (Fifth series 1–13); Je 1, Jl 22, 15 (misdated), Ag 5, 12, 19, 1828 (nos. 17, 20, 21, 24, 25, 26); My 23–S 26, 1829 (nos. 1–13). NIC/MMN: Ja 25, F 8, Mr 1, 1823 (Fifth series 4, 6, 9); My 9, 1828 (1:13). NIC/RHA: Ja 1–Mr 29, 1823 (Fifth series 1–13).

THE COMMUNICATOR see *TOMPKINS COUNTY RURAL NEWS*

THE COMPASS (m) Trumansburg. Ap 1963 to date. *Circ*: 8,000. *Comment*: Issued as supplement to the *Free Press* (q.v.). *Loc*: NT/ Free Press Office: 1963 to date.

THE CONGER'S JOURNAL (semi-m) Groton. Mr 23, 1882–? (1:1–?). *Pub*: C. W. Conger & Company. *Ed*: Mrs. C. W. Conger. *Format*: Four pages 19½″ x 25½″. *Comment*: The Congers, storekeepers, circulated a newspaper devoted to the interests of domestic economy. Although a store paper, it contained news items. The paper was circulated primarily in Genoa, Cayuga County, where the Congers also owned a store. It was printed in the office of the *Groton and Lansing Journal*. *Loc*: NGr/Town Clerk's Office: Mr 23, 1882–Mr 8, 1883 (1:1–24). NIC/MMN: Je 22, 1882 (1:7).

THE COON SKINNER Ithaca. ?–D 9, 1844// (nos. ?–20). *Pol*:
Democrat. *Format*: Four pages 9" x 12". *Comment*: Only one issue
of this newspaper has been located in Tompkins County. No publisher,
editor or printer is indicated in the available issue. *Loc*: NIC/MMN:
D 9, 1844 (no. 20). NIDeW: D 9, 1844 (no. 20).

THE DANBY HERALD (m?) Danby. My 1881–? (1:1–?). *Pub*:
Chester L. Johnson. *Format*: Four pages 11" x 14". *Loc*: NIDeW:
My 1881 (1:1).

DATELINE ITHACA (w) Ithaca. Jl 20, 1967–My 27, 1970// (1–
133). *Pub*: Glad Day Press. *Ed*: Jack Goldman. *Pol*: Independent.
Format: Four to twelve pages 8½" x 11". *Price*: $1.00 per year, 5¢
per issue. *Circ*: 1500. *Comment*: Published from 308 Stewart Avenue,
Ithaca. Founded by students working against the war in Vietnam;
then expanded its scope to deal with community issues. *Loc*: NI/Glad
Day Press: 1967–1970.

DEMOCRATIC FLAG (w) Ithaca. 1840. *Ed*: J. O. Henning. *Pol*:
Democrat. *Format*: Four pages 11" x 14". *Comment*: Campaign paper issued from headquarters in the "Democratic Reading Room, one
door south of Potter's Corner." It carried the slogan "Tompkins
County must be redeemed." *Loc*: NIDeW: O 3, 31, 1840 (nos. 7, 11).

DEPOT DISPATCH (m) Trumansburg. Mr 1965 to date. *Circ*:
4,800. *Comment*: Issued as supplement to the Trumansburg *Free
Press* (q.v.) chiefly for the personnel of the Seneca Ordnance Depot.
Loc: NT/Free Press Office: 1965 to date.

DRYDEN ECHO (w) Dryden. Ag 3, 1889–? (1:1–?). *Pub*: B. M.
Hicks (also proprietor). *Ed*: A. J. Hicks (also business manager).
Pol: Republican. *Format*: Four pages 18" x 24". *Comment*: This
newspaper was published over Wheeler & Co. store in Dryden. *Loc*:
NDrS: [Ag 3, 1889–Je 21, 1890 (1:1–47)]. *See also* p. 290

DRYDEN HERALD (w) Dryden. Jl 7, 1871–My 29, 1919// (1:1–
48:8). *Title changes*: *Dryden Weekly Herald* Jl 7, 1881–S 28, 1881
(1:1–11:11); *Dryden Herald* O 5, 1881–My 29, 1919 (11:12–48:8).
Pub and Ed: William S. Smith Jl 7, 1871–1873; William E. Osmun
1873–1875; William E. Osmun and Clark 1875; A. M. Ford and
C. S. Stowbridge 1876–1877; J. Giles Ford and Walter Ford 1891–
1892; J. Giles Ford 1892–1899; Robert E. Stilwell and Dolph Ross
1899–1919. *Pol*: Neutral. *Format*: Four to ten pages, varying sizes—
15½" x 22", 20" x 25½". *Comment*: Published in Dryden from the
office next to the Lehigh Valley Station, which is no longer standing.
Publication of the *Dryden Herald* was suspended on May 16, 1918
"probably until the end of the war" because of the conditions brought
by the war, namely scarcity of help, shortages of fuel and paper stock.
Publication was resumed March 13, 1919 after a ten month vacation,
but was suspended May 29, 1919. *Loc*: NIDeW: F 11, 1873 (2:28);
Jl 8, 1885 (14:51); [S 21, 1898–F 27, 1901 (28:12–30:35)]; D 7,
1910 (40:24); Ja 25, 1911 (40:31); O 23, 1912 (42:18); [F 3,

1915–Ap 10, 1919 (44:33–48:1)]. NDrS: [Jl 7, 1871–My 29, 1919 (1:1–48:8)]. NIC/RHA: [Ja 2, 1884–My 22, 1919 (13:24–48:7)].*

DRYDEN NEWS see *WEEKLY ITHACAN*

DRYDEN WEEKLY HERALD see *DRYDEN HERALD*

DRYDEN WEEKLY NEWS see *WEEKLY ITHACAN*

THE ECHO (m) Trumansburg. F (?) 1883–? (1:1–?). *Pub*: The Echo Publishing Co. *Format*: Four pages 7″ x 10¼″. *Loc*: NIDeW: My, D 15, 1883 (1:4).

THE ECLECTIC SCALPEL (m?) Trumansburg. Jl 22, 1868–? (1:1–?). *Pub and Ed*: I. W. Hill, M.D. *Format*: Four pages 13½″ x 11½″. *Comment*: This paper was "devoted to the diffusion of a correct knowledge of life and how to preserve health." *Loc*: NIDeW: Jl 22, 1868 (1:1).

THE ENTERPRISE Ithaca. Je 1871–? (1:1–?). *Pub and Ed*: Carnes and Lewis. *Format*: Four pages 13½″ x 19½″. *Comment*: This newspaper was devoted primarily to advertising for the Elias Howe Sewing Machine, but it did contain local news. No indication of frequency of issue. *Loc*: NIDeW: Je 1871 (1:1).

THE FINGER LAKES FARM AND HOME SUPPLEMENT AND AGRICULTURAL NEWS (m) Trumansburg. My 12, 1966 to date. *Circ*: 3,300. *Comment*: Issued as supplement to the *Free Press* (q.v.). *Loc*: NT/Free Press Office: 1966 to date.

FIRESIDE COMPANION see *WEEKLY ITHACAN*.

FLAG OF THE UNION (w) Ithaca. Je 13, 1848– D 20, 1849// (1:1–2:24). *Pub and Ed*: J. B. Gosman. *Pol*: Democrat. *Format*: Four pages 18″ x 24¾″. *Comment*: Published on Tioga Street, four doors north of the Post Office. Gosman sold his interests to J. H. Selkreg, publisher of the *Ithaca Journal* (q.v.). *Loc*: NIDeW: Jl 13, 1848–D 20, 1849 (1:1–2:24). NIC/MMN: Jl 13, 1848–D 20, 1849 (1:1–2:24).

FOREST CITY SPARK (m) Ithaca. Je 1885–? (1:1–?). *Pub*: Amateurs, ages 13–25, National Amateur Press Association. *Ed*: F. A. Partenheimer, Jr. and C. B. Taylor Je 1885. By September 1885 Partenheimer was listed as "Editor, Printer & Publisher." *Format*: Four pages 4½″ x 5″, then 5″ x 7″. *Loc*: NIDeW: Je, S, 1885 (1:1, 4).

FREE PRESS (w) Trumansburg. 1885 to date (1:1 to date). *Title changes*: The Free Press 1885–Ap 6, 1895 (1:1–10:22); *Free Press and Sentinel* Ap 13, 1895–F 19, 1932 (10:23–67:8); *Free Press* F 26, 1932 to date (67:9 to date). *Pub*: Albert F. Allen 1885–Je 28, 1924; M. V. Atwood Jl 4, 1924–Mr 13, 1925; William Heidt, Jr. Mr 20, 1925–Ap 1927; C. Owen Carman Ap 8, 1927–1939; C. Owen Carman & Sons Je 9, 1939–; Robert J. Carman Ja 11, 1955–. On May 4, 1961,

See also p. 290

Duane and Wanda Waid published the paper. 1962–I-T Publishing Corporation, Duane and Wanda Waid Publishers. *Ed*: Albert F. Allen; C. Owen Carman 1927–1939; Robert J. Carman Ja 11, 1955–; Duane and Wanda Waid 1961–. *Pol*: Republican. *Format*: Started as a one-sheet newspaper printed on both sides; soon enlarged to four pages; now up to twelve pages. Size varies from 11″ x 14″ to 12¾″ x 19¾″. *Price*: From 50¢ per year in 1885 to $4.00 per year in 1970. *Circ*: Currently about 1325. *Comment*: The *Trumansburg Leader* (q.v.) established January 6, 1939 by Floyd M. Parke merged with the *Free Press* June 28, 1940. With the January 4, 1968 issue of the *Free Press,* the old volume and numbering was discontinued and the numbering began with issue one. The *Free Press* announced on October 1, 1964, "Five long-established weeklies in Trumansburg, Interlaken, Ovid, Groton and Dryden are now joined through the merger of the Inter-County Publishers, Inc., publishers of the *Tompkins County Rural News* (q.v.) in Dryden and the *Journal and Courier* (q.v.) in Groton with the I-T Corporation, publishers of the Trumansburg *Free Press* and the *Interlaken Review*. The new corporation will use the name of Inter-County Publishers. In addition, the new organization will publish the *Ovid Gazette and Independent*." This corporation ceased to exist July 1, 1965. The *Free Press* issues four supplements per month: *The Finger Lakes Farm and Home Supplement and Agricultural News* (q.v.), *The Window* (q.v.), *The Compass* (q.v.), and the *Depot Dispatch* (q.v.). *Loc*: NIC/MMN: D 19, 1885–F 27, 1886 (1:6–10, 12–16); Ja 7–N 3, 1888 (3:9, 45–46, 48–52); Ja 5, 1889–D 27, 1890 (4:9–5:8); Ja 3, 1891 to date (6:9 to date). NT/Town Clerk's Office: Ja 1, 1887–D 29, 1888 (2:8–4:8). NIDeW: Ja 11, 1896 (11:10); Ag 21, 1897 (12:42); O 8, 1898 (13:49); O 4, 1935 (69:40); Ap 5, 1946 (79:14); O 30, N 20, 1953 (85:44, 47); F 12, 1954 (86:7). NT/Free Press Office: Ja 3, 1957 to date (89:1 to date).

FREE PRESS AND SENTINEL see *FREE PRESS*

THE FREE SOIL ADVOCATE AND REPUBLICAN (w) Ithaca. 1848–? *Comment*: No publisher or editor indicated in issue in hand. *Format*: Four pages 11¼″ x 15¾″. *Loc*: NIDeW: Ag 3, 1848.

FREEVILLE FRIEND (m) Freeville. Mr 1890–? (1:1–?). *Pub*: Freeville Publishing Company. *Pol*: Independent. *Format*: Four pages 14¾″ x 22⅛″. *Comment*: Published in Freeville from headquarters at the corner of Main and Liberal Streets. Issues for 1890 are numbered I; issues for 1891 are also numbered I. *Loc*: NIC/MMN: Ap, Je, S, N, D, 1890 (1:2–4, 7, 9–10); Ja, F, 1891 (1:1–2).

GROTON ADVERTISER Groton. 1864–? *Format*: Four pages 12″ x 17¾″. *Loc*: NIC/MMN: Ap, 1864 (1:3). NIDeW: Jl, 1864 (1:4). *See also* p. 290

GROTON AND LANSING JOURNAL see *JOURNAL AND COURIER*

GROTON AND LANSING JOURNAL AND LOCKE COURIER see *JOURNAL AND COURIER*

GROTON BALANCE see *GROTON DEMOCRAT*

GROTON DEMOCRAT (w) Groton. Ja 31, 1839–S 29, 1840//
(1:1–2:35). *Title changes*: *Groton Balance* Ja 31, 1839–F 1840 (1:1–
2:1); *Groton Democrat* F 11–S 29, 1840 (2:2–2:35). *Pub and Ed*:
H. P. Eels and Co. through 1839; E. S. Keeney O 31, 1839–1840.
Format: Four pages 14½" x 19". *Comment*: The editor stated that
this paper was first called the *Groton Balance* and would not be a
political paper, but would be "devoted to miscellaneous and moral
subjects—agriculture—the mechanical arts—foreign and domestic intelligence." *Loc*: NIC/MMN: F 7, 1839 (1:2). NGr/Town Clerk's
Office [Ja 31, 1839–S 29, 1840 (1:1–2:35)].

GROTON JOURNAL see *JOURNAL AND COURIER*

THE GROTON NEWS (w) Groton. ? *Pub*: Commercial Printing Co.,
M. A. Downing, Manager. *Pol*: Republican. *Format*: Four pages
18" x 24". *Comment*: This paper was published at the "first door
north of the First National Bank" in Groton. *Loc*: NIC/MMN: Mr
31, 1897 (1:15).

THE HEIGHTS WEEKLY (w) Ithaca. My 21–Ag 6, 1959// (1:1–
12). *Pub*: R. T. Cunningham. *Format*: Eight pages 9" x 13" and
8½" x 12¼". *Comment*: Issue for August 6, 1959 indicated a hiatus
in publication but stated paper would be back in print August 20.
No issues have been located beyond August 6. *Loc*: NIC/RHA: My
21–Ag 6, 1959 (1:1–12).

THE HERALD see *TRUMANSBURG HERALD*

HERALD AND RECORD (w) Ithaca. O 22, 1846–? (1:1–?). *Pub*:
Edgar St. John. *Format*: Sixteen pages 6⅛" x 9⅜". *Comment*: Published on Tioga Street over the Post Office, the paper was "devoted
to temperance, the interests of mechanics, etc." Within the paper there
are two sections; one headed the "Temperance Herald"; the other the
"Mechanics' Record." *Loc*: NIC/RHA: Ja 7, 1847 (1:12). NIC/
Rare: N 25, D 3, 17, 1846 (1:6, 7, 9). NIDeW: O 22, 1846–F 18,
1847 (1:1–18).

THE INDEPENDENT TREASURY (w) Ithaca. S 6, 1839–? (1:1–?).
Pub: A. E. Barnaby & Co. *Format*: Four pages 9" x 11½". *Pol*: Campaign paper concerned with Independent Treasury Bill. Readers were
urged to "Examine Thoroughly and Impartially–Then Judge." *Loc*:
NIDeW: S 6, O 11, 1839 (1:1, 6).

THE INDEPENDENT WATCHMAN (w) Ithaca. *Pub and Ed*:
Myron S. Barnes. *Pol*: Republican-Temperance. It carried the slogan
"Moral and legal suasion combined–by these we conquer." *Format*:
Four pages, approximately 17" x 24". *Loc*: NIC/RHA: Ja 11, 18,
Ap 4, 1856 (3:14–15, 26). NIDeW: Mr 28, Ap 4, 1856 (3:25–26).

ITHACA CHRONICLE (w) Ithaca. Mr 3, 1830–1855// (1:1–?).
Title changes: *Ithaca Chronicle* Mr 3, 1830–My 7, 1850; *Ithaca*

Weekly Chronicle My 15, 1850–Ap 12, 1854; *Ithaca Chronicle* Ap 1854–1855. *Pub*: D. D. and A. Spencer 1830–1853; Anson Spencer and Myron Barnes 1854–? *Ed*: Anson Spencer. *Pol*: Republican 1830, Whig 1834 and Democratic Whig 1838. *Format*: Four pages 15¾" x 20" to 19½" x 26". *Comment*: D. D. Spencer remained with the paper for 33 years. Writing his valedictory in the September 7, 1853 issue, Spencer said, "In the year 1820, in connexion with a then young friend, I commenced in this village the publication of the *Republican Chronicle*. With that paper and its successor the *Ithaca Chronicle*, I have been connected as editor and sole or in part proprietor and publisher for 33 years." During this time nobody prosecuted him for libel and only two threatened to strike him but didn't do it. This paper was printed two doors south of the hotel on Aurora Street; the other, four doors west of the hotel on Owego Street. [See also *The American Citizen*.] *Loc*: NIC/MMN: [Mr 3, 1830–Ja 22, 1851 (1:1–21:52)]; Ja 18, 1854–Ja 17, 1855 (25:1–26:1). NIDeW: Ja 22, 1840–F 3, 1847 (10:49–17:52); D 22, 1841 Extra; Jl 12, 1848 (19:24); My 30, Je 13, 27, 1849 (20:16, 18, 21); Ja 9, My 8, 1850 (20:49, 21:14). NIC/RHA: O 15, 1834 (5:34); S 19, 1838 (9:31).*

THE ITHACA CHRONICLE (w) Ithaca. 1888–? *Title changes*: *Mocking Bird Gazette* (m) 1888–F 1889. *Pub and Ed*: J. B. Porter. *Format*: Eight pages 14" x 21¼". *Comment*: *The Mockingbird Gazette* and *The Ithaca Chronicle* were published as monthlies until 1889 when *The Ithaca Chronicle* became a weekly. Published from 18 Hazen Street, Ithaca. A 24-page Hudson-Fulton celebration number was published September 25, 1909. *Loc*: NIDeW: Ja 4–D 27, 1890 (2:29–3:44); S 25, 1909. NIC/MMN: Ja 5–F 2, 1889 (1:11–12); Mr 2–D 28, 1889 (2:28).

ITHACA CHRONICLE AND DEMOCRAT (w) Ithaca. F 25, 1863– Ap 25 1912// (1:1–94:17). *Title changes*: *Ithaca Citizen and Democrat* F 25, 1863–F 13 1868 (1:1–5:52); *The Ithaca Democrat* F 25, 1868–O 25, 1906 (6:1–88:43). Numbering of issues changed with July 9, 1874 issue which became vol. 55 no. 1; *Ithaca Chronicle and Democrat* N 1, 1906–Ap 25, 1912 (88:44–94:17); *Ithaca Weekly Democrat* Ja 23, 1873 (2:4). One issue. *Pub*: Spencer and Williams; Spencer and Gregory 1874–D 21, 1876; Ward Gregory D 1876–Mr 7, 1889; Gregory and Apgar 1889(?)–1906; Atkinson and Mitchell Ap 1906–Jl 1911; Forest City Printing Company Jl 1911–Ap 25, 1912. *Ed*: Anson Spencer and Williams; Spencer and Gregory; Ward Gregory; George Foster; Chester Platt; Bert R. Mitchell Jl 25, 1907– Jl 6, 1911. *Pol*: Democrat. In the January 23, 1896 issue, the newspaper called itself: "The official Democratic paper of Tompkins County." *Format*: Four to twelve pages. Varying sizes 18" x 25", 20" x 26½". *Comments*: *The Ithaca Chronicle and Democrat* had its antecedents in two old newspapers which merged in 1863 and became the *Ithaca Citizen and Democrat*. Although the *Ithaca Citizen and Democrat* officially began publication with vol. 1 no. 1, it also listed itself as being vol. 35 no. 5 of the *American Citizen* (q.v.) and vol. 7 no. 35 of the former *Tompkins County Democrat* (q.v.). This may

See also p. 291

to some extent explain the switch to vol. 55 no. 12 in 1874. First
published at 41 Owego Street over Greenley, Burritt & Co. store (second floor of the DeWitt block), the newspaper moved a number of
times. It went to 69 E. State Street, then to 12 No. Aurora Street,
the Democrat block, and in its later years was published from 122
No. Tioga Street. *Loc*: NIC/MMN: [F 25, 1863–Ap 25, 1912 (1:1–
94:17)]. NIDeW: Jl 12, 1864 (2:21); Ja 25, 1867 (4:49); Je 8–29,
1871 (9:23–26); Jl 6, 1876 (57:27); S 29, O 13, 1881 (62:39, 41);
D 28, 1882 (63:52); N 6, 20, 1884 (65:43, 45); Mr 5, 1885 (66:10);
S 16, 1886 (68:37); My 31, 1888 (70:22); Ap 25, 1889 (71:17);
Mr 29, 1906 (88:13).

ITHACA CITIZEN AND DEMOCRAT see *ITHACA CHRONICLE
AND DEMOCRAT*

ITHACA DAILY CHRONICLE (d) Ithaca. Jl 1846–? (1:–?). *Pub
and Ed*: D. D., A., and S. Spencer; A. Spencer and Co. solely respon-
sible from December 10, 1849. *Pol*: Whig; Whig Democrat. *Format*:
Four pages 11½" x 16½". *Comment*: Published daily from 41 Owego
Street, Ithaca. Many issues misnumbered. *Loc*: NIC/MMN: Jl 14,
1846–My 13, 1850 (1:2–4:236). NIDeW: [F 6, 1847–Ja 12, 1848 (1:
178–2:162)].

ITHACA DAILY DEMOCRAT (d) Ithaca. N 1, 1869–? (no. 1–?).
Title changes: *Ithaca Daily Leader* N 1, 1869–My 7, 1872 (nos. 1–
768); *Ithaca Evening Leader* My 8–D 31, 1872 (nos. 769–971);
Ithaca Daily Democrat Ja 2, 1873–? (no. 972–?). *Pub*: W. A. Burritt
1869–1871; Haines D. Cunningham & Edward D. Norton O 17, 1871–
O 12, 1872; Haines D. Cunningham O 12–D 1872; Spencer & Wil-
liams D 2, 1872–? *Ed*: W. A. Burritt 1869–1871; Haines D. Cun-
ningham 1871–? *Pol*: *Ithaca Daily Leader* "Strictly neutral"; *Ithaca
Evening Leader* ". . . for political reform"; *Ithaca Daily Democrat*
"Democrat." *Format*: Four pages 15½" x 21". *Comment*: Published
in the Grant Block, 14-16 State Street. From 1872 published from 12
Aurora Street. *Loc*: NIDeW: N 1, 1869–My 31, 1871 (nos. 1–479);
[Je 1, 1871–Jl 11, 1873 (no. 480–6:9)]. NIC/RHA: Je 16, 1871.

ITHACA DAILY DEMOCRAT (d) Ithaca. Je 2–N 5, 1884// (1:1–
?). *Pub and Ed*: Ward Gregory. *Pol*: Democrat. *Format*: Four pages
15" x 21½". *Comment*: Published from the first floor of 16 No. Tioga
Street. Ward Gregory inserted the following on June 2, 1884: "We
have the pleasure of greeting our readers today in this first number of
the *Daily Democrat*–an experiment in local journalism that is to
thoroughly test whether Ithaca needs and can support two daily
papers . . . ." On November 14, 1884, Gregory said results justify
withdrawal from the field. Last issue November 5, 1884. Will continue *Weekly Democrat*. *Loc*: NIDeW: Je 2, S 8, O 3, 11, 1884 (1:1,
84, 106, 113).

ITHACA DAILY JOURNAL (d) Ithaca. Je 27–N 14, 1870// (1:1–
1:120). *Pub*: John H. Selkreg, Wesley Hooker and H. D. Cunningham 1870. *Pol*: Republican. *Format*: Four pages 13" x 18"; then four

pages, six columns 16" x 21½". *Comment*: Published from 69 E. State Street, Culver and Bates Block, second floor. *Loc*: NIDeW: S 9–N 14, 1870 (1:64–120). NIC/MMN: Je 27–N 14, 1870 (1:1–1:120).

ITHACA DAILY JOURNAL (1872) see *ITHACA JOURNAL* (d)

ITHACA DAILY LEADER see *ITHACA DAILY DEMOCRAT*

ITHACA DAILY NEWS (d) Ithaca. Ap 6, 1895–N 29, 1919 (1:1–25:277). *Pub*: DeWitt C. Bouton and Merritt M. Dayton, Ap 6, 1895–Ja 16, 1896; M. M. Dayton 1896–1900; Ithaca Publishing Co. (Duncan Campbell Lee, Pres.) 1900–; Forest City Printing Co., later consolidated with Atkinson and Mitchell, publishers of the *Ithaca Chronicle and Democrat* (q.v.). *Ed*: DeWitt C. Bouton and Merritt M. Dayton 1895–1896; Merritt M. Dayton Ap 24, 1896–1899; Duncan C. Lee 1900, with Merritt M. Dayton, business manager and Frank E. Gannett, managing editor; Roe L. Hendrick, managing editor 1906, with E. D. Toohill, city and university editor; Herbert J. Fowler 1907–; Charles E. Westervelt 1915, with Walter E. Williams, associate editor and Gail C. Stover, city editor. *Pol*: Independent; Democrat. *Format*: Issued in a variety of sizes ranging from 15" x 22" to 19¼" x 23¾". Enlarged to eight page coverage in 1899, then to ten page coverage of the news about 1905. Occasionally twelve page spreads were published. Numbering of daily issues was particularly careless. *Comment*: This newspaper was first published at 3 No. Albany Street. On July 5, 1889 it moved to 104-109-111-113 No. Albany where it remained until August 15, 1900, when it moved to the News Building on the corner of No. Tioga and Seneca Streets. *Loc*: NIC/MMN: Ap 6, 1895–N 29, 1919 (1:1–25:277). NIC/RHA: S 7, 1901 (7:130 Death of McKinley issue); My 1, 1919 (Homecoming issue). NIDeW: My 23, 31, Je 1–15, 1898 (4:41, 47–60); Ap 3, 27, 1900 (6:2, 23); D 17, 1901 (7:214).

ITHACA DAILY NEWS (industrial edition) Ithaca. O 1895–? (1:1–?). *Pub and Ed*: DeWitt C. Bouton and Merritt M. Dayton. *Format*: Thirty-two pages 11½" x 15¾". *Comment*: One issue found. *Loc*: NIDeW: O 1895 (1:1).

ITHACA DEMOCRAT see *ITHACA CHRONICLE AND DEMOCRAT*

THE ITHACA ECLECTIC (q) Ithaca. Jl 15, 1868–? (1:1–?). *Pub and Ed*: D. White, M.D. *Format*: Four pages 11¼" x 13¾". *Comment*: This newspaper contained local advertising and local health news. It was published at 75 East State Street in Ithaca over Schuyler & Curtis Drug Store. *Loc*: NIDeW: Jl 15, S 15, 1868 (1:1–2).

ITHACA EVENING LEADER see *ITHACA DAILY DEMOCRAT*

ITHACA GAZETTE AND RELIGIOUS INTELLIGENCER (w) Ithaca. Ag 1816(?)–? (1:1–?). *Pub*: Joseph Benjamin, Ebenezer Reed, Erastus Shepard. *Comment*: The only issue found to date is that of June 5, 1817. Brigham suggests the date of the first issue on the basis of the Tompkins County Court record of mortgages. Brigham states: "According to an article in *The Telegraph* of Newton [Elmira] of September 9, 1817, the *Ithaca Gazette* was succeeded by the *American Journal* in August 1817." *Loc*: NIC/MMN: Je 5, 1817 (1:42).

THE ITHACA HERALD (w) Ithaca. Ag 31, 1836–O 4, 1837// (1:1–2:6). *Pub and Ed*: George H. Freer. *Pol*: Republican. *Format*: Four pages 16½" x 22¾". *Comment*: This newspaper was published in the Brick Building over the jewelry store of J. Burritt, a few doors north of the Hotel on Aurora Street. George H. Freer disposed of the paper to the editor of the *Ithaca Journal and Advertiser* October 4, 1837. *Loc*: NIC/MMN: Ag 31, 1836–O 4, 1837 (1:1–2:6). NIDeW: Ag 2, 1837 (1:49). *See also* p. 291

THE ITHACA INDEPENDENT (w) Ithaca. Je 22, 1907–N 14, 1908// (1:1–42). *Pub*: C. J. Sullivan, President of Ithaca Independent Publishing Company Ap 25, 1908. *Ed*: C. J. Sullivan My 2, 1908–. *Pol*: Independent. *Format*: Four pages 16½" x 23½". *Comment*: The paper was published at 207 S. Meadow Street until April 25, 1908 when it moved to 138 W. State Street. *Loc*: NIC/MMN: Je 22, 1907–N 14, 1908 (1:1–42). NIDeW: N 14, 1908 (1:42).

THE ITHACA ISSUE (bi-m) Ithaca. O 1, 1913–? (1–?). *Pub*: Ithaca Socialist Party. *Pol*: Socialist. *Format*: Four pages 11" x 17⅜". *Comment*: The paper stated that it was "fearless and determined" and "published for a purpose." The available issues located in Ithaca did not list either publisher or editor. Only one person was named, W. J. C. Wismar, who was to receive literary and financial contributions. *Loc*: NIC/RHA: O 1, 18, N 1, 1913 (nos. 1–3).

ITHACA JOURNAL (d) Ithaca. Jl 1, 1872 to date. (1:1 to date). *Title changes*: *Ithaca Daily Journal* Jl 1, 1872–S 26, 1873; *Ithaca Journal* S 27, 1873–Ap 17, 1874; *Ithaca Daily Journal* Ap 18, 1874–·F 26, 1913; *Ithaca Journal* F 27, 1913–N 29, 1919; *Ithaca Journal-News* D 1, 1919–D 30, 1933; *Ithaca Journal* Ja 2, 1934 to date. *Pub*: John Selkreg and D. S. Apgar 1872–1875; Journal Printing Association 1877–; Frank E. Gannett 1912–; Ithaca Journal-News, Inc. 1920–; Harry Stutz 1927–1954; No publisher named 1955–1969; James S. Graham 1970 to date. *Ed*: John H. Selkreg and D. C. Bouton 1872–; George E. Priest and Charles M. Benjamin 1889–; Harry S. Estcourt 1912–1915; John Baker; Harry G. Stutz 1915–1954; William J. Waters 1955–1969; Randall Shew 1969; Jerry Langdon Ja 1, 1970 to date. *Pol*: Republican. *Format*: Started four pages 14½" x 21½"; number of pages now vary (14–27) 15" x 22½". *Comment*: Published at 69 E. State Street, Culver and Bates Brick Block, second floor. In 1872 moved to the Journal Block on S. Tioga Street; in April 1905 moved to Journal Building at 123-125 State Street. *Loc*: NIC/MMN: Jl 1, 1872 to date (1:1 to date), bound and on microfilm. NIDeW: Jl 1, 1872–Je 30, 1873 (1:1–2:152); [Jl 1, 1874–Ja 13, 1912 (1:1–80:11)].

ITHACA JOURNAL (w) Ithaca. Ag 20, 1817–1917(?) (1:1–?). *Title changes*: *American Journal* Ag 20, 1817–Jl 9, 1823; *Ithaca Journal* Jl 16, 1823–N 9, 1825; *Ithaca Journal, Literary Gazette & General Advertiser* N 16, 1825–?; *Ithaca Journal and Advertiser* 1849–Jl 11, 1866; *Ithaca Journal* Jl 18, 1866–1917. *Pub and Ed*: Ebenezer Mack and Erastus Shepard 1817–?; Ebenezer Mack and Augustus P. Searing 1820; Ebenezer Mack, sole proprietor 1821–1823; Ebenezer Mack and Chauncey Morgan 1823–1824; Ebenezer Mack and Andrus 1825–; Nathan Randall 1836; Robbins, Mattison and A. E. Barnaby 1839–1840; Alfred Wells, 1840; Alfred Wells and John H. Selkreg 1845–; John H. Selkreg, sole proprietor except for brief period with D. Bouton and, in 1873, with Apgar; Ithaca Journal Association 1877; Priest and Benjamin 1889–. *Pol*: Democrat; Republican. *Format*: Four pages, varying sizes 12½″ x 20″, 15¼″ x 21″, 18¼″ x 23½″. *Comment*: The *American Journal* (q.v.) was located in the printing office and bookstore of Mack & Andrus and then moved to the brick building opposite the Hotel on Owego Street. From there to Tioga Street, the Journal Block, and then to 69 E. State Street, the Culver and Bates Block. On October 11, 1837, the *Ithaca Herald* united with the *Ithaca Journal and General Advertiser*. For a brief time the running title of the newspaper appearing over the editorial was the *Ithaca Journal and Herald*. *Loc*: NIC/MMN: [Ag 18, 1819–Jl 17, 1839 (3:1–22:52)]; [Jl 20–N 16, 1842 (26:1–18)]; Mr 13–Jl 3, 1844 (27:35–50)]; [Jl 11, 1849–D 30, 1873 (33:46–58:27)]. NIC/RHA: O 17, 1821 (5:10); Ag 3, 1864 (49:6). NIDeW: Ag 20, 1817 (1:1); Mr 22, D 6, 1820 (3:41, 4:17); D 18, 1822 (6:19); Mr 5, 1823 (6:30); Ja 7, 1824 (7:22); Ap 26, Jl 26, 1826 (9:38, 51); My 6, O 11, 1827 (10:10, 39); [Ap 20, 1831–Jl 24, 1833 (14:38, 15:1–16:52)]; Ag 17, 1836 (20:4); F 7, Jl 18, 1838 (21:29, 52); Mr 2, 1842 (25:33); Ag 6, S 17, 1845 (30:4, 10); [My 19, 1847–Ag 28, 1850 (31:44–35:9)]; D 22, 1852 (37:24); Ag 1, 1855 (40:5); [O 22, 1856–F 4, 1857 (41:17–32)]; Ja 11, 1860 (44:28); My 21, 1862 (46:48); My 24, D 6, 1865 (49:44, 50:19); Ja 4–D 27, 1870 (54:21–55:20); Ja 7–D 30, 1873 (57:28–58:27); Ja 4–D 27, 1877 (61:28–62:27); Ja 2–D 25, 1879 (63:29–64:27); Ja 4–D 27, 1883 (67:29–68:28); O 2, 1884 (69:16); Ja 22–D 31, 1885 (69:?–70:29); Ja 3–D 26, 1889 (73:30–74:29); Ap 19, 1894 (79:46); D 12, 26, 1895 (81:28, 30); F 13, Mr 12, 19, Ag 20, 1896 (82: 7, 11, 12, 28?); S 27, 1900 (86:13); My 9, 1901 (87:1).

ITHACA JOURNAL AND ADVERTISER see *ITHACA JOURNAL* (w)

ITHACA JOURNAL AND GENERAL ADVERTISER see *ITHACA JOURNAL* (w)

ITHACA JOURNAL AND HERALD see *ITHACA JOURNAL* (w)

ITHACA JOURNAL, LITERARY GAZETTE AND GENERAL ADVERTISER see *ITHACA JOURNAL*

THE ITHACA MIRROR (semi-m) Ithaca. D 1859. New series Ja

1860–? *Pub*: Miss Helen M. Jay (editress and proprietress) 1859–1862; William A. Burritt 1863–. *Ed*: Miss Helen M. Jay; William A. Burritt. *Pol*: Independent. *Format*: Four pages, varying sizes, 11″ x 17″, 12¾″ x 18½″. *Price*: 50¢ per year. *Circ*: 1300. *Comment*: Motto: "An original, spicy and independent local journal! Devoted to humor, music, literature, commerce, current events, etc." *Loc*: NIC/RHA: Ap 24, My 9, Ag 21, D 11, 25, 1860 (1:9, 11, 16, 22, 23); Ja 8, 1861 (1:24). NIC/MMN: F 21, 1860 (1:5). NIDeW: D 11, 1860 (1:22); D 29, 1863 (3:29).

ITHACA MORNING HERALD (d) Ithaca. O 5, 1894–? (1:1–?). *Pub and Ed*: E. B. Crosby. *Format*: Four pages 17″ x 23¾″. *Comment*: According to an article by Arthur W. Cochran in the June 1, 1938 issue of the *Ithaca Journal* (q.v.), "Two brothers, young men just out of college sought to interest Ithaca readers in a local morning paper. They founded the *Morning Herald*." The public failed to appreciate a morning paper and it was soon sold to Bouton and Dayton who started a daily afternoon paper called the *Ithaca Daily News* (q.v.) on April 6, 1895 at the same address, 3 No. Albany Street, from which the *Morning Herald* had been published. *Loc*: NIC/MMN: O 5, 1894–Ja 4, 1895 (1:1–13, 15–22, 26, 29–73, 75–76).

ITHACA OBSERVER (w) Ithaca. Ja 5–F 2, 1934// (1:1–5). *Pub*: Anthony J. Scales. *Ed*: Thomas R. Mitman. *Pol*: Independent. *Format*: Eight pages 10″ x 14⅜″. *Comment*: Published from 120 E. State Street, Ithaca. *Loc*: NIC/MMN: Ja 5–F 2, 1934 (1:1–5). NIDeW: Ja 5, 12, 19, F 2, 1934 (1:1–3, 5).

ITHACA REPUBLICAN (w) Ithaca. S 6, 1820–? (1:1–?). *Title changes*: *Republican Chronicle* S 6, 1820–Ap 14, 1830 (1:1–10:24). *Pub*: David D. Spencer and Henry R. Stockton; David D. Spencer 1825–; David D. Spencer and S. S. Chatterton 1828(?)–Ag 26, 1829; S. S. Chatterton Ja 20, 1830–. *Ed*: David D. Spencer and Henry R. Stockton; David D. Spencer 1825–; David D. Spencer and S. S. Chatterton Ag 26, 1829; S. S. Chatterton 1829–. *Pol*: Republican. *Format*: Four pages, varying sizes, 12″ x 20½″ (1820), 15″ x 21½″, 30″ x 20⅝″. *Loc*: NIC/MMN: S 6, 1820–Ag 27, 1823 (1:1–3:52); [Ag 31, 1825–Ag 22, 1827 (6:1–7:52)]; Jl 2, 1828 (8:45); Ag 26, 1829–Ja 20, 1830 (10:1–?). NIDeW: D 24, 31, 1823 (4:17–18); My 25, 1825 (5:39); Ap 14, 1830 (10:24 [34?]); Ag 10, 1831 (11:50); Mr 7, 1832 (12:28). NIC/MMN: Ap 21, 1830 (10:35); F 23, O 5, 1831 (11:26, 12:6); Ap 18, 1832 (12:34).

ITHACA SATURDAY UNION (w) Ithaca. ? *Pub*: Central Labor Union. *Ed*: A. J. McElroy. *Format*: Six pages 13½″ x 19½″. *Comment*: Office located corner of State and Aurora Streets. *Loc*: NIDeW: Ag 7, 1897 (4:32); N 12, 1898 (6:43).

THE ITHACA SEMI-WEEKLY (semi-w) Ithaca. 1885–Je 10, 1887// (1:1–2:83). *Pub*: Walter G. Smith and Co. *Pol*: Republican. *Format*: Four pages 18″ x 24″. *Loc*: NIDeW: My 4, 1886 (1:51); Je 10, 1887 (2:83).

ITHACA WEEKLY CHRONICLE see *ITHACA CHRONICLE*

ITHACA WEEKLY DEMOCRAT see *ITHACA CHRONICLE AND DEMOCRAT*

ITHACA WEEKLY NEWS (w) Ithaca. Ag 29, 1895–? (1:1–?). *Pub*: The News Publishing Co. 1895–1896; Merritt M. Dayton, sole proprietor and publisher, Ja 30, 1896–; Ithaca Publishing Co. Je 1900–. *Ed*: DeWitt C. Bouton 1895–Je 1896; Frank E. Gannett N 21, 1900–S 17, 1902. *Pol*: Democrat. *Format*: Eight pages 15" x 22". *Comment*: Newspaper started at 3 No. Albany Street and later moved to the new News Building on the corner of Tioga and Seneca Streets. At this time the Cornell Engraving Company was incorporated into the News business. *Loc*: NIDeW: S 5, 1895– Ag 27, 1896 (1:2–49); Ag 22, 1900–D 27, 1906 (4:43–10:46).

THE ITHACAN (w) Ithaca. N 28, 1868–Je 4, 1870// (1:1–2:27). *Pub*: George C. Bragdon N 28, 1868–Jl 24, 1869; H. D. Cunningham Jl 24, 1869–1870(?). *Ed*: George C. Bragdon N 28, 1868–Jl 24, 1869, with H. D. Cunningham, associate editor; H. D. Cunningham Jl 24, 1869–1870(?). *Pol*: "Independent in politics. Independent in everything." *Format*: Eight pages 13" x 19½". *Comment*: This newspaper was published from the corner of State and Cayuga Streets near the Clinton House. *Loc*: NIDeW: N 28, 1868–Je 4, 1870 (1:1–2:27). NIC/ RHA: My 7, 1870 (2:24).

THE JEFFERSONIAN AND TOMPKINS TIMES (w) Ithaca. 1835–? (1–?). *Pub and Ed*: Charles Robbins. *Pol*: Democrat. *Format*: Four pages 17¼" x 24". *Comment*: This paper was published in the Brick Building over the jewelry store of J. Burritt, a few doors north of the Hotel on Aurora Street. *Loc*: NIC/MMN: N 4, 1835 (1:26); Ja 20–Jl 27, 1836 (1:37–2:12). NIDeW: Mr 30, 1836 (1:47).

JOURNAL AND COURIER (w) Groton. N 9, 1866 to date (1:1 to date). *Title changes*: *Groton Journal* N 9, 1866–O 9, 1879; *Groton and Lansing Journal* O 16, 1879–Mr. 24, 1915; *Groton and Lansing Journal and Locke Courier* Mr 31, 1915–Mr 15, 1916; *Journal and Courier* Mr 22, 1916 to date (50:28 to date). *Pub*: H. C. Marsh, founder and publisher N 9, 1866–; A. T. Lyon; L. N. Chapin D 13, 1872–Jl 17, 1879; The Journal Printing Co. Jl 24, 1879–N 15, 1883 (William H. Allen); L. J. Townley & H. L. Wright N 22, 1883–; L. J. Townley N 26, 1885–1894; Townley & Son (Glen M.) Ja 2, 1895–; L. J. Townley & Sons (Glen M. and Lewis D.) S 27, 1911; Millard V. Atwood O 4, 1911–; William Heidt, Jr. Mr 18, 1925–Ag 4, 1927; Arthur N. Meyers Ag 11, 1927–Mr 29, 1928; Lawrence W. Jacobs Ap 5, 1928–Je 30, 1948; Howard D. & Ruth C. True Jl 7, 1948–S 25, 1952; Arthur E. & Pearl Adams O 2, 1952–N 26, 1959; Arthur Hobbs D 3, 1959–Jl 27, 1961; Everett Rebb Ag 3, 1961–; Inter-County Publishers, Inc. N 15, 1962–. *Ed*: Essentially the same as the publishers. Some years no editor is named. L. J. Townley served as an editor for 28 years, November 22, 1883–September 27, 1911, part of that time also being owner or co-owner with his sons. *Pol*:

Independent until 1874 then Republican. *Format*: Four to eight pages 15" x 21½", 18" x 24". *Comment*: Started in 1866 over the grocery store of Adams Bros., corner of Mill and Cortland Streets. Moved to the New Journal Building in 1868 at the corner of Mill and Main Streets. February 1871 to third story of New Bank Building, Main and Mill Streets; 129 Main Street; 205 Main Street, February 6, 1933. In 1922, M. V. Atwood published the *Weekly Ithacan* (q.v.) and incorporated it in the *Journal and Courier*. On November 16, 1922, he took over the *Dryden-Freeville Press* which since June 29, 1922 was issued by John E. Mansfield at the Print Shop at George Junior Republic. *Loc*: NGr/Town Clerk's Office: N 9, 1866–N 1, 1867 (1:1–52); [D 13, 1872–Ag 29, 1918 (7:7–52:52)]; F 9, 1922–D 27, 1923 (56:24–58:18). NGr: [Ap 12, 1908–N 15, 1917 (43:1–52:15)]; S 6, 1932 to date (52:1 to date). NIDeW: Mr 8, 1867 (1:18); Ag 13, 1869 (3:41); S 19, 1873 (7:47); O 2, 1879 (13:50); S 29, 1881 (15:50). NIC/RHA: [Mr 15, 1867–Ap 17, 1890 (1:19–24:28)]; S 15, 1915 (50:2); 1943 to date. *See also* p. 291

LAKE LIGHT (w) Trumansburg. O 10, 1827–N 19, 1828//(?) (1:1–2:5). *Pub*: W. W. Phelps and R. M. Bloomer 1827; Orasmus B. Clark and Bloomer Mr 19, 1828; O. B. Clark and R. St. John My 7, 1828; R. St. John O 1, 1828. *Ed*: W. W. Phelps and R. M. Bloomer. *Pol*: ". . . a violent political and anti-Masonic sheet." (Pierce, *History of Tioga, Chemung, Tompkins, and Schuyler Counties*). *Format*: Four pages 12" x 20¼". *Comment*: Motto: "Anti-Masonic and True American." On October 28, 1828, the *Lake Light* was removed to D. Trembly's new building east of Riggs and Goddard's store and adjoining the Masonic Hall. It was succeeded by the *Anti-Masonic Sentinel* (q.v.) on February 5, 1829. *Loc*: NIDeW: [1827–1828].

THE LANSING GAZETTE (m?) Ludlowville. ? *Pub and Ed*: Lord & Burr. *Format*: Four pages 9⅜" x 12". *Comment*: Lord and Burr were storekeepers; the newspaper featured advertising rather than news. *Loc*: NIC/MMN: My 1, 1859 (3:1); My 1861 (5:1).

THE LUDLOWVILLE INDEX. Ludlowville. Je 10, 1878–? (1:1–?). *Format*: Four pages 11" x 16". *Loc*: NIC/MMN: Je 10, 1878 (1:1).

THE MAGICIAN (w) Ithaca. 1838–? *Pol*: Democrat. *Format*: Four pages 8¾" x 12½". *Loc*: NIDeW: O 20, 1838 (1:3).

THE MOCKING BIRD GAZETTE see *THE ITHACA CHRONICLE*

THE MONITOR (m) Ithaca Mr 31, 1923–? (1:1–?). *Pub*: J. Elliott Douglass, Jr. *Ed*: J. Elliott Douglass, Jr.; C. O. Wilson April 1923–. *Format*: Eight to sixteen pages 9" x 11⅞". *Comment*: This paper was "Devoted to interests of colored people." No issue for May 1923 because the printer, Chatterton, was too busy. *Loc*: NIC/Rare: Mr, Ap, Je 1923 (1:1–3).

THE MUSEUM AND INDEPENDENT CORRECTOR (bi-m then w) Ithaca. Ap 16–Jl 30, 1824//(?) (1:1–12). *Pub and Ed*: George

Henry Evans and L. B. Butler. *Format*: Four pages 8″ x 9¼″. *Comment*: This paper was printed in the office of A. P. Searing, "just a few rods east of the Hotel Ithaca." There is some question about the final date of publication. The July 30, 1824 issue of the paper stated: "The object of the publication is to afford a weekly fund of amusement, blended with information and to correct those numerous petty vices and follies with which our village, in common with others is infected. . . . We have endeavored to keep as clear of personalities as possible. . . . It was not contemplated that the paper would continue beyond present numbers." An item appearing in the May 21, 1856 issue of the *Ithaca Journal* (q.v.) stated that the editor received from a subscriber in Cortland an old copy of the *Museum* for August 6, 1824. No copy of this issue or issues published after July 30, 1824 have been located. *Loc*: NIC/RHA: Ap 16–Jl 30, 1824 (1:1–12).

THE MUSEUM AND LITERARY REPOSITORY (w) Ithaca. D 1, 1826–? (1:1–?). *Title changes*: *Western Museum and Belles-Lettres Repository* D 1, 1826–Ag 14, 1827 (1:1–36). *Pub*: A. P. Searing & Co. 1826–. *Ed*: A. P. Searing D 1, 1826–Je 13, 1827; A. T. Hopkins Je 20–S 5, 1827. *Pol*: Neutral. *Format*: Eight pages 9″ x 11¾″ (some 9½″ x 12¼″). *Comment*: This newspaper was a literary endeavor. Its motto was "Justice-Truth-Hope-Charity." On June 27, 1827 the office of the newspaper was "removed to a building lately occupied by Messrs. Lessley & Slater directly opposite the old stand." *Loc*: NIDeW: D 1, 1826–D 4, 1827 (1:1–52); Jl 11–O 30, 1827 (1:31–43); D 12, 19, 1827 (2:1–2).

NATIONAL ARCHIVES (w) Ithaca. F 6–Mr 13, 1845// (1:1–6). *Pub*: Samuel C. Clisbee. *Ed*: J. Hunt, Jr. *Pol*: Independent. *Format*: Four pages 14″ x 19½″. *Comment*: This paper was published from the corner of Pearl and Owego Streets, east of the hotel. Motto: "Transmit blessings to posterity: the voice of reason, conscience and the intelligent press." *Loc*: NIC/MMN: F 6–Mr 13, 1845 (1:1–6).

THE NATIONAL REAL ESTATE JOURNAL (m) Ithaca. 1901–? (1:1–?). *Pub*: The National Real Estate Company. *Ed*: J. H. Selkreg. *Format*: Twelve pages 11″ x 15⅝″. *Loc*: NIC/RHA: Je 1901 (1:2).

NEWFIELD ADVERTISER Newfield. 1879. *Pub*: Norton and Conklin. *Format*: Four pages 11½″ x 17½″. *Comment*: This newspaper consists mainly of advertising and humor. Business address was Titus Block, Ithaca. *Loc*: NIC/RHA: Mr 12, 1879.

NEWFIELD HOME NEWS Newfield. Je 7, 1941// (1:1). *Format*: Four pages. *Comment*: Souvenir edition issued for Old Home Day. No indication that subsequent papers would be issued. *Loc*: NIDeW: Je 7, 1941 (1:1).

NEWFIELD TRIBUNE (w) Newfield. Ap 21, 1888–Je 28, 1890// (1:1–3:11). *Pub*: H. M. Wickes and L. E. Kirtland 1888–Ap 24, 1889; L. E. Kirtland and Filkins Ap 24, 1889–1890(?); L. E. Kirtland listed as only publisher in Mr 15, 1890 issue. *Ed*: L. E. Kirtland. *Pol*:

Independent. *Format*: Four pages 11" x 16"; then in 1889, eight pages 13" x 19½". *Price*: Two cents; in 1889 three cents, and by the time the newspaper ceased publication five cents. *Circ*: 620 in 1888. *Comment*: Published on Saturday from quarters over Bailey's meat market in Newfield. *Loc*: NNfPL: Ap 21, 1888–Je 28, 1890 (1:1–3:11). NIDeW: O 13, 1888 (1:26); Je 14, 1890 (3:9).

THE NO-LICENSE ADVOCATE Ithaca. 1881(?)–? *Format*: Four pages 10½" x 13¾". *Comment*: This paper was printed at 54 E. State Street. Only the name of F. P. Rundell, business manager, appears in available issues. *Loc*: NIC/RHA: F 23, 1882 (2:8). NIC/MMN: F 23, 25, 1882 (2:8–9). NIDeW: Ja 21, F 4, 1882 (2:3, 5).

THE OLD CAMPAIGNER Ithaca. 1851? *Pol*: Whig. *Format*: Four pages 11½" x 16½". *Loc*: NIDeW: O 30, 1851 (Third series no. 3).

OLD HICKORY see *THE CASTIGATOR*

THE PHILANTHROPIST (bi-m) Ithaca. 1831–Je 26, 1832// *Pub and Ed*: Orestes Augustus Brownson. *Format*: Sixteen pages, varying sizes, 8½" x 10¾", 5" x 8½". *Loc*: NIDeW: D 3, 1831 (2:3). NIC/Rare: Jl 23, 1831 (1:18); microfilm N 5, 1831–Je 26, 1832 (2:1–16).

THE PROTEST (w) Ithaca. 1834–N 29, 1834// *Format*: Issued as both an eight and four page paper, 6¼" x 9½". *Price*: 25¢ per issue: *Loc*: NIDeW: O 18, N 29, 1834 (nos. 12, 15).

THE REFERENDUM Ithaca. ? *Pol*: Campaign paper of the People's Party of Ithaca endorsing W. K. Cessna for mayor. *Format*: Four pages 7⅝" x 10½". *Comment*: Neither publisher nor editor are cited in issues located. *Loc*: NIC/RHA: F 23, 27, Mr 2, 4, 1895.

REPUBLICAN CHRONICLE see *ITHACA REPUBLICAN*

RUMSEY'S COMPANION see *WEEKLY ITHACAN*

RUMSEY'S FIRESIDE COMPANION see *WEEKLY ITHACAN*

SATURDAY EVENING EXPRESS (w) Ithaca. D 11, 1880–? (1:1–?). *Pub*: Foote and Wright, The Express Printing Co. *Ed*: Foote and Wright 1880–1881. *Pol*: Independent. *Format*: Eight pages 15¼" x 22". *Loc*: NIC/MMN: D 11, 1880 (1:1); F 26, Je 4, 1881 (1:12, 26). NIDeW: D 25, 1880 (1:3); S 24, 1881 (1:42).

THE SATURDAY REVIEW (w?) Trumansburg. Ap 8, 1876–? (1:1–?). *Ed*: "M. and N. Quad, Ye Editors." (The names are puns on printer's terms.) *Pol*: Independent. *Format*: Four pages 8" x 6". *Comment*: Editor's Note: "The subscription price of this paper is 10¢ but for the benefit of those who 'haven't the tin' we will accept farm produce or anything that is valuable. We would like a few potatoes, onions, and dried apples. This offer is made more especially for those who are hard up for cash. A ten cent Havana would come very acceptable, etc." *Loc*: NIDeW: Ap 8, 1876 (1:1).

SEMI-CENTENNIAL NEWS Ithaca. S 8, 1881–?. (1:1–?). *Format*: Four pages. *Comment*: To be published every fifty years. No known record of further issues. Printed at the "Democrat office." *Loc*: NIDeW: S 8, 1881 (1:1).

THE SPY (w) Ithaca. Ja 19–Ap 12, 1828// (1:1–13). *Format*: Four pages 7″ x 9″. No publisher or editor is given for this paper save the tongue-in-cheek reference, "Edited by Launce Gossip and printed by Mr. Printer of Prudent Memory." *Loc*: NIDeW: Ja 19–Ap 12, 1828 (1:1–13).

TEMPLER AND WATCHMAN (w?) Ithaca. 1853–? *Pub*: Orlando Lund and C. F. Williams Mr 3, 1854; C. F. Williams and Co. S 8, 1854; M. S. Barnes and C. F. Williams Mr 23, 1855. *Ed*: Orlando Lund 1853–1854; Myron S. Barnes 1855–. *Format*: Four pages 16⅜″ x 23½″. *Loc*: NIC/RHA: Mr 3, S 8, 1854 (1:23, 50); Mr 23, 1855 (2:24).

TOMPKINS AMERICAN (w) Ithaca. 1833–? *Pub and Ed*: S. S. Chatterton. *Pol*: Whig. *Format*: Four pages 16½″ x 21¾″. *Loc*: NIC/RHA: Jl 4, 1834 (1:33).

TOMPKINS COUNTY DEMOCRAT (w) Ithaca. S 10, 1856–1863 (1:1–?). *Pub*: Timothy Maloney, Samuel C. Clisbe 1861; Clisbe and Williams 1861–1863. *Ed*: J. B. Gosman and H. A. Dowe (Democratic Committee of Publications); Timothy Maloney N 7, 1856–Ap 5, 1861; Samuel C. Clisbe 1861; Clisbe and Williams 1862–1863. *Pol*: Democrat–"Liberty and Union, Now and Forever, One and Inseparable." *Format*: Four pages 17″ x 24″. *Comment*: This newspaper was published in Grant's new block on Owego Street (now State Street). The *Tompkins County Democrat* (q.v.) merged with the *American Citizen* (q.v.) and became the *Ithaca Citizen and Democrat* which changed its title to the *Ithaca Chronicle and Democrat* (q.v.). *Loc*: NIDeW: S 20, 1856–S 11, 1857 (1:1–52); Ja 29, 1858 (2:20); F 3, Je 8, 29, Ag 24, 1860 (4:21, 39, 42, 50); 1862–a one-sheet extra edition. NIC/MMN: S 18 1857–S 6, 1861 (2:1–5:52); Ag 15, D 5, 1862 (6:49, 7:13). NIC/RHA: Ag 21, 1857; Ja 29, 1858; Je 10, 1859; O 31, N 14, D 5–26, 1862; F 6, 1863. NDrS: O 23, 1857 (2:6).

TOMPKINS COUNTY REPUBLICAN (w?) Ithaca. *Pub and Ed*: D. J. Apgar. *Pol*: Republican. *Format*: Four pages 20¼″ x 27″. *Loc*: NIDeW: S 25, 1878.

TOMPKINS COUNTY RURAL NEWS (w) Dryden. Jl 19, 1933 to date (1:1 to date). *Title changes*: The Communicator Jl 19, 1933–Je 27, 1934; *Tompkins County Rural News* Jl 4, 1934 to date. *Pub*: C. Owen Carman Jl 19, 1933–Je 27, 1934; A. K. Fletcher Jl 4, 1934–N 1962; Inter-County Publishers, Inc. N 15, 1962 to date. *Ed*: A. K. Fletcher 1933–; Bernard F. McGuerty and Everett Rebb S 1966 to date. *Pol*: "Official Democratic Newspaper of Tompkins County." *Format*: Four to eight pages 12½″ x 19″. *Loc*: NDrS: Jl 19, 1933 to date: (1:1 to date) NIC/MMN Jl 1, 1936 to date (7:1 to date). NIC/RHA: [My 27, 1936–Je 29, 1949 (6:48–19:1)]. *See also* p. 291

TOMPKINS COUNTY SENTINEL see *TRUMANSBURG SENTINEL*

TOMPKINS DEMOCRAT (w) Ithaca. Ap 11, 1843–D 12, 1844 (1:1–2:34). *Pub and Ed*: J. Hunt, Jr. *Pol*: Democrat. *Format*: Four pages 15″ x 20″. *Comment*: This newspaper was the successor to the *Tompkins Volunteer* (q.v.) and was published over Henning's Hat Store, nearly opposite the hotel. From November 12 to December 12, 1844, no papers were issued, owing to a lack of funds. It ceased after the December 12 issue, misnumbered vol. 2, no. 24 (should have been no. 34). *Loc*: NIC/MMN: Ap 11, 1843–D 12, 1844 (1:1–2:34). NIC/RHA Ap 11, 1843 (1:1). NIDeW: Mr 19, 26, Ap 3, S 19, 1844 (1:50–52, 2:24).

THE TOMPKINS VOLUNTEER (w) Ithaca. N 16, 1841–Ap 4, 1843// (1:1–2:21). *Pub*: J. Gray, Hunt and Gray Mr 1, 1842; J. Hunt, Jr. N 15, 1842. *Ed*: H. C. Goodwin F 22, 1842; Goodwin retired, no editor named; J. Hunt, Jr. N 15, 1842. *Format*: Four pages 14″ x 20½″. *Comment*: Motto: "Truth, justice, liberty, and our country." Published in Ithaca opposite the Farmer's Hotel. On April 4, 1843, the office was removed to the building lately occupied by the *Ithaca Journal* (q.v.) opposite the hotel, over Henning's Hat Store. On April 11, in the first issue of the *Tompkins Democrat* (q.v.), J. Hunt, Jr. wrote the obituary of *The Tompkins Volunteer* as follows: "We therefore, this day, put to death the young volunteer and introduce to our readers an old Democrat. . . . We urge all our editorial brethren who have exchanged with us to strike off the Volunteer and substitute Democrat immediately." *Loc*: NIC/MMN: N 16, 1841–Ap 4, 1843 (1:1–2:21).

THE TOWN CRIER (w) Ithaca. O 29, 1959–O 27, 1969// (1:1–11:43). *Pub*: Howard S. and Helen S. Cogan. *Ed*: Howard S. Cogan. *Pol*: Neutral. *Format*: Eight to fifty-six pages for special issues–8½″ x 11″. *Price*: $1.00 per year. *Comment*: Running title: *The Town Crier and Shoppers Guide*. The offices were located in the Savings Bank Building on Tioga Street and then at S. Albany Street as of September 1965. *Loc*: NI/Cogan Advertising Agency, Ithaca O 29, 1959–O 27, 1969 (1:1–11:43).

TRUMANSBURG ADVERTISER see *TRUMANSBURG ADVERTISER AND TOMPKINS COUNTY WHIG*

TRUMANSBURG ADVERTISER AND TOMPKINS COUNTY WHIG (w) Trumansburg, Jl 4, 1832–? (1:1–?). *Title changes*: *Trumansburg Advertiser* Jl 4, 1832–Je 25, 1834 (1:1–2:52); *Trumansburg Advertiser and Weekly Miscellany* Jl 2, 1834–Je 17, 1835 (3:1–3:51); *Trumansburg Advertiser* Jl 1, 1835–Je 21, 1838 (4:1–6:52); *Trumansburg Advertiser and Tompkins County Whig* Je 27, 1838–? (7:1–?). *Pub and Ed*: David Fairchild Jl 4, 1832–1836; David Fairchild and Erastus S. Palmer 1837(?); E. S. Palmer late 1837–1838; E. S. Palmer and C. M. Maxson 1839–. *Pol*: The *Trumansburg Advertiser, Trumansburg Advertiser and Weekly Miscellany,* and then the *Trumansburg Advertiser* were neutral until June 20, 1838, on which date they stated, "This number closes the volume and with it closes the neutral character of our paper." Whig from 1838. *Format*: Four pages, varying sizes, 13¾″ x 18¾″, 13″ x 20½″, 13½″ x 20½″, 16¼″ x 22½″. *Comment*: This newspaper was published on Main Street opposite the hotel, and in 1839 moved to the upper rooms of the H. Taylor Building over the shoe shop. It is possible that when C. M. Maxson and E. S. Palmer dissolved their partnership on June 17, 1840, the newspaper also came to an end. *Loc*: NIC/RHA: Jl 4, 1832–Je 25, 1834 (1:1–2:52). NIC/MMN: Je 27, 1838–Mr 20, 1839 (7:1–39); [Je 26, 1839–Je 17, 1840 (8:1–52)]. NIDeW: [Jl 25, 1832– Je 22, 1836 (1:3–4:52)]; Jl 19, 1837 (6:4); Ja 30, 1839 (7:32). NT/Town Clerk's Office: Jl 6, 1836–Je 19, 1839 (5:2–7:52).

TRUMANSBURG ADVERTISER AND WEEKLY MISCELLANY see *TRUMANSBURG ADVERTISER AND TOMPKINS COUNTY WHIG*

TRUMANSBURG GAZETTE (w) Trumansburg. O 15, 1843– 1846// (1:1–?). *Pub*: John Creque, Jr. *Format*: Four pages 14″ x 20½″. *Loc*: NIDeW: My 8, 1844 (1:30) [No further vol. and no. given because of frequent errors.] Je 5, 12, Jl 10, 31, Ag 7, 21, 28, S 11–25, O 16, N 27, D 4–18, 1844; Ja 15, F 29, Mr 5–26, Ap 9, 16, 30, My 28, Jl 2, 16–30, Ag 20, 27, S 3, 17, 24, O 1–15, 29, N 5, 19, 26, D 31, 1845; Ja 7, 14, 1846.

TRUMANSBURG HERALD (w) Trumansburg. Mr 7, 1846–F 27, 1847// (1:1–52). *Title changes*: The Herald Mr 7—Ap 18, 1846 (1:1–6). *Pub*: S. Mills Day. *Format*: Four pages 12½″ x 19″. *Comment*: Motto: "To raise the Soul, by tender strokes of Art; to Guide the Genius, and to mend the Heart." *Loc*: NIDeW: [1846–1847 (1:1–29, 31–33, 40, 42–44, 47, 49, 51–52)].

TRUMANSBURG INDEPENDENT (w) Trumansburg. N 1851– 1852//(?) (1:1–?). *Pub and Ed*: W. K. Creque. *Format*: Four pages 18″ x 24½″. *Loc*: NIDeW: D 24, 1851 (1:7).

THE TRUMANSBURG LEADER (w) Trumansburg. Ja 6, 1939– Je 21, 1940// (1:1–2:25). *Pub*: Art Craft Printers (Floyd M. Parke, president). *Format*: Eight pages 15″ x 22″. *Comment*: On June 21, 1940, the paper merged with the *Free Press* (q.v.) *Loc*: NIDeW: Ja 6, 1939–Je 21, 1940 (1:1–2:25). NIC/RHA: F 3, 17, Mr 3–D 29, 1939 (1:5, 7, 9–52); Ja 5, F 23, Mr 15, 1940 (2:1, 8, 11).

THE TRUMANSBURG NEWS (w) Trumansburg. S 7, 1860–? (1:1–?). *Pub*: A. P. Osborn 1860; Edward Himrod D 11, 1861; Hicks and Pasko; A. O. Hicks 1863; J. W. Van Namee 1863; William H. Cuffman 1863. *Ed*: A. P. Osborn, 1860–1861; A. O. Hicks 1860; Edward Himrod 1861; J. W. Van Namee S 1, 1863; William H. Cuffman O 13, 1863. *Pol*: "Independent in all things—neutral in nothing." By 1863 the motto changed slightly to "neutral in religion and politics." *Format*: Four pages issued in varying sizes—18″ x 25¼″, 17″ x 24″, 14″ x 21″. *Comment*: Published over Wickes's Drug Store, Main Street, opposite Elm in Trumansburg. *Loc*: NIDeW: S 14, O 5, 1860 (1:2, 5); Ja 25, My 3, 1861 (1:21, ?); [Ja 9, 1863–F 11, 1864 (3:19–4:23)]. NIC/MMN: S 7, 1860–Ag 30, 1861 (1:1–52); N 28, 1862–O 6, 1863 (3:13–4:5).

TRUMANSBURG SENTINEL (w) Trumansburg. Ap 5, 1866–? (1:1–?). *Title changes*: Tompkins County Sentinel Ap 5, 1866–1895(?). *Pub*: Oscar M. Wilson 1866–1879; Corwin L. Adams F 13, 1879–D 27, 1893; Albert F. Allan; C. Owen Carman; Robert J. Carman. *Ed*: Oscar M. Wilson 1866–1879; Albert F. Allan; C. Owen Carman; Robert J. Carman. *Pol*: Independent. *Format*: Four pages 18″ x 24″. *Loc*: NIC/MMN: Ap 5, 1866–D 31, 1868 (1:1–3:40); My 19, 26, Jl 21, 1870 (5:7, 8, 16); O 26, 1871 (6:30); F 13, 1879–Ap 3, 1895 (13:46–29:44). NIDeW: D 28, 1876 (11:39); Ag 21, 1879 (14:21); S 27, 1882 (17:26); My 26, Je 9, 1886 (21:8, 10); O 18, 1893 (28:28).

THE TRUMANSBURG SUN (w) Trumansburg. D 2, 1840–N 3, 1841// (1:1–49). *Pub and Ed*: John Gray. *Pol*: "Rigid and uncompromising neutrality." *Format*: Four pages 13½″ x 20¼″. *Comment*: This paper lasted about a year—from the time John Gray purchased the printing establishment of the *Trumansburg Advertiser* (q.v.) from Erastus S. Palmer until Gray decided to leave Trumansburg and locate in Ithaca where he planned to publish the *Tompkins Volunteer* (q.v.). *Loc*: NIDeW: D 2–16, 1840 (1:1–3); Ja 20, Mr 31, My 5, 1841 (1:8, 18, 23); Ag 4–18, S 1, N 3, 1841 (1:36–38, 40, 49).

TRUMBULLS CORNERS COURIER Village of Trumbulls Corners (Newfield). *Pub*: G. A. Kresga. *Comment*: The only issue located indicates that the paper was published ca. 1900 by a Trumbulls Corners' merchant. *Loc*: NIDeW: 16:3. [No date given.]

THE WASP (w) Trumansburg. 1875–? *Pub*: Frank Allen 1875. *Ed*: Frank Allen 1875, M. Quad 1875. *Pol*: Neutral. *Format*: Four pages, varying sizes, 3¼″ x 4⅛″, 5⅛″ x 7⅜″. *Price*: 25¢ per six months. *Circ*: 200. *Comment*: Published over Pratt, Seymour & Co. Hardware Store. *Loc*: NIDeW: F 13, Mr 6–20, 1875 (1:2, 5–7).

WEEKLY ITHACAN (w) Dryden; Ithaca. My 7, 1856–? (1:1–?). *Title changes*: Rumsey's Companion My 7, 1856–Ap 8, 1857; *Dryden News* Ap 16, 1857–Jl 1858; *Dryden Weekly News* 1858–Ap 1871; *Weekly Ithacan and Dryden News* 1871–1875; *Weekly Ithacan* 1875–. *Pub*: Henry D. Rumsey My 1856–1858; Asahel Clapp 1858–; Asahel Clapp, Cunningham and Norton 1871; Asahel Clapp, sole proprietor and publisher 1871–; Lewis Clapp 1893–. *Ed*: Henry D. Rumsey 1856–1858; Asahel Clapp 1858–; Lewis Clapp 1893–. *Pol*: *Rumsey's Companion* stated, "Strictly political or sectarian articles cannot be published in this paper." Later papers called themselves independent and fearless. *Format*: Eight pages, varying sizes, 10½" x 16", 16" x 22", 13½" x 21". *Comment*: *Rumsey's Companion,* the *Dryden News* and the *Dryden Weekly* were published from the third story of the Stone Store in Dryden. The *Weekly Ithacan and Dryden News* was published from 17 West Street in Ithaca and then moved to 41 State Street in the Andrus & McChain Building which became the Andrus and Church Building. In 1888 the paper was moved to South Tioga Street. *Loc*: NDrS: [My 7, 1856–S 29, 1870 (1:1–15:13)]. NIDeW: Jl 14, 1871; Mr 7, Ag 8, 1873; Ag 14, D 11, 1874; My 28, 1875; Je 1, 1877; Jl 12, 1878; [Ja 10–Ag 29, 1879]; Je 2, 9, 1882; D 14, 1888; [Ja 1907–Jl 10, 1915]. NIC/RHA: Je 25, Jl 16, D 10, 17, 31, 1856 (1:6, 9, 29, 30, 32); F 25, Mr 4, 1857 (1:40–41); Jl 8, 1858 (3:2); Mr 30–Ap 6, 1865 (9:41–42); F 21, 1867 (11:35); O 20, 1870 (15:16); My 12, 19, 1871; O 9, N 27, 1874; S 17, D 17, 1875; Ja 7, 1876; [Ja 7, 1877–D 26, 1879]; Ja 2–F6, 1885 (14:41–46). NIC/MMN: Je 18, 1857 (2:4); N 28, 1861 (6:23); Jl 16, 30, Ag 6, 23, 27, S 10, N 19, D 10, 1875 (5:14, 16, 17, 18, 20, 22, 32, 35); Mr 22, Ap 5, 12, O 18–D 20, 1878 (7:49, 51, 52, 8:27–36); Ag 8– Ag 29, 1884 (14:22, 23); My 8–My 29, Je 12–Jl 3, Jl 17, Ag 7– O 23, 1885 (15:7–10, 16–19, 21, 24–35); [Ja 21. 1887–Je 28, 1889 (17:3–19:26)]; Ag 11, 25, S 1–D 1, D 22–D 29, 1906 (36:32, 34, 35–48, 51–52); [F 27–O 30, 1909 (39:9, 27, 39, 42, 44)].*

THE WEEKLY ITHACAN AND DRYDEN NEWS see *WEEKLY ITHACAN*

WESTERN MUSEUM AND BELLES-LETTRES REPOSITORY see *THE MUSEUM AND LITERARY REPOSITORY*

THE WINDOW (m) Trumansburg. Ja 1970 to date. *Circ*: 4,850. *Comment*: Issued as supplement to the *Free Press* (q.v.) of Trumansburg. Published for the staff of Willard State Hospital. *Loc*: NT/Free Press Office: 1970 to date.

THE WITNESS Ithaca; Putney, Vt. Ag 20, 1837–? (1:1–?). *Pub*: John H. Noyes Ag 20, 1837–Mr 1, 1839; John H. Noyes and H. A. Noyes Mr 1, 1839; John H. Noyes and John L. Skinner S 6, 1841–. *Ed*: John H. Noyes. *Format*: Eight pages 7⅛" x 10¾". *Comment*: The terms of publication state, "This paper is published not at regular intervals but as often as the Editors think best. We only engage to give our subscribers a Volume of twenty-six numbers, *sooner or later.* While we take this liberty ourselves, we give a corresponding liberty to our subscribers. We shall send the paper to all who apply for it, leaving them free to remunerate us *as* they choose, and *when* they choose. The nominal price of the paper is *one dollar for twenty-six numbers*: but we make not the payment of this, or any other sum, the condition of the subscription." Frequently issues did not appear for two months. No issues appeared between December 20, 1840 and January 20, 1841; none between February 22, 1841 and September

See also p. 291

6, 1841. With January 1, 1839 (1:6), publication transferred to Putney, Vermont. *Loc*: NIC/Rare: Ag 20, 1837–Ja 18, 1843 (1:1–2:26).

YES OR NO? Ithaca. F 22–F 26, 1902. *Comment*: There were possibly no more than two issues of this newspaper published on the question, "Shall Ithaca acquire waterworks?" Neither publisher, editor, nor printer was given. *Loc*: NIC/RHA: F 22, 26, 1902 (1:1, 2). NIDeW: F 22, 1902 (1:1).

YOUTHS' LITERARY GAZETTE (w) Ithaca. Je 5, 1840–? (1:1–?) *Format*: Four pages 9⅞" x 12¾". *Comment*: Neither publishers nor editors are named in the first issue. No other issues located in Tompkins County. *Loc*: NIC/MMN: Je 5, 1840 (1:1).

THE ZEPPELIN Ithaca. O 1915–? (1:1–?). *Format*: Four pages 5¾" x 7⅛". *Comment*: A rabid anti-Catholic newspaper. Only this one issue has been located. No mention of frequency of publication; no editor and no publisher listed. *Loc*: NIC/Rare: O 1915 (1:1).

THE BUNKER HILL CLUB (m) Penn Yan. 1840–? *Pub and Ed*: Abraham H. Bennett and Alfred Reed by 1840–? *Pol*: Democrat. *Format*: Four pages 11″ x 16½″. *Price*: 10¢ per copy. *Loc*: NIC/ RHA: Ag 28, S 18, 1840 (vol. 1, no series no.).

THE CHRONICLE see *CHRONICLE-EXPRESS*

CHRONICLE-EXPRESS (w) Penn Yan. F 28, 1843 to date (1:1 n.s. to date). *Title changes*: *Yates County Whig* F 28, 1843–Jl 1856; *Yates County Chronicle* Jl 5, 1856–?; *The Chronicle* by O 13, 1885– ?; *Yates County Chronicle* ?–Ja 6, 1926; *Chronicle-Express* Ja 13, 1926 to date. *Pub*: Nicholas D. Suydam F 28, 1843–S 18, 1845; Rodney L. Adams by 1845–Je 1852; Stafford C. Cleveland and John B. Look Ag 19, 1852–Mr 31, 1853; Stafford C. Cleveland Ap 7–Ag 11, 1853; Stafford C. Cleveland and Proude Ag 1853–?; Stafford C. Cleveland by 1855–1868; Stafford C. Cleveland and John D. Wolcott Ja 7–D 30, 1869; Stafford C. Cleveland by 1870–D 1873; Stafford C. Cleveland and E. Cleveland Ja 1874–Ap 1875; Stafford C. Cleveland and Isaac C. Cornell Ap 1875–Je 1876; Stafford C. Cleveland 1876(?)–? (died D 3, 1883); Chronicle Publishing Co. (Malcolm D. Mix, Gen. Manager) 1876–1882; Malcolm D. Mix and Steven B. Ayres O 5, 1882– Ap 5, 1883; Steven B. Ayres Ap 12, 1883–1886(?); Samuel P. Burrill 1886–1889; DeWitt C. Ayres 1889–1908; DeWitt C. Ayres and Franklin H. Wilson 1908–1926; Penn Yan Printing Co., Inc. 1927–?; Chronicle-Express Inc. by Ap 6, 1939–?; Greenhow Newspaper Inc. 1972 to date. *Ed*: Nicholas D. Suydam F 28, 1843–S 18, 1845; Rodney L. Adams Ja 1846(?)–Je 1852; Stafford C. Cleveland and John B. Look Ag 19, 1852–Mr 31, 1853; Stafford C. Cleveland Ap 7–Ag 11, 1853; Stafford C. Cleveland and Proude Ag 1853–?; Stafford C. Cleveland by 1855–

The Bunker Hill Club.

"It is not in a splendid government, supported by powerful monopolies, and aristocratical establishments, that the People will find happiness, or their liberties protection ; but in a plain system, void of pomp, protecting all, and granting favors to none."—JACKSON.

VOL. I. —   PENN YAN, N. Y., FRIDAY, OCTOBER 2, 1840.   BY BENNETT, & REED.

ADDRESS,
Of the Democratic State Convention assembled at Syracuse, Sept. 2, 1840.

Republican Electors of New-York !

We believe that you are fully awake to the importance of the crisis. We believe that you are deeply impressed with the conviction, that the contest which you are now waging, is but a renewal of the terrible

sessing abilities like his, could be induced to attend to its active duties.

We feel proud in adding, that his past career, has given the strongest assurance, sonian school ; and as the best evidence of his political faith, he was removed in the year 1813, from the sheriffalty of the county of Schoharie by a federal counell of appointment ; he was then elected to the assembly by the democratic electors of that sterling county, and he first appeared in the halls of our legislature, during the dark pe-

that his excellent common sense will teach him the true interests of the people, his sagacity will enable him to detect and discountenance the plausible schemes of speculating politicians, and his patriotism and purity will lead him to make the public good, the only basis of political action.

Col. BOUCK is a democrat of the Jeffer- which will be, to deprive other sections of the state from participating in the public bounty.

He has recommended that state works be

candidate for re-election. Since his elevation to the presidency, he has been beset with difficulties and embarrassments, yet arising from no fault of his own, which few would thoroughly appreciate; but which would have appalled a head less able, and a hand less true. Two months after his inauguration, all the banks in the United States suspended specie payments. In that hour, when all else were dismayed, he blenched not from his duties.

We speak not as partizans but as free-

1868; Stafford C. Cleveland and John D. Wolcott Ja 7–D 30, 1869; Stafford C. Cleveland by 1870–D 1873; Stafford C. Cleveland and E. Cleveland Ja 1874–Ap 1875; Stafford C. Cleveland and Isaac C. Cornell Ap 1875–Je 1876; Stafford C. Cleveland 1876(?)–?; Steven B. Ayres 1881–1886; Samuel P. Burrill by 1886–1889; DeWitt C. Ayres 1889–?; Sidney E. Ayres by 1926–?; James R. Carberry by 1961–1968; Donald E. Good 1969–?; Mrs. Birdie Tuttle Mr 1972 to date. *Pol*: Whig (1843); Independent; Republican (by 1860 to date). *Format*: Four to twenty-two pages, varying sizes, 18" x 24", 20" x 26", 21" x 28", 20" x 24", 17¾" x 21½". *Price*: $2.50 half yearly in advance (1843); $1.50 per year (1860); $5.00 per year in advance, 15¢ per copy (1972 to date). *Circ*: 1,500 (1884); 1,815 (1891); 3,418 (1910); 3,647 (1912); 4,150 (1919). (Ayer's *Directory* 1884–1972.) *Comment*: Motto: "Where Liberty Dwells, there is my Country." (1843–?); "Thought of Today" (by 1860). Printed in the Brick Building on Elm and Main Streets 1843–1847; by June 1847, published at the Watson, Stark and Co. Building, third story; then in the Brick Building on the West side of Main Street over Bentley and Streeter's Store; and by 1852 in the Bradley Block opposite the American Hotel. The present *Chronicle-Express* is a consolidation of the *Yates County Chronicle* (1824); the *Penn-Yan Express* (1866); the *Rushville Chronicle* (1905); and the *Gorham New Age* (1902). Ayer's states that circa 1919, the *Yates County Chronicle* was printed under the name of *Chronicle and New Age for Rushville and Gorham*. *Loc*: NDun/ Observer: D 23, 1845 (3:44 whole no. 148); Ap 9, 23, 1857 (15:15, 17 whole nos. 737, 739). NIC/MMN: microfilm [F 28, 1843–D 29, 1949 (1:1 n.s.–126:52 whole nos. 1–6555)]. NMn: Mr 21, 1861 (18:12 whole no. 942); S 3, 1863 (20:36 whole no. 1070.) NPyC: microfilm [F 28, 1843 to date (1:1 n.s. to date)]. NPyHi: Ag 29, 1843 (1:27 n.s.). NRu/Mable Blodgett: Je 21, 1860 (18:23 whole no. 903); Ja 6, 1927 (104:1 whole no 5357).

COMMUNITY LEADER (w) Rushville. Mr 8, 1928–S 25, 1930. (1:1–?). *Pub and Ed*: Harry J. Childs. *Format*: Eight to four pages. *Price*: $2.00 per year (Mr 8, 1928–S 12, 1929); $1.00 per year (S 1929–S 1930). *Comment*: "Financed by local business men because they felt advertising in the *Chronicle-Express* was too expensive." (Telephone conversation with Mr. Robert Moody, April 17, 1973.) Unfortunately, in spite of low advertising rates and reduction in the size of the paper from eight to four pages on September 12, 1929, the paper was discontinued. "Not enough advertising to make it pay. About 90% of subscriptions expire October 1; we will refund to all who run beyond October 1." (Editorial, S 25, 1930.) *Loc*: NRu/ Robert Moody: Mr 8, 1928; S 25, 1930.

THE CROCODILE (irr) Penn Yan. D 30, 1842–? (1:1–?). *Pub*: A gentleman called Hooting M. Ses. *Ed*: Nicodemus Mudwalloper, Grand High Priest of the Association. *Comment*: Published "when the morals of this place arrive at such a pass as to call for the interference of men of virtue." Published at the "Cow pasture recess," Penn Yan. *Loc*: NIC/RHA: D 30, 1842 (1:1).

THE DAILY CHRONICLE (d) Penn Yan. F 1876–? (1:1–?). *Pub and Ed*: Stafford C. Cleveland and Isaac C. Cornell 1876–? *Format*: Four pages 9″ x 12″. *Loc*: NIC/MMN: Mr 10, 11, 1876 (1:4, 5).

THE DAILY CHRONICLE (d) Penn Yan. N 20, 1882–? (1:1–?). *Pub and Ed*: Malcolm D. Mix and Steven B. Ayres 1882–? *Pol*: Independent. *Format*: Four pages 9″ x 12″. *Price*: 26¢ per month, 6¢ per week, 1¢ per copy. *Loc*: NIC/MMN: microfilm N 20–D 29, 1882 (1:1–33).

THE DEMOCRATIC ORGAN Penn Yan. ca. 1844. No issues located. "Commenced in 1844, at Penn Yan, by Henry L. Winants, and published two years, when it was abandoned." (*Combination Atlas Map of Yates County, New York, 1876*, p. 22.) Also mentioned in Lewis Cass Aldrich, *History of Yates County, N. Y.* (Syracuse: D. Mason & Co., 1892), p. 210.

THE DEMOCRATIC WHIG (w) Penn Yan. D 1837–1839// (1:1–?). *Pub and Ed*: William Child. *Pol*: Whig. *Format*: Four pages 15″ x 20″. *Comment*: "In 1839, it was published by Nicholas B. Suydam as the *Yates County Whig* [q.v.]." (*Combination Atlas Map of Yates Co., N. Y.*, p. 21.) Four newspapers in the Penn Yan of that day (circa 1833) must have rendered the profit of each rather precarious; at all events three of them shortly died, and it was not till 1837 that a printer was found of sufficient temerity to establish a successor. In that year was begun the publication of the newspaper which ". . . has been the most prosperous, best known, and widely read of all that have been produced in Penn Yan. William Child was the printer and the *Democratic Whig* was the newspaper." (Aldrich, *Yates County*, p. 209.) *Loc*: NIC/MMN: Ap 3, 1838 (1:18).

DIADEM Penn Yan, ca. 1882. No issues located. Established ca. 1882, the *Diadem* was a monthly family newspaper with a claimed circulation of 500. (Ayer's *Directory* of 1883.)

DUNDEE EXPOSITOR (w) Dundee. 1867–1870//(?) (1:1–?). *Pub and Ed*: Thomas Robinson & Bro. *Format*: Four pages 20″ x 26″. *Comment*: "Robinson traded the paper [the *Dundee Expositor*] with D. A. Bridgman [sic] for the *Penn Yan Express* in 1869, and Bridgman finding the publication of the paper unprofitable, suspended it in the Spring of 1870." (Stafford Canning Cleveland, *History and Directory of Yates County, New York*, 1873, II, 1132.) *Loc*: NIC/MMN: D 25, 1868 (2:20 whole no. 72).

DUNDEE HERALD (w) ca. 1867. No issues located. ". . . established in 1867 by Oliver Denison and T. Wm. Hodson. It was a paper of little worth, and the following year was sold to Thomas Robinson who changed its name to the *Dundee Expositor* [q.v.]. "(Cleveland, *Yates County*, II, 1132.)

DUNDEE HOME ADVOCATE see *HOME ADVOCATE*

DUNDEE OBSERVER (w) Dundee. Je 20, 1878 to date (1:1 to

date). *Title changes*: *The Dundee Observer* Je 20, 1878–D 25, 1969; *Viewpoint Finger Lakes* by 1970–Ja 1971; *Dundee Observer* F 25, 1971 to date. *Pub*: Eugene Vreeland 1878–F 1880; Eugene Vreeland and Baker F 25, 1880–S 1881; Eugene Vreeland S 15, 1881–D 1910; J. R. McCormick D 21, 1910–Ja 1913; Mrs. Nellie C. McCormick F 1913–Jl 1914; Mrs. G. Kirk Smith 1914–1916; Harry C. Smith S 1916–O 1955; Lynn H. Carpenter O 20, 1955–1964; Dorothy S. Carpenter 1964–1968; The Dundee Observer Corp. (Rodger Harris, Pub.) 1968–1971; Observer Co. (Michael Backer, Pub.) F 25, 1971 to date. *Ed*: Eugene Vreeland 1878–1880; Eugene Vreeland and Baker 1880–?; Eugene Vreeland S 14, 1881–?; William F. Weich by Jl 2, 1913–?; Harry C. Smith by S 7, 1916–O 1955; Lynn H. Carpenter O 1955–1964; Dorothy S. Carpenter 1964–1968; Mandi Harris 1968–1970; Susan Backer F 1971 to date. *Pol*: Neutral (1878–1882); Republican (1882 to date). *Format*: Four to twelve pages, varying sizes, 20″ x 25½″, 15″ x 22″, 12″ x 16″, 11½″ x 17″. *Price*: $1.00 per year (1890–1915); $1.50 per year (1919–1942); $2.00 per year (by 1947–1958); $2.50 per year (1958–1959); $3.00 per year, 10¢ per copy (1960–1972); $4.00 per year, 15¢ per copy (1973 to date). *Circ*: 1,104 (1884); 1,450 (1910); 1,008 (1926); 988 (1932); 1,280 (1952–1968). (Ayer's *Directory* 1884–1972.) *Loc*: NDun: Ja 3–17, Je 20, Ag 15, 22, S 19, 1883 (5:20, 21, 22; 6:1, 9, 10, 14); F 13, 1884 (6:35); Ap 28, 1921 (43:43); Ag 21, 1947 (70:12). NDun/ Observer: Je 20, 1878 to date (1:1 to date). NIC/MMN: Jl 6, 1887 (9:50). NIC/RHA: [Je 20, 1878–O 7, 1891 (1:1–14:16)]; F 15–D 27, 1893 (15:35–16:27); [Ja 5, 1898–F 23, 1933 (20:29–55:36)]; Mr 16, 1944 to date (66:41 to date).

THE DUNDEE RECORD (w) Dundee. Ja 25, 1844–D 4, 1890// (?) (1:1–46:42). *Pub*: Gifford J. Booth and William Butman 1844–?; William Butman by Ja 1, 1846–?; Gifford J. Booth by 1847–?; E. Hoogland by 1848–?; J. I. Diefendorf and N. Hyatt ?–1854; J. I. Diefendorf by Mr 1854–D 17, 1857; D. S. Bruner 1857–?; James M. Westcott by 1863–?; Spencer and Noble by 1887–?; Miles A. Davis by 1890–? *Ed*: William Butman by Ja 1, 1846–?; E. Hoogland by 1849–?; J. I. Diefendorf and N. Hyatt ?–1854; J. I. Diefendorf by Mr 1854–D 17, 1857; D. S. Bruner 1857–?; James M. Westcott by 1863–?; Spencer and Noble by 1887–?; Miles A. Davis by 1890–? *Pol*: Republican by 1863; Democrat; Independent by 1890. "The writer [Miles A. Davis] recollects when the *Record* was a sturdy exponent and advocate of Republican principles, and dealt some heavy blows under the sledge-hammer wielded by James M. Westcott. On the other hand, it is within the recent remembrance of the patrons of this paper, when, under the able pen of Mr. Churchill, it was a trenchant force in behalf of Dem-ocratic doctrines. Whatever this journal has been in the past, it is not now. . . . It is not a Republican paper. It is not a Democrat. Neither is it a neutral paper. It is non-partisan. Plainly, it is an Independent local newspaper." (Editorial, March 6, 1890). *Format*: Four pages, varying sizes, 15″ x 22″, 16″ x 24″, 18″ x 24″. *Price*: $1.50 per year in advance (1844–?); $1.00 per year in advance, otherwise $1.50 (by

1856); $1.50 per year in advance, otherwise $2.00 (by 1857); $1.00 per year in advance (by 1887). *Circ*: 1,200 (1856–1857); 600 (1880–1884). *Comment*: Motto: "An Independent, Weekly, Family Newspaper: Devoted to that which is Good, Useful, Instructive and Interesting" (?–1856); "A Weekly Family Paper, Impartial and Independent" (1857); "Advocate the Truth and Defend the Right" (by 1863); "Devoted to Local Interest" (1890). ". . . started at Dundee, January 25, 1844 by Gifford J. Booth, it was published by Edward Hoagland [*sic*] in 1847. John Diefendorf suceeded to its editorship in 1853. It was conducted by D. S. Bruner in 1857. It is now published by James M. Westcott." (*Combination Atlas Map*, p. 22.) "After [the death of Westcott] the *Record* came near extinction, but was finally revived by two nephews of Mr. Westcott, sold by them to a syndicate of Democratic politicians, and finally in 1890 was bought by several influential prohibitionists and is now published as a temperance newspaper." (Aldrich, *Yates County*, p. 210.) *Loc*: NCooHi: D 7, 1853 (10:42 whole no. 510); F 20, Mr 5, 1856–D 24, 1857 (12:51; 13:1–14:41). NDun: Ja 1, 1846 (2:49 whole no. 101); O 31, 1849 (6:37 whole no. 297); Ja 30, Jl 24, 1850 (6:50; 7:23 whole nos. 310, 335); D 10, 1856 (13:41 whole no. 661); Ja 4, 1883 (38:51 whole no. 1982); D 2, 1887 (43:41). NDun/Observer: S 12, 1844 (1:33); Mr 20, 1845 (2:8); Mr 31, My 5, Jl 28, O 6, D 15, 29, 1847 (4:8, 13, 24, 34, 43, 45 whole nos. 164, 169, 190, 199, 201); Ja 19, Mr 4, Ag 16, O 11, D 27, 1848 (4:48; 5:2, 26, 34, 45 whole nos. 204, 210, 234, 242, 258); Je 25 1856 (8:17 whole no. 641). NIC/MMN: D 25, 1879 (26:12 whole no. 1839); F 1, 1883 (38:53 whole no. 1984); Jl 1, 1887 (43:19). NIC/RHA: S 14, 1853 (10:30 whole no. 498); D 3, 1863 (fragment whole no. 1002). NPyC: O 29, 1851 (8:36 whole no. 400); Ap 13, N 16, 1853 (10:8, 39 whole nos. 476, 507); Ap 13, N 16, 1853 (10:8, 39 whole no. 476, 507). NPyHi: Mr 22, 1848 (5:5 whole no. 231); S 22, 1852 (9:31 whole no. 477); Mr 28, My 30, S 19, O 31, N 14, 1855 (12:6, 15, 30, 35, 37 whole nos. 578, 587, 602, 607, 609); Ja 23, Ap 2, My 28, 1856 (12:47; 13:5, 13 whole nos. 619, 629, 637); S 3, 1863 (19:52 whole no. 989); D 15, 1864 (21:15 whole no. 1056); N 30, 1865 (22:13 whole no. 1106); S 27, 1866 (23:1 whole no. 1149); F 7, My 30, O 31, 1867 (23:36; 24:?, 10); Mr 25–N 11, 1869 (25:32–26:30 whole nos. 1280–1320); F 16, 23, Mr 23, Ap 13, 1871 (27:25, 26, 30, 33 whole nos. 1377, 1378, 1382, 1385); O 9, 1873 (30:1 whole no. 1515); Ap 23, 1874 (30:29 whole no. 1543); O 19, 1876 (33:2 whole no. 1673); Mr 16, Jl 20, 1882 (38:1, 38 whole nos. 1952, 1969); Ja 4, 1883 (38:51 whole no. 1922); D 4, 1890 (46:42 whole no. ?).

DUNDEE TELEGRAPH (w) Dundee. N 30, 1871–? (1:1–?). *Pub and Ed*: William Drysdale. *Format*: Four pages, varying sizes, 15¼ " x 22½ ", 18" x 24". *Price*: $1.50 per year if paid in 3 months (1871). *Loc*: NDun/Observer: N 30, 1871 (1:1). NIC/MMN: Jl 11, 1872 (1:32).

THE ENQUIRER see *THE PENN YAN ENQUIRER*

GORHAM NEW AGE see *RUSHVILLE CHRONICLE AND GOR-HAM NEW AGE*

HOME ADVOCATE (w) Dundee. D 1890–? (1:1–?). *Pub*: Amendment League, Ltd. (Directors: A. C. Bassett, John Kline, C. P. Mc-Lean, Homer Andrews, George S. Shattuck.) 1890–? *Ed*: Rev. P. J. Bull (also Bus. Mgr.). *Pol*: Temperance. *Format*: Eight pages 13″ x 20″. *Price*: $1.00 per year (1891–1895). *Circ*: 1,000 (1891). *Comment*: Motto: "Protect the Home and the Nation is Safe." *Loc*: NDun/Observer: Ap 7, 21, 1891 (1:16, 18); Mr 21, 1893 (3:14). NIC/MMN: O 18, 1892 (2:44). NIC/RHA: Ja 13–S 1, 1891 (1:4–37); Ja 29, F 5, 1895 (5:6, 7). NMn: O 3–31, 1893 (3:42–46).

THE LITTLE JOKER (m) Dundee. Je 1883–? (1:1–?). *Pub*: F. W. Brace. *Ed*: J. E. Bean. *Format*: Four pages 10″ x 13½″. *Price*: 50¢ per year. *Loc*: NDun/Observer: Je 1883 (1:1).

MIDDLESEX VALLEY CHRONICLE (w) Penn Yan. F 1–N 1893// (1:1–?). *Pub and Ed*: DeWitt C. Ayres 1893–? *Format*: Four pages 13″ x 18″. *Price*: 50¢ per year. *Comment*: "The *Middlesex Valley Chronicle* printed at Penn Yan and circulated in this valley, has been discontinued. The *Chronicle* has served its place well but since the *Valley Review* has come, the publisher, Mr. Ayres has kindly surrendered the field giving his entire time to that well established journal —the *Yates County Chronicle*." (*The Valley Review*, N 18, 1893, p. 3.) *Loc*: NIC/MMN: F 22, Mr 1, 15, N 3, 1893 (1:4, 5, 7, 39); microfilm [F 1–Ag 9, 1893 (1:1–28)].

THE MILO QUESTION (irr) Milo Center. ca. 1915. *Pub*: Committee of One Hundred. *Format*: Four pages 13″ x 20″. *Comment*: Published as a protest paper against licensing. *Loc*: NIC/MMN: O 29, 1915 (no series no.).

THE MISCELLANY Penn Yan. 1883. No issues located. Established by Thomas H. Bassett. Short-lived. (Aldrich, *Yates County*, p. 209.) Also mentioned in *Combination Atlas Map*, p. 21.

NEW AGE. This paper was published in Ontario County. It merged with *The Rushville Chronicle* (q.v.) in 1915. Only one issue has been located in Yates County. Mr. Robert Moody has Ag 26, 1908 (5:40).

NO LICENSE (w) Dundee. F 1890–? (1:1–?). *Pub and Ed*: Stanley B. Roberts and Jesse A. Hungate. *Pol*: Temperance. *Format*: Four pages 10¾″ x 14″. *Comment*: Motto: "For Economy, Sobriety and the Home." *Loc*: NDun/Observer: F 21, 1890 (1:4).

PENN YAN COURIER (w) Penn Yan. My 1818–1950//(?) (1:1 n.s.–?). *Title changes*: *The Penn Yan Herald* My 1818–1820; *Penn Yan Democrat* 1820–Ag 7, 1947; *Penn Yan Courier* Ag 14, 1947–1950(?). *Pub and Ed*: Abraham H. Bennett and P. Youngs by S 1818–Je 8, 1819; Abraham H. Bennett by 1819–?; Abraham H. Bennett and Sutton by 1882–?; Abraham H. Bennett by 1828–?; Abraham H. Bennett and Alfred Reed by 1835–?; Alfred Reed by

1847–1850; Darius A. Ogden by 1850–?; Darius A. Ogden and Reuben Spicer by Je 1, 1852–?; Reuben Spicer and Staton by 1855; Reuben Spicer Jl 1855–?; George D. A. Bridgeman by Ap 8, 1857–?; Eli McConnell by 1866–?; Comings and Harry C. Earles by 1891–?; Walter B. Sheppard by F 1892–1902; Harry C. Earles (Pub.) and Walter B. Sheppard (Prop.) by 1902–?; Harry C. Earles by 1908–?; Kennedy and Morse by 1925–?; The Courier Press by 1947–1950 (Robert H. Clark, Ed.). *Pol*: Democrat. *Format*: Four to twelve pages, varying sizes, 14″ x 20″, 15″ x 22″, 18″ x 24″, 21″ x 26″, 22″ x 28″. *Price*: $2.50 per year in advance (1818–1819); $1.50 per year in advance (1847); $2.00 per year in advance (by 1870); $1.00 per year in advance (1891–1920); $1.25 per year in advance (1920); $1.35 per year in advance (1938). *Comment*: For a brief period from 1826 to 1828, the *Democrat* changed its numbering to n.s. 1 and continuation but by 1828 it resumed the consecutive numbering which established its antecedent as *The Penn Yan Herald*. "In 1818 Penn Yan was a village through which the stages ran once or twice a week on their way from Geneva to Bath, and each stage left here a newspaper or two for the wealthier residents. *The Herald* copied this news matter and disseminated it throughout the county." (Aldrich, *Yates County*, p. 208.) "Till the establishment of the *Democratic Whig* [q.v.] in 1837 by William Child, the *Democrat* lead this field largely by itself. Its chief competition had been the *Yates County Republican* [probably *Yates Republican* q.v.] established by E. J. Fowle in 1824." (Aldrich, *Yates County*, p. 208.) By 1848 office was over Jones and Ells Store, corner of Main and Elm Streets; by 1910 office in Arcade on ground floor. *Loc*: NIC/MMN: microfilm S 29, 1818 (1:21); [Mr 2–N 30, 1819 (1:43–2:81)]; F 1, O 10, 1820 (2:91, 127); My 16–30, 1826 (n.s. 1:20–22 whole nos. 419–421); Ja 29, 1828 (10:fragment); Je 25, Jl 2, 9, 1839 (22:10, 11, 12 whole nos. 1103–1105); Je 9, 1840 (23:9 fragment); Je 9, 1912 (94:41 whole no. 4921). Not filmed Ja 2, 1830 (12:610); Jl 4, O 10, 1855 (39:3, 19 whole nos. 1946, 1960); N 18, 1864 (46:27 whole no. 2419); Ja 5, 1866 (47:35 whole no. 2478); Mr 17, 1876 (56:49 whole no. 3009); Mr 5, 1886 (65:43 whole no. 3529); Je 5, 26, 1891 (72:2, 5 whole nos. 3403, 3406); F 26, 1892 (72:41 whole nos. 3441); Mr 16, 1894 (76:45 whole no. 3956); Ja 7, F 4, 25, 1898 (80:36, 37, 40 whole nos. 4164, 4165, 4168); Je 3, 1902 (83:36 whole no. 4358); F 27, O 30, 1903 (85:43; 86:26); My 3, 1918 (101:1); Jl 18, 1919 (102:12); D 23, 1921 (104:34); Je 3, 23, My 18, 1923 (105:40, 43, 106:3); [Mr 21–My 9, 1924 (106:47–107:2)]. NIC/RHA: S 29, 1818 (1:21); [Mr 2–N 30, 1819 (1:43–2:81)]; F 1, O 10, 1820 (2:91, 127); Ag 27, 1822 (5:225); My 16–30, 1826 (n.s. 1:20–22 whole nos. 419–421); Ja 29, 1828 (10:1 whole no. 508); Je 25, Jl 2, 1839 (22:10, 11 whole nos. 1103, 1104); Je 9, S 15, 1840 (23:9, 22); D 21, 1841 (24:26 whole nos. 1233); F 21, 1843 (25:45 whole no. 1295); Ja 14, 1910 (92:37 whole no. 4813); F 9, 1912 (94:41 whole no. 4921). NPyC: S 19, 1848 (31:37 whole no. 1591); D 4, 25, 1849 (32:42, 45 whole nos. 1654, 1657); [Ja 1, 1850–D 26, 1860 (32:46–43:33 whole nos. 1658–2217)]. NPyCl: [Ja 20, 1899–D 30, 1948

(21:38–131:39)]. NPyHi: My 18, 1847 (30:6 whole no. 1521); Jl 8, 1870 (53:10 whole no. 2712); F 22, 1901 (83:43 whole no. 4313); O 30, 1931 (114:28).

PENN YAN DAILY TELEGRAPH see *PENN YAN TELEGRAPH*

PENN YAN DEMOCRAT see *PENN YAN COURIER*

THE PENN YAN ENQUIRER (w) Penn Yan. 1831–? (1:1–?). *Pub*: B. Tyler and Co. 1831– Ag 14, 1832; B. Tyler and Fowle Ag 21, 1832–1833. *Ed*: J. A. Hadley O 28, 1831–S 12, 1832. *Pol*: Anti-Mason. *Format*: Four pages 15″ x 25″. *Price*: $2.50 per year in advance (1831); $1.50 per year in advance, otherwise $2.00 per year (1832). *Comment*: Motto: "Despotism can no more exist in a Nation, until the Liberty of the Press be destroyed, than might can happen before the sun is set." In an editorial which appeared in the January 18, 1831 issue of the *Yates Republican* (q.v.), Fowle states that he has just sold the newspaper to John Renwick. According to historian Aldrich this transaction took place "in 1834 [and] John Remmich [*sic*] . . . changed its name to the *Enquirer,* and two years later it quietly died and was forgotten." Published in the second story of the building occupied by B. Tyler and Co. on Head St., opposite the Penn Yan Hotel. On March 13, 1833 the paper was "discontinued for a season," in a statement made by Tyler and Fowle. *Loc*: NIC/MMN: microfilm [O 12, 1831–Mr 13, 1833 (1:37–3:9)]. NPyCl: N 23, D 14, 28, 1831 (1:43, 46, 48); Ja 4–S 5, 1831 (1:49–2:34).

THE PENN YAN EXPRESS (w) Penn Yan. 1866–1925// (1:1–?). *Pub and Ed*: George D. A. Bridgeman 1866–?; Reuben A. Scofield by 1873–1923; Print Craft Shop by 1923–1925. *Pol*: Republican (1866–?). *Format*: Four to eight pages, varying sizes, 20″ x 25½″, 17″ x 23″. *Price*: $2.00 per year in advance (by 1871); $1.50 per year in advance (1876); $1.25 per year in advance (by 1899); $1.00 per year in advance (by 1904–1925). *Circ*: 2,050 (1914); 6,000 (1924). (Ayres' *Directory*) *Comment*: Motto: "Devoted to Politics and General Intelligence." (ca. 1870); "Only Continuously Republican Paper in Yates County." (1911). Merged with the *Chronicle-Express* (q.v.) in 1925. ". . . was started in 1866, by G. D. A. Bridgman [*sic*]; in 1869 it was sold to Thomas Robinson, and in 1870 repurchased by Mr. Bridgman. In September, 1872, it was purchased by R[euben] A. Scofield, who is the present publisher. It is Republican in politics, and an ably-edited and influential journal." (*Combination Atlas Map*, p. 22.) *Loc*: NDun/Observer: N 8, 1893 (27:31 whole no. 1440). NIC/MMN: Ja 20, 1875 (9:43 whole no. 459); Je 3, 1891 (26:8 whole no. 1313). NIC/RHA: Ap 12, O 18, 1872 (6:2, 29 whole nos. 262, 289); Mr 8, 15, 1876 (10:50, 51 whole nos. 518, 519); Mr 19, 1879 (13:51 whole no. 676); F 25–Ag 25, 1880 (14:48–15:21 whole nos. 725–751); Ag 30, 1899 (33:21 whole no. 1743); Ja 10, S 5, N 28, 1900 (33:48; 34:22, 34 whole nos. 1762, 1796, 1808); O 29, 1902 (37:30 whole no. 1908); Mr 30, Ap 6, N 9, 1904 (38:51, 52; 39:31 whole no. 1982, 1983, 2014); Je 7, 1911 (46:10 whole no.

2357); [Ap 2–Jl 30, 1913 (47:51–48:16 whole nos. 2452–2619)]; F 14, Ag 2, 1923 (57:45; 58:17 whole nos. 2967, 2991); [Mr 13–Jl 10, 1924 (58:49–59:14 whole nos. 3023–3040)]. NPyC: microfilm Ap 1, 1874–Mr 22, 1876 (9:1–10:52 whole nos. 417–520); [My 2, 1883–D 31, 1925 (18:3–60:39 whole nos. 891–3117)]. NSenHi: Ap 2, 1873 (8:1 whole no. 365); Mr 1, 22, 29, 1876 (10:49, 52; 11:1 whole nos. 517, 520, 521); F 28, 1877 (11:49); Mr 29, Ap 5, 1911 (65:52; 66:1 whole nos. 2347, 2348).

PENN YAN HERALD see *PENN YAN COURIER*

PENN YAN MERCHANTS' STORE NEWS see *YATES COUNTY STORE NEWS*

PENN YAN MYSTERY (w) Penn Yan. Ja 4, 1879// (1:1). *Pub and Ed*: Leon and Harriet Lewis. *Format*: Eight pages 14½ " x 20¾ ". *Price*: $3.00 per year (1879). *Comment*: According to Aldrich's history, only one issue was published. "But of all the journals which have had their incipiency in our county the best known in other localities, the most unprofitable, and the shortest lived was the Penn Yan *Mystery*. It was a mystery indeed. For many years two writers, Leon and Harriet Lewis, had made Penn Yan their home. Their books, and those of Mrs. Lewis in particular, while not indicative of the highest creative power, still were readable and had great vogue among the class who perused with delight the old New York *Ledger* and kindred sheets. Mrs. Lewis died, and unsatisfied with his notoriety the survivor undertook the task of founding a weekly newspaper which should bring him fame and possibly fortune too. It was not an ill advised scheme. A tremendous edition of the first number was sent out on January 4, 1879. It was read and liked. From New Hampshire to Alabama subscriptions and communications flowed in. Had the editor been a different man he might have succeeded. But as it was, discouraged by his financial condition or losing pluck, ere the second edition appeared he left Penn Yan between two days and has never returned." (Aldrich, *Yates County*, p. 211.) *Loc*: NHan: Ja 4, 1879 (1:1).

PENN YAN TELEGRAPH (d, tri-w) Penn Yan. 1846–? (1:1–?). *Title changes*: *Penn Yan Daily Telegraph* 1846–?; *Penn Yan Telegraph* by April 1847. *Pub and Ed*: Rodney L. Adams 1846–? *Pol*: Whig. *Format*: Four pages, varying sizes, 13" x 17", 11¼" x 17". *Price*: $5.50 per year (1846); $3.00 per year, 3¢ per copy (1847). *Comment*: Published at the office of the *Yates County Whig* (q.v.) located at the south-west corner of Main and Elm Streets over Watson, Stark and Co. store, third story. ". . . while its publication was continued longer than expected it succombed in six months. This failure stopped the publication of new journals in Penn Yan for twenty years." (Aldrich, *Yates County*, p. 210.) *Loc*: NIC/MMN: My 7, 1846 (1:97). NIC/RHA: Ap 6, 1847 (2:35).

THE PIONEER (?) Penn Yan. Ag 18, 1886–? (1:1–?). *Pub and Ed*: Samuel P. Burrill 1886–? *Format*: Eight pages. *Price*: $1.25 per year in advance (1886). *Comment*: Printed at the Chronicle Office, Penn Yan. *Loc*: NPyHI: Ag 18, 1886 (1:1).

REPUBLICAN TIMES (w) Rushville. Jl 1856–? (1:1–?). *Pub and Ed*: Cuyler F. Greene. *Pol*: Republican. *Format*: Four pages 18″ x 24″. *Price*: 50¢ per copy. *Comment*: Motto: "Family Newspaper, Devoted to Politics, Agriculture and the Mechanic Arts." May have been established to promote the campaign for Charles Fremont and William L. Dayton Republican candidates for President and Vice-President. Ceased publication when the Republican party lost the election. (According to a phone conversation with Mr. Robert Moody, April 17, 1973.) *Loc*: NRu/Robert Moody: Ag 22, O 17, 31, 1856 (1:9, 17, 19).

RUSHVILLE ARGUS (w) Rushville. Jl 26, 1878–1879// (?) (1:1–?). *Pub and Ed*: J. H. Stewart and Co. *Format*: Four pages 16″ x 21½″. *Price*: $1.25 per year. *Comment*: Motto: "Devoted to the Interests of Rushville and Vicinity." "About a dozen years ago a little sheet started, under the name of the *Rushville Argus,* but it was short lived, and an end came to its existence in less than a year." (*Ontario County Journal,* November 24, 1893.) *Loc*: NRu/Robert Moody: Jl 26, 1878 (1:1).

THE RUSHVILLE CHRONICLE see *RUSHVILLE CHRONICLE AND GORHAM NEW AGE*

RUSHVILLE CHRONICLE AND GORHAM NEW AGE (w) Rushville and Penn Yan. Ap 19, 1905–Ja 1926// (1:1–?). *Title changes*: The Rushville Chronicle Ap 19, 1905–Ja 15, 1915; *Rushville Chronicle and Gorham New Age* Ja 22, 1915–Ja 1926. *Pub*: DeWitt C. Ayres 1905–1908; DeWitt C. Ayres and Frank H. Wilson Ag 21, 1908–1915; Peerless Printing Co. 1915–? *Ed*: DeWitt C. Ayres 1905–1913; DeWitt C. Ayres and Frank H. Wilson 1913–? *Format*: Eight to twelve pages 20″ x 24″. *Price*: $1.25 per year in advance (1905–1913); $1.00 per year (1913–?); $1.50 per year, 4¢ per copy (1919); $2.00 per year (1923). *Comment*: Motto: "Devoted to the Interests of Rushville and the Middlesex Valley." In 1926 the newspaper merged with the *Penn Yan Express* and the *Yates County Chronicle* and together they were published as the *Chronicle-Express* (q.v.) *Loc*: NIC/RHA: [Ap 19, 1905–Jl 10, 1925 (1:1–20:15 whole nos. 1–1003)]. NRu/Robert Moody: S 8, O 13, 27, 1905 (1:20, fragment, 27 whole nos. 20, fragment, 27); Mr 23–Ap 13, 27, Je 29, 1906 (1:48–51, 53; 2:10 whole nos. 48–51, 53, 62).

RUSHVILLE HERALD (w) Rushville. 1880–? (1:1–?). *Pub*: Clark L. Francisco. *Format*: Four pages 13″ x 18½″. *Price*: 75¢ per year in advance, otherwise $1.00. *Circ*: 650 (Ayer's *Directory*.) *Comment*: Office in the Masonic Hall Block. This paper suspended publication when Mr. Francisco moved to Sayre, Pennsylvania. (*Ontario County Journal,* November 24, 1893.) *Loc*: NRu/Robert Moody: Ap 25, 1884 (4:17); Je 11, 1886 (5:24 fragment).

SKYE LOCH VILLAGE BAGPIPER (semi-m, m) Dundee. Jl 1972 to date (1:1 to date). *Pub*: Skye Loch Village Corp. (Printed by Dundee Observer). *Ed*: John Diven. *Comment*: Devoted to local happenings in the retirement colony at Skye Loch Village. *Loc*: NDun/ Observer: Mr 1973.

VALLEY REVIEW (w) Rushville. N 18, 1893–? (1:1–?). *Pub and Ed*: J. K. Smith 1893–? *Pol*: Independent. *Format*: Four to eight pages 15″ x 22″. *Price*: $1.00 per year in advance (1893). *Comment*: Motto: "A Record of Rushville and the Surrounding County." Circulated largely among farmers. *Loc*: NRu/Robert Moody: N 18, 1893 (1:1); N 26, 1898 (6:5).

VIEWPOINT FINGER LAKES see *DUNDEE OBSERVER*

THE VINEYARDIST (bi-w) Penn Yan. No issues located. "This as a bi-weekly, began in 1887 by John H. Butler and Samuel P. Burrill as an exponent of the grape interests on Seneca and Keuka Lakes. Within its limited scope it does good work and is well thought of by its subscribers. Mr. Butler is now [1892] the sole proprietor." (Aldrich, *Yates County*, p. 211.) Ayer's lists its establishment as 1886 and indicates that it was an eight page publication costing $1.00 per year with a circulation of 1,500.

THE WESTERN STAR Penn Yan. 1833. No issues located. Published by H. Gilbert. (*Combination Atlas Map*, p. 21.) Also mentioned in Aldrich, *Yates County*, p. 209.

YATES COUNTY CHRONICLE see *CHRONICLE-EXPRESS*

YATES COUNTY FARM AND HOME BUREAU NEWS (m) Penn Yan. 1918–1936. No issues located. This paper is listed in Ayer's *Directory* as the *Yates County Farm Bureau News* 1918–?; then the *Yates County Farm and Home Bureau News* by 1929–1936. It was published by the Yates County Farm Bureau Association. The editors were A. L. Hollingsworth by 1924–?; C. B. Raymond by 1926–1931; W. C. Stokoe 1932–1936. Ayer's states that a subscription cost 75¢ per year.

YATES COUNTY NEWS (w) Penn Yan. ca. 1923. *Pub*: Print Craft shop, Inc., 1923. *Format*: Eight pages 17″ x 22″. *Price*: 1¢ per copy (1923). *Loc*: NIC/MMN: O 11, 25, 1923 (no vol. or no.).

YATES COUNTY REPUBLICAN (w) Penn Yan. Ag 17, 1855–? (1:1–?). *Pub and Ed*: None listed. *Pol*: Republican. *Format*: Four pages. *Loc*: NIC/MMN: microfilm Ag 17–N 8, 1855 (1:1–13).

YATES COUNTY STORE NEWS (irr) Penn Yan. D 8, 1914–? (1:1–?). *Title changes*: *Penn-Yan Merchants' Store News* 1914–?; *Yates County Store News* by 1915–? *Format*: Six pages 17″ x 24″. *Price*: Free. *Circ*: 6,004 (1914); 7,350 (1915). *Comment*: The paper contained news about the stores in Penn Yan. No publishers or editors are listed. *Loc*: NIC/MMN: D 8, 1914 (1:1); F 10, 1915 (2:2).

YATES COUNTY WHIG (w) Penn Yan. 1839–? (1:1–?). *Pub and Ed*: Andrew Cooper by Ja 6, 1840–? *Pol*: Whig. *Format*: Four pages. *Price*: $2.50 per year in advance. *Comment*: Published in the Brick Building on the corner of Elm and Main Sts. December 15, 1840 contains the official canvass for the offices of Governor, Lt. Governor, Senators and members of Congress. *Loc*: NIC/MMN: microfilm Ja 6, F 25, Jl 14, D 15, 1840 (1:29, 36; 2:4, 26); Ja 5, 12, Ap 13, 20, 1841 (2:29, 30. 43, 44).

YATES COUNTY WHIG (w) Penn Yan. Ag 31, 1841–F 21, 1843 (n.s. 1:1–2:26). *Ed*: Edward J. Fowle. *Pol*: Whig. *Format*: Four pages. *Price*: $2.50 per year in advance. *Comment*: In the February 21, 1843 issue the following statement appears: "the present editors conducted this paper for the last year and a half, under many disadvantages. Their nature were set forth at his commencement—other business at a distant part of the village occupying nearly all his time and attentions and he stated then that he feared (what has proven too true) that the interest of the paper would be neglected. He has in consequence been desirous for some time past to place the publication in other hands . . . The *Yates County Whig* will be conducted from this date for at least a year and a half to come by Mr. Andrew D. Suydam . . ." Signed Edward J. Fowle. Loc: NIC/MMN: microfilm Ag 31, 1841–F 21, 1843 (n.s. 1:1–2:26).

YATES COUNTY WHIG (F 28, 1843–Jl 1856) see *CHRONICLE-EXPRESS*

YATES REPUBLICAN (w) Penn Yan. D 16, 1824–? (1:1–?). *Pub and Ed*: Edward J. Fowle D 16, 1824–Ja 18, 1831. *Pol*: Republican; Anti-Mason. *Format*: Four pages 12″ x 20″. *Price*: $2.50 per year in advance (1824–1831). *Comment*: Motto: "Principia, non Homines." Published in the office of the Republican. The January 18, 1831 issue carried the following editorial: "With this number [7:6] the interest of the undersigned ceases in the establishment of the *Yates Republican*. To those who have sustained us upwards of six years, and enabled us . . . to pursue our avocation with profit—we feel under obligations which we cannot sufficiently express by words. That we should have committed errors was to be expected. We have had much to contend against, and a printer's path lies not altogether among roses. We leave our friends, however, with our best wishes for their success and prosperity; and our political opponents with the remark, that it would be gratifying to us to bury all past differences in oblivion. Mr. John Renwick, the gentleman to whom we have disposed this establishment, comes among us well recommended, and I have no doubt will strive to give satisfaction to his patrons. I wish him god-speed in the commencement of his journey through life." Signed, Edward J. Fowle. Loc: NIC/MMN: microfilm [D 16, 1824–Ja 18, 1831 (1:1–7:6 whole nos. 1–319)]. NIC/RHA: Ag 3, 1830 (6:35 whole no. 295). NPyC: D 16, 1824–D 6, 1825 (1:1–52[?]).

SUPPLEMENT

ALLEGANY COUNTY

THE BELFAST BLAZE (w) Belfast. 1899–Ag 26, 1970// *Loc*: NAngHi: microfilm Ja 11, F 15, 1900 (1:15, 20); Mr 6, 1902 (3:23); Je 1, 1916–Ag 26, 1970 (17:35–68:52).

THE WHITESVILLE NEWS (w) Whitesville. Ap 3, 1895–My 7, 1953// *Loc*: NAngHi: microfilm Ap 3, 1895–My 7, 1953 (1:1–57:51).

BROOME COUNTY

CHENANGO VALLEY CITIZEN (w) Binghamton. 1920(?)–1961(?). No issues located. Published as the English edition of *Obywatel* (q.v.) by the Citizen Publishing Co. Edited by Stanley J. Jankiewicz. Distributed free. Circulation 6,500 (1941). (Information from Ayer's *Directory* 1929–1962.)

DEPOSIT COURIER (w) Deposit. My 31, 1848–S 6, 1862 (1:1–?). *Pub*: M. R. Hulce (Prop.) 1848; C. E. Wright 1848–1855; Sylvester D. Hulce 1855–? *Ed*: C. E. Wright 1848–? *Pol*: Republican although campaigned for Cass and Butler (Democrats) in 1848 and also advocated Free Soil. *Format*: Four pages 13″ x 18¾″. *Comment*: On September 6, 1862, when Sylvester Hulce, publisher and editor of the *Deposit Union Democrat,* merged the latter paper with the *Courier,* he changed the title of both papers to the *Delaware Courier* and renumbered the paper volume 1, number 1 of the *Courier* and volume

The Ostego Republican *on Cooperstown's Main Street, nineteenth century. From the Ward Collection, New York State Historical Association.*

10 of the *Deposit Union Democrat*. The newspaper has gone through a series of numbering changes. Published at 138 Front Street in Deposit. *Loc*: NBiHi: Mr 23, 1849 (1:49).

THE DEPOSIT COURIER (w) Deposit. S 1862 to date (1:1 to date). *Title changes*: *Delaware Courier* 1862–1867; *Deposit Courier* 1867–1905; *Deposit Courier-Journal* 1905–?; *Deposit Courier* ?–1970; *The Deposit Courier* 1970 to date. *Pub*: Allen and Carpenter 1862; Lucius P. Allen 1863–1868; Ambrose Blunt and Joshua Smith 1868–1869; Adrian L. Watson and Charles N. Stow 1869–?; Charles N. Stow and Sons ?–1902; J. Daniel Kellogg 1905–1930; Deposit-Courier Co. (William C. Stow, Pres.) 1930–1937; John J. Stein 1938; G. S. VanRyper 1938; Edward J. Russell, Jr., 1955–1958; William Ryan 1967–1970; Hilton Evans Ag 30, 1970 to date. *Ed*: Lucius P. Allen 1862; Allen and Carpenter 1863–?; Charles N. Stow 1869–1902; John B. Stow 1902–1903; Charles N. Stow's Sons 1905; J. Daniel Kellogg 1905–1930; J. D. and A. B. Kellogg 1919–1920; J. D. and A. B. Kellogg and MacDonald 1921–?; C. H. and J. B. Stow 1935–?; George S. VanRyper 1938–?; J. Daniel Kellogg 1941–1948; William C. Stow 1948–?; Robert S. Gulian 1955–?; James F. Minehan 1955; George R. Venizelos 1955–1957; John O'Dell 1957–?; Ralph Lent 1958–Je 4, 1959; Raymond E. Ruegger Je 4, 1959–S 8, 1960; Charles D. Cook S 26, 1960–1965; George D. Brower 1965–1967; William Ryan 1967–Ag 29, 1970; Hilton Evans Ag 30, 1970 to date. *Pol*: Republican. *Format*: Four to eight pages, varying sizes, 11¾" x 16⅝", 15½" x 22¼", 17½" x 24", 12⅞" x 19", 17½" x 22". *Price*: $1.50 per year (1866); $4.00 per year (1968). *Circ*: 1,730. *Comment*: Published at 138 Front Street in Deposit. *Loc*: NBiHi: Je 30, 1877 (15:44); My 31, 1879 (17:40); Mr 6, 1880 (18:28); [Ja 1, 1881–Mr 2, 1888 (19:19–26:29)]; D 26, 1901 (54:19); Ja 2, 1902 (54:20). NCooHi: S 19, 1901 (54:5). NDeP: [Je 28, 1848–N 13, 1852 (1:5–5:4)]; [S 6, 1862–Jl 27, 1872 (n.s. 1:1–10:47)]; Ag 8, D 12, 1874; N 24, 1877 (16:13); [My 31, 1879–F 11, 1920 (17:38–?)]; Ja 3, N 6, 1929; [Ja 3, 1935 to date]. NHan: O 7, N 1, D 29, 1862 (1:5, 9, 13); Ja 31, F 7, Mr 14, 21, Je 6, Jl 4, S 19, 26, 1863 (1:22, 23, 28, 29, 40, 44; 2:3, 4); O 16, N 18, 27, D 27, 1868 (7:6, 12, 16); F 29, Ag 27, S 18, O 16, D 18, 25, 1869 (7:21, 51; 8:2, 6, 15, 16); Ja 29, Fe 5, 12, Mr 27, Ap 9, 30, Je 11, Jl 9, 16, S 10, O 21, D 2, 1870 (8:21, 22, 23, 29, 31, 34, 40, 44, 45; 9:1; 10:13); [Ja 7–D 7, 1871 (9:18–10:14)]; [Ap 27–S 28, 1872 (10:34–11:?)]; My 31, Je 7, 1873 (11:39, 40). NIC/RHA: O 18, 1862 (1:7); [Ja 10, 1863–Ap 15, 1864 (1:19–2:33)]; F 24, 1865 (3:26); O 23, 1868 (7:7); Jl 9, S 11, 1869 (7:44; 8:1); D 9, 1871 (10:14); Ag 25, 1883 (22:1); O 23, N 13, 1885 (24:10, 13); S 15, 1892 (31:5); N 19, 1896 (35:13); O 14, 1903 (56:9); Mr 27, Ap 3, 1929 (n.s. 26:21, 22); N 6, 1930 (83:22); N 17, 24, D 15, 1938 (91:25, 26, 29); [Ja 14–O 21, 1943 (95:34–96:22)].

HARPURSVILLE BUDGET (w) Harpursville. My 27, 1886–? *Loc*: NHan: Jl 20, 1894 (9:6).

LISLE GLEANER AND NEW ERA (w) Lisle. My 1871–D 1928//
Loc: NCortHi: Je 27, 1883 (13:8). NHan: Ag 12, 1871 (1:12).

OBYWATEL (w) Binghamton. 1919(?)–1958(?). No issues located.
Published originally for Polish immigrants. By 1929 published by the
Citizens Publishing Co. Edited by John A. Polakas (1929–1939) and
M. A. Goffa (1940–1942). The paper sold for $2.00 per year until
1950 and was distributed free of charge thereafter. *The Chenango
Valley Citizen* (q.v.), an English language supplement, was published
from 1941–1961. (Information from Ayer's *Directory 1929–1962*.)

THE SUN-BULLETIN (d) Binghamton. F 23, 1849 to date. *Loc*:
NNoHi: S 20, 1881 (no vol. or no.).

WHITNEY POINT REPORTER (w) Whitney Point. O 1, 1873–O
1960 (1:1–?). *Title changes*: *Nioga Reporter* O 1, 1873–1877; *Whitney's Point Reporter* ?–Mr 4, 1943; *Whitney Point Reporter* Mr 11,
1943–O 6, 1960. *Pub and Ed*: Milo B. Eldredge 1873–1877; Mark D.
Branday 1877–1879; Mark D. and F. C. Branday 1879–1893; F. C.
Branday 1893–My 27, 1948; Charles M. Branday 1948–N 5, 1957;
John H. Gardiner N 1957–O 1960. *Pol*: Independent. *Format*: Four
to twenty-four pages, varying sizes, 20½″ x 26¾″, 15″ x 28½″, 18″ x
24″. *Circ*: 1,500. *Comment*: After the *Broome Gazette* office burned
in 1871, Whitney Point was without a paper for two years. Milo Eldredge called his newspaper the *Nioga Reporter* in order to induce
the people to change the name of the place to Nioga. It remained
Whitney's Point until March 1943, when the Post Office changed the
name to Whitney Point. Published at 510 Main Street in Whitney
Point until a fire in 1897, then moved publishing operation temporarily to Chenango Forks. In 1960 moved to Greene, N. Y., Chenango County, and combined with the *Chenango American,* to form
the *Chenango American and Whitney Point Reporter* (q.v., in Chenango County bibliography.) *Loc*: NBiHi: S 22, 1876 (3:51); My 11,
Ag 17, 1877 (4:32, 46); Ja 4, 11, 1878 (5:14, 15); Mr 11, D 30,
1881 (8:24; 9:14); Ap 27, 1883 (10:31); Je 14, Jl 26, 1889 (16:38,
44); Je 19, 1891 (18:39); My 1, 1897 (24:33). NWhP: N 5, 1873
(1:6); F 28, Mr 21, 1874 (1:21, 24); Je 30, 1876 (3:39); F 2, 1877
(4:18); Ja 4–11, 1878 (5:14, 15); Mr 11, D 30, 1881 (8:24; 9:14);
Ap 27, Je 8, S 7, 1883 (10:31, 37, 50); Ap 19, Je 14; Jl 26, 1889
(16:30, 38, 44); Je 19, 1891 (18:39); Je 2, 1893 (20:37); Ap 23,
1897 (extra); [My 1, 1897 to date (24:33 to date)]. NIC/RHA: Ja
14, 1960 (99:28).

CAYUGA COUNTY

AUBURN (w) Auburn. N 17, 1888–F 16, 1889// (1:1–2:14). *Loc*:
NAub: N 17, 1888–F 16, 1889 (1:1–2:14).

CAYUGA COUNTY COURIER (w) Moravia. O 14, 1863–1871(?)
Loc: NAubHi: O 14, 1863–O 4, 1864 (1:1–52).

CHEMUNG COUNTY

THE FACTS (w) Elmira. 1895–? (1:1–?). *Pub*: Union Publishing Company of Elmira, Ltd. *Ed*: P. J. Bull. *Format*: Two to four pages 15″ x 21½″. *Price*: 2¢ per copy. *Loc*: NDun/Observer: Ja 22, 1897 (2:37).

THE HUSBANDMAN (w) Elmira. Ag 26, 1874–Ag 16, 1893// *Loc*: NCooHi: Ag 26, 1874–Ag 10, 1881 (1:1–7:364).

NEWTOWN TELEGRAPH (w) Newtown Village (Tioga Co., now Elmira, Chemung Co.) N 1815–? (1:1–?). *Title changes*: *The Telegraph* 1815–1818(?); *Newtown Telegraph* by 1819. *Pub*: William Murphy 1815–?; Erastus Shepard by D 1818. *Format*: Four pages, varying sizes, 11½″ x 18″, 12″ x 19½″. *Price*: $1.75 per year in advance; $2.00 at end of each six months, $2.25 at end of year. *Comment*: The office of *The Telegraph* was located in the yellow building, one door east of the Post Office. *Loc*: NEmHi: O 15, 1816 (vol. and no. indistinct). NRU: D 18, 1818 (4:6); Mr 5, Jl 9, 1819 (4:17, 35).

THE SOUTHERN TIER LEADER (w) Elmira. F 28, 1874–? (1:1–?). *Loc*: NCooHi: F 28, 1874–F 19, 1876 (1:1–2:52).

SUNDAY TELEGRAM (w) Elmira. Ap 31, 1879 to date (1:1 to date). *Loc*: NBiHi: Jl 2, 1882 (4:9); My 4, 1884 (6:1); N 1, 1908 (30:27). NNoHi: D 18, 1881 (no vol. or issue no.).

DELAWARE COUNTY

YOUNG AMERICA Crookerville. ca. 1859. No issues located. "*Young America*. This is the title of a new paper just started in Crookerville in the Souncy [*sic*] by our former divel [perhaps, printer's devil], Mr. C. A. Van Vradenburg alias Cobby Pennfuddler. It is democratic in politics but he is trying to print it on old American type." (*The Walton Journal*, Feb. 3, 1859).

OTSEGO COUNTY

HARTWICK SEMINARY MONTHLY (m) Hartwick Seminary. Ja 1880–? (1:1–?). *Title changes*: *Hartwick Seminary Monthly* Ja 1880–?; *Hartwick Seminary Monthly and Eastern Lutheran* by 1887; *The Monthly* by 1909; *Hartwick Seminary Monthly* by 1926. *Pub and Ed*: Willis S. Hinnman and William E. Hull Ja 1880–? *Format*: Four to eight pages, varying sizes, 8½″ x 11″, 7″ x 9″. *Price*: 25¢ per year (1880–?). *Comment*: Issues for volume 1, no. 1 through volume 2, no. 6 were written by the electric pen process. The first printed issue appeared October 1881. The proprietors had hoped to publish on the fifteenth and first of each academic year, but only published ten issues per year. Originally published for alumni and friends of Hartwick Seminary. According to Gary G. Roth, former archivist at Hartwick College, the *Monthly* was succeeded by the *Hartwickian* in 1928. The latter was primarily a school newspaper. *Loc*: NCooHi: [Jl 1880–Ap 1926 (1:7–22:187)]. NOnHC: Ja 1880–Jl 1891; [D 1895–My 1928].

OTSEGO HERALD (w) Cooperstown. Ap 3, 1795–Ja 29, 1821// (1:1–26:1349). *Title changes*: *The Otsego Herald: or, Western Advertiser* Ap 3–Je 5, 1795; *The Otsego Herald; or, Western Advertiser* Je 12–Ag 7, 1795; *Otsego Herald; or, Western Advertiser* Ag 14, 1795–S 12, 1805; *Otsego Herald* S 19, 1805–Ja 29, 1821. *Pub and Ed*: Elihu Phinney Ap 3, 1795–Jl 10, 1813; Henry & Elihu Phinney (died Jl 12, 1813) Jl 17–Ag 7, 1813; Israel W. Clark, For the Proprietors Ag 14, 1813–Mr 12, 1814; Henry & Elihu Phinney Mr 19, 1814–Je 29, 1821. *Pol*: Independent, then Republican. *Format*: Four pages, varying sizes, 11½ " x 19", 10" x 17". *Comment*: Motto: "Historic truth our Herald shall proclaim, the law our guide, the public good our aim!" "On Apr. 3, 1807, the village of Cooperstown was incorporated as Otsego, accordingly with the issue of Apr. 16, 1807, Cooperstown was replaced by Otsego in the imprint. Elihu Phinney died July 12, 1813, and with the issue of July 17, 1813, the paper was published by H. & E. Phinney [Henry and Elihu Phinney, Jr.]. With this issue Otsego was changed to Cooperstown in the imprint, the change having been made by the legislature June 12, 1812. With the issue of Aug. 14, 1813, the paper was published by I[srael] W. Clark, for the Proprietors. Clark withdrew, and with the issue of Mar. 26, 1814, the paper was published by H. & E. Phinney, and was so continued until after 1820." (Clarence S. Brigham, *History and Bibliography of American Newspapers, 1690–1820* [Worcester, Mass.: 1947], p. 568.) Published first door east of the Court House. *Loc*: NCooHi: [Ap 3, 1795–Ja 29, 1821 (1:1–26:1349)].

THE WHARTON VALLEY ECHO Edmeston. No issues examined, but Mr. Emerson Buel of Burlington Flats, New York, in a letter of February 8, 1974 to the editor, reports that the newspaper was founded by Clarence A. and Elba Talbot of Burlington Flats about November 1882. The print shop, located about two miles north of Burlington Flats is now in ruins. Some three years after it was founded, the newspaper was moved to Edmeston, New York, and printed by different owners.

SCHUYLER COUNTY

INDEPENDENT FREEMAN (w) Jefferson. Je 15, 1850–? (1:1–?). *Pub*: William B. Slawson & Co. *Format*: Four pages 18" x 23½". *Price*: $1.00 per year in advance. *Comment*: In 1851 its title was changed to the *Jefferson Eagle,* and continued under that name for only a few months. (Henry B. Pierce and Duane H. Hurd, *History of Tioga, Tompkins, and Schuyler County, New York* [Philadelphia: 1879], p. 568.) *Loc*: NIC/MMN: Mr 21, 1851 (1:41).

WATKINS DEMOCRAT (w) Watkins. Mr 13, 1866–1908//(?) (1:1–?). NDun/Observer: Ja 1, 1891 (26:42).

STEUBEN COUNTY

ERWIN PROGRESS (w) Painted Post. Ag 12, 1972–D 22, 1973// (1:1–2:51). *Pub*: Erwin Board of Supervisors. *Format*: Eight pages 11″ x 18″. *Price*: 10¢ per copy. *Comment*: Contained news primarily of Chemung County reconstruction following the flood July, 1972. *Loc*: NCor/STLS: Ag 12, 1972–D 22, 1973 (1:1–2:51).

TIOGA COUNTY

THE AHWAGA CHIEF (w) Owego. F 23–D 28, 1872// (1:1–38). *Loc*: NHan: S 13, 1872 (1:30).

TOMPKINS COUNTY

THE CORNELL DAILY SUN (d, except Sat. and Sun.) Ithaca. S 16, 1880 to date (1:1 to date). *Title changes*: *The Cornell Sun* S 16, 1880–S 22, 1882; *The Cornell Daily Sun* S 25, 1882 to date. *Pub*: The Students of Cornell University. *Ed*: Changes with each semester. *Format*: Four to twenty-four pages 11″ x 17″. *Price*: 3¢ per copy (1880–?); 5¢ per copy (by 1898–?); 3¢ per copy (by 1939–?); 10¢ per copy (by 1972 to date). *Comment*: Motto: "Ithaca's only Morning Newspaper." Although Cornell's student newspaper, it is considered the only morning newspaper and is subscribed to by Ithaca residents. Suspended publication from November 1943 to September 1946. *Loc*: NIC/MMN: microfilm [S 16, 1880 to date (1:1 to date)]. NIC/RHA: [S 16, 1880 to date (1:1 to date)].

DRYDEN ECHO (w) Ag 3, 1889–? Loc: NCortHi: O 5, 1889 (1:10).

DRYDEN HERALD (w) Dryden. Jl 7, 1871–My 29, 1919// *Loc*: NCortHi: Je 28, 1916 (46:2).

GOOD TIMES (w) Newfield. ca. 1888. No issues located. *Good Times* was an eight page weekly family newspaper. Subscription cost was 50¢ per year. (From an advertisement in the *Newfield Tribune*.)

THE GOOD TIMES GAZETTE (w) Ithaca. Je 28, 1973 to date (1:1 to date). *Format*: Eight to twenty-four pages 11″ x 17″. *Price*: Free. *Comment*: Motto: "Ithaca's Weekly Entertainment Guide." *Loc*: NI/Gazette: Je 28, 1973 to date (1:1 to date).

GROTON ADVERTISER Groton. 1864–? (1:1–?). *Loc*: NAur/ Wells: Jl 1864 (1:4).

ITHACA CHRONICLE (w) Ithaca. Mr 3, 1830–1855// *Loc*: NAub: S 12, 1838 (9:30). NRU: O 16, 1844 (15:36); My 28, 1845 (16:16).

THE ITHACA HERALD (w) Ithaca. Ag 31, 1836–O 4, 1837// *Loc*: NCortHi: Mr 15, 1837 (1:29).

JOURNAL AND COURIER (w) Groton. N 9, 1866 to date. *Loc*: NCortHi: Mr 15, 1877 (11:21); Je 20, 1878 (12:35); S 9, 1880 (14:47); Mr 9, 1898 (32:24).

NEW YORK CONFEDERACY (w) Dryden. O 1857–? (1:1–?). *Pub and Ed*: G. Z. House. *Format*: Four pages 16″ x 22″. *Price*: $1.00 per year. *Comment*: Published from Dwight's Stone Store, third story. *Loc*: NCortHi: O 29, D 24, 1857 (1:3; 2:28); Ja 28, Mr 18, 1858 (2:32, 39).

NEWFIELD NEWS (w) Newfield. F 5, 1973 to date (1:1 to date). *Pub*: Newfield Communications Assoc., Inc. *Ed*: Sam Pizzigati. *Format*: Eight to twenty-four pages 11½″ x 17″. *Price*: $5.50 per year, 20¢ per copy. *Loc*: NNfPL: F 5, 1973 to date (1:1 to date).

TCB TOMPKINS COUNTY BULLETIN (w, bi-w) Ithaca. Jl 3, 1970 to date (1:1 to date). *Title changes*: *TCB Tompkins Chemung Bulletin* Jl 3, 1970 to S 1972; *TCB Tompkins County Bulletin* S 1972 to date. *Format*: Four to twenty pages 11½″ x 17″. *Price*: 15¢ per copy. *Loc*: NI/TCB Office: Jl 3, 1970 to date (1:1 to date). NIC/MMN: Jl 3, 1970 to date (1:1 to date).

TOMPKINS COUNTY RURAL NEWS (w) Dryden. Jl 19, 1933 to date (1:1 to date). *Loc*: NCooHi: Jl 31, 1957 (27:7) Centennial issue.

WEEKLY ITHACAN (w) Dryden, Ithaca. My 7, 1856–? *Loc*: NCort/Mullen: Ja 26, 1865 (9:32). NCortHi: Je 4, 1856 (1:3); S 17, 1857 (2:17); Ja 6, 1859 (3:28); F 9, 1865 (9:34).

Selected Bibliography

Aldrich, Lewis Cass, ed. *History of Yates County, New York.* Syracuse, N.Y.: D. Mason & Co., 1892.

Arnold, William H. "Newspapers of Elmira and Chemung County." Typescript. Steele Memorial Library, Elmira, N.Y.

Ayer Directory of Publications. Philadelphia: Ayer Press, 1869-.

Bacon, Edwin F. *Otsego County, New York, Geographical and Historical . . .* Oneonta, N.Y.: The Oneonta Herald, 1902.

Becker, John E. *A History of the Village of Waterloo, New York, and Thesaurus of Related Facts.* Waterloo, N.Y.: Waterloo Library and Historical Society, 1949.

Biographical Review. Boston: Biographical Review Publishing Co., 1894.

Brigham, Clarence S. *History and Bibliography of American Newspapers, 1690–1820.* 2 vols. Worcester, Mass.: American Antiquarian Society, 1947.

Campbell, Dudley M. *A History of Oneonta from its Earliest Settlement to the Present Time.* Oneonta, N.Y.: G. W. Fairchild & Co., 1906.

————. *A Sketch of the History of Oneonta.* Oneonta, N.Y.: Herald and Democrat Office, 1883.

Child, Hamilton. *Gazetteer and Business Directory of Cortland County, N.Y. for 1869.* Syracuse, N.Y.: Journal Office, 1869.

————. *Gazetteer and Business Directory of Otsego County, New York for 1872-3.* Syracuse, N.Y.: Journal Office, 1872.

————. *Gazetteer and Business Directory of Seneca County, New York for 1867-8.* Syracuse, N.Y.: Journal Office, 1867.

Cleveland, Stafford Canning. *History and Directory of Yates County, New York.* Penn Yan, N.Y.: Stafford C. Cleveland, 1873.

Combination Atlas Map of Yates County, New York. Philadelphia: Everts, Ensign and Everts, 1876.

Doty, Lockwood R. *History of the Genesee Country.* 4 vols. Chicago: S.J. Clark Publishing Co., 1925.

Doty, William J. *Historic Annals of Southwestern New York.* 3 vols. New York: Lewis Historical Publishing Co., 1940.

Farnham, G. Whitfield. *Directory of the Village of Ithaca.* Ithaca, N.Y.: 1869.

Foote, Joyce. *Morris, New York, 1773–1923.* Morris, N.Y.: 1970.

Galpin, Henry Judson. *Annals of Oxford, New York.* Oxford, N.Y.: The Oxford Times, 1906.

Gazetteer and Business Directory of Cayuga County, New York for 1867-8. Syracuse, N.Y.: 1868.

Goodhue, M. P. *Cortland, Homer, McGrawville Directory.* Elmira, N.Y.: 1912.

Goodwin, H. C. "Impressions of Homer," no. 4. Cortland County Historical Society *Bulletin* 24 (June 1970), pp. 1–3.

Gregory, Winifred, ed. *American Newspapers, 1821–1836.* New York: H. W. Wilson Co., 1937.

————. *Union List of Serials in Libraries of the United States and Canada.* 2nd ed. New York: H.W. Wilson Co., 1943.

History of Allegany County, N.Y. New York: F. W. Beers and Co., 1879.

History of Delaware County, N.Y. New York: W. W. Munsell & Co., 1880.

History of Seneca County, New York. Philadelphia: Everts, Ensign and Everts, 1876.

Hopkins, Lazelle R. *Facts Regarding Weedsport, N.Y.* Livingston, N.Y.: Livingston Press, 1933.

Howe, Martha Elson. *A History of the Town of Wellsville.* New York: 1963.

Hurd, Duane H. *History of Otsego County, New York.* Philadelphia: Everts and Fariss, 1878.

Kingman, LeRoy Wilson. *Our County and Its People: A Memorial History of Tioga County, New York.* Elmira, N.Y.: W. A. Fergusson, 1897.

Lawyer, William S., ed. *Binghamton, Its Settlement, Growth and Development, and the Factors in Its History, 1800–1900.* Boston: Central Memorial Publishing Co., 1900.

Littell, W. R. *A History of Cooperstown.* Cooperstown, N.Y.: The Freeman's Journal Co., 1929.

Livermore, William H. "Reminiscences." *Cortland Standard*, supplement, May 3, 1883.

McMaster, Guy H. *History of the Settlement of Steuben County, New York.* Bath, N.Y.: R. S. Underhill & Co., 1853.

Minard, John S. *Allegany County and Its People.* Alfred, N.Y.: W. A. Fergusson & Co., 1896.

More, Carolyn Evelyn, and Irma Mae Griffin. *History of the Town of Roxbury.* Walton, N.Y.: Walton Reporter Co., 1953.

Murray, David, ed. *Delaware County New York: History of the Century, 1797–1897.* Delhi, N.Y.: William Clark, 1898.

Peirce, Henry B. *History of Tioga, Chemung, Tompkins, and Schuyler Counties, New York.* Philadelphia: Everts and Ensign, 1879.

Reynolds, W. O. *Festal Gatherings of the Early Settlers and Present Inhabitants of Virgil . . . August 1853.* Dryden, N.Y.: A. M. Ford, 1878.

Roberts, Millard F. *Historical Gazetteer of Steuben County, New York.* Syracuse, N.Y.: 1891.

Severne, Frank W. "Annual Report of the County Historian." *Proceedings of the Board of Supervisors.* Watkins Glen, N.Y.: 1953.

Seward, William F. *Binghamton and Broome County, New York: A History.* New York and Chicago: Lewis Historical Publishing Co., 1924.

Smith, Henry Perry. *History of Broome County.* Syracuse, N.Y.: D. Mason and Co., 1885.

————. *History of Cortland County.* Syracuse, N.Y.: D. Mason and Co., 1885.

Smith, James H. *History of Chenango and Madison Counties, New York.* Syracuse, N.Y.: D. Mason and Co., 1880.

Spraker, Rowan D., and Frank C. Carpenter, comps. *Supplement to a History of Cooperstown for the Period August 1, 1929–December 31, 1962.* Cooperstown, N.Y.: 1963.

Stilwell, Robert E. "Records: Notebooks." vol. 9. Cortland County Historical Society, Cortland, N.Y.

Storke, Elliot G. *History of Cayuga County, N.Y.* Syracuse, N.Y.: D. Mason and Co., 1879.

_____. "History of the Press." *The Auburn Bulletin*, December 13, 1877.

Towner, Ausburn. *Our County and Its People: A History of the Valley and County of Chemung*. Syracuse, N.Y.: D. Mason and Co., 1892.

Welch, Edgar L. *"Grip's" Historical Souvenir of Cortland*. Cortland, N.Y.: Standard Press, 1899.

_____. *Marathon, New York, and Vicinity*. [*"Grip's" Historical Souvenir of Marathon*]. Fayetteville, N.Y.: Bulletin Publishing Co., 1901.

Winne, Ella L., and Greta G. Hughes. *The Town of Richfield, a Collection of Local History Articles*. Richfield Springs, N.Y.: The Richfield Springs Mercury, 1961.

Index

This index is to all newspaper titles, all counties and other communities, and significant subjects—political parties, religious topics, and the like. Entries citing all newspapers for a particular county or community are set in boldface. If a community had just one newspaper, whose title includes the name of the community, the title of that newspaper is also in boldface.

About Town, Alfred, 1
Academic Gazette, Wellsville, 1
Adams, John Quincy, Newspaper supporting, 86
Addison Advertiser and Woodhull Sentinel, 206
Addison, NY, newspapers, 206-08, 211, 231
Addison Post, 208
Addison Record, 208
Addison Republican, 208
Addison Semi-Weekly Advertiser. See *Addison Advertiser and Woodhull Sentinel*
Addison Tri-Weekly Advertiser. See *Addison Advertiser and Woodhull Sentinel*
Advance, Trumansburg, 251
Advertiser and Free Press, Cortland, 112
Advertiser, Elmira. See *Elmira Advertiser; Weekly Advertiser*
Advertiser, Hancock, 137
Advertiser-Journal, Auburn, 37
Advertising, newspapers devoted to, 14, 61, 80, 112, 114, 121, 134, 135, 167, 217, 223, 254, 259, 264, 265
Advocate. See *Waverly Advocate* (1852)
Advocate of the People, Auburn, 38
Afternoon Advertiser. See *Elmira Advertiser*
Afton Eagle, 89
Afton Enterprise, 89
Afton Enterprise and Harpursville Budget. See *Afton Enterprise*
Afton, NY, newspapers, 89, 99
Afton Sentinel, 89
Afton Weekly Enterprise. See *Afton Enterprise*
Agricultural newspapers, 92, 125-26, 134, 162, 172, 194
Agriculturist. See *Republican Agriculturist*
Ahwaga Chief, Owego, 232, 290
Albany, NY, newspaper, 158
Alfred Centre, NY, newspaper, 14

Alfred, NY, newspapers, 1
Alfred Sun, 1
Allegany County Advocate. See *Allegany Republican*
Allegany County Democrat, Wellsville, 2
Allegany County News. See *Whitesville News*
Allegany County newspapers, 1-16, 285
Allegany County Reporter, Angelica, 2
Allegany County Republican: Angelica, 3; Friendship, see *Friendship Register*
Allegany Democrat. See *Allegany County Democrat*
Allegany Republican, Angelica (1826), 3; (1842), 4
Almond Gleaner, 4
Almond, NY, newspapers, 4, 14
Alumni newspaper, 288
Amateur Courier, Cuba, 4
Amateur newspapers, 148, 254
American Banner, Cherry Vally, 156
American Citizen, Ithaca, 251
American Citizen and Old Ithaca Chronicle. See *American Citizen*
American Constellation, Union, 232
American Farmer. See *American Farmer and Owego Advertiser*
American Farmer and Owego Advertiser, Owego Village, 233
American Freeman. See *Bainbridge Freeman*
American Journal. See *Ithaca Journal*
American Party newspapers: Cayuga Co., 41, 47, 92; Cortland Co., 119; Delaware Co., 148; Seneca Co., 199; Steuben Co., 211; Tioga Co., 236; Tompkins Co., 251. See Also Know Nothing party
American Reveille. See *Seneca Falls-Waterloo Reveille*
American Sabbath Tract Society newspaper, 14
American's Own, Elmira, 68
Andes, NY, newspapers, 137, 138, 152

Andes Recorder (1867), 137; (1892), 138
Andover Advertiser. See *Andover Advertiser and Free Press*
Andover Advertiser and Free Press, 4
Andover News, 5
Andover, NY, newspapers, 4, 5
Andover Weekly Advertiser. See *Andover Advertiser and Free Press*
Angelica Advertiser. See *Allegany County Republican*
Angelica Advocate, 5
Angelica, NY, newspapers, 2, 3, 4, 5, 6, 11
Angelica Reporter, 5
Angelica Reporter and Allegany Republican. See *Allegany County Reporter*
Angelica Republican (1820), 5; (1837), 6; (1871), 6
Angelica Republican and Allegany Whig, 6
Angelica Republican and Farmers' and Mechanics' Press, 6
Anti-Catholic newspaper, 272
Anti-Christian newspaper, 160
Anti-Confederacy newspaper, 50
Anti-Federalist newspaper, 52
Anti-Jacksonian newspaper, 198
Anti-Masonic newspapers: Cayuga Co., 53; Chenango Co., 94; Cortland Co., 121; Otsego Co., 169; Seneca Co., 189, 198; Tompkins Co., 252, 264; Yates Co., 280, 284
Anti-Masonic Republican. See *Cortland County Whig*
Anti-Masonic Sentinel, Trumansburg, 252
Anti-Masonic Telegraph. See *Chenango Telegraph*
Anti-renters newspaper, 153
Anti-slavery newspapers: Cayuga Co., 41, 48, 55, 62; Chenango Co., 93; Cortland Co., 112, 129, 135; Delaware Co., 144; Seneca Co., 195
Anti-trust campaign newspaper, 1902, 139–40
Anti Viet Nam War newspaper, 253
Aquae Gloria, Elmira, 68
Arena Enterprise, Arena, NY, 138
Atlanta News, Atlanta, NY. See *Cohocton Valley Times-Index*
Auburn, 38, 287
Auburn American. See *Auburn Daily Union; Auburn Weekly Union*
Auburn Argus, 38
Auburn Banner, 39
Auburn Banner and Genesee, Oneida, and Black River Conference Record, 39
Auburn Bulletin, 39
Auburn Cayuga Chief. See *Cayuga Chief*

Auburn Citizen, 40
Auburn City News, 40
Auburn Commercial Review, 40
Auburn Daily Advertiser. See *Advertiser-Journal*
Auburn Daily Advertiser and Auburn Union. See *Advertiser-Journal*
Auburn Daily Advertiser and Union. See *Advertiser-Journal*
Auburn Daily American. See *Auburn Daily Union*
Auburn Daily Bulletin. See *Auburn Bulletin*
Auburn Daily Item. See *Evening Auburnian*
Auburn Daily News, 41
Auburn Daily Union, 41
Auburn Democrat. See *Auburn Democrat-Argus*
Auburn Democrat-Argus, 41
Auburn Evening Dispatch. See *Evening Dispatch*
Auburn Free Press, 42
Auburn Gazette, 42
Auburn Herald, 43
Auburnian (1848), 47; (1877), see *Evening Auburnian*
Auburn Idea, 43
Auburn Journal, 43
Auburn Journal and Advertiser. See *Auburn Journal*
Auburn Journal and Weekly Union. See *Auburn Journal*
Auburn Labor Weekly, 44
Auburn Miscellany, 44
Auburn Morning Dispatch, 44
Auburn Morning News (1868), 45; (1872), 45
Auburn News and Bulletin. See *Auburn Bulletin*
Auburn, NY, newspapers, 37–47, 48, 51, 52, 53, 54, 55–57, 58, 59, 61, 62, 63, 64, 65, 67, 287
Auburn Patriot, 45
Auburn Semi-Weekly Journal. See *Auburn Journal*
Auburn State Prison newspaper, 56
Auburn Sunday Dispatch, 46
Auburn True Press, 46
Auburn Weekly American. See *Auburn Weekly Union*
Auburn Weekly Bulletin, 46
Auburn Weekly Dispatch, 46
Auburn Weekly Journal. See *Auburn Journal*
Auburn Weekly News, 46
Auburn Weekly News and Democrat. See *Auburn Democrat-Argus*

Auburn Weekly Union, 47
Aurora Gazette (1805), 47; (1868), 48
Aurora, NY, newspapers, 47, 48
Avoca Advance. See *Avoca Advance Press*
Avoca Advance Press, 208
Avoca Herald, 209
Avoca, NY, newspapers, 208, 209
Axe, Binghamton, 17
Bainbridge Eagle, 90
Bainbridge Express, 90
Bainbridge Freeman, 90
Bainbridge Ledger, 90
Bainbridge News, 90
Bainbridge News and the Bainbridge
   Republican. See *Bainbridge News*
Bainbridge, NY, newspapers, 90–91, 93,
   99, 108
Bainbridge Press, 91
Bainbridge Republican, 91
Bainbridge Republican and Express. See
   Bainbridge Republican
Band fair newspaper, 209
Band Herald, Prattsburgh, 209
Baptist Youth Fellowship newspaper, 1
Barnburner newspaper, 238
Bath Clipper, 209
Bath Echo, 209
Bath Gazette. See *Bath Gazette and*
   Genesee Advertiser
Bath Gazette and Genesee Advertiser, 209
Bath, NY, newspapers, 209–10, 213, 217,
   219, 225–29, 230, 231
Bath Plaindealer, 210
Bath Sunday News, 210
Bath Tri-Weekly Conservative, 210
Bazoo, Elmira (1880), 68; (1877), see
   Elmira Daily Bazoo
Belfast Blaze, 6, 285
Belfast Bulletin, 6
Belfast Champion, 6
Belfast, NY, newspapers, 6, 12, 285
Belfast Patriot. See *Cuba Patriot and*
   Free Press
Belmont Courier, 7
Belmont Dispatch. See *Dispatch*
Belmont, NY, newspapers, 2, 7, 9, 10 12
Belmont Weekly Dispatch. See *Dispatch*
Binghamton Advocate (1895), 17; (1921),
   17
Binghamton Axe. See *Axe*
Binghamton Chronicle, 17
Binghamton Commercial Review, 17
Binghamton Courier, 17
Binghamton Courier and Broome County
   Democrat. See *Binghamton Courier*
Binghamton Daily Democrat, 18

Binghamton Daily Leader. See *Binghamton*
   Leader
Binghamton Daily Republican. See *Sun-Bul-*
   letin
Binghamton Daily Times (1863), 18;
   (1872), 19
Binghamton Democrat, 19
Binghamton Evening Herald. See *Evening*
   Herald
Binghamton Journal, 20
Binghamton Leader, 20
Binghamton Message, 20
Binghamton Morning Herald, 20
Binghamton Morning Republican. See *Sun-*
   Bulletin
Binghamton, NY, newspapers, 17–22, 23,
   26, 28, 29, 30, 31, 32, 33, 34, 35,
   285, 287
Binghamton Phoenix, 20
Binghamton Press. See *Evening Press*
Binghamton Press and Leader. See *Even-*
   ing Press
Binghamton Republican. See *Sun-Bulletin*
Binghamton Republican and Morning Times.
   See *Sun-Bulletin*
Binghamton Republican-Herald. See *Sun-*
   Bulletin
Binghamton Standard, 21
Binghamton Standard and Semi-Weekly
   Republican, 21
Binghamton Sun. See *Sun-Bulletin*
Binghamton Sun and Daily Bulletin. See
   Sun-Bulletin
Binghamton Sunday Tribune, 22
Binghamton Sunday Wasp, 22
Binghamton Times, 22
Binghamton Typographical Union news-
   paper, 17
Binghamton Weekly Herald, 22
Blacks, newspaper devoted to interests
   of, 264
Blade. See *Owego Weekly Blade*
***Bloomville Mirror,* Bloomville, NY.** See
   Mirror-Recorder
Blue Ribbon, Cortland, 112
Bolivar Breeze, 7
Bolivar, NY, newspapers, 7, 11
Boy Scouts of America, Montour Falls,
   newspaper, 183
Breeze, Prattsburgh, 210
Bridge Builder, Groton, 252
Broome County Courier. See *Binghamton*
   Courier
Broome County Courier and Country Lit-
   erary Gazette. See *Binghamton Courier*
Broome County Herald, Chenango Forks, 23

Broome County newspapers, 17–36, 285–87
Broome County Republican. See *Broome Republican*
Broome Gazette, Whitney Point, 23
Broome Republican, Binghamton, 23
Broome Republican and Weekly Times. See *Broome Republican*
Broome Weekly Republican. See *Broome Republican*
Buckeye, Ithaca, 252
Bucktail party newspaper, 82
Budget. See *Elmira Budget.*
Buell's Saturday Review, Cortland, 112
Bunker Hill Club, Penn Yan, 273
Burdett Home Record, 177
Burdett Local Visitor, 177
Burdett, NY, newspapers, 177, 182, 183
Burritt News, Weedsport, 48
Butternut Valley News, Garrattsville, 156
Campaign Daily, Cortland, 112
Campaign newspapers, 35, 51, 102, 106, 132–33, 139–40, 182, 194, 198, 238, 250, 252, 256, 266, 282
Canaseraga Times, **Canaseraga, NY,** 7
Candor Courier, 233
Candor Free Press, 233
Candor Independent, 234
Candor, NY, newspapers, 233–34, 235
Candor Press, 234
Candor Review, 234
Candor Standard, 234
Canisteo Chronicle, 210
Canisteo, NY, newspapers, 210–11
Canisteo Republican, 211
Canisteo Times, 211
Canisteo Valley Journal. See *Canisteo Valley Journal and National American*
Canisteo Valley Journal and National American, Hornellsville, 211
Canisteo Valley Times. See *Hornell Times*
Casket of Gems, Union Springs, 48
Cass, Lewis, 1848 campaign newspapers, 51, 119, 285
Castigator: Auburn and Ithaca, 48, 252; Cooperstown, 156
Cato Citizen, **Cato, NY,** 48
Catskill Mountain News, Margaretville, 138
Cayuga Chief: Auburn, 48; Weedsport, 49
Cayuga Chief-Chronicle, Port Byron, 49
Cayuga County Courier, Moravia, 50, 287
Cayuga County Independent. See *Cayuga County News*
Cayuga County News, Auburn, 51
Cayuga County newspapers, 37–67, 287

Cayuga Democrat: Auburn, 51; Union Springs, 51
Cayuga Lake Herald, Union Springs, 51
Cayuga Lake Record, Union Springs, 52
Cayuga Lake Recorder, Union Springs, 52
Cayuga New Era, Auburn, 52
Cayuga Patriot, Auburn, 52
Cayuga Republican: Auburn, 53; Weedsport, see *Weedsport Republican*
Cayuga Spirit of the Times, Auburn, 53
Cayuga Standard, Auburn, 54
Cayuga Telegraph, Union Springs, 54
Cayuga Tocsin: Auburn, 54; Union Springs, 54
Central Labor Union newspapers: Auburn, 44, 65; Ithaca, 262
Central New Yorker: Auburn, 54; Union Springs, 54
Central Reformer, McGrawville, 112
Century Plant, Auburn, 55
Cessna, W. K., campaign newspaper, Ithaca, 266
Champion, Clifford, anti-trust candidate, Stamford, 140
Charlotte Valley News, East Davenport, 139
Chemung County Democrat. See *Chemung Democrat*
Chemung County Greenbacker. See *Horseheads Journal*
Chemung County Journal, Elmira, 68
Chemung County newspapers, 68–88, 288
Chemung County Patriot and Central Advocate, Horseheads, 68
Chemung County Republican, Horseheads, 69
Chemung Democrat: Elmira, 69; Havana [Montour Falls] and Jefferson [Watkins Glen], 178
Chemung Patriot. See *Chemung County Patriot and Central Advocate*
Chemung Valley Reporter, Horseheads, 69
Chemung Whig, Havana, 178
Chenango American and Whitney Point Reporter: Greene, 91; Whitney Point, 24
Chenango Chronicle, Norwich, 92
Chenango County Democrat, Oxford, 92
Chenango County Farm Bureau News, Norwich, 92
Chenango County newspapers, 89–111
Chenango Democrat: Greene, 92; Oxford, 92
***Chenango Forks Herald,* Chenango Forks, NY.** See *Broome County Herald*
Chenango Free Democrat, Norwich, 93

Chenango Ledger. See *Bainbridge Ledger*
Chenango News, Greene, 93
Chenango, NY, newspaper, 232
Chenango Patriot: Greene, 93; Oxford, 93
Chenango Press, Guilford, 93
Chenango Republican or, Oxford Gazette and People's Advocate, Oxford, 93
Chenango Telegraph, Norwich, 94
Chenango Tribune, Smyrna, 95
Chenango Union, Oxford, 95
Chenango Valley Citizen, Binghamton, 285
Chenango Weekly Advertiser, Norwich, 97
Chenango Whig and Miscellaneous Journal, Oxford, 97
Cherry-Valley Gazette (1818), 156
Cherry Valley Gazette (1832), 156
Cherry Valley Gazette and Richfield Times. See *Cherry Valley Gazette* (1832)
Cherry Valley News, 157
Cherry Valley, NY, newspapers, 156–57, 170, 172, 173, 174, 175
Cherry Valley Temperance Investigator. See *Temperance Investigator*
Christian Ambassador, Auburn, 55
Christian Contributor, McGrawville, 113
Christian Union, Union Springs, 55
Chronicle-Express, Penn Yan, 273
Chronicle Journal, Cattaraugus Star and Rushford Spectator. See *News Time*
Chronicle, Penn Yan. See *Chronicle-Express*
Chronicles, Auburn, 55
Chronicle-Times, Walton, 139
Church Review, Delhi, 139
Cincinnatus Journal, 113
Cincinnatus, NY, newspapers, 103, 113, 132, 134
Cincinnatus Review, 113
Cincinnatus Star, 113
Cincinnatus Times (1898), 113; (1950), 113
Citizen-Advertiser, Auburn, 56
Citizen Press, Elmira, 70
Clarion, Elmira. See *Inter-State Advocate*
Clay, Henry, newspapers supporting, 1824, 86; 1832, 238; 1844–45, 105
Clinton, DeWitt, newspaper supporting, 106
Cohocton Advertiser, 212
Cohocton Herald, 212
Cohocton Journal, 212
Cohocton, NY, newspapers, 210, 212–13, 223
Cohocton Times. See *Cohocton Valley Times-Index*

Cohocton Times Index. See *Cohocton Valley Times-Index*
Cohocton Tribune, 212
Cohocton Valley Times, North Cohocton, 212
Cohocton Valley Times-Index, 213
Columbian Telegraph. See *Telegraph,* Norwich
Commercial newspapers, 40, 61, 63, 121, 131, 194, 283
Commercial Travelers Home, souvenir edition, 20
Communicator, Dryden. See *Tompkins County Rural News*
Community Leader, Rushville, 274
Community News Review, Homer, 113
Compass, Trumansburg, 252
Conference and Family Recorder. See *Auburn Banner and Genesee, Oneida and Black River Conference Record*
Conger's Journal, Groton, 252
Constitutionalist, Bath, 213
Coon Skinner, Ithaca, 253
Cooperstown Federalist. See *Freeman's Journal*
Cooperstown, NY, newspapers, 156, 158, 159, 160, 161, 162, 167, 168, 169, 170, 173, 175, 289
Cornell Daily Sun, Ithaca, 290
Cornell University student newspaper, 290
Corning and Blossburg Advocate, Corning, 213
Corning Daily Democrat. See *Corning Leader*
Corning Daily Journal, 214
Corning Democrat, 214
Corning Democrat Daily Series. See *Corning Leader*
Corning Evening Leader. See *Corning Leader*
Corning Independent, 214
Corning Journal, 215
Corning Leader, 215
Corning News (1939), 216; (1955), 216
Corning, NY, newspapers, 213–16, 218, 222
Corning Sunday News. See *Corning News*
Corona Borealis, Jefferson, 178
Corrector, Auburn, 56
Cortland Advertiser (1860), 114; (1895), 114; (1913), 114
Cortland Advocate, Cortland Village, 114
Cortland American, 114
Cortland Chronicle, 114

Cortland Citizen, 114
Cortland Commerical Review, 115
Cortland County Advertiser, Homer, 115
Cortland County Democrat. See *Cortland Democrat* (1864)
Cortland County Express, McGrawville, 115
Cortland County News, Cortland, 116
Cortland County newspapers, 112–36
Cortland County Republican (1855), see *Homer Republican;* (1897), see *Cortland Republican*
Cortland County Republican and American. See *Cortland Republican* (1897)
Cortland County Sentinel, McGrawville, 116
Cortland County Sentinel and McGrawville News. See *Cortland County Sentinel*
Cortland County Standard. See *Cortland Standard*
Cortland County Whig, Cortland, 117
Cortland Courier, Homer Village, 118
Cortland Daily Journal, 118
Cortland Daily Message. See *Cortland Daily Journal*
Cortland Democrat (1840), 118; (1849), 119; (1864), 119
Cortland Evening Democrat, 120
Cortland Evening Standard. See *Cortland Standard*
Cortland Free Press, 120
Cortland Gazette, Cortland Village, 120
Cortland-Homer Pennysaver, 121
Cortland Journal, Cortland Village, 121. See also *Cortland County Sentinel; Cortland Weekly Journal*
Cortland Liberty Herald. See *Liberty Herald*
Cortland Midlander, 121
Cortland News, 121
Cortland, NY, newspapers, 112, 114, 115, 116, 117, 118, 119, 120, 121, 123–24, 125, 126, 129, 131, 132, 133, 134, 135, 136
Cortland Observer, Homer Village, 121
Cortland Pennysaver, 121
Cortland Repository, Homer Village, 122
Cortland Republican (1815), 122; (1832), see *Cortland County Whig;* (1855), see *Homer Republican;* (1897), 123
Cortland Standard (1867), 123; (1892), 124
Cortland Standard and Cortland Daily Journal. See *Cortland Standard* (1892)
Cortland Standard and Homer Republican.

See *Cortland Standard*
Cortland Standard and Journal. See *Cortland Standard* (1867)
Cortland Tribune, 124
Cortland Tri-Weekly Democrat, 125
Cortland Village, NY, newspapers, 114, 118, 120, 121, 122, 125, 135
Cortland Weekly Journal, Cortland Village, 125
Cortland Weekly Museum, Homer, 125
Courier. See *Binghamton Courier*
Crocodile, Penn Yan, 274
Crookerville, NY, newspaper, 288
Cuba Daily News, 8
Cuba Evening Review, 8
Cuba Free Press, 8
Cuba, NY, newspapers, 4, 8, 9, 10, 13
Cuba Patriot. See *Cuba Patriot and Free Press*
Cuba Patriot and Free Press, 8
Cuba Post, 9
Cuba True Patriot. See *Cuba Patriot and Free Press*
Cuba Weekly Herald. See *Cuba Patriot and Free Press*
Cyclone, Walton. See *People's Press*
Daily Advocate, Bath, 217
Daily Alfred Sun. See *Alfred Sun*
Daily Alleganian, Belmont, 10
Daily Bazoo. See *Elmira Daily Bazoo*
Daily Bulletin: Elmira, 70; Endicott, 25
Daily Cayuga Tocsin, Auburn, 56
Daily Chronicle, Penn Yan (1876), 275; (1882), 275
Daily Democrat: Corning, see *Corning Leader;* Elmira, see *Daily Karlon; Chemung Democrat*
Daily Despatch, Sidney, 139
Daily Free Press and Owego Daily Record, Owego, 234
Daily Gazette. See *Owego Daily Gazette*
Daily Herald. See *Elmira Morning Herald*
Daily Independent, Marathon, 125
Daily Iris. See *Sun-Bulletin,* Binghamton
Daily Item, Auburn. See *Evening Auburnian*
Daily Karlon, Elmira, 70
Daily Leader. See *Binghamton Leader*
Daily Mirrow, Stamford, 139
Daily News and Advertiser, Owego, 235
Daily News, Hornellsville, 217
Daily Owegoan, Owego, 235
Daily Press, Hornellsville, 217
Daily Reporter and Democrat, Wellsville, 10

Daily Reporter: Norwich, 97; Walton, see *Reporter;* Wellsville, see *Wellsville Daily Reporter*
Daily Seneca Observer, Waterloo, 189
Daily Times. See *Hornell Daily Times*
Danby Herald, Danby, NY, 253
D. & H. Canal Railroad, Railway YMCA newspaper, 163
Dateline Ithaca, 253
Davenport Standard. See *Schenevus Free Press Davenport Standard*
Defender, Elmira, 70
Delaware Chief, Hobart, 140
Delaware County Courier, Deposit, 26
Delaware County Dairyman, Franklin, 140
Delaware County Enterprise. See *Tri-Town News*
Delaware County News. See *Delaware Standard*
Delaware County newspapers, 137–55, 288
Delaware Courier. See *Deposit Courier*
Delaware Express, Delhi, 141
Delaware Gazette, Delhi, 141
Delaware Journal, Delhi, 142
Delaware Republican, Delhi (1821), 142; (1830), 142; (1860), see *Delaware Republican Express*
Delaware Republican Express, Delhi, 142
Delaware Standard, 143
Delaware Times. See *Roxbury Times*
Delhi, NY, newspapers, 139, 141–42, 148, 151, 153, 155
Democratic and Independence League newspapers, 114–15, 132–33
Democratic Citizen, Jefferson, 178
Democratic Flag, Ithaca, 253
Democratic Leader, Binghamton. See *Democratic Weekly Reader*
Democratic newspapers: Allegany Co., 2, 5, 7, 10, 11; Broome Co., 19, 20, 26; Cayuga Co., 38, 42, 43, 45, 46, 47, 48–49, 52, 56; Chemung Co., 69, 73, 75, 76, 77; Chenango Co., 92, 93, 95, 101, 104, 106; Cortland Co., 120, 133; Delaware Co., 139–40, 141–42, 146, 148, 149, 150, 153, 154, 155, 288; Otsego Co., 159, 165, 167, 168, 175; Schuyler Co., 177, 182, 183, 184, 187, 188; Seneca Co., 191, 192, 194, 196, 198, 199, 202, 204; Steuben Co., 211, 214, 215, 216, 217, 221, 223, 228, 230; Tioga Co., 233, 238, 241, 242, 245, 247, 249; Tompkins Co., 252, 253, 254, 257, 258, 261, 263, 264, 267, 268; Yates Co., 273, 276, 278–79. See also Hunker newspapers

Democratic Organ, Penn Yan, 275
Democratic Republican newspapers: Cayuga Co., 38, 42, 51, 52, 53, 54, 58; Chenango Co., 101, 106; Cortland Co., 114, 122; Delaware Co., 141–42
Democratic Times, Cuba, 10
Democratic Vidette, Hornell, 217
Democratic Weekly Leader, Binghamton, 26
Democratic Whig newspapers, 257, 258
Democratic Whig, Penn Yan, 275
Democrat, Sidney, 143
Deposit Courier, 26, 143, 285–86
Deposit Courier-Journal. See *Deposit Courier*
Deposit Journal, 27
Deposit, NY, newspapers, 26–28, 143, 285–286
Deposit Times. See *Deposit Times and Democrat*
Deposit Times and Democrat, 143
Deposit Union Democrat, 27
Depot Dispatch, Trumansburg, 253
Diadem, Penn Yan, 275
Diamond, Cayuga County, 56
Dispatch, Belmont, 10
Domestic affairs newspaper, 59
Domestic economy, newspaper devoted to, 252
Downsville Herald, Hancock, 144
Downsville News, Downsville, NY, 144
Drafted Men's Advocate, Cooperstown, 158
Dryden Echo, 253, 290
Dryden Herald, 253, 290
Dryden News. See *Weekly Ithacan*
Dryden, NY, newspapers, 253, 267, 270, 290, 291
Dryden Weekly Herald. See *Dryden Herald*
Dryden Weekly News. See *Weekly Ithacan*
Dundee Expositor, 275
Dundee Herald, 275
Dundee Home Advocate. See *Home Advocate*
Dundee, NY, newspapers, 275–77, 278, 283
Dundee Observer, 275
Dundee Record, 276
Dundee Telegraph, 277
East Davenport, NY, newspaper, 139
Echo: Trumansburg, 254; Waverly, 235
Eclectic Scalpel, Trumansburg, 254
Economist, Hornellsville, 217
Edmeston Local, 158
Edmeston, NY, newspapers, 158, 176, 289
Elmira Advertiser, 70; afternoon edition, 72
Elmira Booster, 72
Elmira Budget, 72
Elmira Daily Bazoo, 72
Elmira Daily Free Press, 73

Elmira Daily Gazette. See *Elmira Gazette and Free Press*

Elmira Daily Herald. See *Elmira Herald;* *Elmira Morning Herald*

Elmira Daily News, 73

Elmira Daily Press, 73

Elmira Daily Republican (1846), 73; (1851), 73

Elmira Enterprise, 74

Elmira Evening Argus, 74

Elmira Evening News, 74

Elmira Evening Star, 74

Elmira Evening Union, 74

Elmira Gazette and Free Press (1828), 75; (1858), 75

Elmira Heights Courier, 76

Elmira Heights, NY, newspapers, 76

Elmira Heights Review, 76

Elmira Herald, 76

Elmira Morning Herald, 76

Elmira Morning Sun, 77

Elmira Morning Telegram. See *Sunday Telegram*

Elmira Morning Tidings. See *Saturday Tidings*

Elmira, NY, newspapers, 68, 69, 70–80, 81, 82, 83–86, 87, 88, 288. See also Newtown, NY; Newtown Village, NY

Elmira Record, 77

Elmira Republican (1831), 77; (1832), 77

Elmira Republican and Canal Advertiser, 78

Elmira Sentinel, 78

Elmira Star-Gazette, 78

Elmira Sunday Herald, 79

Elmira Sunday Morning Examiner, 79

Elmira Sunday Morning Press, 79

Elmira Telegram. See *Sunday Telegram*

Elmira Tidings. See *Saturday Tidings*

Elmira Union. See *Elmira Evening Union*

Elmira Weekly Advertiser. See *Weekly Advertiser*

Elmira Weekly Advertiser and Chemung County Republican. See *Weekly Advertiser*

Elmira Weekly Free Press, 79

Elmira Weekly Gazette. See *Elmira Gazette and Free Press*

Elmira Whig, 80

Endicott Bulletin. See *Daily Bulletin*

Endicott Daily Bulletin. See *Daily Bulletin*

Endicott, NY, newspapers, 25, 28

Endicott Times, 28

Enquirer. See *Penn Yan Enquirer*

Enterprise: Ithaca, 254; Painted Post, 217; Truxton, 125

Entertainment guide, 290

Episcopal newspaper, 58

Era, Hornellsville, 217

Erwin Progress, Painted Post, 290

Evangelical Recorder, Auburn, 56

Evening Auburnian, Auburn, 56

Evening Chronicle, Corning, 218

Evening Dispatch, Auburn, 57

Evening Herald: Binghamton, 28; Elmira, see *Elmira Daily Bazoo*

Evening Journal. See *Waverly Advocate*

Evening Leader and Corning Daily Democrat. See *Corning Leader*

Evening News: Elmira, see *Elmira Evening News;* Oneonta, 158

Evening Press and Sunday Press, Binghamton. See *Evening Press,* Binghamton

Evening Press: Binghamton, 29; Hornellsville, 218

Evening Review, Elmira. See *Saturday Evening Review*

Evening Star. See *Elmira Evening Star*

Evening Sun, Norwich, 97

Evening Tribune and Hornell Daily Times. See *Evening Tribune*

Evening Tribune and Hornell Times. See *Evening Tribune*

Evening Tribune, Hornell, 218

Evening Tribune-Times. See *Evening Tribune*

Evening Union. See *Elmira Evening Union*

Every Week, Angelica, 11

Facts, Elmira, 80, 288

Fair Haven Graphic, 57

Fair Haven, NY, newspapers, 57, 64

Fair Haven Register, 57

Fairman's Daily Advertiser, Elmira, 80

Fair newspapers, 82, 217. See also Band fair

Family Journal and Temperance Advocate, Owego, 235

Family newspapers, 35, 275, 290

Family Visitor. See *Watkins Family Visitor*

Farmer and Seneca Falls Advertiser, Waterloo, 189

Farmer [Interlaken], NY, newspapers, 190, 197

Farmer Review. See *Interlaken Review*

Farmers' Advocate. See *Steuben Advocate Combined with the Keuka Grape Belt and the Prattsburgh News*

Farmers' Advocate and Steuben Advertiser. See *Steuben Advocate Combined with the Keuka Grape Belt and the Prattsburgh News*

Farmers' Gazette, Bath, 219
Farmer's Journal, Cortland, 125
Farmer Village, NY, newspaper, 198
Farmer Village Review. See *Interlaken Review*
Favorite, Elmira, 80
Federalist newspapers, 20, 159
Fillmore Enterprise, Fillmore, NY. See *Northern Allegany Observer*
Finger Lakes Farm and Home Supplement and Agricultural News, Trumansburg, 245
Fire Bell, Cortland, 126
Fireside Companion. See *Weekly Ithacan*
Flag of the Union, Ithaca, 254
Fleischmanns Herald. See *Griffin-Fleischmann Herald*
Fleischmanns Herald-News. See *Griffin-Fleischmann Herald*
Fleischmanns News, Griffin Corners, 144
Fleischmanns, NY, newspapers, 144, 145. See also Griffin Corners, NY
Fleischmanns Press, 144
Flood newspaper, Chemung County, 290
Fly Creek, NY, newspaper, 170
Forest City Spark, Ithaca, 254
Fort Henderson Meddlar, Elmira, 80
Fourth, Cooperstown, 158
Fourth of July newspaper, Cooperstown, 1883, 158
Franklin, NY, newspapers, 140, 144
Franklin Register. See *Delaware County Dairyman*
Franklinville, NY, newspaper, 13
Franklin Visitor, 144
Free Baptist newspaper, 182
Free Democrat. See *Chenango Free Democrat*
Freeman's Journal and Otsego County Advertiser. See *Freeman's Journal*
Freeman's Journal, Cooperstown, 159
Free Press: Auburn, see *Auburn Free Press;* Belfast, see *Genesee Valley Free Press;* Elmira, see *Elmira Weekly Free Press* and *Elmira Gazette and Free Press;* Montour Falls, 178; Trumansburg, 254
Free Press and Sentinel. See *Free Press,* Trumansburg
Free schools newspaper, 238
Free Soil Advocate and Republican, Ithaca, 255
Free Soil newspapers, 27, 119, 200, 245, 255, 285
Free Soil Union. See *Seneca Free Soil Union*
Freeville Friend, Freeville, NY, 255

Fremont, Charles, newspaper supporting, 1856, 282
Friendship Chronicle, 11
Friendship, NY, newspapers, 3, 11, 12, 14; 150th anniversary newspaper, 14
Friendship Register, 11
Friendship Volunteer, 11
Friendship Weekly Register. See *Friendship Register*
Garrattsville, NY, newspapers, 156, 172
Gazette. See *American Banner; Cherry Valley Gazette*
Gazette and Banner, Cortland, 126
Gazette and Examiner, Cherry Valley, 160
Gazette and Seneca Advertiser, Waterloo, 189
Genesee, NY, newspapers, 2, 12
Genesee Valley Free Press, Belfast, 12
Genesee Valley Post. See *Cuba Post*
Geneseo, NY, newspaper, 13
Geneva, NY, newspapers, 58, 197
Genoa Herald. See *Weekly Herald*
Genoa, NY, newspapers, 58, 64, 67
Genoa Spy, 58
Genoa Tribune. See *Southern Cayuga Tribune and the Union Springs News*
German language newspaper, 64
Gilbertsville Eagle and True Democratic and Patriotic Reflector. See *Gilbertsville Eagle and True Religious and Patriotic Reflector*
Gilbertsville Eagle and True Religious and Patriotic Reflector, 160
Gilbertsville, NY, newspapers, 109, 160, 167
Glad Tidings, Seneca Falls, 190
Gleaner: Candor, 235; Poplar Ridge, 58
Glimmerglass, Cooperstown, 160
Globe, Cortland, 126
Golden Rule, Roseboom, 160
Good Times Gazette, Ithaca, 290
Good Times, Newfield, 290
Gorham New Age. See *Rushville Chronicle and Gorham New Age*
Gospel Advocate and Impartial Investigator, Auburn, 58
Gospel Messenger and Church Record of Western New York, Auburn, 58
Grange newspapers, 81, 167–68
Grape interests, newspaper supporting, 283
Greeley, Horace, newspapers supporting, 1872, 146, 153
Greenback Labor Advocate. See *Havana Democrat* (1877)
Greenback Labor Reform party newspaper, Elmira, 72

Greenback newspapers: Chemung Co., 68, 72, 81, 82; Chenango Co., 99, 102, 106; Schuyler Co., 179; Steuben Co., 214-15; Tioga Co., 250

Greene, NY, newspapers, 24, 91, 92, 93, 107

Griffin Corners [Fleischmanns], NY, newspapers, 144, 145

Griffin-Fleischmann Herald, Fleischmanns, 145

Griffin-Fleischmann Herald-News. See *Griffin-Fleischmann Herald*

Griffin's Corners Herald. See *Griffin-Fleischmann Herald*

Groton Advertiser, 255, 290

Groton and Lansing Journal. See *Journal and Courier*

Groton and Lansing Journal and Locke Courier. See *Journal and Courier*

Groton Balance. See *Groton Democrat*

Groton Democrat, 256

Groton Iron Bridge Company newspaper, 252

Groton Journal. See *Journal and Courier*

Groton News, 256

Groton, NY, newspapers, 252, 255, 256, 263, 290, 291

Guilford Mail, 98

Guilford News, 98

Guilford, NY, newspapers, 93, 98

Guilford Wave. See *Chenango Press*

Hammondsport Herald. See *Hammondsport Herald and Bath Plaindealer*

Hammondsport Herald and Bath Plaindealer, 219

Hammondsport, NY, newspapers, 210, 219, 222, 223

Hancock Guardian, 145

Hancock Herald, 145

Hancock, NY, newspapers, 137, 144, 145, 146

Hancock Times, 146

Hancock True Flag, 146

Hancock Weekly Times. See *Hancock Times*

Harpursville Budget, Harpursville, NY, 29, 286

Harpursville-Nineveh Standard, Windsor, 30

Harrison, William H., campaign newspaper, 1836, 252

Hartwick, NY, newspapers, 160, 161

Hartwick Reporter, 160

Hartwick Review, 161

Hartwick Seminary Monthly, 161, 288

Hartwick Seminary, NY, newspapers, 161, 288

Hartwick Visitor, 161

Havana Democrat (1855), 179; (1877), 178

Havana Enterprise, 179

Havana Free Press. See *Free Press,* Montour Falls

Havana Journal (1849), 179; (1853), 180; (1865), 180

Havana [Montour Falls], NY, newspapers, 178, 179-81, 182, 184, 186

Havana Observer, 181

Havana Republican (1837), 181; (1845), 181; (1882), 181

Hayes, Rutherford B., campaign newspaper, 35

Health preservation newspapers, 59, 254, 259

Hector Herald, Burdett, 182

Heights Weekly, Ithaca, 256

Hendryx trial newspaper, Wellsville, 10

Herald and Democrat. See *Oneonta Herald*

Herald and Record, Ithaca, 256

Herald: Cooperstown, see *Otsego Herald;* Newark Valley, see *Tioga County Herald;* Trumansburg, see *Trumansburg Herald*

Highways and bridges newspaper, 252

Hobart Free Press, 146

Hobart Herald, 146

Hobart Independent, 146

Hobart, NY, newspapers, 140, 146, 147, 153

Hobart Times, 147

Home Advocate, Dundee, 278

Home and Abroad, Oneonta. See *Otsego Democrat,* Oneonta

Home and Health, Union Springs, 59

Home News. See *Sherburne News*

Home News or Weekly Advertiser. See *Sherburne News*

Homer Eagle, 126

Homer Herald, Cortland, 126

Homer Independent, 127

Homer, NY, newspapers, 113, 115, 117, 125, 126, 127-28, 132, 134, 135, 136

Homer Post, 127

Homer Republican, 128

Homer Times, 128

Homer Village, NY, newspapers, 118, 121, 122

Home Sentinel, Afton, 99

Home Visitor, Watkins, 182

Hornell Daily Times, 220

Hornell Evening Tribune. See *Evening Tribune*

Hornell, NY, newspapers, 217, 220, 221

Hornellsville Evening Tribune (1873), 221; (1878), see *Evening Tribune*

Hornellsville Morning Times. See *Hornell Daily Times*

Hornellsville, NY, newspapers, 211, 217, 218, 221, 230

Hornellsville Weekly Tribune. See *Hornell Weekly Tribune*

Hornell Times, Hornellsville, 221

Hornell Weekly Tribune, Hornellsville, 221

Hornet, Waterloo, 190

Horseheads Free Press. See *Elmira Weekly Free Press*

Horseheads Independent, 81

Horseheads Journal, 81

Horseheads, NY, newspapers, 68, 69, 79, 81, 83, 88; promotion of as county seat, newspaper, 68

Horseheads Post. See *Post,* Horseheads

Horseheads Weekly Free Press. See *Elmira Weekly Free Press*

Howe, Elias, sewing machine promotional newspaper, 254

Hume Enterprise. See *Northern Allegany Observer*

Humor, newspaper devoted to, 265

Hunker newspaper, 69

Husbandman, Elmira, 81, 288

Hyde Park News, Hartwick Seminary, 161

Illustrated Post, Binghamton, 30

Illustrated Saturday Record, Auburn, 59

Impartial Observer. See *Freeman's Journal*

Independent: Binghamton, 30; Marathon, see *Marathon Independent*

Independent Freeman, Jefferson, 182, 289

Independent newspapers: Allegany Co., 6, 7, 8, 12, 13, 285; Broome Co., 19, 20, 21, 22, 23, 24, 28, 29, 30, 31, 32, 33, 35, 36, 287; Cayuga Co., 39, 42, 44, 46, 48, 51, 52, 55, 56, 57, 59, 63; Chemung Co., 69, 72, 74, 77, 78, 79, 80, 83, 84; Chenango Co., 89, 90, 91, 94, 97, 98, 99, 100, 103, 104, 106, 108, 109, 110; Cortland Co., 112, 113, 115, 116, 121, 122, 124–125, 127, 129, 131, 132; Delaware Co., 140, 141–42, 144, 146, 147, 150, 153, 154; Otsego Co., 156, 158, 160–61, 162, 165, 168, 169, 175; Schuyler Co., 181, 187; Seneca Co., 190, 191, 193, 197, 199; Steuben Co., 207, 208, 210, 214, 216, 218, 221, 225, 226, 227, 229; Tioga Co., 234, 240, 246, 249; Tompkins Co., 253, 255, 259, 260, 262, 263, 264, 265, 266, 269, 271; Yates

Co., 276, 283. See also Neutral newspapers

Independent Republican: Cortland, 129; Elmira, 82

Independent Republican newspapers, 29, 49, 102, 242, 243

Independent Treasury, Ithaca, 256

Independent Villager, Marathon, 129

Independent Watchman, Ithaca, 256

Indian Speaks, Painted Post, 222

Inquirer, Binghamton, 30

Interlaken, NY, newspapers. See Farmer, NY, newspapers

Interlaken Review, Farmer, 190

Inter-State Advocate, Elmira, 82

Investigator, Newtown, 82

Iris, Binghamton, 30

Item. See *Evening Auburnian*

Itemizer, Havana, 182

Ithaca Chronicle (1830), 256, 291; (1888), 257

Ithaca Chronicle and Democrat, 257

Ithaca Citizen and Democrat. See *Ithaca Chronicle and Democrat*

Ithaca Daily Chronicle, 258

Ithaca Daily Democrat (1869), 258; (1884), 258

Ithaca Daily Journal (1870), 258; (1872), see *Ithaca Journal*

Ithaca Daily Leader. See *Ithaca Daily Democrat* (1869)

Ithaca Daily News, 259; industrial edition, 259

Ithaca Democrat. See *Ithaca Chronicle and Democrat*

Ithaca Eclectic, 259

Ithaca Evening Leader. See *Ithaca Daily Democrat* (1869)

Ithaca Gazette and Religious Intelligencer, 259

Ithaca Herald, 260, 291

Ithaca Independent, 260

Ithaca Issue, 260

Ithaca Journal (1817), 261; (1872), 260

Ithaca Journal and Advertiser. See *Ithaca Journal* (1817)

Ithaca Journal and General Advertiser. See *Ithaca Journal* (1817)

Ithaca Journal and Herald. See *Ithaca Journal* (1817)

Ithaca Journal, Literary Gazette and General Advertiser. See *Ithaca Journal* (1817)

Ithaca Mirror, 261

Ithaca Morning Herald, 262

Ithacan, 263

Ithaca, NY, newspapers, 48, 251, 252, 253, 254, 255, 256–63, 264, 265, 266, 267, 268, 270, 271, 272, 290, 291; waterworks newspaper, 272
Ithaca Observer, 262
Ithaca Republican, 262
Ithaca Saturday Union, 262
Ithaca Semi-Weekly, 262
Ithaca Socialist Party newspaper, 260
Ithaca Weekly Chronicle. See *Ithaca Chronicle* (1830)
Ithaca Weekly Democrat. See *Ithaca Chronicle and Democrat*
Ithaca Weekly News, 263
Jefferson Eagle. See *Independent Freeman*
Jeffersonian and Tompkins Times, Ithaca, 263
Jeffersonian, Jefferson, 182
Jeffersonian Democrat newspaper, 118–19
Jefferson [Watkins Glen], NY, newspapers, 178, 182, 289
Johnson City-Endicott Record. See *Record,* Johnson City
Johnson City Journal, 30
Johnson City, NY, newspapers, 30, 31, 32. See also Lestershire, NY
Johnson City Record. See *Record,* Johnson City
Johnson, Richard M., campaign newspaper, 1840, 106
Journal and Courier, Groton, 263, 291
Judge, Cortland, 129
Juniper. See *Quill and Press*
Keuka Grape Belt Combined with the Hammondsport Herald and Bath Plaindealer. See *Keuka Grape Belt,* Hammondsport
Keuka Grape Belt, Hammondsport, 222
King Ferry, NY, newspaper, 64
Kirby harvester newspaper, 61
Kirmessite, Elmira, 82
Kirmessonian, Elmira, 82
Know Nothing party newspapers: Chemung Co., 68, 74, 77, 83; Cortland Co., 114, 119; Seneca Co., 199; Tioga Co., 236; Tompkins Co., 251. See also American Party
Labor newspaper, 84. See also Union newspapers
Labor party newspaper, 218
Lake Light, Trumansburg, 264
Lansing Gazette, Ludlowville, 264
Latest Morning News, Binghamton, 31
Laurens, NY, newspapers, 166, 174
Lawton Talk, Auburn, 59
Leader, Corning, 222, see also *Corning Leader;* Elmira, see *Southern Tier*

Leader
Legal reform newspaper, 191
Lestershire-Endicott Record. See *Record,* Johnson City
Lestershire [Johnson City], NY, newspapers, 31
Lester-Shire News, Lestershire, 31
Lestershire Record. See *Record,* Johnson City
Levana Gazette; or, Onondaga Advertiser, **Levanna [Scipio], NY,** 59
Liberal party newspaper, 135
Liberal Republican newspaper, 232
Liberty Herald, Cortland, 129
Licensing protest newspaper, 278
Life in the Country and Havana Republican. See *Havana Republican* (1845)
Lily, Seneca Falls, 190
Lisle Gleaner and New Era, Lisle, NY, 31, 287
Literary Independent, Norwich, 99
Literary newspapers, 48, 112, 178, 225, 265, 272
Little Joker, Dundee, 278
Living Issue, Cooperstown, 161
Living Question, Auburn, 59
Lodi Christian Advocate, 191
Lodi, NY, newspapers, 191, 201
Louisville [Morris], NY, newspapers, 167, 173
Ludlowville Index, 264
Ludlowville, NY, newspapers, 264
Luminary. See *Waverly Luminary*
McGrawville Advertiser, 129
McGrawville Express. See *Cortland County Express*
McGrawville, NY, newspapers, 112, 113, 115, 116, 129, 131, 134
McGrawville Sentinel. See *Cortland County Sentinel*
Magician, Ithaca, 264
Manuscript newspaper, 134
Marathon Independent, 129
Marathon Leader, 130
Marathon Mirror. See *Marathon Leader*
Marathon News, Cortland, 131
Marathon, NY, newspapers, 125, 129, 130, 131, 132, 134
Marathon Telegraph, 131
Marathon Weekly News. See *Marathon News*
Margaretville Messenger. See *Catskill Mountain News*
Margaretville, NY, newspapers, 138, 147, 153
Margaretville Standard, 147
Masonic newspaper, 168

Memorial, Seneca Falls, 191
Meridian Advertiser, 59
Meridian, NY, newspapers, 59
Meridian Sun, 59
Methodist newspapers, 39, 62, 67, 133–34, 170–71
Mexican War, effect of on newspapers, 225
Midday Sun, Elmira, 82
Middlesex Valley Chronicle, Penn Yan, 278
Midland Times, Sidney Plains, 147
Milford, NY, newspaper, 170
Milford Tidings. See *Otsego Tidings*
***Millport News,* Millport, NY,** 82
***Milo Question,* Milo Center, NY,** 278
Miniature, Oxford, 99
Mirror-Independent, Stamford, 147
Mirror Recorder, Bloomville, 147
Miscellany, Penn Yan, 278
Mocking Bird Gazette. See *Ithaca Chronicle* (1888)
Monday Review, Bainbridge, 99
Monitor: Cortland, 131; Ithaca, 264
Montgomery murder trial newspaper, 147
Monthly. See *Hartwick Seminary Monthly*
Monthly Croaker, Delhi, 148
Montour Falls Free Press. See *Free Press,* Montour Falls
Montour Falls, NY, newspapers, 178, 183, 184. See also Havana, NY
Moravia Citizen. See *Moravia Republican*
Moravia, NY, newspapers, 50, 59–61, 287
Moravia Republican, 59
Moravia Republican-Register, 60
Moravia Valley Register. See *Moravia Republican-Register*
Morning Call, Oneonta, 161
Morning Dispatch. See *Auburn Morning Dispatch*
Morning Echo, Delhi, 148
Morning Star and Binghamton Chronicle. See *Binghamton Chronicle*
Morning Star, McGrawville, 131; Sherburne, 99
Morning Sun, Binghamton, see *Sun-Bulletin;* Norwich, see *Evening Sun*
Morning Sun and Record, Binghamton. See *Sunday Sun and Record*
Morning Times. See *Hornell Daily Times*
Morris Chronicle, 161
Morris, NY, newspapers, 161, 167. See also Louisville, NY
Mt. Vernon, Ohio, newspaper, 190
Museum and Independent Corrector, Ithaca, 264

Museum and Literary Repository, Ithaca, 265
My Lady, Cuba, 13
National Amateur Press Association newspaper, 254
National American. See *Canisteo Valley Journal and National American*
National Archives, Ithaca, 265
National Democratic Union newspaper, 148
National party newspaper, 54
National Real Estate Journal, Ithaca, 265
Neutral newspapers: Chemung Co., 78; Chenango Co., 94, 109; Cortland Co., 115; Delaware Co., 151; Otsego Co., 161, 172, 175; Schuyler Co., 186; Seneca Co., 190; Steuben Co., 210, 231; Tioga Co., 244, 247; Tompkins Co., 253, 258, 265, 268, 269, 270; Yates Co., 276. See also Independent newspapers
New Age, Rushville, 278
***Newark Valley Herald,* Newark Valley, NY.** See *Tioga County Herald*
New Berlin Gazette (1850), 100; (1859), 100
New Berlin Herald, 100
New Berlin, NY, newspapers, 100–101, 108, 109
New Berlin Pioneer. See *New Berlin Gazette*
New Berlin Sentinel, 101
New Berlin Star, 101
New Cortlander, Cortland, 132
New Era, Oneonta, 162
Newfield Advertiser, 265
Newfield Home News, 265
Newfield News, 291
Newfield, NY, newspapers, 265, 290, 291; souvenir newspaper, 265. See also Trumbulls Corners, NY
Newfield Tribune, 265
New Kirby Advertiser, Auburn, 61
News and Wave, Guilford, see *Chenango Press;* Sidney, 149
News-Bulletin-Auburnian. See *Auburn Bulletin*
News-Dispatch, Endicott. See *Endicott Times*
News Time, Rushford, 13
Newtown [Elmira], NY, newspapers, 82, 86, 87
Newton Telegraph, Newtown Village, 82, 288
Newtown Village [Elmira], NY newspaper, 82, 288

New York Confederacy, Dryden, 291
New York Farmer, Cooperstown, 162
New York, NY, newspaper, 55
New York State Fair, 1891, newspaper, 82
New York State Reformatory, Elmira, newspaper, 85
Nichols News, 236
Nichols, NY, newspapers, 236
Nichols Recorder, 236
Nichols Recorder and Agricultural Times. See *Nichols Recorder*
Nioga Reporter. See *Chenango American and Whitney Point Reporter*
No-License Advocate, Ithaca, 266
No License, Dundee, 278
Non-partisan newspapers: Allegany Co., 1; Cayuga Co., 41, 50, 56; Chemung Co., 83, 86; Cortland Co., 113, 121; Seneca Co., 194; Steuben Co., 212, 231; Tioga Co., 236
North Cayuga Times, Port Byron, 61
North Cohocton, NY, newspaper, 212
North Cohocton Times, Cohocton, 223
Northern Advocate. See *Northern Christian Advocate*
Northern Allegany Observer, Fillmore, 13
Northern Christian Advocate, Auburn, 62
Northern Independent, Auburn, 62
Northern Phoenix, Weedsport, 62
Northern Spy, Almond, 14
North Pharsalia, NY, newspaper, 106
Norwich Evening Telegraph, 101
Norwich Journal, 101
Norwich News, 101
Norwich, NY, newspapers, 92, 93, 94, 95, 97, 99, 101–02, 106, 110
Norwich Post, 102
Norwich Sentinel, 102
Norwich Sun. See *Evening Sun*
Nullifier, Cooperstown, 162
Observer and Union. See *Seneca Observer*
Obywatel, Binghamton, 285, 287
Odessa Free Baptist, Odessa, NY, 182
Old Campaigner, Ithaca, 266
Old Hickory. See *Castigator,* Ithaca
Old Home Week Daily, Owego, 236
Old School Democrat, Jefferson, 182
Olive Branch, Sherburne, 102
Oneonta Commercial, 162
Oneonta Daily Local, 162
Oneonta Daily News, 163
Oneonta Daily Star. See *Oneonta Star*
Oneonta Daily Times. See *Oneonta Times*
Oneonta Dispatcher, 163
Oneonta Gazette, 163

Oneonta Herald (1838), 163; (1853), 163
Oneonta Herald and Democrat. See *Oneonta Herald* (1853)
Oneonta Leader, 164
Oneonta, NY, newspapers, 158, 161, 162–65, 166, 167, 168, 172, 173; Normal School controversy newspaper, 166
Oneonta Press and Otsego County Democrat, 164
Oneonta Spy, 165
Oneonta Star, 165
Oneonta Times, 166
Oneonta Weekly Journal, 166
Onondaga Advertiser. See *Levana Gazette; or, Onondaga Advertiser*
Oracle. See *Western Oracle*
Oracle Advertiser, Watkins, 183
Oramel, NY, newspaper, 14
Orphan's Friend, Auburn, 63
Osborne Monthly, Auburn, 63
Otego Literary Record, 166
Otego, NY, newspapers, 166, 168, 172, 173
Otego Record. See *Otego Literary Record*
Otego Times, 166
Otego Valley News, Laurens, 166
O-TE-SA-GA Gazette, Cooperstown, 167
Otsego-Chenango Bee Journal Chronicle, Gilbertsville, 167
Otsego Chronicle. See *Morris Chronicle*
Otsego County Courier, Louisville, 167
Otsego County Democrat, Oneonta, 167
Otsego County Grange News, Cooperstown, 167
Otsego County Leader, Otego, 168
Otsego County newspapers, 156–76, 288–89
Otsego Democrat, Cooperstown, 168; Oneonta, 168
Otsego Examiner, Cooperstown, 168
Otsego Farmer, Cooperstown, 168
Otsego Herald, Cooperstown, 289
Otsego Herald: Or, Western Advertiser. See *Otsego Herald*
Otsego Journal. See *Otsego-Chenango Bee Journal Chronicle*
Otsego Observer. See *Otsego-Chenango Bee Journal Chronicle*
Otsego Republican, Cooperstown (1829), 169; (1855), 169
Otsego Republican Press, Cherry Valley, 170
Otsego Spy, Cooperstown, 170
Otsego Tidings, Milford, 170
Otselic Valley News, South Otselic, 103
Otselic Valley Register, Pitcher, 103, 132

Our Town, Montour Falls, 183
Ovid Bee, 191
Ovid Emporium, 192
Ovid Gazette (1817), 192; (1818), 192; (1894), 192
Ovid Gazette and Independent. See *Ovid Gazette* (1894)
Ovid Gazette and Seneca County Register, 193
Ovid Independent, 193
Ovid, NY, newspapers, 191, 192–93, 197, 201
Ovid Village, NY, newspaper, 194
Owego Advertiser. See *Tioga County Sun-Times and Herald*
Owego American, 236
Owego and Tioga County Gazette. See *Tioga County Courier-Gazette*
Owego Blade. See *Owego Weekly Blade*
Owego Daily Blade, 237
Owego Daily Gazette, 237
Owego Daily News and Advertiser. See *Daily News and Advertiser*
Owego Daily Press, 237
Owego Daily Record. See *Daily Free Press and Owego Daily Record*
Owego Evening Blade. See *Owego Daily Blade*
Owego Free Press, 237
Owego Gazette, (1814), see *Tioga County Courier-Gazette;* (1843), 238
O-We-Go-In, Owego, 239
Owego, NY, newspapers, 232, 234, 235, 236–39, 241–43, 244, 245, 250, 290
Owego Press, 238
Owego Republican, 238
Owego Southern Tier Times. See *Tioga County Sun-Times and Herald*
Owego Times. See *Tioga County Sun-Times and Herald*
Owego Times-Tioga County Herald. See *Tioga County Sun-Times and Herald*
Owego Trade Reporter, 238
Owego Village, NY, newspaper, 233
Owego Weekly Blade, 239
Owego Weekly News, 239
Oxford Gazette, 103
Oxford, NY, newspapers, 92, 93, 95, 97, 99, 103–05, 106, 107
Oxford Press, 104
Oxford Republican, 104
Oxford Republican and Chenango County Democrat, Oxford, 104
Oxford Review. See *Review-Times*
Oxford Review-Times. See *Review-Times*
Oxford Times, 105

Oxford Transcript, 105
Painted Post, NY, newspapers, 217, 222, 223, 231, 290
Painted Post Times, 223
Pastoral Visitor, Fly Creek, 170
Patriot: Auburn, see *Cayuga Patriot;* Cuba, see *Cuba Patriot and Free Press*
Patrons of Husbandry newspaper, 23
Penn Yan Courier, 278
Penn Yan Daily Telegraph. See *Penn Yan Telegraph*
Penn Yan Democrat. See *Penn Yan Courier*
Penn Yan Enquirer, 280
Penn Yan Express, 280
Penn Yan Herald. See *Penn Yan Courier*
Penn Yan Merchants' Store News. See *Yates County Store News*
Penn Yan Mystery, 281
Penn Yan, NY, newspapers, 273, 274, 275, 278–81, 282, 283–84
Penn Yan Telegraph, 281
People's Advocate, Norwich, 106
People's Journal, Marathon, 132
People's Party of Ithaca campaign newspaper, 266
People's Press, Walton, 149
People's Union party newspaper, 92
Philanthropist, Ithaca, 266
Philosopher, Horseheads, 83
Phoenix. See *Binghamton Phoenix*
Pioneer: Cooperstown, see *Weekly Pioneer;* Penn Yan, 281
Pitcher, NY, newspaper, 103, 132
Plainfield, NJ, newspaper, 14
Pleasant Valley Fruit and Wine Recorder, Hammondsport, 223
Polish language newspaper, 287
Political Free Press, Homer, 132
Political reform newspaper, 258
Polk, James K., campaign newspaper, 194
Polk-Wright, Seneca Falls, 194
Poplar Ridge, NY, newspaper, 58
Port Byron Chronicle (1844), see *Port Byron Herald;* (1871), see *Cayuga Chief-Chronicle*
Port Byron Chronicle and Cayuga County News. See *Cayuga Chief-Chronicle*
Port Byron Gazette, 63
Port Byron Herald, 63
Port Byron, NY, newspapers, 49–50, 61, 63, 64
Port Byron Times, 64
Post: Horseheads, 83; Painted Post, 223
Prattsburgh Advertiser (1867), 223; (1921), 224
Prattsburgh Argus, 224

Prattsburgh News (1864), 224; (1872), 224

Prattsburgh, NY, newspapers, 209, 210, 223–25

Prattsburgh Press, 225

President, Oxford, 106

Primitive Christian: Auburn, 64; Bath, 225

Prison newspaper, 56

Prison reform newspaper, 55

Progressive party newspaper, 5

Progress, Spencer, 239

Prohibition newspapers: Allegany Co., 7; Broome Co., 17; Cayuga Co., 54; Chemung Co., 70–71, 80, 82, 87; Cortland Co., 131, 134; Delaware Co., 143; Otsego Co., 162; Steuben Co., 230

Protest, Ithaca, 266

Protestant Sentinel, Homer, 132

Pruning Hook, Norwich, 106

Putney, VT, newspaper, 271

Quill and Press, North Pharsalia, 106

Radical Democratic newspaper, 32

Radical Democrat, Windsor, 32

Railroad newspaper, 163

Reason's Appeal, Cortland, 132

Railroad strike, effect of on newspaper, 1877, 125

Rechabite, Binghamton, 32

Record: Cortland, 133; Johnson City, 32

Recorder. See *Andes Recorder* (1867)

Red Creek, NY, newspaper, 49

Red Hot, Burdett, 183

Referendum, Ithaca, 266

Reformed Methodist Church newspaper, 133

Religious newspapers, 55, 58, 62, 67. See also individual denominations

Reporter, Walton, 149

Republican: Cortland, see *Cortland County Whig* and *Homer Republican;* Ovid Village, 194

Republican Agriculturist, Norwich, 106

Republican and Democrat. See *Otsego Republican* (1855)

Republican and Eagle. See *Cortland County Whig*

Republican and Standard. See *Broome Republican*

Republican Banner, Cortland, 133

Republican Chronicle. See *Ithaca Republican*

Republican Era, Rushford, 14

Republican Herald, Binghamton, 32

Republican Independence newspaper, 12

Republican Messenger, Sherburne, 107

Republican newspapers: Allegany Co., 1, 2, 3, 4, 5, 6, 9, 10, 11, 12, 13, 14, 15, 16; Broome Co., 18, 21, 22, 23, 26, 27, 30, 32, 33, 34, 35; Cayuga Co., 37, 41, 43, 45, 47, 48, 50, 57, 59, 60, 64, 65, 66; Chemung Co., 70–71, 72, 81, 84, 87; Chenango Co., 89, 91, 92, 94, 95, 101, 102, 103, 105, 107, 110; Cortland Co., 112, 123, 124, 126, 127, 128, 129, 133, 134, 135–36; Delaware Co., 137, 138, 140, 141, 143, 144, 145, 146, 147, 149, 151, 153, 154; Otsego Co., 167, 169, 170, 175; Schuyler Co., 179, 180, 181, 183, 185, 187, 188; Seneca Co., 189, 194, 195, 196; Steuben Co., 211, 214, 215, 216, 217, 221, 223, 228, 230; Tioga Co., 233, 234, 237, 239, 240, 244, 246, 247–48, 249; Tompkins Co., 253, 255, 256, 258, 260, 261, 262, 264, 267; Yates Co., 274, 276, 280, 282, 283, 284

Republican Observer, Waterloo, 194

Republican-Temperance newspaper, 256

Republican Times, Rushville, 282

Republican Whig newspaper, 30

Resolute, Owego, 239

Retirement colony newspaper, 283

Reveille. See *Seneca Falls-Waterloo Reveille*

Review Advertiser, Watkins Glen, 183

Review-Times, Oxford, 107

Richfield Springs Daily, 171

Richfield Springs Mercury, 171

Richfield Springs, NY, newspapers, 171

Richmond, IN, newspaper, 190

Rose, Bath, 225

Roseboom, NY, newspapers, 160, 173

Roxbury Times, **Roxbury, NY,** 149

Rumsey's Companion. See *Weekly Ithacan*

Rumsey's Fireside Companion. See *Weekly Ithacan*

Rundshau, Auburn, 64

Rural Critic, Garrattsville, 172

Rural Times: Otego, 172; Sidney, 150

Rushford, NY, newspapers, 13, 14

Rushford Spectator. See *News Time*

Rushville Argus, 282

Rushville Chronicle. See *Rushville Chronicle and Gorham New Age*

Rushville Chronicle and Gorham New Age, 282

Rushville Herald, 282

Rushville, NY, newspapers, 274, 282, 283

Sabbath Recorder, Alfred Centre, 14

Satanic newspaper, 160

Saturday Call. See *Binghamton Chronicle*

Saturday Critic, Oneonta, 172

Saturday Evening Express, Ithaca, 266
Saturday Evening Review, Elmira, 83
Saturday Morning Review. See *Interlaken Review*
Saturday News, Bath, 225
Saturday Review: Bainbridge, 108; Trumansburg, 266
Saturday Sentinel, Binghamton, 33
Saturday Sun. See *Evening Sun*
Saturday Tidings, Elmira, 83
Saturday Visitor, New Berlin, 108
Saturday World, Elmira, 84
Savona Rustler, Bath, 225
Saw-Buck, Cherry Valley, 172
Schenevus Free Press Davenport Standard, 172
Schenevus Monitor, 172
Schenevus, NY, newspapers, 172, 175
Schools, newspaper devoted to, 239. See also Free schools
Schuyler County Chronicle, Watkins Glen, 183
Schuyler County Democrat, Watkins (1864), 183; (1866), see *Watkins Democrat*
Schuyler County newspapers, 177–88, 289–90
Schuyler County Press, Watkins, 183
Schuyler County Times, Watkins, 184
Schuyler County Union, Montour Falls, 184
Science and literature newspaper, 201
Scipio, NY, newspaper. See Levanna, NY
Scipioville, NY, newspaper. See Watkins' Settlement, NY
Scorpion, Solon, 133
Scott, NY, newspaper, 135
Searchlight, Elmira, 84
Semi-Centennial News, Ithaca, 267
Seneca Chief, Waterloo, 194
Seneca County Commercial, Seneca Falls, 194
Seneca County Courier, Seneca Falls (1836), 194; (1839), 194; (1843), 195; (1845), 195; (1848), 195
Seneca County Courier-Journal, Seneca Falls, 196
Seneca County Home Defense Committee newspaper, 198
Seneca County Journal. See *Seneca County Courier-Journal*
Seneca County News, Waterloo, 196
Seneca County Newsletter, Geneva, 197
Seneca County newspapers, 189–205
Seneca County Press, Seneca Falls, 197
Seneca County Sentinel, Ovid, 197
Seneca County Standard. See *Seneca Falls-Waterloo Reveille*

Seneca County War Chest Association, Seneca Falls, 198
Seneca Democrat, Waterloo Village, 198
Seneca Evening Journal, Farmer Village, 198
Seneca Falls Democrat, 198
Seneca Falls Journal, 198
Seneca Falls, NY, newspapers, 189, 190, 191, 194–96, 197, 198–200, 201, 202, 205
Seneca Falls Register, 198
Seneca Falls Reveille. See *Seneca Falls-Waterloo Reveille*
Seneca Falls-Waterloo Reveille, 199
Seneca Farmer. See *Farmer and Seneca Falls Advertiser*
Seneca Farmer and Seneca Falls Advertiser. See *Farmer and Seneca Falls Advertiser*
Seneca Farmer and Waterloo Advertiser. See *Farmer and Seneca Falls Advertiser*
Seneca Free Soil Union, Seneca Falls, 200
Seneca Live Oak, Lodi, 201
Seneca Observer, Waterloo, 201
Seneca Observer and Union. See *Waterloo Observer* (1832)
Seneca Ordnance Depot newspaper, 253
Seneca Patriot, Ovid, 201
Seneca Republican, Ovid, 201
Seneca Sachem, Seneca Falls, 201
Sesquicentennial Times, Friendship, 14
Seventh Day Baptist newspaper, 1
7-Valley Villager. See *Independent Villager*
Sewing machine promotional newspaper, 254
Sherburne Home News. See *Sherburne News*
Sherburne News, 108
Sherburne, NY, newspapers, 99, 102, 107, 108, 109, 111
Sherburne Palladium, 109
Sherburne Transcript, 109
Sherburne Village, NY, newspaper, 109
Sidney Advocate, 150
Sidney Center Transcript, 150
Sidney Enterprise. See *Tri-Town News*
Sidney Herald, Sidney Plains, 150
Sidney, NY, newspapers, 139, 143, 149, 150, 151, 152, 153
Sidney Plains, NY, newspapers, 147, 150
Sidney Record, 150
Sidney Record and Bainbridge News. See *Tri-Town News*
Sidney Record-Enterprise. See *Tri-Town News*

Skye Loch Village Bagpiper, Dundee, 283
Smyrna Citizen, 109
Smyrna, NY, newspapers, 95, 109
Smyrna Press, 109
Socialist party newspaper, 260
Social Visitor, New Berlin, 109
Solon Bugle. See *Scorpion*
Solon, NY, newspaper, 133
Son of Temperance and Schuyler County Union, Watkins, 184
South Cayuga District Temperance Union newspaper, 59–60
***South Cortland Luminary and Reformed Methodist Intelligencer,* South Cort-land, NY,** 133
Southern Cayuga Tribune. See *Southern Cayuga Tribune and the Union Springs News*
Southern Cayuga Tribune and the Genoa Tribune. See *Southern Cayuga Tribune and the Union Springs News*
Southern Cayuga Tribune and the Union Springs News, 64
Southern Tier Greenbacker and Horseheads Journal. See *Horseheads Journal*
Southern Tier Leader, Elmira, 84, 288
Southern Tier Times. See *Tioga County Sun-Times and Herald*
***South New Berlin Bee,* South New Berlin, NY,** 109
South Otselic Gazette, 110
South Otselic, NY, newspapers, 103, 110
Souvenir newspapers, 14, 20, 158, 209, 265
Spanish-American War newspaper, 72
Spectator: Rushford, see *News Time;* Virgil Village, 134
Spencer Herald. See *Spencer Town News*
Spencer Needle, 240
Spencer News, 240
Spencer, NY, newspapers, 239, 240–41
Spencer Town News, 241
Spirit of the Age, Norwich, 110
Spy, Ithaca, 267
Stamford and Bloomville Mirror. See *Mirror Recorder*
Stamford Mirror. See *Mirror Recorder*
Stamford Mirror and Recorder. See *Mirror Recorder*
Stamford Mirror-Recorder. See *Mirror Recorder*
Stamford, NY, newspapers, 139, 147, 151
Stamford Recorder, 151
Standard. See *Margaretville Standard*
Standard and Journal, Junior, Cortland, 134

Star-Gazette and Advertiser, Elmira, 84
Star-Gazette, Elmira, 84
Star of Delaware, Delhi, 151
Star, Sidney, 151
Steuben Advocate. See *Steuben Advocate Combined with the Keuka Grape Belt and the Prattsburgh News; Steuben Courier-Advocate*
Steuben Advocate and the Keuka Grape Belt. See *Steuben Advocate Combined with the Keuka Grape Belt and the Prattsburgh News*
Steuben Advocate Combined with the Keuka Grape Belt and the Prattsburgh News, Bath, 225
Steuben Advocate with which is Combined the Keuka Grape Belt. See *Steuben Advocate Combined with the Keuka Grape Belt and the Prattsburgh News*
Steuben Agricultural Society newspaper, 217
Steuben American, Bath, 227
Steuben and Allegany Patriot, and Spirit of Agriculture and Manufactures, Bath, 227
Steuben County Democrat, Bath, 227
Steuben County Fair, 1880, newspaper, 217
Steuben County newspapers, 206–31, 290
Steuben Courier. See *Steuben Courier-Advocate*
Steuben Courier-Advocate, Bath, 228
Steuben Democrat, Bath, 229
Steuben Farmers' Advocate. See *Steuben Advocate Combined with the Keuka Grape Belt and the Prattsburgh News*
Steuben Farmers' Advocate and the Prattsburgh News. See *Steuben Advocate Combined with the Keuka Grape Belt and the Prattsburgh News*
Steuben Messenger, Bath, 229
Steuben Patriot. See *Steuben and Allegany Patriot and Spirit of Agriculture and Manufactures*
Steuben Patriot and Spirit of Agriculture and Manufactures. See *Steuben and Allegany Patriot and Spirit of Agriculture and Manufactures*
Steuben Republican, Bath, 230
Steuben Sentinel, Woodhull, 230
Steuben Signal, Hornellsville, 230
Steuben Times, Atlanta, 230
Steuben Whig, Bath, 230
Strikers, newspaper started by, 74–75
Strikes, effect of on newspaper, 125
Student, Andes, 152

Student newspapers, 253, 290
Subsoiler, Homer, 134
Summary, Elmira, 85
Sun, Binghamton. See *Sun-Bulletin*
Sun-Bulletin, Binghamton, 33, 287
Sunday Message, Binghamton, 34
Sunday Morning Republican, Binghamton, 34
Sunday Morning Star and Binghamton Chronicle. See *Binghamton Chronicle*
Sunday Morning Telegram, Elmira. See *Sunday Telegram*
Sunday Morning Tidings, Elmira. See *Saturday Tidings*
Sunday Press, Binghamton. See *Evening Press*
Sunday Press, Elmira. See *Elmira Sunday Morning Press*
Sunday Republican, Elmira, 85
Sunday Sun and Record, Binghamton, 34
Sunday Telegram, Elmira, 85, 288
Sunday Tidings, Elmira. See *Saturday Tidings*
Sunday Times: Elmira, 86; Norwich, 110
Susquehanna Independent, Oneonta, 173
Susquehanna Journal, Binghamton, 34
Susquehanna News, Unadilla, 173
Susquehanna Wave, Otego, 173
Swamp Angel, Fair Haven, 64
Switch, Cooperstown, 173
Syracuse, NY, newspaper, 62
TCB Tompkins County Bulletin, Ithaca, 291
Telegraph: Elmira, see *Young American;* Louisville, 173; Newtown, see *Newtown Telegraph;* Norwich, 110
Telephone, McGrawville, 134
Temperance Advocate, Norwich, 110
Temperance Canoe, Roseboom, 173
Temperance Gem, Bath, 231
Temperance Investigator, Cherry Valley, 174
Temperance newspapers: Allegany Co., 6, 11; Broome Co., 32; Cayuga Co., 41, 43, 46, 48–49, 58, 59, 62, 64, 65; Chemung Co., 69, 70, 84; Cortland Co., 112, 133, 135; Otsego Co., 160, 161, 173, 174; Steuben Co., 231; Tioga Co., 235, 239; Tompkins Co., 256; Yates Co., 276–77, 278
Temperance Union, Union Springs, 65
Templer and Watchman, Ithaca, 267
Times: Canisteo, see *Canisteo Times;* Oxford, see *Oxford Times*
Times-Herald. See *Tioga County Sun-Times and Herald*
Times-Republican. See *Canisteo Times*

Tinkle, Binghamton, 35
Tioga and Bradford Democrat, Waverly, 241
Tioga County Courier-Gazette. See *Tioga County Gazette & Times*
Tioga County Gazette & Times, Owego, 241
Tioga County Greenbacker, Owego, 243
Tioga County Herald, Newark Valley, 243
Tioga County newspapers, 232–50, 290
Tioga County Record, Owego, 244
Tioga County Sun-Times and Herald, Owego, 244
Tioga Freeman, Owego, 245
Tioga Patriot, Havana, 184
Tioga Register, Newtown, 86
Tioughniogian, Marathon, 134
Tocsin. See *Otsego Republican* (1829)
Tocsin for the Tourist, Laurens, 174
Tompkins American, Ithaca, 267
Tompkins County Democrat, Ithaca, 267
Tompkins County newspapers, 251–72, 290–91
Tompkins County Republican, Ithaca, 267
Tompkins County Rural News, Dryden, 267, 291
Tompkins County Sentinel. See *Trumansburg Sentinel*
Tompkins Democrat, Ithaca, 268
Tompkins Volunteer, Ithaca, 268
Tourist newspapers, 160, 171, 174
Town and Country: Arctic Series, Cortland, 134
Town and Country Pennysaver, Cincinnatus, 134
Town Crier, Ithaca, 268
Town Meeting, Homer, 134
Tribune. See *Hornell Weekly Tribune*
Tri-County Journal. See *Deposit Journal*
Tri-County Pennysaver, Homer, 135
Tri-Town News, Sidney, 152
Tri-Weekly Conservative. See *Bath Tri-Weekly Conservative*
True American. See *True American and Religious Examiner*
True American and Religious Examiner, Cortland, 135
True Patriot. See *Cuba Patriot and Free Press*
True Reformer, Scott, 135
Trumansburg Advertiser. See *Trumansburg Advertiser and Tompkins County Whig*
Trumansburg Advertiser and Tompkins County Whig, 268
Trumansburg Advertiser and Weekly Miscellany. See *Trumansburg Advertiser and Tompkins County Whig*

Trumansburg Gazette, 269
Trumansburg Herald, 269
Trumansburg Independent, 269
Trumansburg Leader, 269
Trumansburg News, 269
Trumansburg, NY, newspapers, 251, 252,
    253, 254, 264, 266, 268–70, 271
Trumansburg Sentinel, 270
Trumansburg Sun, 270
***Trumbulls Corners Courier,* Trumbulls**
    Corners [Newfield], NY, 270
Truxton Courier, 135
Truxton, NY, newspapers, 125, 135
Unadilla Advertiser, 174
Unadilla Herald, 174
Unadilla News, 174
Unadilla, NY, newspapers, 173, 174, 175
Unadilla Times, 175
Unahanna, Sidney, 153
Union Advertiser, Wayland, 231
Union Democrat newspaper, 27
Union-Endicott News. See *Endicott Times*
Union News: Auburn, 65; Endicott, see
    Endicott Times
Union newspapers, 17, 44, 65, 262. See
    also Labor newspapers
Union, NY, newspaper, 232
Union party newspapers, 70–71, 87, 92,
    144, 237
Union Republican newspapers, 94, 126,
    180
Union Springs Advertiser, 65
Union Springs Herald. See *Cayuga Lake*
    Herald
Union Springs Ledger, 65
Union Springs News, 65
Union Springs, NY, newspapers, 48, 51,
    52, 54, 55, 57, 59, 65
Union Springs sanitarium newspaper, 59
Urbana, NY, newspaper, 219
Utica, NY, newspaper, 58
Utilitarian, Margaretville, 153
Valley Breeze, Van Etten, 86
Valley News: Schenevus, 175; Sidney, 153
Valley Review, Rushville, 283
Van Buren, Martin, campaign newspaper,
    1840, 106
Van Etten, NY, newspaper, 86
Vedette, Newtown, 87
***Vestal News,* Vestal, NY,** 35
Viet Nam War, newspaper against, 253
Viewpoint Finger Lakes. See *Dundee*
    Observer
Village Museum, Cortland Village, 135
Village Record, Hobart, 153
Village Republican, Cortland, 136

Vineyardist, Penn Yan, 283
Virgil Village, NY, newspaper, 134
Voice of the Nation, Addison, 231
Voice of the People, Delhi, 153
Volunteer, Norwich, 110
Walton Blade. See *Walton Journal*
Walton Chronicle, 153
Walton Chronicle-Times. See *Chronicle-*
    Times
Walton Journal, 154
Walton, NY, newspapers, 139, 149, 153,
    154, 155
Walton Reporter, 154
Walton Star. See *Walton Reporter*
Walton Times, 155
Walton True Press, 155
Wasp: Trumansburg, 270; Waterloo, 202
Watch-Tower, Cooperstown, 175
Water Bucket, Seneca Falls, 202
Waterloo Enterprise, 202
Waterloo Enunciator, 202
Waterloo Evening Register, 202
Waterloo Gazette, 202
Waterloo, NY, newspapers, 189, 190, 194,
    196, 201, 202–04, 205
Waterloo Observer (1828), 203; (1832), 203
Waterloo Register, 204
Waterloo Republican, 204
Waterloo Reveille, Seneca Falls, 205
Waterloo Village, NY, newspaper, 198
Waterworks newspaper, Ithaca, 272
Watkins Daily Record, 184
Watkins Democrat, 184, 290
Watkins Express, 185
Watkins Family Visitor, 186
Watkins Glen, NY, newspapers, 178, 183,
    187. See also Jefferson, NY
Watkins Herald, Havana, 186
Watkins Independent, 186
Watkins, NY, newspapers, 182, 183, 184,
    185–86, 187, 188, 290
Watkins Republican, 187
Watkins Review, Watkins Glen, 187
Watkins' Settlement [Scipioville], NY,
    newspaper, 67
Watkins Weekly Union, 188
Waverly Advocate (1852), 245; (1895),
    246
Waverly and Athens Democrat, Waverly,
    246
Waverly Daily Review, 246
Waverly Democrat, 246
Waverly Enterprise, 247
Waverly Evening Journal, 247
Waverly Free Press. See *Waverly Free*
    Press and Tioga County Record

Waverly Free Press and Tioga County Record, 247

Waverly Luminary, 248

Waverly, NY, newspapers, 234, 235, 241, 245–52

Waverly Review, 249

Waverly Sun, Nichols Recorder and Valley News, Waverly, 249

Waverly Tribune, 249

Wayland, NY, newspapers, 231

Wayland Register, 231

Weedsport Advertiser (1827), 66; (1850), 66

Weedsport Cayuga Chief. See *Cayuga Chief*

Weedsport Cayuga Chief-Port Byron Chronicle. See *Cayuga Chief-Chronicle*

Weedsport Monitor, 66

Weedsport, NY, newspapers, 48, 49, 62, 66, 67

Weedsport Republican, 66

Weedsport Sentinel, 66

Weedsport Times, 67

Weekly Advertiser, Elmira, 87

Weekly Auburnian. See *Auburn Weekly Bulletin*

Weekly Bulletin, Horseheads, 88

Weekly Courier, Unadilla, 175

Weekly Free Press. See *Elmira Weekly Free Press*

Weekly Herald, Genoa, 67

Weekly Ithacan, 270, 291

Weekly Monitor, Painted Post, 231

Weekly News and Democrat. See *Auburn Democrat-Agus*

Weekly Pioneer: Cooperstown, 175; Norwich, 110

Weekly Telegraph, Elmira. See *Young American*

Weekly True Press. See *Auburn True Press*

Weekly Union. See *Auburn Weekly Union*

Weekly Visitor. See *Franklin Visitor*

Wellsville Daily Free Press, 15

Wellsville Daily Reporter, 15

Wellsville Free Press. See *Genesee Valley Free Press*

Wellsville, NY, newspapers, 1, 2, 10, 12, 15

Wellsville Times, 15

Western Banner, Auburn, 67

Western Courier, Homer, 136

Western Federalist, Auburn, 67

Western Luminary, Watkins' Settlement, 67

Western Museum and Belles-Lettres Repository. See *Museum and Literary Repository*

Western Oracle and Chenango Weekly Maga-
zine, Sherburne, 111

Western Republican, Bath, 231

Western Star, Penn Yan, 283

Western Times, Waterloo, 205

Westford, NY, newspaper, 170

Wharton Valley Echo, Edmeston, 289

Whig and Advocate. See *Allegany Republican*

Whig newspapers: Allegany Co., 6; Cayuga Co., 37, 43; Chemung Co., 74, 77, 80, 94, 97, 105; Cortland Co., 114, 117, 121; Delaware Co., 141; Schuyler Co., 179, 180; Seneca Co., 189, 195; Steuben Co., 213, 215, 228, 230; Tioga Co., 237, 238, 244; Tompkins Co., 252, 257, 258, 266, 267, 268; Yates Co., 275, 281, 284

Whig Republican newspaper, 208

White's American Greenbacker. See *Quill and Press*

Whitesville News, Whitesville, NY, 16, 285

Whitney Point, NY, newspapers, 23, 24, 35, 287

Whitney Point Reporter, 35, 287. See also *Chenango American and Whitney Point Reporter*

Whitney's Point Reporter. See *Chenango American and Whitney Point Reporter*

Willard State Hospital staff newspaper, 271

Window, Trumansburg, 271

Windsor, NY, newspapers, 30, 32, 35, 36

Windsor Standard, 35

Windsor Times, 36

Witness, Ithaca, 271

Women's Christian Temperance Union newspapers, 6, 11

Women's newspaper, 45

Women's rights newspaper, 190–91

Woodhull, NY, newspaper, 230

Woodhull Sentinel. See *Addison Advertiser and Woodhull Sentinel*

Worcester, NY, newspapers, 176

Worcester Times, 176

Worcester Times and Schenevus Monitor, 176

Workingman, Owego, 250

Workingman's newspapers, 70, 72

World War I, effect of on newspapers, 13, 115, 253

World War II, effect of on newspapers, 7, 65

Wreath and Ladies Literary Repository, Waterloo, 205

Wright, Silas, campaign newspaper, 1844, 194

Wyoming Conference newspaper, 246
Yates County Chronicle. See *Chronicle-Express*
Yates County Farm and Home Bureau News, Penn Yan, 283
Yates County News, Penn Yan, 283
Yates County newspapers, 273–84
Yates County Republican, Penn Yan, 283
Yates Country Store News, Penn Yan, 283
Yates County Whig, Penn Yan (1839), 284; (1841), 284; (1843), see *Chronicle-Express*
Yates Republican, Penn Yan, 284
Yes or No?, Ithaca, 272
Young America, Crookerville, 288
Young American, Elmira, 88
Young Patriot, Delhi, 155
Young Pioneer, Norwich. See *Weekly Pioneer*
Youth newspapers, 202, 254, 272
Youths' Literary Gazette, Ithaca, 272
Zeppelin, Ithaca, 272